Aslib Directory

VOLUME ONE

Aslib Directory
Volume 1

Information Sources in Science, Technology and Commerce

Edited by
ELLEN M. CODLIN, F.L.A.

Aslib
LONDON
1977

First edition 1928
Second edition 1957
Third edition 1968
Reprinted, with minor corrections, 1970
Fourth edition 1977

SBN 0 8 5142 104 0

Produced by computer-controlled phototypesetting
using OCR input techniques and printed offset by
UNWIN BROTHERS LIMITED
The Gresham Press, Old Woking, Surrey
A member of the Staples Printing Group

CONTENTS

FOREWORD

It is fifty years since Sir Ernest Rutherford, then President of the Royal Society, wrote an Introduction to the first Aslib Directory to sources of specialized information. "While the expert", he wrote, "may be assumed to be cognizant of sources of importance in his own field, it is clearly desirable if not essential that there should be a general key indicating where one should turn for information in any sphere of knowledge".

Even though Sir Ernest's assumption itself may be open to challenge as a result of the tremendous changes in the number, variety and nature of information sources during this period, the need for a general guide that crosses the frontiers of individual disciplines is clearly one that remains as persistent today as it was then. Successive versions of the Aslib Directory have proved invaluable reference tools for all those who from time to time need to track down information over a wide range of subjects. Now Aslib presents an entirely new compilation, confident that, like its predecessors, it too will ease the labours of its users and point the way surely to the information for which they search.

Leslie Wilson
Director of Aslib
September 1977

INTRODUCTION

IT IS now nearly ten years since the publication of the last edition of volume I of the Aslib Directory and I estimate that 70 per cent of the sources then listed have changed their names, addresses or responsibilities, or disappeared altogether. Many new bodies, of course, have come into being. For the present edition, over 5000 questionnaires were distributed to organizations, selected from some eighty general and special directories, and including most of the bodies given in the last edition. Second forms were sent to those who did not respond; Post Office returns of those no longer at recorded addresses were resubmitted when new addresses could be found. Even so, this edition has still less than three thousand entries.

The main consideration for inclusion was the propensity of an organization to make information available, whether freely, by subscription, as consultants, or by publications, even if, in some cases, they had no formal information services. It follows that every entry has a purpose and none is included by reason of institutional prestige only. A few organizations, proper to volume 2, have been included for the convenience of those with business or industrial interests. Every entry has been arranged to identify exactly the organization it represents, its place in a large or complex system, its previous and/or alternative name or designation and its connections, when known, with other or broader institutions (including EEC or international bodies). Such pointers to European or international sources have been regarded as important, although only UK and Eire organizations comprise the Directory.

The organizations include the very large and the very small; commercial, scientific and research, learned and academic, service, governmental, negotiating, standardizing, qualifying, professional and amateur; producers of data, statistics and abstracts; experts in specialized technologies; repositories of vast collections of books and holders of single special collections.

The arrangement of the new edition is a break with the traditional geographical listing and is in alphabetical order of carefully identified organizations, with generous references from changed or alternative names. Limited geographical approach to the Directory is possible because the place names of public libraries, universities, polytechnics and chambers of commerce are given in the alphabetical sequence.

Consistency of style has had to be abandoned. Organizations cannot be treated as documents and cannot be controlled by cataloguing rules. It has not been possible to achieve consistency in the form of organizational name used. Some bodies have registered the acronym of their full name and no longer wish to use the latter; some are variously known by both or by even more than two names; some acronyms are of names now long forgotten. Again, a particular problem arose in the Public Library sector, both because of the recent local government reorganization and because of the wishes of some authorities to be themselves the only entry and of others to have full entries for their area or district libraries. Such directives or preferences have been followed where possible and have resulted in unevenness of the Public Library coverage and references only where full entries might be expected.

Another break with tradition is the omission in this edition of details of library holdings of books and pamphlets. In my experience, the existence or size of a library is not necessarily an indication of willingness or ability in information-giving, and even the claims as to numbers of books are subject to argument or to severe fluctuation.

The subject index is a key to the numbered list of organizations, according to subject fields they have themselves selected as within their competence. The constraints in compiling the index stem from these selections and from the terms used; such an index cannot be a schedule of all knowledge in science, technology and commerce, but it has been devised for and dedicated to that amorphous creature, the average user, who is compounded of all levels of intellectual condition, many professional and technical requirements, patience, impatience, and desperation.

In the introduction to the last edition, Brian Wilson appealed for the application of commonsense in the use of the index. May I echo this appeal and add that sources should be sought under the most specific head which defines the query. Two-word subjects such as Marine engineering should not be inverted and Objects is not the heading to consult for unidentified flying objects.

I would like to thank all those who took time to complete questionnaires; all those who patiently answered telephone enquiries; all those, particularly Government Department librarians, who explained the make-up or hierarchy of their organizations; the very co-operative Printer; and my long-suffering husband, Ronald, critic and assistant proof-reader.

ELLEN M. CODLIN
August 1977

ABERCONWY AREA LIBRARY *see* **GWYNEDD LIBRARY SERVICE**

ABERDARE CENTRAL LIBRARY *now* **CYNON VALLEY BOROUGH LIBRARIES,** *q.v.*

1 ABERDEEN AND NORTH OF SCOTLAND LIBRARY AND INFORMATION CO-OPERATIVE SERVICE (ANSLICS)
The Library, Robert Gordon's Institute of Technology, St. Andrew Street, Aberdeen AB1 1BG — Tel. 0224 22338
Interlibrary Co-operative Scheme

Enquiries to the Secretary

Subject coverage
general, scientific, technical and commercial

Publications
Oil: a bibliography. 2nd ed., 1973
Directory of Resources

2 ABERDEEN ANGUS CATTLE SOCIETY
6 Kings Place, Perth PH2 8AD — Tel. 0738 22477
Breed Society

Enquiries to the Secretary

Subject coverage
pedigree Aberdeen Angus cattle

Publications
Aberdeen Angus Review (annual)
Aberdeen Angus Herdbook (annual)

3 ABERDEEN CHAMBER OF COMMERCE
15 Union Terrace, Aberdeen AB9 1HF — Tel. 0224 29222, Telex 73315

Chamber of Commerce

Enquiries are accepted from members only

Subject coverage
business information

Publication
Journal (monthly)

4 ABERDEEN CITY LIBRARIES
Rosemount Viaduct, Aberdeen AB9 1GU — Tel. 0224 28991
Public Library

Enquiries to the City Librarian

Subject coverage
international business, trade, and finance

5 ABERDEEN COLLEGE OF COMMERCE
Holburn Street, Aberdeen AB9 2YT — Tel. 0224 572811
College of Further Education, Grampian Region

Enquiries to the Librarian

Subject coverage
business and commerce

ABERDEEN COUNTY LIBRARY *now* **NORTH EAST OF SCOTLAND LIBRARY SERVICE,** *q.v.*

6 ABERDEEN FISHING VESSEL OWNERS ASSOCIATION LIMITED
5 Albert Quay, Aberdeen AB1 2QA Tel. 0224 29283
Trade Association; Member of the Scottish Trawlers Federation; houses the Aberdeen Fish Producers Organisation Limited

Enquiries to the Secretary

Subject coverage
landing of fishing vessels at Aberdeen; training

ABERDEEN PUBLIC LIBRARY *see* **NORTH EAST OF SCOTLAND LIBRARY SERVICE**

7 ABERDEEN TECHNICAL COLLEGE
Gallowgate, Aberdeen AB9 1DN Tel. 0224 50366
Technical College

Enquiries to the Principal

Subject coverage
building; engineering; food technology; management; paper making; sciences; telecommunications

8 ABERDEEN UNIVERSITY LIBRARY
Kings College, Aberdeen AB9 2UB Tel. 0224 40241
Telex 73458
University Library; includes Science Library, Marischal College Library, School of Agriculture Library

Enquiries to the Librarian

Subject coverage
General; science including engineering and agriculture

Special collections
Gregory Collection on the History of Science and Medicine
O'Dell Collection on Railways

Publications
University Studies Series

ABERYSTWYTH/CEREDIGION DISTRICT LIBRARY *see* **DYFED COUNTY LIBRARY**

9 ACCIDENT RESEARCH UNIT
Birmingham University, Edgbaston, Birmingham B15 2TT Tel. 021-472 1301 ext. 2579
Telex 338938
Research and Consulting Organization

Enquiries to the Head of the Accident Research Unit

Subject coverage
investigation and reconstruction of road and other transport accidents; injury research; causes of injury; biomechanics; product liability litigation

Publications
Project Reports
Reprints of publications
Lists of research projects
Lists of publications

10 ACOUSTICAL INVESTIGATION & RESEARCH ORGANISATION LIMITED
26–28 Bedford Row, London WC1R 4HS Tel. 01-242 0391
Company, wholly-owned subsidiary of Hall-Thermotank Limited

Enquiries to the Chief Consulting Engineer

Subject coverage
architectural acoustics; noise measurement and assessment; noise control; electronic control of auditorium acoustics

ACCRINGTON PUBLIC LIBRARY *now* **HYNDBURN DISTRICT CENTRAL LIBRARY**

11 ACTION FOR DISASTER

3 Queen Margaret Road, Glasgow G20 6DP — Tel. 041-946 4263

Voluntary, Charitable Organization

Enquiries, by letter only, to the Secretary

Subject coverage

planning for disasters; disaster management; high altitude study of hypothermia; study of hazards of North Sea oil operations; co-ordination of emergency services; emergency communications; human blood bank for burn casualties

Publications

Proceedings of two international Conferences:

1. Guide to Disaster Management (1974)
2. Developments in Disaster Management (1976)

12 ACTON DISTRICT LIBRARY

High Street, London W3 6NA — Tel. 01-992 6991, Telex 24363

Public Library; District Library of the London Borough of Ealing Library Service; includes the Borough Commercial and Technical Reference Library; Administrative Headquarters of CICRIS (Co-operative Industrial and Commercial Reference and Information Service, West London), *q.v.*

Enquiries, by letter or telex, to the District Librarian; by telephone, to the Commercial and Technical Librarian

Subject coverage

general; commerce; science; technology; electronics; atomic energy

Special collections

UK and foreign directories

Atomic Energy reports

13 ACTON TECHNICAL COLLEGE

High Street, London W3 6RD — Tel. 01-993 2344 ext. 2335

Technical College

Enquiries to the Librarian

Subject coverage

technical education; production engineering; automobile repair and garage management; electronic engineering; office and secretarial skills

Special collection

British Standards

ADAM SMITH LIBRARY *see* **GLASGOW UNIVERSITY**

ADHESIVE MANUFACTURERS ASSOCIATION *now* **BRITISH ADHESIVE MANUFACTURERS ASSOCIATION,** *q.v.*

14 ADHESIVE TAPE MANUFACTURERS ASSOCIATION

15 Tooks Court, London EC4A 1LA — Tel. 01-831 7581, Telex 23485

Trade Association

Enquiries to the Secretary

Subject coverage

manufacture of pressure-sensitive tapes

Publication

List of members

15 ADMINISTRATIVE STAFF COLLEGE
Greenlands, Henley-on-Thames, Oxfordshire RG9 3AU Tel. 049-166 454
Independent Organization recognized as a Charity; associated with Brunel University

Enquiries to the Librarian or Registrar

Subject coverage
management (general, office, production, personnel, marketing and selling); public administration, national and local, British and foreign; economics, money and banking; industrial relations; statistical method and operational research

Publications
books and monographs on management
Occasional Papers
College Papers
Publications list available

16 ADMIRALTY COMPASS OBSERVATORY
Ditton Park, Slough, Berkshire SL3 7JE Tel. 75 42231
Telex 847181
Government Department; Division of the Admiralty Surface Weapons Establishment, *q.v.*

Enquiries to the Head of ACO

Subject coverage
navigation; tribological aspects of gas bearings

ADMIRALTY DISTILLING EXPERIMENTAL STATION *now* **ADMIRALTY MARINE ENGINEERING ESTABLISHMENT (P),** *q.v.*

17 ADMIRALTY EXPERIMENTAL DIVING UNIT
HMS Vernon, Portsmouth, Hampshire PO1 3ER Tel. 0705 22351 ext. 872376
Government Research Unit, part of the Admiralty Underwater Weapons Establishment, *q.v.*

Enquiries to the Officer in Charge

Subject coverage
diving and associated equipment, underwater activities in connection with hydrocarbon exploitation

18 ADMIRALTY MARINE ENGINEERING ESTABLISHMENT
Haslar, Gosport, Hampshire PO12 2AF Tel. 0705 22351
Telex 86145
Government Department, of the Procurement Executive, Ministry of Defence, Ship Department; associated with an Establishment of the same name at Portland, Dorset, *q.v.*

Enquiries to the Deputy Superintendent

Subject coverage
development and testing of all marine engineering machinery other than internal combustion engines and gas turbines; boiler combustion equipment and refractories; air treatment machinery; pumps and compressors; desalination and waste disposal equipment; fire hazards in ships and firefighting systems

Publications
Annual Review/Technical Reports: enquiries to Procurement Executive, Ministry of Defence, Ship Department, Section 201, Block G Foxhill, Bath, Somerset BA1 5AB

19 ADMIRALTY MARINE ENGINEERING ESTABLISHMENT (P)
H.M. Naval Base, Portland, Dorset
Government Department, of the Procurement Executive, Ministry of Defence, Ship Department; formerly Admiralty Distilling Experimental Station, Portland

Enquiries to the Officer in Charge

Subject coverage
development and evaluation of desalination of seawater machinery applicable to shipboard use; reverse osmosis as a means of obtaining potable water from the sea

20 ADMIRALTY MATERIALS LABORATORY
Holton Heath, Poole, Dorsetshire BH16 6JU — Tel. 020-122 2711
Telex 41392

Government Department, of the Ministry of Defence, Procurement Executive

Enquiries to the Information Officer

Subject coverage
materials, mainly for marine use; related metallurgy and chemistry; organic materials

21 ADMIRALTY RESEARCH LABORATORY
Queens Road, Teddington, Middlesex TW11 0LN — Tel. 01-977 3231
Government Research Laboratory, of the Ministry of Defence, Procurement Executive

Enquiries to the Librarian

Subject coverage
hydrodynamics; oceanography; underwater acoustics; vibration

22 ADMIRALTY SURFACE WEAPONS ESTABLISHMENT
Portsdown, Cosham, Portsmouth, Hampshire PO6 4AA — Tel. 07018 79411
Telex 86132

Government Research and Development Establishment, of the Ministry of Defence, Procurement Executive; Divisions include the Admiralty Compass Observatory, *q.v.*, and a gunnery division at Bath; there are three other laboratories of the Establishment and two trials sites

Enquiries to the Librarian

Subject coverage
naval surface weapons, communications and navigation systems; radars; harbours navigational equipment

Publications
Technical Reports

23 ADMIRALTY UNDERWATER WEAPONS ESTABLISHMENT
Portland, Dorset DT5 2JS — Tel. 0305 820381
Government Research Unit, of the Ministry of Defence; including the Admiralty Experimental Diving Unit, *q.v.*

Enquiries to the Head of Library and Information Services

Subject coverage
underwater research and development; underwater acoustics; fluid dynamics; oceanography; mathematics; physics; electronics; materials

24 ADVERTISEMENT TYPESETTING AND FOUNDRY EMPLOYERS FEDERATION
Treasure House, 19/21 Hatton Garden, London EC1N 8PS — Tel. 01-405 5746 and 0910
Employers Trade Federation

Enquiries to the Secretary

Subject coverage
typesetting, hot metal and photo composition; platemaking, electrotype and stereotypes

25 ADVERTISING ASSOCIATION
Abford House, 15 Wilton Road, London SW1V 1NJ — Tel. 01-828 2771
Trade Association; houses the National Federation of Publicity Associations and the Incorporated Advertising Management Association

Enquiries to the Information Officer

Subject coverage
advertising; marketing; public relations; communications

Special collection
Old advertisements

Publications
Advertising Quarterly
Standards and Codes of Practice
Research Monographs
Bibliographies
Reading List for Students
Statistics
Films
Publications List

26 ADVERTISING STANDARDS AUTHORITY LIMITED
15–17 Ridgmount Street, London WC1E 7AW Tel. 01-580 0801
Telex 28905
Regulatory Body; Secretariat is shared with the Code of Advertising Practice Committee, *q.v.*

Enquiries to the Director

Subject coverage
constraints on advertisement content in the U.K., and, to a lesser extent, in Europe

Publications
Monthly Lists of Complaints Resolved
The A.S.A.: How It Can Help You
British Code of Advertising Practice
British Code of Sales Promotion Practice

27 ADVISORY, CONCILIATION AND ARBITRATION SERVICE
Cleland House, Page Street, London SW1P 4ND Tel. 01-222 4383
Independent Statutory Body; formerly Conciliation and Arbitration Service

Enquiries to the Librarian

Subject coverage
industrial relations; personnel management

Publications
ACAS Guides
ACAS Reports
Codes of Practice under the Employment Protection Act

28 ADVISORY COUNCIL ON CALIBRATION AND MEASUREMENT
26 Chapter Street, London SW1P 4NS Tel. 01-834 7032 ext. 8
Government Department, of the Department of Prices and Consumer Protection

Enquiries to the Secretary

Subject coverage
calibration and calibration services; measurement

AEI LIMITED *now* **MARCONI RADAR SYSTEMS LIMITED,** *q.v.*

29 AERODROME OWNERS ASSOCIATION
18 Orchard Street, Bristol, Avon BS1 5DX Tel. 0272 292480
Trade Assocation

Enquiries to the Association

Subject coverage
airport operation and finance

Publication
Newsletter (bi-monthly)

30 AERONAUTICAL RESEARCH COUNCIL

National Physical Laboratory, Teddington, Middlesex TW11 0LW — Tel. 01-977 3222 ext. 3254

Advisory Council to the Ministries of Defence and of Industry

Enquiries to the Librarian

Subject coverage

aerodynamics; aircraft structures; materials; propulsion

Publications

ARC Reports, Papers and Memoranda

31 AEROPLANE AND ARMAMENT EXPERIMENTAL ESTABLISHMENT

Boscombe Down, Salisbury, Wiltshire SP4 0JF — Tel. 09802 3331, Telex 47681

Government Department, of the Procurement Executive, Ministry of Defence

Enquiries to the Information Officer

Subject coverage

aircraft flight testing; aeronautical engineering

32 AGREMENT BOARD

Lord Alexander House, Waterhouse Street, Hemel Hempstead HP1 1DH

Assessment Board for Construction Industry products; grant-aided by the Department of the Environment

Enquiries, by letter only, to the Information Officer

Subject coverage

construction industry products assessed and approved by the Board

Publications

Agrément Certificates

Methods of Assessment and Testing documents

33 AGRICULTURAL AVIATION RESEARCH UNIT (CIBA-GEIGY)

Cranfield Institute of Technology, Cranfield, Bedfordshire MK43 0AL — Tel. 0234 750851, Telex 825437

Research Unit, of Ciba-Geigy Limited, Basle, and Ciba-Pilatus Aerial Spraying Company Limited

Enquiries to the Director

Subject coverage

bio-aeronautics, including aerial transport of biologically significant matter (including insects); atomisation physics and related aerodynamics; meteorology relative to bio-aeronautics; aerial spraying of crops and forests; aerial spraying in public health

34 AGRICULTURAL CO-OPERATION & MARKETING SERVICES LIMITED

Agriculture House, 25–31 Knightsbridge, London SW1X 7NJ — Tel. 01-235 7853

Trade Association; linked with the National Farmers Union, the British Agricultural Council, and the Federation of Agricultural Cooperatives (U.K.) Limited; formerly the Agricultural Cooperative Association

Enquiries to the Press and Information Officer

Subject coverage

agricultural cooperation and marketing

Publications

Annual Report

Broadsheet (bi monthly)

AGRICULTURAL DEVELOPMENT AND ADVISORY SERVICE *see* **EAST MALLING RESEARCH STATION**

AGRICULTURAL ECONOMICS BUREAU *see* **INSTITUTE OF AGRICULTURAL ECONOMICS**

AGRICULTURAL ECONOMICS RESEARCH INSTITUTE *now* **INSTITUTE OF AGRICULTURAL ECONOMICS,** *q.v.*

AGRICULTURAL ECONOMICS UNIT *see* **CAMBRIDGE UNIVERSITY, Department of Land Economy**

AGRICULTURAL MACHINERY TRACTOR DEALERS ASSOCIATION LIMITED *now* **BRITISH AGRICULTURAL AND GARDEN MACHINERY ASSOCIATION,** *q.v.*

35 AGRICULTURAL RESEARCH COUNCIL

160 Great Portland Street, London W1N 6DT Tel. 01-580 6655

Independent Body—Government Financed by Department of Education and Science

Enquiries to the Information Officer

Subject coverage

agriculture; horticulture; food science

Publications

Annual Report
Index of Agricultural and Food Research
ARC Research Review
Agricultural Research Service
ARC News

AGRICULTURAL RESEARCH COUNCIL INSTITUTES *see*

ANIMAL BREEDING RESEARCH ORGANISATION
FOOD RESEARCH INSTITUTE
INSTITUTE FOR RESEARCH ON ANIMAL DISEASES
INSTITUTE OF ANIMAL PHYSIOLOGY
LETCOMBE LABORATORY
MEAT RESEARCH INSTITUTE
POULTRY RESEARCH CENTRE
WEED RESEARCH ORGANISATION

AGRICULTURAL RESEARCH COUNCIL STATE-AIDED INSTITUTES *see*

ANIMAL DISEASES RESEARCH ASSOCIATION
ANIMAL VIRUS RESEARCH INSTITUTE
EAST MALLING RESEARCH STATION
GLASSHOUSE CROPS RESEARCH INSTITUTE
GRASSLAND RESEARCH INSTITUTE
HANNAH RESEARCH INSTITUTE
HILL FARMING RESEARCH ORGANISATION
HOUGHTON POULTRY RESEARCH ORGANISATION
JOHN INNES INSTITUTE
LONG ASHTON RESEARCH STATION
MACAULAY INSTITUTE FOR SOIL RESEARCH
NATIONAL INSTITUTE FOR RESEARCH IN DAIRYING
NATIONAL INSTITUTE OF AGRICULTURAL ENGINEERING
NATIONAL VEGETABLE RESEARCH STATION
PLANT BREEDING INSTITUTE
ROTHAMSTED EXPERIMENTAL STATION
ROWETT RESEARCH INSTITUTE
SCOTTISH HORTICULTURAL RESEARCH INSTITUTE
SCOTTISH SOCIETY FOR RESEARCH IN PLANT BREEDING
WELSH PLANT BREEDING STATION
WYE COLLEGE DEPARTMENT OF HOP RESEARCH

AGRICULTURAL RESEARCH COUNCIL UNITS *see*
PLANT GROWTH SUBSTANCES AND SYSTEMIC FUNGICIDES UNIT
STATISTICS GROUP
UNIT OF ANIMAL GENETICS
UNIT OF MUSCLE MECHANISM AND INSECT PHYSIOLOGY
UNIT OF NITROGEN FIXATION
UNIT OF SOIL PHYSICS
UNIT OF STATISTICS

36 AGRICULTURAL TRAINING BOARD
Bourne House, 32 Beckenham Road, Beckenham, Kent BR3 4PB Tel. 01-650 4890
Government Department; formerly Agricultural, Horticultural and Forestry Industry Training Board; of the Training Services Agency, Manpower Services Commission

Enquiries to the Librarian

Subject coverage
training in agriculture

Publication
Annual Report (including list of published research reports)

AGRICULTURE CO-OPERATIVE MANAGERS ASSOCIATION *see* **PLUNKETT FOUNDATION FOR CO-OPERATIVE STUDIES**

AIR POLLUTION RESEARCH UNIT *now* **ENVIRONMENTAL HAZARDS UNIT,** *q.v.*

AIR REGISTRATION BOARD *now* **CIVIL AVIATION AUTHORITY,** *q.v.*

37 AIR SAFETY GROUP
5 Chalfont House, Chesham Street, London SW1
Voluntary, Informal Association

Enquiries to the Honorary Secretary

Subject coverage
most aspects of aviation safety connected with civil air transport

Publications
occasional reports

38 AIR TRANSPORT AND TRAVEL INDUSTRY TRAINING BOARD
158–162 High Street, Staines, Middlesex TW18 4AS Tel. 81 57171
Industrial Training Board, of the Training Services Agency, Manpower Services Commission; formerly the Civil Air Transport Industry Training Board

Enquiries to the Board Secretary

Subject coverage
staff training in the air transport and travel industries

Publications
Training Guides and Recommendations
Manpower Survey (annual)
Training Research Bulletin (2 per annum)
Training World (quarterly, newsletter)
Guide to Levy Exemption and Grants etc., list available

AIR TRANSPORT LICENSING BOARD *now* **CIVIL AVIATION AUTHORITY,** *q.v.*

39 AIRCRAFT RESEARCH ASSOCIATION LIMITED
Manton Lane, Bedford MK41 7PF Tel. 0234 50681
Telex 825056

Association of Major Companies

Enquiries to the Librarian

Subject coverage
aerodynamics; wind tunnel testing of aircraft models; mathematical analysis and computing in related fields

AIRDRIE PUBLIC LIBRARY *now* **MONKLANDS DISTRICT LIBRARIES,** *q.v.*

40 AIRFLOW DEVELOPMENTS LIMITED
Lancaster Road, High Wycombe, Buckinghamshire HP12 3QP Tel. 0494 25252
Telex 83288

Manufacturing company

Requests to the Sales Office Manager

Subject coverage
air and gas flow and pressure measurement instruments; flue gas and dust measurement and monitoring; air blowers; extractor units

Publications
trade and installation instruction literature

41 AIRLIE ASSOCIATES
80 Roewood Lane, Macclesfield, Cheshire SK10 2PQ Tel. 0625 25065
Telex 667156

Company

Enquiries to the Information Officer

Subject coverage
textiles

Publications
Textile Manufacturer (monthly)
Knitting World (monthly)

42 ALBRIGHT & WILSON LIMITED
1 Knightsbridge Green, London SW1X 7QD Tel. 01-589 6393
Company; Divisions at Whitehaven and Oldbury

No enquiry service

Subject coverage
detergents and chemicals

43 ALCAN BOOTH SHEET LIMITED
Castle Works, Rogerstone, Newport, Gwent NP1 9YA Tel. 0633-43 2722
Telex 497381
Company; division of Alcan Booth Industries, part of Alcan Aluminium (U.K.) Limited; formerly Alcan Industries Limited

Enquiries to the Sales Director, the Technical Services Manager, or the Industrial Editor

Subject coverage
rolling and extruding aluminium; sheet and plate and strong alloy extrusions; painted products

44 ALCAN INTERNATIONAL LIMITED
Research Centre, Southam Road, Banbury, Oxfordshire OX16 7SP Tel. 0295 2821
Company Development and Research Section; formerly Alcan Research and Development Limited

Enquiries to the Librarian

Subject coverage
aluminium; other metals

45 ALCOA OF GREAT BRITAIN LIMITED
Alcoa House, P.O. Box 15, Corbett Avenue, Droitwich, Worcestershire WR9 7BG — Tel. 090-57 3411, Telex 338518
Company; formerly Imperial Aluminium Company Limited
No enquiry service
Subject coverage
aluminium industry

ALDRIDGE DISTRICT LIBRARY *see* **WALSALL LIBRARY AND MUSEUM SERVICES**

46 ALGINATE INDUSTRIES LIMITED
22 Henrietta Street, London WC2E 8NB — Tel. 01-240 5161, Telex 23815
Company
Enquiries to the Information Officer
Subject coverage
alginic acid, its salts and esters; extraction from brown seaweeds (phaeophycae); properties and applications
Publications
publicity and technical documentation

ALKALI AND CLEAN AIR INSPECTORATE *see* **HEALTH AND SAFETY EXECUTIVE**

47 P.W. ALLEN & COMPANY
253 Liverpool Road, London N1 1NA — Tel. 01-607 4665
Company
Enquiries to the Sales Department
Subject coverage
visual inspection equipment, including illuminated magnifiers; ultraviolet lights; equipment for viewing inside hollow components such as pipes and cylinders; fibre optic equipment; periscopes; bomb disposal equipment
Publications
Product catalogues and information sheets

48 W.H. ALLEN SONS AND COMPANY LIMITED
Queens Engineering Works, P.O. Box 43, Bedford MK40 4JB — Tel. 0234 67400, Telex 82486
Company
No enquiry service
Subject coverage
manufacture of prime movers in heavy engineering

49 ALLEN & HANBURYS RESEARCH LIMITED
Research Division, Priory Street, Ware, Hertfordshire SG12 0DJ — Tel. 32 54567, Telex 81144
Company, subsidiary of the Glaxo Group; formerly Allen and Hanburys Limited
Enquiries to the Librarian
Subject coverage
chemistry, biochemistry, medicine, pharmacy, veterinary science, pharmacology

50 ALLIED BREWERIES (PRODUCTION) LIMITED
Research Department, Station Street, Burton-on-Trent, Staffordshire DE14 1BZ — Tel. 0283 45320
Company

Enquiries to the Librarian

Subject coverage
brewing, malting, microbiology, yeasts, hops, biochemistry, analytical methods

51 ALLIED BREWERY TRADERS ASSOCIATION
392 New Cross Road, London SE14 6UA — Tel. 01-691 3950
Trade Association; houses the Plastics Crate Manufacturers Association

Enquiries to the Secretary

Subject coverage
supply of goods and services to the brewing industry

ALNWICK LIBRARY *see* **NORTHUMBERLAND COUNTY LIBRARY**

ALTRINCHAM PUBLIC LIBRARY *see* **TRAFFORD BOROUGH LIBRARY SERVICE**

ALUMINIUM EXTRUDERS ASSOCIATION *see* **ALUMINIUM FEDERATION LIMITED**

52 ALUMINIUM FEDERATION LIMITED
Broadway House, Calthorpe Road, Birmingham B15 1TN — Tel. 021-455 0311, Telex 338024
Trade Association; sub-groups: Aluminium Extruders Association, Aluminium Forging Group, Aluminium Powder and Paste Association, Aluminium Primary Producers Association

Enquiries to the Librarian

Subject coverage
aluminium and its alloys; technical and commercial aspects; smelting, rolling, extrusion, drawing, forging, and casting

ALUMINIUM FOIL CONTAINER MANUFACTURERS ASSOCIATION *see* **BRITISH ALUMINIUM FOIL ROLLERS ASSOCIATION**

ALUMINIUM FORGING GROUP *see* **ALUMINIUM FEDERATION LIMITED**

ALUMINIUM POWDER AND PASTE ASSOCIATION *see* **ALUMINIUM FEDERATION LIMITED**

ALUMINIUM PRIMARY PRODUCERS ASSOCIATION *see* **ALUMINIUM FEDERATION LIMITED**

53 ALUMINIUM STOCKHOLDERS ASSOCIATION
P.O. Box 360, 75 Harborne Road, Birmingham B15 3DH — Tel. 021-454 6171 ext. 290
Trade Association

Enquiries to the Secretary

Subject coverage
aluminium stockholding

54 ALUMINIUM WINDOW ASSOCIATION
26 Store Street, London WC1E 7EL — Tel. 01-637 3578
Trade Association; member of the Metal Window Federation Limited, *q.v.*

Enquiries to the Director or Secretary

Subject coverage
aluminium windows, doors, curtain walling

55 ALUMINIUM WIRE & CABLE COMPANY LIMITED
Port Tennant, Swansea SA1 8PS Tel. 0792 52251
Telex 48191
Company, associated with Tube Investments Limited and Hawker Siddeley Group Limited

Enquiries to the Librarian

Subject coverage
aluminium wire; conductors and cables

ALYN AND DEESIDE AREA LIBRARY *see* **CLWYD COUNTY LIBRARY SERVICE**

56 AM & S EUROPE LIMITED
Group Library and Information Service, St Andrews Road, Avonmouth, Bristol BS11 9HP Tel 027-52 3646
Telex 449178
Company, formerly Imperial Smelting Corporation, and variations of that title and initials; subsidiary of Rio Tinto Zinc Corporation

Enquiries to the Library and Information Executive

Subject coverage
zinc and lead smelting

57 AMALGAMATED POWER ENGINEERING LIMITED
Queens Engineering Works, Bedford MK40 4JB Tel 0234 51621
Telex 826265
Company

Enquiries to the Publicity Manager

Subject coverage
heavy machinery, mechanical, hydraulic and pneumatic, for public services, industry and ships

58 AMALGAMATED SOCIETY OF WIREDRAWERS AND KINDRED WORKERS
Prospect House, Alma Street, Sheffield S3 8SA Tel. 0742 21674
Trade Union

No enquiry service

Subject coverage
trade union services within the industry

59 AMATEUR ENTOMOLOGISTS SOCIETY
355 Hounslow Road, Hanworth, Feltham, Middlesex TW13 5JH
Scientific Society, affiliated to the Council for Nature

Enquiries, if specific, to the Advisory Panel; if general, to the Secretary

Subject coverage
entomology

Publications
Amateur Entomologist (originally an annual publication, now a serial title for Handbooks)
Bulletin of the Amateur Entomologists Society (annual)
Leaflets and pamphlets on collection and study of insects

60 AMATEUR YACHT RESEARCH SOCIETY
Hermitage, Newbury, Berkshire RG16 9RW Tel. 0635 200668
Educational Charity

Enquiries to the Administrator

Subject coverage
yachting, mainly sailing craft

Publications
bound books and paperbacks: list available e.g.
Self Steering
Rudder Design
Design for Fast Sailing

61 AMERICAN EMBASSY COMMERCIAL LIBRARY
Grosvenor Square, London W1A 1AE — Tel. 01-499 9000, Telex 266777

Government Department

Enquiries to the Librarian

Subject coverage
commerce, industry and trade only

62 AMPEX GREAT BRITAIN LIMITED
Acre Road, Reading RG2 0QR — Tel. 0734 85200, Telex 848345

Company

Enquiries to the Press Officer

Subject coverage
broadcast video; industrial video; instrumentation; computer peripherals; professional audio; magnetic tape

AMUSEMENT CATERERS ASSOCIATION *now* **BRITISH AMUSEMENT CATERING TRADES ASSOCIATION,** *q.v.*

AMUSEMENT TRADES ASSOCIATION LIMITED *now* **BRITISH AMUSEMENT CATERING TRADES ASSOCIATION,** *q.v.*

63 ANBAR PUBLICATIONS LIMITED
P.O. Box 23, 65 Wembley Hill Road, Wembley, Middlesex HA9 8DJ — Tel. 01-902 4489, Telex 935779

Company; also having the trade name Anbar Management Services

Enquiries (generally from subscribers only) to the Company

Subject coverage
management; accounting; data processing; marketing; distribution; personnel management and training; work study; organization and method

Publications
Accounting and Data Processing Abstracts
Marketing and Training Abstracts
Top Management Abstracts
Work Study and O & M Abstracts
Personnel and Training Abstracts

ANDERSONIAN LIBRARY *see* **STRATHCLYDE UNIVERSITY LIBRARY**

64 ANDOVER LIBRARY
Chantry Way, Andover, Hampshire SP10 1LT — Tel. 0264 2807, 0264 66540

Public Library; Branch of Hampshire County Library *q.v.*, and central library of Hampshire's Test Valley District

Enquiries to the Librarian

Subject coverage
general; printing and publishing

ANGLESEY AREA LIBRARY *see* **GWYNEDD LIBRARY SERVICE**

65 ANGLIAN REGIONAL MANAGEMENT CENTRE
Danbury Park, Danbury, Chelmsford, Essex CM3 4AT

Management College; associated with a Centre of the same name, at Asta House, 156/164 High Road, Chadwell Heath, Romford, Essex RM6 6LX; both parts of North East London Polytechnic, *q.v.*

Enquiries to the Librarian

Subject coverage
management

66 ANGUS DISTRICT LIBRARY SERVICE
Library Administration Unit, County Buildings, Forfar DD8 3LG — Tel. 0307 3661
Public Library, formed by the amalgamation of the Burgh Libraries of Arbroath, Brechin, Carnoustie, Forfar and Montrose with Angus Country Library

Enquiries to the Director of Libraries and Museums

Subject coverage
general

ANIMAL BREEDING LIBRARY *see* **COMMONWEALTH BUREAU OF ANIMAL BREEDING AND GENETICS**

ANIMAL BREEDING RESEARCH ORGANISATION *see* **COMMONWEALTH BUREAU OF ANIMAL BREEDING AND GENETICS**

67 ANIMAL DISEASES RESEARCH ASSOCIATION
Moredun Institute, Gilmerton Road, Edinburgh EH17 7JH — Tel. 031-664 3262
State-aided Research Institute

Enquiries to the Librarian

Subject coverage
veterinary aspects of microbiology, biochemistry, pathology, physiology, physical chemistry, parasitology

Publication
Annual Report

68 ANIMAL HEALTH TRUST
24 Portland Place, London W1N 4HN — Tel. 01-636 1707
Registered Charity; with the Equine Research Station, *q.v.*, and the Small Animals Centre

Enquiries to the Secretary

Subject coverage
animal health

Publication
Animal Health (annual)

69 ANIMAL VIRUS RESEARCH INSTITUTE
Pirbright, Woking, Surrey GU24 0NF — Tel. 048-631 2441
Grant-aided Institute, of the Agricultural Research Council; houses the World Reference Laboratory for Foot and Mouth Disease

Enquiries to the Librarian

Subject coverage
animal virology, particularly foot and mouth disease and swine vesicular disease

Special collection
Collection of reprints on foot and mouth disease

ANSLICS *see* **ABERDEEN AND NORTH OF SCOTLAND LIBRARY AND INFORMATION CO-OPERATIVE SERVICE**

70 ANSWERS RESEARCH LIMITED
Algarve House, 140 Borden Lane, Sittingbourne, Kent ME9 8HR — Tel. 0795 23778
Company

Enquiries to the Director

Subject coverage
market research; advertising research; consultancy for advice and problem solving

71 ANTIFERENCE LIMITED
Bicester Road, Aylesbury, Buckinghamshire HP19 3BJ Tel. 0296 82511
Telex 83666

Company, member of Antiference Group Limited

Enquiries to the Technical Director

Subject coverage
aerials and accessories, including television distribution systems; electronic components

ANTI-LOCUST RESEARCH CENTRE *now* **CENTRE FOR OVERSEAS PEST RESEARCH,** *q.v.*

ANTRIM COUNTY LIBRARY *now* **NORTHERN IRELAND, NORTH EASTERN EDUCATION AND LIBRARY BOARD,** *q.v.*

72 APPAREL AND FASHION INDUSTRY'S ASSOCIATION OF GREAT BRITAIN AND NORTHERN IRELAND
81 Wimpole Street, London W1M 7DB Tel. 01-935 2915
Trade Association and Employers Organization

Enquiries, from within the industry only, to the Secretary

Subject coverage
British clothing industry; dressmaking; statutory provisions, wages, terms and conditions of employment; import and export regulations

73 APPAREL INDUSTRIES FEDERATION
Confederation House, Kildare Street, Dublin 2 Tel. Dublin 779801
Telex 4711 EI

Trade Association; member of the Confederation of Irish Industry and of MAILLEUROP (EEC Knitting Industry Association)

Enquiries to the Director

Subject coverage
clothing industry including tariffs, wages, customs duties, licensing, EEC legislation, industrial training

74 APPLE AND PEAR DEVELOPMENT COUNCIL
Union House, The Pantiles, Tunbridge Wells, Kent TN4 8HF Tel. 0892 20255/6
Statutory Body

Enquiries to the Marketing Director

Subject coverage
availability of major varieties; work studies on aspects of the industry, for example: Bramley processing; packaging; dessert apple planting; production in U.K. and abroad; imports

Publications
publicity material

75 APPLETON LABORATORY
Ditton Park, Slough, Berkshire SL3 9JX Tel. 75 44234
Telex 848369

Government Research Laboratory, formerly Radio and Space Research Station; of the Science Research Council

Enquiries to the Librarian

Subject coverage
propagation of radiowaves at all lengths, physics of the atmosphere at all heights, astronomy, and use of rockets and satellites to study those subjects; tracking and control of satellites and processing of data therefrom

Publication
Triennial Report (H.M.S.O.)

APPLIED GEOCHEMISTRY RESEARCH GROUP *see* **ROYAL SCHOOL OF MINES**

76 APPLIED SCIENCE DEVELOPMENTS LIMITED
153 Hull Road, York YO1 3JX Tel. 0904 55801
Company, formerly Applied Science Associates

Enquiries to the Chairman

Subject coverage
physical sciences, lasers, thin film technology, electronics, optics, electron spectroscopy

77 APPLIED SCIENTIFIC INSTRUMENTS LIMITED
268 High Street, Boston Spa, Wetherby, Yorkshire LS23 6AJ Tel. 0904 59861
Company; associated with Applied Science Developments Limited, *q.v.*

Enquiries to the Secretary

Subject coverage
design and construction of scientific instruments; lasers and their control; optical devices; electron optical devices

78 APV COMPANY
P.O. Box 4, Manor Royal, Crawley, Sussex RH10 2QB Tel. 0293 27777
Telex 87237

Company, subsidiary of APV Holdings Limited

Enquiries to the Librarian

Subject coverage
manufacture of process plant for food and chemical industries; heat transfer; metallurgy; dairy science; brewing science; corrosion

79 AQUATIC SCIENCES AND FISHERIES INFORMATION SYSTEM
The Library, Marine Biological Association of the U.K., Citadel Hill, Plymouth, Devonshire PL1 2PB Tel. 0752 21761
International Information System, coordinated by Food and Agriculture Organization of the United Nations (FAO) and the Intergovernmental Oceanographic Commission (IOC)

Enquiries to the Librarian, Marine Biological Association

Subject coverage
science and technology of marine and freshwater environments by a computer-orientated system compatible with UNISIST

Publication
Aquatic Sciences and Fisheries Abstracts (monthly) (formerly Aquatic Biology Abstracts)

80 ARBORICULTURAL ASSOCIATION
Merrist Wood Agricultural College, Worplesdon, Guildford, Surrey GU3 3PE Tel. 048-631 2424
Professional/Charity Organization; incorporating the former Association of British Tree Surgeons and Arborists; member of the Tree Council; has five regional branches

Enquiries to the Secretary, passed to Consultants and Contractors

Subject coverage
production, selection, planting and maintenance of ornamental trees, shrubs and amenity woodlands; tree surveys, inspection, pathology; legal matters

Publications
Journal of Arboriculture (twice per annum)
Advisory booklets

ARBOVIRUS UNIT of the Medical Research Council *see* **LONDON SCHOOL OF HYGIENE AND TROPICAL MEDICINE**

ARBROATH PUBLIC LIBRARY *see* **ANGUS DISTRICT LIBRARY SERVICES**

81 ARCHITECTURAL ASSOCIATION
36 Bedford Square, London WC1 Tel. 01-636 0974
Professional Association and School of Architecture

Enquiries from Members of the Association only

Subject coverage
architecture; building; planning

Publications
Guide to the Architectural Association Library (annual)
Architectural Association Quarterly
Architectural Association Notes (quarterly)
Events Lists (weekly)
Architectural Association Papers (irregular)
Bibliographies
Periodicals and Serial Holdings

ARCHITECTURAL GRANITE ASSOCIATION *now* **FEDERATION OF STONE INDUSTRIES,** *q.v.*

82 ARCHITECTURAL METALWORK ASSOCIATION
Greenhills, Tydcombe, Warlingham, Surrey Tel. 01-820 3131
Trade Association, formerly Architectural Metal Craftsmen's Assocation

Enquiries to the Director

Subject coverage
all applications of decorative, builders' and structural sheet metal and castings; for buildings, ceilings, doors, windows, flooring, furniture, gates, lifts, electrical fittings, railings, screens, staircases, statues, etc.

ARFON/DWYFOR AREA LIBRARY *see* **GWYNEDD LIBRARY SERVICE**

83 ARGYLL AND BUTE DISTRICT LIBRARY
Argyll House, Alexandra Parade, Dunoon, Argyll PA23 8AJ Tel. Dunoon 4000
Public Library, by reorganisation of Argyll County Library, Bute County Library, Tulloch Library Dunoon and Campbeltown Public Library

Enquiries to the District Librarian

Subject coverage
Local and general reference information

Special collection
Clyde steamers (books, pamphlets, photographs)

ARMAGH COUNTY LIBRARY *now* **NORTHERN IRELAND, SOUTHERN EDUCATION AND LIBRARY BOARD,** *q.v.*

84 ARMITAGE & ASSOCIATES
P.O. Box RNM4, Rainham, Gillingham, Kent ME8 7EZ Tel. 0634 31384
Telex 24224

Management Consultants

Enquiries to the Librarian

Subject coverage
management, business and personnel consultancy in Western Europe, parts of Eastern Europe, and other countries world wide, in all industries and professions

85 Alan ARMSTRONG & ASSOCIATES LIMITED
8 Queen Victoria Street, Reading, Berkshire RG1 1TG Tel. 0734 56007
Telex 27461

Company; includes the London Business School Bookshop and the Ashridge Management College Bookshop

Enquiries to the Information Officer at the above address or at the London Business School Bookshop

Subject coverage
sources of commercial and business information; Middle East business information sources

Publications
Library and Information News (on subscription)
Next month's Directories and New Business Books (on subscription)

ARTHUR D. LITTLE RESEARCH INSTITUTE *now* **INVERESK RESEARCH INTERNATIONAL,** *q.v.*

86 Ove ARUP & PARTNERS
13 Fitzroy Street, London W1P 6BQ — Tel. 01-636 1531, Telex 263935

Company

Enquiries to the Librarian

Subject coverage
architecture; engineering (structural, civil, mechanical and electrical); trade literature

Publications
Arup Journal (quarterly)
Newsletter (bi-monthly)

87 ASBESTOS CEMENT MANUFACTURERS ASSOCIATION
602 Castle Lane West, Bournemouth BH8 9UF
Trade association

Enquiries to member companies

Subject coverage
asbestos cement products

88 ASBESTOS FIBRE LABORATORY
Turner and Newall, Ltd., c/o TAC Construction Materials Limited, P.O. Box 22, Trafford Park, Manchester M17 1RU — Tel. 061-872 2181, Telex 667638
Company Laboratory

Enquiries to the Director

Subject coverage
geology and mineralogy of asbestos; identification of asbestos fibres; mechanical properties of asbestos fibres; assessment of quality of graded asbestos

89 ASBESTOS INFORMATION COMMITTEE
2 Old Burlington Street, London W1X 2LH — Tel. 01-734 0081
Information and Advisory Body, industry-sponsored

Enquiries to the Secretary, or Information Officer

Subject coverage
asbestos and health; asbestos mining and product manufacture; safety and control

Publications
Asbestos—its Special Attributes and Uses
Asbestos Safety and Control
Asbestos and health: eight publications, various titles
Safety of Buildings Incorporating Asbestos
Factory posters

90 ASBESTOSIS RESEARCH COUNCIL
P.O. Box 40, Rochdale, Lancashire OL12 7EQ Tel. 0706 47422
Research Organization

Enquiries to the Secretary to the Council, or to the Secretary Environmental Control Committee, P.O. Box 18, Cleckheaton, West Yorkshire BD19 3UJ

Subject coverage
all aspects of asbestos and health; dust measurements; control of airborne asbestos environments

Publications
Codes of Practice (for handling and disposal of asbestos materials)
Technical Notes (for measurement and sampling of dusts)
Control and Safety Guides (for applications and manufacturing processes)
Safety posters

ASBESTOSIS RESEARCH FOUNDATION *see* **INSTITUTE OF OCCUPATIONAL MEDICINE**

ASHFIELD DISTRICT LIBRARY *see* **NOTTINGHAMSHIRE COUNTY LIBRARY**

ASHFORD DIVISIONAL LIBRARY *see* **KENT COUNTY LIBRARY**

91 ASHORNE HILL COLLEGE
Ashorne Hill, Leamington Spa, Warwickshire CV33 9QW Tel. 092-685 321
Telex 311750

Management College, Registered Charity and Subsidiary of British Steel Corporation

Enquiries to the Librarian/Information Officer

Subject coverage
management; industrial relations; (some material relates specifically to the British Steel industry)

92 ASHRIDGE MANAGEMENT COLLEGE
Berkhamsted, Hertfordshire HP4 1NS Tel. 044 284 3491
Telex 28604

College of Management Education

Enquiries to the Registrar, the Director of Research, or the Librarian

Subject coverage
behavioural sciences; general management; management science; personnel and industrial relations; finance; marketing; economics; shift working; product development

Publications
Papers in Management Studies

93 ASKHAM BRYAN COLLEGE OF AGRICULTURE AND HORTICULTURE
Askham Bryan, Yorkshire YO2 3PR Tel. 0904 66232
Agricultural College, with Centres at Bedale, Easingwold, Pickering and Guisborough, *q.v.*

Enquiries to the Tutor Librarian

Subject coverage
agriculture, horticulture, landscape technology; homecrafts such as upholstery, corn dollies, spinning, weaving; country crafts such as hedging, stonewalling, ditching, thatching

94 ASLIB
3 Belgrave Square, London SW1X 8PL Tel. 01-235 5050
Telex 23667

Research Association

Enquiries to the Librarian

Subject coverage
all aspects of information management, including: library and information science, documentation, reprography, translations, mechanised systems for information handling; information sources through the Aslib subject-based Groups

Publications
Journal of Documentation (quarterly)
Aslib Proceedings (monthly)
Aslib Information (monthly)
Aslib Booklist (monthly)
Program: news of computers in libraries (quarterly)
Forthcoming International Scientific and Technical Conferences (quarterly)
Technical Translations Bulletin (3 times per annum)
Index to Theses accepted for higher degrees by the Universities of Great Britain and Ireland and the Council for National Academic Awards (semi-annual)
Aslib Directory:
volume 1, information sources in science technology and commerce
volume 2, information sources in medicine, the social sciences and the humanities
Handbook of Special Librarianship

95 ASPHALT AND COATED MACADAM ASSOCIATION LIMITED
25 Lower Belgrave Street, London SW1W 0LS Tel. 01-730 0761
Trade Association, formed by the former Asphalt Roads Association and the former Federation of Coated Macadam Industries; member of the European Asphalt Pavement Association; thus part of an exchange-of-information scheme of twelve national trade associations of asphalt road contractors

Enquiries, technical, to the Technical Officer; others, to the Public Relations Executive

Subject coverage
asphalt; bitumen, macadam and tarmacadam used for paving; commercial and statistical information on the industry, but *not* labour relations or wage rates, etc.

Special collections
bound collections of asphalt & bitumen journals of Denmark, Holland, France, Germany and U.S.A.

Publications
ACMA Newsletter
Queens Highway (or King's Highway as appropriate)

96 ASSOCIATED DAIRIES LIMITED
Craven House, Kirkstall Road, Leeds LS3 1JE Tel. 0532 36151
Company; includes ASDA Stores Limited Telex 556201

Enquiries to the Group Public Relations Officer

Subject coverage
dairy operation; superstore retailing

97 ASSOCIATED ENGINEERING LIMITED
Ince House, 60 Kenilworth Road, Leamington Spa, Warwickshire CV32 6JZ Tel. 0926 21351
Telex 311259
Company and Group of Companies divided into: Bearings Division, Covrad Limited, Cylinder Components Division, Replacement Parts Division, Turbine Components, Group Research and Development Centre

Enquiries to the Group Publicity Manager

Subject coverage
manufacture and distribution of precision mechanical components; bearings; castings; metallic packings and seals; heat exchangers; automobile radiators; heaters and air conditioners; piston and cylinder components; turbine blades

ASSOCIATED INDUSTRIAL CONSULTANTS LIMITED *now* **INBUCON/AIC MANAGEMENT CONSULTANTS LIMITED,** *q.v.*

98 ASSOCIATED LEAD MANUFACTURERS LIMITED
Central Research Laboratories, 7 Wadsworth Road, Perivale, Greenford, Middlesex UB6 7JQ — Tel. 01-997 5635
Company Research Laboratories

Enquiries, by letter, to the Librarian

Subject coverage
Metallurgy of lead and its alloys and antimony; chemistry of compounds of lead, antimony and zirconium; stabilisers for polyvinyl chloride; flameproofing; ceramic colours

99 ASSOCIATED MASTER PLUMBERS AND DOMESTIC ENGINEERS
Longwood, Kenley Lane, Kenley CR2 5DR — Tel. 01-660 3336
Employers Association, affiliated to the National Association of Plumbing, Heating and Mechanical Services Contractors

Enquiries to the Secretary

Subject coverage
the plumbing industry

100 ASSOCIATED OCTEL COMPANY LIMITED
P.O. Box 17, Oil Sites Road, Ellesmere Port, Wirral, Cheshire L65 4HF — Tel. 051-355 3611, Telex 62384

Company

Enquiries to the Information Officer

Subject coverage
motor gasolines; antiknock compounds

Publications
booklets on the use and handling of anti-knock compounds, etc.

101 ASSOCIATED OCTEL COMPANY LIMITED
Engine Laboratory, Watling Street, Bletchley, Milton Keynes MK1 1EZ — Tel. 0908 72611
Company

Enquiries to the Information Officer

Subject coverage
petrol, petrol additives, anti-knock compounds, internal combustion engines, exhaust gas pollution and its prevention

Publications
Exhaust Gas Air Pollution Abstracts (monthly, with annual and five-yearly indexes)
Brief British Passenger Car Data booklet (annual)

ASSOCIATED PLANNING CONSULTANTS *see* **S.B. TIETZ & PARTNERS**

102 ASSOCIATED PORTLAND CEMENT MANUFACTURERS LIMITED
Research Department, Greenhithe, Kent DA9 9JQ — Tel. 0322 842244, Telex 896335

Company, part of the Blue Circle Group

Enquiries to the Librarian

Subject coverage
cement and concrete, chemical engineering, fuel, refractories, clay technology, paints

103 ASSOCIATED SOCIETY OF LOCOMOTIVE ENGINEERS AND FIREMEN
9 Arkwright Road, London NW3 6AB Tel. 01-435 6300 and 2160
01-794 7220

Trade Union

Enquiries to the General Secretary

Subject coverage
conditions of employment of footplate staff on British Railways and trainmen on London Transport

Publication
Locomotive Journal (monthly)

104 ASSOCIATION FOR PROGRAMMED LEARNING AND EDUCATIONAL TECHNOLOGY
33 Queen Anne Street, London W1M 0AL Tel. 01-636 5791
Educational and Training Association, associated with the Network of Programmed Learning Centres; houses the National Committee for Audio-Visual Aids in Education

Enquiries to the Administrator

Subject coverage
educational and instructional technology, programmed learning

Publications
Programmed Learning & Educational Technology (quarterly)
Aspects of Educational Technology (annual conference proceedings)
Educational and Instructional Technology (biennial)

105 ASSOCIATION FOR RADIATION RESEARCH
Department of Pharmacy, The University, Manchester M13 9PL Tel. 061-273 7121 ext. 149
Scientific Association; affiliated to the International Association for Radiation Research

Enquiries to the Honorary Secretary

Subject coverage
radiation physics; radiation chemistry; radiation biology

106 ASSOCIATION FOR SCIENCE EDUCATION
College Lane, Hatfield, Hertfordshire AL10 9AA Tel. 30 67411
Educational Charity

Enquiries to the General Secretary

Subject coverage
science education, primary, secondary and further education; study for its improvement

Publications
School Science Review (quarterly)
Education in Science (5 times per annum)
Occasional Papers
ASE Study Series

107 ASSOCIATION OF ADVERTISERS IN IRELAND LIMITED
44 Lower Leeson Street, Dublin 2 Tel. Dublin 761016
Trade Association, member of International Union of Advertisers Associations

Enquiries to the Administrator

Subject coverage
advertising, its practice and standards; agency services; media conditions

108 ASSOCIATION OF AGRICULTURE
78 Buckingham Gate, London SW1E 6PE Tel. 01-222 6115/6
Educational Charity

Enquiries to the General Secretary

Subject coverage
agriculture and the countryside; (Farm Open Days for the general public)

Publications
Journal (twice per annum)

109 ASSOCIATION OF APPLIED BIOLOGISTS
c/o Department of Agricultural Botany, University College of Wales, Aberystwyth, Dyfed SY23 3DD — Tel. 0970 3111
Learned Society; linked with the Federation of British Plant Pathologists, *q.v.*

Enquiries to the Association

Subject coverage
general biology; plant pathology; plant virology

Publication
Annals of Applied Biology (quarterly)

110 ASSOCIATION OF BEE APPLIANCE MANUFACTURERS OF GREAT BRITAIN
Austin Canons, The Street, Leonard Stanley, Stonehouse, Gloucestershire GL10 3NR — Tel. 045-382 3220
Trade Association, member of the British Beekeepers Association

Enquiries to the Secretary

Subject coverage
appliances for beekeeping

111 ASSOCIATION OF BRITISH CHAMBERS OF COMMERCE
6/14 Dean Farrar Street, London SW1H 0DX — Tel. 01-222 0201
Association of 88 Chambers of Commerce in England, Scotland, Wales and Northern Ireland

Enquiries, for research purposes, from Governmental organizations or from members, to the Association

Subject coverage
current and future operations of British industry; commerce and the economy within a world context

112 ASSOCIATION OF BRITISH DIRECTORY PUBLISHERS
Imperial House, 17 Kingsway, London WC2B 6UN — Tel. 01-836 7111
Trade Association; member of the Periodical Publishers Association and of the European Association of Directory Publishers (Brussels)

Enquiries to the Chairman

Subject coverage
compilation and publication of directories and advertising in directories; problems created by activities of fraudulent directory promoters

Publication
Handbook and List of Members

113 ASSOCIATION OF BRITISH GEODESISTS
c/o Department of Land Surveying, North East London Polytechnic, Forest Road, London E17 4JB — Tel. 01-527 2272
Professional Association

Enquiries to the Secretary

Subject coverage
geodesy

ASSOCIATION OF BRITISH MANUFACTURERS OF MINERAL INSULATING FIBRES *see* **EURISOL-UK**

114 ASSOCIATION OF BRITISH PHARMACEUTICAL INDUSTRY
162 Regent Street, London W1R 6DD Tel. 01-734 9061
Trade Association, associated with the National Association of Pharmaceutical Distributors, *q.v.* and the Office of Health Economics of the same address; affiliated to the Chemical Industries Association Limited

Enquiries to the Information Services (O.H.E. enquiries to the Librarian)

Subject coverage
ABPI: pharmaceutical industry and exports; veterinary products
OHE: economic aspects of medical care; other health and social problems; comparison with other countries

Publications
OHE Studies of Current Health Problems (series)
Reports of OHE Symposia
OHE Information Sheets *and* Briefings
Compendium of Health Statistics
ABPI occasional booklets

115 ASSOCIATION OF BRITISH PICTURE RESTORERS
Berries, Littlewick Green, near Maidenhead. Berkshire SL6 3RA Tel. 062-882 3288
Voluntary Association

Enquiries to the Secretary

Subject coverage
restoration and conservation of paintings, professional training

116 ASSOCIATION OF BRITISH ROOFING FELT MANUFACTURERS LIMITED
London Chamber of Commerce and Industry, 69 Cannon Street, Tel. 01-248 4444
London EC4N 5AB Telex 888941
Trade Association

Enquiries to the Secretary

Subject coverage
roofing felt

ASSOCIATION OF BRITISH SAILMAKERS *see* **SHIP AND BOAT BUILDERS NATIONAL FEDERATION**

ASSOCIATION OF BRITISH TREE SURGEONS AND ARBORISTS *now* **ARBORICULTURAL ASSOCIATION,** *q.v.*

ASSOCIATION OF BRITISH YACHT AGENTS *see* **SHIP AND BOAT BUILDERS NATIONAL FEDERATION**

117 ASSOCIATION OF BRONZE AND BRASS FOUNDERS
136 Hagley Road, Edgbaston, Birmingham B16 9PN Tel. 021-454 4141
Trade Association; member of the British Metal Castings Council

Enquiries to the Secretaries, Heathcote & Coleman, of the above address

Subject coverage
supply of bronze and brass castings for all purposes

Publication
Guide to the Reduction of Metal Losses in Foundries

118 ASSOCIATION OF BUILDERS HARDWARE MANUFACTURERS

5 Greenfield Crescent, Birmingham B15 3BE Tel. 021-454 2177

Trade Association; member of the National Building and Allied Hardware Manufacturers Federation, *q.v.*; houses the Timber Packaging and Pallet Confederation, *q.v.* and the British Institute of Embalmers

Enquiries to the Director

Subject coverage

industrial relations; wages; working conditions; trade information; interpretation of government legislation

ASSOCIATION OF BUILDING TECHNICIANS *now* **UNION OF CONSTRUCTION, ALLIED TRADES AND TECHNICIANS,** *q.v.*

119 ASSOCIATION OF BUTTER BLENDERS AND BUTTER AND CHEESE PACKERS

20 Eastbourne Terrace, London W2 6LE Tel. 01-262 6722
Telex 262027

Trade Association; member of National Association of Creamery Proprietors, and of Dairy Trade Federation

Enquiries to the Secretary

Subject coverage

butter industry consultations with Ministry of Agriculture, Fisheries, and Food, with the Department of Prices and Consumer Protection, with European Trade Association, and with the EEC Commission

120 ASSOCIATION OF CERTIFIED ACCOUNTANTS

22 Bedford Square, London WC1B 3HS Tel. 01-636 2103
Telex 24381

Professional Association; incorporated by Royal Charter; formerly Association of Certified and Corporate Accountants; supporting Irish, Scottish and 42 other district societies; housing the Institute of Accounting Staff; member of the Consultative Committee of Accountancy Bodies, Union Européenne des Experts Comptables Economiques et Financiers, International Co-ordination Committee for the Accountancy Profession and International Accounting Standards Committee

Enquiries,

policy, to the Secretary
general, to the Director of Information
technical, to the Secretary—Technical
membership, to the Secretary—Membership
students, education, training, to the Secretary—Education
post-qualifying training, to the Secretary—Training
examinations, to the Registrar

Subject coverage

accountancy: pre and post qualifying education and examinations; practical training; professional ethics and conduct; members providing general or specialized services

Publications

List of Members
Certified Accountant
Certified Accountants Students Newsletter
Annual Report
Members Handbook
Technical publications

121 ASSOCIATION OF CHEESE PROCESSORS

20 Eastbourne Terrace, London W2 6LE Tel. 01-262 6722
Telex 262027

Trade Association, formerly Processed Cheese Section of Food Manufacturers Federation; member of National Association of Creamery Proprietors and of Dairy Trade Federation

Enquiries to the Secretary

Subject coverage
cheese industry consultations with Ministry of Agriculture, Fisheries, and Food, with European Trade Association and with EEC Commission

ASSOCIATION OF CLINICAL BIOCHEMISTS *see* **ROYAL INSTITUTE OF CHEMISTRY**

122 ASSOCIATION OF CLOTHING CONTRACTORS
22 Osborn Street, London E1 6TE Tel. 01-247 8255
Trade Association

Enquiries to the Secretary

Subject coverage
legislation in connection with the ladies clothing industry, including statutes governing employment, etc.; other matters relating to the making-up side of the industry

123 ASSOCIATION OF CONFERENCE EXECUTIVES
8 St. Johns Street, Huntingdon, Cambridgeshire PE18 6DD Tel. 0480 57595
Conference Association

Enquiries to the Secretary-General

Subject coverage
meetings and conferences

Publication
ACE News

124 ASSOCIATION OF CONSULTING ACTUARIES
Metropolis House, 39/45 Tottenham Court Road, London W1P 0JL Tel. 01-636 7777
Professional Association

Enquiries to the Secretary

Subject coverage
consultancy in retirement benefits and pension arrangements; sickness and hospital benefit schemes; investment policy; financial planning of funds; operational research and other statistical applications; mergers

Publication
List of members and Association's activity

125 ASSOCIATION OF CONSULTING ENGINEERS
Hancock House, 87 Vincent Square, London SW1P 2PH Tel. 01-222 6557
Professional Association, affiliated to the International Federation of Consulting Engineers (FIDIC), the Hague

Enquiries to the Secretary

Subject coverage
engineering consultancy worldwide

Publications
List of Members (annual)
Brochure of Overseas Work entrusted to Members (annual)

126 ASSOCIATION OF CONSULTING ENGINEERS OF IRELAND
22 Clyde Road, Dublin 4 Tel. Dublin 684341
Professional Association, member of CEDIC/European Committee of Engineers and of FIDIC/International Federation of Consulting Engineers

Enquiries to the Secretary

Subject coverage
civil engineering; electrical engineering; heating, ventilating and air conditioning; marine engineering; mechanical engineering; structural engineering; traffic engineering

127 ASSOCIATION OF CONSULTING SCIENTISTS
47 Belgrave Square London SW1X 8QX Tel. 01-235 0640
Voluntary Association/Scientific and Technical Services; including the Testing and Analytical Laboratories Group and comprising over fifty specialist organisations

Enquiries to the Secretary

Subject coverage
consulting, laboratory and research services in physical, and biological sciences and technology; forensic matters, patents, market research, statistical services; analysis and testing; safety; toxicology; materials of all kinds; pollution; mining and all engineering disciplines

Publications
List of Members and Services Offered, includes Code of Practice
Register of Consulting Scientists and Contract Research Organisations (3rd ed., in association with Fulmer Institute)

128 ASSOCIATION OF CONTACT LENS PRACTITIONERS
5 Branksome Way, Kenton, Harrow, Middlesex HA3 9SH Tel. 01-226 8316
Professional Body

Enquiries to the Secretary or Chairman

Subject coverage
contact lens practice

Publications
Newsletter (for members)
Introduction to Contact Lenses

129 ASSOCIATION OF CONTRACTORS IN TELEVISION AND FILM LIGHTING EQUIPMENT
Admin House, Market Square, Leighton Buzzard, Bedfordshire Tel. 05253 75251
Trade Assoication

Enquiries to the Secretary

Subject coverage
television and film lighting contracting

130 ASSOCIATION OF CONTROL MANUFACTURERS
Leicester House, 8 Leicester Street, London WC2H 7BN Tel. 01-437 0678
Trade Association; member of BEAMA, *q.v.*

Enquiries to the Director

Subject coverage
manual and automatic switches; thermal and time controls for household, commercial and industrial uses

131 ASSOCIATION OF COST ENGINEERS
33 Ovington Square, London SW3 1LJ Tel. 01-589 9648
Professional Association

Enquiries to the Honorary Secretary

Subject coverage
engineering estimating; methods of measurement of engineering works; cost indices; cost control systems

Publication
Cost Engineer (bi-monthly)

132 ASSOCIATION OF ELECTRICAL MACHINERY TRADES
24 Ormond Road, Richmond, Surrey Tel. 01-948 4151
Trade Association

Enquiries, in writing, to the Secretary

Subject coverage
repair and reconditioning of industrial electrical machinery; geographic location of members providing these services

ASSOCIATION OF ENGINEERING DISTRIBUTORS *see* **FEDERATION OF WHOLESALE AND INDUSTRIAL DISTRIBUTORS**

133 ASSOCIATION OF EUROPEAN MACHINE TOOL MERCHANTS
2A North End Road, Golders Green, London NW11 7PH Tel. 01-455 3424/5
Telex 923060

Trade Association, formerly British Association of Machine Tool Merchants

Enquiries to the Secretary

Subject coverage
machine tool merchandising: the sources of new and used tools

Publications
Annual Directory
Pocket Serial Number Book of Metalworking Machinery

134 ASSOCIATION OF EXHIBITION ORGANISERS
10 Manchester Square, London W1M 5AB Tel. 01-486 1951
Trade Association

Enquiries to the Director

Subject coverage
exhibitions and trade fairs, U.K. and overseas

ASSOCIATION OF EXHIBITORS AND CONFERENCE MANAGERS LIMITED *now* **NATIONAL ASSOCIATION OF EXHIBITORS,** *q.v.*

135 ASSOCIATION OF EXPORT SUBSCRIPTION NEWSAGENTS
Regent House, 89 Kingsway, London WC2B 6RH Tel. 01-242 3458
Trade Association

Enquiries to the Secretary

Subject coverage
commercial information in the export subscription trade

ASSOCIATION OF FRANCHISED DISTRIBUTORS OF ELECTRONIC COMPONENTS *see* **FEDERATION OF WHOLESALE AND INDUSTRIAL DISTRIBUTORS**

ASSOCIATION OF GLASS CONTAINER MANUFACTURERS *see* **GLASS MANUFACTURERS FEDERATION**

ASSOCIATION OF GREEN CROP DRIERS LIMITED *now* **BRITISH ASSOCIATION OF GREEN CROP DRIERS LIMITED,** *q.v.*

136 ASSOCIATION OF HEAVY TEXTILE PROOFERS OF GREAT BRITAIN
135 Buchanan Street, Glasgow G1 2JQ Tel. 041-221 7236
Trade Association, affiliated to the Canvas Consultative Committee

Enquiries to the Secretary

Subject coverage
heavy textile proofing

137 ASSOCIATION OF HOME ECONOMISTS LIMITED
307 Uxbridge Road, London W3 9QU Tel. 01-992 3532
Professional Association, member of the United Kingdom Federation for Education in Home Economics and therefore of the International Federation of Home Economics

Enquiries to the Honorary Secretary, are directed to specialists

Subject coverage
home economics, careers, qualification, freelance work, etc.

Publications
Newsletter (members only)
Leaflets on careers and training courses, work of home economists in the social services
Money Sense: a guide to budgeting

138 ASSOCIATION OF HYDRAULIC EQUIPMENT MANUFACTURERS LIMITED
54 Warwick Square, London SW1V 2AW Tel. 01-834 0855
Trade Association

Enquiries to the Director

Subject coverage
technical and commercial information in the hydraulic equipment manufacturing industry

Publications
Directory of Members
List of Publications

ASSOCIATION OF INDEPENDENT BUSINESSES *see* **SBA—ASSOCIATION OF INDEPENDENT BUSINESSES**

139 ASSOCIATION OF INDEPENDENT CONTRACT RESEARCH ORGANISATIONS
7 Catherine Place, London SW1E 6EB Tel. 01-834 0292
Trade Association, comprising the Electrical Research Association, the Fulmer Research Institute, the Huntingdon Research Centre, International Research and Development, Inveresk Research International, Ricardo Consulting Engineers and Robertson Research International, *qq.v.*

Enquiries to the particular member firm directly

Subject coverage
refer to the entries for the member firms

ASSOCIATION OF INSPECTORS OF WEIGHTS AND MEASURES *now* **ASSOCIATION OF TRADING STANDARDS OFFICERS,** *q.v.*

140 ASSOCIATION OF INSURANCE BROKERS
157 High Street, Colchester, Essex CO1 1PG Tel. 0206 44343
Trade Association, member of the British Insurance Brokers Association, the United Kingdom Insurance Brokers European Committee and the Bureau International des Producteurs d'Assurances et de Réassurances

Enquiries to the Secretary

Subject coverage
insurance

Publications
Brokers Chronicle
List of Insurance Brokers

ASSOCIATION OF LAND VALUATION ASSESSORS OF SCOTLAND *now* **SCOTTISH ASSESSORS ASSOCIATION,** *q.v.*

141 ASSOCIATION OF MANUFACTURERS ALLIED TO THE ELECTRICAL AND ELECTRONIC INDUSTRY
Leicester House, 8 Leicester Street, London WC2H 7BN Tel. 01-437 0678
Trade Association

Enquiries to the Director

Subject coverage
market or product interests within the electrical industry for which there is no other BEAMA association or section, *e.g.*, cable connectors; emergency lighting

142 ASSOCIATION OF MANUFACTURERS AND SUPPLIERS FOR THE GRAPHIC ARTS
Honeycrock Lane, Salfords, Redhill, Surrey RH1 5LX Tel. 0737 68644
Trade Association

Enquiries to the Secretary

Subject coverage
photomechanical matters relating to films, plates, processes, etc., used in the printing industry for the production of offset and letterpress printing plates and gravure cylinders

143 ASSOCIATION OF MANUFACTURERS OF DOMESTIC ELECTRICAL APPLIANCES (AMDEA)
AMDEA House, 593 Hitchin Road, Stopsley, Luton, Bedfordshire LU4 7UN Tel 0582 411001 Telex 825363
Trade Association, formerly BEAMA Domestic Appliance Division, now independent

Enquiries, trade only, to the Director

Subject coverage
domestic electrical appliance industry, industrial policy, technology, servicing, statistics

Publications
Industry statistics
Code of Practice: appliance servicing

ASSOCIATION OF MANUFACTURING CHEMISTS LIMITED *see* **BRITISH MERCANTILE AGENCY LIMITED**

144 ASSOCIATION OF MARINE ENGINEERING SCHOOLS
Department of Marine Engineering and Communications, Faculty of Maritime and Engineering Studies, Hull College of Higher Education, Queens Gardens, Hull HU1 3DG
Educational Association

Enquiries to the Honorary Secretary

Subject coverage
marine engineering education and training

145 ASSOCIATION OF MASTER UPHOLSTERERS
4 Sutherland Avenue, London W9 2QE Tel. 01-965 3565
Trade Association

Enquiries to the Administrative Secretary

Subject coverage
conditions of employment and general information on the upholstery trade

146 ASSOCIATION OF METAL SPRAYERS
P.O. Box 360, 75 Harborne Road, Birmingham B15 3DH Tel. 021-454 6171 ext. 290
Trade Association

Enquiries to the Secretary

Subject coverage
anti-corrosive coatings; engineering coatings; hardfacing; metal spraying

Publications
Directory of Members
Information Sheets
Symposia papers
Aluminium & Zinc Inspection Guides

147 ASSOCIATION OF MUSICAL INSTRUMENT INDUSTRIES
62 Park View, Hatch End, Pinner, Middlesex HA5 4LN Tel. 01-428 4700
Trade Association; member of the Federation of Wholesale and Industrial Distributors, *q.v.*

Enquiries to the Consultant; not generally accepted from the public

Subject coverage
information on manufacturers, wholesalers and importers; interests of musical instrument retailers

148 ASSOCIATION OF NATIONAL HEALTH SERVICE SUPPLIES OFFICERS
Signal House, Lyon Road, Harrow, Middlesex HA1 2EL Tel. 01-863 9111
Professional Association; formerly National Association of Hospital Supplies Officers

Enquiries to the Honorary Secretary

Subject coverage
sources of supply for hospital equipment; organization of procurement for the National Health Service

Publication
Annual Yearbook

149 ASSOCIATION OF OFFICIAL ARCHITECTS
66 Portland Place, London W1N 4AD Tel. 01-580 5533
Trade Union

Enquiries, by letter only, to the Secretary

Subject coverage
employment conditions and prospects for architects employed by central and local government, health service, and nationalised industries

150 ASSOCIATION OF ORIENTAL CARPET TRADERS OF LONDON
54 Baker Street, London W1M 1DJ Tel. 01-486 5888
Telex 267716

Trade Association

Enquiries to the Secretary

Subject coverage
names and addresses of London wholesale oriental carpet merchants

151 ASSOCIATION OF PATTERNMAKERS AND ALLIED CRAFTSMEN
15 Cleve Road, Hampstead, London NW6 1YA Tel. 01-624 7085
Trade Union

Enquiries to the General Secretary

Subject coverage
trade union services and the engineering industry

Publication
Patternmaker (monthly)

152 ASSOCIATION OF PROFESSIONAL, EXECUTIVE, CLERICAL AND COMPUTER STAFF
22 Worple Road, London SW19 4DF Tel. 01-947 3131/6
Trade Union, formerly Clerical and Administrative Workers Union

Enquiries to Head of Research

Subject coverage
industrial relations; all aspects of employment of white collar staff, including salaries, terms and conditions, legal matters, pensions, holidays, job evaluation

153 ASSOCIATION OF PROFESSIONAL FORESTERS
Brokerswood House, Brokerswood. Westbury, Wiltshire BA13 4EH Tel. 0373 822238
Professional Association

Enquiries to the Secretary

Subject coverage
afforestation; management of forests; matters relating to trees

Publication
Newsletter (quarterly)

154 ASSOCIATION OF PUBLIC ANALYSTS
30 Russell Square, London WC1B 5DT Tel. 01-580 3482
070-18 78749

Professional Association/Limited Company

Enquiries to the Honorary Information Officer, Canynge Hall, Whatley Road, Bristol or to the Honorary Secretary, 18 Hilltop Crescent, Cosham, Portsmouth PO6 1BD

Subject coverage
analysis of, and legal problems relating to food and drugs, medicines, fertilizers and feeding stuffs, toys, enamelware; environmental analysis, toxicology, analytical chemistry, microscopy, water analysis

Publications
Journal of the Association of Public Analysts (quarterly)
Occasional papers on food analysis

ASSOCIATION OF PUBLIC HEALTH INSPECTORS *now* **ENVIRONMENTAL HEALTH OFFICERS ASSOCIATION,** *q.v.*

155 ASSOCIATION OF PUBLIC LIGHTING ENGINEERS
28 Buckingham Court, 78 Buckingham Gate, London SW1E 6PF Tel. 01-834 3655
Professional Association

Enquiries to the Secretary

Subject coverage
public lighting, its science, efficient use, and planning

Publications
Public Lighting (quarterly)
Annual Conference and Exhibition Catalogue
Technical Reports

ASSOCIATION OF RIVER AUTHORITIES *now* **NATIONAL WATER COUNCIL,** *q.v.*

156 ASSOCIATION OF ROAD TRAFFIC SIGN MAKERS
33 Constable Road, Eaton Rise, Norwich NR4 6RW Tel. 0603 51876
Trade Association

Enquiries to the Director

Subject coverage
manufacture of road traffic signs and components

157 ASSOCIATION OF SCIENTIFIC, TECHNICAL AND MANAGERIAL STAFFS
10–26a Jamestown Road, London NW1 7DT Tel. 01-267 4422
Telex 25226

Trade Union

Enquiries to Director of Research

Subject coverage
trade union service in electrical engineering, food, chemicals, oil, textile industry, general engineering, vehicle building, aircraft, steel, glass industry, tobacco, civil airlines, insurance, finance, shipping, tailoring, carpet manufacturing, rubber industry, metal manufacture, computer industries

Publications
Finance News
Quarterly Economic Review
Union Journal

158 ASSOCIATION OF SEA AND AIR PORT HEALTH AUTHORITIES
Health Department, P.O. Box 270, Guildhall, London EC2P 2EJ Tel. 01-606 3030
Health Organization

Enquiries to the Honorary Secretary

Subject coverage
public health legislation, etc., relating to sea ports and air ports; standards of administration of health matters in connection with air port, sea port, and riparian areas; international cooperation in port health administration

159 ASSOCIATION OF SHELL BOILERMAKERS
Spicer and Pegler (Secretaries), P.O. Box 498, 12 Booth Street, Manchester M6O 2ED Tel. 061-236 9721
Trade Association

Enquiries, other than statistical, to the Secretaries

Subject coverage
shell boilers; water treatment

Publications
ASB Review (2 per annum, confidential)
Treatment of Water for Shell Boilers (book)

160 ASSOCIATION OF STREET LIGHTING ERECTION CONTRACTORS
140 Sloane Street, London SW1X 9AY Tel. 01-730 0341
Trade Association

Enquiries to the Secretary

Subject coverage
street lighting

Publication
Code of Practice for the Erection of Street Lighting Equipment

161 ASSOCIATION OF SUPERVISORY AND EXECUTIVE ENGINEERS
Wix Hill House, West Horsley, Surrey KT24 6DZ Tel. 0483 222383
Professional Association; formerly Association of Supervising Electrical Engineers; affiliated to the Electrical Power Engineers Association

Enquiries, from members only, to the Technical Secretary

Subject coverage
engineering and engineering management

Publications
Executive Engineer *incorporating* The Electrical Supervisor
ASEE Illustrated Guide to the IEE Regulations for the Electrical Equipment of Buildings.
ASEE Year Book and Technical Guide (annual)
Lending Library Catalogue.

ASSOCIATION OF TAR DISTILLERS *now* **BRITISH TAR INDUSTRY ASSOCIATION,** *q.v.*

162 ASSOCIATION OF TOY AND FANCY GOODS FACTORS AND IMPORTERS
69 Cannon Street, London EC4N 5AB Tel. 01-248 4444
Trade Association

Enquiries accepted from members only

Subject coverage
toys, fancy goods

163 ASSOCIATION OF TOY AND FANCY GOODS WHOLESALERS
41 Tothill Street, London SW1H 9LG Tel. 01-930 6524
Trade Association

Enquiries to the Secretary, normally from members only

Subject coverage
manufacturers and sources of supply

164 ASSOCIATION OF TRADING STANDARDS OFFICERS
Abberley House, Granhams Road, Great Shelford, Cambridgeshire Tel. 022-04 3367
Professional Association, formerly Association of Inspectors of Weights and Measures

Enquiries to the Honorary Secretary

Subject coverage
professional standing of officers in consumer protection and trading standards departments of local authorities

165 ASSOCIATION OF UNDERWATER CONTRACTORS
First Floor, 251 Brompton Road, London SW3 2EP Tel. 01-584 5552
Trade Association

Enquiries to the Secretary

Subject coverage
diving operations for civil engineering, and salvage

166 ASSOCIATION OF WATER OFFICERS LIMITED
15 Market Place, South Shields, Tyne & Wear NE33 1JQ Tel. 08-943 63882
Professional Association, formerly Association of Waterworks Officers Ltd.

No enquiry service

Subject coverage
water supply

Publication
AWO Journal (quarterly)

ASSOCIATION OF WHOLESALE WOOLLEN MERCHANTS LIMITED *see* **FEDERATION OF WHOLESALE AND INDUSTRIAL DISTRIBUTORS**

167 ASSOCIATION OF X-RAY EQUIPMENT MANUFACTURERS
Leicester House, 8 Leicester Street, London WC2 7BN Tel. 01-437 0678
Telex 263536
Trade Association; formerly X-ray Apparatus Division of the Control and Automation Manufacturers Association, affiliated to BEAMA, *q.v.*

Enquiries to the Director

Subject coverage
commerce and technology of the X-ray apparatus field

Publications
specifications, standards, guides

168 ASTBURY DEPARTMENT OF BIOPHYSICS
Leeds University, Leeds LS2 9JT Tel. 0532 31751 ext. 6130
University Department

Enquiries to the Head of Department

Subject coverage
three-dimensional structure of proteins and other biological macromolecules; relationship between molecular structure and biological function; biological structure at the cellular level and its interpretation in terms of molecular assembly; physical techniques for the study of molecular structure, including X-ray crystallography, electron microscopy and spectroscopy

169 ASTON COLLEGE
Mold Road, Wrexham, Clwyd Tel. 0978 56601-5
College of Higher Education, of the North East Wales Institute of Higher Education; formerly Wrexham Technical College and Denbighshire Technical College

Enquiries to the Librarian

Subject coverage
engineering; business studies; building; catering

170 ASTON in BIRMINGHAM, UNIVERSITY
Department of Civil Engineering, Gosta Green, Birmingham B4 7ET Tel. 021-359 3611
University Department

Enquiries to the Information Officer

Subject coverage
geotechnical engineering; water resources; fluid mechanics; remote sensing; transportation; highway materials and construction

Publication
List of Research Activities

171 ASTON in BIRMINGHAM, UNIVERSITY LIBRARY
Gosta Green, Birmingham B4 7ET Tel. 021-359 3611
Telex 336997
University Library. The University houses the Biodeterioration Information Centre and the Wolfson Heat Treatment Centre, *qq.v.*

Enquiries to the University Librarian

Subject coverage
applied psychology; architectural planning and urban studies; biological sciences; building; chemical engineering; chemistry; civil engineering; computer studies; electrical engineering and electronics; geophysical sciences; management; mathematics; mechanical engineering; metallurgy; ophthalmic optics; pharmacy; physics; production engineering; safety and hygiene

Special collection
British Standard Specifications

Publications
List of Theses

ASTON IN BIRMINGHAM UNIVERSITY *see also*
ASTON TECHNICAL MANAGEMENT AND PLANNING SERVICES LIMITED
BIODETERIORATION INFORMATION CENTRE
WOLFSON HEAT TREATMENT CENTRE

172 ASTON TECHNICAL, MANAGEMENT & PLANNING SERVICES LIMITED
Alexander Parkes Building, 200 Aston Brook Street, Birmingham B6 4SY Tel. 021-359 4647/8/9
Company, within University of Aston in Birmingham; formerly Small Business Centre

Enquiries to the Director

Subject coverage
management development and training; management consultancy; prototype development; building; chemical engineering; civil engineering; electrical and electronic engineering; mechanical engineering; metallurgy; production engineering including metrology; biology including biodeterioration; computing; chemistry; pharmacy; physics; environmental planning; safety and health in industry

Publications
Study of Terotechnological Practices of Small Firms
West Midlands Automotive Component Industry
Industrial Training Act and Management Training

173 ASTRONOMICAL SOCIETY OF EDINBURGH
City Observatory, Calton Hill, Edinburgh EH7 5AA Tel. 031-447 2381
Registered Charity

Enquiries to the Director

Subject coverage
teaching of astronomy

Special collection
antiquarian astronomical telescopes and clocks

Publications
Occasional Papers

174 W.S. ATKINS GROUP LIMITED
Woodcote Grove, Ashley Road, Epsom, Surrey KT18 5BW Tel. 03727 26140
Telex 23497

Company, Consulting Engineers

Enquiries to the Librarian

Subject coverage
engineering: civil, structural, mechanical, offshore, electrical; mining; metallurgy; heating and ventilating; architecture; landscape planning; town planning; environmental studies including noise, air, water pollution; planning including transportation, financial, management, computing; quality control; non-destructive testing

175 ATLANTIC SALMON RESEARCH TRUST LIMITED
Morley House, 29 South Street, Farnham, Surrey GU9 7RE Tel. 02513 24400
Voluntary organisation

Enquiries to the Director

Subject coverage
North Atlantic salmon and sea-trout: environment, biology, control of fishing, methods of exploitation and their levels; management of salmon fisheries

Publications
Newsletters, which include research projects lists

ATLAS COMPUTING DIVISION LABORATORY *see* **RUTHERFORD LABORATORY**

176 ATOMIC ENERGY RESEARCH ESTABLISHMENT
Harwell, Didcot, Oxfordshire OX11 0R Tel. 0235 24141 ext. 2032/2252
Telex 83135

Government Research Establishment, of the United Kingdom Atomic Energy Authority; Headquarters of the Research Group; Service Centres at Harwell are: the Hazardous Materials Service, the Heat Transfer and Fluid Flow Service, the Materials Technology Bureau, the Non-Destructive Testing Centre, the Separation Processes Service, and the Marine Technology Support Unit, *qq.v.*

Enquiries, preferably by letter, to the Information Officer or Librarian

Subject coverage
Nuclear science and technology, particularly in support of the UK nuclear power programme, and associated material sciences. This embraces: nuclear physics; reactor science and technology, metallurgy, ceramics and materials generally; non-destructive testing; isotope technology; chemical engineering, heat transfer, fluid flow, separation processes; theoretical physics; health physics and medicine; environmental science, pollution, hazardous materials; inorganic and analytical chemistry; particle accelerators; radiation effects; mathematics, computers; contract research

Publications
Harwell Reports and Memoranda (H.M.S.O. or open literature)
Harwell Information Bulletin (weekly)
UKAEA List of publications (monthly, free)

ATOMIC ENERGY RESEARCH ESTABLISHMENT *see also*
HAZARDOUS MATERIALS SERVICE
HEAT TRANSFER AND FLUID FLOW SERVICE
MARINE TECHNOLOGY SUPPORT UNIT
MATERIALS TECHNOLOGY BUREAU
NON-DESTRUCTIVE TESTING CENTRE
SEPARATION PROCESSES SERVICE
WASTE MANAGEMENT INFORMATION BUREAU

177 ATOMIC WEAPONS RESEARCH ESTABLISHMENT
Aldermaston, Reading, Berkshire RG7 4PR Tel. 073-56 4111
Telex 848104/5
Government Department, of the Procurement Executive, Ministry of Defence, to which it was transferred from the United Kingdom Atomic Energy Authority; having a Branch at Foulness, Southend; and housing the Mass Spectrometry Data Centre, *q.v.*

Enquiries, 'unclassified' only, to the Chief Librarian

Subject coverage
science, technology and engineering supporting the Establishment's programme

Publications
Research Reports (on sale, from H.M.S.O.)
Mass Spectrometry Data Bulletin (from the Data Centre)

178 ATV NETWORK LTD
Elstree Studios, Eldon Avenue, Borehamwood, Hertfordshire WD6 1JF Tel. 01-953 6100
Public Company, part of Associated Television Corporation

Enquiries to the Librarian

Subject coverage
television; television engineering; theatre and entertainment

Special collection
black-and-white photograph collection

179 AUDIO VISUAL LANGUAGE ASSOCIATION
97 Heslington Road, York YO1 5AX
Association of Language Teachers; member of the Joint Council of Language Associations

Enquiries to the Honorary Secretary

Subject coverage
language teaching; applied linguistics

Publication
Audio-Visual Language Journal (3 times per annum)

180 AUSTRALIAN AND NEW ZEALAND MERCHANTS AND SHIPPERS ASSOCIATION
Town Hall Chambers, 32/34 Borough High Street, London SE1 1XU Tel. 01-403 0601
Trade Association, having a reciprocal affiliation with the British Shippers Council

Enquiries (trade) to the Secretary

Subject coverage
export to Australia and New Zealand

Publications
Annual Report
Freight Amendments

181 AUTOMATIC VENDING ASSOCIATION OF BRITAIN
50 Eden Street, Kingston-upon-Thames, Surrey KT1 1EE Tel. 01-549 7311
Trade Association

Enquiries to the Information Officer

Subject coverage
availability and suitability of automatic vending machines systems for catering or retailing services

Publications
Booklet on vending
Annual Membership List/Buyers Guide

AUTOMOTIVE DESIGN ADVISORY UNIT *see* **INSTITUTE OF SOUND AND VIBRATION RESEARCH**

182 AUTOMOTIVE PRODUCTS LIMITED
Tachbrook Road, Leamington Spa, Warwickshire CV31 3ER Tel. 0926 27000
Telex 31518

Company, formerly Lockheed Hydraulic Brake Company Limited

Enquiries to the Information Officer

Subject coverage
brakes; clutches; automatic gearboxes; aircraft hydraulics; industrial hydraulics; filters

Publications
Product catalogues

183 AVERY RESEARCH ADMINISTRATION LIMITED
Alan Pond House, 366–370 Soho Road, Handsworth, Birmingham B21 9QL Tel. 021-523 9296
Company, part of Averys Limited

Enquiries to the Information Officer

Subject coverage
weighing machines; materials testing machines; petrol pumps; posture seating; shopfitting

184 AVICULTURAL SOCIETY
20 Bourdon Street, London W1X 9HX
Scientific Society/Charity

Enquiries to the Information Officer

Subject coverage
aviculture; identification of species of birds; study and breeding of British and foreign birds in the wild and in captivity

Special collection
Avicultural Library, housed at the Linnaean Society

Publication
Avicultural Magazine (quarterly, free to members, or by subscription)

185 AVON COUNTY LIBRARY
Headquarters, Avon House, P.O. Box 11, The Haymarket, Bristol BS99 7DE Tel. 0272 29077
Public Library Service; Regional District Libraries at Bristol, *q.v.*, Bath, *q.v.*, Yate (Kingswood/Northavon) and Weston-super-Mare

Enquiries to the Librarians

Subject coverage
general

186 AVON RUBBER COMPANY LIMITED
P.O. Box 2, Melksham, Wiltshire SN12 8AA Tel. 0225 703101 ext. 231 or 239
Telex 44142

Company

Enquiries to the Manager, Information and Library Service

Subject coverage
rubber technology, chemistry and physics; polymer chemistry and physics; management

Publication
Printed catalogue of books (loose-leaf, classified)

AYLESBURY DIVISIONAL LIBRARY *see* **BUCKINGHAMSHIRE COUNTY LIBRARY**

187 AYR TECHNICAL COLLEGE
Dam Park, Ayr KA8 0EU Tel. 0292 65184/5
Technical College

Enquiries to the Librarian

Subject coverage
general

AYRSHIRE COUNTY LIBRARY *now* **KYLE AND CARRICK DISTRICT COUNCIL LIBRARY SERVICES,** *q.v.*

188 BABCOCK AND WILCOX (OPERATIONS) LIMITED
165 Great Dover Street, London SE1 4YB Tel. 01-407 8383
Telex 884151/2/3

Company; an associated Research Station at Renfrew, *q.v.*

Enquiries to the Librarian

Subject coverage
conventional and nuclear boilers; steam generation and allied subjects

189 BABCOCK AND WILCOX (OPERATIONS) LIMITED
Research Station, Renfrew PA4 8UW Tel. 041-886 2201 *and* 3704
Telex 779072

Company; member of Babcock & Wilcox Limited, Power and Process Engineering Group

Enquiries to the Librarian

Subject coverage
power and process engineering, but no special resources

190 BACUP PUBLIC LIBRARY
St James Square, Bacup, Lancashire OL13 9AH Tel. 070-683 3324
Public Library, part of the Lancashire Library, and District Branch in the Rossendale District

Enquiries to the Librarian

Subject coverage
specialist subjects include environmental hygiene; food and drug control; sanitation; aircraft equipment and instruments; leather and fur industries; manufacture of leather goods; cemetery planning

191 BAKELITE XYLONITE LIMITED
8 Grafton Street, London W1A 2LR Tel. 01-629 8100
Telex 22201

Manufacturing Company, subsidiary of Union Carbide Corporation (USA)

Enquiries to the Communications Officer

Subject coverage
plastics raw materials, specifically polyethylene and thermosetting materials; decorative laminates; plastics packaging; framed plastics; plastics film

Publications
Technical Data Sheets
Product catalogues

192 G.G. BAKER AND ASSOCIATES
54 Quarry Street, Guildford, Surrey GU1 3UF Tel. 048-68 6653
Partnership; providing Secretariat and information resources for the Microfilm Association of Great Britain, *q.v.*

Enquiries to the Senior Partner (complex enquiries may involve fees)

Subject coverage
micrographics, including computer output microfilm

Publications
Guide to Computer Output Microfilm, 2 vols
Guide to Microfilm Readers and Reader Printers
Guide to the Production of Microforms
VAT Record Storage on Microfilm
Slides and Notes for Introduction to Microfilm
Slides and Notes for Cost of C.O.M.
Slides and Notes for Access Methods for Microfilm Systems

193 BAKERS UNION
Stanborough House, Great North Road, Stanborough, Welwyn Garden City, Hertfordshire AL8 7TA Tel. 30 60150
Trade Union

Enquiries to the Secretary

Subject coverage
bakery, confectionery, meat pie and biscuit industry

Publication
Bakery Worker

194 HENRY BALFOUR & COMPANY LIMITED
Leven, Fife KY8 4RW Tel. 033-32 23500
Company; member of Sybron Corporation U.S.A.

Enquiries to the Information Officer/Librarian

Subject coverage
chemical engineering

BALFOUR AND NEWTON LIBRARIES *see* **CAMBRIDGE UNIVERSITY Department of Zoology**

195 BALFOUR BEATTY ENGINEERING LIMITED
Information Centre, Marlowe House, Station Road, Sidcup, Kent DA15 7AU Tel. 01-300 3355 Telex 25588
Company, of the Balfour Beatty Group, formerly Engineering and Power Development Consultants Limited and EPDC Limited

Enquiries to the Information Services Manager

Subject coverage
power developments, hydro, nuclear, fossil fuels; civil, mechanical, electrical and process engineering consultancy; mineral and metals developments; hydraulics; tidal power and hydro schemes; design and setting up of overseas libraries/information units

Publications
Bibliographies
Group Serials List
Group Information Manual

BALHAM PUBLIC LIBRARY *see* **WANDSWORTH PUBLIC LIBRARIES**

BAMEX LIMITED *see* **BRITISH ARTMETAL MANUFACTURING EXPORT GROUP**

BANBURY DISTRICT LIBRARY *see* **OXFORDSHIRE COUNTY LIBRARIES**

BANFF COUNTY LIBRARY *see* **NORTH EAST OF SCOTLAND LIBRARY SERVICE**

196 BANK OF ENGLAND
Threadneedle Street, London EC2R 8AH — Tel. 01-601 4444, Telex 885001

Central Bank

Enquiries to the Librarian

Subject coverage
U.K. and overseas banking and financial economics; history of British banking

Special collections
collections include United Kingdom 17th-19th century economic tracts and 19th century government reports in banking and finance; sets include Acts of Parliament from 1693 and the Course of the Exchange (Castaing, Shergold, Lutyens and Wetenhall) from 1698-1898.

Publications
Bank of England Report (annual)
Bank of England Quarterly Bulletin
Bank of England Statistical Abstracts (no. 1 1970, no. 2 1975)

BANK OF LONDON & SOUTH AMERICA LIMITED *now* **LLOYDS BANK INTERNATIONAL LIMITED,** *q.v.*

197 BANKING INFORMATION SERVICE
10 Lombard Street, EC3V 9AR — Tel. 01-626 8486, Telex 888364

Trade Association; affiliated to the Committee of London Clearing Bankers and the Committee of Scottish Clearing Bankers; includes the Bank Education Service

Enquiries to the Information Service

Subject coverage
domestic banking policy and practice

198 BARBOUR INDEX LIMITED
New Lodge, Drift Road, Windsor, Berkshire SL4 4RQ — Tel. 03447 4121
Company

Enquiries to the Research, Records, or Marketing Managers

Subject coverage
design, editorial and production of formulated technical product data, computer stored and retrieved, or otherwise; information distribution techniques, sophisticated and manual; building materials product information

Special collection
complete trade literature collection of building products and materials

Publications
Catalogue and Data Sheet for manufacturers
Product Journal
Comprehensive Index
Compendium of Building Products, U.K., Canada, S. Africa, individually

199 BARCLAYS BANK INTERNATIONAL LIMITED
Group Economic Intelligence Unit, Barclays House, Poole, Dorset BH15 2BB — Tel. 020-13 71212, Telex 417221/3

Bank; the Unit was formerly known as Barclays Bank Limited Economic Intelligence Department

Enquiries, from Bank customers, to the Librarian

Subject coverage
economics; industries; banking; finance; international trade; European Community law

Special collection
European Community Documentation Centre (Tel. 01-283 8989)

200 BARING BROTHERS AND COMPANY LIMITED
88 Leadenhall Street, London EC2A 3DT — Tel. 01-588 2830, Telex 883622

Merchant Bank

Enquiries to the Librarian

Subject coverage
banking

201 BARKING COLLEGE OF TECHNOLOGY
Dagenham Road, Romford, Essex RM7 0XU — Tel. 70 66841 ext. 39
College of Further Education; formerly Rush Green Technical College; includes an Industrial Liaison Centre

Enquiries to the Librarian

Subject coverage
construction; science and mathematics; printing and design; engineering; bakery; business studies

202 BARKING PUBLIC LIBRARIES
Central Library, Axe Street, Barking, Essex IG11 7NB — Tel. 01-594 9135/9, Telex 897605

Public Library

Enquiries to the Reference Librarian

Subject coverage
general; journalism, publishing and newspapers

Publication
Barking Record (quarterly)

203 BARNET LIBRARY SERVICES
Ravensfield House, The Burroughs, Hendon, London NW4 4BE — Tel. 01-202 5625, Telex 25665

Public Library

Enquiries to the Borough Librarian

Subject coverage
general

204 BARNSLEY COLLEGE OF TECHNOLOGY
Church Street, Barnsley, Yorkshire S70 2AN — Tel. 0226 84066
College of Technology

Enquiries to the Librarian

Subject coverage
engineering; mining; commerce; management; construction; sciences

205 BARNSLEY METROPOLITAN BOROUGH CENTRAL LIBRARY
Shambles Street, Barnsley, South Yorkshire S70 2JF — Tel. 0226 83241, Telex 547369

Public Library

Enquiries to the Librarian

Subject coverage
general

206 BARNSTAPLE CENTRAL LIBRARY
The Square, Barnstaple, Devonshire EX32 8LN — Tel. 0271 2813, Telex 46214

Public Library; the North Devon Area Library of the Devon Library Services, *q.v.*

Enquiries to the Area Librarian

Subject coverage
general

207 BARROW-IN-FURNESS PUBLIC LIBRARY
Ramsden Square, Barrow-in-Furness, Cumbria Tel. 0229 20650
Telex 65240
Public Library, part of Cumbria County Library and its main technical information service
Enquiries to the Librarian
Subject coverage
general technical and commercial subjects

BASEEFA *see* **BRITISH APPROVALS SERVICE FOR ELECTRICAL EQUIPMENT IN FLAMMABLE ATMOSPHERES**

208 BASINGSTOKE LIBRARY
19/20 Westminster House, Potters Walk, Basingstoke, Tel. 0256 3901/2
Hampshire RG21 1LS Telex 858391
Public Library; Branch of Hampshire County Library, *q.v.*
Enquiries to the Librarian
Subject coverage
general
Special collection
British Standards

209 BASINGSTOKE TECHNICAL COLLEGE
Worting Road, Basingstoke, Hampshire RG21 1TN Tel. 0256 65551
College of Further Education
Enquiries to the Librarian
Subject coverage
engineering; building; business studies; catering; general
Special Collection
British Standards

BASSETLAW DISTRICT LIBRARY *see* **NOTTINGHAMSHIRE COUNTY LIBRARY**

210 BATH REFERENCE LIBRARY
18 Queen Square, Bath, Somerset BA1 2HN Tel. 0225 28144
Public Library; formerly Bath Municipal Library, now part of Avon County Library system
Enquiries to the Reference Librarian
Subject coverage
public health; water supply; domestic sanitation

211 BATH TECHNICAL COLLEGE
Avon Street, Bath, Avon BA1 1UP Tel. 0225 64191
College of Further Education
Enquiries to the Principal
Subject coverage
electrical and mechanical engineering; construction industries; catering; management

212 BATH UNIVERSITY LIBRARY
Claverton Down, Bath, Somerset BA2 7AY Tel. 0225 6941
University Library; houses the Library of Bath, West and Southern Agricultural Society
Enquiries to the Librarian
Subject coverage
science and technology

Special collection
Pitman Collection (history of orthography and shorthand)

Publication
Research projects

BATH UNIVERSITY *see also* **WOLFSON MOBILE RADIO PROJECT**

BATHGATE TECHNICAL COLLEGE *now* **WEST LOTHIAN COLLEGE OF FURTHER EDUCATION,** *q.v.*

BATLEY DISTRICT LIBRARY *see* **KIRKLEES LIBRARIES AND MUSEUMS SERVICE**

213 BATTELLE INSTITUTE LIMITED
15 Hanover Square, London W1R 9AJ Tel. 01-493 0184
Telex 23773

Company, Subsidiary of Battelle Memorial Institute, Columbus, Ohio, U.S.A.; operating not-for-profit; associated laboratories in Frankfurt and Geneva

Enquiries to the Administrative Assistant

Subject coverage
scientific research and development in the physical, life, and behavioural sciences

Publications
Report and Annual Review
Information upon the laboratories' activities
Battelle Information (quarterly, published in Germany)

BATTERSEA DISTRICT LIBRARY *see* **WANDSWORTH PUBLIC LIBRARIES**

214 BBA GROUP LIMITED
P.O. Box 20, Whitechapel Road, Cleckheaton, West Yorkshire BD19 6HP Tel. 0274 874444
Telex 51106

Company

Enquiries to the Librarian

Subject coverage
automotive industry; materials technology, materials handling; management; mining; industrial medicine, personnel and welfare; data processing and computers; statistics

BBC *see* **BRITISH BROADCASTING CORPORATION**

215 BCIRA (BRITISH CAST IRON RESEARCH ASSOCIATION)
Alvechurch, Birmingham B48 7QB Tel. 073-92 66414
Telex 337125

Research Association

Enquiries to the Head of Information Services and Librarian

Subject coverage
cast iron; foundry industry

Publication
Abstracts of Foundry Literature

BDH PHARMACEUTICALS LIMITED *now* **DUNCAN, FLOCKHART AND COMPANY LIMITED,** *q.v.*

216 BEAMA (BRITISH ELECTRICAL AND ALLIED MANUFACTURERS ASSOCIATION LIMITED)
Leicester House, 8 Leicester Street, London WC2H 7BN Tel. 01-437 0678
Telex 263536
Trade Association; a federation of fifteen associations; other (independent) organizations resident in Leicester House are the British Compressed Air Society, Electronic Engineering Association, *q.v.* National Association of Lift Makers, *q.v.*

Enquiries normally to the Federated Association appropriate to the subject concerned; or, from members only, to the BEAMA communications department

Subject coverage
see the subject areas given under the titles of the federated associations; contract conditions; contract price adjustment; materials; standards

Publications
BEAMA Handbook (annual)
BEAMA Buyers Guide to the products and services of the Electrical and Electronic Industry

BEAMA *see also*
ASSOCIATION OF CONTROL MANUFACTURERS
ASSOCIATION OF MANUFACTURERS ALLIED TO THE ELECTRICAL AND ELECTRONIC INDUSTRY
ASSOCIATION OF X-RAY EQUIPMENT MANUFACTURERS
BEAMA METER ASSOCIATION
BEAMA TRANSMISSION AND DISTRIBUTION ASSOCIATION
BRITISH ELECTRICAL SYSTEMS ASSOCIATION
CONTROL AND AUTOMATION MANUFACTURERS ASSOCIATION
ELECTRICAL AND ELECTRONIC INSULATION ASSOCIATION
ELECTRICAL INSTALLATION EQUIPMENT MANUFACTURERS ASSOCIATION LIMITED
INDUSTRIAL CLEANING MACHINE MANUFACTURERS ASSOCIATION
POWER GENERATION ASSOCIATION
ROTATING ELECTRICAL MACHINES ASSOCIATION
SCIENTIFIC INSTRUMENT MANUFACTURERS ASSOCIATION OF GREAT BRITAIN
WATER-TUBE BOILERMAKERS ASSOCIATION
WELDING MANUFACTURERS ASSOCIATION

217 BEAMA METER ASSOCIATION
Leicester House, 8 Leicester Street, London WC2H 7BN Tel. 01-437 0678
Trade Association; member of BEAMA, *q.v.*

Enquiries to the Director

Subject coverage
all classes of a.c. integrating electricity meters

218 BEAMA TRANSMISSION AND DISTRIBUTION ASSOCIATION
Leicester House, 8 Leicester Street, London WC2H 7BN Tel. 01-437 0678
Trade Association; member of BEAMA, *q.v.*

Enquiries to the Director

Subject coverage
technical and commercial matters relating to power switchgear; industrial switchgear and associated equipment; power transformers; capacitors; instrument transformers; protective gear and relays

219 BEATSON INSTITUTE FOR CANCER RESEARCH
Wolfson Laboratory for Molecular Pathology, Garscube Estate, Switchback Road, Bearsden, Glasgow G61 1BD Tel. 041-942 9361
Independent Research Institute

Enquiries to the Director

Subject coverage
molecular biology; somatic cell genetics; molecular pathology; cancer research

Publication
Biennial Report

220 F.E. BEAUMONT LIMITED
480–482 Rathgar Road, London SW9 7ER Tel. 01-274 4066
Telex 25837

Company

Enquiries to the Director

Subject coverage
industrial stack chimneys, design, fabrication and erection; gas solids collection

BEBINGTON AREA LIBRARY *see* **WIRRAL PUBLIC LIBRARIES**

BECKENHAM DISTRICT LIBRARY *see* **BROMLEY PUBLIC LIBRARIES**

BECTIS *see* **BELL COLLEGE OF TECHNOLOGY**

221 BEDALE AGRICULTURAL CENTRE
Benkhill Drive, Bedale, Darlington DL8 2EA
Agricultural Centre

Enquiries to the Head of the Centre

Subject coverage
home economics and country crafts

222 BEDFORD CENTRAL LIBRARY
Harpur Street, Bedford, Bedfordshire MK40 1PG Tel. 0234 50931
Public Library; formerly Bedford Public Library; now the North Bedfordshire District Library of the Bedfordshire County Library system

Enquiries to the District Librarian

Subject coverage
general and commercial

223 BEDFORD COLLEGE
Regents Park, London NW1 4NS Tel. 01-486 4400
University Institution, of the University of London

Enquiries to the Librarian

Subject coverage
biochemistry; botany; chemistry; geography; biology; mathematics; physics; physiology; zoology

Special collection
Library of the Remote Sensing Society

224 BEDFORDSHIRE COUNTY LIBRARY
County Hall, Bedford MK42 9AP Tel. 0234 56181
Telex 82244

Public Library, with District Libraries at Bedford and Luton, *qq.v.*

Enquiries to the County Librarian

Subject coverage
subject specialization in aeronautics; agricultural technology; automobile engineering

BEE RESEARCH ASSOCIATION *now* **INTERNATIONAL BEE RESEARCH ASSOCIATION,** *q.v.*

225 BEECHAM PHARMACEUTICALS RESEARCH DIVISION
Brockham Park, Betchworth, Surrey RH3 7AJ Tel. 939 3202
Company Research Division, formerly Beecham Research Laboratories

Enquiries to the Information Officer or Librarian

Subject coverage
organic chemistry; medicine; pharmacy; pharmacology; biology; biochemistry; physical chemistry; chemical engineering

226 BEECHAM PHARMACEUTICALS RESEARCH DIVISION
Coldharbour Road, Fourth Avenue, The Pinnacles, Harlow, Essex CM9 5AD — Tel. 0279 32131
Company Research Division; formerly Beecham Research Division
Enquiries to the Librarian or Information Officer
Subject coverage
medicinal research
Publication
Safety Bulletin

227 BEECHAM PHARMACEUTICALS RESEARCH DIVISION
Clarendon Road, Worthing, Sussex BN14 8QH — Tel. 0903 39900, Telex 87418
Company Research Division, formerly Beecham Research Laboratories
Enquiries to the Information Officer or Librarian
Subject coverage
pharmaceutical chemistry; chemistry; medicine; microbiology

228 BEECHAM PHARMACEUTICALS RESEARCH DIVISION
Nutritional Research Centre, Walton Oaks, Dorking Road, Tadworth, Surrey KT20 7NT — Tel. 01-823 2444
Company Research Centre, formerly Beecham Research Laboratories, and, before that, Vitamins Limited
Enquiries to the Librarian
Subject coverage
animal feedstuffs; nutritional biochemistry

229 BEECHAM PRODUCTS RESEARCH DEPARTMENT
Randalls Road, Leatherhead, Surrey KT22 7RX — Tel. 53 77601
Company Research Department
Enquiries to the Manager, Information Services
Subject coverage
cosmetics; toiletries; food and drink; proprietary medicines

230 BELFAST CENTRAL LIBRARY
Royal Avenue, Belfast, Northern Ireland BT1 1EA — Tel. 0232 43233, Telex 747359
Public Library; Headquarters of the Belfast Education and Library Board
Enquiries to the Librarian
Subject coverage
general

231 BELFAST HARBOUR COMMISSIONERS
Harbour Office, Corporation Square, Belfast BT1 3AL — Tel. 0232 34422, Telex 74204
Port Authority
Enquiries to the Commercial Manager
Subject coverage
port facilities and statistics

232 BELFAST MARINE ENGINEERING EMPLOYERS ASSOCIATION
Queens Road, Belfast BT3 9DU Tel. 0232 58456
Employers Association; member of the Engineering Employers Federation, London *q.v.*

Enquiries to the Secretary

Subject coverage
industrial relations in the marine engineering industry; scientific, technical or commercial information only by courtesy and permission of separate members

BELFAST UNIVERSITY *see* **QUEENS UNIVERSITY OF BELFAST**

233 BELGIAN EMBASSY
103 Eaton Square, London SW1W 9AB Tel. 01-235 5422
Diplomatic Mission; heads or is associated with Belgian and Anglo-Belgian organizations in London, notably the Belgian Chamber of Commerce, the Anglo-Belgian Centre, the Belgian Tourist Office

Enquiries, educational or private, to the Information Section

Subject coverage
general (no market research information)

Publications
Bulletin of Belgian Cultural Events in Great Britain (6 times per annum)
N.B. The Belgian National Tourist Office
and the Belgian Chamber of Commerce each issue Bulletins

234 BELL & HOWELL LIMITED
Alperton House, Bridgewater Road, Wembley HA0 1EG Tel. 01-902 8812
Company; subsidiary of Bell & Howell Company of Chicago, U.S.A.

Enquiries to the Press and Publications Officer

Subject coverage
audio-visual equipment including closed circuit television; paging equipment

235 BELL COLLEGE OF TECHNOLOGY
Almada Street, Hamilton ML3 0JB Tel. 069-82 29221 ext. 231, 242
College of Further Education; Library includes the Bell College Technical Information Service (BECTIS)-069-82 58901

Enquiries to the Technical Information Officer

Subject coverage
mechanical, electrical and electronic engineering; metallurgy; materials science; physics; chemistry; biology; mathematics and computer science; civil engineering and construction technology; management; business administration

Special collection
Sir Andrew McCance Collection (metallurgical subjects, especially steel)
British Standards

Publications
BECTIS Bulletin (abstracts)
Bell College of Technology Library Bulletin (abstracts)
Computerised Listing of British Standards

236 BERK SPENCER ACIDS LIMITED
Abbey Mills Chemical Works, Canning Road, Stratford, London E15 3NX Tel. 01-534 5162
Company, subsidiary of the Steetley Company Limited; another installation at Pentrepoeth Chemical Works, Morriston, Swansea, Glamorgan

Enquiries to the Company

Subject coverage
supply of sulphuric, hydrochloric and nitric acids and safe bulk handling of them

Publications
Bulk Handling of Sulphuric Acid
Bulk Handling of Hydrochloric Acid

237 BERKELEY NUCLEAR LABORATORIES
Berkeley, Gloucestershire GL13 9PB Tel. 045-381 451
Research Laboratory of the Central Electricity Generating Board, *q.v.*

Enquiries to the Information Officer

Subject coverage
properties of reactor materials, including radiation chemistry, oxidation behaviour and mutual compatibility of reactor structural materials, and the effect of reactor environment, particularly irradiation, on the properties of materials; performance and properties of reactor fuels; nuclear engineering, including heat transfer and vibration studies; the physics of reactors including safety, system optimization and health; applied physics including instrumentation, gas circuit physics, tribology and sodium technology; structural mechanics, especially analysis of power plant components and behaviour

Publications
several hundred research reports per year (about half openly available)

238 BERKSHIRE COUNTY LIBRARY
Abbey Mill House, Abbey Square, Reading, Berkshire RG1 3BH Tel. 0734 55981
Public Library service; six regional/district libraries: Newbury, Reading, *q.v.*, Wokingham, Maidenhead/Windsor, *q.v.*, Slough, Bracknell, *q.v.*

Enquiries to the Librarian

Subject coverage
local government topics, including law and public administration

BERWICK-UPON-TWEED DISTRICT LIBRARY *see* **NORTHUMBERLAND COUNTY LIBRARY**

BETHNAL GREEN AREA LIBRARY *see* **TOWER HAMLETS LIBRARIES DEPARTMENT**

239 BEVERLEY PUBLIC LIBRARY
North Divisional Library, Humberside County Leisure Services Department, 10 Lord Roberts Road, Beverley, North Humberside HU17 9BE Tel. 0482 885167
Public Library, comprising the former East Riding County Library, Beverley Public Library, Goole Public Library and Bridlington Public Library

Enquiries to the Divisional Leisure Services Officer

Subject coverage
general

240 BEXLEY LIBRARIES AND MUSEUMS DEPARTMENT REFERENCE LIBRARY
1 Townley Road, Bexleyheath, Kent DA6 7HJ Tel. 01-303 4672
Reference Library and Information Service; local contact point of SEAL (South East Area Library Information Service)

Enquiries to the Reference Librarian

Subject coverage
general

Special collections
British Standards
Government publications

241 BHRA FLUID ENGINEERING
Cranfield, Bedford MK43 0AJ Tel. 0234 750422
Telex 825059
Research Association; formerly the British Hydromechanics Research Association

Enquiries, free of charge for members, to the Head of Information Group; other enquiries accepted at discretion of the Group

Subject coverage
All aspects of fluid engineering, more specifically:— pumps and other fluid machines; fluid power (oil hydraulics and pneumatics); fluidics; noise in hydraulic systems; tribology; bearings; jet cutting; fluid sealing; pressure losses in pipe systems and fittings; flow in pipes; pressure surges; cavitation; flow measurement and control; hydraulic and pneumatic transport of solid materials in pipelines; open channel flow; dredging; civil engineering hydraulic structures (dams, spillways, flood defences, cooling systems etc.) and physical and mathematical models of them; wind and wave effects on structures; non-aeronautical industrial aerodynamics; ventilation of tunnels

Publications
Civil Engineering Hydraulics Abstracts
Pumps and other Fluids Machinery Abstracts
Solid-liquid Flow Abstracts
Fluid Flow Measurements Abstracts
Tribos (Tribology Abstracts)
Fluid Sealing Abstracts
Fluid Power Abstracts
Fluidics Feedback
Industrial Aerodynamics Abstracts
International Dredging Abstracts
Proceedings of conferences organized by BHRA
Reviews and Bibliographies
Research Reports, (available to public 2 years after publication)

242 BICTON COLLEGE OF AGRICULTURE
East Budleigh, Budleigh Salterton, Devon EX9 7BY Tel. 039 56 353
Agricultural College
Enquiries to the Librarian
Subject coverage
agriculture; horticulture

243 BICYCLE ASSOCIATION OF GREAT BRITAIN LIMITED
Starley House, Eaton Road, Coventry CV1 2FH Tel. 0203 27427
Trade Association; together with the Motor Cycle Association of Great Britain Limited, of the same address, formed the original Cycle and Motor Cycle Association now dissolved
Enquiries to the Director
Subject coverage
British bicycle industry, manufacture, statistics, imports, accessories

244 BINNIE & PARTNERS
Artillery House, Artillery Row, Westminster, London SW1P 1RX Tel. 01-222 7755
Telex 24552
Consulting Services Company
Enquiries to the Research and Information Engineer
Subject coverage
water resource engineering, including water supply, water treatment, sewerage and sewage disposal, hydroelectric works, irrigation, drainage, water recreation and offshore technology; secondary but allied subjects such as hydrology, geology, soil mechanics, hydraulics, pumping machinery and structural design
Special collection
Journal of the Institution of Civil Engineers from 1872

245 BIOCHEMICAL SOCIETY
7 Warwick Court, London WC1R 5DP Tel. 01-242 1076
Learned Society
Enquiries to the Secretarial Assistant

Subject coverage
organization of British biochemistry; career prospects in biochemistry

Publications
Biochemical Journal
Biochemical Society Transactions
Clinical Science & Molecular Medicine
Essays in Biochemistry
Essays in Medical Biochemistry
Symposia

246 BIODETERIORATION INFORMATION CENTRE
University of Aston, 80 Coleshill Street, Birmingham B14 7PF Tel. 021-359 3611 ext. 229
University Department, Information Centre; the address also houses the Biodeterioration Society

Enquiries to the Information and Service Officer

Subject coverage
biodeterioration (attack by organisms on materials of economic importance); waste materials biodegradation; biological treatment of wastes and biodegradation of waste materials in nature

Publications
Biodeterioration Research Titles (quarterly)
Waste Materials Biodegradation Research Titles (quarterly)
International Biodeterioration Bulletin (quarterly)

BIODETERIORATION SOCIETY *see* **BIODETERIORATION INFORMATION CENTRE, Aston University**

BIODETERIORATION UNIT *see* **CENTRE FOR INDUSTRIAL INNOVATION, Strathclyde University**

247 BIOLOGICAL COUNCIL
Institute of Biology, 41 Queens Gate, London SW7 5HU Tel. 01-589 9076
Confederation of biological societies

Enquiries to the Secretary

Subject coverage
biology; drug action

Publications
Suggestions for Speakers and Standards for Slides
List of Abbreviated Titles of Biological Journals
Calendar of Meetings

248 BIOLOGICAL ENGINEERING SOCIETY
Biophysics Department, Faculty of Medical Sciences, University College, Gower Street, London WC1E 6BT Tel. 01-387 7050 ext. 288
Scientific Learned Society; affiliated to the International Federation for Medical and Biological Engineering

Enquiries to the Honorary Secretary

Subject coverage
physical sciences; biomedical engineering; biological systems; physiological systems; medical techniques; electronic, mechanical and instrument engineering; materials science; computing and mathematics; education and training

Publications
Sets of Abstracts of Annual Conferences
Education, Training and Careers in Bio-medical Engineering
Proceedings of Conferences and Symposia

BIOLOGICAL INFORMATION SERVICE *see* **UNITED KINGDOM CHEMICAL INFORMATION SERVICE**

249 BIOMEDICAL INFORMATION SERVICE
University of Sheffield, Western Bank, Sheffield S10 2TN Tel. 0742 78555
Telex 54348

University Library Service; formerly Biomedical Information Project

Enquiries to the Director

Subject coverage
cell biology and physiology

Publications
Current Awareness Bulletins (25 titles, monthly; cell membranes and intestinal absorption are important examples)
Economy Bulletins (60 titles)

250 BIOMEDICAL INSTRUMENTATION ADVISORY SERVICE (BIAS)
Bioengineering Division, Clinical Research Centre, Watford Road, Harrow, Middlesex HA1 3UJ Tel. 01-864 5311 ext. 2151
Telex 923410
Information Section of Research Centre, of the Medical Research Council

Enquiries to the Information Officer (fees chargeable)

Subject coverage
commercially available biomedical instrumentation, equipment and materials; sources of supply (over 4000 suppliers indexed); electronic, analytical and general laboratory apparatus; aids for disabled; hospital equipment

251 BIOMETRIC SOCIETY
C/o British Regional Secretary, Department of Statistics, St. Andrews University, North Haugh, St. Andrews, Fife KY16 9SS

Scientific Society; headquarters: the Institute of Statistics, Box 5962, Raleigh, North Carolina, U.S.A.

Enquiries to the Regional Secretary

Subject coverage
applications of mathematical and statistical techniques in any aspect of biological science, including agriculture and medicine

Publication
Biometrics (quarterly)

BIONICS RESEARCH LIMITED *see* **TETRONICS RESEARCH AND DEVELOPMENT COMPANY LIMITED**

252 BIRKENHEAD COLLEGE OF TECHNOLOGY
Borough Road, Birkenhead, Merseyside L42 9QD Tel. 051-652 1521 ext. 16
College of Further Education, formerly Birkenhead Technical College; Open University Study Centre for Wirral

Enquiries to the Librarian or Principal

Subject coverage
building; business studies; chemical engineering; electrical engineering; food technology; mechanical engineering; chemistry; physics; biology

Special collections
British Standards
Open University publications

BIRKENHEAD PUBLIC LIBRARY *see* **WIRRAL PUBLIC LIBRARIES**

253 BIRMINGHAM AND WEST MIDLANDS FURNITURE MANUFACTURERS ASSOCIATION
67 Newhall Street, Birmingham B3 1NU Tel. 021-236 7711
Trade Association, member of the British Furniture Manufacturers Federated Associations

Enquiries to the Secretary

Subject coverage
industrial relations in the industry, work conditions; exhibitions

Publication
Bulletin (monthly)

254 BIRMINGHAM CHAMBER OF INDUSTRY AND COMMERCE
Box 360, 75 Harborne Road, Birmingham B15 3DH Tel. 021-454 6171
Trade Association

Enquiries to the Information Officer

Subject coverage
general commercial intelligence

255 BIRMINGHAM COLLEGE OF FOOD AND DOMESTIC ARTS
Summer Row, Birmingham B3 1JB Tel. 021-235 2774
College of Further Education

Enquiries to the Tutor-Librarian

Subject coverage
hotel and catering; food technology; nursery nursing

256 BIRMINGHAM ENVIRONMENTAL HEALTH AND SAFETY ASSOCIATION LIMITED
22 Summer Road, Acocks Green, Birmingham B27 7UU Tel. 021-706 8121
Company; affiliated to RoSPA; formerly Birmingham and District Industrial Safety Group Limited

Enquiries to the Secretary

Subject coverage
occupational safety and health

257 BIRMINGHAM LIBRARY AND INFORMATION NETWORK (B-LINK)
Science and Technology Department, Central Libraries, Tel. 021-235 4537
Birmingham B3 3HQ Telex 337655
Interlibrary Cooperative Scheme; formerly Birmingham Works Libraries Loan Scheme

Enquiries to B-Link

Subject coverage
all fields of science and technology

258 BIRMINGHAM METALLURGICAL ASSOCIATION
Metallurgy Department, Aston University, Birmingham B4 7ET Tel. 021-359 3611
Company; linked with the Institution of Metallurgists and the Metals Society, *qq.v.*

Enquiries to the Honorary Secretary of the Association c/o Department of Mechanical and Production Engineering, City of Birmingham Polytechnic, Franchise Street, Perry Barr B42 2SU

Subject coverage
extraction, processing and use of metals and non-metals

Publications
Papers presented at Meetings and Conferences e.g. Metals and the Motor Car (1976)

259 BIRMINGHAM POLYTECHNIC, NORTH CENTRE
Franchise Street, Perry Barr, Birmingham B42 2SU Tel. 021-356 6911
College of Technology; formerly North Birmingham Technical College, then Birmingham Polytechnic (Science and Technology)

Enquiries to the Reader Services Librarian

Subject coverage
construction technology; quantity surveying; mechanical and production engineering; electrical engineering; computer studies; mathematics; chemistry; physics; biomedical sciences; architecture; planning

260 BIRMINGHAM PRODUCTIVITY SERVICE LIMITED
Chamber of Commerce House, 75 Harborne Road, Edgbaston, Birmingham B15 3DW — Tel. 021-454 5778
Advisory Service of the West Midlands Productivity Association

Enquiries to the Executive Director

Subject coverage
productivity improvement

Publications
Explanatory guides on current industrial legislation

261 BIRMINGHAM PUBLIC LIBRARIES
Quick Reference and Commercial Information Department, Paradise Circus, Birmingham B3 3HQ — Tel. 021-235 4531, Telex 337655
Public Library Service

Enquiries to the Librarian

Subject coverage
commercial and general; geographical, biographical, and market research; statistics

Special collection
Trade names index (since 1934)

262 BIRMINGHAM PUBLIC LIBRARIES
Science and Technology Department, Paradise Circus, Birmingham B3 3HQ — Tel. 021-235 4537, Telex 337655
Public Library Service; includes B-LINK (Birmingham Library and Information Network, *q.v.*; houses Weslink (West Midlands Library and Information Network), *q.v.*

Enquiries to the Librarian

Subject coverage
nuclear science and technology; chemistry and chemical technology; ornithology; horticulture; electronics; firearms; metallurgy; metal manufactures; automobile engineering; building; history of science and technology

Publications
Technical bibliographies

263 BIRMINGHAM SMALL FIRMS INFORMATION CENTRE
53 Stephenson Street, Birmingham B2 4DH — Tel. 021-643 3344, Telex 337919

Government Information Centre of the Department of Industry

Enquiries to the Manager

Subject coverage
business studies and problems; management

Publications
Pamphlets on financial and business subjects

264 BIRMINGHAM UNIVERSITY
Department of Electronic and Electrical Engineering, P.O. Box 363, Edgbaston, Birmingham B15 2TT — Tel. 021-472 1301
University Department

Enquiries to the Administrative Officer

Subject coverage
electrical engineering in general; electronics; radar; radio; underwater acoustics; solid state; microelectronics

Publications
Prospectus
Research Reports

265 BIRMINGHAM UNIVERSITY LIBRARY
P.O. Box 363, Edgbaston, Birmingham B15 2TT Tel. 021-472 1301
Telex 338160

University Library

Enquiries to the Librarian

Subject coverage
mathematical sciences (including pure mathematics, mathematical statistics, mathematical physics, and computer science); physics; space research; chemistry; biological sciences (including bacteriology, botany, genetics, microbiology, zoology and comparative physiology); psychology; geology; geography; mechanical engineering; engineering production; civil engineering; transportation and environmental planning; electronic and electrical engineering; chemical engineering; physical metallurgy and science of metals; industrial metallurgy; minerals engineering; biochemistry (including malting and brewing)

Publications
Series of Quick Lists
Library Guides
Other papers, list available

BIRMINGHAM UNIVERSITY *see also*
ACCIDENT RESEARCH UNIT
GAS KINETICS DATA COMPILATION AND EVALUATION GROUP

BIRMINGHAM WORKS LIBRARIES LOAN SCHEME *now* **BIRMINGHAM LIBRARY AND INFORMATION NETWORK (B-Link),** *q.v.*

BIRNIEHILL INSTITUTE *now* **NATIONAL ENGINEERING LABORATORY.** *q.v.*

266 BIS MARKETING RESEARCH LIMITED
79–80 Blackfriars Road, London SE1 8HP Tel. 01-928 9511
Telex 919642

Company, part of the BIS Group, formerly Business Intelligence Services Marketing Research Division; consultants

Enquiries to the Director

Subject coverage
paper and pulp, packaging, printing, catering, food, building and construction, chemicals. In the Group, interests include data processing consultancy, in-house training systems and consumer market research

Publications
multi-client surveys, mainly for the paper, printing, packaging and allied industries

267 BISHOP AUCKLAND TECHNICAL COLLEGE
Woodhouse Lane, Bishop Auckland, Co. Durham DL14 6JZ Tel. 0388 3052/3
Technical College

Enquiries to the Librarian

Subject coverage
engineering; construction; business studies

268 BISHOP BURTON COLLEGE OF AGRICULTURE
Bishop Burton, Beverley, North Humberside
College of Agriculture; formerly East Riding College of Agriculture; its Library is part of the North Humberside County Library

Enquiries to the Librarian

Subject coverage
agriculture (student level and practical only)

269 BISHOPSGATE INSTITUTE LIBRARY
230 Bishopsgate, London EC2M 4QH Tel. 01-247 6844
Public Reference Library of the Bishopsgate Foundation; houses the London & Middlesex Archaeological Society and the London Topographical Society

Enquiries to the Librarian

Subject coverage
except for trade unionism, the special subjects of this library are more relevant to volume II of the Directory

BLACK BOLT AND NUT ASSOCIATION OF GREAT BRITAIN *see* **BRITISH INDUSTRIAL FASTENERS FEDERATION**

270 BLACKBURN COLLEGE OF TECHNOLOGY AND DESIGN
Feilden Street, Blackburn, Lancashire BB2 1LH Tel. 0254 64321
College of Technology

Enquiries to the Head of the Library and Information Department

Subject coverage
management; textiles; computers; pure and applied science; electrical engineering; mechanical engineering; construction

BLACKBURN DISTRICT CENTRAL LIBRARY *see* **LANCASHIRE LIBRARY**

271 BLACKPOOL COLLEGE OF TECHNOLOGY AND ART
Ashfield Road, Bispham, Blackpool FY2 0HB Tel. 0253 52352
College of Further Education; formerly Blackpool Technical College

Enquiries to the Librarian

Subject coverage
practical aspects and management of hotels and catering

BLACKPOOL DISTRICT CENTRAL LIBRARY *see* **LANCASHIRE LIBRARY**

272 B.H. BLACKWELL LIMITED
Broad Street, Oxford OX1 3BQ Tel. 0865 49111
Booksellers

Enquiries to the Library Service Adviser

Subject coverage
books service; periodicals subscriptions; microforms; cataloguing support services

Publications
catalogues
advisory/information cards

BLAENAU REGIONAL LIBRARY *see* **GWENT COUNTY LIBRARY**

273 BLAIR BELL RESEARCH SOCIETY
C/o Royal College of Obstetricians and Gynaecologists, 27 Sussex Place, Regents Park, London NW1 4RG
Scientific Research Society

Enquiries to the Honorary Secretary

Subject coverage
research in obstetrics, gynaecology and reproductive physiology

BLEACHERS ASSOCIATION *now* **WHITECROFT LIMITED,** *q.v.*

BLEACHING TRADE ASSOCIATION *now* **WHITECROFT LIMITED,** *q.v.*

BLETCHLEY DIVISIONAL LIBRARY *see* **BUCKINGHAMSHIRE COUNTY LIBRARY**

B-LINK *see* **BIRMINGHAM LIBRARY AND INFORMATION NETWORK**

BLOXWICH DISTRICT LIBRARY *see* **WALSALL LIBRARY AND MUSEUM SERVICES**

BLUE CIRCLE GROUP *see* **ASSOCIATED PORTLAND CEMENT MANUFACTURERS LIMITED**

BLYTH LIBRARY *see* **NORTHUMBERLAND COUNTY LIBRARY**

274 BMES GROUP LIMITED
Hammersmith Grove, London W6 7EN
Company, subsidiary of George Wimpey & Company Limited

Enquiries to the Manager, Tanjon Limited, Cheam Road, Sutton, Surrey, Tel. 01-642 0191

Subject coverage
feasibility reports and budget costs for mechanical and electrical services in industrial and commercial buildings, including fire prevention; design and installation of such services

Publications
Sprinkler Fire Protection brochures

275 BNF METALS TECHNOLOGY CENTRE
Grove Laboratories, Denchworth Road, Wantage, Berkshire OX12 9BJ Tel. 023-57 2992
Research Association; formerly the British Non-Ferrous Metals Research Association; houses the British Brazing and Soldering Association and the International Environmental Bureau

Enquiries to the Head of Information & Library Department

Subject coverage
refining; melting; casting (shapes for further working especially by continuous casting, shapes by sand casting – pressure diecasting and gravity diecasting); all metalworking processes, metal finishing and coatings; uses of non-ferrous metals; environmental protection from emissions, effluents, noise and toxic hazards; market appraisals and industrial studies; process measurement and control; instrumentation; testing; computer applications; analysis; metallographic studies; mechanical testing for creep and fatigue; furnace development; energy saving

Publication
BNF Abstracts (monthly, free to members, or by subscription)

276 BOC INTERNATIONAL LIMITED
Hammersmith House, London W6 9DX Tel. 01-748 2020
Telex 934664

Public Company; formerly the British Oxygen Company Limited

Enquiries to the Archivist

Subject coverage
production and uses of industrial gases; low temperature techniques and equipment; cryogenic engineering; chemical engineering; welding and cutting; anaesthesia and resuscitation; offshore services; underwater techniques

BOC LIMITED *see also*
BRITISH OXYGEN CHEMICALS
EDWARDS HIGH VACUUM
HIRST ELECTRIC INDUSTRIES LIMITED

277 BOC MEDISHIELD LIMITED
Springfield Road, Chesham, Buckinghamshire HP5 1PW Tel. 024-05 75251
Telex 83473

Company; member of BOC International Group

Enquiries to the Marketing Support Manager

Subject coverage
medical equipment for hospitals; servicing of such equipment; consultancy service for hospitals

Publications
"This is BOC Medishield"
Product catalogues

278 BOC MUREX
Research and Development Laboratories, Waltham Cross, Hertfordshire EN8 7RP — Tel. 0992 23636, Telex 21498
Company, formerly Murex Welding Processes Limited
Enquiries to the Information Officer/Librarian
Subject coverage
welding electrodes, rods and wires
Publication
The Welder (quarterly)

279 BODLEIAN LIBRARY
Oxford OX1 3BG — Tel. 0865 44675, Telex 83656
University Library and Copyright Library; scientific section is the Radcliffe Science Library, *q.v.*
Enquiries, bibliographical, by letter only, to the Librarian
Subject coverage
comprehensive, general
Special Collections
John Johnson Collection of Printing Ephemera
UN and EEC documents
Publications
Current Foreign and Commonwealth Periodicals in the Bodleian Library and in other Oxford Libraries
Union List of Serials in the Science Area, Oxford
Many general and catalogue publications proper to volume 2 of the Aslib Directory

BODMIN DISTRICT LIBRARY *see* **CORNWALL COUNTY LIBRARY**

280 BOEHRINGER INGELHEIM LIMITED
Southern Industrial Estate, Bracknell, Berkshire RG12 4YS — Tel. 0344 24600, Telex 847634
Company
Enquiries to the Librarian
Subject coverage
pharmaceuticals; cardiovascular, respiratory and pharmaceutical medicine; clinical pharmacology; toxicology

BOLLAND LIBRARY *see* **BRISTOL POLYTECHNIC**

281 BOLTON AND DISTRICT TEXTILE EMPLOYERS ASSOCIATION
Lloyds Bank Chambers, Howell Croft North, Bolton BL1 1QY — Tel. 0204 21511
Employers Association; merged with the former Bolton and District Textile Manufacturers Association and the Darwen Textile Manufacturers Association; member of the British Textile Employers Association
Enquiries to the Secretary and Executive Officer
Subject coverage
wages and conditions of work in the textile industry; industrial relations, negotiations, consultations; factory agreements; commercial information
Publication
Annual Report

282 BOLTON INSTITUTE OF TECHNOLOGY
Deane Road, Bolton, Lancashire BL3 5AB — Tel. 0204 28851
College of Technology

Enquiries to the Librarian

Subject coverage
civil, electrical, mechanical engineering; science; textiles; business studies

283 BOLTON METROPOLITAN BOROUGH CENTRAL LIBRARY
Civic Centre, Le Mans Crescent, Bolton BL1 1SD — Tel. 0204 22311
Telex 635001
Public Library (Scientific and Technical Library and Central Reference Library); District Libraries at Farnworth, Harwood and Westhoughton

Enquiries to the Principal Librarian

Subject coverage
all fields of science and technology; building, building materials, architecture of public buildings, churches, educational and scientific buildings; textile technology; diseases of the cardio-vascular system

Special collections
British Standards, complete set
Comprehensive collection of commercial and technical dictionaries and directories

284 BOLTON TECHNICAL COLLEGE
Manchester Road, Bolton, Greater Manchester BL2 1ER — Tel. 0204 31411
College of Further Education

Enquiries to the Librarian

Subject coverage
mechanical engineering; electrical engineering; welding and fabrication; food preparation and service; food technology; industrial safety; building

BOOK TOKENS LIMITED *see* **BOOKSELLERS ASSOCIATION OF GREAT BRITAIN AND IRELAND**

BOOK TRADE IMPROVEMENT LIMITED *see* **BOOKSELLERS ASSOCIATION OF GREAT BRITAIN AND IRELAND**

285 BOOKBINDING AND ALLIED TRADES MANAGEMENT ASSOCIATION
4 Jenton Avenue, Bexley Heath, Kent DA7 4SP — Tel. 01-304 4653
Trade Association

Enquiries to the Honorary Technical Representative or Secretary

Subject coverage
bookbinding and allied trades; training and management; machinery and materials

286 BOOKSELLERS ASSOCIATION OF GREAT BRITAIN & IRELAND
152–154 Buckingham Palace Road, London SW1W 9TZ — Tel. 01-730 8214
Trade Association; housing Book Tokens Limited, Booksellers Clearing House and Book Trade Improvement Limited

Enquiries, from members only, to the Information Officer

Subject coverage
book trade; negotiation with publishers; training; shopfitting; bibliographical information; legislation; conditions of employment

Publications
Bookselling News (6 times per annum, to members only)
Directory of British Publishers (to bookseller or publishers only)
List of Members of the Booksellers Association
Various books and pamphlets (given in a List of Publications)

BOOTLE LIBRARY *see* **SEFTON METROPOLITAN BOROUGH LIBRARIES**

287 BOOTS COMPANY LIMITED
Nottingham NG2 3AA — Tel. 0602 56255, Telex 37128

Company; formerly Boots Pure Drug Company

Enquiries to the Chief Librarian

Subject coverage
medicine; biology; pharmacy; pharmacology; biochemistry; chemistry; chemical engineering; agriculture; horticulture; animal science; commerce; economics; management; marketing; retailing; engineering; food science; packaging, cosmetics; toiletries

288 BOOZ, ALLEN & HAMILTON INTERNATIONAL B.V.
New Bond Street House, 1–5 New Bond Street, London W1Y 0DB — Tel. 01-499 8971, Telex 261884

Management Consultants

Enquiries to the Managing Director

Subject coverage
operations and profit improvement; financial analysis; capital budgeting; long range planning; growth planning through new products and services, diversification, acquisition or divestiture; market appraisal; distribution rationalization; manufacturing systems; production and inventory control; personnel services; manpower planning; executive selection and compensation

Publications
Brochures and reports

289 BORAX CONSOLIDATED LIMITED
Research Centre and Laboratories, Cox Lane, Chessington, Surrey KT9 1SJ — Tel. 01-397 5141, Telex 929612

Company; subsidiary of RTZ Borax Limited; houses Geomet Services, *q.v.*

Enquiries to the Chief Information Officer

Subject coverage
chemistry of boron and its compounds; their uses in industry and agriculture

Publications
Boron in Glass
Boron in Agriculture

290 BORDEN (UK) LIMITED
North Baddesley, Southampton SO5 9ZB — Tel. 042-123 2131, Telex 47212

Private Company, formerly Borden Chemical Company (UK) Limited

Enquiries to the Librarian

Subject coverage
adhesives; packaging film; foundry binders

291 BORDER UNION AGRICULTURAL SOCIETY
30 The Square, Kelso, Roxburghshire TD5 7HL — Tel. 057-32 2188

Agricultural Society

Enquiries are not accepted

Subject coverage
agriculture; agricultural shows and sales

292 BORDERS REGIONAL LIBRARY
Headquarters, Galashiels Library, Lawyers Brae, Galashields, Selkirkshire TD1 3JQ — Tel. 0896 2512
Public Library Service; comprises the former Berwickshire, Roxburghshire, and Peebleshire County Libraries; District Libraries at Galashiels (Ettrick and Lauderdale Area), Duns (Berwickshire Area), Roxburgh (Roxburghshire Area) and Peebles (Tweeddale Area), *q.v.*

Enquiries to the Librarians

Subject coverage
general

293 BOROUGH ROAD COLLEGE
P.O. Box 239, Borough Road, Isleworth, Middlesex TW7 5DU — Tel. 01-560 5991
College of Education

Enquiries to the Librarian

Subject coverage
pure science and mathematics

294 BOTANICAL SOCIETY OF EDINBURGH
Royal Botanic Garden, Inverleith Row, Edinburgh EH3 5LR — Tel. 031-552 7171
Voluntary Society, incorporating the Cryptogamic Society of Scotland

Enquiries to the General Secretary

Subject coverage
all fields of botany; taxonomic problems; nomenclature and bibliography

Special collections
letters and personal files of several early plant collectors

Publications
Transactions of the Botanical Society of Edinburgh
BSE News

295 BOTANICAL SOCIETY OF THE BRITISH ISLES
C/o Department of Botany, British Museum (Natural History), Cromwell Road, London SW7 5BD
Learned Society/Registered Charity

Enquiries to the Honorary General Secretary

Subject coverage
British flowering plants and ferns; conservation of the British flora; identification of wild plants

Publications
Watsonia: Journal and Proceedings of the Botanical Society of the British Isles (2 parts annually)
BSBI Abstracts (annual)
Conference Reports
Atlas of the British Flora
Handbooks on Identification, etc.

296 BOULTON AND PAUL LIMITED
Riverside Works, Norwich NR1 1EB — Tel. 0603 60133
Telex 97326
Company; subsidiary of the British Electric Traction Company Limited

Enquiries to the Group Publicity Manager, Boulton & Paul Ltd., Eversley Road, Norwich NR6 6SX

Subject coverage
standard joinery; structural steelwork; mechanical handling plant; aluminium windows, doors, entrances and curtain walling; builders plant for contract and hire; aluminium and timber ladders and steps

BOURNEMOUTH AREA LIBRARY *see* **DORSET COUNTY LIBRARY**

297 BOVRIL LIMITED
Wellington Road, Burton-on-Trent, Staffordshire DE14 2AB Tel. 0283 62881
Telex 34322

Company

Enquiries to the Technical Services Officer

Subject coverage
food technology, particularly yeast and meat extract manufacture; biochemistry; nutrition; analysis

298 BOWATER TECHNICAL SERVICES LIMITED
Callybank House, Northfleet, Gravesend, Kent DA11 9AQ Tel. 0474 64444
Telex 96449

Consultant Company, of Bowater Paper Corporation

Enquiries to the Technical Information Officer

Subject coverage
wood; pulp; paper; printing; packaging

299 BOWHURST LIMITED
Chronicle House, 72–78 Fleet Street, London EC4Y 1HY Tel. 01-353 2106/7
Company

Enquiries to the Managing or other Directors

Subject coverage
quantitative and qualitative research and feasibility studies in industrial, commercial and financial markets, U.K. and overseas; acquisition, advertising, distribution, diversification, image and attitude, market investigation, inter-company comparison, new products, product investigation, promotion and marketing; sales analyses, forecasting, sales structure

BP CHEMICALS LIMITED *see* **BRITISH PETROLEUM COMPANY LIMITED BP Chemicals Limited**

BP COMPANY LIMITED *see* **BRITISH PETROLEUM COMPANY LIMITED**

BP OIL LIMITED *see* **BRITISH PETROLEUM COMPANY LIMITED BP Oil Limited**

BPB INDUSTRIES (RESEARCH & DEVELOPMENT) LIMITED *now* **BRITISH GYPSUM LIMITED,** *q.v.*

300 BRACKNELL LIBRARY
Town Square, Bracknell, Berkshire RG12 1BH Tel. 0344 23149
Telex 849317

Public Library, of Berkshire County Library system

Enquiries to the Reference Librarian

Subject coverage
general; computers and electronics

301 BRADFORD COLLEGE
Great Horton Road, Bradford, Yorkshire BD7 1AY Tel. 0274 34844
College of Further and Higher Education; comprising the former Technical College, Regional College of Art, Margaret McMillan College of Education and Bolton Royd College; includes an Industrial Enquiry Centre

Enquiries to the Librarian or the Manager of the Industrial Enquiry Centre

Subject coverage
textiles, dyeing; engineering (electrical & electronic, mechanical & auto fabrication, civil & construction, production); management & supervisory studies; business studies; public administration; banking; accountancy; industrial design; advertising; display; photography; printing

& publicity; food technology; hairdressing; optical dispensing; metallurgy; jewellery; technical problem definition in management and production in the manufacturing and service industries

Special collection
British Standards

302 BRADFORD LIBRARIES
Library of Commerce, Science and Technology, Princes Way, Bradford, West Yorkshire BD1 1NN — Tel. 0274 33081, Telex 51480
Public Library Service

Enquiries to the Chief Librarian

Subject coverage
business management; commerce; science; technology with emphasis on textiles; trade and production statistics; U.K. and foreign trade directory information

Special collections
Lees Botanical Collection (19th century flora)
British Standards
DIN Standards in English
API Standards

303 BRADFORD SCIENTIFIC TECHNICAL AND COMMERCIAL SERVICE (BRASTACS)
Central Library, Prince's Way, Bradford BD1 1NN — Tel. 0274 33081 ext. 36, Telex 51480

Enquiries to the Librarian

Subject coverage
general, commercial, scientific and technical

Special collections
British Standards
British Patents
DIN and API standards

Publications
List of Members
List of Local Translators

304 BRADFORD UNIVERSITY LIBRARY
Richmond Road, Bradford, West Yorkshire BD7 1DP — Tel. 0274 33466, Telex 51309
University Library

Enquiries to the Librarian

Subject coverage
history of science and technology; mathematics; physics; chemistry; astronomy; geology; palaeontology; anthropology; biology; botany; zoology; medicine; pharmacy; ophthalmic optics; control engineering; mechanical engineering; transport engineering; electrical engineering; surveying; civil engineering; town and country planning; chemical engineering; dyeing; metallurgy; textiles; plastics technology

Publication
ACE: Articles in Civil Engineering (current awareness service available on subscription)

BRADFORD UNIVERSITY *see also* **DISASTER RESEARCH UNIT MANAGEMENT CENTRE**

305 BRANDED HAND KNITTING ASSOCIATION LIMITED
Lloyds Bank Chambers, Hustlergate, Bradford, West Yorkshire, BD1 1NU — Tel. 0274 22652
Trade Association; the Knitting Craft Group of P.O. Box 2, Richmond, North Yorkshire DL10 7DT is linked with the Association

Enquiries to the Secretary

Subject coverage
hand knitting yarns

BRASTACS *see* **BRADFORD SCIENTIFIC TECHNICAL AND COMMERCIAL SERVICE**

306 BRAZILIAN EMBASSY
Commercial Section, 15 Berkeley Street, London W1X 5AE — Tel. 01-499 6706, 01-499 1533
Telex 25814

Brazilian Diplomatic Service of the Brazilian Foreign Office

Enquiries to the Commercial Attaché

Subject coverage
exports from, investment in, and commercial contracts in Brazil; statistics

307 Ronald BRECH INCORPORATED
Guild House, 32 Worple Road, Wimbledon, London SW19 4EF — Tel. 01-946 8641/2
Company; associated with Ronald Brech Partnership Limited and Brech-Rivett Business Services

Enquiries to the Librarian

Subject coverage
economic and business advice under contract; design of dynamic information systems incorporating forecasts and risk assessment; economic forecasts; econometrics; statistics; accounting; in-company development

Publication
Economic Commentary (3 times per annum)

BRECHIN PUBLIC LIBRARY *see* **ANGUS DISTRICT LIBRARY SERVICE**

BRECON AREA LIBRARY *see* **POWYS COUNTY LIBRARIES**

308 BRENT LIBRARY SERVICE
Central Library, 95 High Road, Willesden Green, London NW10 2ST — Tel. 01-459 5242
Telex 923595

Public Library service

Enquiries to the Borough Librarian & Curator

Subject coverage
general; mathematics

Publication
Management: a select booklist 1974

309 BREWERS ASSOCIATION OF SCOTLAND
6 St Colme Street, Edinburgh EH6 4AD — Tel. 031 225 4681
Trade Association, affiliated to the Brewers Society

Enquiries to the Secretary

Subject coverage
brewing industry in Scotland

310 BREWERS SOCIETY
42 Portman Square, London W1H 0BB — Tel. 01-486 4831
Telex 261946

Trade Association

Enquiries to the General Secretary

Subject coverage
brewing industry and retail licensed trade

Publications
Brewing Review (monthly)
Statistical Handbook (annual)

311 BREWING RESEARCH FOUNDATION
Lyttel Hall, Nutfield, Redhill, Surrey RH1 4HY Tel. 682 2272
Non-profit-making Company; formerly Brewing Industry Research Foundation; associated with the Brewers Society and the Institute of Brewing
Enquiries, from responsible organizations, to the Librarian; concerning use of the Library, to the Director
Subject coverage
brewing; malting; flavour; fermentation; yeast technology; biochemistry; microbiology; biophysics; analytical techniques
Special collection
National Collection of Yeast Cultures
Publication
Bulletin of Current Literature (monthly)

BREWOOD DISTRICT LIBRARY *see* **STAFFORDSHIRE COUNTRY LIBRARY**

312 BRICK DEVELOPMENT ASSOCIATION
19 Grafton Street, London W1X 3LE Tel. 01-409 1021
Trade Association, affiliated to National Council of Building Materials Producers, and housing also Southern Brick Federation; its Advisory Centre is at the London Building Centre
Enquiries, general, to the Information Department; technical, to the Technical Department
Subject coverage
bricks and brickwork
Publications
Brick Bulletin
Technical Notes
Research Notes
Practical Notes
List of publications is available

BRIDGEND PUBLIC LIBRARY *see* **MID-GLAMORGAN COUNTY LIBRARY**

BRIDGNORTH DISTRICT LIBRARY *see* **SHROPSHIRE COUNTY LIBRARY**

313 BRIDGWATER COLLEGE
Broadway, Bridgwater, Somerset Tel. 0278 55464
Tertiary College, formerly Bridgwater Technical College
Enquiries to the Tutor Librarian
Subject coverage
general; business management

BRIDGWATER DISTRICT LIBRARY *see* **SOMERSET COUNTY LIBRARY**

314 BRIDLINGTON TECHNICAL INSTITUTE
West Street, Bridlington, North Humberside YO15 3EA Tel. 0262 2676
Further Education Establishment
Enquiries to the Librarian
Subject coverage
general
Publication
Prospectus

BRIERLEY HILL DISTRICT LIBRARY *see* **DUDLEY PUBLIC LIBRARIES**

BRIGHOUSE PUBLIC LIBRARY *see* **CALDERDALE METROPOLITAN DISTRICT LIBRARIES**

315 BRIGHTON AREA LIBRARIES
Church Street, Brighton, Sussex BN1 1UE — Tel. 0273 691195, Telex 87167

Public Library; Area Library of East Sussex County Library

Enquiries to the Area Librarian

Subject coverage
history of architecture; bicycle history; railway history; general; printing

316 BRIGHTON POLYTECHNIC
Moulsecoomb, Brighton BN2 4GJ — Tel. 0273 67304
Polytechnic

Enquiries to the Deputy Head of Learning Resources

Subject coverage
engineering and science

Publication
Union List of Periodicals in Libraries in the Brighton area

317 BRIGHTON TECHNICAL COLLEGE
Pelham Street, Brighton BN1 4FA — Tel. 0273 685971
College of Further Education

Enquiries to the Librarian

Subject coverage
applied biology and ecology to a higher level than remaining subjects in science and technology, commerce and catering

318 BRISTOL AND WEST OF ENGLAND ENGINEERING MANUFACTURERS ASSOCIATION
Royal London House, Queen Charlotte Street, Bristol BS1 4EZ — Tel. 0272 25930, 0272 28404

Trade Association, member of the Engineering Industries Association, *q.v.*

Enquiries to the Secretary

Subject coverage
engineering capacity; location of materials; expertise in engineering; advice on Government legislation; record of national wage agreements

Publications
Directory of Members
Register of Available Capacity

319 BRISTOL CENTRAL LIBRARY
Library of Commerce and Industry, College Green, Bristol BS1 5TL — Tel. 0272 26121, Telex 44200

Public Library, part of Avon County Library system; formerly Bristol Public Libraries

Enquiries to the Librarian

Subject coverage
commerce and industry with emphasis on management

Special collection
British Patent abridgements

320 BRISTOL CHAMBER OF COMMERCE INDUSTRY AND SHIPPING
16 Clifton Park, Bristol BS8 3BY — Tel. 0272 37081
Chamber of Commerce, formerly Bristol Incorporated Chamber of Commerce and Shipping

Enquiries to the Trade Information Officer

Subject coverage
industrial, commercial and financial affairs in Bristol and region; overseas trade, travel and marketing; overseas trade documentation, transport and shipping procedures; general business information

Publications
Directory of Members
Quarterly business magazine

321 BRISTOL CHANNEL TIMBER TRADES ASSOCIATION
27 Heol Hir, Llanishen, Cardiff CF4 5AA Tel. 0222 752779
Trade Association; affiliated to the Timber Trade Federation

Enquiries to the Secretary

Subject coverage
timber; plywood and other board materials; saw-milling

322 BRISTOL POLYTECHNIC
Bolland Library, Coldharbour Lane, Bristol BS16 1QY Tel. 0272 656261
College of Further Education; separate addresses for the Engineering and the Surveying & Town Planning Libraries

Enquiries to the Site Librarian

Subject coverage
management

323 BRISTOL POLYTECHNIC
Engineering Library, Ashley Down Road, Bristol BS7 9BU Tel. 0272 41241
College of Further Education

Enquiries to the Site Librarian

Subject coverage
engineering

324 BRISTOL POLYTECHNIC
Surveying and Town Planning Library, 3 Unity Street, Bristol BS1 5MP Tel. 0272 23016
College of Further Education

Enquiries to the Site Librarian

Subject coverage
surveying and town planning

325 BRISTOL SMALL FIRMS INFORMATION CENTRE
Colston Centre, Colston Avenue, Bristol BS1 4UB Tel. 0272 294546
Telex 449650

Government Information Centre of the Department of Industry

Enquiries to the Manager

Subject coverage
business studies and problems; management

Publications
pamphlets on financial and business subjects

326 BRITISH ACADEMY OF FORENSIC SCIENCES
Department of Forensic Medicine, London Hospital Medical College, Turner Street, London E1 2AD Tel. 01-377 9201
Learned Society

Enquiries to the Secretary-General

Subject coverage
forensic sciences; problems in medicine, science and the law; provision of names of experts prepared to advise

Publication
Medicine Science and the Law (official journal)

BRITISH ACETYLENE ASSOCIATION *now* **BRITISH COMPRESSED GASES ASSOCIATION,** *q.v.*

327 BRITISH ADHESIVE MANUFACTURERS ASSOCIATION
20 Pylewell Road, Hythe, Southampton SO4 6YW — Tel. 0703 842765
Trade Association, formed by the merger of the Adhesive Manufacturers Association and the British Rubber & Resin Adhesive Manufacturers Association

Enquiries to the Secretary

Subject coverage
selection and use of adhesives

328 BRITISH AEROSOL MANUFACTURERS ASSOCIATION
93 Albert Embankment, London SE1 7TU — Tel. 01-582 1115
Telex 916672

Trade Association, affiliated to the Chemical Industries Association Limited

Enquiries to the Director

Subject coverage
aerosol industry

Publications
Annual Report
Aerosol Memorandum
Aerosol ABC
Slide Kit, Notes and Booklet for Teachers

329 BRITISH AGRICULTURAL & GARDEN MACHINERY ASSOCIATION
Church Street, Rickmansworth, Hertfordshire WD3 1RQ — Tel. 87 77241
Trade Association, formerly Agricultural Machinery Tractor Dealers Association Limited

Enquiries to the Association

Subject coverage
agricultural and/or garden machinery industry

330 BRITISH AGRICULTURAL AND HORTICULTURAL PLASTICS ASSOCIATION
47 Piccadilly, London W1V 0DN — Tel. 01-734 2041
Telex 267746

Trade Association, affiliated to the British Plastics Federation, *q.v.*

Enquiries to the Secretary

Subject coverage
manufacture, supply and application of plastic products in all areas of agriculture and horticulture

Publication
Buyers Guide

331 BRITISH AGRICULTURAL EXPORT COUNCIL
Agriculture House, 25–31 Knightsbridge, London SW1X 7NJ — Tel. 01-245 9819/0
Telex 22255/6

Export Promotion Body

Enquiries to the Marketing Information Executive

Subject coverage
commercial/exporting information and consultancy in any branch of agriculture; livestock; poultry; equipment; buildings; animal feedstuffs; veterinary products; agricultural chemicals; irrigation and drainage; seeds; machinery; food processing (milk, meat, grain, oil seeds, vegetables, sugar, cold storage)

Publications
Livestock and Bloodstock of Great Britain
Poultry Exports—Great Britain
Animal Feeds
Introduction to British Consultancy in Agriculture
British Agricultural Export Council (for British Companies)
British Agricultural Export Council (for overseas organizations)

332 BRITISH AGROCHEMICALS ASSOCIATION
93 Albert Embankment, London SE1 7TU — Tel. 01-735 8471, Telex 916672

Trade Association, affiliated to the Chemical Industries Association Limited

Enquiries to the Information Officer

Subject coverage
pests and pesticides

Publications
Directory of Members and their Products
Why Feed Pests?
Safety of New Pesticides in the Environment

333 BRITISH AIRCRAFT CORPORATION LIMITED
Commercial Aircraft Division, Filton House, Bristol BS99 7AR — Tel. 0272 693831 ext. 254, Telex 44163

Manufacturing Company; formerly BAC (Operating) Limited; Head Office: 100 Pall Mall, London SW1

Enquiries to the Librarian

Subject coverage
aircraft manufacture; aerodynamics; aeronautical engineering; history of aero engineering

334 BRITISH AIRCRAFT CORPORATION LIMITED
Guided Weapons Division, P.O. Box 77, Filton House, Bristol BS99 7AR — Tel. 0272 693831, Telex 44188

Industrial Company; having another factory at Stevenage, *q.v.*

Enquiries to the Chief Librarian

Subject coverage
general; missile systems; target aircraft; ground support equipment; satellites; advanced electronic equipment, especially aerodynamics; automatic control (particularly missiles and satellite attitude control); electronics; environmental testing; guidance; holography; human factors; hybrid computing; instruments; mechanisms; microwaves; physical optics; reliability; statistical analysis; structures

335 BRITISH AIRCRAFT CORPORATION LIMITED
Guided Weapons Division, Six Hills Way, Stevenage, Hertfordshire SG1 2DA — Tel. 0438 2422, Telex 82125

Industrial Company

Enquiries to the Librarian

Subject coverage
guided weapons; precision instruments; electronics; microwave equipment

336 BRITISH AIRCRAFT CORPORATION LIMITED
Military Aircraft Division, Warton Aerodrome, Preston, Lancashire PR4 1AX — Tel. 0772 633333, Telex 67627

Company

Enquiries to the Technical Librarian

Subject coverage
military aircraft descriptions; design; engineering (aerodynamics, structures, materials, propulsion); manufacture; operations

337 BRITISH AIRPORTS AUTHORITY
2 Buckingham Gate, London SW1E 6JL Tel. 01-834 6621
Telex 919039

Airport Authority

Enquiries to External Relations Department

Subject coverage
airports in U.K.

Publications
Airport Information Bulletins
Annual Report
Consultancy Brochure

338 BRITISH AIRWAYS
Victoria Terminal, Buckingham Palace Road, London SW1W 9SR Tel. 01-834 2323
Telex 22531
Airline; including British Airways Helicopters Limited, British Airways Associated Companies Limited, British Airways Engine Overhaul Limited and International Aeradio Limited

Enquiries to the Chief of Information Services

Subject coverage
airlines and civil aviation in general; British Airways in particular

339 BRITISH AIRWAYS EUROPEAN DIVISION LIBRARY
Engineering Base, London (Heathrow) Airport, Hounslow, Middlesex TW6 2JR Tel. 01-759 3131 ext. 4459
Airline; the library was formerly known as the British European Airways Library

Enquiries to the Librarian

Subject coverage
aircraft engineering; airline management

Publication
British Airways News (produced by Public Relations Department)

340 BRITISH ALUMINIUM FOIL ROLLERS ASSOCIATION
24 Portland Place, London W1N 4AU Tel. 01-580 3529
Trade Association; affiliated to the Aluminium Federation; the Aluminium Foil Container Manufacturers Association is at this address

Enquiries to the Information Officer

Subject coverage
technical aspects of the uses of aluminium foil

Publications
Handbooks on the uses of aluminium foil

341 BRITISH AMUSEMENT CATERING TRADES ASSOCIATION
122 Clapham Common North Side, London SW4 9SP Tel. 01-228 4107
Trade Association

Enquiries to the General Secretary

Subject coverage
operation of coin-operated machines and of fairground games and riding devices

342 BRITISH AND IRISH ASSOCIATION OF LAW LIBRARIANS
c/o The Inner Temple Library, The Temple, London EC4Y 7DA Tel. 01-353 2959
Professional Association

Enquiries to the Honorary Secretary

Subject coverage

legal bibliographical matters; careers in law librarianship; general information **(but not legal advice)** relating to the history of the law and the courts

Publications

Report of the Committee on Co-operation 1970
Community Law 1973 (now out of print)
Directory of Law Libraries in the British Isles 1976

343 BRITISH ANTARCTIC SURVEY

Madingley Road, Cambridge CB3 0ET Tel. 0223 61188

Government Department, of the Natural Environment Research Council of the Department of Education and Science

Enquiries to the Information Officer

Subject coverage

Antarctic research as follows:
Atmospheric Sciences: Upper air and surface meteorology (including ozone observations), geomagnetism, aurora and airglow, ionosphere and whistlers
Earth Sciences: Glaciology and physical oceanography, marine and land geophysics (including seismology), geology, topographical survey, hydrography and hydrographic surveys, Quaternary studies.
Life Sciences: Taxonomy, biogeography, bioclimatology, marine biology, freshwater biology, pedology, terrestrial ecology, physiology (including human physiology), Quaternary studies.
Also: polar equipment and travel techniques, including the operation of ships, aircraft and vehicles

Special collections

Sea ice records and field data of all scientific work carried out
BAS Herbaria—Code: AAS (Antarctic and Sub-Antarctic plants)

Publications

British Antarctic Survey Scientific Reports—(monographs)
British Antarctic Survey Bulletins (collections of shorter papers)

344 BRITISH APPROVALS SERVICE FOR ELECTRICAL EQUIPMENT IN FLAMMABLE ATMOSPHERES (BASEEFA)

Harpur Hill, Buxton, Derbyshire SK17 9SS Tel. 0298 6211

Government Department, part of the Health and Safety Executive

Enquiries to the Director

Subject coverage

certification of electrical equipment for use in flammable atmospheres

Publications

BASEEFA Guide
BASEEFA Standards
List of Certified Equipment

345 BRITISH ARCHITECTURAL LIBRARY

Royal Institute of British Architects, 66 Portland Place, London W1N 4AD Tel. 01-580 5533

Special Library; comprising the Sir Bannister Fletcher Library, the Drawings Collection and the Heinz Gallery, the latter two units at 21 Portman Square, London W1H 9HF; formerly known as the Royal Institute of British Architects Library

Enquiries to the Senior Information Librarian

Subject coverage

architecture of all periods and all countries, theory, design, building types, interiors; construction industry, building methods and materials; sociology and management in relation to architecture; planning and environment, landscape

Special collections

3,500 works published before 1840
Handley-Read Collection on 19th century architecture

Major Collection of International Modern Movement books and periodicals
Archives of the Design and Industries Association
Substantial manuscript holdings
Extensive biographical files

Publications
Architectural Periodicals Index (quarterly with annual cumulation)
RIBA Book List (annual)
Catalogue of RIBA Drawings Collection
Catalogue of pre-1840 books (in preparation)

346 BRITISH AROMATIC COMPOUND MANUFACTURERS ASSOCIATION
London Chamber of Commerce and Industry, 69 Cannon Street, London EC4N 5AB — Tel. 01-248 4444, Telex 888941
Trade Association

Enquiries to the Secretary

Subject coverage
aromatic compounds

347 BRITISH ARTMETAL MANUFACTURERS EXPORT GROUP (BAMEX LIMITED)
82–84 Moseley Street, Birmingham B12 0RT — Tel. 021-622 1556
Company and Trade Association

Enquiries to the Director

Subject coverage
domestic, ornamental and reproduction articles manufactured of brass and copper, for export

348 BRITISH ASSOCIATION FOR COMMERCIAL AND INDUSTRIAL EDUCATION (BACIE)
16 Park Crescent, London W1N 4AP — Tel. 01-636 5351
Educational Charity

Enquiries, from members only, to the Information Department

Subject coverage
training; personnel management, manpower planning; business studies

Publications
BACIE Bibliography (annotated list of books, 3 vols.)
BACIE Journal (monthly, not August)
Textbooks
Monographs, Lectures, Occasional Papers
List of publications

349 BRITISH ASSOCIATION FOR THE ADVANCEMENT OF SCIENCE
Fortress House, 23 Savile Row, London W1X 1AB — Tel. 01-734 6010
Registered Charity, having sixteen specialist sections

Enquiries to the Secretary

Subject coverage
physics and mathematics; chemistry; geology; zoology; geography; economics; engineering; anthropology; biomedical sciences; psychology; botany; forestry; education; agriculture; sociology

Publications
BA Record (quarterly, for members)
Advancement of Science (annual)
Reports, monographs, and specialist publications (list available)

350 BRITISH ASSOCIATION IN FORENSIC MEDICINE
c/o Honorary Secretary, Sub-Department of Forensic Pathology, University of Sheffield, Western Bank, Sheffield S10 2TN — Tel. 0742 20617
Professional Association

Enquiries to the Honorary Secretary

Subject coverage
forensic pathology; forensic science; paternity testing

351 BRITISH ASSOCIATION OF COLLIERY MANAGEMENT
317 Nottingham Road, Old Basford, Nottingham NG7 7DP Tel. 0602 76949
Management Trade Union

Enquiries to the General Secretary

Subject coverage
representation of senior management up to Board level in the coal industry

352 BRITISH ASSOCIATION OF CONFERENCE TOWNS
6 Falsgrave Road, Scarborough, North Yorkshire YO12 5AT Tel. 0723 68735
Local Authority Association

Enquiries to the Director

Subject coverage
facilities for and planning of conferences at home and overseas, for the tourist and travel trade and meetings planners

Publication
Brochure on member towns

BRITISH ASSOCIATION OF CONSULTANTS IN AGRICULTURE AND HORTICULTURE *now* **BRITISH INSTITUTE OF AGRICULTURAL CONSULTANTS,** *q.v.*

353 BRITISH ASSOCIATION OF FISHING TACKLE MAKERS & DISTRIBUTORS
145 Oxford Street, London W1R 1TB Tel. 01-437 7281
Trade Association; the words '& Distributors' were recently added to its title; affiliated to the Federation of British Manufacturers of Sports and Games

Enquiries to the Secretary

Subject coverage
manufacture and manufacturers of types of fishing tackle

Publication
Trade Directory (in preparation)

354 BRITISH ASSOCIATION OF GRAIN SEED FEED AND AGRICULTURAL MERCHANTS LIMITED
3 Whitehall Court, London SW1A 2EQ Tel. 01-930 3611
Telex 917868
Trade Association; includes ICAM (the former Institute of Corn and Agricultural Merchants Limited), which constitutes the training and educational arm of the Association; merger of the Association with the Compound Animal Feeding Stuffs Manufacturers National Association, *q.v.*, to form the United Kingdom Agricultural Supply Trades Association, is proposed

Enquiries to the Secretary

Subject coverage
agricultural merchanting industry; careers, technical training, management, legislation

Publications
Agricultural Merchant
ICAM Technical Newscast
MAS Bulletin
Specific Studies

355 BRITISH ASSOCIATION OF GREEN CROP DRIERS LIMITED
Agroup House, 16 Lonsdale Gardens, Tunbridge Wells, Kent TN1 1PD Tel. 0892 37777
Telex 95114
Trade Association; formerly Association of Green Crop Driers Limited

Enquiries to the Chief Executive

Subject coverage
production and utilization of dried forages from green crops (grass, lucerne, maize) for animal feeding

Publications
Grass (3 times per annum)

356 BRITISH ASSOCIATION OF INDUSTRIAL EDITORS
2a Elm Bank Gardens, Barnes, London SW13 0NT Tel. 01-876 6283
Professional Association; member of the Federation of European Industrial Editors Association and the International Association of Business Communicators, U.S.A.

Enquiries to the Secretary General

Subject coverage
education and careers in industrial editing; consultancy and assessment for house journals

Special collection
library of current house journals

Publications
BAIE News (monthly, for members)
Editing for Industry (standard text)
BAIE House Journals 1973 (statistical survey)

BRITISH ASSOCIATION OF MACHINE TOOL ASSOCIATIONS *now* **ASSOCIATION OF EUROPEAN MACHINE TOOL MERCHANTS,** *q.v.*

BRITISH ASSOCIATION OF NUMISMATIC SOCIETIES *see* **ROYAL NUMISMATIC SOCIETY**

BRITISH ASSOCIATION OF OVERSEAS FURNITURE REMOVERS *now* **BRITISH ASSOCIATION OF REMOVERS,** *q.v.*

357 BRITISH ASSOCIATION OF REMOVERS
279 Grays Inn Road, London WC1X 8SY Tel. 01-837 3088
Trade Association, affiliated to the Federation of International Furniture Removers (Brussels, Belgium); formerly the National Association of Furniture Warehousemen and Removers *and* the British Association of Overseas Furniture Removers; houses the Institute of the Furniture Warehousing and Removing Industry

Enquiries to the General Secretary; answers only possible under certain conditions

Subject coverage
domestic and international removal work; removal staff training

Publication
Removals and Storage (monthly)

BRITISH ASSOCIATION OF SYNTHETIC RUBBER MANUFACTURERS *see* **CHEMICAL INDUSTRIES ASSOCIATION LIMITED**

BRITISH ASTRONOMICAL ASSOCIATION *see* **ROYAL ASTRONOMICAL SOCIETY**

358 BRITISH BACON CURERS FEDERATION
Icknield Way, Tring, Hertfordshire HP23 4JY Tel. 044-282 4124
Trade Association; houses the Offices of Bacon Curing Industry National Joint Industrial Council

Enquiries to the Marketing and Publicity Manager

Subject coverage
bacon, ham, and pig meat processing; technical and statistical information

359 BRITISH BANKERS ASSOCIATION
10 Lombard Street, London EC3V 9EL Tel. 01-623 4001
Telex 888364

Bankers Association

Enquiries to the Secretary-General

Subject coverage
banking, including U.K. and E.E.C.

Publications
Annual Report
Occasional publications on specific banking subjects, e.g. Prudential Regulation of Banks in the E.E.C.

BRITISH BANTAM ASSOCIATION *see* **POULTRY CLUB OF GREAT BRITAIN**

360 BRITISH BATH MANUFACTURERS ASSOCIATION LIMITED
Fleming House, Renfrew Street, Glasgow G3 6TG Tel. 041-332 0826/7/8
Telex 779433

Trade Association

Enquiries to the Information Officer

Subject coverage
light metals trades

361 BRITISH BATTERY MAKERS SOCIETY
46 Park Street, London W1Y 4DJ Tel. 01-491 7966
Telex 25386

Trade Association

Enquiries, limited, to the Secretary

Subject coverage
lead-acid storage battery manufacture, (*not* primary batteries)

362 BRITISH BIOPHYSICAL SOCIETY
c/o Biochemical Society, 7 Warwick Court, High Holborn, Tel. 01-242 1076
London WC1R 5DP
Learned Society

Enquiries to the Secretary

Subject coverage
biophysics research and education

363 BRITISH BLIND AND SHUTTER ASSOCIATION
First Floor, 251 Brompton Road, London SW3 2EZ Tel. 01-584 5552
Trade Association

Enquiries to the Secretary

Subject coverage
window blinds and rolling shutters

Publication
Blinds and Shutters (quarterly)

BRITISH BOLT, NUT, AND SCREW FEDERATION *now* **BRITISH INDUSTRIAL FASTENERS FEDERATION,** *q.v.*

BRITISH BRAZING AND SOLDERING ASSOCIATION *see* **BNF METALS TECHNOLOGY CENTRE**

364 BRITISH BROADCASTING CORPORATION
Research Department, Kingswood Warren, Tadworth, Surrey Tel. 604 2361
Public Corporation Research Department

Enquiries to the Librarian

Subject coverage
electronics; radio and television engineering

365 BRITISH BRONZE & BRASS INGOT MANUFACTURERS ASSOCIATION
136 Hagley Road, Edgbaston, Birmingham B16 9PN Tel. 021-454 4141
Trade Association

Enquiries to the Secretaries, Heathcote & Coleman, of the above address

Subject coverage
supply of copper alloy ingots

Publication
Specifications for Cast Copper Alloys

366 BRITISH BRUSH MANUFACTURERS ASSOCIATION
Baptist Church House, 4 Southampton Row, London WC1B 4AB Tel. 01-242 1799
Trade Association; houses also the British Brush Manufacturers Research Association, the Brush Export Group, the National Joint Committee for the Brush & Broom & Hair, Fibre & Bass Industries, *qq.v.*

Enquiries to the Secretary

Subject coverage
brooms and brushes and painting rollers

367 BRITISH BRUSH MANUFACTURERS RESEARCH ASSOCIATION
Baptist Church House, 4 Southampton Row, London WC1B 4AB Tel. 01-242 1799
Research Association; houses also the British Brush Manufacturers Association and the Brush Export Group, *qq.v.*

Enquiries to the Director

Subject coverage
design and manufacture of brushes; characteristics, quality and processing of brush filling materials; adhesives and all other components and materials

368 BRITISH BRYOLOGICAL SOCIETY
Department of Botany, National Museum of Wales, Cardiff, CF1 3NP Tel. 0222 397951/3
Learned Society

Enquiries to the Honorary Secretary

Subject coverage
bryology (mosses and liverworts); conservation

Special collection
herbarium of approximately 28,000 dried specimens of bryophytes

Publications
Journal of Bryology
Bulletin

BRITISH BUREAU OF NON-FERROUS METALS STATISTICS *now* **WORLD BUREAU OF METAL STATISTICS,** *q.v.*

369 BRITISH BUSINESS GRADUATES SOCIETY
84 Moorgate, London EC2M 6SQ Tel. 01-287 1030 ext. 327
Trade Association

Enquiries to the Secretary

Subject coverage
business studies

370 BRITISH BUTTON MANUFACTURERS ASSOCIATION
P.O. Box 5, Berkhamsted, Hertfordshire HP4 3UG Tel. 024-029 437
Telex 268205

Trade Association, affiliated to the European Button Industries Federation

Enquiries to the Secretary

Subject coverage
sources of supply

371 BRITISH CALIBRATION SERVICE
26 Chapter Street, London SW1P 4NS Tel. 01-834 7032
Government Department, of the Metrology, Quality Assurance and Standards Division of the Department of Prices and Consumer Protection; certificates of approval granted to over seventy laboratories

Enquiries to the Director

Subject coverage
calibration; measurement; metrology; measuring instruments

Publications
BCS List of publications gives the general, guidance and miscellaneous documents and a film
List of Approved Laboratories (booklet)
Directory of Approved Laboratories (full details of laboratories and measurements); updated five times per year (on subscription only)

372 BRITISH CARBONIZATION RESEARCH ASSOCIATION
Wingerworth, Chesterfield, Derbyshire S42 6JS Tel. 0246 76821
Research Association; formerly British Coke Research Association *and* Coal Tar Research Association

Enquiries to the Information Officer

Subject coverage
coke (from coal) and coal tar-production, properties, testing and uses; air pollution, control and measurement; liquid effluent treatment and analysis

Publication
BCRA Review (quarterly abstracts journal)

BRITISH CARPET CLASSIFICATION SCHEME *see* **BRITISH CARPET MANUFACTURERS ASSOCIATION TECHNICAL COMMITTEE**

BRITISH CARPET INDUSTRY TECHNICAL ASSOCIATION *now* **BRITISH CARPET MANUFACTURERS ASSOCIATION TECHNICAL COMMITTEE,** *q.v.*

373 BRITISH CARPET MANUFACTURERS ASSOCIATION
Dorland House, 14–16 Regent Street, London SW1Y 4PL Tel. 01-930 8711
Telex 338526
Trade Association; formed by the merger of the Federation of British Carpet Manufacturers and the Tufted Carpet Manufacturers Association; houses the British Carpet Export Council

Enquiries, commercial, to the Association, Dorland House

Subject coverage
pile carpets, trade and commercial aspects

Publication
Technical Bulletin (members and subscribers only)

374 BRITISH CARPET MANUFACTURERS ASSOCIATION TECHNICAL COMMITTEE
Technical Centre, Ackroyd House, Hoo Road, Kidderminster, Worcestershire DY10 1NB Tel. 0562 4053
Trade Association, Technical Section; formerly the British Carpet Industry Technical Association; includes the British Carpet Classification Scheme

Enquiries, technical, to the Technical Centre

Subject coverage
pile carpet technology

375 BRITISH CARTOGRAPHIC SOCIETY
11 Hope Terrace, Edinburgh EH9 2AP Tel. 031-447 6261
Learned Society/Registered Charity; Library, *see next entry*

Enquiries to the Honorary Secretary

Subject coverage
cartography; history of cartography; map curatorship; technical developments and automation in cartography; education and careers in cartography

Publications
Cartographic Journal (six-monthly)
Careers in Cartography (booklet)
Automated Cartography
Newsletter (quarterly, to members only)

376 BRITISH CARTOGRAPHIC SOCIETY LIBRARY
c/o Central Library, George IV Bridge, Edinburgh EH1 1EG   Tel. 031-225 5584
Learned Society's Library

Enquiries to the Librarian (loans to members only)

Subject coverage
geography; cartography; aerial photography; surveying; navigation

Special collection
atlases (housed at John Bartholomew & Sons Limited, 12 Duncan Street, Edinburgh EH9)

Publications
Catalogue, 1971; Supplement 1972

BRITISH CAST IRON PRESSURE PIPE ASSOCIATION *now* **DUCTILE IRON PIPE ASSOCIATION,** *q.v.*

BRITISH CAST IRON RESEARCH ASSOCIATION *see* **BCIRA**

377 BRITISH CATTLE VETERINARY ASSOCIATION
c/o Honorary Secretary, Meat and Livestock Commission, P.O. Box 44, Queensway House, Bletchley, Milton Keynes MK2 2EF   Tel. 0908 74941
Professional Association; affiliated to the British Veterinary Association, *q.v.*

No enquiry service

Subject coverage
veterinary science

378 BRITISH CAVE RESEARCH ASSOCIATION
Bethel Green, Calderbrook Road, Littleborough, Lancashire OL15 9ND   Tel. 061-764 6911
Learned Society, registered charity, affiliated to the International Union of Speleology and National Caving Association

Enquiries to Secretary, (address as above), or to the Librarian, 7 Parkinson Lane, Halifax, W. Yorkshire

Subject coverage
cave science (speleology) world-wide, archaeology, biology, geology of limestone, limestone geomorphology, limestone (Karst) hydrology, cave survey, cave photography, caving expeditions abroad, cave research

Publications
Transactions of the British Cave Research Association (quarterly)
Bulletin of the British Cave Research Association (quarterly)
Both free to members

379 BRITISH CELLOPHANE LIMITED
Bath Road, Bridgewater, Somerset TA6 4PA   Tel. 0278 4321
Telex 4666

Company

Enquiries to the Information Officer

Subject coverage
packaging films technology

380 BRITISH CERAMIC PLANT AND MACHINERY MANUFACTURERS ASSOCIATION
P.O. Box 9, Sunbury, Middlesex TW16 6BX Tel. 76 83280/87352
Trade Association

Enquiries to the Secretary

Subject coverage
plant and machinery and/or turnkey projects for the manufacture of the complete range of ceramic products, including building bricks; sewer pipes; roofing, wall and floor tiles; tableware; sanitary ware; art pottery; porcelain insulators; refractories; etc

Publication
British Ceramic Review (quarterly)

381 BRITISH CERAMIC RESEARCH ASSOCIATION
Queens Road, Penkhull, Stoke-on-Trent, Staffordshire ST4 7LQ Tel. 0782 45431
Research Association

Enquiries, by letter, to the Director of Research; by telephone, to the Information Officer (service not necessarily free or unrestricted)

Subject coverage
production and service behaviour of ceramic materials and pottery (tableware, sanitary ware, tiles, electrical porcelain); refractories; technical ceramics for engineering and electrical applications; clay and calcium silicate-based building products (bricks, sewer pipes) and their behaviour in structures; evaluation of properties and physical and chemical testing methods

Special collections
Mellor Memorial Library (the Association's Library)
Graves Library (on bricks and building)

Publications
British Ceramics Abstracts (monthly)
In Fact
Conference Proceedings
Research reports

382 BRITISH CERAMIC TILE COUNCIL
Federation House, Station Road, Stoke-on-Trent, Staffordshire ST4 2RU Tel. 0782 45147
Trade Association

Enquiries to the Publicity Manager

Subject coverage
manufacture, supply and installation of ceramic glazed tiles and ceramic unglazed floor tiles

Publications
Compendium of literature on the range of wall and floor tiles manufactured by members
Technical literature on installation

BRITISH CHEMICAL AND DYESTUFFS TRADERS ASSOCIATION LIMITED *see* CHEMICAL INDUSTRIES ASSOCIATION LIMITED

383 BRITISH CHEMICAL ENGINEERING CONTRACTORS ASSOCIATION
1–3 Regent Street, London SW1Y 4NR Tel. 01-839 6514
Trade Association

Enquiries to the Director

Subject coverage
chemical engineering contracting work of the Association; the qualifications and experience of member companies

Publication
Directory of member companies and their capabilities

BRITISH COKE RESEARCH ASSOCIATION *now* **BRITISH CARBONIZATION RESEARCH ASSOCIATION,** *q.v.*

384 BRITISH COLOUR MAKERS ASSOCIATION
Alembic House, 93 Albert Embankment, London SE1 7TU Tel. 01-735 3001
Telex 916672

Trade Association, affiliated to the Chemical Industries Association Limited

Enquiries to the Secretary

Subject coverage
coloured pigment manufacture

385 BRITISH COMBUSTION EQUIPMENT MANUFACTURERS ASSOCIATION
The Fernery, Market Place, Midhurst, Sussex GU29 9DP Tel. 073-081 2782
Trade Association; formerly British Oil and Gas Firing Equipment Manufacturers Association

Enquiries to the Secretary

Subject coverage
combustion equipment and its ancillaries for all kinds of combustible fuel

Publications
British Combustion (quarterly)
Register of Members (biennial)

386 BRITISH COMPRESSED GASES ASSOCIATION
93 Albert Embankment, London SE1 7TU Tel. 01-735 3001
Telex 916672

Trade Association; formerly the British Acetylene Association; affiliated to the Chemical Industries Association Limited

Enquiries to the Secretary

Subject coverage
U.K. manufacture of compressible gases, cylinders, valves, etc., and the uses thereof

Publications
Codes of Practice CP1 pressure regulators
CP2 blowpipes

387 BRITISH COMPUTER SOCIETY
29 Portland Place, London W1N 4HU Tel. 01-637 0471
Telex 28319

Scientific Society

Enquiries, library, to the Librarian, British Computer Society Library, at the City University Library, q.v.; other enquiries to the Society's address

Subject coverage
all aspects of computers and their applications; commercial data processing; management of data processing (but hardware manuals and software are *not* kept)

Publications
Computer Journal (quarterly)
Computer Bulletin (monthly)
Monographs and conference papers

388 BRITISH COPYRIGHT COUNCIL
29–33 Berners Street, London W1P 3DB Tel. 01-580 5544
Consultative Council of organizations representing copyright interests

Enquiries to the Secretary (tel. 01-930 1911); (no full-time enquiry staff)

Subject coverage
copyright

Publications
Comment on Copyright

Photocopying and the law

BRITISH CONSTRUCTIONAL STEELWORK ASSOCIATION LIMITED *see* **COMMITTEE OF ASSOCIATIONS OF SPECIALIST ENGINEERING CONTRACTORS**

389 BRITISH CONSULTANTS BUREAU
55–58 Pall Mall, London SW1Y 5LH — Tel. 01-839 7687
Telex 916469

Company limited by guarantee/Consultants

Enquiries to the Director

Subject coverage
overseas projects in agriculture; architecture; economics; engineering; management; planning; surveying and costing

Publication
BCB Brochure (directory)

390 BRITISH CONTRACT FURNISHING ASSOCIATION
116 Bermondsey Street, London SE1 — Tel. 01-403 0231
Trade Association; formerly Contract Furnishing Association

Enquiries to the Director

Subject coverage
all aspects of contract furnishing (*i.e.* non-domestic furnishing)

Publications
Contract Directory (annual)
Newsletter (monthly)

BRITISH COTTON WASTE ASSOCIATION *now* **BRITISH TEXTILE BY-PRODUCTS ASSOCIATION,** *q.v.*

391 BRITISH COUNCIL OF MAINTENANCE ASSOCIATIONS
c/o Instron Limited, Coronation Road, High Wycombe, Buckinghamshire HP12 3SY — Tel. 0494 33333
Voluntary Association; member of the European Federation of National Maintenance Societies

Enquiries to the Honorary General Secretary

Subject coverage
maintenance engineering (terotechnology); reliability; use of computers in maintenance management decisions

Publications
Newsletter
Pamphlet on the Council's work

BRITISH COUNCIL OF PRODUCTIVITY ASSOCIATIONS *see* **BRITISH PRODUCTIVITY COUNCIL**

392 BRITISH CRYOGENICS COUNCIL
c/o Institution of Chemical Engineers, 165–171 Railway Terrace, Rugby CV21 3HQ — Tel. 0788 78214
Voluntary Council; affiliated to a number of the major chemical, metallurgical and engineering institutions

Enquiries to the Secretary

Subject coverage
low temperature engineering; superconductivity; low temperature physics; cryogenics; safety

Publications
Monographs
Cryogenics Safety Manual
Vacuum insulated lines
Cryogenic Equipment: buyers guide

393 BRITISH DECORATORS ASSOCIATION
6 Haywra Street, Harrogate, North Yorkshire HG1 5BL Tel. 0423 67292
Employers/Trade Association, member of the Federation of Associations of Specialists and Sub-Contractors and founder member of the Paint and Painting Industries Liaison Committee; formerly National Federation of Master Painters and Decorators of England and Wales

Enquiries, limited unless from Members, to the Director or Secretary

Subject coverage
members' service relating to the decorating trade, in materials breakdown investigation, arbitration, insurance, training and education

Publications
British Decorator (periodical)
Reference Handbook (annual)

394 BRITISH DEER SOCIETY
Forge Cottage, Askham, Penrith, Cumbria CA10 2PF Tel. Hackthorpe 400
National Society, having nine English branches and seven Scottish branches

Enquiries to the General Secretary and Educational Director

Subject coverage
natural history of deer, world-wide; control and management, veterinary advice

Special collections
photographs and colour transparencies, films, library and archive material

Publication
Deer (3 times per annum)

395 BRITISH DIRECT MAIL MARKETING ASSOCIATION
11 New Burlington Street, London W1X 1FD Tel. 01-437 4485
Trade and Professional Association; formerly British Direct Mail Advertising Association; affiliated to the Advertising Association, *q.v.*

Enquiries to the Secretary

Subject coverage
direct marketing (direct mail and mail order)

396 BRITISH DISINFECTANT MANUFACTURERS ASSOCIATION
93 Albert Embankment, London SE1 7TU Tel. 01-582 1115
Telex 916672
Trade Association, affiliated to the Chemical Industries Association Limited

Enquiries to the Secretary

Subject coverage
all aspects of the disinfectant industry

Publications
Annual Report
Directory of Members' Products

BRITISH DRUG HOUSES LIMITED *see*
BDH CHEMICALS LIMITED
BDH PHARMACEUTICALS LIMITED

397 BRITISH ECOLOGICAL SOCIETY
Harvest House, 62 London Road, Reading RG1 5AS Tel. 0734 861345
Scientific Society/Charity

Enquiries to the Council Secretary, Department of Zoology, University of Manchester, Manchester M13 9PL

Subject coverage
Ecology in the widest sense; conservation; pollution; land use

Publications
Journal of Ecology
Journal of Animal Ecology
Journal of Applied Ecology
Proceedings of Symposia

398 BRITISH EDUCATIONAL EQUIPMENT ASSOCIATION LIMITED
Sunley House, Gunthorpe Street, London E1 7RW Tel. 01-247 9320
Trade Association; formerly Educational Equipment Association; associated with the Educational Contractors Group and the British Educational Furniture Manufacturers Council

Enquiries to the Director

Subject coverage
educational equipment and materials

Publications
List of Members
Annual Report
Memorandum and Articles of Association

BRITISH EDUCATIONAL FURNITURE MANUFACTURERS COUNCIL *see* **BRITISH EDUCATIONAL EQUIPMENT ASSOCIATION LIMITED**

399 BRITISH EGG PRODUCTS ASSOCIATION
No. 1 London Bridge, London SE1 9SZ Tel. 01-407 0738
Trade Association; formerly British Egg Products Distributors Association

Enquiries to the Secretary

Subject coverage
frozen and liquid whole egg; dried egg; separated egg

BRITISH ELECTRIC TRACTION COMPANY LIMITED *see*
BOULTON AND PAUL LIMITED
INTERNATIONAL SYSTEMS RESEARCH LIMITED

BRITISH ELECTRICAL AND ALLIED MANUFACTURERS ASSOCIATION LIMITED *see* **BEAMA**

BRITISH ELECTRICAL CONDUIT SYSTEMS MANUFACTURERS ASSOCIATION *now* **BRITISH ELECTRICAL SYSTEMS ASSOCIATION,** *q.v.*

400 BRITISH ELECTRICAL SYSTEMS ASSOCIATION
Leicester House, 8 Leicester Street, London WC2H 7BN Tel. 01-437 0678
Telex 263536
Trade Association; member of BEAMA, *q.v.*; formerly British Electrical Conduit Systems Manufacturers Association

Enquiries to the Director

Subject coverage
electrical conduit; cable trunking and associated fittings

401 BRITISH ELECTRO-CERAMIC MANUFACTURERS ASSOCIATION
Federation House, Stoke-on-Trent ST4 2SA Tel. 0782 48631
Trade Association; member of the British Ceramic Manufacturers Federation

Enquiries to the Secretary

Subject coverage
supplies of electro-ceramics

402 BRITISH ELECTROTECHNICAL APPROVALS BOARD FOR HOUSEHOLD EQUIPMENT
Mark House, The Green, 9/11 Queens Road, Hersham, Surrey KT12 5LU Tel. 093-22 44401
Independent National Organization, formerly British Electrical Approvals Board for Household Appliances

Enquiries to the Office Administrator

Subject coverage
electrical household equipment approvals

Publications
BEAB List of Approved Household Electrotechnical Equipment (annual, quarterly supplements)
"Shop Safe"

403 BRITISH ENGINEERING BRICK ASSOCIATION
Grove House, Sutton New Road, Birmingham B23 6QY Tel. 021-373 7445
Trade Association

Enquiries to the Secretary

Subject coverage
engineering brick industry: members names and addresses; other subject enquiries referred to Research Associations

404 BRITISH ESSENCE MANUFACTURERS ASSOCIATION
1/2 Castle Lane, Buckingham Gate, London SW1E 6DN Tel. 01-828 7822
Telex 918095
Trade Association, linked with the Food Manufacturers Federation Incorporated

Enquiries to the Executive Secretary

Subject coverage
pertinent U.K. and E.E.C. legislation affecting the flavouring industry for food manufacturing

BRITISH EXECUTIVE SERVICE OVERSEAS *see* **INSTITUTE OF DIRECTORS**

405 BRITISH FARM PRODUCE COUNCIL
Agriculture House, Knightsbridge, London SW1X 7NJ Tel. 01-235 4964
Council

Enquiries to the Information Officer

Subject coverage
quality, availability, and use by the consumer of all British edible agricultural and horticultural produce

BRITISH FEDERATION OF MASTER PRINTERS *now* **BRITISH PRINTING INDUSTRIES FEDERATION,** *q.v.*

BRITISH FELT HAT MANUFACTURERS FEDERATION *now* **BRITISH HEADWARE INDUSTRIES FEDERATION,** *q.v.*

406 BRITISH FILTERS LIMITED
Thames Industrial Estate, Fieldhouse Lane, Marlow, Buckinghamshire SL7 1TD Tel. 062-84 73131
Company; member of the Tecalemit Group

Enquiries to the Technical Sales Department

Subject coverage
filtration; hydraulics; bulk liquid filtration (beer, chemicals, pharmaceuticals)

407 BRITISH FIRE PROTECTION SYSTEMS ASSOCIATION LIMITED
21 Whitefriars Street, London EC4Y 8AL Tel. 01-583 8121
Trade Association, affiliated to the Council of British Fire Protection Equipment Manufacturers (CBFPEM) and to the European Association of Fire Alarm Manufacturers (EURALARM)

Enquiries, by letter only, to the General Manager

Subject coverage
automatic fire detection; manual alarm systems; fire warning signalling; automatic sprinkler installations; inert gas and chemical extinguishing systems; fire fighting equipment

Publications

Code of Practice for Low Pressure CO_2 Systems
Code of Practice for Fire Detectors incorporating radioactive material
Standard for CO_2 Fire Extinguishing Systems
Report on the Performance of Fire Alarm Systems in Britain

408 BRITISH FIRE SERVICES ASSOCIATION

86 London Road, Leicester LE2 0QR — Tel. 0533 542879

Professional Association, member of the Federation of British Fire Organizations; created by the merger of the Professional Fire Brigades Association and the National Fire Brigades Association

Enquiries to the General Secretary

Subject coverage

organization of fire brigades in industry; fire protection in industry and commerce; training of fire brigade personnel

Publication

Journal (quarterly)

409 BRITISH FLAME RESEARCH COMMITTEE

140 Battersea Park Road, London SW11 4LZ — Tel. 01-622 5511
Telex 918917

Research Association; affiliated to the International Flame Research Foundation, Ijmuiden, Netherlands

Enquiries to the Secretary

Subject coverage

fundamental aspects and basic mechanisms of combustion and heat transfer; physics and physico-chemistry of large flames; performance of industrial furnaces; burner systems; reduction of noise and pollution

Publication

Annual Report

BRITISH FLOWER INDUSTRY ASSOCIATION *see* **COVENT GARDEN AUTHORITY**

410 BRITISH FOOD EXPORT COUNCIL

World Trade Centre, Europe House, East Smithfield, London E1 9AA — Tel. 01-480 6594
Telex 884671

Trade Association

Enquiries to the Council

Subject coverage

promotion of British processed foods exports in overseas markets

Publications

periodic Market Reports

411 BRITISH FOOD MANUFACTURING INDUSTRIES RESEARCH ASSOCIATION

Randalls Road, Leatherhead, Surrey KT22 7RY — Tel. 53 76761
Telex 929846

Research Association

Enquiries from Members only

Subject coverage

food science; nutrition; catering; hygiene; pollution; quality control; microbiology; analytical chemistry; polymer science; biochemistry; microscopy

Publications

Research Reports and Technical Circulars (for members only)
Scientific and Technical Surveys
Abstracts Journal
Literature Surveys
Layman's Guides
Symposium Proceedings
Computerized Bibliographies

412 BRITISH FOOTWEAR MANUFACTURERS FEDERATION
Royalty House, 72 Dean Street, London W1V 5HB Tel. 01-437 5573
Trade Association

Enquiries to the Director General

Subject coverage
footwear manufacture

413 BRITISH FRICTION MATERIALS COUNCIL
99 Aldwych, London WC2B 4JY Tel. 01-242 0211
Telex 268002

Trade Association

Enquiries to the Secretaries, Baker, Rooke & Amsdons, of the same address, who will refer questions to members

Subject coverage
general and technical information on the friction materials industry

414 BRITISH FROZEN FOOD FEDERATION
Honeypot Lane, Colsterworth, Grantham, Lincolnshire NG33 5LX Tel. 0476 84414
Trade Association, formerly the National Association of Wholesale Distributors of Frozen Foods

Enquiries to the Secretary

Subject coverage
frozen food industry

BRITISH FUR TRADE ASSOCIATION *see* **INTERNATIONAL FUR TRADE FEDERATION**

BRITISH FURNITURE MANUFACTURERS FEDERATED ASSOCIATIONS *see* **BIRMINGHAM AND WEST MIDLANDS FURNITURE MANUFACTURERS ASSOCIATION**

415 BRITISH GAS CORPORATION
HQ, 59 Bryanston Street, London W1A 2AZ Tel. 01-723 7030
Telex 261710

Nationalised Industry, formerly Gas Council

Enquiries to the Librarian

Subject coverage
gas (towns, natural or synthetic); its production, distribution and uses (via appropriate departments, *q.v.*)

Publications
List of Tested and Approved Domestic Gas Appliances
List of Tested and Approved Commercial Gas Appliances
List of Approved and Certificated Catering Gas Appliances
Film Catalogue
British Gas Educational Aids
Britain's Natural Gas
Discovering Gas
Natural Gas on Target
Safe use of Gas

416 BRITISH GAS CORPORATION
Research and Development Division Headquarters, Tel. 01-242 0789
National Westminster House, 326 High Holborn, London WC1V 7PT Telex 28645
Nationalised Industry, Research HQ

Enquiries to the Assistant Research Secretary

Subject coverage
gas industry research in general; patents information; international consultancy service

417 BRITISH GAS CORPORATION
Research and Development Division, Engineering Research Station, Tel. 0632 684828
Killingworth, P.O. Box 1LH, Newcastle upon Tyne NE99 1LH Telex 53470
Nationalised Industry

Enquiries to Assistant Division Manager/Information

Subject coverage
gas supply engineering; mechanical engineering; gas/natural gas; metallurgy; materials science; high and low pressure gas pipelines; gas storage installations and associated equipment including compressors, valves, flow meters, instrumentation and maintenance equipment

418 BRITISH GAS CORPORATION
Research and Development Division, London Research Station, Tel. 01-736 3344
Michael Road, London SW6 2AD Telex 24670
Nationalised Industry, Division formerly the London Research Station of the Gas Council

Enquiries to the Leader, Library and Information

Subject coverage
mathematical and computing techniques and services; chemical and microbiological aspects of gas production, treatment, storage, and distribution; chemical and physical methods of analysis; basic physics and chemistry in relation to natural and manufactured gas, including combustion, chemical kinetics, catalysis and thermophysical properties; appliance testing; production, installation and quality control standards; properties of metals, ceramics and polymers; energy conservation; novel energy processes

419 BRITISH GAS CORPORATION
Research and Development Division, Midlands Research Station, Tel. 021-705 7581
Wharf Lane, Solihull, West Midlands B91 2JW Telex 339128
Nationalised Industry

Enquiries to the Head of Information and Publications

Subject coverage
production of substitute natural gas; combustion and heat transfer; burner design; automated control systems; gas firing in boilers; furnaces; some low temperature processes; safety, noise and anti-pollution studies

Publication
Publications List

420 BRITISH GAS CORPORATION
Scientific Information Centre, Research and Development Division, Tel. 01-736 1212
Watson House, Peterborough Road, Fulham, London SW6 3HN
Nationalised Industry

Enquiries to the Leader, Scientific Information

Subject coverage
domestic and small scale commercial utilisation of gas; reliability; preparation of standards; design and development of components such as ignition controls, thermostats and burners

421 BRITISH GAS SCHOOL OF FUEL MANAGEMENT
Midlands Research Station, Wharf Lane, Solihull, Tel. 021-705 7581
West Midlands B91 2JW Telex 339128
Unit of British Gas Corporation, *q.v.*; formerly the School of Industrial Gas Engineering

Enquiries to the Head of the School

Subject coverage
all aspects of fuel management

422 BRITISH GEAR MANUFACTURERS ASSOCIATION
301 Glossop Road, Sheffield S10 2HN Tel. 0742 21071
Telex 54170
Trade Association; member of the European Committee of Associations of Manufacturers of Gears and Transmission Parts

Enquiries to the Secretaries

Subject coverage
gears and ancillary equipment and services

Publication
Buyers Guide

423 BRITISH GEOTECHNICAL SOCIETY
Institution of Civil Engineers, Great George Street, London SW1P 3AA Tel. 01-839 3611 ext. 266
Learned Society, member of the International Society for Soil Mechanics and Foundation Engineering, *q.v.* and of the International Society for Rock Mechanics

Enquiries, limited, to the Secretary

Subject coverage
soil mechanics; foundation engineering, rock and ice mechanics; details of conferences and proceedings in the field; no careers information

Publication
Geotechnique (quarterly)

424 BRITISH GLASS INDUSTRY RESEARCH ASSOCIATION
Northumberland Road, Sheffield S10 2UA Tel. 0742 686201
Telex 54208
Research Association

Enquiries to the Information Officer

Subject coverage
glass technology

Publication
Digest of Information and Patent Review

425 BRITISH GOAT SOCIETY
Lion House, Rougham, Bury St. Edmunds, Suffolk IP30 9LJ Tel. 035-97 351
Breed Society

Enquiries to the Society

Subject coverage
goat management; details of goats registered

Publications
Monthly Journal
Year Book
Herd Book
Various booklets

BRITISH GRANITE AND WHINSTONE FEDERATION *now* **BRITISH QUARRYING & SLAG FEDERATION,** *q.v.*

426 BRITISH GYPSUM LIMITED
Research and Development Department, East Leake, Loughborough, Leicestershire Tel. 0602 214321
Company Research & Development Department; of BPB Industries Limited

Enquiries to the Research and Development Librarian

Subject coverage
gypsum and plaster technology; wood wool

427 BRITISH HACKSAW MAKERS ASSOCIATION
Light Trades House, Melbourne Avenue, Sheffield S1Q 2QJ Tel. 0742 663084
Trade Association; member of the National Federation of Engineers' Tool Manufacturers

Enquiries to the Secretary

Subject coverage
manufacture of hacksaws

428 BRITISH HARD METAL ASSOCIATION
Light Trades House, Melbourne Avenue, Sheffield S10 2QJ Tel. 0742 663084
Trade Association; member of the National Federation of Engineers' Tool Manufacturers

Enquiries to the Secretary

Subject coverage
hard metal industry

BRITISH HARDWARE FEDERATION *see* **GUILD OF ARCHITECTURAL IRONMONGERS**

429 BRITISH HEADWEAR INDUSTRIES FEDERATION
27 Higher Hillgate, Stockport SK1 3EU Tel. 061-480 8731
Trade Association; formerly British Felt Hat Manufacturers Federation

Enquiries to the Secretary

Subject coverage
headwear in general

430 BRITISH HELICOPTER ADVISORY BOARD LIMITED
Knowles House, Cromwell Road, Redhill, Surrey RH1 1LW Tel. 91 62371
Trade Association

Enquiries to the Chief Executive

Subject coverage
all aspects of helicopter operations

Publications
Annual Information Handbook
Code of Flight Conduct for Helicopter Pilots

431 BRITISH HERPETOLOGICAL SOCIETY
Zoological Society of London, Regents Park, London NW1 4RY Tel. 01-205 7635
Scientific Society

Enquiries, by letter accompanied by SAE, to the Secretary

Subject coverage
conservation of reptiles and amphibians; their care in captivity; import restrictions

Publication
Journal of Herpetology (twice per annum)

BRITISH HIRE CRUISER FEDERATION *see* **SHIP AND BOAT BUILDERS NATIONAL FEDERATION**

BRITISH HOSIERY AND KNITWEAR EXPORT GROUP *now* **BRITISH KNITTING EXPORT COUNCIL,** *q.v.*

432 BRITISH HOSPITAL EQUIPMENT DISPLAY CENTRE
22 Newman Street, London W1P 3HB Tel. 01-637 9948
Permanent Exhibition and Information Centre

Enquiries to the Manager

Subject coverage
equipping of hospitals, nursing homes and medical centres

Publications
catalogues and brochures

BRITISH HYDROMECHANICS RESEARCH ASSOCIATION *now* **BHRA FLUID ENGINEERING,** *q.v.*

433 BRITISH IMPORTERS CONFEDERATION
69 Cannon Street, London EC4N 5AB Tel. 01-248 4444
Telex 888941
Trade Association, including Clothing and Textiles Sub-Committee and Small Tools Sub-Committee

Enquiries to the Secretary

Subject coverage
importing

Publication
Directory of British Importers

434 BRITISH INDUSTRIAL BIOLOGICAL RESEARCH ASSOCIATION
Woodmansterne Road, Carshalton, Surrey SM5 4DS Tel. 01-643 4411
Research Association

Enquiries, from members only, to the Information Officer

Subject coverage
toxicology and safety-in-use of food additives; contaminants, including packaging migrants, processing aids, pesticides, feed additives and other agricultural chemicals; cosmetics and toiletries; surgical dressings; tobacco additives; industrial chemicals and other possible environmental hazards; toxicological tests and testing; legislation

Publications
Food and Cosmetics Toxicology
Toxicology

435 BRITISH INDUSTRIAL FASTENERS FEDERATION
Queen's House, Queen's Road, Coventry CV1 3EG Tel. 0203 22325
Trade Federation; formerly the British Bolt, Nut, and Screw Federation; houses the Black Bolt and Nut Association of Great Britain; the Rolled Thread Screw Association and the Small Rivet Association are Product Groups of the Federation

Enquiries to the Director

Subject coverage
industrial fasteners including bolts, screws, rivets, nuts, aerospace fasteners

Publication
Metrication Brochure

436 BRITISH INDUSTRIAL MEASURING AND CONTROL APPARATUS MANUFACTURERS ASSOCIATION
20 Peel Street, London W8 7PD Tel. 01-727 2614
Trade Association

Enquiries to the Secretary

Subject coverage
process control and instrumentation

437 BRITISH INDUSTRIAL PLASTICS LIMITED
P.O. Box 6, Oldbury, Warley, West Midlands B69 4PD Tel. 021-552 1551
Telex 337261
Company, formerly BIP Chemicals Limited; subsidiary of Turner and Newall Limited

Enquiries to the Technical Information Officer

Subject coverage
plastics technology

438 BRITISH INDUSTRIAL PLASTICS LIMITED
Sheet and Film Division, Brantham, Manningtree, Essex CO11 1NJ — Tel. 020-639 2401, Telex 98201

Company, subsidiary of Turner and Newall Limited

Enquiries to the Librarian

Subject coverage
plastic sheet and film

439 BRITISH INSTITUTE OF AGRICULTURAL CONSULTANTS
25 Market Place, Newark, Nottinghamshire NG24 1EA — Tel. 0636 4773, 72491

Professional Institute, formerly British Association of Consultants in Agriculture and Horticulture

Enquiries to the Secretary

Subject coverage
agriculture; horticulture; forestry; silviculture; arboriculture; crop production; livestock production; mechanisation; land drainage and reclamation; landscape planning; chemicals and fertilizers; plant pathology; farm and estate management; farm buildings; pollution; soils; management; finance; planning appeals; agricultural education and law

Publications
List of members and their specialist services
Curricula vitae of overseas & international consultants

BRITISH INSTITUTE OF EMBALMERS *see* **ASSOCIATION OF BUILDERS HARDWARE MANUFACTURERS**

440 BRITISH INSTITUTE OF INTERIOR DESIGN
162 Derby Road, Stapleford, Nottingham NG9 7AY — Tel. 0602 397250
Professional Institute, formerly Incorporated Institute of British Decorators and Interior Designers

Enquires to the Secretary

Subject coverage
interior design, architectural design, textiles, fashion, sign design, advertising, printing, publicity, display, shop fitting; education and training in the foregoing subjects

441 BRITISH INSTITUTE OF MANAGEMENT
Management House, Parker Street, London WC2B 5PT — Tel. 01-405 3456
Professional Body, having a Management Education Information Unit and a Management Consultancy Services Information Unit

Enquiries, usually from members only, to the Information Officer or the Librarian

Subject coverage
management; industrial relations; marketing; office planning; production and productivity; training; etc

Publications
Management Review and Digest (quarterly)
Guidelines for Smaller Businesses
Bibliographies and reading lists
Salary surveys
Reports

442 BRITISH INSTITUTE OF NON-DESTRUCTIVE TESTING
53–55 London Road, Southend-on-Sea, Essex SS1 1PF — Tel. 0702 354252
Professional Institute, formerly Non-destructive Testing Society of Great Britain

Enquiries to the Secretary

Subject coverage
non-destructive testing applications

Publication
British Journal of Non-destructive Testing (quarterly)

443 BRITISH INSTITUTE OF RADIOLOGY
32 Welbeck Street, London W1M 7PG Tel. 01-935 6237
Scientific/Learned Society

Enquiries to the General Secretary

Subject coverage
medical radiology and allied subjects

Publications
list available

444 BRITISH INSURANCE ASSOCIATION
Box 538, Aldermary House, Queen Street, London EC4P 4JD Tel. 01-248 4477
Trade Association

Enquiries to the Information Officer, Public Relations Department

Subject coverage
insurance; insurance statistics

Publications
Insurance facts and figures
Guide to motor insurance
Insurance film library, a list of films for sale, free loan or hire
Pamphlets on various aspects of insurance
Educational packs for schools

BRITISH INSURANCE BROKERS ASSOCIATION *see*
ASSOCIATION OF INSURANCE BROKERS
FEDERATION OF INSURANCE BROKERS
LLOYDS INSURANCE BROKERS ASSOCIATION

445 BRITISH INTERNAL COMBUSTION ENGINE MANUFACTURING ASSOCIATION (BICEMA)
127 Regent Street, London W1R 7HA Tel. 01-734 8368
Trade Association, also housing the Secretariat for the British National Committee of the International Council on Combustion Engines

Enquiries to the Chief Executive

Subject coverage
internal combustion engines

Publications
British Engines: BICEMA catalogue
BICEMA Metric Medium Pitch Screw Threads Standard

446 BRITISH INTERNAL COMBUSTION ENGINE RESEARCH INSTITUTE LIMITED
111 Buckingham Avenue, Slough, Berkshire SL1 4PH Tel. 75 27371/4
Research and Development Organization; title formerly Association, now Institute

Enquiries to Librarian, Information Officer or Director of Research

Subject coverage
diesel engines and ancillary equipment; petrol engines and ancillary equipment; exhaust emissions; engine control equipment; torsional vibration; stress analysis

Publications
Weekly Abstracts to trade and technical press

447 BRITISH INTERPLANETARY SOCIETY
12 Bessborough Gardens, London SW1V 2JJ Tel. 01-828 9371
Learned Society, member of the International Astronautical Federation

Enquiries to the Librarian

Subject coverage
astronautics

Publication
Spaceflight (monthly)

448 BRITISH INVESTMENT CASTERS TECHNICAL ASSOCIATION
117–121 Charles Street, Sheffield S1 2ND Tel. 0742 737816
Professional Association

Enquiries to the Secretary

Subject coverage
investment casting process and equipment, materials, components; suppliers of castings and equipment

Special collections
technical publications on investment castings; Conference proceedings

Publications
Abstracts (for members only)

449 BRITISH IRON AND STEEL CONSUMERS COUNCIL
Rotaflex House, 241 City Road, London EC1P 1ET Tel. 01-253 1200
Telex 263084
Steel Consumer Body; formerly a Government body called Iron and Steel Consumers Council

Enquiries to the Director

Subject coverage
supply of steel to U.K. users

BRITISH IRON AND STEEL RESEARCH ASSOCIATION *now* **BRITISH STEEL CORPORATION Corporate Engineering Laboratory,** *q.v.*

BRITISH JERSEY FABRIC BOARD *see* **KNITTING INDUSTRIES FEDERATION LIMITED**

450 BRITISH KINEMATOGRAPH, SOUND & TELEVISION SOCIETY
110 Victoria House, Vernon Place, London WC1B 4DJ Tel. 01-242 8400
Professional Society

Enquiries to the Secretary

Subject coverage
technical fields of film, sound, television and audio visuals industries

Publications
BKSTS Journal (monthly)
Technical Manuals (list available)

451 BRITISH KNITTING EXPORT COUNCIL
Academy House, 26–28 Sackville Street, London W1X 1DA Tel. 01-734 6277
Telex 25149
Trade Association, formerly British Hosiery and Knitwear Export Group

Enquiries to the Director

Subject coverage
(for buyers overseas) British manufacturers of knitwear, hosiery, knitted fabrics interested in export contacts and sources of supply
(for member firms) details of export markets, regulations tariffs, export statistics, potential customers and methods of marketing; trade promotions; exhibitions; trade representation

Publication
Information Bulletin (fortnightly)

452 BRITISH LABORATORY WARE ASSOCIATION LIMITED
28 Worple Road, Wimbledon, London SW19 4EE Tel. 01-946 2548
Trade Association; includes Labware Promotions, a department for organizing Exhibitions

Enquiries, normally from members only, or concerning members' products, to the Association

Subject coverage
laboratory apparatus and equipment

Publication
Membership Directory (free to users of laboratory equipment, etc.)

BRITISH LAMPBLOWN SCIENTIFIC GLASSWARE MANUFACTURERS ASSOCIATION LIMITED *see* **GLASS MANUFACTURERS FEDERATION**

453 BRITISH LAUNDERERS RESEARCH ASSOCIATION
Hill View Gardens, Hendon, London NW4 2JS Tel. 01-203 2143
Research Association

Enquiries, from members, and from non-members in certain circumstances, to the Information Officer

Subject coverage
washing processes; laundering equipment; examination of goods damaged during laundering; energy conservation; effluent treatment

Publications
Clean Up to Date
Newsletter
Data Link
Process and Equipment News (includes Patents)

454 BRITISH LAWNMOWER MANUFACTURERS FEDERATION
99 Aldwych, London WC2B 4JY Tel. 01-242 0211
Telex 268002
Trade Association; formerly British Lawn Mower and Grass Cutter Makers Federation

Enquiries to the Secretaries, Baker Rooke & Amsdons, of the above address, who will refer them to members

Subject coverage
general and technical information on the lawnmower industry

455 BRITISH LEAD MANUFACTURERS ASSOCIATION
Vernon House, Sicilian Avenue, Bloomsbury Square, London WC1A 2QH Tel. 01-242 5021
Trade Association; housing the Lead Smelters and Refiners Association, Red Lead and Litharge Manufacturers Association, White Lead Manufacturers Association, Lead Sheet and Pipe Export Group

Enquiries to the Director

Subject coverage
lead manufacture; sources of supply of products; use, characteristics and performance of products; sources of technical information

456 BRITISH LEATHER MANUFACTURERS RESEARCH ASSOCIATION
Milton Park, Egham, Surrey TW20 9UQ Tel. 01-389 3086/7
Trade Association

Enquiries to the Information Officer

Subject coverage
manufacture and use of leather in all aspects, including raw hides and skins; fellmongering; treatment and disposal of industrial wastes; chemical testing of leather and tanning; physical and mechanical testing of leather; leather dyes and surface coatings

Publications
BLMRA Journal (monthly, confidential to members)
Hides, Skins, and Leather under the Microscope
Leather clothing, its Make-up and Dry Cleaning
Microscopical Examination of Leather: a guide line for forensic scientists
Translations and Abstracts for Staff and Members

457 BRITISH LEYLAND (UK) LIMITED

BL Cars, Engineering and Development, Longbridge, Birmingham B31 2TB — Tel. 021-475 2101 ext. 151, Telex 33491

Manufacturing Company

Enquiries to the Information Officer

Subject coverage

automobile, mechanical and production engineering; management

458 BRITISH LIBRARY BIBLIOGRAPHIC SERVICES DIVISION

Store Street, London WC1E 7DG — Tel. 01-636 0755, Telex 22787

Government Department; the Bibliographic Services Division was formed using the Council of the British National Bibliography as base and including the Copyright Receipt Office and the U.K. National Serials Data Centre, linked to the UNESCO-sponsored International Serials Data Centre, Paris

Enquiries to the Customer Relations Officer

Subject coverage

British publishing in general; bibliographic searches; legal deposit and copyright; cataloguing; classification; location of serials; registration for ISSN's

Publications

British National Bibliography (weekly; quarterly and annual cumulations)
Books in English (catalogue on microfiche)
U.K. MARC Manual
Precis Manual

459 BRITISH LIBRARY LENDING DIVISION

Boston Spa, Wetherby, West Yorkshire LS23 7BQ — Tel. 0937 843434, Telex 557831

National Library; the Division was formed by the merger of the former National Central Library and the National Lending Library for Science and Technology; houses the U.K. Medlars Service Centre

Enquiries, for loans or photocopies, by the printed requisition forms, to the Loans Enquiry Office

Subject coverage

science, technology, industry; specially medicine and allied subjects (through the Medlars Service); Russian scientific and technical literature (much in English translation)

Special collections

Conference Proceedings (over 56,000)
Theses and Dissertations (about 150,000, U.K., U.S., and some European)
Research Reports (over 1,000,000, mainly U.S.)
Translations (over 300,000)
All British Official Publications since 1962
All E.E.C. official Publications since 1973

Publications

BLL review (annual)
Current Serials Received, 1975
BLL Conference Index, 1964–1973
Index of Conference proceedings received (Annual cumulations from 1974)
BLLD Announcement Bulletin
Keyword Index of Guides to the Serial Literature
Serial publications of the European Communities and its institutions held by the BLLD (gratis)
BLLD brief guides (U.K. and overseas versions available gratis)
IFLA Office for International Lending. Brief guide to centres of international lending and photocopying
Annual Report
British Library News (gratis)

460 BRITISH LIBRARY NEWSPAPER LIBRARY
130 Colindale Avenue, Hendon, London NW9 5HE — Tel. 01-205 6039, 01-205 4788

Part of the Reference Division of the British Library; formerly British Museum Newspaper Library

Enquiries to the Superintendent

Special collections

National Collection of Newspapers, including London newspapers and journals from 1801 onwards
English Provincial, Scottish and Irish newspapers from 1700 onwards
Commonwealth and foreign newspapers

Publications

Catalogue of the Newspaper Library, 8 volumes, (obtainable from British Museum Publications Ltd)

461 BRITISH LIBRARY SCIENCE REFERENCE LIBRARY
25 Southampton Buildings, London WC2A 1AW — Tel. 01-405 8721

National Library; a unit of the British Library Reference Division; formerly National Reference Library of Science and Invention, and, before that, the Patent Office Library; comprises the Holborn Branch (address above), a Kean Street annexe, and the Bayswater Branch at 10 Porchester Gardens, Queensway, London W2 4DE

Enquiries to the Director (Services)

Subject coverage

all physical and life sciences and technologies (except social science and economics); at Holborn: national patents and trademarks, chemistry, physics, engineering; at Kean Street: trade catalogues and report series; at Bayswater: natural resources, biology and health; linguistic help in fifteen languages

Special collections

National Patents collection including overseas holdings and trade mark literature
U.K. Copyright deposit holdings in science and technology
Trade catalogues and technical House Journals
Abstracting journals supported by on-line bibliographic data bases
Spectroscopic data

Publications

Periodicals News
Occasional Publications: guides to patent literature in various countries, lists of abstract journals, etc
Guidelines: introductions to sources of information
Industrial property news: Latest publications on patents, trade marks and designs

462 BRITISH LIBRARY OF POLITICAL AND ECONOMIC SCIENCE
Houghton Street, London WC2A 2AE — Tel. 01-405 7686

Library, of which the Court of Governors of the London School of Economics is the Sole Trustee, serving as the Library of the School; houses the Edward Fry Library of International Law

Enquiries to the Librarian

Subject coverage

bibliographical information on politics; economics; sociology; public administration

Special collections

a large number of collections made by or concerning prominent people in economics and politics
Bell Collection on early railways
Nadel Collection on anthropological work in Nigeria and the Sudan

Publications

London Bibliography of the Social Sciences
Classified Catalogue of a Collection on Publishing & Bookselling
Outline of the Resources of the Library
Annual Report

463 BRITISH LICHEN SOCIETY
Department of Botany, British Museum (Natural History), Cromwell Road, London SW7 5BD — Tel. 01-589 6323 ext. 552
Learned Society; member of the Council for Nature, the Biological Council *q.v.* and the International Mycological Association

Enquiries to the Secretary

Subject coverage
lichens; air pollution

Special collection
a lichen herbarium

Publications
The Lichenologist (journal of research)
British Lichen Society Bulletin (news)

464 BRITISH LOCK MANUFACTURERS ASSOCIATION
91/93 Tettenhall Road, Wolverhampton WV3 9PE — Tel. 0902 26726, Telex 338490

Trade Association

No enquiry service

Subject coverage
wage rates and service conditions within the industry

465 BRITISH MAN-MADE FIBRES FEDERATION
Bridgewater House, 58 Whitworth Street, Manchester M1 6LS — Tel. 061-236 3777
Trade Association, member of the British Textile Confederation; houses the office of the Secretary of the British Throwsters Association; (London Office of the Federation, 41–42 Dover Street, London W1, houses the Secretary of the Home Laundering Consultative Council)

Enquiries to the Information Officer, with stamped addressed envelope

Subject coverage
sources of product supplies and statistical information on the fibre producing and using sectors of the U.K. textiles industry

466 BRITISH MARINE EQUIPMENT COUNCIL LIMITED
111/112 Whitechapel High Street, London E1 7PT — Tel. 01-247 7566, Telex 886593

Trade Association

Enquiries to the Director

Subject coverage
marine equipment; from main engine to galley stove; radar and control equipment

Publications
Contact Lists
Market Information
Directory

467 BRITISH MASONRY DRILL ASSOCIATION
Light Trades House, 3 Melbourne Avenue, Sheffield S10 2QJ — Tel. 0742 663084
Trade Association

Enquiries to the Secretary

Subject coverage
masonry drill industry

468 BRITISH MERCANTILE AGENCY LIMITED
Sidcup House, 12–18 Station Road, Sidcup, Kent DA15 7EH Tel. 01-300 6815
Telex 262859

Trade Association; including the Association of Manufacturing Chemists Limited, Textiles Credit Protection Limited, Paper Trade Protection Agency, *q.v.*, Grocery Trade Protection Agency, Palatine Trade Protection Office, Photographic Trade Protection Agency

Enquiries to the Director

Subject coverage
commercial debt collection and status information

BRITISH METAL CASTINGS COUNCIL *see* **COUNCIL OF IRONFOUNDRY ASSOCIATIONS**

469 BRITISH METAL SINTERINGS ASSOCIATION
Windsor House, Temple Row, Birmingham B2 5LD Tel. 021-236 0201
Association

Enquiries to the Secretary

Subject coverage
powder metallurgy

470 BRITISH METALWORKING PLANT MAKERS ASSOCIATION
7 Ludgate Broadway, London EC4V 6DX Tel. 01-248 1543
Telex 8812908

Trade Association; member of the Metallurgical Plantmakers Federation, *q.v.*

Enquiries to the Secretary

Subject coverage
steelworks plant, *i.e.* casting, forming and processing machinery for ferrous and non-ferrous metals, including rolling mills and ancillary equipment; continuous casting machines; process, treatment and cut-up lines; drawing machines; tube making machinery

Publication
List of Members

471 BRITISH MUSEUM (NATURAL HISTORY)
Cromwell Road, London SW7 5BD Tel. 01-589 6323

Taxonomic Research Institution; administers also the library of the Zoological Museum at Tring (specializing in ornithology)

Enquiries to the Librarian

Subject coverage
zoology; entomology; botany; palaentology, including physical anthropology; mineralogy; oceanography

Special collections
Linnaeus Collection (binomial nomenclature system in botanical classification; works on plants and animals
Richard Owen (anatomy)
Robert Brown (botany, including material from the Australian expedition 1801–1805)
Sydney Parkinson (natural history; drawings)
Walsingham (entomology)
John Murray (oceanography)
Albert Gunther (zoology, 16th/17th century, including European animals and fish)
Walter Rothschild (zoology)
Sowerby (natural history, especially botany; the family were artists and publishers)
Joseph Banks (natural history, note-books, etc from Cook's first voyage around the world)
Sloane (natural history and collection of curiosities and artifacts of c. 1753. Sloane's collection was the foundation of the British Museum)
Tweeddale Library (zoology)

Publications

Bulletin of the British Museum (Natural History): Zoology series, Entomolgy series, Botany series, Palaeontology series, Mineralogy series, Historical series
Monographs, handbooks, guide books
Catalogue of the Works of Linnaeus
Catalogue of the Books and Manuscripts, Maps and Drawings in the British Museum (Natural History)
List of Serials in the British Museum (Natural History)

BRITISH MUSEUM (ETHNOLOGY DEPARTMENT) *see* **MUSEUM OF MANKIND**

472 BRITISH NATIONAL COMMITTEE FOR ELECTROHEAT
30 Millbank, London SW1P 4RD Tel. 01-834 2333
Telex 23385 & 261130
Independent Body; member of L'Union Internationale d'Electrothermie, Paris

Enquiries to the Executive

Subject coverage
industrial process heating by electricity

473 BRITISH NATIONAL COMMITTEE FOR NON-DESTRUCTIVE TESTING
53–55 London Road, Southend-on-Sea, Essex SS1 1PF Tel. 0702 354252
Liaison Committee

Enquiries to the Secretary

Subject coverage
applications of non-destructive testing techniques in industry

474 BRITISH NATIONAL COMMITTEE ON MATERIALS
c/o 12 High March, Long March Industrial Estate, Daventry, Northamptonshire NN11 4HB Tel. 032-72 2964 & 3004
Consultative Body

Enquiries to the Secretary

Subject coverage
materials application and conservation

475 BRITISH NATURALISTS ASSOCIATION
Willowfield, Boyneswood Road, Four Marks, Alton, Hampshire GU34 5EA Tel. 0420 63659
Voluntary organisation, affiliated to the Council for Nature

Enquiries to the Honorary Secretary

Subject coverage
natural history

Publication
Countryside (3 times per annum)

476 BRITISH NON-FERROUS METALS FEDERATION
Crest House, 7 Highfield Road, Edgbaston, Birmingham B15 3ED Tel. 021 454 7766
Telex 339161
Trade Association; housing the Copper Tube Fittings Manufacturers Association and the Non-Ferrous Hot Stampers Association

Enquiries to the Secretary

Subject coverage
production and supply of semi-manufactures in copper and copper alloys

Publication
Annual Report

BRITISH NON-FERROUS METALS RESEARCH ASSOCIATION *now* **BNF METALS TECHNOLOGY CENTRE,** *q.v.*

477 BRITISH NUCLEAR ENERGY SOCIETY

Institution of Civil Engineers, 1–7 Great George Street, London SW1P 3AA — Tel. 01-839 3611

Forum of eleven Constituent Bodies as follows: the Institutions of Civil Engineers, Mechanical Engineers, Electrical Engineers, Electronic and Radio Engineers and Chemical Engineers; the Institute of Physics, the Metals Society, the Royal Institute of Chemistry, the Institute of Fuel, the Joint Panel on Nuclear Marine Propulsion, and the Institute of Measurement and Control

Enquiries to the Executive Officer

Subject coverage

nuclear energy; reactor systems; fuel; safety

Publications

BNES Journal (quarterly)
List of Books (about 25 titles)

478 BRITISH NUCLEAR FORUM

1 St. Albans Street, London SW1Y 4SL — Tel. 01-930 6888/9
Telex 22565

Industrial Association, affiliated to FORATOM (European Association of Atomic Forums)

Enquiries to the Director

Subject coverage

nuclear energy

Publications

Monthly Bulletin
News Letter
Specialised reports

479 BRITISH NUCLEAR FUELS LIMITED

Capenhurst Works, Capenhurst, Chester CH1 6ER — Tel. 051-339 4101

Nationalised Industrial Company, wholly owned by UKAEA, formerly UKAEA Production Group

Enquiries to the Librarian/Information Officer

Subject coverage

uranium enrichment, especially by gaseous diffusion and gas centrifuge; chemistry and chemical engineering; electrical and mechanical engineering; mathematics and computers

480 BRITISH NUMERICAL CONTROL SOCIETY

Rochester House, 66 Little Ealing Lane, London W5 4XX — Tel. 01-579 9411 ext. 35

Professional Society; associated with the Institution of Production Engineers, *q.v.*

Enquiries to the Secretary

Subject coverage

numerical control systems for machine tools and machinery; programming of N.C. systems; machine tools suitable for N.C. and the interface between the machines and their controls; education and training; design of parts for production by N.C. and production planning; investment appraisal and costing considerations

Publications

BNCS News
BNCS Buyers Guide (biennial)
Proceedings of Annual Technical Conferences

481 BRITISH NUMISMATIC SOCIETY

Warburg Institute, Woburn Square, London WC1H 0AB

Learned Society; its Library is combined with that of the Royal Numismatic Society, *q.v.*

Enquiries to the Honorary Librarian

Subject coverage
coins, currency, medals and tokens of Great Britain and Ireland and the English-speaking world from the earliest times; history of minting techniques

Publication
British Numismatic Journal (annual)

482 BRITISH NUTRITION FOUNDATION
Alembic House, 93 Albert Embankment, London SE1 7TY Tel. 01-735 8201
Registered Charity, formerly British Nutrition Foundation Limited

Enquiries to the Secretary

Subject coverage
nutrition in general

Publications
BNF Bulletin (3 times per annum)
Leaflets
Teachers Food and Nutrition Kit

483 BRITISH OCCUPATIONAL HYGIENE SOCIETY
c/o Esso Research Centre, Abingdon, Oxfordshire
Learned Society

Enquiries to the Honorary Secretary

Subject coverage
occupational hygiene; recognition, evaluation, and control of stresses in the environment, affecting the health or well-being of workers or the community; emphasis on health hazards at work

Publications
Annals of Occupational Hygiene (Pergamon Press)
BOHS Newsletter

BRITISH OCEANOGRAPHIC DATA SERVICE *see* **INSTITUTE OF OCEANOGRAPHIC SCIENCES**

BRITISH OIL AND GAS FIRING EQUIPMENT MANUFACTURERS *now* **BRITISH COMBUSTION EQUIPMENT MANUFACTURERS ASSOCIATION,** *q.v.*

484 BRITISH OPTICAL ASSOCIATION
65 Brook Street, London W1Y 2DT Tel. 01-629 3382
Professional Body

Enquiries to the Secretary and Director of Examinations or to the Librarian

Subject coverage
ophthalmic and dispensing optics; professional qualifications

Special collection
museum of optical and ophthalmic instruments and appliances

Publications
British Journal of Physiological Optics
Ophthalmic Optician

485 BRITISH ORNITHOLOGISTS UNION
Zoological Society of London, Regents Park, London NW1 4RY Tel. 01-586 4443
Scientific Society, member of the Council for Nature, and the Biological Council, *q.v.*; houses the British Ornithologists Club

Enquiries to the Union will be channelled to bodies best able to deal with them

Subject coverage
ornithology (the Union has Corresponding Members in all areas of the world; but no information officer or libary on the premises)

Publications
The Ibis (quarterly)
Status of Birds in Britain and Ireland 1971
Checklists
Bulletin (variable number per annum) issued by the Club

486 BRITISH OVERSEAS TRADE BOARD
1 Victoria Street, London SW1H 0ET — Tel. 01-215 7877, Telex 8811074

Government-sponsored Body, associated with the Department of Trade; includes the Export Intelligence Service, Export Services and Promotions Division, Exports to Japan Unit and Overseas Tariffs and Regulations Section, *q.v.*

Enquiries to the Publicity Unit, Room 231A (tel. 01-215 3221)

Subject coverage
Government services for existing and potential exporters

Publications
Annual Report
Export Handbook
Report on Education and Training for Overseas Trade
Foundation Course in Overseas Trade
Leaflets on the services
Special Market Reports
Publications list available

487 BRITISH OVERSEAS TRADE GROUP FOR ISRAEL
British Overseas Trade Board, Michael House, Baker Street, London W1A 1DN — Tel. 01-935 4422, Telex 267141

Voluntary Group; formerly the Israel Committee of the British National Export Council

Enquiries to the Executive Secretary

Subject coverage
Anglo-Israel trade

488 BRITISH OXYGEN CHEMICALS
Vigo Lane, Chester-le-Street, County Durham DH3 2RB — Tel. 0894 242631, Telex 53163

Company; part of BOC Limited, *q.v.*

Enquiries to the Technical Information Officer

Subject coverage
chemistry and chemical technology; uses of tall oil and derived fatty acids and rosin; dicyandiamide; melamine; aqueous acrylic dispersions for pressure-sensitive adhesives

BRITISH OXYGEN COMPANY LIMITED *see* **BOC LIMITED**

489 BRITISH PAPER AND BOARD INDUSTRY FEDERATION
3 Plough Place, Fetter Lane, London EC4A 1AL — Tel. 01-583 0686, Telex 24854

Employers/Trade Association, formerly British Paper and Board Makers Association which merged with Employers Federation of Papermakers and Boardmakers; list of sectional and affiliated associations follows

Enquiries to the Information Officer

Subject coverage
U.K. paper and board industry

Publications
A wide range of fact sheets and other publications (technical and commercial)—list available

BRITISH PAPER AND BOARD INDUSTRY FEDERATION *see also*
ASSOCIATION OF BOARD MAKERS
ASSOCIATION OF MAKERS OF NEWSPRINT
ASSOCIATION OF MAKERS OF PACKAGING PAPERS
ASSOCIATION OF MAKERS OF PRINTING AND WRITING PAPERS
ASSOCIATION OF MAKERS OF SOFT TISSUE PAPERS
ASSOCIATION OF OFFICE MACHINE PAPERS COATERS AND LAMINATORS
ASSOCIATION OF PAPER FINISHERS
ASSOCIATION OF U.K. WOOD PULP PRODUCERS
CORRUGATED CASE MATERIALS ASSOCIATION

490 BRITISH PEST CONTROL ASSOCIATION
Alembic House, 93 Albert Embankment, London SE1 7TU — Tel. 01-582 8268, Telex 916672

Trade Association, formerly Industrial Pest Control Association; member of the Chemical Industries Association Limited

Enquiries to the Director

Subject coverage
industrial pesticide usage; rodent control; timber and wood preservation treatment; fumigation

Publications
British Pest Control Conference Proceedings
British Pest Control Association Directory

491 BRITISH PETROLEUM COMPANY LIMITED
BP Chemicals Limited, Devonshire House, Mayfair Place, London W1X 6AY — Tel. 01-629 8867, Telex 266883

Company; BP Chemicals Limited was formerly BP Chemicals International Limited

No enquiry service

Subject coverage
economics; plastics; petrochemicals

Publications
technical leaflets and catalogues

492 BRITISH PETROLEUM COMPANY LIMITED
BP Oil Limited, BP House, Victoria Street, London SW1E 5NJ — Tel. 01-821 2000, Telex 8811151

Company; BP Oil Limited was formerly BP Refineries Limited

Enquiries to the Library

Subject coverage
petroleum refining; oil products distribution and marketing

493 BRITISH PETROLEUM COMPANY LIMITED
Central Information and Library Service, Brittanic House, Moor Lane, London EC2Y 9BU — Tel. 01-920 8000, Telex 888811

Company

Enquiries to the Librarian

Subject coverage
petroleum industry

Publications
educational, technical and promotional literature

494 BRITISH PETROLEUM COMPANY LIMITED
Exploration and Production Research Division, BP Research Centre, Chertsey Road, Sunbury-on-Thames, Middlesex TW16 7LN — Tel. 76 85533

Company

No enquiry service

Subject coverage
geology; geophysics; petroleum engineering, geochemistry

495 BRITISH PHARMACOLOGICAL SOCIETY
Department of Pharmacology, Royal College of Surgeons, Lincolns Inn Fields, London WC2A 3PN — Tel. 01-405 3474
Learned Society

Enquiries to the Honorary General Secretary

Subject coverage
pharmacology

Publications
British Journal of Pharmacology
British Journal of Clinical Pharmacology

496 BRITISH PHARMACOPOEIA COMMISSION
8 Bulstrode Street, London W1M 5FT — Tel. 01-487 2665
Government Department, of the Department of Health and Social Security

Enquiries to the Secretary

Subject coverage
standards for the purity, identity, and potency of medicinal products; nomenclature of medicinal products

Publications
British Pharmacopoeia (H.M.S.O.)
Approved Names (H.M.S.O.)

497 BRITISH PHOTOGRAPHIC EXPORT GROUP
76 Vine Lane, Hillingdon, Middlesex UB10 0BE — Tel. 89 33372
Trade Association

Enquiries to the Secretary

Subject coverage
photographic supplies; exporting

498 BRITISH PHOTOGRAPHIC IMPORTERS ASSOCIATION
8 St. Bride Street, London EC4A 4DA — Tel. 01-353 3020, Telex 24276
Trade Association

No enquiry service

Subject coverage
information about the photographic industry is issued to Members only; the Association is the industry's link with the Government

499 BRITISH PLASTICS FEDERATION
47 Piccadilly, London W1V 0DN — Tel. 01-734 2041, Telex 267746
Trade Association; houses the British Agricultural and Horticultural Plastics Association, *q.v.*

Enquiries to the Information Bureau

Subject coverage
all sectors of the plastics industry, commercial and technical; economic trends and statistics; environmental considerations; fire hazards and prevention; industrial health and safety; plastics in building; processing and moulding; reinforced plastics; thermoplastics

Publications
Business Trends Survey
Journalists Guide to Plastics
British Machinery and Equipment for Plastics Processing

Many other papers, etc., from specialist Groups and Committees in, for example, safety, environment, fire, health, PVC, reinforced plastics

500 BRITISH POLAROGRAPHIC RESEARCH INSTITUTE
55Oriental Road, Woking, Surrey GU22 7AL
Private Charity/Research Foundation

Enquiries, from supporting Organizations and Trusts only, to Director

Subject coverage
polarisational phenomena, gas phase and liquid phase; polarography, analogue and electrochemical; polarophilosophy, environmental and medical; polarovision science; polaro-engineering

Publications
Occasional Research Papers (to supporting bodies only)

501 BRITISH PORTS ASSOCIATION
3 Queen Square, London WC1N 3AR — Tel. 01-278 6995
Trade Association, formerly Dock and Harbour Authorities Association

Enquiries to the Secretary

Subject coverage
port operations

Publications
Port Statistics for the Foreign Trade of the United Kingdom, parts 1, 2, and 3 (annual)

502 BRITISH POSTAL EQUIPMENT ENGINEERING ASSOCIATION
9 Catherine Place, London SW1E 6DX — Tel. 01-834 1426
Trade Association

Enquiries to the Secretary

Subject coverage
postal equipment industry (*not* labour relations)

503 BRITISH POTTERY MANAGERS ASSOCIATION
c/o Department of Ceramic Technology, North Staffordshire Polytechnic, College Road, Stoke-on-Trent ST4 2DE — Tel. 0782 45531
Professional Association

Enquiries to the Secretary

Subject coverage
production of pottery; supplies of materials

504 BRITISH POULTRY BREEDERS AND HATCHERIES ASSOCIATION LIMITED
High Holborn House, 52/54 High Holborn WC1V 6SX — Tel. 01-242 4683/4, Telex 28479
Trade Association; formerly Poultry Stock Association Limited; member of the British Poultry Federation, *q.v.*

Enquiries to the Information Officer

Subject coverage
poultry breeding; hatching; rearing; sources of supply of stock for eggs and poultry meat

505 BRITISH POULTRY FEDERATION
52–54 High Holborn, London WC1V 6SX — Tel. 01-242 4683/4, Telex 28479

Trade Association, affiliated to the Employers Federation of Trade Associations

Enquiries to the Director-General

Subject coverage
poultry industry

BRITISH POULTRY FEDERATION *see also*
BRITISH EGG PRODUCTS ASSOCIATION
BRITISH POULTRY BREEDERS AND HATCHERIES ASSOCIATION LIMITED
BRITISH POULTRY MEAT ASSOCIATION LIMITED
COMPOUND ANIMAL FEEDING STUFFS MANUFACTURERS NATIONAL ASSOCIATION
DUCK PRODUCERS ASSOCIATION
NATIONAL EGG PACKERS ASSOCIATION LIMITED

506 BRITISH POULTRY MEAT ASSOCIATION LIMITED
52–54 High Holborn, London WC1V 6SX Tel. 01-242 4683
Telex 28479
Trade Association, formed by merger of the National Association of Poultry Packers Limited and the British Chicken Association Limited; member of the British Poultry Federation

Enquiries to the Secretary

Subject coverage
the poultry industry; production statistics; identification of poultry processors; recipe service

Publications
Background Paper on the British Chicken Industry
Newsletters (for members only; irregular)
Code of Practice

BRITISH POWER PRESS MANUFACTURERS ASSOCIATION LIMITED *now* **METAL FORMING MACHINERY MAKERS ASSOCIATION,** *q.v.*

507 BRITISH PRECAST CONCRETE FEDERATION LIMITED
60 Charles Street, Leicester LE1 1FB Tel. 0533 28627
Trade Association; member Associations of the following titles: Autoclaved Aerated Concrete Product, Box Culvert Manufacturers, Concrete Brick Manufacturers, Cladding and Cast Stone, Concrete Block, Federation of Concrete Specialists, Flag and Kerb Product, Interlocking Paving, Lighting Column, Pipe Products, Prestressed Concrete, and Roofing Tile

Enquiries to the Secretary, the Research Officer or the Technical Administrator

Subject coverage
precast concrete industry (as indicated by member associations above); technical services, research, training, contract advice, industrial relations, economics, international developments

Publication
Newsletter (to members only)

508 BRITISH PRESSURE GAUGE MANUFACTURERS ASSOCIATION
67 Newhall Street, Birmingham B3 1NU Tel. 021-236 7711
Trade Association

Enquiries to the Secretary

Subject coverage
pressure gauge standards

509 BRITISH PRINTING INDUSTRIES FEDERATION
11 Bedford Row, London WC1R 4DX Tel. 01-242 6904
Telex 8811566
Employers Federation; formerly the British Federation of Master Printers; houses the Institute of Printing, *q.v.* and the London Printing Industries Association, to which latter the Federation is allied; affiliated to the International Master Printers Association

Enquiries to the Librarian

Subject coverage
the printing industry

Publications
Printing Industries (monthly, for members only)
Printing Industries Annual

510 BRITISH PRINTING MACHINERY ASSOCIATION
12 Clifford's Inn, Fetter Lane, London EC4A 1DX Tel. 01-405 9610
Trade Association

Enquiries to the Secretary

Subject coverage
machinery and equipment for the printing and allied trades

Publication
Handbook of Members and Products

511 BRITISH PRODUCTIVITY COUNCIL
16 South Molton Street, London W1Y 1DE Tel. 01-629 4254
Company, non-profit making, registered as a Charity; 47 local Productivity Associations are affiliated and the Organization may also be known as the British Council of Productivity Associations

Enquiries to the Secretarial Staff

Subject coverage
the promotion of higher productivity in industry; all levels of management; industrial relations; the assistance of firms with their problems; representation of local Associations at national level; training

Publications
Film Catalogue
Newsletter (quarterly)
Annual Report
Posters and Publications are also issued by the Member Associations

512 BRITISH PTERIDOLOGICAL SOCIETY
46 Sedley Rise, Loughton, Essex IG10 1LT Tel. 01-508 4601
Scientific Society, member of the Council for Nature

Enquiries, (if from non-members), accompanied by the information fee of 50p, to the Secretary

Subject coverage
identification of ferns; sources of supply; guidance for students; botanical and horticultural information on ferns

Publications
Fern Gazette (scientific journal)
Bulletin (growers information journal)

513 BRITISH QUARRYING & SLAG FEDERATION
14 Waterloo Place, London SW1Y 4AR Tel. 01-930 7107
Trade Association; formed by the merger of the British Granite and Whinstone Federation, the British Slag Federation, the Limestone Federation and the Federated Quarry Owners of Great Britain

Enquiries to the Technical Officer

Subject coverage
sources and uses of products derived from crushed hard rocks and slags; igneous rocks, sandstone, limestone, chalk, blastfurnace and steel slags; quicklime

Publications
Annual Report
Technical Review (quarterly)
Members Directory
Books and booklets on the technology & applications (list available)

514 BRITISH RABBIT COUNCIL
Purefoy House, 7 Kirkgate, Newark on Trent, Tel. 0636 6042
Nottinghamshire NG24 1AD
Trade Council

Enquiries to the Secretary

Subject coverage
exhibition rabbits; control and licence of shows

Publications
Annual Handbook
Breed Standards Handbook (5-yearly)

515 BRITISH RADIO CABINET MANUFACTURERS ASSOCIATION
1 Lincolns Inn Fields, London WC2A 3AA — Tel. 01-242 5671
Trade Association

Enquiries to the Secretary

Subject coverage
manufacture and supply of radio and television cabinets

516 BRITISH RADIO EQUIPMENT MANUFACTURERS ASSOCIATION
20th Century House, 31 Soho Square, London W1V 5DG — Tel. 01-734 7471
Telex 27869

Trade Association; member of the Radio Industry Council, *q.v.*; housing the Federation of British Audio

Enquiries to the Secretary

Subject coverage
general information on the television, radio and audio manufacturing industry

517 BRITISH RAIL HOVERCRAFT LIMITED
22 Finsbury Square, London EC2P 2BR — Tel. 01-628 3050
Telex 883339

Company, wholly-owned subsidiary of British Railways Board

Enquiries to the Commercial and Planning Manager

Subject coverage
operation of hovercraft, world-wide; consultancy

518 BRITISH RAILWAYS BOARD
Research and Development Division Library, London Road, Derby DE2 8UP — Tel. 0332 49203
Telex 37367
Nationalized Industry

Enquiries to the Librarian

Subject coverage
railway technology

Publication
Review of technical literature (monthly)

519 BRITISH RATE AND DATA
76 Oxford Street, London W1N 0HH — Tel. 01-637 7511
Telex 24555

Publishing House; part of Maclean-Hunter Limited

Enquiries to the Publisher or Editor, from subscribers or advertisers only

Subject coverage
advertisement media facts relating to the British market and also to the French, German, Italian, Swiss and Austrian markets; information on advertising agencies, newspapers and magazines publishers, television and commercial radio companies and most other media which accept advertising

Publications
BRAD Advertiser and Agency List
BRAD Directories and Annuals
BRAD Digest

520 BRITISH REINFORCEMENT TEXTILES ASSOCIATION
12 Booth Street, Manchester M60 2ED Tel. 061-236 9721
Trade Association, formerly the Cotton Canvas Manufacturers Association

Enquiries to the Secretary

Subject coverage
reinforcement textiles, tyre cord fabrics, belting and hose ducks in both cotton and man-made fibres

BRITISH RESIN MANUFACTURERS ASSOCIATION *see* **CHEMICAL INDUSTRIES ASSOCIATION LIMITED**

521 BRITISH ROAD FEDERATION
26 Manchester Square, London W1M 5RF Tel. 01-935 0221
Trade Association, member of International Road Federation

Enquiries to the Information Officer

Subject coverage
roads and road transport

Publications
Basic Road Statistics (annual)
Britain's Road Progress (twice per annum, map)
Occasional reports, etc

BRITISH ROAD TAR ASSOCIATION *now* **BRITISH TAR INDUSTRY ASSOCIATION,** *q.v.*

522 BRITISH ROLL TURNERS TRADE SOCIETY
44 Collingwood Avenue, Corby, Northamptonshire Tel. 053-66 2617
Trade Union

Enquiries to the General Secretary

Subject coverage
industrial relations within the steel industry

BRITISH RUBBER AND RESIN ADHESIVE MANUFACTURERS ASSOCIATION *now* **BRITISH ADHESIVE MANUFACTURERS ASSOCIATION,** *q.v.*

523 BRITISH RUBBER MANUFACTURERS ASSOCIATION LIMITED
90–91 Tottenham Court Road, London W1P 0BR Tel. 01-580 2794
Trade Association, formerly Federation of Rubber Manufacturers

Enquiries to the Information Officer

Subject coverage
rubber manufacturing trade

Publications
Technical and safety books and pamphlets
Codes of practice
Directory of the British Rubber Industry

524 BRITISH SALT LIMITED
Cledford Lane, Middlewich, Cheshire CW10 0JP Tel. 0606 84 2881
Telex 669235
Limited Company, formerly British Soda Company Limited, part of Staveley Industries Limited

Enquiries to the Sales Manager

Subject coverage
salt

BRITISH SCIENTIFIC INSTRUMENT RESEARCH ASSOCIATION *now* **SIRA INSTITUTE LIMITED,** *q.v.*

525 BRITISH SCRAP FEDERATION
16 High Street, Brampton, Huntingdon, Cambridgeshire PE18 8TU Tel. 0480 55249
Telex 32546

Trade Association; houses the Reclamation Association, the Federation of Reclamation Industries, the Reclamation Industries Council, and the Independent Waste Paper Processors Association, *q.v.*

Enquiries to the Secretary

Subject coverage
reclamation and recycling of ferrous and non-ferrous metals

526 BRITISH SECURITY INDUSTRY ASSOCIATION LIMITED
14–22 Tottenham Street, London W1P 0AA Tel. 01-637 8889

Trade Association, of four sections: Alarms, Safe and Lock, Guard and Patrol, and Transport

Enquiries to the Director-General

Subject coverage
security equipment and services as indicated by the Association's Sections, given above; assistance to industry, the public, police and government in the prevention of crime; information on reliable/responsible security companies

527 BRITISH SHIP RESEARCH ASSOCIATION
Marine Coatings (ROSCM) Laboratory, New Quay Road, Poole, Dorset BH15 4AF Tel. 02013 4447

Research Association; part of British Ship Research Association, Wallsend, Tyne and Wear; formerly Research Organisation of Ships Compositions Manufacturers Limited

Enquiries to the Head of Materials Section

Subject coverage
marine biological research as applied to marine paint manufacture and testing; corrosion in the marine environment; metallurgical investigations associated with the failure of structures and machinery

528 BRITISH SHIP RESEARCH ASSOCIATION
Wallsend Research Station, Wallsend, Tyne and Wear NE28 6UY Tel. 0632 625242
Telex 53476

Research Association

Enquiries to the Technical Information Division

Subject coverage
design, construction and operation of ships and machinery; materials; corrosion; offshore structures; underwater engineering; instrumentation and measurement

Publications
Journal of Abstracts (monthly)
Research Reports
Recommended Practice for the Protection and Painting of Ships
Recommended Code of Procedure for Marine Instrumentation and Control Equipment

BRITISH SHIPBUILDING EXPORTS *now* **MARITIME TRANSPORT RESEARCH,** *q.v.*

529 BRITISH SHIPPERS COUNCIL
21 Tothill Street, London SW1H 9LW Tel. 01-930 6711 ext. 226
Telex 21332

Trade Association/Independent Body; comprised of many trade associations, CBI and individual companies; associated with the 14 other Shippers Councils of Western Europe, through an International Secretariat in the Hague

Enquiries to the Director/Secretary or Assistant Secretary

Subject coverage
interests of importers or exporters concerning overseas transportation of goods by sea or air; shipping and air freighting; international trade documentation and procedures; international law on carriage of goods and ports matters; negotiation and consultation with Government Departments, agencies, shipping and airlines, port authorities, etc

BRITISH SHIPPING FEDERATION *see* **GENERAL COUNCIL OF BRITISH SHIPPING**

BRITISH SLAG FEDERATION *now* **BRITISH QUARRYING & SLAG FEDERATION,** *q.v.*

530 BRITISH SOCIETY FOR CELL BIOLOGY

c/o Department of Human Morphology, University of Nottingham, Medical School, Clifton Boulevard, Nottingham NG7 2UH — Tel. 0602 700111 ext. 3191

Scientific Society/Learned Body; affiliated to the European Cell Biology Organization

Enquiries to the Secretary

Subject coverage

research and teaching in the field of cell biology; sources of supply of permanent cell lines

Publications

Bi-annual Series of British Society of Cell Biology Symposia (Cambridge University Press, vol. 1 1976)
Laboratory Manual of Cell Biology (English Universities Press, 1975)

531 BRITISH SOCIETY FOR DEVELOPMENTAL BIOLOGY

c/o Department of Developmental Biology, Marischal College, University of Aberdeen AB9 1AS — Tel. 0224 40241 ext. MC 238

Scientific Society

Enquiries to the Secretary

Subject coverage

developmental biology

Publications

Occasional Symposia on selected topics

532 BRITISH SOCIETY FOR STRAIN MEASUREMENT

281 Heaton Road, Newcastle upon Tyne NE6 5QB — Tel. 0632 655273

Technical Society

Enquiries to the Administration Officer

Subject coverage

strain measurement by strain gauges, brittle lacquers, photoelasticity, strain transducers, and any form of experimental stress analysis; associated instrumentation and theoretical analysis

Publication

Strain: Journal of the BSSM (quarterly)

BRITISH SOCIETY FOR THE HISTORY OF SCIENCE *see* **INSTITUTE OF PHYSICS**

533 BRITISH SOCIETY OF ANIMAL PRODUCTION

c/o Meat and Livestock Commission, P.O. Box 44, Queensway House, Bletchley, Milton Keynes MK2 2EF — Tel. 0908 74941

Learned Society

Enquiries to the Honorary Secretary

Subject coverage

animal production

Publication

Animal Production

BRITISH SOCIETY OF AUDIOLOGY *see* **INSTITUTION OF MECHANICAL ENGINEERS**

534 BRITISH SOCIETY OF COMMERCE LIMITED

25 Bridgeman Terrace, Wigan WN1 1TD — Tel. 0942 43572

Professional Society

Enquiries to the General Secretary

Subject coverage
industry and commerce

Publication
Quarterly Journal

535 BRITISH SOCIETY OF DOWSERS
19 High Street, Eydon, Daventry, Northamptonshire N11 6PP Tel. 0327 60525
Charity

Enquiries to the Secretary

Subject coverage
location of underground water, minerals, oil, etc. and animate and inanimate objects, for geophysical, agricultural and medical purposes

Publications
Quarterly Journal
Elementary Radiesthesia

536 BRITISH SOCIETY OF RHEOLOGY
67 Daniells, Welwyn Garden City, Hertfordshire AL7 1QT Tel. 958 29928
Learned Society

Enquiries to the Secretary

Subject coverage
deformation and flow of materials

BRITISH SODA COMPANY LIMITED *now* **BRITISH SALT LIMITED,** *q.v.*

BRITISH SOLUBLE COFFEE MANUFACTURERS ASSOCIATION *see* **FOOD MANUFACTURERS FEDERATION INCORPORATED**

BRITISH SPINNERS AND DOUBLERS ASSOCIATION *now* **BRITISH TEXTILE EMPLOYERS ASSOCIATION,** *q.v.*

537 BRITISH STANDARDS INSTITUTION
2 Park Street, London W1A 2BS Tel. 01-629 9000
Telex 266933
Independent Institution incorporated under Royal Charter; member of the International Organization for Standardization (ISO), the International Electrotechnical Commission (IEC), the European Committee for Standardization (CEN) and the European Committee for Electrotechnical Standardization (CENELEC); controls BSI Centre, Hemel Hempstead, *q.v. and* BSI Sales Department, 101 Pentonville Road, London N1 9ND

Enquiries to the Secretary

Subject coverage
standardization, British and International

Special collection
BSI standards and those of other national standards bodies

Publication
BSI Yearbook (lists and indexes of the Standards)

538 BRITISH STANDARDS INSTITUTION
Maylands Avenue, Hemel Hempstead, Hertfordshire HP2 4SQ Tel. 0442 3111
Telex 82424
Department of British Standards Institution, London, *q.v.*; housing the Quality Assurance Department, the Inspectorate, the Test House and Technical Help to Exporters, *q.v.*

Enquiries to the Group Manager of the appropriate section

Subject coverage
British Standards approval schemes; manufacturers quality control; testing; technical requirements overseas

Publications
Kitemark Buyers Guide
T.H.E. Quarterly Bulletin

BRITISH STATIONERY AND OFFICE PRODUCTS FEDERATION *see* **FEDERATION OF WHOLESALE AND INDUSTRIAL DISTRIBUTORS**

539 BRITISH STEAM SPECIALTIES GROUP LIMITED
Fleet Street, Lee Circle, Leicester LE1 3QQ — Tel. 0533 23232, Telex 34589

Company

Enquiries to the Technical Department

Subject coverage
industrial heating and pipeline equipment, including tube fittings and flanges; pipeline plastics; pipeline valves; steam and air traps; heat exchange equipment; instruments and meters, strainers and filters; heat emitters

Publications
product catalogues

540 BRITISH STEEL CORPORATION
Corporate Engineering Laboratory, 140 Battersea Park Road, London SW11 1AA — Tel. 01-622 5511, Telex 918917

Nationalised Industry/Research, formerly British Iron and Steel Research Association

Enquiries to the Information Officer/Librarian

Subject coverage
steel disciplines, relating to conservation engineering; environmental control; mechanical engineering; machines and systems; materials handling; terotechnology; design; tribology; ergonomics; instrumentation; control and computing systems; energy; steel applications

541 BRITISH STEEL CORPORATION
Sheffield Laboratories, Information and Library Services, Swinden House, Moorgate, Rotherham, South Yorkshire *and* Hoyle Street, Sheffield S3 7EY — Tel. Rotherham 64901, Sheffield 28941, Telex 457279 *and* 547013

Company Research and Development Laboratories; formerly United Steel Companies Limited; housing, at Rotherham, the special Steels User Advisory Centre, *q.v.*

Enquiries to the Information Officer or Librarian

Subject coverage
iron and steel; all processes and production; special carbon, alloy and stainless steels; physical metallurgy and machinability; steel specifications (Hoyle Street); electroslag remelting; powder metallurgy; iron and steel roll technology

Special collections
Steel specifications
Steel grades with analyses and properties

542 BRITISH STEEL CORPORATION
Technical Information Systems, Research Centre, Port Talbot, West Glamorgan SA13 2NG — Tel. 063-984 3161, Telex 48431

Nationalised Industry Company, formerly Steel Company of Wales; Technical Information Systems includes those of the BSC Tinplate Group, Swansea and the Orb Works, Newport; houses also the Steel Sheet Information Centre

Enquiries to the Technical Information Officer

Subject coverage
production, properties, and uses of strip and sheet steel products; press forming and welding of steel sheet

Publications
Environmental studies
Literature surveys and bibliographies
Open technical reports

BRITISH STEEL CORPORATION *see also*
SPECIAL STEELS USER ADVISORY CENTRE
STANTON AND STAVELEY LIMITED
STEEL SHEET INFORMATION CENTRE

BRITISH STONE FEDERATION *now* **FEDERATION OF STONE INDUSTRIES,** *q.v.*

543 BRITISH STONEWARE POTTERS ASSOCIATION
102 Friar Gate, Derby DE1 1FH — Tel. 0332 363321, Telex 377724

Trade Association; formerly Stoneware Potters Association

Enquiries to the Secretary

Subject coverage
manufacture and marketing of British stoneware pottery

544 BRITISH SUB-AQUA CLUB
70 Brompton Road, London SW3 1HA — Tel. 01-584 7163
Non-profit-making Governing Body

Enquiries to the Director General

Subject coverage
underwater swimming and diving; coaching

Publications
Diving Manual
Diving Officer's Handbook
Snorkel Manual
Science Diving: proceedings 3rd Symposium
Oceans 2000 Report
BSAC scientific papers

BRITISH SULPHATE OF AMMONIA FEDERATION LIMITED *see* **CHEMICAL INDUSTRIES ASSOCIATION LIMITED**

BRITISH TAPE INDUSTRY ASSOCIATION *now* **EUROPEAN TAPE INDUSTRY ASSOCIATION,** *q.v.*

545 BRITISH SULPHUR CORPORATION LIMITED
Parnell House, Wilton Road, London SW1V 1NH — Tel. 01-828 5581
Consultancy Organization

Enquiries to the Information Department

Subject coverage
fertilizers; phosphate rock; nitrogen; sulphur

Publications
Fertilizer International (monthly)
Nitrogen (6 issues per annum)
Phosphorus and Potassium (6 issues per annum)
Sulphur (6 issues per annum)
World Surveys and Guides (list available)

546 BRITISH TAR INDUSTRY ASSOCIATION
132–135 Sloane Street, London SW1X 9BB Tel. 01-730 5212
Telex 21574
Trade Association; formed by the merger of the British Road Tar Association and the Association of Tar Distillers; Member of the Chemical Industries Association

Enquiries, technical, to the Scientific Officer or the Technical Officer; commercial, to the Director

Subject coverage
supply and use of the products of the tar industry, particularly bulk products for road construction, timber preservation and as fuel

Publications
Road Tar (twice per annum, for tar users)

547 BRITISH TAXPAYERS ASSOCIATION LIMITED
34 Grand Parade, Brighton, Sussex B22 2QA Tel. 0273 682235
Tax Consultants

Enquiries to the Directors

Subject coverage
personal taxation

BRITISH TECHNOLOGY INDEX *see* **LIBRARY ASSOCIATION**

548 BRITISH TEXTILE BY-PRODUCTS ASSOCIATION
12 Booth Street Manchester M60 2ED Tel. 061-236 9721
Trade Association; formerly British Cotton Waste Association Limited

Enquiries to the Secretary

Subject coverage
conditions of trade, arbitration, availability of supplies

549 BRITISH TEXTILE CONFEDERATION
65 Victoria Street, London SW1H 0HW Tel. 01-222 5996
Association of eleven trade associations and seven trade unions; includes 4 associate members; see the list of members following this entry

Enquiries to the Secretary

Subject coverage
textile industry, legislation, technology, design, exports, research; through the membership, lace, man-made fibres, linen, knitwear, wool textiles, clothing, dyeing

BRITISH TEXTILE CONFEDERATION
- **BRITISH INTERLINING MANUFACTURERS' ASSOCIATION**
- **BRITISH LACE FEDERATION**
- **BRITISH MAN-MADE FIBRES FEDERATION**
- **BRITISH TEXTILE EMPLOYERS' ASSOCIATION,** *q.v.*
- **CENTRAL COUNCIL OF THE IRISH LINEN INDUSTRY**
- **CORDAGE MANUFACTURERS' INSTITUTE**
- **OVERALL MANUFACTURERS' ASSOCIATION OF GREAT BRITAIN,** *q.v.*
- **SCOTTISH KNITWEAR COUNCIL**
- **SHIRT COLLAR AND TIE MANUFACTURERS' FEDERATION LIMITED**
- **TEXTILE CONVERTERS' ASSOCIATION**
- **WOOL TEXTILE DELEGATION,** *q.v.*
- **AMALGAMATED SOCIETY OF TEXTILE WORKERS AND KINDRED TRADES**
- **AMALGAMATED TEXTILE WORKERS' UNION**
- **GENERAL WORKERS' GROUP OF THE TRANSPORT AND GENERAL WORKERS' UNION**
- **NATIONAL ASSOCIATION OF UNIONS IN THE TEXTILE TRADE**
- **NATIONAL UNION OF DYERS, BLEACHERS AND TEXTILE WORKERS**
- **NATIONAL UNION OF GENERAL AND MUNICIPAL WORKERS**
- **NATIONAL UNION OF HOSIERY AND KNITWEAR WORKERS**

ASSOCIATE MEMBERS
CLOTHING EXPORT COUNCIL OF GREAT BRITAIN
SOCIETY OF DYERS AND COLOURISTS
TEXTILE INSTITUTE, *q.v.*
TEXTILE RESEARCH COUNCIL, *q.v.*

550 BRITISH TEXTILE EMPLOYERS ASSOCIATION (COTTON, MAN-MADE AND ALLIED FIBRES)
Fifth Floor, Royal Exchange, Manchester M2 7ED Tel. 061-834 7871
Trade Employers Association; formed by the amalgamation of the former British Spinners and Doublers Association, the United Kingdom Textile Manufacturers Association and the Textile Finishing Trades Association

Enquiries to the Assistant to the Director (Administration and Finance)

Subject coverage
industrial relations; wages and conditions; commercial and tariff matters; water and effluent; safety, health and welfare, all relating to the cotton, man-made, and allied fibres textile industry

Publications
Annual Report
Newsletter (every 2 or 3 weeks)

551 BRITISH TEXTILE MACHINERY ASSOCIATION
444–446 Royal Exchange, Manchester M2 7EP Tel. 061-834 2991
Trade Association; formerly Textile Machinery and Accessory Manufacturers Association

Enquiries to the Director

Subject coverage
textile machinery

BRITISH THROWSTERS ASSOCIATION *see* **BRITISH MAN-MADE FIBRES FEDERATION**

552 BRITISH TIMKEN
Duston, Northamptonshire NN5 6UL Tel. 0604 52311
Company; subsidiary of Timken Company (U.S.A)

Enquiries to the Information Officer

Subject coverage
roller bearing technology; lubrication; tribology; workshop technology; industrial management and training

553 BRITISH TOY MANUFACTURERS ASSOCIATION LIMITED
80 Camberwell Road, London SE5 Tel. 01-701 7271
Trade Association; with subsidiary British Toy Fairs (International) Limited

Enquiries to the Assistant Secretary

Subject coverage
British toy industry in general; toy safety

Publications
British Toys (monthly, controlled circulation)
Annual Directory

554 BRITISH TOYMAKERS GUILD
32–34 Ridgway, Wimbledon Village, London SW19 4QW Tel. 01-947 5662
Trade Association

Enquiries to the Secretary

Subject coverage
craft toymaking

Special collection
British Toymakers Guild Exhibition

Publication
Craft Membership List (annual)

555 BRITISH TRANSPORT DOCKS BOARD
Melbury House, Melbury Terrace, London NW1 6JY Tel. 01-486 6621
Telex 23913

Port Authority, with the British Transport Docks Board Research Station, *q.v.*; state-owned

Enquiries to the Information Officer or the Press Officer

Subject coverage
the ports industry, organisation, administration and operation; cargo liner services

Publications
Docks (monthly house journal)
List of cargo liner services operating from Board ports
Annual report

556 BRITISH TRANSPORT DOCKS BOARD RESEARCH STATION
Hayes Road, Southall, Middlesex UB2 5ND Tel. 01-573 0136
State-controlled Sector of the Ports Industry

Enquiries to the Director of Research

Subject coverage
dock and harbour engineering; maritime hydraulics; hydrographic surveying; port operations

Publication
Research Station Annual Report

BRITISH TRANSPORT HISTORICAL RECORDS *see* **PUBLIC RECORD OFFICE**

557 BRITISH TRANSPORT STAFF COLLEGE LIBRARY
Hook Heath Road, Woking, Surrey GU22 0QH Tel. 048-62 5444
Staff College

Enquiries to the Librarian

Subject coverage
transport management; British and European transport

BRITISH TRAWLERS FEDERATION *see* **HULL FISHING VESSEL OWNERS ASSOCIATION LIMITED**

558 BRITISH TRUST FOR ORNITHOLOGY
Beech Grove, Tring, Hertfordshire HP23 5NR Tel. 044-282 3461
Company limited by Guarantee

Enquiries to the Trust

Subject coverage
British birds, especially population levels, breeding season, mortality, migration

Publications
Bird Study (quarterly)
Ringing and Migration (annual)
Occasional technical guides

BRITISH UNIDENTIFIED FLYING OBJECTS RESEARCH ASSOCIATION *see* **BUFORA LIMITED**

559 BRITISH UNITED PROVIDENT ASSOCIATION LIMITED
24–27 Essex Street, London WC2 3AX Tel. 01-353 9451
Insurance Company

Enquiries to switchboard for relevant department

Subject coverage
private medical insurance

560 BRITISH UNITED SHOE MACHINERY COMPANY LIMITED
P.O. Box 88, Union Works, Belgrave Road, Leicester LE4 5BX Tel. 0533 61551
Telex 34445
Company

Enquiries to the Librarian

Subject coverage
shoe machinery; shoe materials; adhesives; fasteners; general mechanical and electrical engineering

Special collection
British, American and foreign shoe trade journals

561 BRITISH URBAN AND REGIONAL INFORMATION SYSTEMS ASSOCIATION

Berkshire County Council Planning Department, Alpha House, Kings Road, Reading, Berkshire RG1 3DN Tel. 0734 55981 ext. 164
Loose Association of individuals with common interest

Enquiries to the Secretary, answering capacity limited

Subject coverage
information systems

Publication
Newsletter (bimonthly)

BRITISH VACUUM COUNCIL *see* **INSTITUTE OF PHYSICS**

562 BRITISH VALVE MANUFACTURERS ASSOCIATION LIMITED
3 Buckingham Gate, London SW1E 6JH Tel. 01-834 1496/7
Trade Association

Enquiries to the Information Officer

Subject coverage
commercial and technical aspects of industrial valves

Publication
BVMA Technical Reference Book on valves for the control of fluids

563 BRITISH VETERINARY ASSOCIATION
7 Mansfield Street, London W1M 0AT Tel. 01-636 6541/5
Professional Association; houses Eurovet (a Group interested in European veterinary matters)

Enquiries to the Secretary

Subject coverage
veterinary science; including animal welfare and public health

Publications
Veterinary Record (weekly)
Research in Veterinary Science (bi-monthly)
Handbooks, etc.

564 BRITISH WATCH AND CLOCK MAKERS GUILD
65 Clyde Road, London N15 4LS
Trade Association

Enquiries, by letter only, to the Honorary Secretary

Subject coverage
horological and allied crafts

Publication
Jeweller (monthly)

565 BRITISH WATER AND EFFLUENT TREATMENT PLANT ASSOCIATION
27 Crendon Street, High Wycombe, Buckinghamshire HP13 6LG Tel. 0494 444544
Trade Association; member of the British Mechanical Engineering Confederation

Enquiries to the Secretary, for reference to Staff or Members

Subject coverage
water and effluent treatment and plant

Publications
Annual Report
Membership List including products and services

566 BRITISH WATERFOWL ASSOCIATION
111–113 Lambeth Road, London SE1 Tel. 01-582 0185
Trade and Technical Association

Enquiries to the Secretary

Subject coverage
rearing and breeding of domestic and ornamental waterfowl

Publications
Waterfowl (quarterly)
Yearbook and Buyers Guide

567 BRITISH WATERWAYS BOARD
Melbury House, Melbury Terrace, London NW1 6JX Tel. 01-262 6711
Telex 263605
Government Agency, of the Department of the Environment; having offices and depots throughout England, Wales and Scotland; housing also the Inland Waterways Amenity Advisory Council

Enquiries to the Board

Subject coverage
canals and rivers; navigation; reservoirs; leisure aspects of waterways; commercial freight on the waterways; barges; provision of water for cooling for industrial processes

Publications
Annual Report
Waterways Guides, by regions
Waterway Environment Handbook
Waterway News (periodical)
Waterway Users Companion 1976
Canal Architecture in Britain

BRITISH WATERWORKS ASSOCIATION *now* **NATIONAL WATER COUNCIL,** *q.v.*

BRITISH WELDING RESEARCH ASSOCIATION *now* **WELDING INSTITUTE,** *q.v.*

568 BRITISH WHITING FEDERATION
11 White Lion House, Town Centre, Hatfield, Hertfordshire AL10 0JL Tel. 30 71580
Trade Association

Enquiries to the Secretary

Subject coverage
production and uses of chalk whiting

BRITISH WHOLESALE JEWELLERS ASSOCIATION *see* **FEDERATION OF WHOLESALE AND INDUSTRIAL DISTRIBUTORS**

569 BRITISH WOMEN PILOTS ASSOCIATION
P.O. Box 13, British Airways, London SW1W 9SR — Tel. 821 4073
Trade Association, affiliated to the Women's Engineering Society

Enquiries to the Honorary Secretary

Subject coverage
careers for women in aviation; sporting flying, leisure flying, etc.

Publication
House magazine (3 issues per annum)

570 BRITISH WOOD TURNERS ASSOCIATION
C/o James Constance & Sons Limited, Sawmills and Turnery Works, Longhope, Gloucestershire GL17 0LB — Tel. 0452 830297
Trade Association

Enquiries to the Honorary Secretary

Subject coverage
hand-turned wood products

Publication
Directory of Members and their Products

571 BRITISH WOOL MARKETING BOARD
Kew Bridge House, Kew Bridge Road, Brentford, Middlesex TW8 0EL — Tel. 01-560 0551
Agricultural Marketing Board

Enquiries to the Director of Administration

Subject coverage
wool production and marketing; uses of British wools

Special collections
British wool types (in the Board's Bradford Offices)

572 BRITISH WOOL TEXTILE INDUSTRY PRESS OFFICE
5th Floor, Lloyds Bank Chambers, Hustlergate, Bradford BD1 1PE — Tel. 0274 25631, Telex 517086
Trade Organisation Press Office

Enquiries to the Chief Press Officer

Subject coverage
commercial and industrial information on the British wool textile industry and its export trade

573 BRIXHAM LABORATORY ICI LIMITED
Freshwater Quarry, Overgang, Brixham, Devonshire TQ5 8BA — Tel. 080-45 6411, Telex 42812
Company, formerly Brixham Research Laboratory

Enquiries to the Information Officer

Subject coverage
environmental pollution; effluent and waste treatment; fish toxicity; biodegradability; fish bioassays; ecology; oceanography; hydrography

Special collection
RAE Society publications

Publications
Reports on the flora and fauna of estuaries
Mercury Bibliographies (over 3500 references on mercury as an environmental pollutant)

BRIXTON SCHOOL OF BUILDING *now* **POLYTECHNIC OF THE SOUTH BANK,** *q.v.*

574 BROMLEY INSTITUTE OF HIGHER EDUCATION

Rookery Lane, Bromley BR2 8HE Tel. 01-462 6331

College of Higher Education; formerly Bromley Technical College, then Bromley College of Technology; merged with Stockwell College of Education and Ravensbourne College of Art and Design

Enquiries to the Librarian

Subject coverage

science including biology; business studies; engineering

575 BROMLEY PUBLIC LIBRARIES

Tweedy Road, Bromley, Kent BR1 1EX Tel. 01-460 9955 Telex 896712

Public Libraries; regional/district libraries at Beckenham and Orpington

Enquiries to the Borough Librarian

Subject coverage

general

576 BROOKLYN TECHNICAL COLLEGE

Aldridge Road, Great Barr, Birmingham B44 8NE Tel. 021-360 3543

Technical College

Enquiries to the Librarian

Subject coverage

building trades; management; town planning

577 BROOM'S BARN EXPERIMENTAL STATION

Higham, Bury St. Edmunds, Suffolk IP28 6NF Tel. 0284 810363

Research Establishment, affiliated to Rothamsted Experimental Station *q.v.*

Enquiries to the Director

Subject coverage

cultivation of sugar beet, particularly agronomic practices, use of fertilisers, control of pests and diseases, seed production

BROTHERTON LIBRARY *see* **LEEDS UNIVERSITY LIBRARY**

BROWN AND POLSON LIMITED *now* **CPC (UNITED KINGDOM) LIMITED** *q.v.*

578 BROWN-FIRTH RESEARCH LABORATORIES

Attercliffe Road, Sheffield S4 7UY Tel. 0742 20081 Telex 54279

Company, part of Firth Brown Limited

Enquiries to the Librarian

Subject coverage

metallurgy (ferrous)

Publications

Product and process brochures

BROWNHILLS DISTRICT LIBRARY *see* **WALSALL LIBRARY AND MUSEUM SERVICES**

BRUNDRETT TRUST *see* **PLUNKETT FOUNDATION FOR CO-OPERATIVE STUDIES**

579 BRUNEL UNIVERSITY LIBRARY

Kingston Lane, Uxbridge, Middlesex UB8 3PH Tel. 0895 37188 Telex 261173

University Library

Enquiries to the Librarian

Subject coverage
biology, chemistry, physics, materials science, metallurgy, engineering, building technology, production technology, cybernetics, mathematics, computer science, statistics, economics

Special collections
I.K. Brunel photographs; British Standards

BRUNEL UNIVERSITY *see also* **INSTITUTE OF INDUSTRIAL TRAINING**

580 BRUSH EXPORT GROUP
Baptist Church House, 4 Southampton Row, London WC1B 4AB Tel. 01-242 1799
Trade Association; part of the British Brush Manufacturers Association

Enquiries to the Secretary

Subject coverage
export of brushes, painting rollers and pads

581 BRYNMOR JONES LIBRARY
Hull University, Cottingham Road, Hull HU6 7RX Tel. 0482 46311
Telex 52530

University Library, formerly University of Hull Library

Enquiries to the Librarian

Subject coverage
pure sciences; social sciences; law

Publications
Abstracts of Theses for Higher Degrees

BRYOPHYTE PROJECT GROUP *see* **INSTITUTE OF TERRESTRIAL ECOLOGY, Edinburgh Laboratories (Bush)**

582 BTP TIOXIDE LIMITED
Central Laboratories, Portrack Lane, Stockton, Tel. 0642 63571
Cleveland TS18 2NQ Telex 58540
Company, part of the Tioxide Group; formerly British Titan Products Company Limited

Enquiries, in writing, to the Librarian

Subject coverage
chemistry of titanium compounds; their manufacture and use and related subjects; titanium dioxide pigment technology

Publications
Technical Booklets

583 BTR LIMITED
Silverton House, Vincent Square, London SW1P 2PL Tel. 01-834 3848
Company; formerly BTR Leyland Industrial Limited

Enquiries to the Publicity Controller

Subject coverage
engineering including offshore materials handling; conveyor belting, hose; glass reinforced plastic technology; hydraulic hose, assemblies and components; automotive mouldings and extrusions; aerospace engineering components; rubber mouldings and extrusions; electrical insulation and composites; automotive and domestic carpets; steel fabrication; lining vessels, tanks and pipes; sports equipment; medical equipment; roll coverings for the paper making, etc., industries

Publications
Quarterly Newspaper
Brochure on the Companies, and Directory
GRP technology and Practice

BUCKINGHAM, UNIVERSITY COLLEGE *see* **UNIVERSITY COLLEGE AT BUCKINGHAM**

584 BUCKINGHAMSHIRE COLLEGE OF HIGHER EDUCATION
Queen Alexandra Road, High Wycombe, Buckinghamshire Tel. 0494 22141
College of Higher Education; formerly High Wycombe College of Technology and Art and Newland Park College of Education; an Open University Study Centre

Enquiries to Chief Librarian/Head of Learning Resources

Subject coverage
general; specialization in furniture, timber technology, art and management

585 BUCKINGHAMSHIRE COUNTY LIBRARY
County Offices, Walton Street, Aylesbury, Buckinghamshire HP20 1UU Tel. 0296 4671 Telex 83101
Public Library Service; three Divisional Libraries at Aylesbury, Bletchley, High Wycombe

Enquiries to the County Librarian

Subject coverage
general; law

Publications
Union List of Periodicals

586 BUFORA LIMITED
6 Cairn Avenue, London W5 Tel. 01-723 0305 01-579 3796
Non-profit Company; the British Unidentified Flying Objects Research Association; linked with the Direct Investigation Group on Aerial Phenomena, *q.v.*

Enquiries, general only, to the Director, 15 Freshwater Court, Crawford Street, London W1H 1HS

Subject coverage
unidentified flying objects; investigation of current reports

Publications
BUFORA Journal (bimonthly)
Guide to the UFO Phenomenon
Investigators Handbook

587 BUILDER GROUP
4 Catherine Street, London WC2B 5JN Tel. 01-836 6251 Telex 268312
Company; including 1. Building Management & Marketing Consultants Limited, *q.v.*, 2. National Building Commodity Centre Limited, *q.v.*, and 3. Building (Publishers) Limited

Enquiries to the Librarian; in the case of the above company (1.) to the Director and of the above company (2.) to the General Manager

Subject coverage
construction industry

Publications
Lists of research projects
Weekly Journal (Building (Publishers) Ltd.)

588 BUILDING ADVISORY SERVICE
18 Mansfield Street, London W1M 9FG Tel. 01-636 2862 Telex 265763
Training and Consultancy Service, of the National Federation of Building Trades Employers

Enquiries to the Director

Subject coverage
building and construction industry in many aspects including planning, organization, marketing, safety, recruitment, salaries, working conditions, management training

Publications
Construction Safety Manual
VAT Manual for the Construction Industry

Construction Key Facts
Builders Overheads and Labour Rates
Survey of Salaries and Fringe Benefits in the Construction Industry

589 BUILDING CENTRE
26 Store Street, London WC1E 7BT Tel. 01-637 8361 (trade)
01-637 9001 (public)
Telex 261446

Information service and permanent Exhibition of materials and products; part of the Building Centre Group (London, Bristol, Cambridge, Durham, Glasgow, Manchester and Southampton); also of the National Association of Building Centres; houses ten organizations which are listed following this entry

Enquiries to the Chief Information Officer

Subject coverage
building materials and products

Publications
catalogue available

BUILDING CENTRE allied organizations:
ALUMINIUM WINDOW ASSOCIATION, *q.v.*
ASSOCIATION OF BUILDING COMPONENT MANUFACTURERS
BRICK DEVELOPMENT ASSOCIATION, *q.v.*
BRITISH WOODWORK MANUFACTURERS ASSOCIATION
BUILDING BOOKSHOP
BUILDING MATERIALS EXPORT GROUP, *q.v.*
NATIONAL COUNCIL OF BUILDING MATERIALS PRODUCERS, *q.v.*
NATIONAL HOME IMPROVEMENT COUNCIL STEEL WINDOW ASSOCIATION, *q.v.*
TIMBER RESEARCH AND DEVELOPMENT ASSOCIATION, *q.v.*

590 BUILDING CENTRE, BRISTOL
Stonebridge House, Colston Avenue, Bristol BS1 4TW Tel. 0272 27002
Product Information Service, independent; affiliated to the National Association of Building Centres; formerly Bristol Building and Design Centre; houses the Regional Office of the Timber Research and Development Association, *q.v.*

Enquiries to the Information Officer

Subject coverage
proprietary technical data relating to material, elements, components, fittings, services and finishes used in all forms of building construction, excluding civil engineering and mechanical plant operations; service for non-commercial areas of information, (research, bibliographies, etc.), is subscription-based

591 BUILDING CENTRE SCOTLAND
6 Newton Terrace, Glasgow G3 7PF Tel. 041-248 6212
Trade Association; member of the Building Centre Group, *q.v.*; houses the Scottish Regional Office of the Timber Research and Development Association, *q.v.*

Enquiries to the Director

Subject coverage
manufacturers and sources of supplies of all building materials and components

592 BUILDING INFORMATION CENTRE
Cauldon College of Further Education, Stoke Road, Shelton, Stoke-on-Trent, Staffordshire ST4 2DG Tel. 0782 24651 ext. 229
Information Centre for the construction industry, affiliated to the Association of Building Centres

Enquiries to the Building Information Officer

Subject coverage
building materials and equipment; physical testing of building materials (fees chargeable)

593 BUILDING MANAGEMENT AND MARKETING CONSULTANTS LIMITED
Waldorf House, 18 Exeter Street, London WC2E 7LT Tel. 01-836 9484
Telex 268312
Company, part of The Builder Limited (publishers), Builder Group
Enquiries to the Company
Subject coverage
construction industry; building materials
Publications
Marketing Research
Forest Products
Project Management
Construction Consultants International

594 BUILDING MATERIALS EXPORT GROUP
26 Store Street, London WC1E 7BT Tel. 01-636 6920
Trade Association, part of the National Council of Building Material Producers, *q.v.*
Enquiries, from members only, to the Secretary
Subject coverage
world-wide export promotion
Publications
List of Members
Reports of Sales Missions

595 BUILDING REGULATIONS ADVISORY COMMITTEE
Department of the Environment, Becket House, Lambeth Palace Road, London SE1 7ER Tel. 01-928 7855
Statutory Committee
Enquiries to the Secretary
Subject coverage
building regulations (advisory to the Secretary of State)

596 BUILDING RESEARCH ESTABLISHMENT
Bucknalls Lane, Garston, Watford, Hertfordshire WD2 7JR Tel. 47 74040
Telex 923220
Government Research Establishment of the Department of the Environment; formerly Building Research Station; includes Fire Research Station and Princes Risborough Laboratory, *qq.v.*
Enquiries to the Librarian
Subject coverage
building; civil engineering; materials; fire protection and prevention; timber
Publications
Research Programme
Information Directory
Current Papers (reports)
Digests
Building Research Thesaurus

BUILDING SERVICES ENGINEERING SOCIETY *see* **INSTITUTION OF CIVIL ENGINEERS**

597 BUILDING SERVICES RESEARCH AND INFORMATION ASSOCIATION
Old Bracknell Lane, Bracknell, Berkshire RG12 4AH
Research Association, formerly Heating and Ventilating Research Association
No enquiry service
Subject coverage
mechanical and electrical services of buildings, including heating, ventilating, air conditioning; heat transfer and fluid flow; industrial aerodynamics and acoustics

Publications
Thermal Abstracts (bi-monthly)
Application Guides
Technical Notes
Bibliographies

598 BUILDING SERVICES RESEARCH UNIT
Department of Mechanical Engineering, Glasgow University, Tel. 041-334 2269
3 Lilybank Gardens, Glasgow G12 8RZ 041-339 8855
University Department; formerly Hospital Engineering Research Unit

Enquiries to the Leader of the Unit

Subject coverage
building services engineering; heating, ventilating, water, electricity and gas services for all types of building but especially for hospitals

Publications
Research Reports and Papers
List of publications
List of research projects

BUILDING SURVEYORS INSTITUTE *now* **CONSTRUCTION SURVEYORS INSTITUTE,** *q.v.*

599 BULGARIAN EMBASSY
12 Queens Gate Gardens, London SW7 5NA Tel. 01-584 4948
Government Department, having a connection with the Committee for Science and Technical Progress, 8 Slavyanska Street, Sofia, Bulgaria

Enquiries to the Embassy

BUPA *see* **BRITISH UNITED PROVIDENT ASSOCIATION LIMITED**

600 BURDEN NEUROLOGICAL INSTITUTE
Stoke Lane, Stapleton, Bristol BS16 1QT Tel. 0272 56744
Scientific Institute

Enquiries to the Director

Subject coverage
brain science, particularly physiology and psychology

Publication
Annual Report

601 BUREAU OF ANALYSED SAMPLES LIMITED
Newham Hall, Newby, Middlesbrough, Cleveland TS8 9EA Tel. 0642 37216
Company

Enquiries to the Sales Manager

Subject coverage
Certified Reference materials, sources of supply

Publication
Catalogue of Reference materials produced by the Bureau

602 BUREAU OF ENGINEER SURVEYORS
71 Sandhurst Drive, Ilford, Essex IG3 9DD Tel. 01-590 5114
Company/Professional Institution; constituent member of the Engineers Registration Board; formerly National Register of Engineer Surveyors

Enquiries to the Honorary Secretary

Subject coverage
engineering inspection of pressure vessels, lifts and cranes, and electrical engineering installations coming under the Statutory Regulations of the Health and Safety at Work Act

Publication
Verifact (quarterly)

BUREAU OF HYGIENE AND TROPICAL DISEASES *see* **LONDON SCHOOL OF HYGIENE AND TROPICAL MEDICINE**

603 BURMAH-CASTROL COMPANY LIMITED
Burmah Refinery, Ellesmere Port, Wirral, Cheshire L65 4ES — Tel. 051-355 3737
Company, subsidiary of Burmah Oil Company Limited

Enquiries to the Information Officer

Subject coverage
petroleum refining

604 BURMAH CASTROL COMPANY LIMITED
Castrol Research Laboratories, Whitchurch Hill, Pangbourne, Reading, Berkshire RG8 7QR — Tel. 073 57 4321
Company, part of Burmah Oil Trading Limited

Enquiries to the Information Officer

Subject coverage
lubrication; lubricating oils and oil additives; lubricating greases; hydraulic and other specialised fluids, *e.g.* brake fluids

Publication
Current Awareness Bulletin (abstracts, monthly)

605 BURNLEY COLLEGE OF ARTS AND TECHNOLOGY
Ormerod Road, Burnley, Lancashire BB11 2RX

College of Technology; formerly Burnley Municipal College; its Library is part of the Lancashire Library system

Enquiries to the Librarian

Subject coverage
engineering; arts and technology; textiles; building

BURNLEY DISTRICT CENTRAL LIBRARY *see* **LANCASHIRE LIBRARY**

606 BURTON GROUP LIMITED
Hudson Road Mills, Leeds LS9 7DN — Tel 0532 36373
Telex 55111

Group of Companies, formerly Montague Burton Limited

Enquiries to the Secretary

Subject coverage
retailing & manufacturing of clothing and other products

BURTON UPON TRENT DISTRICT LIBRARY *see* **STAFFORDSHIRE COUNTY LIBRARY**

607 BURTON UPON TRENT TECHNICAL COLLEGE
Lichfield Street, Burton upon Trent, Staffordshire DE14 3RL — Tel. 0283 61041
College of Further Education

Enquiries to the Principal or the Tutor Librarian

Subject coverage
electrical, mechanical and automobile engineering; building; rubber and plastics technology; mathematics and pure sciences; economics; business and management studies; welding

608 BURY METROPOLITAN BOROUGH CENTRAL LIBRARY
Manchester Road, Bury, Lancashire BL9 0DG — Tel. 061-764 4110
061-761 4021

Public Library; District Libraries at Prestwich, Radcliffe, Ramsbottom

Enquiries to Director of Libraries and Arts

Subject coverage
office organization, inventories, paper manufactures, bookbinding, heating, ventilation, plumbing, domestic architecture

609 BURY METROPOLITAN COLLEGE OF FURTHER EDUCATION
Market Street, Bury BL9 0BG Tel. 061-764 1960
College of Further Education; formerly Bury College

Enquiries to the Vice-Principal

Subject coverage
general, for Further Education

BURY ST EDMUNDS DISTRICT LIBRARY *see* **SUFFOLK COUNTY LIBRARY**

610 BUSH BOAKE ALLEN LIMITED
Blackhorse Lane, London E17 5QP Tel. 01-531 4211
Company, Division of Albright & Wilson Limited

Enquiries to the Librarian/Information Officer

Subject coverage
flavour; fragrance; chemicals

611 BUSINESS AIRCRAFT USERS ASSOCIATION LIMITED
75 Victoria Street, London SW1H 0HZ Tel. 01-222 5315
Voluntary Association

Enquiries to the Chief Executive

Subject coverage
business aviation

612 BUSINESS ARCHIVES COUNCIL
37–45 Tooley Street, London Bridge, London SE1 Tel. 01-407 6110
Voluntary Society; with the Business Records Advisory Service

Enquiries to the Honorary Secretary

Subject coverage
records management; business history

Special collection
Library of Business Histories

Publications
Business Archives

613 BUSINESS EQUIPMENT TRADE ASSOCIATION
109 Kingsway, London WC2B 6PU Tel. 01-405 6233
Trade Association; member of the European Association of Manufacturers of Business Machines and Data Processing Equipment, the European Federation of Importers of Office Machines, and the European Steel Office Furniture Federation

Enquiries to the Secretary

Subject coverage
General information on the industry's products together with the names and addresses of the principal suppliers of the different types of business equipment available in the U.K., including office machines and systems, computers and associated peripheral equipment and also office furniture.

Publications
Guides to users, e.g. on microfilm, dictating machines, etc.

BUSINESS INTELLIGENCE SERVICES *now* **BIS MARKETING RESEARCH LIMITED,** *q.v.*

614 BUSINESS STATISTICS OFFICE
Cardiff Road, Newport, Gwent NPT 1XG Tel. 0633 56111 ext. 2973
Telex 497121/2

Government Department of the Department of Industry

Enquiries to the Librarian

Subject coverage
business statistics on the manufacturing, distributive and service industries; UK Government statistics

Special collection
G.R. Porter collection of early statistical material

Publications
Business Monitors, listed in HMSO Sectional List 3
List of the G.R. Porter Collection

BUTE COUNTY LIBRARY *now* **ARGYLL AND BUTE DISTRICT LIBRARY,** *q.v.*

BUXTON PUBLIC LIBRARY *see* **DERBYSHIRE COUNTY LIBRARY**

615 CABLE TELEVISION ASSOCIATION OF GREAT BRITAIN
295 Regent Street, London W1R 7YA Tel. 01-637 4591
Trade Association, housed with the National Television Rental Association Limited, *q.v.;* formerly Relay Services Association of Great Britain

Enquiries to the Association

Subject coverage
cable television industry

Publication
Cablevision News

CADIG *see* **COVENTRY AND DISTRICT INFORMATION GROUP**

616 CADMIUM ASSOCIATION
34 Berkeley Square, London W1X 6AJ Tel. 01-499 6636
Telex 261286

Trade Association; affiliated to the Zinc Development Association, *q.v.*, and served by the Zinc/Lead Library

Enquiries to the Information Officer

Subject coverage
all uses of cadmium; environmental and industrial hygiene problems

Publications
Cadmium: a guide to the literature
Cadmium Abstracts

CAERPHILLY DISTRICT LIBRARY *now* **RHYMNEY VALLEY DISTRICT LIBRARY** *see* **MID-GLAMORGAN COUNTY LIBRARY**

CAITHNESS COUNTY LIBRARY *now* **HIGHLAND REGION LIBRARY SERVICE,** *q.v.*

617 CAKE AND BISCUIT ALLIANCE LIMITED
Westmorland House, 127–131 Regent Street, London W1R 7HA Tel. 01-734 2843
Trade Association; associated with the Joint Industrial Council for the Biscuit Industry

Enquiries, generally from members only, to the Secretary

Subject coverage
production and marketing of biscuits and cakes

Publication
Annual Report

618 CALCIUM SILICATE BRICK ASSOCIATION LIMITED
11 White Lion House, Town Centre, Hatfield, Hertfordshire AL10 0JL Tel. 30 71580
Trade Association, formerly the Sandlime Brick Manufacturers Association

Enquiries to the Association

Subject coverage
calcium silicate bricks, manufacture and uses

Publications
Calcium Silicate Bricks
Movement in Brickwork

619 CALDERDALE INFORMATION SERVICE (CALDIS)
Percival Whitley College of Further Education Library, Tel. 0422 58221 ext. 15
Francis Street, Halifax, West Yorkshire HX1 3UZ
Interlibrary Cooperative Scheme, in cooperation with Calderdale Libraries Department, Calderdale Development Services and Huddersfield Polytechnic; formerly Halifax and District Information Service for Business and Industry

Enquiries to the Secretary or Tutor Librarian

Subject coverage
public and company commercial, technical and management resources

Special collection
British Standards

620 CALDERDALE METROPOLITAN DISTRICT LIBRARY
Wellesley Park, Gibbet Street, Halifax HX2 0BA Tel. 0422 63561
Public Library Service; Regional Libraries: East Calderdale at Brighouse, Mid-Calderdale at Halifax, West Calderdale at Hebden Bridge

Enquiries to the Librarians

Subject coverage
general

CALDIS *see* **CALDERDALE INFORMATION SERVICE**

621 CALOR GAS LIMITED
Central Laboratories, Coombelands, Addlestone, Weybridge, Tel. 97 43244
Surrey KT15 1JW Telex 23543
Company, part of Imperial Continental Gas Ltd

Enquiries to the Librarian

Subject coverage
liquid petroleum gases, applications and distribution

622 CALTEX (UK) LIMITED
29 Old Burlington Street, London W1X 2AR Tel. 01-437 9876
Telex 265031

Company; service company to Caltex Services Limited

Enquiries, book loans only, to the Technical Librarian

Subject coverage
petroleum engineering, including materials selection, corrosion, maintenance, instrumentation, etc.

623 CAMBORNE SCHOOL OF MINES
Trevenson, Pool, Redruth, Cornwall TR15 3SE Tel. 02092 714866
Specialist College; formerly Camborne School of Metalliferous Mining

Enquiries to the Librarian

Subject coverage
metalliferous mining, mineral processing, extractive metallurgy, geology

624 CAMBRIDGE CONSULTANTS LIMITED
Bar Hill, Cambridge CB3 8EZ Tel. 0954 80461
Telex 81481

Company; associated with Arthur D. Little Limited

Enquiries to the Director

Subject coverage
contract research and development; instrumentation and equipment design; theoretical studies

Publications
Interface (house journal)
Some Projects performed by Cambridge Consultants

CAMBRIDGE DIVISIONAL LIBRARY *see* **CAMBRIDGESHIRE LIBRARIES**

625 CAMBRIDGE UNIVERSITY
Applied Biology Library, Downing Street, Cambridge CB2 3DX Tel. 0223 58381
University Department Library

Enquiries to the Librarian

Subject coverage
agriculture; nutrition; soil science; plant breeding; plant pathology; ecology; entomology

Publications
Memoir (annual)
Guides for Readers
List of Current Periodicals

626 CAMBRIDGE UNIVERSITY
Botany School Library, Downing Street, Cambridge CB2 3EA Tel. 0223 61414 ext. 34
University Department Library

Enquiries, from bona fide research workers only, to the Librarian

Subject coverage
all aspects of botany, except agriculture and forestry; radiocarbon dating; history of quaternary vegetation

Special collections
Simpson Collection of early local floras
Early herbals

627 CAMBRIDGE UNIVERSITY
Chemical Laboratory Joint Library, Lensfield Road, Cambridge CB2 1EW Tel. 0223 66499
University Department Library

Enquiries to the Librarian

Subject coverage
all branches of chemistry, physical to biological

628 CAMBRIDGE UNIVERSITY
Department of Applied Economics Library, Sidgwick Avenue, Cambridge CB3 9DE Tel. 0223 58944
University Department Library

No enquiry service

Subject coverage
economics

Publications
Monograph Series and Occasional papers (C.U.P.)

629 CAMBRIDGE UNIVERSITY
Department of Applied Mathematics and Theoretical Physics, Library, Tel. 0223 51645
Old Press Site, Silver Street, Cambridge CB3 9EW
University Department Library

Enquiries to the Librarian

Subject coverage
Mathematical methods; mechanics; control theory; optimization; biomechanics; physiology; general continuum mechanics; elasticity; solid mechanics; sound; acoustics; fluid mechanics; geophysics; magnetohydrodynamics; plasma physics; electromagnetism; optics; thermodynamics; heat transfer; quantum mechanics; nuclear physics; elementary particles; atomic physics; statistical physics; structure of matter; solid state physics; physical chemistry; relativity; astrophysics; numerical analysis; computer techniques

630 CAMBRIDGE UNIVERSITY
Department of Biochemistry, Biochemistry (Colman) Library, Tel. 0223 51781
Tennis Court Road, Cambridge CB2 1QW
University Department Library; includes the former Oliver Gatty Library

Enquiries to the Librarian

Subject coverage
biochemistry; colloid science

Special collection
Hopkins reprints

Publications
Annual Report
List of Research Projects

631 CAMBRIDGE UNIVERSITY
Department of Chemical Engineering, the Chemical Engineering Library, Tel. 0223 58231
Pembroke Street, Cambridge CB2 3RA
University Department Library

Enquiries to the Librarian

Subject coverage
fluid flow related to chemical engineering; chemical reactor design; polymers; fluidisation and two-phase flow; flow of granular materials; optimisation

632 CAMBRIDGE UNIVERSITY
Department of Clinical Veterinary Medicine, Veterinary Library, Tel. 0223 55641
Madingley Road, Cambridge CB3 0ES
University Department Library; the Department was formerly the School of Veterinary Medicine

Enquiries to the Librarian

Subject coverage
veterinary medicine; some agricultural subjects

Special collection
Hammond Collection, of material on nutrition in animals and man

633 CAMBRIDGE UNIVERSITY
Genetics Library, Department of Genetics, Downing Street,
Cambridge CB2 3DH
University Department

Enquiries to the Librarian

Subject coverage
genetics; cytology; relevant parts of biochemistry, cell biology and ecology

634 CAMBRIDGE UNIVERSITY
Department of Geodesy and Geophysics, the Library, Madingley Road, Cambridge CB3 0EZ — Tel. 0223 51686
University Department Library

Enquiries to the Librarian

Subject coverage
geophysics of the solid earth

Publication
Annual Report

635 CAMBRIDGE UNIVERSITY
Department of Geography Library, Downing Place, Cambridge CB2 3EN — Tel. 0223 53809 ext. 33
University Department Library

Enquiries to the Librarian

Subject coverage
geography

Special collection
Clark collection (books, some very old, mainly on exploration)

636 CAMBRIDGE UNIVERSITY
Department of Geology, Sedgwick Geology Library, Downing Street, Cambridge CB2 3EQ
University Department Reference Library

Enquiries are not accepted

Subject coverage
geology

637 CAMBRIDGE UNIVERSITY
Department of Land Economy, 19 Silver Street, Cambridge CB3 9EP — Tel. 0223 55262
University Department, including the Agricultural Economics Unit

Enquiries to the Librarian, Land Economy Library, Faculty Rooms, Laundress Lane, Cambridge

Subject coverage
land values, use and tenure; rural sociology; agricultural economics; forestry; town and country planning

Publications
Research and publications (annual)

638 CAMBRIDGE UNIVERSITY
Department of Metallurgy and Materials Science Library, Pembroke Street, Cambridge CB2 3QZ — Tel. 0223 65151
University Department Library

Enquiries to the Librarian

Subject coverage
metallurgy; materials science

639 CAMBRIDGE UNIVERSITY
Department of Mineralogy and Petrology Library, Downing Place, Cambridge CB2 3EW — Tel. 0223 64131 ext. 287
University Department Library

Enquiries to the Librarian

Subject coverage
petrology; mineralogy; physical and structural crystallography; geochemistry; geophysics; lunar studies

Special collections
Harker Collection
Tilley collection

640 CAMBRIDGE UNIVERSITY
Department of Pathology, Kanthack Library, Tennis Court Road, Cambridge CB2 1QP Tel. 0223 58251
University Department Library

Enquiries to the Librarian

Subject coverage
pathology; bacteriology; virology; immunology; histology; cryobiology; some general medicine; cancer; surgery

641 CAMBRIDGE UNIVERSITY
Department of Pure Mathematics and Statistics, Statistical (Wishart) Library, 16 Mill Lane, Cambridge CB2 1SB Tel. 0223 65621 ext. 245
University Department Library; linked with the Pure Mathematics Library

No enquiry service

642 CAMBRIDGE UNIVERSITY
Department of Zoology, Balfour and Newton Libraries, Downing Street, Cambridge CB2 3EJ Tel. 0223 58717
University Department Libraries

Enquiries to the Librarian

Subject coverage
zoology

Special collections
Newton Library on ornithology
Strickland Collection on conchology
Norman Reprint Collection

643 CAMBRIDGE UNIVERSITY
Engineering Department Library, Trumpington Street, Cambridge CB2 1PZ
University Department Library

No enquiry service

Publication
Annual Report

644 CAMBRIDGE UNIVERSITY
Institute of Astronomy Library, The Observatories, Madingley Road, Cambridge CB3 0HA Tel. 0223 62204
University Department Library; formerly Library of the Observatories and Institute of Theoretical Astronomy

Enquiries to the Librarian

Subject coverage
astronomy and astrophysics

Special collection
John Couch Adams Collection of astronomy books, mostly pre-1850

Publication
Annual Report of the Institute of Astronomy

645 CAMBRIDGE UNIVERSITY
Marshall Library of Economics, Sidgwick Avenue, Cambridge CB3 9DB — Tel. 0223 58944
University Faculty Library

Enquiries to the Librarian

Subject coverage
economics

646 CAMBRIDGE UNIVERSITY
Physiological Laboratory Library, Downing Street, Cambridge CB2 3EG — Tel. 0223 64131
University Department Library

Enquiries to the Librarian

Subject coverage
physiology; biophysics

647 CAMBRIDGE UNIVERSITY
Whipple Library, Free School Lane, Cambridge CB2 3RH — Tel. 0223 58381 ext. 383
University Department Library, Cambridge University

Enquiries to the Librarian

Subject coverage
history and philosophy of science; history of medicine

Special collections
Works of Robert Boyle
Scientific Works of 16th–19th centuries
Phrenology

648 CAMBRIDGE UNIVERSITY
Whipple Museum of the History of Science, Department of History and Philosophy of Science, Free School Lane, Cambridge CB2 3RH — Tel. 0223 58381 ext. 360
University Department Museum

Enquiries to the Curator

Subject coverage
scientific instruments and instrument-makers, (Middle Ages to 19th century); history of science

649 CAMBRIDGE UNIVERSITY LIBRARY
West Road, Cambridge CB3 9DR — Tel. 0223 61441
Telex 81395

University and Copyright Library; separate Medical Library

Enquiries, in writing only, to the Librarian

Subject coverage
general

Publications
Medical Abstracts and Indexes, 1975: a bibliography
Current Serials
Classified List of Current Serials

CAMBRIDGE UNIVERSITY Library of the Observatories *now* **CAMBRIDGE UNIVERSITY Institute of Astronomy Library,** *q.v.*

CAMBRIDGE UNIVERSITY *see also*
CAVENDISH LABORATORY
SCIENTIFIC PERIODICALS LIBRARY
SCOTT POLAR RESEARCH INSTITUTE
UNIVERSITY BOTANIC GARDEN

650 CAMBRIDGE UNIVERSITY PRESS
The Pitt Building, Trumpington Street, Cambridge CB2 1RP — Tel. 0223 58331, Telex 817256

University Department; London office, 200 Euston Road, London NW1 2DB

Enquiries to the Chief Executive

Subject coverage
The Press publishes in all main subject areas, from schoolbooks to advanced monographs and reference books

Publications
about 400 titles per annum
over 50 learned journals
Annual complete catalogue available; also seasonal lists, subject lists, lists of journals

651 CAMBRIDGESHIRE COLLEGE OF ARTS AND TECHNOLOGY
Collier Road, Cambridge CB1 2AJ — Tel. 0223 63271
College of Technology, of Cambridgeshire County Council

Enquiries to the Librarian

Subject coverage
general

652 CAMBRIDGESHIRE LIBRARIES
County Library Headquarters, Princes Street, Huntingdon, Cambridgeshire PE18 6NS — Tel. 0480 52181, Telex 32180
Public Libraries; district libraries at Cambridge, Huntingdon, March, and Peterborough, *q.v.*

Enquiries to the Information Librarian

Subject coverage
general; science and technology; commerce, especially local

Special collections
Peterborough Technical Library

CAMDEN LIBRARIES *see*
HOLBORN LIBRARY
ST PANCRAS LIBRARY
SWISS COTTAGE LIBRARY

653 CAMEROON EMBASSY
84 Holland Park, London W11 — Tel. 01-727 0771, Telex 25176

Governmental Embassy

Enquiries to the Information Officer

Subject coverage
tourism; commerce; transport; statistics

CAMPBELTOWN PUBLIC LIBRARY *see* **ARGYLL AND BUTE DISTRICT LIBRARY**

654 CAMPDEN FOOD PRESERVATION RESEARCH ASSOCIATION
Chipping Campden, Gloucestershire GL55 6LD — Tel. 0386 840319
Research Association, formerly Fruit and Vegetable Preservation Research Association

Enquiries to the Librarian and Information Officer

Subject coverage
chemistry, physics, biochemistry, microbiology, and technology of food preservation by thermal processing, including cans, glass jars, sterilizable flexible packaging materials, freezing and dehydration; horticulture in relation to the raw materials for processing, including quality standards; food production, export, and import statistics; EEC food legislation

Publications
Abstracts of Current Literature
Research reports
Annual Report
Bibliographies
Processed Food Statistics

655 CAMPING TRADE ASSOCIATION OF GB LIMITED
76 Vine Lane, Hillingdon, Middlesex UB10 0BE Tel. 89 33372
Trade Association

Enquiries to the Secretary

Subject coverage
camping equipment trade

656 W. CANNING & COMPANY LIMITED
Great Hampton Street, Birmingham B18 6AS Tel. 021-236 8621
Telex 33241

Company

Enquiries to the Librarian

Subject coverage
electroplating plant and materials

Publications
Canning Journal
Canning Handbook

657 CANNOCK CHASE TECHNICAL COLLEGE
Stafford Road, Cannock, Staffordshire WS11 2AE Tel. 05435 5811/3
College of Further Education

Enquiries to the Librarian

Subject coverage
mining; engineering

CANNOCK DISTRICT LIBRARY *see* **STAFFORDSHIRE COUNTY LIBRARY**

658 CANTERBURY COLLEGE OF TECHNOLOGY
New Dover Road, Canterbury, Kent CT5 2LJ Tel. 0227 66081
College of Technology; formerly Canterbury Technical College

Enquiries to the Tutor Librarian

Subject coverage
business studies; electrical engineering; coal mining; welding; automobile engineering; mechanical engineering; radio and television; building construction; catering

CANTERBURY DIVISIONAL LIBRARY *see* **KENT COUNTY LIBRARY**

CANVAS CONSULTATIVE COMMITTEE *see* **ASSOCIATION OF HEAVY TEXTILE PROOFERS OF GREAT BRITAIN**

CANVAS GOODS AND MADE-UP TEXTILES ASSOCIATION LIMITED *now* **MADE-UP TEXTILES ASSOCIATION LIMITED,** *q.v.*

659 CAPE BOARDS & PANELS LIMITED
Uxbridge, Middlesex UB8 2JQ Tel. 89 37111
Telex 23471

Company

Enquiries to the Manager

Subject coverage
asbestos board

660 CAPE INSULATION LIMITED
Stirling, Scotland FK7 7RW — Tel. 0786 3100
Telex 77228

Company; part of Cape Industries

Enquiries to Head of Public Relations

Subject coverage
application of thermal insulation materials; fire protection materials; acoustic control materials

Publications
Catalogues

661 CARBOLITE COMPANY LIMITED
Bamford Mill, Bamford, Sheffield S30 2AU — Tel. 043-34 551
Telex 54524

Company, in association with Industrial Plant (Combustion) Ltd and Eurascience Limited

Enquiries to the Director of Sales

Subject coverage
electric resistance heated furnaces; heating, ventilating and electrical contracting; laboratory equipment

662 CARDIFF NATURALISTS SOCIETY
National Museum of Wales, Cathays Park, Cardiff CF1 3NP — Tel. 0222 397951
Voluntary Society

Enquiries to the Librarian

Subject coverage
natural history; zoology; ornithology; botany; geology

Publications
Transactions of the Cardiff Naturalists Society
Birds of Glamorgan

CARDIFF PUBLIC LIBRARIES *now* **SOUTH GLAMORGAN COUNTY LIBRARIES,** *q.v.*

663 CARDIFF SMALL FIRMS INFORMATION CENTRE
16 St Davids House, Wood Street, Cardiff CF1 1ER — Tel. 0222 396116
Telex 497515

Government Information Centre of the Department of Industry

Enquiries to the Manager

Subject coverage
business studies and problems; management

Publications
Pamphlets on financial and business subjects

664 CARDIFF UNIVERSITY COLLEGE SCIENCE LIBRARY
P.O. Box 78, Cathays Park, Cardiff CF1 1XL — Tel. 0222 44211
Telex 49635

University Library, of the University of Wales; Cardiff University College was formerly the University College of South Wales and Monmouthshire; it houses the Cardiff University Industry Centre and the Wolfson Centre for Magnetics Technology, *qq.v.*; the Applied Sciences Library is at Newport Road, Cardiff

Enquiries to the Librarians

Subject coverage
physical and life sciences; microbiology; minerals; metallurgy; engineering

Publications
Readers' Guides

665 CARDIFF UNIVERSITY INDUSTRY CENTRE
University College, P.O. Box 78, Cardiff CF1 1XL — Tel. 0222 44211 ext. 2645
University Unit; includes the Wolfson Laboratory for the Biology of Industry and the Wolfson Centre for Magnetics Technology, *q.v.*

Enquiries to the Manager

Subject coverage
analytical and testing facilities for engineering, metallurgy, mineral exploitation and geology, and chemical, physical and biological sciences; industrial research in science, technology and management; waste use/recycling; pollution, effluent treatment; biodeterioration; pest control; solar energy; energy conservation; consultancy

666 CARGILL ATTWOOD AND THOMAS LIMITED
11–12 The Green, London W5 5EA — Tel. 01-567 4745
Consultancy Company; houses the International Consultants Foundation

Enquiries to the Managing Director

Subject coverage
organization development; planning and implementation of change; people development; communications; marketing

667 CARLISLE PUBLIC LIBRARY
17 Castle Street, Carlisle, Cumbria — Tel. 0228 24166
Telex 64317
North East Division HQ of Cumbria County Library, and the main reference and local history collection

Enquiries to the Librarian

Subject coverage
general

668 CARLISLE TECHNICAL COLLEGE
Victoria Place, Carlisle, Cumberland CA1 1HS — Tel. 0228 24464
College of Further Education

Enquiries to the Librarian

Subject coverage
general

CARMARTHEN DISTRICT LIBRARY *see* **DYFED COUNTY LIBRARY**

CARNARVON COUNTY LIBRARY *now* **GWYNEDD LIBRARY SERVICE**

CARNOUSTIE PUBLIC LIBRARY *see* **ANGUS DISTRICT LIBRARY SERVICE**

669 CARPET INDUSTRY TRAINING BOARD
32 Alderley Road, Wilmslow, Cheshire SK9 1NX — Tel. 099-64 27118
Industrial Training Board, of the Training Services Agency, Manpower Services Commission

Enquiries to the Secretary

Subject coverage
manpower and industrial training in the carpet industry; employment, safety and legislation

Publications
Annual Report
Pamphlets on training and safety
Training Recommendations

CARSHALTON PUBLIC LIBRARY *see* **SUTTON LIBRARIES AND ARTS SERVICES**

CASTLEFORD PUBLIC LIBRARY *see* **WAKEFIELD METROPOLITAN DISTRICT LIBRARIES**

CASTROL COMPANY *see* **BURMAH CASTROL COMPANY LIMITED**

670 CATHODEON CRYSTALS LIMITED
Linton, Cambridge CB1 6JU Tel. 0223 891501
Telex 81212

Company; Subsidiary of Pye of Cambridge Limited

Enquiries to the Technical Director

Subject coverage
frequency control and selection; quartz crystal oscillators; crystal and LC bandpass filters

671 CAULDON COLLEGES OF FURTHER EDUCATION
Stoke Road, Shelton, Stoke-on-Trent, Staffordshire ST4 2DG Tel. 0782 24651
Colleges of Further Education, including the Elms Technical College of the same address; served by the Concourse Library; Cauldon College was formerly the College of Building and Commerce of the same address; houses the Building Information Centre, *q.v.*

Enquiries to the Tutor Librarian

Subject coverage
building; quantity surveying; business studies

672 CAV LIMITED
P.O. Box 36 Warple Way, Acton, London W3 7SS Tel. 01-743 3111
Company, subsidiary of Joseph Lucas Limited

Enquiries to the Librarian

Subject coverage
mechanical engineering, particularly fuel injection equipment for diesel engines; electrical engineering; automotive equipment

673 CAVENDISH LABORATORY
Madingley Road, Cambridge CB3 0HE Tel. 0223 66477 ext. 562
University Research Department, within Cambridge University Department of Physics; includes the Rayleigh Library and the Napier Shaw Library (meteorology)

Enquiries to the Librarian

Subject coverage
physics; meteorology; radio astronomy

Publication
Current Research at the Cavendish Laboratory

674 CBD RESEARCH LIMITED
154 High Street, Beckenham, Kent BR3 1EA Tel. 01-650 7745
Private Limited Company, Publishers

Enquiries to the Director

Subject coverage
sources of business and technical information; directories and guides to associations, societies and institutions of all kinds in Great Britain and Europe

Publications
Current British Directories (8th ed 1976; triennially)
Directory of British Associations (5th ed 1976; biennially)
Directory of European Associations
European Companies: A Guide to Sources of Information (3rd ed 1972)
Current European Directories (2nd ed 1976)
Statistics—Europe: Sources for social, economic & market research. (3rd ed 1976)
and numerous related titles

675 CBMPE (COUNCIL OF BRITISH MANUFACTURERS AND CONTRACTORS SERVING THE PETROLEUM AND PROCESS INDUSTRIES)
178–202 Great Portland Street, London W1N 6DU Tel. 01-637 8841
Trade Association; formerly Council of British manufacturers of Petroleum Equipment

Enquiries to the Director

Subject coverage
equipment for the oil industry

Special collection
API (American Petroleum Institute) standards

Publication
British Petroleum Equipment and Services

676 CCI LIMITED
Productivity House, Rectory Road, Shelton, Stoke on Trent ST1 4PW
Company Independent Consultancy; formerly Ceramic Consultants International

Enquiries to the Managing Director

Subject coverage all fields of ceramics

677 CEMENT ADMIXTURES ASSOCIATION
Dickens House, 15 Tooks Court, London EC4A 1LA Tel. 01-831 7581
Telex 23485

Trade Association

Enquiries to the Secretary

Subject coverage
admixtures, waterproofers, pigments, renders and surface treatments for concrete and mortars; superplasticisers for concrete

Publications
Data Sheet

678 CEMENT AND CONCRETE ASSOCIATION
Wexham Springs, Wexham, Slough SL3 6PL Tel. 395 2727
Telex 848352

Research Association/Technical Advisory Service

Enquiries to the Head of the Library Information Service

Subject coverage
Portland cement; concrete technology; training in the industry

Publications
Concrete (monthly)
Magazine of Concrete Research (quarterly)
Precast Concrete (monthly)
Concrete Technology
Concrete Quarterly
Research Reports
Catalogue of Publications in Print

679 CEMENT MAKERS FEDERATION
52 Grosvenor Gardens, London SW1W 0AH Tel. 01-730 2148

Trade Association

Enquiries to the Secretary

Subject coverage
statistics relating to the manufacture, distribution and sale of Portland cement in the U.K.

680 CEMENTATION RESEARCH LIMITED
Denham Way, Maple Cross, Rickmansworth, Hertfordshire WD3 2SW Tel. 87 76666
Telex 922102

Company; subsidiary of Trafalgar House Investment Limited, *q.v.*

Enquiries to the Librarian

Subject coverage
ground engineering; piling; foundations; instrumentation of structures; excavation support; cement and concrete technology; bentonite mud technology; cement and chemical grouting

681 CENTRAL COUNCIL FOR AGRICULTURAL AND HORTICULTURAL CO-OPERATION
Market Towers, New Covent Garden Market, Nine Elms Lane, London SW8 5NQ — Tel. 01-720 2144
Government Agency

Enquiries to the Information Officer

Subject coverage
agricultural and horticultural cooperation and marketing; administration of Government Grants Scheme

Publications
Farming Business (quarterly)
Series of technical publications (list available)

682 CENTRAL ELECTRICITY GENERATING BOARD
Sudbury House, 15 Newgate Street, London EC1A 7AU — Tel. 01-248 1202
Nationalised Industry; includes the Berkeley Nuclear Research Laboratories, the Central Electricity Research Laboratories and the Marchwood Engineering Laboratories, *qq.v.*; administers five regional units and the Generation, Development and Construction Division

Enquiries to the Information Services

Subject coverage
all aspects of power generation; electrical engineering; mechanical engineering; environmental matters

Special collection
early works on power generation

Publication
CEGB Digest (abstracting bulletin)

683 CENTRAL ELECTRICITY GENERATING BOARD
Scientific Services Department, Portishead, Bristol BS20 9DH — Tel. 0272 843551, Telex 449673
Nationalised Industry

Enquiries to the Librarian

Subject coverage
electrical engineering; steam and combustion engineering; mechanical engineering; power generation and power plant; nuclear engineering; materials, metallurgy and welding; environmental science; non-destructive testing; instrument and control engineering; physics; chemical engineering

CENTRAL ELECTRICITY GENERATING BOARD *see also*
BERKELEY NUCLEAR LABORATORIES
MARCHWOOD ENGINEERING LABORATORIES

684 CENTRAL ELECTRICITY RESEARCH LABORATORIES
Kelvin Avenue, Leatherhead, Surrey KT22 7SE — Tel. 5374488 ext. 248, Telex 917338
Nationalized Industry Research Establishment, of the Central Electricity Generating Board

Enquiries to the Information Officer/Librarian

Subject coverage
planning, generation and transmission of electricity; environmental aspects; control and communications; electrical engineering; materials; superconductivity

Publications
CEGB Research (house journal)
Guide to the Laboratories
Annual List of CERL Staff Papers

685 CENTRAL FILM LIBRARY
Government Building, Bromyard Avenue, London W3 7JB — Tel. 01-743 5555
Government Department within the Central Office of Information, *q.v.*

Enquiries to the Librarian

Subject coverage
documentary and instructional films on a wide range of subjects illustrating the British way of life

Publications
Lists of films

686 CENTRAL OFFICE OF INFORMATION
Hercules Road, Westminster Bridge Road, London SE1 7DU — Tel. 01-928 2345
Telex 915444

Government Department; responsible for the Central Film Library

Enquiries, export publicity to the Overseas Coordination Unit; films, to the Central Film Library; photographs, to the Photographs Librarian; pamphlets, etc., to the Reference Distribution Unit; list of publications, to the Publications Circulation Section

Subject coverage
export publicity; British way of Life

Publications
Britain: an official handbook (annual)
Survey of Current Affairs (monthly)
Film Catalogues
List of Reference Pamphlets
List of Publications
List of Photo-posters

CENTRAL PUBLIC HEALTH LABORATORY *see* **PUBLIC HEALTH LABORATORY SERVICE**

687 CENTRAL STATISTICAL OFFICE
Great George Street, London SW1P 3AQ — Tel. 01-233 6135
Telex 27582

Government Department

Enquiries to the Press and Information Service

Subject coverage
Government statistics in general; specialised information on national income and expenditure, balance of payments, index of industrial production, financial statistics, input/output statistics, social and regional statistics

Publications
Monthly Digest of Statistics (monthly) and Supplement (annual) HMSO
Statistical News (quarterly)
Abstract of Regional Statistics (annual) HMSO
Annual Abstract of Statistics
Studies in Official Statistics
Studies in Official Statistics, Research Series

688 CENTRAL VETERINARY LABORATORY
New Haw, Weybridge, Surrey KT15 3NB — Tel. 91 41111
Telex 262318

Government Department Research Laboratory, of the Ministry of Agriculture, Fisheries and Food; connected with the Veterinary Laboratory, Lasswade, Midlothian and with the Cattle Breeding Centre, Shinfield, Reading, *qq.v.*; houses also the Commonwealth Bureau of Animal Health, *q.v.*

Enquiries to the Librarian

Subject coverage
investigation and control of diseases of farm animals; animal husbandry; biochemistry

Publication
Research in Progress (irregular)

689 CENTRAL WATER PLANNING UNIT
Reading Bridge House, Reading, Berkshire RG1 8PS Tel. 0734 57551
Government Department, of the Department of the Environment; formerly Water Resources Board; houses the Water Data Unit, *q.v.*, and the Hydrogeological Enquiry Service

Enquiries to the Librarian; or, for the Hydrogeological Enquiry Service, to the Secretary of the Service

Subject coverage
water resources management and planning

Publication
Annual Report

690 CENTRE FOR AGRICULTURAL STRATEGY
Reading University, Earley Gate, Reading, Berkshire RG6 2AT Tel. 0734 85123 ext. 6231
University Research Centre; Nuffield Foundation unit

Enquiries to the Information Officer

Subject coverage
long-term planning for British agriculture, including food, horticulture, forestry and fishing

Publications
Discussion documents and critical reviews are envisaged

691 CENTRE FOR ENVIRONMENTAL STUDIES
62 Chandos Place, London WC2N 4HH Tel. 01-240 3424 ext. 281
Research Organization

Enquiries to the Librarian

Subject coverage
urban and regional planning; economics; housing, demography

Publications
Annual Report
Newsletter
Research papers
Conference papers
Information papers

692 CENTRE FOR EUROPEAN AGRICULTURAL STUDIES
Wye College, Wye, Ashford, Kent TN25 5AH Tel. 0233 812181
University Research Unit, of the University of London; designated European Documentation Centre

Enquiries to the Director

Subject coverage
agricultural finance; regional and rural planning; agricultural marketing; relationship between European and Third World agricultures

Publications
Brochure on the Centre and its work
List of publications (reports and occasional papers)

693 CENTRE FOR INDUSTRIAL CONSULTANCY AND LIAISON
Edinburgh University, 14 George Square, Edinburgh EH8 9JZ
University Consultancy Unit

Enquiries to the Director

Subject coverage
laboratory measurement; agriculture; architecture; astronomy; bacteriology; biochemistry; biological sciences; chemical engineering; civil engineering; dermatology; forestry; machine intelligence; microbiology

694 CENTRE FOR INDUSTRIAL INNOVATION

Strathclyde University, 100 Montrose Street, Glasgow G4 0LZ Tel. 041-551 4400
Telex 77472

University Department for Contract Research and Development; includes the Division for optical strain recording in engineering components, Optecord; also the Biodeterioration Unit, and the Division for the study of micro-organism growth

Enquiries to the Director

Subject coverage

materials; thermodynamics; fluid mechanics; dynamics and control; bioengineering; engineering strain recording; applied microbiology; food science; biochemistry; chemical engineering; electrical engineering; electronic science; computer technology; fibre science; metallurgy; environmental problems

Publications

Improvement and Protection of the Environment
Reports

695 CENTRE FOR INDUSTRIAL RESEARCH AND CONSULTANCY

The University, 1 Cross Row, Dundee DD1 4HN Tel. 0382 23936
University Department

Enquiries to the Director

Subject coverage

design, development and manufacture of special purpose machines; test facilities; analytical facilities; geophysical and hydrographic surveys; management consultancy

696 CENTRE FOR INFORMATION SCIENCE

City University, St John Street, London EC1V 4PB Tel. 01-253 4399 ext. 556
University Department

No enquiry service

Subject coverage

training and research in information science

697 CENTRE FOR INTERNATIONAL BRIEFING

The Castle, Farnham, Surrey GU9 0AG Tel. 02513 21194
Independent Company/Charity

Enquiries to the Director

Subject coverage

living and working conditions in over 70 countries in Africa, Middle East, Latin America, Caribbean, Asia and the Pacific; international marketing

Special collection

audio-visual material and documentation on the developing world

698 CENTRE FOR OVERSEAS PEST RESEARCH

College House, Wrights Lane, London W8 5SJ Tel. 01-937 8191

Government Department, of the Ministry of Overseas Development; created by the amalgamation of the Anti-Locust Research Centre, the Tropical Pesticides Headquarters and Information Unit, the Tropical Pesticides Research Unit and the Termite Research Unit

Enquiries to the Head, Scientific Information and Library Service

Subject coverage

problems of agriculture and public health in developing countries, mainly tropics, *e.g.* rodents, birds (like weaver birds), insects (like locusts, armyworm, mosquitoes, tse-tse flies; flies (like *Simulium damnosum*, vector of river blindness), and snails (vectors of bilharzia); pests of crops such as rice, cotton, maize, millet, citrus, coconut, etc.; biology of pests; taxonomy of locusts, grasshoppers and termites; population dynamics of pests; economics of pest control operations and crop loss; tropical meteorology and ecology; pesticides development and environmental effects; radar entomology; statistics

Special collections

the former Anti-Locust Research Centre Collection
the former Termite Research Centre Collection
Sir B.P. Uvarov Collection of Orthopteran literature
H.B. Johnston Collection of Orthopteran literature
Desert Locust Information Service Archives
E. Brown Collection of Armyworm literature
Theses on Pest Biology and Control
Photographic collection of locusts, grasshoppers and other pests

Publications

Acridological Abstracts
Anti-Locust Bulletin
Anti-Locust Memoir
Miscellaneous reports and proceedings series
Tropical Pest Bulletin
Annual Report
PANS manuals on crop protection
Books, many and varied (list available)

CENTRE FOR TROPICAL VETERINARY MEDICINE *see* **ROYAL (DICK) SCHOOL OF VETERINARY STUDIES LIBRARY**

699 CERAMIC AND ALLIED TRADES UNION

5 Hillcrest Street, Hanley, Stoke-on-Trent ST1 2AB — Tel. 0782 24201
Trade Union; formerly National Society of Pottery Workers

Enquiries to the General Secretary

Subject coverage

industrial conditions and relations in the ceramic trades

CERAMIC CONSULTANTS INTERNATIONAL *now* **CCL LIMITED,** *q.v.*

700 CERAMICS, GLASS & MINERAL PRODUCTS INDUSTRY TRAINING BOARD

Bovis House, Northolt Road, Harrow, Middlesex HA2 0EF — Tel. 01-422 7101
Training Board

Enquiries to the Information Officer

Subject coverage

training in the ceramics, glass and minerals industries

CERTIFICATION SCHEME FOR WELDMENT INSPECTION PERSONNEL *see* **WELDING INSTITUTE**

701 CEYLON TEA CENTRE

22 Regent Street, London SW1Y 4QD — Tel. 01-930 8632
Promotional Organization

Enquiries to the Centre

Subject coverage

tea, particularly from Sri Lanka

702 J.W. CHAFER LIMITED

19 Thorne Road, Doncaster, Yorkshire DN1 2HQ — Tel. 0302 67371
Telex 547132

Company, subsidiary of ICI Limited

Enquiries to the Information Officer

Subject coverage
agricultural chemicals and machinery; liquid fertilizer production, transportation and storage; agronomic advice

Publications
Technical Sales manuals
Farmers Guide

703 CHAIN TESTERS ASSOCIATION OF GREAT BRITAIN
430 Barking Road, London E13 8HJ Tel. 01-476 2958
Trade Association; houses the Secretariat of the Lifting Equipment Manufacturers Association, *q.v.*

Enquiries to the Secretary; research in depth may be chargeable

Subject coverage
design of lifting gear from the mathematical angle; sources of supply; metallurgical problems

Publications
Chain Testers' Handbook (important technical and safety manual)
Training Manuals (8 titles)
Codes of Practice
Tables and other publications on safe working loads
List of publications

704 CHAIR FRAME MANUFACTURERS ASSOCIATION
4 Sutherland Avenue, London W9 2QE Tel. 01-965 3561
Trade Association

Enquiries to the Administrative Secretary

Subject coverage
chair frame manufacture; wages and conditions in the furniture industry

705 CHALLENGER SOCIETY
Dunstaffnage Marine Research Laboratory, P.O. Box 3, Oban, Argyllshire PA34 4AD Tel. 0631 2244
Learned Society

No enquiry service

Subject coverage
oceanography and marine biology

Publication
Quarterly Newsletter

CHARD DISTRICT LIBRARY *see* **SOMERSET COUNTY LIBRARY**

CHARLES MYERS LIBRARY *see* **NATIONAL INSTITUTE OF INDUSTRIAL PSYCHOLOGY**

CHARLES TREVELYAN TECHNICAL COLLEGE *now* **NEWCASTLE UPON TYNE COLLEGE OF ARTS AND TECHNOLOGY,** *q.v.*

CHARTERED AUCTIONEERS AND ESTATE AGENTS INSTITUTE *now* **ROYAL INSTITUTION OF CHARTERED SURVEYORS,** *q.v.*

CHARTERED ENGINEERS INSTITUTE *see* **INSTITUTE OF MARINE ENGINEERS**

706 CHARTERED INSTITUTE OF PATENT AGENTS
Staple Inn Buildings, High Holborn, London WC1V 7PZ Tel. 01-405 9450
Professional Body

Enquiries to the Secretary

Subject coverage
patent agency and patent matters as they affect inventors

Publications
CIPA: the Journal of the Chartered Institute of Patent Agents (monthly)
Register of Patent Agents (annual)

CHARTERED INSTITUTE OF SECRETARIES *now* **INSTITUTE OF CHARTERED SECRETARIES AND ADMINISTRATORS,** *q.v.*

707 CHARTERED INSTITUTE OF TRANSPORT
80 Portland Place, London W1N 4DP Tel. 01-580 5216
Professional Institute, formerly Institute of Transport

Enquiries to the Librarian

Subject coverage
economics and operation of all forms of transport by land, sea, and air

Special collection
the Reinohl Collection of Bus Tickets

Publication
Journal of the Chartered Institute of Transport

708 CHARTERED INSURANCE INSTITUTE
20 Aldermanbury, London EC2V 7HY Tel. 01-606 3835
Professional Institute/Qualifying Body

Enquiries to the Librarian or to the Secretary General

Subject coverage
insurance, U.K. and overseas

Publications
Journal of the Chartered Insurance Institute (annual)
Yearbook
List of Fellows and Associates
Bibliographies

CHARTERED LAND AGENTS SOCIETY *now* **ROYAL INSTITUTION OF CHARTERED SURVEYORS,** *q.v.*

709 CHARTERHOUSE GROUP LIMITED
1 Paternoster Row, St. Pauls, London EC4M 7DH Tel. 01-248 3999
Telex 884276

Industrial Holding Company

Enquiries to the Librarian

Subject coverage
company information (U.K. quoted and unquoted companies); industrial and economic information (press reports); City and general financial topics

CHATHAM PUBLIC LIBRARY *now* **MEDWAY DIVISIONAL LIBRARY**
see **KENT COUNTY LIBRARY**

CHEADLE BRANCH LIBRARY *see* **STOCKPORT CENTRAL LIBRARY**

710 CHELSEA COLLEGE
Manresa Road, London SW3 6LX Tel. 01-352 6421
University Department, of London University; formerly Chelsea College of Science and Technology

Enquiries to the Librarian

Subject coverage
biochemistry; botany; chemistry; geology; mathematics; physiology; zoology; pharmacy and pharmacology; physics; electronics; applied biology; microbiology

Special collection
Darwin Collection

CHELMSFORD DISTRICT LIBRARY *see* **ESSEX COUNTY LIBRARY**

CHELSEA PUBLIC LIBRARY *see* **KENSINGTON & CHELSEA CENTRAL LIBRARY**

CHELTENHAM PUBLIC LIBRARY *see* **GLOUCESTER COUNTY LIBRARY**

711 CHEMICAL AND ALLIED PRODUCTS INDUSTRY TRAINING BOARD
158–162 High Street, Staines, Middlesex TW18 4AT Tel. 90 51366
Industrial Training Board, of the Training Services Agency, *q.v.*

Enquiries to the Information Officer

Subject coverage
training within the chemical and allied products industry

Publications
Training Recommendations, numbers 1–29
Information Papers, 1–16
Instrument Training Manuals, 1–10
Publications for Smaller Companies
Career Patterns and Training Needs of Engineers, Scientists and Technologists
Levy Extension Arrangements
Publications list available

712 CHEMICAL AND INSULATING COMPANY LIMITED
West Auckland Road, Darlington, Co. Durham DL3 0UR Tel. 0325 53881
Telex 58542
Manufacturing Company; member of the Darlington Group of Companies, whose Holding Company is Darchem Limited, *q.v.*

Enquiries to the Technical Information Officer

Subject coverage
science and technology of thermal insulation, including silica fibre; chemistry and technology of light basic magnesium carbonate, light magnesium oxide and magnesium hydroxide

713 CHEMICAL BUILDING PRODUCTS LIMITED
Cleveland Road, Hemel Hempstead, Hertfordshire HP2 7DH Tel. 91 2101
Telex 82252

Company, part of Foseco Minsep Group

Enquiries, on products sold, to the Technical Manager

Subject coverage
concrete admixtures; concrete surface treatments; grouts; anchoring systems; mortars and repair compounds; flooring materials; protective surface coatings; sealants and adhesives

Publications
Product Data Sheets

714 CHEMICAL DEFENCE ESTABLISHMENT
Porton Down, Salisbury, Wiltshire SP4 0JQ Tel. 0980 610211
Government Research Centre, of the Ministry of Defence, Procurement Executive; formerly Chemical Defence Experimental Establishment

Enquiries to the Information Officer

Subject coverage
chemical, physical and meteorological problems of defence against chemical agents; design and development of protective equipment, respirators and protective clothing; physiological effects, toxicology and biochemistry of poisonous substances and the development of therapeutic and prophylactic procedures

Publications
Technical Papers
Technical Notes

715 CHEMICAL INDUSTRIES ASSOCIATION LIMITED
Alembic House, 93 Albert Embankment, London SE1 7TU — Tel. 01-735 3001
Telex 916672

Trade Association; (a list of affiliated Associations follows this entry)

Enquiries to the Economic Intelligence Officer or Information Officer

Subject coverage
chemical and allied industries economic aspects, *e.g.* production, investment, employees and employment, safety, law, trade, tariffs, statistics; *not* information on individual companies; technical information limited to the extent of staff expertise

Publications
U.K. Chemical Industry Statistics (annual)
Many various manuals, codes of practice, etc., (list available)

CHEMICAL INDUSTRIES ASSOCIATION LIMITED
ASSOCIATION OF BRITISH PHARMACEUTICAL INDUSTRY, *q.v.*
BRITISH AEROSOL MANUFACTURERS ASSOCIATION, *q.v.*
BRITISH AGROCHEMICALS ASSOCIATION, *q.v.*
BRITISH ASSOCIATION OF SYNTHETIC RUBBER MANUFACTURERS
BRITISH CHEMICALS AND DYESTUFFS TRADERS ASSOCIATION LIMITED
BRITISH COLOUR MAKERS ASSOCIATION, *q.v.*
BRITISH COMPRESSED GASES ASSOCIATION, *q.v.*
BRITISH DISINFECTANT MANUFACTURERS ASSOCIATION, *q.v.*
BRITISH PEST CONTROL ASSOCIATION, *q.v.*
BRITISH RESIN MANUFACTURERS ASSOCIATION
BRITISH SULPHATE OF AMMONIA FEDERATION LIMITED
BRITISH TAR INDUSTRY ASSOCIATION, *q.v.*
FERTILISER MANUFACTURERS ASSOCIATION LIMITED
HYDROCARBON SOLVENTS MANUFACTURERS ASSOCIATION LIMITED, *q.v.*
NATIONAL SULPHURIC ACID ASSOCIATION LIMITED
SOCIETY OF BRITISH PRINTING INK MANUFACTURERS, *q.v.*

716 CHEMICAL SOCIETY
Burlington House, London W1V 0BN — Tel. 01-734 9971
Telex 268001

Learned Society; its Analytical Division formerly the Society of Analytical Chemistry, its Faraday Division formerly the Faraday Society; the Dalton Division (inorganic area), the Perkin Division (organic area), the Education Division and the Industrial Division are all new Divisions since 1972; the Royal Institute of Chemistry will also become part of the Society

Enquiries to the Librarian

Subject coverage
chemistry; chemical engineering; biochemistry

Special collection
Alchemy and Chemistry to 1850 (2000 volumes)

Publications
Analytical Abstracts (monthly)
Large number of journals, transactions, reviews, periodical reports, books and monographs (list available)

717 CHEMICAL RECOVERY ASSOCIATION
Petrol House, Hepscott Road, London E9 5HD — Tel. 01-985 5500

Trade Association; having also a Midlands Office at 6 Kingscote Road, Dorridge, Solihull B93 8RA, Tel. 056-45 6699

Enquiries to the Liaison Executive, at the Midlands Office address

Subject coverage
recovery of chemical wastes from industry

Publications
Code of Practice for the Recovery of Mineral Oils
Code of Practice for the Recovery of Chlorinated Solvents and other Halogenated Organic Compounds
Other Codes in preparation

CHEMISTS DEFENCE ASSOCIATIONS LIMITED *see* **NATIONAL PHARMACEUTICAL UNION**

718 CHESHIRE COUNTY LIBRARY
Headquarters, 91 Hoole Road, Chester CH2 3NG Tel. 0244 20055
Public Library system; main libraries at Chester, Crewe, Ellesmere Port, Macclesfield, *q.v.*, Runcorn, Warrington *q.v.* Widnes and Wilmslow; *see also* Cheshire County Local Government Information Service and Cheshire Information Service

Enquiries to the Director

Subject coverage
specialization in agriculture

719 CHESHIRE COUNTY LOCAL GOVERNMENT INFORMATION SERVICE
Research Library, Room 264, County Hall, Chester CH1 1SF Tel. 0244 602246
Information Service, part of Cheshire County Library, *q.v.*

Enquiries to the Research Librarian

Subject coverage
local government; planning; social services; architecture; management; finance; highways and transportation

Publications
Today's Press (daily)
Weekly subject Bulletins
Monthly Research Review

720 CHESHIRE INFORMATION SERVICE
Research Library, Room 264, County Hall, Chester CH1 1SF Tel. 0244-60 2247
Interlibrary Co-operative Scheme, comprising 88 information centres and public libraries

Enquiries to the Senior Librarian

Subject coverage
general; exhibitions; local government; public utilities

721 CHESTER LIBRARY
St John Street, Chester CH1 1DH Tel. 0244 21938 & 43427
Public Library, part of the Cheshire County Library, *q.v.*

Enquiries to the Librarian

Subject coverage
military science (excluding air and naval forces); military engineering

Publication
Chester Newspaper Index (every 5 years, 1955–)

722 CHESTERFIELD COLLEGES OF ART & TECHNOLOGY
Infirmary Road, Chesterfield, Derbyshire S41 7NG Tel. 0246 70271
College of Technology

Enquiries to the Tutor Librarian, Library and Resources Centre

Subject coverage
mechanical and electrical engineering, foundry technology, construction, industrial design, printing, painting and decorating, dress design; economics, commerce, management, accountancy, computing; mathematics, chemistry, physics, biology

Special collection
British Standard Codes of Practice

Publication
Bank Reviews Index

CHESTERFIELD PUBLIC LIBRARY *see* **DERBYSHIRE COUNTY LIBRARY**

CHESTERFORD PARK RESEARCH STATION *see* **FISONS LIMITED, Agrochemical Division**

CHICHESTER DIVISIONAL LIBRARY *see* **WEST SUSSEX COUNTY COUNCIL LIBRARY SERVICE**

CHIGWELL DISTRICT LIBRARY *see* **ESSEX COUNTY LIBRARY**

723 CHINA CLAY ASSOCIATION
14 High Cross Street, St. Austell, Cornwall PL25 4AB Tel. 0726 4101
Trade Association

Enquiries to the Secretary

Subject coverage
production and sales of china clay

CHIPPENHAM DIVISIONAL LIBRARY *see* **WILTSHIRE COUNTY LIBRARY**

CHISWICK DISTRICT LIBRARY *see* **HOUNSLOW LIBRARY SERVICE**

CHISWICK POLYTECHNIC *see*
HOUNSLOW BOROUGH COLLEGE
WEST LONDON INSTITUTE OF HIGHER EDUCATION

724 CHLORIDE TECHNICAL LIMITED
Wynne Avenue, Swinton, Manchester M27 2HB Tel. 061-794 4266
Telex 668041
Company, part of the Chloride Group Limited; formerly Electric Power Storage Limited, R & D Division, and then Chloride Technical Centre

Enquiries to the Information Officer or Librarian

Subject coverage
secondary rechargeable batteries; electrochemistry and applications; battery-related products such as chargers, security systems, etc.

CHORLEY CENTRAL LIBRARY *see* **LANCASHIRE LIBRARY**

725 CHROMATOGRAPHY DISCUSSION GROUP
Trent Polytechnic, Burton Street, Nottingham NG1 4BU Tel. 0602 48248 ext. 2187
Scientific Society

Enquiries to the Executive Secretary

Subject coverage
all aspects of gas and liquid chromatography techniques

Publication
Gas and Liquid Chromatography Abstracts (quarterly)

726 CHUBB AND SON LIMITED
Totfield House, Tottenham Street, London W1P 0AA Tel. 01-637 2377
Holding Company; some U.K. Subsidiaries are as follows: Chubb and Son's Lock and Safe Company, Chubb Alarms Group, Chubb Fire Security, Chubb Integrated Systems, Gross Cash Register Company

Enquiries to the Director of Public Relations, Chubb Security Services, 44–45 Chancery Lane, London WC2A 1JP (Tel. 01-242 9861)

Subject coverage
physical security: locks, safes, strongrooms; intruder alarms: CCTV, wardens; fire engineering, fire extinguishers, fire vehicles; foam and dry powder; anti-bandit screens and equipment; personal safety

equipment, including spectacles, eye shields, ear defenders, breathing apparatus; emergency cutting equipment; architectural ironmongery; cash dispensers and cash transaction systems; coin counting machines; paper shredding machines; cash registers

Publications

Catalogues

CIBA-GEIGY AGRICULTURAL AVIATION RESEARCH UNIT *see* **AGRICULTURAL AVIATION RESEARCH UNIT**

CICRIS *see* **CO-OPERATIVE INDUSTRIAL AND COMMERCIAL REFERENCE AND INFORMATION SERVICE**

CINDERFORD PUBLIC LIBRARY *see* **GLOUCESTER COUNTY LIBRARY**

CIRENCESTER PUBLIC LIBRARY *see* **GLOUCESTER COUNTY LIBRARY**

CIRIA UNDERWATER ENGINEERING GROUP *see* **CONSTRUCTION INDUSTRY RESEARCH AND INFORMATION ASSOCIATION**

CIS *see* **CORNWALL INFORMATION SERVICE**

727 CITY AND EAST LONDON COLLEGE

Pitfield Street, London N1 6BX — Tel. 01-253 6883

College of Further Education, formerly City College, Tower Hamlets College, Walbrook College

Enquiries to the Site Librarian

Subject coverage

optics; electrical engineering

728 CITY BUSINESS LIBRARY

Gillett House, Basinghall Street, London EC2V 5BX — Tel. 01-638 8215/6
Telex 887955

Public Reference Library; one of the City of London Libraries

Enquiries to the Librarian

Subject coverage

management; finance; banking; insurance; employment; commercial law; product, industry and area data; market research; statistics; company data

Special collections

British and overseas trade directories
Company data card services

Publication

City Business Courier

CITY OF LONDON LIBRARIES *see*
CITY BUSINESS LIBRARY
ST BRIDE PRINTING LIBRARY
GUILDHALL LIBRARY (entry in Volume 2 of the Directory)

729 CITY OF LONDON POLYTECHNIC LIBRARY

Calcutta House Precinct, Old Castle Street, London E1 7NT — Tel. 01-283 1030
Telex 8812073

Polytechnic, having units at Moorgate Precinct, Moorgate; Central House Library, Whitechapel; School of Navigation Library, Tower Hill, all East London; formerly known as Sir John Cass College Library and then the City of London College Library

Enquiries to the Librarian

Subject coverage
business studies; law; science; metallurgy; silversmithing; accounting; navigation; transport

Publication
Research Review

730 CITY UNIVERSITY SKINNERS LIBRARY
St. John Street, London EC1V 4PB Tel. 01-253 4399
Telex 263896

University Library; houses the Library of the British Computer Society, *q.v.*

Enquiries to the Librarian

Subject coverage
engineering; management; ophthalmic optics

Publications
Quest, Journal of the City University
Research Memoranda
Annual Report

CITY UNIVERSITY *see also* **GRADUATE BUSINESS CENTRE**

731 CIVIL AVIATION AUTHORITY
Aviation House, 129 Kingsway, London WC2B 6NN Tel. 01-405 6922 ext. 440
Telex 27464

Independent Statutory Body; carries out the functions of the former Air Transport Licensing Board and the Air Registration Board; its Library was formerly the Civil Aviation Library of the Department of Trade and Industry

Enquiries, quick reference only, to the Reader Services Librarian; Library available to outside researchers by arrangement

Subject coverage
electronics; telecommunications; air transport statistics

Publications
CAA publications list available
ICAO publications agency

732 CIVIL SERVICE COLLEGE
11 Belgrave Road, London SW1V 1RB Tel. 01-834 6644 ext. 250
Government Department

Enquiries to the Librarian

Subject coverage
economics, sociology, statistics

733 CIVIL SERVICE COLLEGE
17 Atholl Crescent, Edinburgh EH3 8HB Tel. 031-229 8911 ext. 284
Government Department

Enquiries to the Librarian

Subject coverage
general

734 CIVIL SERVICE COLLEGE
Sunningdale Park, Ascot, Berkshire SL5 0QE Tel. 0990 23444 ext. 307
Government Department

Enquiries to the Librarian

Subject coverage
public administration, local government, management, personnel management

735 CIVIL SERVICE DEPARTMENT
Information Division, Whitehall, London SW1A 2AZ — Tel. 01-839 7848, Telex 918322

Government Department; houses the Central Computer Agency

Enquiries to the Librarian, Central Management Library

Subject coverage
general management, public administration, British civil service

Special collection
history of the British civil service

Publication
"Published by CSD, 1968–" (annual cumulation)

736 CIVIL SERVICE UNION
14–21 Hatton Wall, London EC1N 8JP — Tel. 01-242 2991, 01-405 5371

Trade Union

No enquiry service

CJB LIMITED *see* **CONSTRUCTORS JOHN BROWN LIMITED**

737 CLACKMANNAN DISTRICT LIBRARY
17 Mar Street, Alloa, Clackmannanshire FK10 1HT — Tel. Alloa 2160 ext. 269
Public Library, formerly Clackmannan County Library

Enquiries to the District Librarian

Subject coverage
general

738 C & J CLARK LIMITED
Intelligence Department, 40 High Street, Street, Somerset BA16 0YA — Tel. 045-84 3131, Telex 44102

Private Company

Enquiries to the Information Officer

Subject coverage
Shoe-making and allied trades technology; footwear markets

739 CLARKE CHAPMAN-JOHN THOMPSON LIMITED
Thompson Wolverhampton Division, Friction Welding/Mechanical Unit, Spring Road, Ettingshall, Wolverhampton WV4 6JX — Tel. 0902 41121, Telex 33212

Company Division

Enquiries to the General Manager

Subject coverage
friction welding; special machines

740 CLAY PIPE DEVELOPMENT ASSOCIATION LIMITED
Drayton House, 30 Gordon Street, London WC1 0AN — Tel. 01-388 0025/6
Trade Association

Enquiries to the Director General

Subject coverage
design and construction of drains and sewers; specialised advice on hydraulic and chemical drainage; vitrified clay pipes

Publications
Technical literature on the properties and performance of vitrified clay pipes and similar products

741 CLEAN AIR COUNCIL
Department of the Environment, Queen Annes Chambers, 28 Broadway, London SW1H 9JU — Tel. 01-930 4300
Statutory Body

Enquiries are not accepted; advisory services only to the Secretary of State for the Environment

Subject coverage
all aspects of air pollution

742 CLEVELAND COUNTY LIBRARY
Victoria Square, Middlesbrough TS1 2AY — Tel. 0642 45294/6
Telex 58439

Public Library Service; three District Libraries: Hartlepool, *q.v.*, Redcar, Stockton; Headquarters for LIST (Library Information Service for Teesside); formerly Teesside Public Library

Enquiries to the County Librarian

Subject coverage
general science, technology & commerce; metallurgy

Special collection
British Standards
British Patent Abridgements

Publications
see "LIST"

743 CLEVELAND SCIENTIFIC INSTITUTION
70 Corporation Road, Middlesbrough, Yorkshire TS1 2RG — Tel. 0642 42303
Headquarters and Library of local branches of the professional and semi-professional societies

Enquiries to the Secretary

Subject coverage
civil, electrical, mechanical and structural engineering; welding; metallurgy; shipbuilding; chemistry; transport; insurance; commerce; management

CLIMATIC RESEARCH UNIT *see* **EAST ANGLIA UNIVERSITY**

CLINICAL RESEARCH CENTRE *see* **BIOMEDICAL INSTRUMENTATION ADVISORY SERVICE FAST ACCESS INFORMATION RETRIEVAL PROJECT**

744 CLOTH PRESSERS SOCIETY
34 Southgate, Honley, Huddersfield, Yorkshire HD1 1RL — Tel. 0484 61175
Trade Union

Enquiries to the Secretary

Subject coverage
trade union matters and services

745 CLOTHING AND ALLIED PRODUCTS INDUSTRY TRAINING BOARD
Tower House, Merrion Way, Leeds LS2 8NY — Tel. 0532 41331
Industrial Training Board, of the Training Services Agency, Manpower Services Commission

Enquiries to the Information Services Department

Subject coverage
manpower, management and training in the clothing industry; careers; recruitment

Publications
Handcraft Tailors Guidelines
Sewing Machinist Guidelines
Cutting Room Trainee Guidelines
Metrication and Pattern Cutting Guidelines

746 CLOTHING INSTITUTE
Albert Road, Hendon, London NW4 Tel. 01-203 0191
Professional and Technological Body

Enquiries to the Director and Secretary or the Deputy Director and Technical Officer

Subject coverage
clothing manufacture and technology

Publications
Clothing Institute Journal (bimonthly, free to members)
Clothing Research Journal (three times per annum)
Report (quarterly, free to members)
Many other publications: reports, information sheets, etc. (list available)

747 CLWYD COUNTY LIBRARY SERVICE
County Civic Centre, Mold, Clwyd CH7 6NW Tel. 0352 2121 ext. 587
Telex 61454
Public Library service; six Area Libraries: Alyn and Deeside, Colwyn Bay, Delyn, Glyndwr, Rhuddlan, Wrexham Maelor

Enquiries to the Librarian, Technical and Commercial Library

Subject coverage
technical and commercial; jewellery, canal engineering and forestry at Wrexham Area Library

748 CLYDEBANK DISTRICT LIBRARIES
Dumbarton Road, Clydebank G81 1XH Tel. 041-952 1416
Public Libraries, formerly Clydebank Public Libraries

Enquiries to the Chief Librarian

Subject coverage
general

COAL PREPARATION SOCIETY *now* **MINERALS ENGINEERING SOCIETY,** *q.v.*

749 COAL RESEARCH ESTABLISHMENT
Stoke Orchard, Cheltenham, Gloucestershire GL52 4RZ Tel. 024-267 3361
Telex 43568
Research Establishment, of the National Coal Board

Enquiries to the Information Officer or Librarian

Subject coverage
coal processing and combustion

COAL TAR RESEARCH ASSOCIATION *now* **BRITISH CARBONIZATION RESEARCH ASSOCIATION,** *q.v.*

COALVILLE LIBRARY *see* **LEICESTERSHIRE LIBRARIES AND INFORMATION SERVICES**

750 COATBRIDGE BRANCH LIBRARY
Academy Street, Coatbridge, Lanarkshire ML5 3AT Tel. 0236 24150
Public Library, part of Monklands District Libraries, *q.v.*

Enquiries to the Librarian

Subject coverage
general

751 COATBRIDGE TECHNICAL COLLEGE
Kiodonan Street, Coatbridge, Lanarkshire ML5 3LS Tel. 0236 22316/7/8
Technical College

Enquiries to the Librarian

Subject coverage
economics; mathematics; physics; chemistry; mechanical engineering; electrical engineering; commerce

752 COATES BROTHERS & COMPANY LIMITED
New Arterial Road, St. Mary Cray, Orpington, Kent BR5 3PP Tel. 66 27080
Telex 25898

Company

Enquiries, by telex or letter, to the Information Officer

Subject coverage
polymer chemistry in the surface coatings industry; paint technology; ink technology

753 J. and D. COATS (UK) LIMITED
Research Laboratory, Anchor Mills, Paisley, Renfrewshire PA1 1JR Tel. 041-887 7666
Company; subsidiary of Coats Paton Limited

Enquiries to the Librarian

Subject coverage
thread manufacture

COCKERMOUTH PUBLIC LIBRARY *now* **CUMBRIA COUNTY LIBRARY,** *q.v.*

754 COCOA, CHOCOLATE & CONFECTIONERY ALLIANCE
11 Green Street, London W1Y 3RF Tel. 01-629 8971
Telex 24738
Trade Association; member of the Food and Drink Industries Council and of CAOBISCO, the corresponding E.E.C. professional organization

Enquiries to the Director

Subject coverage
cocoa, chocolate, and confectionery products

Publications
Annual Report
Occasional publications for members only

755 CODE OF ADVERTISING PRACTICE COMMITTEE
15–17 Ridgmount Street, London WC1E 7AW Tel. 01-580 0801
Telex 27950
Self-regulatory Body of the advertising industry; under general supervision of the Advertising Standards Authority, *q.v.*

Enquiries, from within the advertising industry only, to the Secretariat; from the general public, to the Advertising Standards Authority

Subject coverage
policy-making for the advertising industry; advice to, and complaint-investigation for, anyone involved in advertising business

Publications
British Code of Advertising Practice (5th ed.)
Code of Advertising Practice Committee: how it works, with particular reference to the investigation of complaints

756 COFFEE TRADE FEDERATION
69 Cannon Street, London EC4N 5AB Tel. 01-248 4444
Trade Association

Enquiries are only accepted in connection with the Federation's function as representatives of the trade

Subject coverage
coffee trade

757 COLCHESTER DISTRICT LIBRARY
Shewell Road, Colchester, Essex COL 1JB — Tel. 0206 70378
Public Library, district library of Essex County Library

Enquiries to the District Librarian

Subject coverage
general; some coverage of advertising and commercial art

758 COLCHESTER INSTITUTE OF HIGHER EDUCATION
Sheepen Road, Colchester, Essex CO3 3LL — Tel. 0206 70271
College of Higher Education, formerly North East Essex Technical College and School of Art; merged with St. Osyth College of Education

Enquiries to the Librarian

Subject coverage
mechanical, electrical, and production engineering; building; printing; business studies; management; hotel and catering management

759 COLD ROLLED SECTIONS ASSOCIATION
King Edward House, New Street, Birmingham B2 4QP — Tel. 021-643 5494
Trade Association

Enquiries, in writing, to the Secretary

Subject coverage
manufacturers of cold formed sections and activities within the industry

COLERAINE DIVISIONAL LIBRARY *see* **NORTHERN IRELAND, NORTH EASTERN EDUCATION AND LIBRARY BOARD**

760 COLGATE-PALMOLIVE LIMITED
371 Ordsall Lane, Salford, Lancashire M5 3FS — Tel. 061-872 3321
Company

Enquiries to the Technical Information Officer

Subject coverage
dentistry and oral health; soaps and detergents; aerosols; cosmetics; perfumery; analytical chemistry; toxicology; packaging; non-woven fabrics; pet foods

761 COLLEGE FOR THE DISTRIBUTIVE TRADES
30 Leicester Square, London WC2H 7LG — Tel. 01-839 1547 ext. 37
Specialist College; having a Department of Display, 107 Charing Cross Road, London WC2H 0DX and a Department of Food Commodities, Briset House, 6–9 Briset Street, London EC1M 5SL

Enquiries to the Librarian

Subject coverage
retailing, advertising, marketing, textiles; display techniques; meat technology

COLLEGE OF FOOD TECHNOLOGY AND COMMERCE *now* **SOUTH GLAMORGAN INSTITUTE OF FURTHER AND HIGHER EDUCATION,** *q.v.*

COLLEGE OF MARKETING *see* **INSTITUTE OF MARKETING**

COLLEGE OF THE SEA *see* **MARINE SOCIETY**

COLMAN LIBRARY *see* **CAMBRIDGE UNIVERSITY, Department of Biochemistry**

762 COLOMBIAN EMBASSY
Flat 3a, 3 Hans Crescent, London SW1X 0LR — Tel. 01-589 9177
Telex 916468

Embassy

Enquiries to the Commercial Section

Subject coverage
Colombian trade and investment opportunities; imports and exports

COLQUHOUN LIBRARY *see* **GLASGOW CHAMBER OF COMMERCE AND MANUFACTURES**

COLWORTH/WELWYN LABORATORY *see* **UNILEVER RESEARCH LABORATORY (Colworth/Welwyn)**

COLWYN BAY AREA LIBRARY *see* **CLWYD COUNTY LIBRARY SERVICE**

763 COMMERCIAL AND FORENSIC LABORATORIES
220–222 Elgar Road, Reading RG2 0DG Tel. 0734 82428/9
Company, chemical and microscopical laboratories

Enquiries to the Principal or Secretary

Subject coverage
chemical analysis; infrared spectroscopy analysis of plastics, cosmetics, etc.; atomic absorption analysis of metals and plating solutions; dust analysis; asbestos materials analysis; surfactants and detergents; formulation development; forensic science; starches; horticulture—agriculture trials; effluents and wastes examination; quality control

Publication
Starch Literature Survey (six times per annum)

764 COMMERCIAL RABBIT ASSOCIATION
Tyning House, Shurdington, Cheltenham GL51 5XF Tel. 0242 862387
Trade Association

Enquiries to the Secretary

Subject coverage
meat rabbit production and marketing

765 COMMERCIAL UNION ASSURANCE COMPANY LIMITED
P.O. Box 420, St Helens, 1 Undershaft, London EC3P 3DQ Tel. 01-283 7500 ext. 2132
Company

Enquiries to the Librarian, P.E.A.U. Library

Subject coverage
all aspects of insurance, economics, statistics, worldwide

Publications
Concord
Hand-in-hand (3 times per annum)
News journals issued by overseas branches

766 COMMITTEE OF ASSOCIATIONS OF SPECIALIST ENGINEERING CONTRACTORS
ESCA House, 34 Palace Court, Bayswater, London W2 4JG Tel. 01-229 2488
Trade Association

Enquiries to the Director

Subject coverage
policy matters only, in the commercial and contractual field

Publications
CASEC Annual Report
CASEC Statement on Nomination
Onerous Contract Clauses

COMMITTEE OF ASSOCIATIONS OF SPECIALIST ENGINEERING CONTRACTORS *see also*
BRITISH CONSTRUCTIONAL STEELWORK ASSOCIATION LIMITED
ELECTRICAL CONTRACTORS ASSOCIATION
ELECTRICAL CONTRACTORS ASSOCIATION OF SCOTLAND

HEATING AND VENTILATING CONTRACTORS ASSOCIATION
METAL WINDOW FEDERATION LIMITED
NATIONAL ASSOCIATION OF LIFT MAKERS
NATIONAL ASSOCIATION OF PLUMBING, HEATING AND MECHANICAL SERVICES CONTRACTORS

767 COMMITTEE OF DIRECTORS OF RESEARCH ASSOCIATIONS
47 Victoria Street, London SW1H 0EQ Tel. 01-222 0589
Association of Industrial Research Associations; houses the Federation of European Industrial Cooperative Research Organisations; supports 8 Working Groups: (may assume the name CDRA Limited)

Enquiries to the Director or Secretary

Subject coverage
cooperative and contract industrial research and matters relating to the Associations in the United Kingdom

COMMITTEE OF EXPERTS ON MAJOR HAZARDS *see* **HEALTH AND SAFETY EXECUTIVE**

768 COMMITTEE ON MIDDLE EAST TRADE
33 Bury Street, London SW1Y 6AX Tel. 01-839 1170
01-839 2137

Area Advisory Group of the British Overseas Trade Board

Enquiries to the Secretary

Subject coverage
exports to the Middle East

COMMITTEE ON SAFETY OF DRUGS *now* **DEPARTMENT OF HEALTH AND SOCIAL SECURITY, Medicines Division,** *q.v.*

769 COMMODITIES RESEARCH UNIT LIMITED
55 Gower Street, London WC1E 6HJ Tel. 01-637 2886
Telex 264008

Company

Enquiries, on a fee-paying basis, to the Director

Subject coverage
commodities (minerals and metals); theory and practice of markets and buffer stock operations; econometric and simulation modelling; data storage and retrieval; economic forecasting; foreign exchange analysis

Publications
consultancy reports
multi-client reports
regular market reports

770 COMMONWEALTH AGRICULTURAL BUREAUX
H.Q., Farnham House, Farnham Royal, Slough SL2 3BN Tel. 9764 2281
Quasi-Government/Commonwealth Agency/Research Information and Documentation Services; composed of four Institutes and ten Bureaux, *qq.v.*

Enquiries to the Secretary or to the Institutes or Bureaux

Subject coverage
agricultural and other subjects given in the entries for the component Institutes and Bureaux listed and following this entry

Publications
Abstract journals, bibliographies, etc., given in the entries for the component Institutes and Bureaux and associated organizations, Weed Research Organization and International Food Information Service

COMMONWEALTH AGRICULTURAL BUREAUX *see also*
COMMONWEALTH BUREAU OF AGRICULTURAL ECONOMICS
COMMONWEALTH BUREAU OF ANIMAL BREEDING AND GENETICS
COMMONWEALTH BUREAU OF ANIMAL HEALTH
COMMONWEALTH BUREAU OF DAIRY SCIENCE AND TECHNOLOGY
COMMONWEALTH BUREAU OF HORTICULTURE AND PLANTATION CROPS
COMMONWEALTH BUREAU OF NUTRITION
COMMONWEALTH BUREAU OF PASTURES AND FIELD CROPS
COMMONWEALTH BUREAU OF PLANT BREEDING AND GENETICS
COMMONWEALTH BUREAU OF SOILS
COMMONWEALTH FORESTRY BUREAU
COMMONWEALTH INSTITUTE OF ENTOMOLOGY
COMMONWEALTH INSTITUTE OF HELMINTHOLOGY
COMMONWEALTH MYCOLOGICAL INSTITUTE
N.B. Commonwealth Institute of Biological Control is not included because it operates in Trinidad

771 COMMONWEALTH BUREAU OF AGRICULTURAL ECONOMICS
Dartington House, Little Clarendon Street, Oxford OX1 2HH Tel. 0865 59829
Unit of the Commonwealth Agricultural Bureaux, *q.v.*

Enquiries to the Director

Subject coverage
agricultural economics, policy, and products; marketing and distribution; international trade; co-operatives and collectives; land use; pollution

Publications
Annotated bibliographies
World Agricultural Economics and Rural Sociology Abstracts (monthly)

772 COMMONWEALTH BUREAU OF ANIMAL BREEDING AND GENETICS
Animal Breeding Research Organisation, The King's Buildings, West Mains Road, Edinburgh EH9 3JX Tel. 031-667 6901
Unit of the Commonwealth Agricultural Bureaux, *q.v.*; with the Animal Breeding Library

Enquiries to the Director

Subject coverage
genetics and reproduction of farm animals, and related species, laboratory mammals, poultry and fur-bearers; non-genetic aspects of performance, excluding nutrition; theoretical genetics; effects of environmental factors

Publications
Animal Breeding Abstracts (monthly)
Annotated Bibliographies

773 COMMONWEALTH BUREAU OF ANIMAL HEALTH
Central Veterinary Laboratory, New Haw, Weybridge, Surrey KT15 3NB Tel. 29 42826
Unit of the Commonwealth Agricultural Bureaux, *q.v.*

Enquiries to the Director

Subject coverage
veterinary science; animal health; diseases of animals; effects of air and water pollution

Publications
Index Veterinarius (monthly)
Veterinary Bulletin (monthly)
Review Series (occasional)

774 COMMONWEALTH BUREAU OF DAIRY SCIENCE AND TECHNOLOGY
Lane End House, Shinfield, Reading, Berkshire RG2 9BB Tel. 0734 883895
Telex 847204
Unit of the Commonwealth Agricultural Bureaux, *q.v.*

Enquiries to the Director

Subject coverage
milk production and processing; milk products; mammary gland and lactation in all mammals; milk composition and constituents; contamination of products; treatment of waste products

Publications
Dairy Science Abstracts (monthly)
Annotated bibliographies

775 COMMONWEALTH BUREAU OF HORTICULTURE AND PLANTATION CROPS
East Malling Research Station, near Maidstone, Kent ME19 6BJ   Tel. 0732 843833
Unit of the Commonwealth Agricultural Bureaux, *q.v.*

Enquiries to the Director

Subject coverage
horticulture, including temperate tree fruits and nuts; temperate, tropical and greenhouse vegetables; ornamental plants; minor temperate and tropical industrial crops; tropical and sub-tropical fruit and plantation crops; land use; air and water pollution

Publications
Horticultural Abstracts (monthly)
Ornamental Horticulture (monthly)
Annotated Bibliographies
Technical Communications and Research Reviews

776 COMMONWEALTH BUREAU OF NUTRITION
Rowett Research Institute, Bucksburn, Aberdeen AB2 9SB   Tel. 022-471 2162
Unit of the Commonwealth Agricultural Bureaux, *q.v.*

Enquiries to the Director

Subject coverage
nutrition of man and animals; pesticides in foods; pesticide residues

Publications
Nutrition Abstracts and Reviews (monthly)
Annotated Bibliographies

777 COMMONWEALTH BUREAU OF PASTURES AND FIELD CROPS
Grassland Research Institute, Hurley, Maidenhead,   Tel. 062-882 3457
Berkshire SL6 5LR
Unit of the Commonwealth Agricultural Bureaux, *q.v.*

Enquiries to the Director

Subject coverage
grasslands; rangelands; herbage; annual field crops; air and water pollution; land use

Publications
Field Crop Abstracts (monthly)
Herbage Abstracts (monthly)
Occasional Publications

778 COMMONWEALTH BUREAU OF PLANT BREEDING AND GENETICS
Department of Applied Biology, Downing Street, Cambridge CB2 3BX   Tel. 0223 58381 ext. 63
Unit of the Commonwealth Agricultural Bureaux, *q.v.*

Enquiries to the Director

Subject coverage
plant breeding for adaptation to particular environmental and soil conditions, atmosphere, pollution, etc.

Publications
Plant Breeding Abstracts (monthly)
Technical Communications

779 COMMONWEALTH BUREAU OF SOILS

Rothamsted Experimental Station, Harpenden, Hertfordshire AL5 2JQ — Tel. 058-27 4671

Unit of the Commonwealth Agricultural Bureaux, *q.v.*

Enquiries to the Director

Subject coverage

soil conservation and reclamation; all materials, including environmentally harmful materials, in or entering soil or water and affecting nutrition of crops

Publications

Soils and Fertilizers (monthly)
Annotated Bibliographies

780 COMMONWEALTH FORESTRY ASSOCIATION

11 Keble Road, Oxford OX1 3QG — Tel. 0865 50156

Charity

Enquiries to the Editor/Secretary

Subject coverage

forestry

Publications

Quarterly Review
Handbook

781 COMMONWEALTH FORESTRY BUREAU

Commonwealth Forestry Institute, South Parks Road, Oxford OX1 3RD — Tel. 0865 57185

Unit of the Commonwealth Agricultural Bureaux; *q.v.*

Enquiries to the Director

Subject coverage

forestry; factors of the environment, biology; silviculture; harvesting; logging; forest engineering; forest injuries and protection; mensuration; increment and yield; surveying and mapping; forest economics; forest products and their utilization; pollution damage and control

Publications

Forestry Abstracts (monthly)
Annotated Bibliographies
Card Title Service of Abstracts (weekly)
Oxford System of Decimal Classification for Forestry
Technical Communications

782 COMMONWEALTH FORESTRY INSTITUTE

South Parks Road, Oxford OX1 3RD — Tel. 0865 511431

University Department; houses also Commonwealth Forestry Bureau, *q.v.*

Enquiries to the Librarian

Subject coverage

forestry and ancillary subjects

Special collection

world catalogues of forestry literature, 1822–present (about 1½ million cards)

Publications

Annual Report
Institute Papers and Monographs
Conference Proceedings
Catalogues of World Forestry Literature on microfilm
Theses on microfilm

783 COMMONWEALTH INDUSTRIES ASSOCIATION LIMITED
55 Park Lane, London W1Y 3DH Tel. 01-222 4120
Company

Enquiries to the Director

Subject coverage
U.K.—Commonwealth and Commonwealth—U.K. markets, investments, transport, technical cooperation

Publication
Quarterly Journal—Britain and Overseas

784 COMMONWEALTH INSTITUTE AND RESOURCE CENTRE
Kensington High Street, London W8 6NQ Tel. 01-602 3252
Educational and Publicising Body; having also a Centre in Edinburgh

Enquiries (bibliographical and current information on the Commonwealth) to the Librarian; or, (activities within the Institute) to the Public Relations Officer

Subject coverage
the Commonwealth countries, race relations, immigration and emigration, aid and development, education; exhibitions and displays

Special collections
Commonwealth Literature Collection
Commonwealth Periodicals and Newspapers
Audio-visual materials

Publications
Bibliographies
Schedules of Information

785 COMMONWEALTH INSTITUTE OF ENTOMOLOGY
56 Queen's Gate, London SW7 5JR Tel. 01-584 0067
Institute, of the Commonwealth Agricultural Bureaux, *q.v.*

Enquiries to the Librarian

Subject coverage
entomology, mainly insects, mites or ticks of importance in agricultural, medical and veterinary fields; correct forms of insect names; distribution of specific insects; pesticides and control

Special collection
of older Russian agricultural journals

Publications
Review of Applied Entomology, Series A Agricultural. Series B Medical and Veterinary (both abstract journals monthly)
Bulletin of Entomological Research (quarterly)
Distribution Maps of Pests

786 COMMONWEALTH INSTITUTE OF HELMINTHOLOGY
The White House, 103 St Peters Street, St. Albans, Hertfordshire AL1 3EW Tel. 56 52126
Research Institute, of the Commonwealth Agricultural Bureaux; formerly Commonwealth Bureau of Helminthology

Enquiries to the Director

Subject coverage
animal and human helminthology; plant nematodes; identification of animal helminths and plant parasitic nematodes

Special collection
R.T. Leiper Collection (old parasitological literature)

Publications
Helminthological Abstracts, series A, Animal and Human Helminthology
Helminthological Abstracts, series B, Plant Nematology

CIH Descriptions of Plant Parasitic Nematodes
CIH Keys to the Nematode Parasites of Vertebrates
Annotated Bibliographies
Occasional Publications

787 COMMONWEALTH MYCOLOGICAL INSTITUTE
Ferry Lane, Kew, Surrey TW9 3AF Tel. 01-940 4086
Research Institute, of the Commonwealth Agricultural Bureaux; houses the Library of the British Mycological Society

Enquiries, by letter, to the Director

Subject coverage
mycology, plant and animal including man; identification services

Special collections
National Collection of 200,000 dried micro-fungi
Culture collection, 6,000 species

Publications
Bibliography of Systematic Mycology
Catalogue of the Culture Collection
CMI/AAB Descriptions of Plant Viruses
CMI Descriptions of Pathogenic Fungi and Bacteria
Distribution Maps of Plant Diseases
Herbarium Duplicate Collection Catalogue
Index of Fungi
Mycological Papers
Phytopathological Papers
Review of Medical and Veterinary Mycology (quarterly)
Review of Plant Pathology (monthly)

788 COMPANIES REGISTRATION OFFICE
Companies House, Crown Way, Maindy, Cardiff CF4 3UZ Tel. 0222 388588
Government Department, of the Department of Trade; London Search Room at 55–71 City Road, London EC1Y 1BB (tel. 01-253 9393); *see also* the Registry of Business Names

Enquiries, on services or general matters, to the Administration Section; on individual companies, by personal inspection of records in Cardiff or London

Subject coverage
statutory records of all registered limited and unlimited companies

Publication
Annual Report (H.M.S.O.)

789 COMPOUND ANIMAL FEEDING STUFFS MANUFACTURERS NATIONAL ASSOCIATION LIMITED
58 Southwark Bridge Road, London SE1 0AS Tel. 01-261 1955
Telex 918160
Trade Association; a merger with the British Association of Grain, Seed, Feed and Agricultural Merchants, *q.v.* is proposed; member of the British Poultry Federation, *q.v.*

Enquiries to the Director-General or to the Secretary

Subject coverage
animal feeding stuffs legislation (domestic and E.E.C.); feeding stuffs raw materials; supplies and prices situation

790 COMPUTER AIDED DESIGN CENTRE
Madingly Road, Cambridge CB3 0HB Tel. 0223 63125
Telex 81420

Industrial Research Establishment, of the Department of Industry

Enquiries to the Head of Promotions

Subject coverage
development and application of computer aided design techniques in all branches of engineering and design, particularly electrical engineering, chemical engineering, industrial design, construction industry, mechanical engineering

791 COMPUTER ANALYSTS & PROGRAMMERS LIMITED
CAP House, 14 Great James Street, London WC1N 3DY — Tel. 01-242 0021, Telex 267152

Company (consultants)

Enquiries to the Librarian

Subject coverage
computer systems design and implementation, computer software, management, programming

792 CONCHOLOGICAL SOCIETY OF GREAT BRITAIN AND IRELAND
51 Wychwood Avenue, Luton, Bedfordshire LU2 7HT — Tel. 0582 24801
Registered Charity, affiliated to the Council for Nature

Enquiries to the Honorary Secretary

Subject coverage
all aspects of conchology, world-wide; marine, non-marine and fossil molluscs; distribution maps for all British species

Publications
Journal of Conchology (2 per annum)
Conchologists Newsletter (4 per annum)
Papers for Students (infrequent, irregular)
List of Members (annual)
Programme of Events (annual)

CONCILIATION AND ARBITRATION SERVICE *see* **ADVISORY, CONCILIATION AND ARBITRATION SERVICE**

CONCOURSE LIBRARY *see* **CAULDON COLLEGES OF FURTHER EDUCATION**

793 CONCRETE PIPE ASSOCIATION
Brenchley, Tonbridge, Kent TN12 7BX — Tel. 089-272 2881
Trade Association

Enquiries to the Secretary

Subject coverage
pre-cast concrete pipe products

794 CONCRETE SOCIETY
Terminal House, Grosvenor Gardens, London SW1W 0AJ — Tel. 01-730 8252, Telex 261700

Voluntary Association

Enquiries are preferably dealt with by the Cement and Concrete Association, q.v.

Subject coverage
cements in the construction industry

Publications
Concrete (monthly)
Technical Reports
Data sheets
Proceedings of Symposia

795 CONFEDERATION FOR THE REGISTRATION OF GAS INSTALLERS (CORGI)
St. Martins House, 140 Tottenham Court Road, London W1P 9LN — Tel. 01-387 9185
Trade Confederation

Enquiries to the Advisory Services Officer

Subject coverage
safety in the installation and/or servicing of gas appliances, in the domestic, commercial or industrial fields

Publications
Guides to Mandatory Regulations
Lecture Notes
Technical Aids to Members

796 CONFEDERATION OF BRITISH INDUSTRY
21 Tothill Street, London SW1H 9LP Tel. 01-930 6711
Telex 21332

Representative Organization for member companies, employers organizations and trade associations

Enquiries, principally from members, to the Information Officer or Librarian

Subject coverage
industrial policy, international, national and regional; economic situation and trends; taxation; industrial relations; conditions of employment; education and training; research and development; overseas affairs; commercial and company law and practice; industrial property law; industrial effluent; energy and water resources

Publications
many and various on subjects given above (list available)
CBI Members Bulletin (fortnightly)

797 CONFEDERATION OF HEALTH SERVICE EMPLOYEES
Glen House, High Street, Banstead, Surrey SM7 2LH Tel. 25 53322
Telex 944245

Trade Union

Enquiries to the Research Officer

Subject coverage
National Health Service in general, and conditions of employment, economic considerations and development

Publication
Health Services Monthly Journal

798 CONFEDERATION OF IRISH INDUSTRY
Confederation House, Kildare Street, Dublin 2 Tel. Dublin 779801
Telex 4711

Trade Association; formerly Federation of Irish Industries (see following entry for affiliated associations and federations within the Confederation)

Enquiries to the Information Officer

Subject coverage
all matters affecting Irish industry, excepting industrial relations

Publications
Newsletter (weekly)
Euroletter (fortnightly)
Economic Trends (monthly)
CII/ESRI Business Forecast (monthly)
Occasional Papers

CONFEDERATION OF IRISH INDUSTRY—Affiliated Bodies
ASSOCIATION OF DUBLIN STEVEDORES
ASSOCIATION OF MANAGEMENT CONSULTING ORGANISATIONS
ASSOCIATION OF WOOLLEN AND WORSTED MANUFACTURERS OF IRELAND
IRISH HOTELS FEDERATION
IRISH MINERAL EXPLORATION GROUP
IRISH OFFSHORE SERVICES ASSOCIATION
IRISH PACKAGING INSTITUTE

IRISH PETROLEUM EXPLORATION GROUP
IRISH PRINTING BOARD
IRISH SHIPPERS COUNCIL
MERCHANT LORRY OWNERS ASSOCIATION
PHARMACEUTICAL, CHEMICAL AND ALLIED INDUSTRIES ASSOCIATION

CONFEDERATION OF IRISH INDUSTRY—Federations
APPAREL INDUSTRIES
BUILDING MATERIALS
ENGINEERING INDUSTRY ASSOCIATION
FOOD DRINK AND TOBACCO
IRISH TEXTILES
PLASTICS INDUSTRIES ASSOCIATION

CONSERVATION CORPS *see* **ZOOLOGICAL SOCIETY OF LONDON**

799 CONSOLIDATED GOLD FIELDS LIMITED
49 Moorgate, London EC2R 6BQ Tel. 01-606 1020
Telex 883071

Mining Finance House

Enquiries to the Librarian

Subject coverage
historical, commercial and statistical information on gold and on tin; mining

Publication
Gold Survey (annual)

CONSTANTINE COLLEGE OF TECHNOLOGY *now* **TEESSIDE POLYTECHNIC,** *q.v.*

800 CONSTRUCTION HEALTH AND SAFETY GROUP
Enfield Skillcentre, Bilton Way, Enfield, Middlesex 3NQ 7NZ Tel. 01-804 2756
Training Organization, of the Training Services Agency; formerly London Construction Safety Group; member of the Royal Society for the Prevention of Accidents, *q.v.* and of the International Social Security Association

Enquiries to the Centre Manager

Subject coverage
all areas of construction safety; safety training

Publications
Crane Teams Handbook
"Infor 3" (summary of reports from a Colloquium on the prevention of accidents in public and building works, held in Stockholm)
Proceedings of the Second Assembly of the International Committee of ISSA on the prevention of occupational risks in the building industry and public works

801 CONSTRUCTION INDUSTRY INFORMATION GROUP
26 Store Street, London WC1E 7BT Tel. 01-637 4522
Information Group; formerly Building Industry Information Group

Enquiries to the Honorary Secretary

Subject coverage
construction industry

Publications
CIIG Newsletter
Occasional Review

802 CONSTRUCTION INDUSTRY RESEARCH AND INFORMATION ASSOCIATION
6 Storeys Gate, London SW1P 3AU Tel. 01-839 6881
Research Association; includes CIRIA Underwater Engineering Group

Enquiries to the Information Officer

Subject coverage
structural design; civil engineering construction; building design and construction; earthworks and foundations; hydraulic engineering; public health engineering; underground construction; underwater engineering; offshore engineering

Publications
Annual Report
Miscellaneous reports, technical notes, etc.

803 CONSTRUCTION INDUSTRY TRAINING BOARD
Radnor House, London Road, London SW16 4EL Tel. 01-764 5060
Training Board, of the Training Services Agency, Manpower Services Commission

Enquiries to the Information Services Officer, Glen House, Stag Place, London SW1E 5AL (tel. 01-828 7384)

Subject coverage
training for all levels of employees in civil engineering; building, electrical engineering services; mechanical engineering services

Publications
Training recommendations
Notes for guidance

804 CONSTRUCTION SURVEYORS INSTITUTE
Wellington House, 203 Lordship Lane, East Dulwich, London SE22 8HA Tel. 01-693 0219/0210
Professional Institute; formerly Building Surveyors' Institute

Enquiries to the Executive Director

Subject coverage
surveying in all aspects *except* house surveying for building societies

Publications
Construction Surveyor (3 times per annum)
Guide for the Education and Training of Construction Surveyors
Code of Professional Conduct and Scale of Fees
Private Practice Members Directory
Examination Syllabus and Past papers, etc.

805 CONSTRUCTORS JOHN BROWN LIMITED
CJB House, Eastbourne Terrace, London W2 6LE Tel. 01-262 8080
Telex 263521

Company, part of the John Brown Group

Enquiries to the Information Officer; loan requests to the Librarian

Subject coverage
chemical engineering and all aspects of chemical plant construction; offshore engineering and design

Publications
Monthly Abstracting Bulletin
Bibliographies

CONSUMER CREDIT LICENCES REGISTER *see* **OFFICE OF FAIR TRADING**

806 CONSUMERS ASSOCIATION
14 Buckingham Street, London WC2N 6DS Tel. 01-839 1222
Research Association; houses the Research Institute for Consumer Affairs, and the Good Food Club

Enquiries to the Chief Librarian (fees chargeable)

Subject coverage
consumer affairs; product testing; consumer law; standards

Publications
Which?
Motoring Which?
Money Which?
Handyman Which?
Holiday Which?
Daily Consumer News
Drug and Therapeutics Bulletin

807 CONTRACT CLEANING AND MAINTENANCE ASSOCIATION
142 Strand, London WC2R 1HH Tel. 01-240 1577
01-836 6044

Trade Association

Enquiries to the Secretary

Subject coverage
cleaning and maintenance industry; member companies and specialized cleaning processes

Publications
Newsletter (bi-monthly, for members)
Publications on Management, current legislation etc (for members)

CONTRACT FURNISHING ASSOCIATION *now* **BRITISH CONTRACT FURNISHING ASSOCIATION,** *q.v.*

808 CONTRACTORS MECHANICAL PLANT ENGINEERS
48 Colburn Avenue, Hatch End, Pinner, Middlesex HA5 4PF Tel. 01-428 4795
Trade Association

No enquiry service

Subject coverage
mechanical plant contracting and engineering

809 CONTRACTORS PLANT ASSOCIATION
28 Eccleston Street, London SW1W 9PY Tel. 01-730 7117
Trade Association

Enquiries to the Secretary

Subject coverage
conditions of contract for plant hire; working conditions; industrial relations

Publications
Annual Handbook
Hire Rate Schedule
Operating Cost Studies
Monthly Bulletin

810 CONTROL AND AUTOMATION MANUFACTURERS ASSOCIATION
BEAMA, 8 Leicester Street, London WC2H 7BN Tel. 01-437 0678
Telex 263536

Trade Association; member of BEAMA; formerly the ICE Division of BEAMA, *q.v.*

Enquiries to the Director

Subject coverage
commerce and technology related to the control and automation field

Publications
specifications, standards, guides

811 CONTROL SYSTEMS CENTRE
Manchester University Institute of Science and Technology, Tel. 061-236 3311
P.O. Box 88, Sackville Street, Manchester M60 1QD
University Unit, within the Institute of Science and Technology (UMIST)

Enquiries to the Director; reports queries to the Departmental Librarian

Subject coverage
computer control of processes; machine tool control; control of automotive power plants, aircraft gas turbines, lift systems; stochastic, optimal, and multivariable control; composite systems; computer-aided design of control systems; medical engineering; econometric and environmental studies; stability of non-linear systems; modelling and identification of dynamical systems

Publication
Control System Centre Reports

812 CONTROL THEORY CENTRE
Warwick University, Coventry, Warwickshire CV4 7AL Tel. 0203 24011
University Department

Enquiries to the Director

Subject coverage
control theory

Publications
Control Theory Centre Reports

813 COOKRIDGE RADIATION RESEARCH CENTRE
Cookridge Hospital, Leeds LS16 6QB Tel. 0532 672511
University Department, of Leeds University; formerly Cookridge High Energy Radiation Research Centre

Enquiries to the Director

Subject coverage
effects of radiation of materials; radiation chemistry

814 COOLING WATER ASSOCIATION
74 Queensway, London W2 3RW Tel. 01-229 0155
Professional/Educational Association

Enquiries to the Secretariat

Subject coverage
correct use and re-use of national water resources; cooling water treatment; cooling towers

Publications
Code of Practice for Cooling Water Treatment
Guide to Mechanical Draught Evaporative Cooling Towers

COOPER TECHNICAL BUREAU *now* **WELLCOME RESEARCH LABORATORIES,** *q.v.*

815 COOPERATIVE INDUSTRIAL COMMERCIAL REFERENCE AND INFORMATION SERVICE (CICRIS)
Acton District Library (Ealing Library Service), High Street, Tel. 01-992 5566 ext. 2105, 2101 *or* 2102
Acton, London W3 6NA
Interlibrary Co-operative Scheme, of 104 members

Enquiries to the Honorary Secretary

Subject coverage
technical and commercial

Publications
Directory of Members
Union List of Periodicals
Union List of Interlingual Dictionaries
Annual Report

816 COOPERS AND ALLIED WORKERS FEDERATION OF GREAT BRITAIN
13 Gayfield Square, Edinburgh EH1 3NX Tel. 031-556 2109
Trade Union; formerly Coopers Federation of Great Britain

Enquiries to the General Secretary

Subject coverage
trade union functions and services to the industry

817 COPPER DEVELOPMENT ASSOCIATION
Orchard House, Mutton Lane, Potters Bar, Tel. 77 50711
Hertfordshire EN6 3AP Telex 27711
Non-trading organisation, sponsored by copper producers and fabricators

Enquiries to the Information Officer

Subject coverage
copper, its alloys and compounds; market development and technical data

Publications
International Copper Information Bulletin (quarterly)
Technical Notes

COPPER TUBE FITTINGS MANUFACTURERS ASSOCIATION *see* **BRITISH NON-FERROUS METALS FEDERATION**

CORBY DISTRICT LIBRARY *see* **NORTHAMPTONSHIRE LIBRARIES**

818 CORDWAINERS TECHNICAL COLLEGE
Mare Street, Hackney, London E8 3RE Tel. 01-985 0273
Technical College

Enquiries to the Librarian

Subject coverage
footwear production; leathergoods production and technology

819 CORK INDUSTRY FEDERATION
73 Kingswood Road, Shortlands, Bromley, Kent BR2 0NL Tel. 01-460 5378
Trade Association; formerly Cork Trade Association

Enquiries to the Secretary

Subject coverage
cork and cork products

Publication
Cork in the 20th Century

820 CORK MANUFACTURING COMPANY LIMITED
Langite Works, Hall Lane, Chingford, London E4 8JB Tel. 01-529 1101
Telex 21883

Company, subsidiary of Turner & Newall Limited

Enquiries to the Assistant General Manager

Subject coverage
use of composition cork and rubber/cork in gasketing applications

Publications
technical data sheets

CORK TRADE ASSOCIATION *now* **CORK INDUSTRY FEDERATION,** *q.v.*

821 CORNING LIMITED

Process Plant Division, Newstead Industrial Estate, Stoke-on-Trent ST4 8JG — Tel. 0782 658521, Telex 36120

Company Division; Corning Limited was formerly James A. Jobling Limited, and before that, QVF Limited; it has a Laboratory Division at Stone, Staffordshire

Enquiries to the Market Services Manager

Subject coverage

process plant and pipeline in glass and laboratory drainage systems in glass (QVF brand); glass for use in process plant and laboratories

Publications

Catalogues of process plant, pipeline and drainline components and applications for such equipment

822 CORNWALL COUNTY LIBRARY

Old County Hall, Station Road, Truro, Cornwall TR1 3HG — Tel. 0872 4282

Public Library; District Libraries: (East) Bodmin; (Central) St. Austell; (West) Penzance

Enquiries to the County Librarian

Subject coverage

general; landscape gardening and metalliferous mining in Cornwall

823 CORNWALL INFORMATION SERVICE (CIS)

Cornwall Technical College, Pool, Redruth, Cornwall TR15 3RD — Tel. 020-92 2911

Interlibrary Cooperative Scheme

Enquiries, technical, to CIS Librarian, Cornwall Technical College; commercial, to CIS Librarian, Cornwall County Library

Subject coverage

commercial, technical, general

Publication

Annual Report

824 CORNWALL TECHNICAL COLLEGE

Pool, Redruth, Cornwall TR15 3RD — Tel. 020-92 712911, Telex 45482

Technical College

Enquiries to the Librarian, Headquarters, Cornwall Information Service (Technical)

Subject coverage

engineering; environmental studies

Special collection

British Standards

CORY LIBRARY *see* **UNIVERSITY BOTANIC GARDEN**

825 COSSOR ELECTRONICS LIMITED

The Pinnacles, Harlow, Essex CM19 5BB — Tel. 02796 26862, Telex 81228

Company, subsidiary of Raytheon Company, (U.S.A.); formerly A.C. Cossor Limited

Enquiries to the Librarian

Subject coverage

electronics; radar; displays

826 Richard COSTAIN LIMITED

111 Westminster Bridge Road, London SE1 7UE — Tel. 01-928 4977, Telex 8811804

Group of Companies

Enquiries to the Public Relations Department

Subject coverage
construction; civil engineering and allied subjects, world-wide

Publication
Costain Enterprise

827 COTTON AND ALLIED TEXTILES INDUSTRY TRAINING BOARD
10th Floor, Sunlight House, Quay Street, Manchester M3 3LH Tel. 061-832 9656
Industrial Training Board, of the Training Services Agency

Enquiries to the Information Officer

Subject coverage
textile industry training, safety, industrial relations, recruitment

Publications
Recommendations and Guides for training of operatives, technicians, supervisors, managers

COTTON CANVAS MANUFACTURERS ASSOCIATION *now* **BRITISH REINFORCEMENT TEXTILES ASSOCIATION,** *q.v.*

828 COTTON SILK & MAN-MADE FIBRES RESEARCH ASSOCIATION
Shirley Institute, Didsbury, Manchester M20 8RX Tel. 061-445 8141
Telex 668417
Research Association

Enquiries to the Librarian or Information Officer

Subject coverage
textile science, technology, and management; polymer science; effluent treatment; industrial safety

Publications
World Textile Abstracts
Digest of English Language Textile Literature
Textiles
Summaries of Foreign-language Articles (SOFA Series)
Keyterm Index 1970–75
Other serial and individual publications

829 COUNCIL FOR EDUCATIONAL TECHNOLOGY FOR THE UNITED KINGDOM
3 Devonshire Street, London W1N 2BA Tel. 01-636 4186
Educational Charity; formerly National Council for Educational Technology; state-aided

Enquiries to the Information Officer

Subject coverage
application and development of education technology; media and methods; audio-visual materials; design of schools, etc.

Publications
British Journal of Educational Technology (3 times per annum)
Books and Studies for example:
Directory of Information Sources and Advisory Services
Film in Medical Education
Design of Lecture Theatres
Catalogues of audio-visual materials

830 COUNCIL FOR NATIONAL ACADEMIC AWARDS
344–354 Grays Inn Road, London WC1X 8BP Tel. 01-278 4411
Autonomous Educational Organization

Enquiries to the Publications Officer; enquiries concerning theses to the candidates' sponsoring establishments

Subject coverage
approval of courses of study or research to be offered at institutions in the U.K., other than universities; the courses include science and technology

COUNCIL FOR NATURE *see*
AMATEUR ENTOMOLOGISTS SOCIETY
BRITISH NATURALISTS ASSOCIATION
BRITISH ORNITHOLOGISTS ASSOCIATION
BRITISH PTERIDOLOGICAL SOCIETY
CONCHOLOGICAL SOCIETY OF GREAT BRITAIN AND IRELAND

831 COUNCIL FOR SCIENCE AND SOCIETY
3–4 St Andrews Hill, London EC4V 5BY Tel. 01-236 0032
Charity

No enquiry service

Subject coverage
study of the effects of science and technology on human society

Publications
Reports of the Council's Working Parties

832 COUNCIL FOR SMALL INDUSTRIES IN RURAL AREAS (COSIRA)
Queen's House, Fish Row, Salisbury, Wiltshire SP1 1EX Tel. 0722 24411
Telex 477638
Government-sponsored Advisory Service, of the Development Commission; formerly Rural Industries Bureau

Enquiries to the Secretariat at above address, or to the Librarian, 35 Camp Road, Wimbledon Common, London SW19 4UP

Subject coverage
technical and business management advisory service; rural development; marketing; building; engineering; tourism; woodworking and furniture restoring; plastics; thatching; saddlery; wrought iron work; other underwood and rural industries; grant and loan facilities

Publications
How COSIRA helps small firms
Newsletter
Bibliographies
Technical books and pamphlets lists

COUNCIL FOR TECHNICAL EDUCATION AND TRAINING FOR OVERSEAS COUNTRIES *now* **TECHNICAL EDUCATION AND TRAINING ORGANIZATION FOR OVERSEAS COUNTRIES,** *q.v.*

COUNCIL OF BRITISH FIRE PROTECTION EQUIPMENT MANUFACTURERS *see*
BRITISH FIRE PROTECTION SYSTEMS ASSOCIATION LIMITED
FIRE EXTINGUISHING TRADES ASSOCIATION

COUNCIL OF BRITISH MANUFACTURERS AND CONTRACTORS SERVING THE PETROLEUM AND PROCESS INDUSTRIES *see* **CBMPE**

COUNCIL OF COMMONWEALTH MINING AND METALLURGICAL INSTITUTIONS *see* **INSTITUTION OF MINING AND METALLURGY**

833 COUNCIL OF ENGINEERING INSTITUTIONS
2 Little Smith Street, London SW1P 3DL Tel. 01-799 3912
Chartered Institute; formerly Engineering Institutions Joint Council; houses the Engineers Registration Board; a list of constituent bodies follows this entry

Enquiries to the Secretary

Subject coverage
engineering profession, education, qualification, careers, salary surveys

Publications
Lectures
Annual Report
Rules and Syllabuses
Survey of Professional Engineers
Publications lists

COUNCIL OF ENGINEERING INSTITUTIONS
INSTITUTE OF MARINE ENGINEERS
INSTITUTION OF CHEMICAL ENGINEERS
INSTITUTION OF CIVIL ENGINEERS
INSTITUTION OF ELECTRICAL ENGINEERS
INSTITUTION OF ELECTRONIC AND RADIO ENGINEERS
INSTITUTION OF GAS ENGINEERS
INSTITUTION OF MECHANICAL ENGINEERS
INSTITUTION OF MINING AND METALLURGY
INSTITUTION OF MINING ENGINEERS
INSTITUTION OF MUNICIPAL ENGINEERS
INSTITUTION OF PRODUCTION ENGINEERS
INSTITUTION OF STRUCTURAL ENGINEERS
ROYAL AERONAUTICAL SOCIETY
ROYAL INSTITUTION OF NAVAL ARCHITECTS

COUNCIL OF INDUSTRIAL DESIGN *now* **DESIGN COUNCIL,** *q.v.*

834 COUNCIL OF IRONFOUNDRY ASSOCIATIONS (CFA)
14 Pall Mall, London SW1Y 5LZ Tel. 01-930 7171
Trade Association; a Federation of seven associations; member of the British Metal Castings Council

Enquiries to the Council's switchboard, will be referred to appropriate officer

Subject coverage
iron castings; iron foundries; representation for the industry, materials supplies; health and safety; environmental pollution; properties of cast irons

Publications
Monthly Bulletin (to members only)
Technical publications (list available)
Films (list available)

COUNCIL OF SCIENCE AND TECHNOLOGY INSTITUTES *see* **INSTITUTE OF PHYSICS**

835 COUNCIL OF UNDERGROUND MACHINERY MANUFACTURERS
301 Glossop Road, Sheffield S10 2HN Tel. 0742 21071
Telex 54170

Trade Association

Enquiries to the Secretaries

Subject coverage
underground mining machinery

COUNTY COMPUTER CENTRES (OXFORD) LIMITED *see* **ECONOMIC FORESTRY GROUP**

COUNTY SEELY LIBRARY *now* **ISLE OF WIGHT COUNTY LIBRARY,** *q.v.*

836 COURTAULDS LIMITED
18 Hanover Square, London W1 Tel. 01-629 9080
Company

Enquiries to the Commercial Librarian

Subject coverage
textile industries, commercial information

837 COURTAULDS LIMITED
NTDU, Droylsden, Manchester M35 7AJ Tel. 061-370 2621
Telex 667625

Company; formerly Droylsden Research Laboratory

Enquiries to the Information Officer

Subject coverage
textile dyeing and finishing; fibre properties

838 COURTAULDS LIMITED
Patent and Technical Information Department, P.O. Box 16, Foleshill Road, Coventry, West Midlands CV6 5AE Tel. 0203 88771
Telex 31538
Company

Enquiries to the Information Officer

Subject coverage
polymer chemistry; plastics, pulp and paper; textiles

839 COURTAULDS LIMITED
Textile Development Department, P.O. Box 5, Spondon, Derbyshire DE2 7BP Tel. 0332 61422
Telex 37221
Company Department, formerly Textile Research Laboratory

Enquiries to the Librarian

Subject coverage
textile technology and processing; textile fibres

840 COVENT GARDEN MARKET AUTHORITY
Market Towers, 1 Nine Elms Lane, London SW8 5NX Tel. 01-720 2211
Statutory Body; market tenants include the British Flower Industry Association; Fruit Importers Association; Covent Garden Tenants Association Limited

Enquiries to the Information Officer

Subject coverage
wholesaling of horticultural produce

841 COVENTRY AND DISTRICT INFORMATION GROUP (CADIG)
Reference Library, Bayley Lane, Coventry CV1 5RG Tel. 0203 25555 exts. 2115, 2116 and 2165
Telex 31469

Interlibrary Co-operative Scheme

Enquiries to the Liaison Officer, CADIG Liaison Centre

Subject coverage
technical and commercial

Publications
publicity material and constitution
Newsletter
Directory of Membership and Resources
Index to Bus Timetables of Great Britain
Various subject bibliographies
Union List of Members Periodicals Holdings (9,000 titles; twice yearly)

842 COVENTRY CITY LIBRARIES
Reference Library, Bayley Lane, Coventry, Warwickshire CV1 5RG Tel. 0203 25555 ext. 2115
Telex 31469

Public Library, houses the Coventry and District Information Group

Enquiries to the Director of Libraries, Arts and Museums

Subject coverage
automobile engineering; history of automobiles; car workshop practice (collection of manuals); local industry

Special collections
Bartleet collection on development of the bicycle
Waring Brown collection of newscuttings on engineering

Publications
CADIG publications:
Union List of Periodicals
Directory of Members
Range of subject bibliographies

843 COVENTRY TECHNICAL COLLEGE
The Butts, Coventry, Warwickshire CV1 3GD Tel. 0203 57221
Technical College

Enquiries to the Librarian

Subject coverage
mechanical and electrical engineering; construction; life sciences; management; home economics; training of technical teachers

844 COW AND GATE BABY FOODS
42 Stoke Road, Guildford, Surrey GU1 4HS Tel. 0483 68181
Company, part of Unigate Foods Limited; formerly Cow and Gate Limited

Enquiries to the Chief Chemist

Subject coverage
infant nutrition; general nutrition; food technology; milk technology

Publications
teaching aids and films on infant nutrition

845 CPC (UNITED KINGDOM) LIMITED
Technical Information Centre, Trafford Park, Manchester M17 1PA Tel. 061-872 2571
Telex 667022

Company; formerly Brown and Polson Limited

Enquiries to the Technical Director

Subject coverage
corn (maize) and its derived products, *e.g.* starch, glucose, animal feed, corn oil, etc

846 CRAFER ASSOCIATES
Lopen Laboratory, Lopen, Somerset TA15 5LT Tel. 0460 40836
Independent Practice; affiliated to Trisil Laboratories Limited

Enquiries to the Director

Subject coverage
fire, ignition, propagation; reactions to fire of materials and constructions; investigation of fires in buildings, ships and aircraft; assessment of fire hazards; design of fire precautions schemes; regulations and insurance rules; standard and special fire tests on constructions; automatic fire detection systems and automatic fire extinguishing systems

Publications
Occasional papers for architects

847 CRAFTS ADVISORY COMMITTEE
12 Waterloo Place, Lower Regent Street, London SW1Y 4AU Tel. 01-839 1917
Independent Government-funded Organization, of the Department of Education and Science; includes the British Crafts Centre of 43 Earlham Sttreet, London WC2 and a crafts shop in the Victoria and Albert Museum

Enquiries to the Index Librarian or Press Officer

Subject coverage
all aspects of contemporary crafts; exhibitions; grants and loans; sources of supplies; courses, etc.

Special collections
Slide Library
Index of Craftsmen
National Collection of contemporary crafts

Publications
Crafts (bi-monthly)
Exhibition Catalogues
Occasional specialist books
Films, slidepacks, postcards and posters

CRAMLINGTON LIBRARY *see* **NORTHUMBERLAND COUNTY LIBRARY**

848 CRANFIELD INSTITUTE OF TECHNOLOGY
Cranfield, Bedfordshire MK43 0AL — Tel. 0234 750111
Telex 825072

University; formerly College of Aeronautics; includes the Cranfield School of Management, the National College of Agricultural Engineering, Silsoe, *q.v.*; houses the Agricultural Aviation Research Unit, and the National Materials Handling Centre, *qq.v.*

Enquiries to the Librarian

Subject coverage
aeronautics; agricultural engineering; automobile engineering; management

Publications
research reports

CRANFIELD SCHOOL OF MANAGEMENT *see* **CRANFIELD INSTITUTE OF TECHNOLOGY**

849 CRANFIELD UNIT FOR PRECISION ENGINEERING
Cranfield Institute of Technology, Cranfield, — Tel. 0234 750111
Bedfordshire MK43 0AL — Telex 825072
University Industrial Unit

Enquiries to the Chief Engineer or the Office and Contracts Manager

Subject coverage
design, prototype manufacture and development of high performance machines, e.g. CNC machine tools, high precision measuring machines and instruments; design, development and application of metrological systems and methods to science and manufacture; design, development and evaluation of high performance servo drive systems and components

CRAWLEY DIVISIONAL LIBRARY *see* **WEST SUSSEX COUNTY LIBRARY SERVICE**

850 CRC INFORMATION SYSTEMS LIMITED
83 Clerkenwell Road, London EC1R 5HP — Tel. 01-242 0747
Telex 261171

Company; part of ICFC Limited; associated with Scan Limited, Cybernetics Research Consultants Limited, Quotel Limited and Cybernet Timesharing Limited

Enquiries to the Technical Director

Subject coverage
daily stockmarket information; company reports; press and T.V. media data; life and motor insurance rates

CREAMERY PROPRIETORS ASSOCIATION *see* **STILTON CHEESE MAKERS ASSOCIATION**

CREPE SOLE RUBBER ASSOCIATION OF LONDON *see* **RUBBER GROWERS ASSOCIATION LIMITED**

851 CREWE LIBRARY
Prince Albert Street, Crewe, Cheshire CW1 2DH Tel. 0270 2156
Public Library, part of the Cheshire County Library, *q.v.*

Enquiries to the Librarian

Subject coverage
nuclear engineering

852 CRONER PUBLICATIONS LIMITED
46–50 Coombe Road, New Malden, Surrey KT3 4QL Tel. 01-942 9615
Company

Enquiries to the Editorial Department

Subject coverage
employment law; exporting; importing; road transport; freight (shipping) conferences; VAT; air transport

Publications
Croner's Reference Book for Employers
Croner's Reference Book for Exporters
Croner's Reference Book for Importers
Croner's Road Transport Operation
Croner's World Directory of Freight Conferences
Croner's Reference Book for VAT
Croner's Air Transportation Guide

CROOK BRANCH LIBRARY *see* **DURHAM COUNTY LIBRARY**

CROSBY DISTRICT LIBRARY *see* **SEFTON METROPOLITAN BOROUGH LIBRARIES AND ARTS SERVICES**

853 CROWN AGENTS FOR OVERSEAS GOVERNMENTS AND ADMINISTRATIONS
4 Millbank, London SW1P 3JD Tel. 01-222 7730
Telex 916205

Agents for Overseas Governments; Millbank Technical Services Limited, *q.v.* is a subsidiary

Enquiries to the Information Officer

Subject coverage
supply of goods and services to Third World countries

854 CROYDON COLLEGE OF DESIGN AND TECHNOLOGY
Fairfield, Croydon, Surrey CR9 1DX Tel. 01-688 9271 ext. 128/9
Technical College; created by the merger of the former Croydon Technical College and Croydon College of Art and Design

Enquiries to the Librarian

Subject coverage
building; business studies; electrical and radio engineering; food trades; management studies; mechanical engineering; ceramics; graphic design; print making; textile design

855 CROYDON PUBLIC LIBRARIES
Katharine Street, Croydon, Surrey CR9 1ET Tel. 01-688 3627
Public Library

Enquiries to the Librarian

Subject coverage
general; economics; labour economics

CRYPTOGAMIC SOCIETY OF SCOTLAND *see* **BOTANICAL SOCIETY OF EDINBURGH**

856 CRYSTALLOGRAPHIC DATA CENTRE
University Chemical Laboratory, Lensfield Road, Cambridge CB2 1EW — Tel. 0223 66499
Telex 81240

University Research Group

Enquiries to the Honorary Director or Assistant Director

Subject coverage
information including numeric data on the structure of organic and organometallic compounds determined by X-ray diffraction methods; structure of proteins

Special collections
Structural data, chemical connectivity, and bibliographic data files on magnetic tape
Reprint Collection
Structural diagrams (cards)

Publications
Molecular Structures and Dimensions Series (bibliographies and Interatomic Distances) list available

857 CULHAM LABORATORY
Abingdon, Oxfordshire OX14 3DB — Tel. 0235 21840
Telex 83189

Public Corporation, of the United Kingdom Atomic Energy Authority; houses the Astrophysics Division of the Appleton Laboratory, *q.v.*

Enquiries to the Librarian

Subject coverage
plasma physics; controlled thermonuclear fusion; laser applications; electrotechnology

Publication
Library Guide (in preparation)

858 CULTURE CENTRE FOR ALGAE AND PROTOZOA
36 Storeys Way, Cambridge CB3 0DT — Tel. 0223 61378

Research Unit, of the Institute of Terrestrial Ecology, *q.v.*, within the Natural Environment Research Council; formerly Culture Collection of Algae and Protozoa, Botany School, Cambridge University

Enquiries to the Director

Subject coverage
algae, other than the large seaweeds; free-living protozoa; culture methods

Publications
List of strains

CUMBERLAND COUNTY LIBRARY *now* **CUMBRIA COUNTY LIBRARY,** *q.v.*

859 CUMBRIA COUNTY LIBRARY
1 Portland Square, Carlisle CA1 1PS — Tel. 0228 32161
Telex 64316

County Library Service; constituted from the Public Libraries of Cumberland, Westmorland, Carlisle, Barrow, Workington, Whitehaven, Cockermouth, Windermere and parts of Lancashire and West Riding; North East Divisional Library at Carlisle, *q.v.*, Western at Barrow, *q.v.*, Southern at Workington

Enquiries to Assistant County Librarian; bibliographical services, or to local librarians

Subject coverage
general; geology

Special collections
Jackson Collection (local history, at Carlisle)
Geology Collection (geology, at Kendal)

860 CURTIS AND COMPANY
Green Lane, Challock, Ashford, Kent TN25 4BL — Tel. 023-374 387
Company, member of the Land Advisory Group, *q.v.*

Enquiries to the Director

Subject coverage
farm management

CUSTOMS AND EXCISE *see* **H.M. CUSTOMS AND EXCISE**

861 CUTLERY AND ALLIED TRADES RESEARCH ASSOCIATION
Henry Street, Sheffield S3 7EQ — Tel. 0742 79736
Trade Association; carries out the work of the now disbanded File Research Council

Enquiries to the Director or the Information Officer

Subject coverage
heat treatment and working of steel, particularly stainless steel; grinding and polishing; corrosion resistance; metallography; surface finish measurement

Publication
Annual Report

CYBERNETICS RESEARCH CONSULTANTS LIMITED *see* **CRC INFORMATION SYSTEMS LIMITED**

CYCLE AND MOTOR CYCLE ASSOCIATION LIMITED *now*
BICYCLE ASSOCIATION OF GREAT BRITAIN LIMITED, *q.v.*
MOTOR CYCLE ASSOCIATION OF GREAT BRITAIN LIMITED, *q.v.*

862 CYNON VALLEY BOROUGH LIBRARIES
Central Public Library, Aberdare, Mid-Galmorganshire CF44 7AG — Tel. 068-588 2441
Public Libraries, formerly Aberdare Urban District Council Central Library

Enquiries to the Borough Librarian

Subject coverage
photography; transport; (Welsh Libraries Subject Allocation Scheme responsibility for those subjects)

863 CZECHOSLOVAK EMBASSY
Commercial Section, 26 Kensington Palace Gardens, London W8 4QQ — Tel. 01-229 1255
Telex 28276

Governmental Department

Enquiries to Ustředí vědeckých, technických a ekonomických informaci, 113 57 Praha 1, Konviktska 5, Czechoslovakia

Subject coverage
science, technology and economics in CSSR

864 DAIRY TRADE FEDERATION
20 Eastbourne Terrace, London W2 6LE — Tel. 01-262 6722
Telex 262027

Trade Association; affiliated to the Food and Drink Industries Council, and member of the National Milk Publicity Council

Enquiries to the Secretary

Subject coverage
milk and milk products

DAIRY TRADE FEDERATION *see also*
ASSOCIATION OF CHEESE PROCESSORS
ASSOCIATION OF BUTTER BLENDERS AND BUTTER AND CHEESE PACKERS
STILTON CHEESE MAKERS ASSOCIATION

865 DARCHEM LIMITED
West Auckland Road, Darlington, Co. Durham DL3 0UP Tel. 0325 66762
Telex 58542

Group of companies, U.K. and European; formerly Darlington Chemicals Limited

Enquiries to the Information Officer

Subject coverage
insulation (thermal and acoustic); tank linings; pipe fittings; high precision press tools, dies, etc.; heat treatment; resistance welding equipment; antifriction metals and non-ferrous alloys; electrically-operated actuators for hydraulic and pneumatic control systems

DARCHEM LIMITED *see also* **CHEMICAL AND INSULATING COMPANY LIMITED**

866 DARESBURY LABORATORY
Daresbury, Warrington WA4 4AD Tel. 0925 65000
Telex 62609
Government Research Establishment, of the Science Research Council; formerly Daresbury Nuclear Physics Laboratory

Enquiries to the Information Officer

Subject coverage
high energy physics; atomic, molecular, and solid state physics; synchrotron radiation; nuclear structure accelerator physics

Publications
Annual Report
Research reports

DARLASTON DISTRICT LIBRARY *see* **WALSALL LIBRARY AND MUSEUM SERVICES**

DARLINGTON BRANCH LIBRARY *see* **DURHAM COUNTY LIBRARY**

867 DARLINGTON COLLEGE OF TECHNOLOGY
Cleveland Avenue, Darlington, Co. Durham DL3 7BB Tel. 0325 67651
College of Further Education

Enquiries to the Tutor Librarian

Subject coverage
economics; business management; accountancy; engineering; building; catering; domestic science; mathematics; physics; chemistry; metallurgy

DARTFORD DIVISIONAL LIBRARY *see* **KENT COUNTY LIBRARY**

DARWEN TEXTILE MANUFACTURERS ASSOCIATION *see* **BOLTON AND DISTRICT TEXTILE EMPLOYERS ASSOCIATION**

868 DATRON RESEARCH LIMITED
3–11 Edgedale Road, Sheffield S7 2BQ Tel. 0742 582184
Telex 54395

Company

Enquiries to the Managing Director

Subject coverage
trade with Sweden, South Africa and Germany; construction market in those countries

DAVENTRY DISTRICT LIBRARY *see* **NORTHAMPTONSHIRE LIBRARIES**

DAVID KEIR LIBRARY *now* **QUEENS UNIVERSITY OF BELFAST SCIENCE LIBRARY,** *q.v.*

869 G.C. DAVIS AND COMPANY LIMITED
61 High Street, Barnet, Hertfordshire EN5 5UR — Tel. 01-449 3580, Telex 264880

Company; also houses Hazard Control Limited, *q.v.*

Enquiries to the Technical Director

Subject coverage
gas control and detection; control of environmental hazards

870 DAVY INTERNATIONAL LIMITED
15 Portland Place, London W1A 4DD — Tel. 01-637 2821, Telex 22604

Company, formerly Davy-Ashmore Limited

Enquiries to the Public Relations Officer

Subject coverage
engineering and technology in and for the following industries: oil, natural gas, chemicals/petrochemicals, fertilizers, roll-making, water treatment, synthetic fibres, plastics, base metals, iron and steel, electronic weighing, industrial control and pollution control

Publications
Annual Report
Brochures and Catalogues

871 DAVY-LOEWY LIMITED
Mills Division, Prince of Wales Road, Sheffield S9 4EX — Tel. 0742 49971, Telex 54296

Company, affiliated to Davy International Limited, and formerly Davy & United Engineering Company Limited

Enquiries to the Librarian

Subject coverage
steelworks plant, rolling mills

872 DAWE INSTRUMENTS LIMITED
Concord Road, Western Avenue, Acton, London W3 0SD — Tel. 01-992 6751, Telex 934848

Company; subsidiary of Joseph Lucas Industries Limited

Enquiries to the Librarian

Subject coverage
ultrasonics; measurement of acoustic noise

873 William DAWSON & SONS LIMITED
Cannon House, Folkestone, Kent CT19 5EE — Tel. 0303 57421, Telex 96392

Company; London Office, 10–14 Macklin Street WC2B 5NG Tel. 01-242 5111

Enquiries to the Manager, Sales Development Department

Subject coverage
journal subscriptions; back issues of scientific and technical and scholarly journals; advertising; publishing

Publications
Book Auction Records (annual)
BAR Quarterly

874 DECCA RADAR LIMITED
Hersham Division, Lyon Road, Hersham, Walton-on-Thames, Surrey KT12 3PS — Tel. 98 28851 ext. 217, Telex 928478

Company

Enquiries to the Librarian

Subject coverage
radar and radar systems; microwave theory and applications; applications of semiconductors; electronics circuitry; printed circuit boards; thin film technology. *Also* mathematics; physics; management; computer programming; reliability and quality control

875 DECORATIVE LIGHTING ASSOCIATION
Tyn-Pwll, Moelfre, Anglesey LL72 8LN Tel. 024-888 396
Trade Association

No enquiry service

Subject coverage
lighting

Publication
Show Catalogue

876 DEFENCE RESEARCH INFORMATION CENTRE
Station Square House, St. Mary Cray, Orpington, Kent BR5 3RE Tel. 66 32111
Telex 896866

Government Department, of the Ministry of Defence, Procurement Executive

Enquiries to the Centre; technical, ext. 249; Defence Research Abstracts and DRA Digests, ext. 21; specifications, ext. 110; British reports, ext. 107; Overseas reports, ext. 40; all services primarily for the Ministry and Government Contractors

Subject coverage
unpublished R and D reports, U.K. and overseas; emphasis on aerospace, naval science and technology; U.S. military specifications

Publications
Defence Research Abstracts
DRA Digests
Standard Profiles
Bibliographies
all with limited distribution

877 DELTA MATERIALS RESEARCH LIMITED
P.O. Box 22, Hadleigh Road, Ipswich IP2 0EG Tel. 0473 57494
Company, of Delta Metal Company Limited; formerly Delta Metals Research Limited

Enquiries to the Information Officer

Subject coverage
materials science; noise control

DELYN AREA LIBRARY *see* **CLWYD COUNTY LIBRARY SERVICE**

878 DEMOLITION AND DISMANTLING INDUSTRY REGISTER
141 London Road, Leicester LE2 1EF Tel. 0533 536155
Government-approved Register

No enquiry service

Subject coverage
record of demolition and dismantling contractors

DENBIGHSHIRE TECHNICAL COLLEGE *now* **ASTON COLLEGE,** *q.v.*

879 DENT & HELLYER LIMITED
Walworth Road, Andover, Hampshire SP10 5AA Tel. 0264 62111
Telex 47430

Company, subsidiary of Thomas Tilling Intermed Group

Enquiries to the Marketing Advisor

Subject coverage
hospital sterilization systems; hospital sanitary control equipment; steam disinfection

DENTON PUBLIC LIBRARY *see* **TAMESIDE LIBRARIES**

DEPARTMENT OF AGRICULTURE AND FISHERIES FOR SCOTLAND *see*
ROWETT RESEARCH INSTITUTE
ROYAL BOTANIC GARDEN

880 DEPARTMENT OF AGRICULTURE FOR NORTHERN IRELAND
Dundonald House, Upper Newtonards Road, Belfast BT4 3SB Tel. 0232 650111
Telex 74578

Government Department

Enquiries to the Information Officer or the Press Officer

Subject coverage
agriculture, fisheries, forestry, horticulture

Publications
Annual Report
Agriculture in Northern Ireland (monthly)
Angling Guide (annual)
Outline of Northern Ireland Agriculture
Outdoors in Ulster's Forests
Record of Agricultural Research
Annual Report on Research and Technical Work
Statistical Review

881 DEPARTMENT OF ENERGY
Thames House South, Millbank, London SW1P 4QJ Tel. 01-211 3000
01-211 4679 (Library)
Telex 918777

Government Department, formerly of the Department of Trade and Industry; includes the Offshore Supplies Office, *q.v.* and the Offshore Energy Technology Board

Enquiries, public relations matters, to the Director of Information; press matters, to the Chief Press Officer; subject queries, to the Librarian

Subject coverage
energy policy, economics and technology of energy, (coal, gas, electricity, nuclear power, oil, new sources of energy); offshore industry

Special collection
United Kingdom Continental Shelf Well Records

Publications
Digest of United Kingdom Energy Statistics (annual)
Development of the Oil and Gas Resources of the U.K. (annual)
Energy Papers Series
Energy Trends (monthly)
Publications listed in H.M.S.O. Sectional List 3

882 DEPARTMENT OF HEALTH AND SOCIAL SECURITY
Main Library, Alexander Fleming House, Elephant and Castle, London SE1 6BY Tel. 01-407 5522 ext. 6363
Telex 883669

Government Department; formed by the merger of the Ministry of Health and the Ministry of Social Security; Library Branches: John Adam Street Library, Supply Library, Health Building Library, Medicines Division Library, *qq.v.* immediately following this entry

Enquiries to the Librarian

Subject coverage
health services; hospitals; public health; social services and security

Publications
Hospital Abstracts, (H.M.S.O., monthly)
Current Literature on Health Services

883 DEPARTMENT OF HEALTH AND SOCIAL SECURITY
Health Building Library, Euston Tower, 286 Euston Road, London NW1 3DN — Tel. 01-388 1188 ext. 206, Telex 27722
Government Department, Branch Library (*see also* Main Library)
Enquiries to the Librarian
Subject coverage
architectural, engineering and related aspects of buildings for the health and social services

884 DEPARTMENT OF HEALTH AND SOCIAL SECURITY
John Adam Street Library, 10 John Adam Street, London WC2N 6HD — Tel. 01-217 5250, Telex 22843
Government Department, Branch Library (*see also* Main Library)
Enquiries to the Librarian
Subject coverage
social security, including national insurance, supplementary benefits, family allowances, war pensions and industrial injuries insurance

885 DEPARTMENT OF HEALTH AND SOCIAL SECURITY
Medicines Division Library, Finsbury Square House, 33–37A Finsbury Square, London EC2A 1PP — Tel. 01-638 6020 ext. 328
Government Department, Branch Library (*see also* Main Library); the Division took over the work of the former Committee on Safety of Drugs, and houses the Committee on Safety of Medicines and the Medicines Commission
Enquiries to the Librarian
Subject coverage
pharmacology; pharmaceutics; safety, quality and efficacy of medicines
Publications
Annual Report of the Medicines Commission, the Committee on the Safety of Medicines and of the Division
Medicines Act leaflets

886 DEPARTMENT OF HEALTH AND SOCIAL SECURITY
Supply Library, 14 Russell Square, London WC1B 5EP — Tel. 01-636 6811 ext. 3258, Telex 23514
Government Department, Branch Library (*see also* Main Library)
Enquiries to the Librarian
Subject coverage
medical supplies and equipment

DEPARTMENT OF HEALTH AND SOCIAL SECURITY *see also* **PUBLIC HEALTH LABORATORY SERVICE**

887 DEPARTMENT OF INDUSTRIAL AND FORENSIC SCIENCE
Department of Commerce, Government of Northern Ireland, 180 Newtownoreda Road, Belfast BT8 4QR — Tel. Belfast 645421
Government Department
Enquiries to the Librarian
Subject coverage
applied science and technology; forensic science

888 DEPARTMENT OF INDUSTRY
1 Victoria Street, London SW1H 0ET — Tel. 01-215 7877, Telex 8811074
Government Department, formerly Board of Trade, then Ministry of Technology
Enquiries to the appropriate Division, Section or Unit; see other entries

Subject coverage
industrial policy; financial assistance to industry; sponsorship of individual manufacturing industries including iron and steel, aircraft, shipbuilding, British Steel Corporation and the Post Office; technical services to industry and industrial research and development

Publications
listed in H.M.S.O. Sectional List 3

889 DEPARTMENT OF INDUSTRY
Central Library, 1 Victoria Street, London SW1H 0ET Tel. 01-215 7877
Telex 918779
Government Department Library; Library services include the Department of Industry Marine Library, Department of Industry Technology Library and the Statistics and Market Intelligence Library, *q.v.*

Enquiries to the Head of Reader Services

Subject coverage
current trade, economic and commercial affairs

Publication
Contents of Recent Economics Journals (weekly, H.M.S.O.)

890 DEPARTMENT OF INDUSTRY
Marine Library, Sunley House, 90 High Holborn, London WC1V 6LP Tel. 01-405 6911
Telex 264084
Government Department Library, part of the Library Services

Enquiries to the Librarian

Subject coverage
marine safety, including aspects of ship construction and equipment; employment, safety and health of seamen; safety of navigation; search and rescue; oil pollution

Special collections
Historical material on the administration of the Merchant Shipping Acts from c. 1855, including wreck reports and boiler explosion reports

Publications
Merchant Shipping: a guide to Government Publications
Principal Regulations on Merchant Shipping (annual, free)
Merchant Shipping Notices current (annual, free)

891 DEPARTMENT OF INDUSTRY
Regional Development Grants Division, Millbank Tower, Millbank London SW1P 4QU Tel. 01-211 3000
Telex 918829
Government Department, formerly the Investment Grants Division of the Board of Trade and then of the Department of Trade and Industry; Regional offices at Billingham, Bootle, Cardiff, Glasgow and London

Enquiries to the Offices: Billingham (tel. 0642 553671); Bootle (tel. 051-922 4030); Cardiff (tel. 0222 42611); Glasgow (tel. 041-221 9833); London (tel. 01-211 5518)

Subject coverage
administration of regional development grants under the Industry Act 1972 and residual work on investment grants under the Industrial Development Act 1966

892 DEPARTMENT OF INDUSTRY
Overseas Technical Information Unit, Abell House, John Islip Street, London SW1P 4LN Tel. 01-211 3000
Telex 918829
Government Department Information Unit

Enquiries to the Unit, tel. 01-211 4431, Room 214

Subject coverage
developments in science and technology abroad

Publications

Series of newsletters on behalf of Scientific Counsellors in British Embassies and High Commissions abroad

893 DEPARTMENT OF INDUSTRY

Technology Library, Abell House, John Islip Street, London SW1P 4LN — Tel. 01-211 3475

Government Department Library, formerly of the Department of Trade and Industry

Enquiries to the Librarian

Subject coverage

technology and industry; industrial development; management of research and development; science policy

894 DEPARTMENT OF INDUSTRY, Regional Organisation

North: Wellbar House, Gallowgate,	Tel. 0632 27575
Newcastle upon Tyne NE1 4TR	Telex 53178
North West: Sunley Building, Piccadilly Plaza,	Tel. 061-236 2171
Manchester M1 4BA	Telex 667104
Yorkshire and Humberside: Priestley House, 1 Park Row,	Tel. 0532 443171
Leeds LS1 5LF	Telex 557925
West Midlands: Ladywood House, Stephenson Street,	Tel. 021-632 4111
Birmingham B2 4DT	Telex 337021
East Midlands: Severns House, 20 Middle Pavement,	Tel. 0602 56181
Nottingham NG1 7DW	Telex 37143
London & South East: Charles House, 375 Kensington High Street,	Tel. 01-603 2060
London W14 8QH	Telex 25991
South West: The Pithay,	Tel. 0272 291071
Bristol BS1 2PB	Telex 44214
East: Charles House, 375 Kensington High Street,	Tel. 01-603 2070
London W14 8QH	Telex 25991

Regional Offices of Government Department

Enquiries to the Regional Offices

Subject coverage

representation of the Department in its dealings with local authorities, Offices of other Departments, other local bodies; administration of assistance to industry in Assisted Areas; regional industrial development; some activities on behalf of Departments of Trade and of Energy

DEPARTMENT OF INDUSTRY *see also*
BUSINESS STATISTICS OFFICE
COMPUTER AIDED DESIGN CENTRE
LABORATORY OF THE GOVERNMENT CHEMIST
NATIONAL COMPUTING CENTRE
NATIONAL CORROSION CENTRE
NATIONAL ENGINEERING LABORATORY
NATIONAL MARITIME INSTITUTE
NATIONAL PHYSICAL LABORATORY
PROGRAMMES ANALYSIS UNIT
SMALL FIRMS INFORMATION CENTRES (and entries under names of towns)
STATISTICS AND MARKET INTELLIGENCE LIBRARY

895 DEPARTMENT OF PRICES AND CONSUMER PROTECTION

1 Victoria Street, London SW1H 0ET — Tel. 01-215 7877, Telex 8811074

Government Department; formerly part of Department of Trade and Industry; includes the Advisory Council on Calibration and Measurement, the British Calibration Service, the Metrication Board, *qq.v.* and the Weights and Measures Service

Enquiries to the appropriate Division

Subject coverage
policy on prices, including food prices and subsidies, except for those of the nationalized industries; consumer affairs generally, including fair trading, consumer safety, weights and measures, monopolies, mergers and restrictive practices

Publications
listed in HMSO Sectional List 3

896 DEPARTMENT OF THE ENVIRONMENT *and* DEPARTMENT OF TRADE
2 Marsham Street, London SW1P 3EB Tel. 01-212 3434
01-212 4816 or 4822 (direct)
Telex 22801

Government Department, formed 1970, by merger of Ministry of Housing and Local Government, Ministry of Transport, and Ministry of Public Building and Works; six regional libraries; six information offices; nine sub-libraries

Enquiries to the Chief Librarian

Subject coverage
housing (all aspects); town, country, and regional planning; new towns; environmental health; pollution; water supply; sewage disposal; refuse and radioactive waste disposal; transport of dangerous goods; countryside; land use; roads; bridges; inland waterways; ports; Channel Tunnel; road safety; traffic; mineral workings (sand, gravel, aggregates)

Publications
DOE Library Bulletin (Abstracts) (fortnightly)
DOE Annual List of Publications
DOE Register of Research (4 vols)
Bibliography Series
Information Series
Occasional Papers series
HMSO Sectional Lists 5, 22, and 27

DEPARTMENT OF THE ENVIRONMENT *see also*
AGREMENT BOARD
BRITISH WATERWAYS BOARD
BUILDING RESEARCH ESTABLISHMENT
CENTRAL WATER PLANNING UNIT
CLEAN AIR COUNCIL
FIRE RESEARCH STATION
HYDRAULICS RESEARCH STATION
ORDNANCE SURVEY
PRINCES RISBOROUGH LABORATORY
PROPERTY SERVICES AGENCY
RESEARCH MANAGEMENT DIVISION
TRANSPORT AND ROAD RESEARCH LABORATORY
WATER DATA UNIT

897 DEPARTMENT OF TRADE
1 Victoria Street, London SW1H 0ET Tel. 01-215 7877
Telex 8811074

Government Department; formerly Board of Trade and then Department of Trade and Industry

Enquiries to the appropriate Division, Unit or Section

Subject coverage
commercial and overseas trade policy; promotion of exports; sponsorship of shipping, civil aviation, tourism, hotel, newspaper, printing, publishing, film, and distributive industries; administration of statutes governing company affairs, insolvency, insurance, patent, trade mark and copyright matters

Publications
listed in HMSO Sectional List 3

DEPARTMENT OF TRADE *see also*
BRITISH OVERSEAS TRADE BOARD
COMPANIES REGISTRATION OFFICE
EXPORT SERVICES AND PROMOTIONS DIVISION
PATENT OFFICE
REGISTRY OF BUSINESS NAMES

898 DERBY CENTRAL LIBRARY
Wardwick, Derby DE1 1HF Tel. 0332 31111
Telex 377596

Public Library, of Derbyshire County Library system

Enquiries to the Reference or Local Studies Librarians

Subject coverage
local industries

Publication
Index of Statistical Sources (general)

899 DERBY COLLEGE OF ART AND TECHNOLOGY
Kedleston Road, Derby DE3 1GB Tel. 0332 47181
College of Technology; formerly the Derby and District College of Technology and the Derby and District College of Art

Enquiries to the Librarian

Subject coverage
engineering; biological sciences; earth sciences; management sciences; physical sciences

Special collection
British Standards

900 DERBYSHIRE COLLEGE OF AGRICULTURE
Morley, Nr Derby DE7 6DN Tel. 0332 831345
Agricultural College

Enquiries to the Librarian

Subject coverage
agriculture and horticulture at the practical level

901 DERBYSHIRE COUNTY LIBRARY
County Offices, Smedley Street, Matlock, Derbyshire DE4 3AG Tel. 0629 3411
Public Library Service; District Libraries at Buxton, Chesterfield, Derby, *q.v.*, and Ilkeston

Enquiries to the County Librarian

Subject coverage
local industrial history, especially lead mining

Publications
List and Index of Lead-mining Section, Wolley MSS (B.M.)
Derbyshire County and College Libraries Periodicals List

DERRITRON GROUP *see* **TECHNICAL INDEXES LIMITED**

902 DERWENT PUBLICATIONS LIMITED
128 Theobalds Road, London WC1X 8RP Tel. 01-242 5823/6
Telex 267487

Company, subsidiary of the Thomson Organisation Limited

Enquiries to the Managing Director

Subject coverage
patents information in all technologies; journal information in pharmaceutical and related technologies

Publications
Central Patents Index
World Patents Index
Patents Abstracts Journals
RINGDOC Pharmaceutical Literature Documentation *and* Profile Booklets
PESTDOC Pesticidal Literature Documentation
VETDOC Veterinary Literature Documentation
Chemical Reactions Documentation Service
Descriptive literature on all the above services

903 DESIGN AND INDUSTRIES ASSOCIATION
12 Carlton House Terrace, London SW1Y 5AL Tel. 01-940 4925
Voluntary Association

Enquiries to the Secretary

Subject coverage
conference and study, home and abroad, connected with design topics

Publication
DIA Yearbook

904 DESIGN COUNCIL
Design Centre, 28 Haymarket, London SW1Y 4SU Tel. 01-839 8000
Telex 8812963
Grant-aided Body, of the Department of Industry; formerly the Council of Industrial Design; member of the International Council of Societies of Industrial Design, Brussels

Enquiries, on the Design Centre, to the Centre; on the Record of Industrial Expertise, to the Head of Engineering Division; on the Designer Selection Service, to the Head of Industrial Division; on the Slide Library of well-designed products, to the Librarian

Subject coverage
high standards of design of goods manufactured by British industry; consumer products such as furniture, fabrics, household appliances, toys, sports, gardening equipment, jewellery, etc. as well as engineering design

Publications
Engineering Design Guides
Booklets, Catalogues

905 DEVELOPMENT CORPORATION FOR WALES
15 Park Place, Cardiff CF1 3DQ Tel. 0222 21208
Telex 497i90

Industrial Development Association

Enquiries to the Chef Executive

Subject coverage
industrial development and trade promotion in Wales

Publications
Progress Wales (quarterly)
Industrial Directory of Wales

906 DEVON LIBRARY SERVICES
Administrative Centre, Barley House, Isleworth Road, Exeter EX4 1RQ Tel. 0392 74142
Telex 42933
Public Library Service, having four Area Central Libraries: North at Barnstaple, South at Torquay, East at Exeter, and West at Plymouth, *qq.v.*; incorporating Torbay Library Service, Devon County Library, Bideford Free Library, and Newton Abbot Public Library

Enquiries to the County Librarian or to Area Librarians

Subject coverage
general

907 DEWSBURY AND BATLEY TECHNICAL COLLEGE
Halifax Road, Dewsbury, Yorkshire — Tel. 0924 465916
College of Further Education

Enquiries to the Librarian

Subject coverage
textiles

DEWSBURY DISTRICT LIBRARY *see* **KIRKLEES LIBRARIES AND MUSEUMS SERVICE**

908 DIAMOND, PEARL AND PRECIOUS STONE TRADE SECTION
London Chamber of Commerce, 69 Cannon Street, London EC4N 5AB — Tel. 01-248 4444, Telex 888941
Trade Association; includes the Gem Testing Laboratory

Enquiries to the Secretary

Subject coverage
diamonds, pearls and gem trade; gem testing

909 DIAMOND PRODUCTS DIVISIONAL R & D LABORATORY
Tuffley Crescent, Gloucester GL1 5NG — Tel. 0452 28521, Telex 43116
Company Division Laboratory, of Unicorn Industries Limited, formerly Universal Grinding Limited. The Laboratory was formed by the merger of L.M. van Moppes and Sons Limited and Impregnated Diamond Products Limited

Enquiries to the R & D manager

Subject coverage
industrial diamond and cubic boron nitride tooling

910 DICKINSON ROBINSON LIMITED
1 Redcliffe Street, Bristol BS99 7QY — Tel. 0272 294294, Telex 44276

Public Company, formerly E.S. and A. Robinson Limited

Enquiries to the Information Officer

Subject coverage
packaging; plastics; paper/stationery; commercial information

Publications
House journal
Sales literature

DIECASTING SOCIETY *see* **INSTITUTION OF MECHANICAL ENGINEERS**

911 DIESEL ENGINEERS AND USERS ASSOCIATION
18 London Street, London EC3R 7JR — Tel. 01-481 2393
Professional Association

Enquiries to the Secretary

Subject coverage
manufacture, design, maintenance and supplies of diesel engines and gas turbine plant

Publication
Journal (5 or 6 per annum)

DINGWALL DIVISIONAL LIBRARY *see* **HIGHLAND REGION LIBRARY SERVICE**

912 DIRECT INVESTIGATION GROUP ON AERIAL PHENOMENA
24 Bent Fold Road, Unsworth, Bury BL9 8NG Tel. 061-766 4560
Amateur Club, affiliated to the British UFO Research Association (BUFORA LIMITED) *q.v.*

Enquiries to the Secretary

Subject coverage
unidentified flying objects

913 DIRECTORATE OF FISHERIES RESEARCH
Fisheries Laboratory, Lowestoft, Suffolk NR33 0HT Tel. 0502 62244
Telex 97470
Government Department, of the Ministry of Agriculture, Fisheries and Food; comprised of formerly separate Laboratories as follows: Fisheries Radiobiological Laboratory Lowestoft, Fisheries Laboratory Burnham-on-Crouch, *q.v.*, Fisheries Experiment Station Conwy, Salmon and Freshwater Fisheries Laboratory London, Fish Diseases Laboratory Weymouth, *q.v.*

Enquiries to the Information Officer

Subject coverage
fisheries and fishing; marine biology; oceanography

DIRECTORATE OF OCCUPATIONAL SAFETY AND HEALTH *now* **HEALTH AND SAFETY EXECUTIVE,** *q.v.*

914 DIRECTORATE OF RADIO TECHNOLOGY
Waterloo Bridge House, Waterloo Road, London SE1 8UA Tel. 01-275 3270
Government Department

Enquiries to the Director

Subject coverage
frequency spectrum engineering; radio interference; International Radio Consultative Committee work

Publications
Home Office Radio Equipment Type Approval Specifications (HMSO)

915 DISASTER RESEARCH UNIT
Bradford University, Bradford, West Yorkshire BD7 1DP Tel. 0274 33466 ext. 8287
Telex 51309
University Research Group, part of the Project Planning Centre for Developing Countries, of the University of Bradford

Enquiries to the Director

Subject coverage
natural disaster occurrence; precautionary planning; specific precautions (construction, logistics, financial, developmental); economic analysis of disaster impact; social implications; commissioned research projects

Publications
Bibliography of Disaster Reference Material
Series of Occasional Papers

916 DISTA PRODUCTS LIMITED
Fleming Road, Speke, Liverpool L24 9LN Tel. 051-486 3939
Telex 627178

Company; part of Lilly Industries Limited

Enquiries to the Information Officer

Subject coverage
pharmaceutical industry

917 DISTILLERS COMPANY LIMITED
Glenochil Research Station, Menstrie, Clackmannanshire FK11 7ES Tel. Menstrie 481
Company; formerly Scottish Grain Distillers Limited

Enquiries to the Librarian

Subject coverage
fermentation; malting; distillation; general biochemistry and enzymology; microbiology; chemical engineering; food technology

918 DISTRIBUTIVE INDUSTRIES TRAINING BOARD
MacLaren House, Talbot Road, Stretford, Manchester M32 0FP Tel. 061-872 2494
Industrial Training Board, part of the Training Services Agency

Enquiries to the Librarian

Subject coverage
distributive trades, training, wholesaling, retailing and mail order

919 DISTRICT HEATING ASSOCIATION
Bedford House, Stafford Road, Caterham, Surrey CR3 6JA Tel. 0883 42323
Trade Association, formerly District Heating Association Limited

Enquiries to the Controller

Subject coverage
district heating

Publications
Quarterly Journal
Annual Handbook

DOCK AND HARBOUR AUTHORITIES ASSOCIATION *now* **BRITISH PORTS ASSOCIATION,** *q.v.*

920 DOMESTIC COAL CONSUMERS COUNCIL
Dean Bradley House, 52 Horseferry Road, London SW1P 2AG Tel. 01-212 0093/0119
Consumer Council

Enquiries to the Secretary

Subject coverage
advice to consumers of solid fuel relating to its price and availability

Publication
Annual Report

DOMESTIC REFRIGERATION DEVELOPMENT COMMITTEE *now* **FOOD FREEZER AND REFRIGERATOR COUNCIL,** *q.v.*

921 DONCASTER METROPOLITAN BOROUGH LIBRARY SERVICE
Waterdale, Doncaster, Yorkshire DN1 3JE Tel. 0302 69123
Telex 54425
Public Library and Information Services; member of SINTO (Sheffield Interchange Organization); supporting a Medical and Technical Library and Information Service at Doncaster Royal Infirmary

Enquiries to the Chief Librarian

Subject coverage
general; commerce, science and technology; coal mining; railways

Publications
Search (daily, newspaper abstracts, for local government current awareness)
Analysis (weekly, periodical abstracts for a similar purpose)

922 DONCASTER METROPOLITAN INSTITUTE OF HIGHER EDUCATION (Mexborough Site)
Park Road, Mexborough, South Yorkshire S64 9PJ Tel. 070-988 2306 & 3389
Institute of Higher Education; formerly Mexborough Technical College and merged with Doncaster College of Technology; the Library is at the Institute's Waterdale Site, *q.v.*

Enquiries to the Librarian

Subject coverage
technology

923 DONCASTER METROPOLITAN INSTITUTE OF HIGHER EDUCATION (Waterdale Site)
Waterdale, Doncaster DN1 3EX Tel. 0302 66881
College of Further and Higher Education; formerly Doncaster Technical College; *see also* the Institute's Mexborough Site

Enquiries to the Librarian

Subject coverage
business studies; management; engineering as follows: construction, mechanical, production, electrical, mining and mineral

DORCHESTER PUBLIC LIBRARY *see* **DORSET COUNTY LIBRARY**

924 DORSET COUNTY LIBRARY
Colliton Park, Dorchester, Dorset DT1 1XJ Tel. 0305 3131
Telex 417201
Public Library; main Area libraries: Bournemouth (East), Poole (Central) and Dorchester (West)

Enquiries to the Librarian

Subject coverage
general

925 DOUGLAS PUBLIC LIBRARY
Ridgeway Street, Douglas, Isle of Man Tel. 0624 23021
Public Library

Enquiries to the Borough Librarian

Subject coverage
general; Manx subjects

DOUNREAY EXPERIMENTAL REACTOR ESTABLISHMENT *see* **UNITED KINGDOM ATOMIC ENERGY AUTHORITY, Reactor Group**

926 DOVE MARINE LABORATORY
Cullercoats, North Shields, Tyne and Wear NE30 4PZ
University Department, of Newcastle University

Enquiries to the Librarian or the Director

Subject coverage
oceanography; fisheries

Publications
Contributions and Reports of the Laboratory

DOVER DIVISIONAL LIBRARY *see* **KENT COUNTY LIBRARY**

927 DOVER HARBOUR BOARD
Harbour House, Dover, Kent CT17 9BU Tel. 0304 206560
Telex 965619

Statutory Board

Enquiries to General Manager

Subject coverage
port administration, particularly cross-channel passenger trade and roll-on roll-off traffic

Publications
Annual Report
Statistical Digests
Service Brochures

928 DOWEL AND WOODWARE IMPORTERS ASSOCIATION
163 London Road, Croydon, Surrey CR9 2RP Tel. 01-686 5644
Trade Association

No enquiry service

Subject coverage
woodware imports

929 DOWTY ROTOL LIMITED
Cheltenham Road, Gloucester GL2 9QH Tel. 0452 712424
Telex 43246/7
Company

Enquiries to the Information Engineer

Subject coverage
aircraft engineering; aerodynamics; applied hydraulics; materials

DREDGING INVESTIGATIONS LIMITED *now* **OSIRIS SURVEY PROJECTS LIMITED,** *q.v.*

930 H.P. DREWRY (SHIPPING CONSULTANTS) LIMITED
Palladium House, 1–4 Argyll Street, London W1V 1AD Tel. 01-434 3771
Publishers and Consultants

Enquiries to the Company Secretary

Subject coverage
shipping economics and bulk trade flows; statistics; trade and shipping of oil, liquefied gases, chemicals, bulk commodities; tankers, drilling rigs, bulk carriers and other cargo ships; ports and terminals; pipelines; shipbuilding, repairing and scrapping; etc.

Publications
Studies (50 titles)
Surveys (7 titles)
World Shipping Statistics (annual, 1975 first year)

DRILLING TECHNOLOGY TRAINING CENTRE *see* **PETROLEUM INDUSTRY TRAINING BOARD**

DROP FORGING TRAINING GROUP *see* **NATIONAL ASSOCIATION OF DROP FORGERS AND STAMPERS**

DROYLSDEN PUBLIC LIBRARY *see* **TAMESIDE LIBRARIES**

931 DRY LINING AND PARTITION ASSOCIATION LIMITED
15 South Street, Lancing, Sussex BN15 8AE Tel. 090-63 5700
Trade Association; member of the Federation of Specialist Sub-contractors

Enquiries to the Secretary

Subject coverage
dry internal finishing of buildings; internal walls, partitions, party walls and soffites

932 DUCK PRODUCERS ASSOCIATION LIMITED
High Holborn House, 52–54 High Holborn, Tel. 01-242 4683
London WC1V 6SX Telex 28479
Trade Association; member of the British Poultry Federation, *q.v.*

Enquiries to the Secretary

Subject coverage
general information on duck production levels and processes

933 DUCTILE IRON PIPE ASSOCIATION
14 Pall Mall, London SW1Y 5LZ Tel. 01-930 7171
Trade Association, formerly the British Cast Iron Pressure Pipe Association; member of the Council of Ironfoundry Associations, *q.v.*

Enquiries to the Secretary

Subject coverage
applications of ductile iron pipes

Publication
Pipeline (quarterly, free on request)

934 DUDLEY PUBLIC LIBRARIES
Central Library, St James Road, Dudley, Worcestershire DY1 1HR Tel. 0384 56321
Telex 339831
Public Library; District Libraries at Brierley Hill, Halesowen, Kingswinford, Sedgley and Stourbridge

Enquiries to the Information Department

Subject coverage
general

Special collections
British Standards
Extel Service

935 DUDLEY TECHNICAL COLLEGE
The Broadway, Dudley, West Midlands DY1 4AS Tel. 0384 53585
Technical College, formerly Dudley and Staffordshire Technical College

Enquiries to the Librarian or Heads of Departments

Subject coverage
materials testing (especially crushing strength of brick, concrete and related materials); design of components; testing for high alumina cement; analysis for lead pollution; metallurgical analysis; advisory and testing services, by arrangement within those fields and in electrical installations problems

DULWICH DISTRICT LIBRARY *see* **SOUTHWARK LIBRARY SERVICES**

936 DUMBARTON DISTRICT LIBRARIES
Levensford House, Helenslee Road, Dumbarton G82 4AJ Tel. 0389 65100 ext. 233
Public Library Service; incorporating the former Helensburgh Public Library (the Templeton Library), Dumbarton Public Library and part of Dunbarton County Library

Enquiries to the Librarian

Subject coverage
general, and local history and commerce

937 DUMFRIES AND GALLOWAY COLLEGE OF TECHNOLOGY
Heathhall, Dumfries DG1 3QZ Tel. 0387 6126115
College of Further Education, formerly Dumfries Technical College

Enquiries to the Head of Learning Resources

Subject coverage
mechanical and electrical engineering; building; commerce; safety

938 DUMFRIES AND GALLOWAY REGIONAL LIBRARY SERVICE
Ewart Library, Catherine Street, Dumfries DG1 1JB Tel. 0387 3820 & 2070
Public Library; formerly Dumfries County Library

Enquiries to the Librarian

Subject coverage
general

939 DUNCAN, FLOCKHART AND COMPANY LIMITED
P.O. Box 46, Birkbeck Street, London E2 6LA Tel. 01-739 3451
Telex 264566

Company, formerly BDH Pharmaceuticals Limited; member of the Glaxo Group

Enquiries to the Professional Services Department

Subject coverage
pharmaceutical specialities

940 DUNDEE CITY DISTRICT LIBRARIES
Albert Institute, Albert Square, Dundee DD1 1DB Tel. 0382 24938/9
Public Libraries; official title is City of Dundee District Libraries; formerly Dundee Public Libraries

Enquiries to the Chief Librarian

Subject coverage
general; specialist subjects are textiles; architecture; insurance

Special collections
Sir James Ivory Collection of Mathematical Books
Ower Collection of Architectural Books

941 DUNDEE COLLEGE OF TECHNOLOGY
Bell Street, Dundee DD1 1HG Tel. 0382 27225
Telex 76453

College of Technology

Enquiries to the Principal Librarian

Subject coverage
accountancy, economics and business studies; building and surveying, civil engineering, electrical and electronic engineering, mathematics and computer studies, mechanical and industrial engineering, molecular and life sciences, physics, textile science

942 DUNDEE UNIVERSITY LIBRARY
Dundee DD1 4HN Tel. 0382 23181
Telex 76293

University Library

Enquiries to the Librarian

Subject coverage
Law, science, engineering and applied science, environmental studies, medicine and dentistry

Special collection
Thoms mineralogical collection

DUNDEE UNIVERSITY *see also* **CENTRE FOR INDUSTRIAL RESEARCH AND CONSULTANCY**

943 DUNFERMLINE DISTRICT COUNCIL CENTRAL LIBRARY
1 Abbot Street, Dunfermline, Fife KY12 7NW Tel. 23661/2
Public Library, formerly Dunfermline Public Libraries

Enquiries to the Director of Libraries, Museums and Art Galleries

Subject coverage
general

944 DUNLOP HOLDINGS LIMITED
Dunlop House, Ryder Street, St. James's, Tel. 01-930 6700
London SW1X 6PX Telex 915864
Company, formerly Dunlop Company Limited and Dunlop Rubber Company Limited

Enquiries to the Public Relations Department

Subject coverage
rubber production; tyres; automotive industry; products for sport, fire-fighting, bedding, flooring, belting, footwear

Publications
catalogues and data sheets

DUNS DISTRICT LIBRARY *see* **BORDERS REGIONAL LIBRARY**

945 DURHAM AGRICULTURAL COLLEGE
Houghall, Durham DH1 3SG — Tel. 0385 61351/4 (college) 0385 4020 (farm)

Agricultural College

Enquiries to the Librarian

Subject coverage
agriculture and horticulture

946 DURHAM CHEMICALS LIMITED
Birtley, Chester-le-Street, County Durham DH3 1QX — Tel. 0894-24 2361 Telex 53618

Company, subsidiary of Harrisons & Crosfield Limited

Enquiries to the Information Officer

Subject coverage
chemicals for the plastics, paint, rubber, paper, pharmaceutical and chemical industries, e.g. zinc chemicals, metal soaps, stabilisers and plasticisers for PVC, driers and fungicides for paints

Publication
List of Products

947 DURHAM COUNTY LIBRARY
County Hall, Durham DH1 5TY — Tel. 0385 64411
Public Library; Branches at Darlington, Durham, Easington, Stanley, Sedgfield, Crook

Enquiries to the County Librarian

Subject coverage
general

Special collection
Collection devoted to railway history

948 DURHAM UNIVERSITY LIBRARY
Science Section, Science Laboratories, South Road, Durham DH1 3LE — Tel. 0385 64971 Telex 537351

University Library

Enquiries to the Keeper of Science Books, preferably by letter

Subject coverage
anthropology, applied physics, botany, chemistry, computing, engineering science, geography, geological sciences, mathematics, physics, psychology, zoology

Special collections
Stock of 50,000 pre-1850 books, some scientific mathematical journals of Sir Edward Collingwood, the remainder of whose library is housed in the Department of Mathematics

Publication
Durham University Journal

949 DUST CONTROL EQUIPMENT LIMITED
Humberstone Lane, Thurmaston, Leicester LE4 8HP — Tel. 053723 3333 Telex 34500

Company; member of the Thomas Tilling Group

Enquiries to the Technical Librarian

Subject coverage
design, manufacture and application of industrial dust control equipment; unit collectors; insertable filters; automatic reverse jet filters; tubular bag filters; wet collectors; complete plant installations

950 DYFED COUNTY LIBRARY
H.Q., St. Peters Street, Carmarthen, Dyfed Tel. 0267 7488/9
Public Library Service; Bibliographical and Cultural Service, Corporation Street, Aberystwyth; District libraries at Aberystwyth/Ceridigion, Carmarthen and Pembroke

Enquiries to the Librarian

Subject coverage
general

951 DYSON PERRINS LABORATORY
University of Oxford, South Parks Road, Oxford OX1 3QY Tel. 0865 57809
UNiversity Department

No enquiry service

Subject coverage
organic chemistry

EA SPACE AND ADVANCED MILITARY SYSTEMS LIMITED *now* **EASAMS LIMITED,** *q.v.*

952 EALING TECHNICAL COLLEGE
St. Mary's Road, London W5 5RF Tel. 01-579 4111
Technical College; see also next entry; the Thomas Huxley College is to be merged with Ealing Technical College

Enquiries to the Librarian

Subject coverage
business studies; home and catering studies; photography; printing

953 EALING TECHNICAL COLLEGE
Woodlands Avenue, Acton, London W3 9DN Tel. 01-992 6944
Technical College Department; see previous entry

Enquiries to the Librarian

Subject coverage
librarianship; management

954 EALING LIBRARY SERVICE
Central Library, Walpole Park, London W5 5EQ Tel. 01-567 3656
Telex 262289
Public Library: formerly (London Borough of) Ealing Public Libraries; District Libraries at Acton and Southall, Technical Services Library at Ealing Town Hall, *qq.v.*

Enquiries, by letter or telex, to the Borough Librarian; by telephone, to the Central Reference Librarian

Subject coverage
general, including science and technology

Special collections
Selborne Society Library (hundreds of editions of Gilbert White's "Natural History")
Pearl Natural History collection

955 EALING TECHNICAL SERVICES GROUP
Technical Services Library, Room 136, 22/24 Uxbridge Road, London W5 2BP Tel. 01-579 2424 ext. 2218
Borough Council Department

Enquiries to the Technical Services Librarian

Subject coverage
engineering; architecture; town planning

Special collections
Trade literature
Building Research Establishment papers
Transport Research Laboratory papers
"Architects Journal" information library

956 EASAMS LIMITED
Lyon Way, Frimley Road, Camberley, Surrey GU16 5EX — Tel. 0276 63377 — Telex 858115

Company, formerly E-A Space and Advanced Military Systems Limited; independent management company within GEC-Marconi Electronics Limited

Enquiries to the Librarian

Subject coverage
aerodynamics; avionics; communications; computing; development economics; electronics; ergonomics; infrared; management; materials handling; military operational research; missile technology; navigation; oceanography; port management; project management; radar systems; systems analysis; systems design; systems engineering; telecommunications; transportation; underwater systems; weapon systems

EASINGTON BRANCH LIBRARY *see* **DURHAM COUNTY LIBRARY**

957 EASINGWOLD AGRICULTURAL CENTRE
Handleton Way, Easingwold, Yorkshire YO6 3EF
Agricultural Centre

Enquiries to the Head of the Centre

Subject coverage
home economics and country crafts

958 EAST ANGLIA UNIVERSITY
School of Environmental Sciences, University Plain, Norwich, Norfolk NR4 7TJ — Tel. 0603 56161
University Department; includes the Climatic Research Unit

Enquiries to the Dean

Subject coverage
research and teaching in environmental sciences

Publications
Climatic Research Unit Research Publications (CRURP)
Climatic Research Unit Monthly Bulletin (CRUMB)
List of Publications (annual)

959 EAST ANGLIA UNIVERSITY LIBRARY
University Plain, Norwich, Norfolk NR4 7TJ — Tel. 0603 56161 — Telex 97154

University Library

Enquiries to the Librarian

Subject coverage
biological, chemical, environmental, mathematical, physical and computing sciences

Publication
Union Catalogue of Periodicals

960 EAST ANGLIAN SHIP AND BOAT BUILDING EMPLOYERS ASSOCIATION
Ipswich Chamber of Commerce and Shipping, 17/19 Museum Street, Ipswich, Suffolk IP1 1HF — Tel. 0743 59201 — Telex 987703
Employers Association

Enquiries to the Secretary

Subject coverage
ship and boat building industry; employment conditions

961 EAST EUROPEAN TRADE COUNCIL
21 Tothill Street, London SW1H 9LP Tel. 01-930 6711
Telex 21332
Government grant-aided, Independent Advisory Group, of the British Overseas Trade Board
Enquiries to the Executive Secretary
Subject coverage
stimulation of British trade and economic cooperation with Albania, Bulgaria, Czechoslovakia, German Democratic Republic, Hungary, Mongolia, Poland, Romania, and the Soviet Union
Publications
Contracts with Eastern Europe
Various publications on conditions of trade with E. European countries
Lists of E. European Chambers of Trade, Commercial Counsellors, etc.

962 EAST HAM COLLEGE OF TECHNOLOGY
High Street South, London E6 4ER Tel. 01-472 1480
College of Further Education, formerly East Ham Technical College
Enquiries to the Librarian
Subject coverage
building; gas engineering; mechanical and production engineering

963 EAST LOTHIAN DISTRICT LIBRARY
Victoria Road, Haddington, East Lothian EH41 4DU Tel. 062-082 2370
Public Library, formerly East Lothian County Library
Enquiries to the District Librarian
Subject coverage
general

964 EAST MALLING RESEARCH STATION
East Malling, Maidstone, Kent ME19 6BJ Tel. 0732 843833
Research Institute, of the Agricultural Research Council; houses the Commonwealth Bureau of Horticulture and Plantation Crops, *q.v.*, and some Officers of the Agricultural Development and Advisory Service
Enquiries, library services, to the Librarian; scientific matters, to the Scientific Liaison Officer
Subject coverage
horticulture and plant sciences; fruit culture, including pomology, plant physiology, fruit nutrition, fruit storage; fruit breeding, plant pathology, entomology, plant protective chemistry; statistics; the Station's own research includes diseases of hops; the East Malling fruit-tree rootstocks
Publication
Annual Report

EAST OF SCOTLAND COLLEGE OF AGRICULTURE *see* **EDINBURGH SCHOOL OF AGRICULTURE**

EAST RIDING COLLEGE OF AGRICULTURE *see* **BISHOP BURTON COLLEGE OF AGRICULTURE**

EAST RIDING COUNTY LIBRARY *now* **NORTH YORKSHIRE COUNTY LIBRARY,** *q.v.*

EAST SHEEN DISTRICT LIBRARY *see* **RICHMOND UPON THAMES LIBRARIES SERVICE**

965 **EAST SUSSEX COUNTY LIBRARY**
Southdown House, 44 St. Annes Crescent, Lewes, East Sussex BN7 1SQ Tel. 079-16 5400
Telex 877515

Public Library; major libraries at Brighton, Eastbourne, Hastings and Hove, *qq.v.*

Enquiries to the Chief Librarian

Subject coverage
general

EAST SUSSEX SCHOOL OF AGRICULTURE *now* **PLUMPTON AGRICULTURAL COLLEGE,** *q.v.*

966 **EASTBOURNE CENTRAL PUBLIC LIBRARY**
Grove Road, Eastbourne, Sussex BN21 4TL Tel. 0323 22834
Public Library, part of East Sussex County Library

Enquiries to the Area Librarian

Subject coverage
general

Publication
Catalogue of the Local Collection

EASTLEIGH LIBRARY *see* **HAMPSHIRE COUNTY LIBRARY**

967 **EASTLEIGH TECHNICAL COLLEGE**
Cranbury Road, Eastleigh, Hampshire SO5 5HT Tel. 042-126 4444
Technical College

Enquiries to the Librarian

Subject coverage
general; economics; business studies; engineering and science

EBBW VALE DISTRICT LIBRARY *see* **GWENT COUNTY LIBRARY**

ECCLES CENTRAL AREA LIBRARY *see* **SALFORD CITY LIBRARIES**

968 **ECOLOGICAL ENGINEERING LIMITED**
Hulley Road, Macclesfield, Cheshire Tel. 0625 26238
Company (engineering and research)

Enquiries to the Sales Manager

Subject coverage
electrochemistry; electrochemical engineering; recovery of metals from solutions; treatment of metal-contaminated effluents; design and construction of electrochemical cells for organic synthesis, metal winning, etc.

Publications
catalogues

ECONOMIC ASSOCIATES LIMITED *see* **PRS GROUP LIMITED**

969 **ECONOMIC CONSULTANTS LIMITED**
36–38 West Street, London WC2H 9NA Tel. 01-836 7064
Telex 28604

Company/Consultancy

Enquiries to the Deputy Managing Director

Subject coverage
economic aspects of development, especially: industrial development and location; regional and urban planning; mineral and agricultural development; water and sewerage; transport; tourism; industrial product markets

970 ECONOMIC DEVELOPMENT COMMITTEE FOR FOOD AND DRINK MANUFACTURE
National Economic Development Office, Millbank Tower, Tel. 01-211 3577
21–41 Millbank, London SW1P 4QX
Tripartite Committee of the National Economic Development Council; formerly Economic Development Committee for the Food Manufacturing Industry

Enquiries to the Secretary

Subject coverage
general information on the food & drink industries

Publication
First Report to the Council (NEDO)

971 ECONOMIC DEVELOPMENT COMMITTEE FOR INTERNATIONAL FREIGHT MOVEMENT
National Economic Development Office, Millbank Tower, Tel. 01-211 3922
21–41 Millbank, London SW1P 4QX
Industrial Committee of the National Economic Development Council; formerly the Economic Development Committee for the Movement of Exports

Enquiries to the Secretary

Subject coverage
international movement of goods by all modes; representative interests of users and providers of transport facilities, the Unions concerned and the Government Departments

Publications
Committee studies, such as:
United Kingdom Air Cargo (1975)
Cut out Queues: vehicle appointment schemes (1974)
Packing for Profit (1973)
all available from NEDO Books

972 ECONOMIC DEVELOPMENT COMMITTEE FOR THE AGRICULTURE INDUSTRY
National Economic Development Office, Millbank Tower, Tel. 01-211 3000
21–41 Millbank, London SW1P 4QX
Industrial Committee of the National Economic Development Council

Enquiries to the Clerk (Tel. 01-211 3756)

Subject coverage
economic prospects and performance of the U.K. agricultural industry

Publications
Reports

973 ECONOMIC DEVELOPMENT COMMITTEE FOR THE BUILDING INDUSTRY
National Economic Development Office, Millbank Tower, Tel. 01-211 3000
21–41 Millbank, London SW1P 4QX
Industrial Committee of the National Economic Development Council

Enquiries to the Secretary

Subject coverage
economic forecasts; the industry's structure, productivity, markets, etc.

Publications
Construction Forecasts (2 per annum, on subscription)
Reports on research projects (list available)

974 ECONOMIC DEVELOPMENT COMMITTEE FOR THE CLOTHING INDUSTRY
National Economic Development Office, Millbank Tower, Tel. 01-211 5209 *or* 5709
21–24 Millbank, London SW1P 4QX
Industrial Committee of the National Economic Development Council

Enquiries to the Secretary

Subject coverage
economic, statistical and financial data; productivity; management of the clothing industry

Publications
Your Future in Clothing
Technology and the Garment Industry
Made to measure [guide to organizations providing research and management services to the industry]
Financial Tables for the Clothing Industry
For other publications and updating, see NEDO in Print

975 ECONOMIC DEVELOPMENT COMMITTEE FOR THE ELECTRICAL ENGINEERING INDUSTRY
National Economic Development Office, Millbank Tower, 21–41 Millbank, London SW1P 4QX — Tel. 01-211 6854
Industrial Committee of the National Economic Development Council

Enquiries to the Secretary

Subject coverage
electrical engineering products generally, including turbine generators; transformers and switchgear; electric motors; starting and control equipment; stand-by generators; domestic electrical equipment

976 ECONOMIC DEVELOPMENT COMMITTEE FOR THE HOTEL & CATERING INDUSTRY
National Economic Development Office, Millbank Tower, 21–41 Millbank, London SW1P 4QX — Tel. 01-211 3000
Industrial Committee of the National Economic Development Council

Enquiries to the Administrative Assistant (Tel. 01-211 7327)

Subject coverage
hotel and catering industry: manpower, hotel development, catering, investment, prospects for grants

Publications
This is the Hotels and Catering EDC
Manpower Policy in the Hotels and Catering Industry
Trends in Catering
Hotel Prospects to 1985
Catering Supply Industry
For other publications and updating, see NEDO in Print

ECONOMIC DEVELOPMENT COMMITTEE FOR THE MOVEMENT OF EXPORTS *now* **ECONOMIC DEVELOPMENT COMMITTEE FOR INTERNATIONAL FREIGHT MOVEMENT,** *q.v.*

977 ECONOMIC DEVELOPMENT COMMITTEE FOR THE RUBBER INDUSTRY
National Economic Development Office, Millbank Tower, 21–41 Millbank, London SW1P 4QX — Tel. 01-211 3000
Industrial Committee of the National Economic Development Council

Enquiries to the Secretary, Rubber Processing Sector Working Party

Subject coverage
rubber processing; plastics processing; synthetic rubber; plastics materials

978 ECONOMIC DEVELOPMENT COMMITTEE FOR THE WOOL TEXTILE INDUSTRY
National Economic Development Office, Millbank Tower, 21–24 Millbank, London SW1P 4QX — Tel. 01-211 4163
Industrial Committee of the National Economic Development Council

Enquiries to the Secretary

Subject coverage
economic, statistical and financial data; productivity; management of the wool textile industry

Publications
Noise Control in the Wool Textile Industry
U.K. Textile Industry 1968–70 (wall chart)

Employment Practices in EEC Textile Industries, 1973
Finance and Profitability in Wool Textile Industry, 1970/71, 1972/73, 1974/75
For other publications and updating, see NEDO in Print

979 ECONOMIC FORESTRY GROUP
Forestry House, Great Haseley, Oxford OX9 7PG Tel. 084-46 571/6
Telex 837410
Group of Companies, including units in Scotland and Wales, EFG (Nurseries) Ltd and EFG (Consultancy) Ltd; houses County Computer Centres (Oxford) Limited and Rural Planning Services Limited

Enquiries to the Group Secretary

Subject coverage
forestry and agriculture investment, consultancy, management and contracting; supply of forestry, farm and horticultural products

Publication
Group Magazine

980 ECONOMIC STUDY ASSOCIATION LIMITED
60 York Road, Acomb, Yorkshire YO2 5LW Tel. 0904 7191905
Company/Registered Charity

Enquiries to the Director

Subject coverage
national income and value-added analysis; public finance; employment; location

Publications
ESA Papers: no. 1, Enquiry into Prices and Incomes
no. 2, Local Government Finance
no. 3, Fanfare to Action
no. 4, Social Justice or Unbridled Government

981 ECONOMISTS ADVISORY GROUP
54b Tottenham Court Road, London W1P 9RE Tel. 01-323 4923
Partnership, unlimited liability

Enquiries to the Office Manager

Subject coverage
budgeting; business finance; econometrics; economics; financial analysis and management; forecasting; market research and consultancy; planning; programming; technology transfer studies

Publications
A series of business research studies (with the Financial Times)
Reports, at request of clients

982 EDINBURGH CITY LIBRARIES
George IV Bridge, Edinburgh EH1 1EG Tel. 031-225 5584
Public Library Service, formerly Edinburgh Public Libraries

Enquiries to the City Librarian

Subject coverage
advertising; architecture; engraving; industrial design; silverwork; local studies: banking; insurance; medicine; technology; science; transport; water supply

Special collections
British Cartographic Society Library, *q.v.*
Scottish Beekeepers Association, Moir Library, *q.v.*

EDINBURGH COLLEGE OF COMMERCE *now* **NAPIER COLLEGE OF COMMERCE AND TECHNOLOGY (Sighthill Court),** *q.v.*

983 EDINBURGH MATHEMATICAL SOCIETY
Department of Mathematics, University of Edinburgh, Edinburgh Tel. 031-667 1011
Learned Society

Enquiries to the Honorary Secretary

Subject coverage
pure and applied mathematics and the teaching thereof

Publication
Proceedings of the Edinburgh Mathematical Society

984 EDINBURGH SCHOOL OF AGRICULTURE
Edinburgh University, West Mains Road, Edinburgh EH9 3JG Tel. 031-667 1041
School of Agriculture and Advisory Service; combines the East of Scotland College of Agriculture and the Agriculture Department of the University of Edinburgh

Enquiries to the Librarian

Subject coverage
all aspects of agriculture excluding fisheries, particularly relating to the East of Scotland

Publications
Bulletins and Conference Reports
Advisory leaflets

985 EDINBURGH UNIVERSITY
Department of Forestry and Natural Resources and Molecular Biology Library, Kings Buildings, Mayfield Road, Edinburgh EH9 3JU Tel. 031-667 1011
University Departmental Library; housing the Library of the Royal Scottish Forestry Society

Enquiries to the Librarian

Subject coverage
forestry, ecology, wildlife management; fisheries research; land use; hydrology; agricultural economics; meteorology; climatology; biometeorology; molecular biology; molecular genetics, etc.; botany

Special collection
Thane Ringy Collection of Wildlife Management Papers

Publications
Lists of Research Projects
Current advances in Ecological Research (past interest)

986 EDINBURGH UNIVERSITY LIBRARY
George Square, Edinburgh EH8 9LJ Tel. 031-667 1011
University Main Library

Enquiries to the Librarian

Subject coverage
general and scientific

Special collections
Bruce Collection (oceanography)
Geikie Collection (geology)
Murray Collection (zoology, geography, geology)
Cleghorn Bequest (forestry)
Collection of 18th and 19th century books on agriculture
Royal Physical Society of Edinburgh Library
Theses from British and foreign Universities

Publications
Catalogue of the Printed Books in the Library of the University, 3 vols (to 1923)
Index to Manuscripts 2 vols
Inaugural Lectures
Publications on Science

EDINBURGH UNIVERSITY *see also*
EDINBURGH SCHOOL OF AGRICULTURE
ROYAL (DICK) SCHOOL OF VETERINARY STUDIES
SCOTTISH BUSINESS SCHOOL
UNIT OF ANIMAL GENETICS
WOLFSON MICROELECTRONICS LIAISON UNIT

EDMONTON MAIN LIBRARY *see* **ENFIELD LIBRARY SERVICE**

EDUCATIONAL CONTRACTORS GROUP *see* **BRITISH EDUCATIONAL EQUIPMENT ASSOCIATION LIMITED**

EDUCATIONAL EQUIPMENT ASSOCIATION *now* **BRITISH EDUCATIONAL EQUIPMENT ASSOCIATION LIMITED,** *q.v.*

EDUCATIONAL FILMS OF SCOTLAND *see* **SCOTTISH COUNCIL FOR EDUCATIONAL TECHNOLOGY**

987 EDWARDS HIGH VACUUM
Manor Royal, Crawley, West Sussex RH10 2LW — Tel. 0293 28844
Company; Subsidiary of BOC Limited

Enquiries to the Information Officer

Subject coverage
vacuum technology

988 EEC INFORMATION UNIT
Department of Industry, 1 Victoria Street, London SW1H 0ET — Tel. 01-215 4301
Information Unit for the Government Departments of Industry, Trade and Prices and Consumer Protection; formerly EFTA Information Centre and later the EFTA/EEC Information Unit

Enquiries to the Unit

Subject coverage
EEC aspects of all matters for which the above Government Departments are responsible

Publication
EEC – Your Questions Answered

EFTA INFORMATION CENTRE *now* **EEC INFORMATION UNIT** *q.v.*

989 EKCO INSTRUMENTS LIMITED
Ekco Works, Priory Crescent, Southend-on-Sea, Essex SS2 6PS — Tel. 0702 30851
Telex 99167
Company, formerly Ekco Electronics Limited; subsidiary of Pye of Cambridge Limited

Enquiries to the Director and General Manager, Marketing Manager, or Technical Sales Manager

Subject coverage
crane safety equipment

990 ELECTRIC BATTERY MANUFACTURERS ASSOCIATION
c/o Car Battery Service of Liverpool Limited, Wharf Road, Sale, Trafford MA33 2AF — Tel. 061-973 2232/3
Trade Association

Enquiries are not accepted from the public

Subject coverage
lead acid storage batteries; starting, lighting and ignition; stationary lighting; industrial/traction cells

991 ELECTRIC CABLE MAKERS CONFEDERATION
Regent Arcade House, 252–260 Regent House, London W1R 5DA Tel. 01-734 9651
Telex 24893

Trade Association

Enquiries to the Confederation

Subject coverage
manufacture of electric cables

ELECTRIC POWER STORAGE LIMITED *now* **CHLORIDE TECHNICAL LIMITED,** *q.v.*

992 ELECTRIC TRANSPORT DEVELOPMENT SOCIETY
37 Wellesley Road, Ilford IG1 4JX Tel. 01-554 2293
Professional Society; member of Transport 2000

Enquiries to the Honorary Secretary

Subject coverage
electric transport organization and operation; urban transport planning

Publication
News sheet

993 ELECTRIC VEHICLE ASSOCIATION OF GREAT BRITAIN
30 Millbank, London SW1P 4RD Tel. 01-834 2333
Telex 261130

Trade Association

Enquiries to the Secretary or Press Officer

Subject coverage
battery electric road vehicles; industrial trucks; batteries and chargers and ancillary equipment

Publications
Brochures on types of vehicles available, current developments, etc.

994 ELECTRICAL AND ELECTRONIC INSULATION ASSOCIATION
BEAMA, 8 Leicester Street, London WC2H 7BN Tel. 01-437 0678
Telex 263536

Trade Association; formerly the Insulation Section of BEAMA, *q.v.* and now one of the BEAMA federated companies

Enquiries to the Secretary

Subject coverage
electrical or electronic insulation

995 ELECTRICAL CONTRACTORS ASSOCIATION
ESCA House, 34 Palace Court, Bayswater, London W2 4HY Tel. 01-229 1266
Telex 27929

Trade Association; a merger of three former associations: Electrical Contractors Association, National Federated Electrical Association and NECTA Limited

Enquiries, normally from members only, to the Press and Information Officer

Subject coverage
electrical installation work

Publications
Electrical Contractor (monthly)
ECA Year Book Desk Diary

996 ELECTRICAL CONTRACTORS ASSOCIATION OF SCOTLAND
23 Heriot Row, Edinburgh EH3 6EW Tel. 031-225 7221/2/3
Trade Assocation

Enquiries to the Director

Subject coverage
industrial relations and employment matters; commercial and contractual matters; education and training; management; technical questions

Publications
Contract Manual
Quarterly Journal

997 ELECTRICAL INSTALLATION EQUIPMENT MANUFACTURERS ASSOCIATION
BEAMA, 8 Leicester Street, London WC2H 7BN Tel. 01-437 0678
Telex 263536
Trade Association; affiliated to British Electrical and Allied Manufacturers Association (BEAMA), *q.v.*
Enquiries to the Director
Subject coverage
electrical accessories; fuses; switch and fusegear, miniature, earth leakage and moulded case circuit-breakers

998 ELECTRICAL REMOTE CONTROL COMPANY LIMITED
P.O. Box 10, Bush Fair, Harlow, Essex CM18 6LZ Tel. 0279 24285
Telex 81284
Manufacturing Company
Enquiries, commercial, to the Sales Manger; technical, to the Director of Research and Engineering
Subject coverage
electro-mechanical, electronic, electro-pneumatic and pneumatic timing equipment; fixed installation and portable gas detectors; soldering irons including models with electronic temperature control
Publications
Catalogue
Installation and maintenance manuals

ELECTRICAL RESEARCH ASSOCIATION *now* **ERA LIMITED,** *q.v.*

ELECTRICAL WHOLESALERS FEDERATION *see* **FEDERATION OF WHOLESALE AND INDUSTRIAL DISTRIBUTORS**

999 ELECTRICITY COUNCIL INTELLIGENCE SECTION
30 Millbank, London SW1P 4RD Tel. 01-834 2333
Telex 23385
Central Council of a Nationalized Industry; Advisory Body to the Department of Energy
Enquiries to the Head of Intelligence; bibliographical requests to the Librarian
Subject coverage
administrative, commercial and economic aspects of electricity supply and utilisation; distribution engineering
Publications
Library Bulletin
Library Reading Lists
List of Periodicals
Select Abstracts Bulletins
Summaries of Reports of Major Interest
Bibliographies
Handbook of Electricity Supply Statistics (annual)

1000 ELECTRICITY COUNCIL MARKETING DEPARTMENT
Information Centre, 30 Millbank, London SW1P 4RD Tel. 01-834 2333 ext. 6297
Nationalised Industry Department; houses the Electric Vehicle Association of Great Britain and the British National Committee for Electroheat
Enquiries to the ECMD Information Centre

Subject coverage
industrial utilization of electricity; data on industrial electrical products, equipment and manufacturers

Publication
Catalogue of slides

1001 ELECTRICITY COUNCIL RESEARCH CENTRE
Capenhurst, Cheshire CH1 6ES Tel. 051-339 4181
Telex 627124

Nationalised Industry Research Centre

Enquiries to the Information Officer

Subject coverage
applications of electricity; distribution of electricity (132 kV and below)

1002 ELECTRICITY SUPPLY INDUSTRY COMMITTEE
The Electricity Council, 30 Millbank, London SW1P 4RD Tel. 01-834 2333
Telex 23385

Training Organization; formerly Electricity Supply Industry Training Board

Enquiries to the Secretary

Subject coverage
training recommendations and their implementation according to the requirements within the electricity supply industry

Publications
Training Recommendations
Bulletins

1003 ELECTRO-AUTOMAT LIMITED
104 Hazelhurst Road, Worsley, Manchester M28 4SP Tel. 061-794 4110
Company

Enquiries to the Director

Subject coverage
transformers and rectifiers; specialised electronic equipment

Publications
catalogues

1004 ELECTRONIC COMPONENTS BOARD
222 Regent Street, London W1R 5EE Tel. 01-437 4127
Trade Association; includes the Radio and Electronic Component Manufacturers Federation

Enquiries to the Secretary

Subject coverage
electronic components

1005 ELECTRONIC ENGINEERING ASSOCIATION
8 Leicester Street, London WC2H 7BN Tel. 01-437 0678
Telex 263536

Trade Association

Enquiries to the Information Officer

Subject coverage
capital electronic equipment and components industry for aviation/space, radio communication, computers, maritime purposes; legislation, design, education & training, standardization within the industry

Publications
Annual Report
Product Guide
Guides on new techniques or codes of practice

ELECTRONIC RENTALS ASSOCIATED LIMITED *now* **NATIONAL TELEVISION RENTAL ASSOCIATION LIMITED,** *q.v.*

ELECTROSTATIC PRECIPITATORS ASSOCIATION *now* **INDUSTRIAL GAS CLEANING ASSOCIATION,** *q.v.*

ELEY GAME CONSERVANCY STATION *now* **GAME CONSERVANCY,** *q.v.*

1006 ELGA PRODUCTS LIMITED
Lane End, High Wycombe, Buckinghamshire HP14 3JH Tel. 0494 881393
Company

Enquiries to the Publicity Manager

Subject coverage
water purification; deionisation and reverse osmosis

Publications
reprints on deionisation, reverse osmosis and applications for water purification in industry and research

1007 ELLESMERE PORT LIBRARY
Civic Way, Ellesmere Port, Cheshire L65 0BG Tel. 051-355 8101
Public Library, part of the Cheshire County Library *q.v.*

Enquiries to the Librarian

Subject coverage
civil engineering; industrial chemicals; oils and petroleum technology

ELLIOTT FLIGHT AUTOMATION *now* **MARCONI ELLIOTT AVIONIC SYSTEMS LIMITED, Rochester,** *q.v.*

ELMS TECHNICAL COLLEGE *see* **CAULDON COLLEGES OF FURTHER EDUCATION**

1008 ELSON AND ROBBINS LIMITED
Bennett Street, Long Eaton, Nottingham NG10 4HL Tel. 060 76 2225
Telex 37112

Public Company

Enquiries to the Director

Subject coverage
cellular plastics

Publications
Technical Bulletins 14 and 18 PVC Granules
Technical Bulletin 26 Hot Cured Moulded Urethane Foam
Data Sheets on Duflex vinyl foam and chipfoam; compress packaging; and foams for indoor bowling rinks

ELTON LIBRARY *see* **OXFORD UNIVERSITY Elton Library**

1009 EMI LIMITED
Blyth Road, Hayes, Middlesex UB3 1BP Tel. 01-573 3888
Company, for research, design and development; formerly E.M.I. Electronics Limited; also at Victoria Road, Feltham, Middlesex

Enquiries to the Information Assistant or Librarian, preferably by letter

Subject coverage
electronics; physics, particularly of electricity; analytical chemistry; properties of materials; data processing; computers and related mathematical techniques; sound production; medical electronics

EMPLOYMENT AGENTS FEDERATION *now* **FEDERATION OF PERSONNEL SERVICES OF GREAT BRITAIN**

1010 EMPLOYMENT MEDICAL ADVISORY SERVICE
Health and Safety Executive, Baynards House, Chepstow Place, London W2 4TF — Tel. 01-229 3456 ext. 14
Government Department, formerly Medical Services Division of the Department of Employment

Enquiries to the Advisory Service D

Subject coverage
occupational medicine, hygiene and safety; industrial diseases

Publications
are listed in the HMSO Sectional List no. 18

ENFIELD COLLEGE OF TECHNOLOGY *now* **MIDDLESEX POLYTECHNIC,** *q.v.*

1011 ENFIELD LIBRARY SERVICE
Central Library, Cecil Road, Enfield, Middlesex EN2 6TW — Tel. 01-366 2244
Public Library Service; District Libraries at Edmonton, and Palmers Green

Enquiries to the Director of Libraries

Subject coverage
general

1012 ENGINEERING AND BUILDING CENTRE
Broad Street, Birmingham B1 2DB — Tel. 021-643 1914, Telex 336701

Permanent Exhibition Centre

Enquiries to the Chief, Information Service

Subject coverage
mechanical and production engineering; building construction industry and materials

ENGINEERING AND POWER DEVELOPMENT CONSULTANTS LIMITED *now* **BALFOUR BEATTY ENGINEERING LIMITED,** *q.v.*

ENGINEERING AND RESOURCES CONSULTANTS LIMITED *see* **SOIL MECHANICS LIMITED**

1013 ENGINEERING EMPLOYERS ASSOCIATION OF SOUTH WALES
2 Stanwell Road, Penarth, South Glamorgan CF6 2YH — Tel. 0222 708632/4, 0222 703934

Trade Association

Enquiries to the Association

Subject coverage
industrial relations

1014 ENGINEERING EMPLOYERS FEDERATION
Broadway House, Tothill Street, London SW1H 9NQ — Tel. 01-930 6314
Employers Organization

Enquiries, limited, to the Public Relations Department

Subject coverage
engineering industry employment terms and conditions

Publications
Annual Review
Annual Economic Report
Monthly Newsletter

1015 ENGINEERING EMPLOYERS NORTHERN IRELAND ASSOCIATION
451 Antrim Road, Belfast BT15 3BJ — Tel. 0232 779358/9
Employers Association, member of the Engineering Employers Federation

Enquiries to the Secretary

Subject coverage
engineering industry industrial relations; all aspects of engineering employment, conditions, negotiations

1016 ENGINEERING EQUIPMENT USERS ASSOCIATION
20 Grosvenor Place, London SW1X 7HZ Tel. 01-235 5316/7
Trade Association

Enquiries to the Director

Subject coverage
mechanical, chemical, instrumentation, control equipments

Publications
EEUA Publications Lists
Technical Handbooks and Documents
Rules
Details of suppliers, etc.

1017 ENGINEERING INDUSTRIES ASSOCIATION
Equitable House, Lyon Road, Harrow, Middlesex HA1 2HG Tel. 01-863 9188
Trade Association; also administering the Mechanical Handling Engineers Association as a Special Product Group

Enquiries, generally from members, to the Secretary

Subject coverage
engineering industry

1018 ENGINEERING INDUSTRY ASSOCIATION
Confederation House, Kildare Street, Dublin 2 Tel. Dublin 779801
Telex E14711
Trade Association

Enquiries to the Librarian

Subject coverage
engineering industry in Ireland

1019 ENGINEERING INDUSTRY TRAINING BOARD
54 Clarendon Road, Watford, Hertfordshire WD1 1LB Tel 92 38441
Training Board, of the Training Services Agency, *q.v.* Manpower Services Commission

Enquiries to the Librarian

Subject coverage
industrial training; engineering industry

Publications
list available

1020 ENGINEERING RESEARCH AND APPLICATION LIMITED
London Road, Dunstable, Bedfordshire LU6 3UR Tel. 0582 62301
Company, subsidiary of Zenith Carburettor Company Limited

Enquiries to the Director

Subject coverage
carburettor technology; petrol engine exhaust emission control; petrol engine design

1021 ENGINEERING SCIENCES DATA UNIT LIMITED
251–259 Regent Street, London W1R 7AD Tel. 01-437 4894
Telex 916168
Company, owned by the Royal Aeronautical Society, and operated in association with the Institutions of Chemical, Mechanical and Structural Engineers; a marketing unit operates from 34 Haymarket, London SW1Y 4HZ

Enquiries to the Head of External Affairs

Subject coverage
aeronautical, chemical, mechanical and structural engineering; particularly aerodynamics, acoustic fatigue, dynamics, fatigue, fluid mechanics; heat transfer, machine design, noise, performance of aircraft; transonic aerodynamics; wind properties and loading; hydrodynamics; stress analysis, welding

Publications
Data Items
ESDU Index (annual)

ENGINEERS HAND TOOL ASSOCIATION *see* **FEDERATION OF BRITISH HAND TOOL MANUFACTURERS**

ENGINEERS REGISTRATION BOARD *see* **COUNCIL OF ENGINEERING INSTITUTIONS**

1022 ENGLISH CLAYS LOVERING POCHIN & COMPANY LIMITED
Research Department, John Keay House, St Austell, Cornwall Tel. 0726 2381
Telex 45526/7
Company; four autonomous information centres within the Research Department: corporate planning, exploration, overseas and engineering

Enquiries to the Director

Subject coverage
statistics; economics; geology; engineering; chemistry; physics; rheology; ceramics; mining; mineralogy; paper; print; clay science and technology

Publication
Monitor (quarterly, technical marketing review)

ENGLISH COUNTRY CHEESE COUNCIL *see* **NATIONAL MILK PUBLICITY COUNCIL**

ENGLISH ELECTRIC LIMITED *now* **GEC POWER ENGINEERING LIMITED.** *q.v.*

ENGLISH ELECTRIC DIESELS LIMITED *now* **RUSTON DIESELS LIMITED,** *q.v.*

1023 ENGLISH INDUSTRIAL ESTATES CORPORATION
Kingsway, Team Valley, Gateshead, Tyne and Wear NE11 0NA Tel. 0632 876071
Telex 53645
Statutory Corporation under the Department of Industry

Enquiries to the Public Relations Officer

Subject coverage
industrial estates, their layout and factory buildings

1024 ENGLISH SEWING LIMITED
Thread Division, 56 Oxford Street, Manchester M60 1HJ Tel. 061-228 1144
Telex 667791

Company, subsidiary of the Tootal Group

Enquiries to the Technical Information Officer

Subject coverage
properties of all types of sewing threads and their use in all industries

1025 ENGLISH TOURIST BOARD
4 Grosvenor Gardens, London SW1 0DU Tel. 01-730 3400
Telex 919041

Government Department

Enquiries to the Correspondence Department on English holidays, etc.; the Library does not deal with outside enquiries

Subject coverage
development, promotion and improvement of tourism; financing of tourist projects; research and planning; publicity; hotel registration

Special collections
ETB Information Library
ETB Research Library (includes statistics)

Publications
Tourism in England (quarterly)
Publications Information Sheet available

1026 ENGLISH VINEYARDS ASSOCIATION LIMITED
York House, 199 Westminster Bridge Road, London SE1
Trade Association; affiliated to the Agricultural Cooperative Association

Enquiries, by letter, to the Secretary, The Vineyards, Cricks Green, Felsted, Essex CM6 3JT

Subject coverage
cultivation of vines in England

Publications
Annual News Journal
Information Leaflets (to members only)

1027 ENVIRONMENT ANALYSIS LIMITED
Commercial Road, Bromborough, Wirral, Cheshire — Tel. 051-334 2643
Company

Enquiries to the Director

Subject coverage
organic and inorganic analysis; mass spectroscopy; gas chromatography; environment analysis, i.e. air and water pollution, etc.; asbestos and dust measurement; geochemical analysis, specifically North Sea Basin; isotopic analysis for geochemical and geological functions; high pressure liquid chromatography

1028 ENVIRONMENTAL HAZARDS UNIT
St Bartholomew's Hospital Medical College, Charterhouse Square, London EC1M 6BQ
Government Research Unit, of the Medical Research Council; formerly Air Pollution Research Unit

Enquiries to the Librarian/Information Officer

Subject coverage
medical aspects of air pollution and of other environmental hazards

Publications
List of publications
List of publications suitable for school projects

1029 ENVIRONMENTAL HEALTH OFFICERS ASSOCIATION
19 Grosvenor Place, London SW1X 7HU — Tel. 01-235 5158
Professional Association; formerly Association of Public Health Inspectors

Enquiries to the Secretary; this service is mainly for members, but may be extended to others in special cases

Subject coverage
environmental health; food safety and hygiene; noise; air pollution; housing; health and safety

Publications
Environmental health reports

1030 ENVIRONMENTAL RESOURCES LIMITED
35a Thayer Street, London W1M 5LH — Tel. 01-486 8277
Telex 21879/25247

Consulting Company

Enquiries to the Managing Director or Research Director

Subject coverage
environment and pollution (air, water, noise, land); pollution control technology and economics; waste disposal technology and economics; resource recovery and product planning

1031 EQUINE RESEARCH STATION
Animal Health Trust, Balaton Lodge, Snailwell Road, Newmarket, Suffolk CB8 7DW — Tel. 0638 2241
Private Research Laboratory, of the Animal Health Trust *q.v.*

Enquiries to the Director

Subject coverage
study of the health and wellbeing of horses; the only U.K. laboratory devoted solely to that study, which includes haematology, immunology, clinical chemistry, microbiology, mycology, pathology, radiography, surgery and epidemiology; research upon and provision of haematological standards

Publications
Annual Report
Animal Health (two issues per annum)

EQUIPMENT LEASING ASSOCIATION LIMITED *see* **FINANCE HOUSES ASSOCIATION LIMITED**

1032 ERA LIMITED
Cleeve Road, Leatherhead, Surrey KT22 7SA — Tel. 53 74151
Research Association; formerly the Electrical Research Association; houses the National Terotechnology Centre, *q.v.*

Enquiries to the Information Officer or Librarian

Subject coverage
electrical machines; power systems; cables; thermal engineering; switch and control gear; electrochemistry; power control; electronics; materials science; metallurgy; computers and automation; computer systems and operation

Publications
News of ERA
List of published reports
List of ongoing projects
Translations List

1033 ERGONOMICS INFORMATION ANALYSIS CENTRE
Department of Engineering Production, Birmingham University, P.O. Box 363, Birmingham B15 2TT — Tel. 021-472 1301 ext. 2731
University Department

Enquiries to the Information Officer

Subject coverage
ergonomics; human factors

Publications
Ergonomics Abstracts (quarterly)
Specialised Bibliographies (list of some 90 titles is available)

1034 ERGONOMICS RESEARCH SOCIETY
Ergonomics Branch, Institute of Occupational Medicine, c/o National Coal Board, Mining Research and Development Establishment, Ashby Road, Stanhope Bretby, Burton-on-Trent, Staffordshire DE15 0QD — Tel. 0283 216161, Telex 341741
Professional Society

Enquiries to the Honorary General Secretary

Subject coverage
ergonomics and human factors; work design; environmental science; equipment design

Publications
Ergonomics (quarterly)
Applied Ergonomics (quarterly)
Ergonomic Abstracts (quarterly)

ERIC MENSFORTH LIBRARY *see* **SHEFFIELD CITY POLYTECHNIC**

1035 ESSEX COUNTY LIBRARY
Goldlay Gardens, Chelmsford, Essex CM2 0EW — Tel. 0245 51141, Telex 99223

Public Library system; its Technical Library Service is the Headquarters for the Co-operative Information Service for firms in Essex; agency libraries at Chelmsford, Chigwell, Colchester, and Southend

Enquiries to the Librarian or Information Officer

Subject coverage
specialisation in chemistry; metallurgy

Special collections
British, American and German Standards
Workshop Manuals
Extel cards

Publication
Union List of Serials

ESSEX INSTITUTE OF AGRICULTURE *now* **WRITTLE AGRICULTURAL COLLEGE,** *q.v.*

1036 ESSEX TECHNICAL AND COMMERCIAL LIBRARY SERVICE
County Library Headquarters, Goldlay Gardens, Chelmsford, Essex CM2 0EW — Tel. 0245 51141, Telex 99223
Interlibrary Cooperative Scheme

Enquiries to the County Librarian

Subject coverage
Technical and commercial; statistics

Special collections
British Standards and Government Department Standards
DIN Standards (in English translation)

Publications
Essex Union List of Periodicals (six-monthly)

1037 ESSEX UNIVERSITY LIBRARY
P.O. Box 24, Wivenhoe Park, Colchester CO4 3UA — Tel. 0206 44144, Telex 98440

University Library

Enquiries to the Librarian

Subject coverage
biology; chemistry; electrical engineering; mathematics; computing science

1038 ESSO CHEMICAL LIMITED
Arundel Towers, Portland Terrace, Southampton SO9 2GW — Tel. 0703 34191, Telex 47437

Manufacturing and Marketing Company, part of Exxon Chemical Company, which in turn is a subsidiary of Exxon Corporation (US)

Enquiries to the Information Officer

Subject coverage
petrochemicals and downstream industries, i.e. plastics, synthetic fibres, synthetic rubbers

1039 ESSO PETROLEUM COMPANY LIMITED
Victoria Street, London SW1E 5JW Tel. 01-834 6677
Company; wholly-owned subsidiary of Exxon Corporation (US)
Enquiries to the Information and Library Service
Subject coverage
oil industry, management, economics, planning and marketing; North Sea exploration; history of the oil industry

1040 ESSO PETROLEUM COMPANY LIMITED
Esso Refinery, Fawley, Southampton SO4 1TX Tel. 0703 892511
Telex 24942
Company, subsidiary of Exxon Corporation (US)
No enquiry service
Subject coverage
oil refining

1041 EURISOL - UK (ASSOCIATION OF BRITISH MANUFACTURERS OF MINERAL INSULATING FIBRES)
7 Montagu Mansions, London W1H 1LD Tel. 01-935 5492
Trade Association, affiliated to EURIMA/European Insulation Manufacturers Association, Denmark
Enquiries to the Secretary-General or the Information Officer
Subject coverage
thermal and sound insulation of buildings of all types, with particular reference to energy conservation
Publications
Newsletters on insulation topics

1042 EUROLEC
Little Waltham, Chelmsford, Essex CM3 3NU Tel. 0245 360344
Publishing Company, formerly David Rayner Associates
Enquiries to the Manager
Subject coverage
electronics industry in the U.K.
Publications
Electronic Components on offer in the U.K. (7th ed.)
Communications Equipment on offer in the U.K. (in preparation)
Directories of electronic manufacturers and instrument manufacturers

EUROPEAN ASSOCIATION OF FIRE ALARM MANUFACTURERS *see* **BRITISH FIRE PROTECTION SYSTEMS ASSOCIATION LIMITED**

EUROPEAN ASSOCIATION OF MANUFACTURERS OF BUSINESS MACHINES AND DATA PROCESSING *see* **BUSINESS EQUIPMENT TRADE ASSOCIATION**

EUROPEAN BUTTON INDUSTRIES FEDERATION *see* **BRITISH BUTTON MANUFACTURERS ASSOCIATION**

EUROPEAN CARAVAN FEDERATION *see* **NATIONAL CARAVAN COUNCIL LIMITED**

EUROPEAN CELL BIOLOGY ORGANIZATION *see* **BRITISH SOCIETY FOR CELL BIOLOGY**

1043 EUROPEAN COLLEGE OF MARKETING AND MARKETING RESEARCH
9 Aston Road, Nuneaton, Warwickshire Tel. 0682 67161
Training and Educational Foundation; part of the European Marketing Association
Enquiries to the Director

Subject coverage
marketing; marketing research

Publications
Manual of Industrial Marketing Research
Sampling in Industrial Markets
Statistical Forecasting Techniques
Marketing Intelligence

EUROPEAN COMMITTEE OF PAINT, PRINTING INK AND ARTISTS COLOURS MANUFACTURERS ASSOCIATIONS *see* **SOCIETY OF BRITISH PRINTING MANUFACTURERS**

EUROPEAN ECONOMIC COMMUNITY *see* **EEC**

1044 EUROPEAN FEDERATION OF DAIRY RETAILERS
20 Eastbourne Terrace, London W2 6LE Tel. 01-262 6722
Telex 262027

Trade Association; formerly based in Germany; member of the European Committee of Traders, Brussels and of the International Confederation of Dairy Retailers

Enquiries to the General Secretary

Subject coverage
European and EEC consultation upon dairy industry matters

EUROPEAN FEDERATION OF FINANCIAL ANALYSTS SOCIETIES *see* **SOCIETY OF INVESTMENT ANALYSTS**

EUROPEAN FEDERATION OF IMPORTERS OF OFFICE MACHINES *see* **BUSINESS EQUIPMENT TRADE ASSOCIATION**

EUROPEAN FEDERATION OF NATIONAL MAINTENANCE SOCIETIES *see* **BRITISH COUNCIL OF MAINTENANCE ASSOCIATIONS**

EUROPEAN FREE TRADE AREA *now* **EEC,** *q.v.*

EUROPEAN GLASS CONTAINER MANUFACTURERS ASSOCIATION *see* **GLASS MANUFACTURERS FEDERATION**

1045 EUROPEAN INDUSTRIAL MARKETING RESEARCH SOCIETY
9 Aston Road, Nuneaton, Worcester CV11 5EL Tel. 0682 67161

Professional Association; part of the European Marketing Association, *q.v.*, corporate member of the Conseil Européen pour le Marketing and the Commission Internationale de Marketing; affiliated to the International Market Research Association; comprises the European College of Marketing and Marketing Research

Enquiries to the Regional Director

Subject coverage
industrial marketing research; market intelligence

Publications
European Marketing Newsletter
Marketing Intelligence Service
see also the European Marketing Association's publications

1046 EUROPEAN MARKETING ASSOCIATION
9 Aston Road, Nuneaton, Warwickshire CV11 5EL Tel. 0682 67161

Professional Association; formerly European Association for Industrial Marketing and Marketing Management; houses the European College of Marketing and Marketing Research

Enquiries to the Regional Director

Subject coverage
marketing research, management and training

Publications
Journal of International Marketing and Marketing Research
International Marketing Directory
Directory and Year Book of Industrial Marketing Research in Europe

EUROPEAN STEEL OFFICE FURNITURE FEDERATION *see* **BUSINESS EQUIPMENT TRADE ASSOCIATION**

1047 EUROPEAN TAPE INDUSTRY ASSOCIATION
8 St. Bride Street, London EC4A 4DA Tel. 01-353 3020
Telex 24276

Trade Association; formerly British Tape Industry Association

Enquiries to the Secretary

Subject coverage
blank tape

EUROPEAN TRADE UNION CONFEDERATION *see* **TRADES UNION CONGRESS**

1048 EVANS, ADLARD & COMPANY LIMITED
Postlip Mills, Winchcombe, Cheltenham, Gloucestershire GL54 5BB Tel. 0242 602227
Telex 43316

Company, part of Imperial Group

Enquiries to the Technical Director

Subject coverage
production of high quality technical papers

1049 EVANS MEDICAL LIMITED
Speke, Liverpool L24 9JD Tel. 051-486 1881
Telex 62673

Company, part of the Glaxo Group Limited; formerly Evans Medical Research Laboratories

Enquiries to the Librarian

Subject coverage
pharmacy; virology; veterinary science; biological sciences; chemistry; medicine

1050 EVER READY COMPANY (HOLDINGS) LIMITED
Central Laboratories, St Ann's Road, London N15 3TJ Tel. 01-800 1101
Telex 261070

Company

Enquiries to the Information Officer

Subject coverage
primary and rechargeable electrochemical power sources; battery materials and components; battery applications

EWELL BRANCH LIBRARY *see* **SURREY COUNTY LIBRARY**

EWELL COUNTY TECHNICAL COLLEGE *now* **NORTH EAST SURREY COLLEGE OF TECHNOLOGY,** *q.v.*

1051 EXCHEQUER AND AUDIT DEPARTMENT
Audit House, Victoria Embankment, London EC4Y 0DS Tel. 01-353 8901
Government Department

Enquiries to the Information Services

Subject coverage
audit of Government accounts

1052 EXECUTIVE AND OPERATIVE TRAINING ASSOCIATES
80 Whitelands Avenue, Chorleywood, Nr Rickmansworth, Hertfordshire WD3 5RG — Tel. 260 2878
Company

Enquiries to the Senior Consultant

Subject coverage
human resources problems, *e.g.* recruitment, training, industrial relations, organisation development, manpower planning, retirements

1053 EXETER CENTRAL LIBRARY
Castle Street, Exeter, Devonshire EX4 3PQ — Tel. 0392 73047, Telex 42691
Public Library; the East Devon Area Library of the Devon Library Services; formerly Exeter City Library

Enquiries to the Area Librarian

Subject coverage
general

Special collections
Bequest of early shorthand books
British Standards

1054 EXHIBITIONS BULLETIN
London Bureau, 226–272 Kirkdale, London SE26 4RZ — Tel. 01-778 2888
Company

Enquiries to the Information Officer

Subject coverage
world trade fairs and exhibitions

Publication
Exhibition Bulletin (monthly)

1055 EXPANDED POLYSTYRENE PRODUCT MANUFACTURERS ASSOCIATION
1 Keymer Road, Hassocks, West Sussex BN6 8AE — Tel. 07918 5568
Trade Association; member of the British Plastics Federation, *q.v.*

Enquiries to the Technical Director, Advisory Service Centre

Subject coverage
packaging; D-I-Y; construction (insulation); expanded polystyrene

EXPLOSIVES INSPECTORATE *see* **HEALTH AND SAFETY EXECUTIVE**

1056 EXPLOSIVES RESEARCH AND DEVELOPMENT ESTABLISHMENT
Powdermill Lane, Waltham Abbey, Essex EN9 1BP — Tel. 0992 713030, Telex 267455
Government Department, of the Procurement Executive, Ministry of Defence; formerly of the Ministry of Aviation, and before that, of the Ministry of Technology

Enquiries to the Director, by letter only

Subject coverage
explosives; propellants; materials; chemistry

Special collection
History of gunpowder and early explosives

1057 EXPORT CREDITS GUARANTEE DEPARTMENT
Aldermanbury House, Aldermanbury, London EC2P 2EL — Tel. 01-606 6699, Telex 883601

Government Department, responsible to Secretary of State for Trade

Enquiries to the Information Officer, Publicity Branch

Subject coverage
export credits insurance; overseas investments insurance; export finance guarantees for banks

Publications
Booklets on ECGD services
Leaflets on various facilities

1058 EXPORT INTELLIGENCE SERVICE (EIS)
Export House, 50 Ludgate Hill, London EC4M 7HU — Tel. 01-248 5757
Telex 886143

Information service, of the British Overseas Trade Board, Department of Trade, and a Section of the Export Data Branch of the Export Services and Promotions Division

Enquiries, EIS subscriptions and accounts, to the Service, ext. 7118; alterations to subscribers' requirements to ext. 610; other enquiries to extensions 7016, 7017, 7025

Subject coverage
computer-based selective export information for British exporters on opportunities overseas

Publications
EIS Selective Card Service
Daily Gazette
World Economic Comments (quarterly)

1059 EXPORT SERVICES AND PROMOTIONS DIVISION
Department of Trade, Export House, 50 Ludgate Hill, London EC4M 7HU — Tel. 01-248 5757
Telex 886143

Government Department, under the direction of the British Overseas Trade Board; formerly Export Services Branch; includes the Fairs and Promotions Branch, *and* the Overseas Tariffs and Regulations Section

Enquiries to the Head of the Division, London or regional offices

Subject coverage
exporting

EXPORT SERVICES AND PROMOTIONS DIVISION *see also*
EXPORT INTELLIGENCE SERVICE
FAIRS AND PROMOTIONS BRANCH
OVERSEAS TARIFFS AND REGULATIONS SECTION
STATISTICS AND MARKET INTELLIGENCE LIBRARY

1060 EXPORTS TO JAPAN UNIT
Department of Trade, Hillgate House, 26 Old Bailey, London EC4M 7HU — Tel. 01-248 5757 (exts. 613 and 7162)
Telex 886143

Branch of the Government-sponsored British Overseas Trade Board, *q.v.*

Enquiries to the Unit

Subject coverage
the Japanese market in general and specialized sections of that market; advice on approaching and tackling the Japanese market

Publications
Commissioned Market Research Reports (mainly in connection with officially-sponsored exhibitions in Tokyo)
Tokyo market Research Reports
Trading with Japan (booklets)

1061 EXTEL STATISTICAL SERVICES LIMITED
37–45 Paul Street, London EC2A 4PB — Tel. 01-253 4500
Telex 23721

Company, subsidiary of Exchange Telegraph Company (Holdings) Limited

Enquiries to the Sales Office

Subject coverage
information on U.K. and foreign companies, quoted and unquoted; dividends; capital issues; analyses and comparisons; international bonds; etc

Special collection
Ten-year files of company reports and accounts

Publications
Card services, home and overseas, giving information on above subjects and related affairs
Annual and other books in similar subjects

FACTORY INSPECTORATE *see* **HEALTH AND SAFETY EXECUTIVE**

1062 FACULTY OF ACTUARIES IN SCOTLAND
23 St. Andrews Square, Edinburgh EH2 1AQ Tel. 031-556 6791
Professional Body

Enquiries to the Secretary

Subject coverage
actuarial science, studies and research

Publication
Transactions of the Faculty of Actuaries

1063 FACULTY OF ARCHITECTS AND SURVEYORS LIMITED
68 Gloucester Place, London W1H 3HL Tel. 01-935 9966
Professional Association; with which the Institute of Registered Architects merged in 1974

Enquiries to the Secretary
Subject coverage
architecture and surveying

Publication
Portico (quarterly, to members and others)

1064 FACULTY OF BUILDING
10 Manor Way, Boreham Wood, Hertfordshire WD6 1QQ Tel. 01-953 7053
Multi-professional Society; eleven regional branches

Enquiries to the Secretary

Subject coverage
There are one hundred and seven technical advice panels covering a very wide range of building and civil engineering, and related subjects, including for example acoustics, asphalt technology, bridge construction, building construction and maintenance, ceramics, contract law and procedure, demolition, district and group heating, drainage, gas engineering and technology, geodetic engineering, lift installation, materials handling, testing and purchasing, piling, quarrying, sewerage technology, timber technology

Publications
Register of members
Newsletter
Annual Lectures, etc.

1065 FACULTY OF THE BUILT ENVIRONMENT
Polytechnic of the South Bank, Wandsworth Road, London SW8 2JZ Tel. 01-928 8989 ext. 7158
Higher Education Establishment; formerly Brixton School of Building

Enquiries to the Faculty Librarian

Subject coverage
architecture; town planning; civil and structural engineering; land surveying; building construction; land and building economics; estate management; interior design

1066 FAIREY SURVEYS LIMITED
Reform Road, Maidenhead, Berkshire SL6 8BU Tel. 0628 21371
Telex 847352
Company, part of the Fairey Company Limited; branches in Livingston, West Lothian, Scotland and Dublin, Ireland

Enquiries to the Commercial Manager

Subject coverage
aerial and ground surveys; photogrammetric mapping; orthophotography; terrain modelling; resource surveys; airborne geophysics; cartographic and reprographic services

Special collection
Film library

Publications
Company brochures and leaflets
Project Lists
Newsletters

FAIRS AND PROMOTIONS BRANCH *see* **EXPORT SERVICES AND PROMOTIONS DIVISION**

1067 FALKIRK COLLEGE OF TECHNOLOGY
Grangemouth Road, Falkirk FK2 9AD Tel. 0324 24981
College of Technology; formerly Falkirk Technical College

Enquiries to the College Librarian

Subject coverage
automobile, construction and building, electrical and electronic, foundry, mechanical, plant, and mining engineering; chemistry; food technology; health; business studies; management; computer studies

1068 FALKIRK DISTRICT DEPARTMENT OF LIBRARIES AND MUSEUMS
Hope Street, Falkirk FK1 5AU Tel. 0324 24911
Public Libraries; formerly Falkirk Public Library

Enquiries to the Librarian

Subject coverage
general

1069 FARADAY DIVISION OF THE CHEMICAL SOCIETY
Chemical Society, Burlington House, London W1V 0BN Tel. 01-734 9971
Telex 268001
Learned society, formerly the Faraday Society

Enquiries to the Assistant Secretary

Subject coverage
physical chemistry, including electrochemistry; sciences lying between chemistry, physics, and biology

Publications
Faraday Discussions (biannually)
Faraday Symposia (annually)
Faraday Transactions of the Chemical Society I and II (monthly)

FARADAY SOCIETY *now* **FARADAY DIVISION OF THE CHEMICAL SOCIETY,** *q.v.*

FAREHAM DISTRICT LIBRARY *see* **HAMPSHIRE COUNTY LIBRARY**

1070 FARM BUILDINGS INFORMATION CENTRE
National Agricultural Centre, Stoneleigh, Kenilworth, Warwickshire CV8 2LG Tel. 0203 22345/6
Information Service/Publishing Company

Enquiries to the Secretary, primarily from subscribers

Subject coverage
economics, layout, design, materials and construction of farm buildings, equipment and machinery

Publications
Farm Buildings Digest (quarterly)
Infill (newsletter)
Progress (quarterly, published by Scottish Farm Buildings Investigation Unit)

1071 FARMERS UNION OF WALES
Llys Amaeth, Queens Square, Aberystwyth, Dyfed SY23 2EA — Tel. 0970 2755
Agricultural Union

Enquiries to the Information Officer

Subject coverage
agriculture in Wales; farming, land use, etc.

Publication
Y Tir and Welsh Farmers (journal)

1072 FARMING AND WILDLIFE ADVISORY GROUP
The Lodge, Sandy, Bedfordshire SG19 2DL — Tel. 0767 80551
Independent Group

Enquiries to the Adviser

Subject coverage
management of natural habitats on farmland, related to progressive and profitable farming and land-owning

1073 FARNBOROUGH LIBRARY
Pinehurst Avenue, Farnborough, Hampshire GU14 7JZ — Tel. 0252 513838, Telex 858695

Public Library; Branch of Hampshire County Library, *q.v.*

Enquiries to the Librarian

Subject coverage
general; British aviation

FARNWORTH PUBLIC LIBRARY *see* **BOLTON METROPOLITAN BOROUGH CENTRAL LIBRARY**

1074 FAST ACCESS INFORMATION RETRIEVAL [Project FAIR]
Bioengineering Division, Clinical Research Centre, Watford Road, Harrow, Middlesex HA1 3UJ — Tel. 01-864 5311 ext. 2500 *or* 2847, Telex 923410
Information Centre, of Research Centre, of the Medical Research Council

Enquiries to the Information Officer (fees chargeable)

Subject coverage
bioengineering; medical engineering; medical instrumentation

Publications
BECAN—Biomedical Engineering Current Awareness Notification (bi-weekly)
IRBEL—Indexed References to Biomedical Engineering Literature, 1968— (annual subscription; booklets each of 640 numbered references; subject index on punched feature cards)
Bibliographies (50 titles)

1075 FASTENERS AND TURNED PARTS INSTITUTE
136 Hagley Road, Edgbaston, Birmingham B16 9PN — Tel. 021-454 4141
Trade Association

Enquiries to the Secretary

Subject coverage
fasteners turned from the bar; turned parts

1076 FAUNA PRESERVATION SOCIETY
Zoological Society of London, Regents Park, London NW1 4RY Tel. 01-586 0872
Voluntary Society

Enquiries to the Honorary Secretary

Subject coverage
wildlife conservation, especially of endangered species

FEDERATION OF AGRICULTURAL COOPERATIVES (UK) LIMITED *see* **AGRICULTURAL COOPERATION AND MARKETING SERVICES LIMITED**

FEDERATION OF ASSOCIATIONS OF SPECIALISTS AND SUB-CONTRACTORS *see*
MASTIC ASPHALT COUNCIL AND EMPLOYERS FEDERATION
NATIONAL FEDERATION OF ROOFING CONTRACTORS
NATIONAL FEDERATION OF TERRAZZO-MOSAIC SPECIALISTS

FEDERATION OF BRITISH CARPET MANUFACTURERS *now* **BRITISH CARPET MANUFACTURERS ASSOCIATION** *q.v.*

FEDERATION OF BRITISH FIRE ORGANISATIONS *see*
BRITISH FIRE SERVICES ASSOCIATION
INSTITUTION OF FIRE ENGINEERS

1077 FEDERATION OF BRITISH HAND TOOL MANUFACTURERS
Light Trades House, Melbourne Avenue, Sheffield S10 2QJ Tel. 0742 663084
Telex 54208
Trade Association; comprising Engineers Hand Tool Association, File Association, Horticultural and Contractors Tool Association, Power Actuated Systems Association, Saw Association, *q.v.*

Enquiries to the Federation

Subject coverage
hand tools industry; trade marks; supply sources; production; exports and imports

Publication
British Tools Directory

1078 FEDERATION OF BRITISH MANUFACTURERS OF SPORTS AND GAMES LIMITED
145 Oxford Street, London W1R 1TB Tel. 01-437 7281
Trade Association, housing also the British Association of Fishing Tackle Makers and Distributors, *q.v.*, and the Golf Ball Manufacturers Conference

Enquiries to the General Secretary

Subject coverage
sports manufacturers

1079 FEDERATION OF BRITISH PLANT PATHOLOGISTS
c/o the Secretary, Rothamsted, Harpenden,
Hertfordshire AL5 2LQ
Learned Society; associated with the British Mycological Society and the Association of Applied Biologists, *q.v.*

Enquiries to the Secretary

Subject coverage
plant pathology

1080 FEDERATION OF BRITISH UMBRELLA INDUSTRIES
52 Hermiston Avenue, London N8 8NP Tel. 01-340 1014
Trade Association

Enquiries to the Secretary

Subject coverage
British umbrella industry

1081 FEDERATION OF CIVIL ENGINEERING CONTRACTORS
Romney House, Tufton Street, London SW1P 3DU Tel. 01-222 2544-6
Trade Association; eight Area Sections covering England, Scotland and Wales, and a General Section

Enquiries to the Information Officer

Subject coverage
the civil engineering contracting industry and its conditions of contract, industrial relations, plant dayworks schedules; training; safety; conditions for hiring of plant

Publication
Handbook (annual)

FEDERATION OF COATED MACADAM INDUSTRIES *see* **ASPHALT AND COATED MACADAM ASSOCIATION LIMITED**

1082 FEDERATION OF ENGINE RE-MANUFACTURERS
31 Caryl Road, St. Annes, Lytham St. Annes, Lancashire FY8 2QB Tel. 039-15 729438
Trade Association

Enquiries to the Secretary

Subject coverage
engine reconditioning/remanufacturing

1083 FEDERATION OF ENGINEERING DESIGN COMPANIES LIMITED
156 London Road, Mitcham, Surrey CR4 3LD Tel. 01-640 2113
Employers Organization; formerly Federation of Engineering Design Consultants Limited

Enquiries to the General Secretary

Subject coverage
contract drawing office operations in all branches of engineering

FEDERATION OF EUROPEAN INDUSTRIAL CO-OPERATIVE RESEARCH ASSOCIATIONS *see* **COMMITTEE OF DIRECTORS OF RESEARCH ASSOCIATIONS**

FEDERATION OF EUROPEAN INDUSTRIAL EDITORS ASSOCIATION *see* **BRITISH ASSOCIATION OF INDUSTRIAL EDITORS**

FEDERATION OF HARDWARE FACTORS *see* **FEDERATION OF WHOLESALE AND INDUSTRIAL DISTRIBUTORS**

1084 FEDERATION OF INSURANCE BROKERS
1 Queen Victoria Road, Coventry CV1 3JG Tel. 0203 21999
Professional Organization; Member of the British Insurance Brokers Council and of Bureau International de Producteurs d'Assurance et Réassurance

Enquiries to the General Secretary

Subject coverage
insurance broking

Publication
Change (official magazine)

1085 FEDERATION OF LONDON WHOLESALE NEWSPAPER DISTRIBUTORS
Regent House, 89 Kingsway, London WC2B 6RH Tel. 01-242 3458
Trade Association

Enquiries to the Secretary

Subject coverage
commercial and labour matters within the newspaper industry

1086 FEDERATION OF MANUFACTURERS OF CONSTRUCTION EQUIPMENT AND CRANES
8 St Bride Street, London EC4A 4DA Tel. 01-353 3020
Telex 24276

Trade Association

No enquiry service

Subject coverage
information about the construction equipment and cranes industry is issued to members only; the Federation is the industry's link with the Government

1087 FEDERATION OF MERCHANT TAILORS
Admin House, Market Square, Leighton Buzzard, Bedfordshire Tel. 05253 75251
Trade Association

Enquiries to the General Secretary

Subject coverage
retail bespoke tailoring trade, including export

FEDERATION OF NATIONAL ASSOCIATIONS OF SHIPBROKERS AND AGENTS *see* **INSTITUTE OF CHARTERED SHIPBROKERS**

1088 FEDERATION OF PERSONNEL SERVICES OF GREAT BRITAIN
120 Baker Street, London W1M 2DE Tel. 01-487 5250
Trade Association; formerly Employment Agents Federation

Enquiries to the Secretary General

Subject coverage
employment agencies; their conduct, ethics, laws relating thereto

Publications
occasional surveys, *e.g.* temporary and permanent office workers; agency nurses; job-centres

FEDERATION OF RECLAMATION INDUSTRIES *see* **BRITISH SCRAP FEDERATION**

FEDERATION OF REGISTERED HOUSEBUILDERS *now* **HOUSE-BUILDERS FEDERATION,** *q.v.*

FEDERATION OF RUBBER MANUFACTURERS *now* **BRITISH RUBBER MANUFACTURERS ASSOCIATION LIMITED,** *q.v.*

1089 FEDERATION OF STONE INDUSTRIES
Admin House, Market Square, Leighton Buzzard, Bedfordshire Tel. 05253 75252
Trade Association; amalgamating the former British Stone Federation, the Marble and Granite Association and the Architectural Granite Association

Enquiries to the Secretary

Subject coverage
the natural stone industry; use of natural stone

Publication
Code of Practice on stone cleaning and restoration

1090 FEDERATION OF WHOLESALE AND INDUSTRIAL DISTRIBUTORS
Conway House, 212 Croydon Road, Caterham, Surrey CR3 6QG Tel. 22 43617
01-387 9611

Trade Association, representing some 20 distributors associations which are listed following this entry; formerly Federation of Wholesale Organisations

Enquiries to the Secretary or Director

Subject coverage
wholesale and industrial distribution

FEDERATION OF WHOLESALE AND INDUSTRIAL DISTRIBUTORS Members:
ASSOCIATION OF ENGINEERING DISTRIBUTORS
ASSOCIATION OF FRANCHISED DISTRIBUTORS OF ELECTRONIC COMPONENTS
ASSOCIATION OF MUSICAL INSTRUMENT INDUSTRIES, *q.v.*
ASSOCIATION OF TOY AND FANCY GOODS WHOLESALERS, *q.v.*
ASSOCIATION OF WHOLESALE WOOLLEN MERCHANTS LIMITED
BRITISH STATIONERY AND OFFICE PRODUCTS FEDERATION
BRITISH WHOLESALE JEWELLERS ASSOCIATION
CYCLE AND MOTOR CYCLE ASSOCIATION LIMITED
ELECTRICAL WHOLESALERS FEDERATION
ELECTRONIC ORGAN DISTRIBUTORS ASSOCIATION
FEDERATION OF HARDWARE FACTORS
MILLINERY DISTRIBUTORS ASSOCIATION
MOTOR FACTORS ASSOCIATION
NATIONAL ASSOCIATION OF ROPE AND TWINE MERCHANTS, *q.v.*
NATIONAL TYRE DISTRIBUTORS ASSOCIATION
POTTERY AND GLASS WHOLESALERS ASSOCIATION, *q.v.*
RADIO WHOLESALERS FEDERATION
TEXTILE DISTRIBUTORS ASSOCIATION
WATCH AND CLOCK IMPORTERS ASSOCIATION OF GREAT BRITAIN LIMITED
WHOLESALE FLOORCOVERING DISTRIBUTORS ASSOCIATION
WHOLESALE FOOTWEAR DISTRIBUTORS ASSOCIATION, *q.v.*
WHOLESALE HORTICULTURAL ASSOCIATION

1091 FEDERATION OF WIRE ROPE MANUFACTURERS OF GREAT BRITAIN
301 Glossop Road, Sheffield S10 2HN Tel. 0742 21071
Telex 54170

Trade Association

Enquiries to the Information Officer

Subject coverage
wire rope manufacture

1092 FELT ROOFING CONTRACTORS ADVISORY BOARD
Maxwelton House, Boltro Road, Haywards Heath, Tel. 0444 51835
West Sussex RH16 1BJ
Trade Association

Enquiries to the Secretary

Subject coverage
roof weatherproofing specifications; built-up bituminous roofings systems

Publication
Built-up Roofing: information, techniques and specifications

FELTHAM DISTRICT LIBRARY *see* **HOUNSLOW LIBRARY SERVICE**

1093 FENNING ENVIRONMENTAL PRODUCTS LIMITED
112 Leagrave Road, Luton, Bedfordshire Tel. 0582 26538-30
Telex 826335

Company

Enquiries to the Information Officer

Subject coverage
supply and repair of geophysical equipment; applicability of geophysical equipment to various geological problems

1094 FERODO LIMITED
Chapel-en-le-Frith, Stockport, Cheshire SK12 6JP Tel. 029 881 2520
Company, member of the Turner & Newall Group

Enquiries to the Information Officer

Subject coverage
friction materials for automotive, agricultural and industrial applications; flooring materials

Publications
Ferodo International Technical News
Friction Materials for Engineers
Trade catalogues

FERTILISER MANUFACTURERS ASSOCIATION LIMITED *see* **CHEMICAL INDUSTRIES ASSOCIATION LIMITED**

1095 FIBRE BUILDING BOARD DEVELOPMENT ORGANISATION LIMITED
6 Buckingham Street, London WC2N 6BZ Tel. 01-839 1122
Trade Association, with a Hardboard Advisory Service and an Insulating Board Advisory Service

Enquiries to the Information Officer

Subject coverage
industrial or do-it-yourself use of hardboard or insulating board

Publications
Series of data sheets
Technical papers and standards on physical properties; insect and fungal attack; thermal and acoustic performance; applications

1096 FIBREGLASS LIMITED
St Helens, Lancashire WA10 3TR Tel. 074 24022
Company; member of the Pilkington Group

Enquiries, by letter only, to the Information Officer

Subject coverage
glass fibres and their applications

1097 FIELD STUDIES COUNCIL
9 Devereux Court, Strand, London WC2R 3JR Tel. 01-583 7471
Company Limited by Guarantee/Registered Charity with the Department of Education and Science

Enquiries to the Information Officer, Preston Montford, Montford Bridge, Shrewsbury SY4 1HW

Subject coverage
biology; geography; ecology; photography; birds (all subjects as one-week courses)

Publications
Field Studies (annual)
Course Programmes
Annual Report

1098 FIELDEN HOUSE PRODUCTIVITY CENTRE LIMITED
Fielden House, Mersey Road, West Didsbury, Manchester M20 8QA Tel. 061-445 2426
Company

Enquiries to the Chief Executive

Subject coverage
industrial training; safety in industry; personnel management; industrial relations; inflation accounting; capital investment; supervisory training; work study; organization and method; production control; stock control

FIFE COUNTY LIBRARY *now* **KIRKCALDY AND NORTH EAST FIFE DISTRICT LIBRARIES,** *q.v.*

FIGHTING VEHICLES RESEARCH AND DEVELOPMENT ESTABLISHMENT *now* **MILITARY VEHICLES AND ENGINEERING ESTABLISHMENT,** *q.v.*

FILE ASSOCIATION *see* **FEDERATION OF BRITISH HAND TOOL MANUFACTURERS**

FILE RESEARCH COUNCIL *now* **CUTLERY AND ALLIED TRADES RESEARCH ASSOCIATION,** *q.v.*

1099 FILTON TECHNICAL COLLEGE
Filton Avenue, Filton, Bristol BS12 7AT — Tel. 0272 694217 ext. 37
Technical College

Enquiries to the Librarian

Subject coverage
economics; geography; mathematics; chemistry; physics; photography

1100 FILTRATION SOCIETY
1 Katharine Street, Croydon CR9 1LB — Tel. 01-686 6339
Technical Society; its Library is housed at the Institution of Chemical Engineers' Library

Enquiries to the Honorary Secretary

Subject coverage
filtration and separation technology and equipment

Publication
Filtration & Separation (six times per annum)

1101 FINANCE HOUSES ASSOCIATION LIMITED
14 Queen Annes Gate, London SW1H 9AG — Tel. 01-930 3391
Trade Association; houses the Equipment Leasing Association Limited; affiliated to the European Federation of Finance House Associations

Enquiries to the Director-Secretary

Subject coverage
instalment credit

Publications
List of members
Introduction to the Consumer Credit Act
Credit (quarterly)
Annual Report
About Instalment Credit

1102 FINANCIAL TIMES LIMITED
Bracken House, 10 Cannon Street, London EC4P 4BY — Tel. 01-248 8000
Telex 886341/2
Newspaper; includes Financial Times Business Enterprises, and the Financial Times Business Information Centre

Enquiries to the Manager, Information Services

Subject coverage
companies, industries, marketing, countries, law and tax, personalities, scientific and technical subjects, statistics

Special collection
annual Reports and accounts of all U.K. public quoted companies (in microfiche)

Publications
Newsletters
Yearbooks and Business Studies
Catalogue of publications (available from Business Enterprises)

1103 FINISHING PUBLICATIONS LIMITED
179B High Street, Hampton Hill, Middlesex TW12 1NL — Tel. 01-979 7559
Publishing Company; includes the Metal Finishing Book Centre

Enquiries to the Director

Subject coverage
protection and decoration of metals; spraying; coating; waste treatments; corrosion; health and safety

Publications
Metal Finishing Abstracts (bi-monthly)
Metal Finishing Plant and Processes (bi-monthly)

1104 FINNISH PLYWOOD DEVELOPMENT ASSOCIATION
21 Panton Street, London SW1Y 4DR Tel. 01-930 3282
Trade Association, member of the Association of Finnish Plywood Industry, Helsinki

Enquiries to the Technical or Commercial Manager

Subject coverage
roofing; farm building; flooring; vehicle building; concrete formwork; industrial uses and strength properties of Finnish plywood; surfaced plywoods; fixing

Publications
technical publications, specifications and design data (list available)

FIRA *see* **FURNITURE INDUSTRY RESEARCH ASSOCIATION**

1105 FIRE EXTINGUISHING TRADES ASSOCIATION
Beech House, 39 London Road, Reigate, Surrey RH2 9QE Tel. 073-72 41841
Trade Association; affiliated to the Council of British Fire Protection Equipment manufacturers; formerly Fire Extinguisher Trades Association

Enquiries to the Secretary

Subject coverage
development, protection and promotion of fire extinguishers of all types, portable fire fighting equipment and fittings; information and advice on all technical aspects of the trade

FIRE FIGHTING VEHICLE MANUFACTURERS ASSOCIATION *see* **SOCIETY OF MOTOR MANUFACTURERS AND TRADERS LIMITED**

1106 FIRE INSURERS RESEARCH AND TESTING ORGANISATION
Melrose Avenue, Borehamwood, Hertfordshire WD6 2BJ Tel. 01-207 2345
Company

Enquiries to the Secretary

Subject coverage
fire tests on building materials and structures; tests on fire-fighting equipment and fire protection systems; approval of fire appliances, equipment and systems for insurance purposes; fire protection in general and of high-racked storage in particular

Special collection
Fire Officers Committee Collection of sprinkler heads

Publications
Occasional publications on subjects as above and on fire research

1107 FIRE PROTECTION ASSOCIATION
Aldermary House, Queen Street, London EC4N 1TJ Tel. 01-248 5222
Central Advisory Organization

Enquiries to the Information Officers

Subject coverage
fire; fire prevention; fire protection

Publications
books and booklets
technical data sheets
planning guides
films

1108 FIRE RESEARCH STATION
Boreham Wood, Hertfordshire WD6 2BL Tel. 01-953 6177
Government Department, part of the Building Research Establishment of the Department of the Environment; formerly Joint Fire Research Organization; affiliated to the Fire Offices Committee

Enquiries to the Head of Fire Research

Subject coverage
fire statistics; ignition and growth of fire; structural aspects of fire in buildings; detection, extinction and suppression of fire; fire hazards in industries and materials

Special collection
Late 19th and early 20th century books and journals of the British Fire Prevention Committee

Publications
Fire Research Notes
Current Papers (BRE series)
U.K. Fire and Loss Statistics
References to Scientific Literature on Fire (a 6-monthly bibliography)
Special bibliographies

1109 FIRE SERVICE STAFF COLLEGE
Wotton House, Abinger Common, Dorking, Surrey RH5 6HT Tel. 0306 730441
Government Department College, of the Home Office

Enquiries to the Librarian

Subject coverage
fire fighting and fire brigade management; fire extinguishing apparatus and fire alarm systems; fire engineering in general; fire prevention, including inspections and surveys; hazardous conditions of buildings, transport, and materials; codes of practice and legislation; history of the fire service, fire insurance and fire marks; arson and pyromania; command and management training for Local Authority Fire Services

1110 FISH DISEASES LABORATORY
The Nothe, Weymouth, Dorsetshire DT4 8UB Tel. 030-5772137/8/9
Government Department, formerly the Fish Pathology Unit, Ministry of Agriculture, Fisheries and Food; part of the Directorate of Fisheries Research, Lowestoft

Enquiries to the Director

Subject coverage
control and prevention of disease of marine and freshwater fish and shellfish in culture systems

Publications
Occasional Technical Reports

FISHERIES EXPERIMENT STATION *see* **DIRECTORATE OF FISHERIES RESEARCH**

FISHERIES HELMINTHOLOGY RESEARCH UNIT *now* **INSTITUTE FOR MARINE ENVIRONMENTAL RESEARCH,** *q.v.*

1111 FISHERIES LABORATORY
Remembrance Avenue, Burnham-on-Crouch, Essex Tel. 0621 782658
Government Department, Ministry of Agriculture, Fisheries and Food; connected with the main laboratory at Lowestoft, the Directorate of Fisheries Research

Enquiries to the Information Scientist

Subject coverage
non-radioactive marine pollution

1112 FISHERIES LABORATORY
Pakefield Road, Lowestoft, Suffolk NR33 0HT Tel. 0502 4251
Government Research Laboratory, Ministry of Agriculture, Fisheries and Food; headquarters of the Directorate of Fisheries Research

Enquiries to the Information Officer or Librarian

Subject coverage
fish and shellfish; hydrography; radiobiology; marine pollution

Publications
Annual Report
Fishing Prospects (annual)
List of Staff Publications (quarterly)
Fishery Investigations, Laboratory Leaflets and Technical Reports (irregular)

1113 FISHERIES ORGANIZATION SOCIETY LIMITED
558 London Road, North Cheam, Sutton, Surrey SM3 9AA Tel. 01-644 4666
Grant-aided National Organization; 116 coastal federal societies and associations are affiliated; the National Commercial Salmonmen's Circle is also associated

Enquiries, preferably in writing, to the General Secretary; research, statistical or advisory requests may only be undertaken on a consultative basis

Subject coverage
inshore fishing industry; fisheries including shellfisheries and marine fish farming; formation of co-operatives; marketing; technical education and training; supplies, marine insurance; vessel construction and gear; conservation; pollution; fishing limits and fishing legislation

Publications
Official Yearbook and Report (annual)
FOS Newsletter (about 5 times per annum)

FISHERIES RADIOBIOLOGICAL LABORATORY *see* **DIRECTORATE OF FISHERIES RESEARCH**

1114 FISHERIES SOCIETY OF THE BRITISH ISLES
Secretary, c/o Department of Biological Sciences, The University, Exeter EX4 4PS Tel. 0392 77911
Professional/Scientific Society

Enquiries to the Secretary

Subject coverage
any scientific aspect of freshwater or marine fisheries; *not* the economics of fisheries, fish farming or commercial fisheries

Publication
Journal of Fish Biology (monthly)

1115 FISHERY ECONOMICS RESEARCH UNIT
White Fish Authority, 10 Young Street, Edinburgh EH2 4JQ Tel. 031-225 2515
Telex 727225
Statutory Body, of the White Fish Authority and Herring Industry Board; houses the Secretariat of the forthcoming Fisheries Economics Newsletter (international, biennial)

Enquiries to the Economist

Subject coverage
fisheries economics and statistics; fisheries resource management; consumer research; investment appraisal, employment, marketing and trade studies

Publications
Fish Retailer Purchase Study (monthly)
Occasional papers (list available)

FISHING BOAT BUILDERS ASSOCIATION *see* **SHIP AND BOAT BUILDERS NATIONAL FEDERATION**

FISHMONGERS COMPANY *see* **SHELLFISH ASSOCIATION OF GREAT BRITAIN**

1116 FISONS LIMITED
Agrochemical Division, Chesterford Park Research Station, Saffron Walden, Essex CB10 1XL — Tel. 0799 23542, Telex 817300
Company Division; also at Hauxton, Cambridge; formerly Fisons Pest Control Limited

Enquiries to the Information Officer

Subject coverage
pesticides; agriculture; horticulture, and related topics

Special collection
Flora (worldwide)

Publications
Summary of the Official Recommendations (for safe use) MAFF
Pesticide Trade Names (normally, internal use only)

1117 FISONS LIMITED
Fertilizer Division, Harvest House, Felixstowe, Suffolk 1P11 7LP — Tel. 039-42 4444, Telex 98273

Company

Enquiries to the Manager, Public Relations Department

Subject coverage
Fertilizers and their use in agriculture; fertilizer research and related aspects

Publications
occasional papers on fertilizer research

1118 FISONS LIMITED
Pharmaceutical Division, R. & D. Laboratories, Bakewell Road, Loughborough, Leicestershire LE11 0QY — Tel. 0509 66361, Telex 34341
Company

Enquiries to the Librarian

Subject coverage
medicinal, analytical and organic chemistry; pharmacology; pharmaceutics; pharmaceutical packaging; medicine; life sciences; toxicology; biochemistry

FISONS LIMITED *see also* **LEVINGTON RESEARCH STATION**

1119 FLAT GLASS ASSOCIATION
6 Mount Row, London W1Y 6DY — Tel. 01-629 8334
Trade Association

Enquiries to the Information Officer

Subject coverage
glazing; flat glass processing and decoration including mirror manufacture

Publications
Glazing manual
Numerous other publications

1120 FLAT GLASS MANUFACTURERS ASSOCIATION
Prescot Road, St Helens, Merseyside, WA10 3TT — Tel. 0744 28882 ext. 2585, Telex 627441

Trade Association

Enquiries to the Secretary; information should also be sought from Pilkington Brothers, q.v.

Subject coverage
flat glass used in the construction industry

FLEET LIBRARY *see* **HAMPSHIRE COUNTY LIBRARY**

1121 FLEETWOOD NAUTICAL COLLEGE
Broadwater, Fleetwood, Lancashire FY7 8JZ Tel. 03917 2772
College

Enquiries to the Tutor Librarian

Subject coverage
maritime sciences and technology including marine electronics

FLEETWOOD PUBLIC LIBRARY *now* **WYRE DISTRICT CENTRAL LIBRARY** *see* **LANCASHIRE LIBRARY**

1122 FLIGHT SAFETY COMMITTEE
Building 209, Epsom Square, Heathrow, London Airport, Middlesex TW6 2ET Tel. 01-759 1024
Independent Committee of aircraft operators, manufacturers, commanders, insurers and aviation authorities

Enquiries to the Secretary

Subject coverage
flight safety

Publication
Flight Safety Focus

FLINTSHIRE COLLEGE OF TECHNOLOGY *now* **NORTH EAST WALES INSTITUTE OF HIGHER EDUCATION,** *q.v.*

1123 FLOOR QUARRY ASSOCIATION
Federation House, Station Road, Stoke-on-Trent, Staffordshire ST4 2RU Tel. 0782 45147
Trade Association

Enquiries to the Secretary

Subject coverage
manufacture, supply and installation of clay floor quarries

Publication
Clay Floor Quarry Manual

1124 FLOUR MILLING AND BAKING RESEARCH ASSOCIATION
Chorleywood, Rickmansworth, Hertfordshire WD3 5SH Tel. 09278 4111
Research Association

Enquiries to the Information Officer

Subject coverage
cereals and their milled products; bakery raw materials and products; milling and baking processes; botany and biochemistry of wheat grain; milling process control and machinery; wheat and flour quality and improvement; industrial uses of flour; bread, biscuits and flour confectionery; baking machinery, measurement and control; product keeping quality; nutritional and toxicological studies; domestic and overseas food legislation

Special Collection
R.B. Seville Collection of British Patent Abridgements and Specifications on Bakery Machinery 1635–1955

Publications
Annual Report
Abstracts free to members (on subscription to non-members)

Gazette confidential to members
Bulletin confidential to members
Research reports confidential to members

FOLKESTONE CENTRAL LIBRARY *now* **SHEPWAY DIVISIONAL LIBRARY**
see **KENT COUNTY LIBRARY**

FOOD AND DRINK INDUSTRIES COUNCIL *see*
COCOA, CHOCOLATE AND CONFECTIONERY ALLIANCE
DAIRY TRADE FEDERATION
UNITED KINGDOM ASSOCIATION OF FROZEN FOOD PRODUCERS

FOOD AND NUTRITION LIBRARY *now* **MINISTRY OF AGRICULTURE, FISHERIES AND FOOD, Whitehall Place,** *q.v.*

1125 FOOD, DRINK & TOBACCO INDUSTRY TRAINING BOARD
Barton House, Barton Street, Gloucester GL1 1QQ — Tel. 0452 28621
Industrial Training Board, of the Training Services Agency

Enquiries to the Manager, Library/Information Services

Subject coverage
industrial training, including management training in the food, drink and tobacco industries

Publications
Training guides and recommendations
FDT News (occasional)

1126 FOOD FREEZER AND REFRIGERATOR COUNCIL
25 North Row, London W1R 2B7 — Tel. 01-499 0414
Telex 267531
Promotional Body; formed by a merger of the former Domestic Refrigeration Development Committee and the Food Freezer Committee

Enquiries to the Secretary

Subject coverage
refrigerators; food freezers; food freezer packaging materials; frozen food centres; frozen food; freezer insurance (domestic only)

Publication
Consumer Booklet: a pre-shopping guide on buying a refrigerator or freezer

1127 FOOD MANUFACTURERS FEDERATION INCORPORATED
1–2 Castle Lane, London SW1E 6DN — Tel. 01-828 7822
Trade Association of thirteen affiliated societies, providing Library and information services for all of them and the Secretariat for all save one (the Meat Manufacturers Association)

Enquiries to the Librarian

Subject coverage
general information on the U.K. food industry; E.E.C. legislation (proposed regulations, directives, etc.) relating to food and agriculture; developments in E.E.C. matters which could affect the food industry

FOOD MANUFACTURERS FEDERATION INCORPORATED
BRITISH ESSENCE MANUFACTURERS' ASSOCIATION *q.v.*
BRITISH SOLUBLE COFFEE MANUFACTURERS' ASSOCIATION
FOOD MANUFACTURERS' INDUSTRIAL GROUP
FRUIT AND VEGETABLE CANNERS' ASSOCIATION
ICE CREAM FEDERATION
LARD ASSOCIATION
MARGARINE AND SHORTENING MANUFACTURERS' ASSOCIATION
MEAT MANUFACTURERS ASSOCIATION
NATIONAL EDIBLE OIL DISTRIBUTORS ASSOCIATION

PET FOOD MANUFACTURERS ASSOCIATION
PRE PACKED FLOUR ASSOCIATION
SEED CRUSHERS & OIL PROCESSORS ASSOCIATION
U.K. ASSOCIATION OF MANUFACTURERS OF BAKERS' YEAST

1128 FOOD RESEARCH INSTITUTE
Colney Lane, Norwich NR4 7UA — Tel. 0603 56122
Research Institute, of the Agricultural Research Council

Enquiries to the Liaison Officer

Subject coverage
biochemistry, chemistry and microbiology of foods, particularly fruits, vegetables, eggs, poultry, edible fats and oils; refrigerated stores for primary produce

1129 FOOTWEAR DISTRIBUTORS FEDERATION
69 Cannon Street, London EC4N 5AB — Tel. 01-248 4444
Telex 888941

Trade Association

Enquiries to the Secretary

Subject coverage
availability of footwear in the U.K.; information on the Voluntary Code of Practice for Footwear; marketing of footwear; broad statistical information

1130 FOOTWEAR, LEATHER & FUR SKIN INDUSTRY TRAINING BOARD
29 Birmingham Road, Sutton Coldfield, West Midlands B72 1QE — Tel. 021-355 3511
Industrial Training Board, of the Training Services Agency

Enquiries to the Senior Technical Officer, Information Unit

Subject coverage
training in general and specifically for footwear, leather and fur skin industries

Publications
Annual Report
Training Recommendations
Grant Schemes

1131 FORD MOTOR COMPANY LIMITED
Eagle Way, Brentwood, Essex CM13 3BW — Tel. 0277 253000
Telex 882121

Company

Enquiries to the Secretary

Subject coverage
motor vehicle manufacture; tractors; industrial engines; parts and accessories

1132 FORD MOTOR COMPANY LIMITED
Research and Engineering Centre, Laindon, Basildon SS15 6EE — Tel. 0268 3020
Telex 882121

Enquiries to the Technical Librarian

Subject coverage
automobile engineering

1133 FORENSIC SCIENCE SOCIETY
P.O. BOX 41, Harrogate, North Yorkshire HG1 2LF — Tel. 0423 56068
Scientific Society

Enquiries to the Secretary

Subject coverage
forensic sciences and medicine

Publications
Journal of the Forensic Science Society
World List of Forensic Science Laboratories

FOREST PRODUCTS RESEARCH LABORATORY *now* **PRINCES RISBOROUGH LABORATORY,** *q.v.*

1134 FORESTRY COMMISSION
Forest Research Station, Alice Holt Lodge, Wrecclesham, near Farnham, Surrey GU10 4LH — Tel. 042-04 2255
Government Department

Enquiries to the Librarian

Subject coverage
forestry

Publications
listed in H.M.S.O. Sectional List No. 31 and in the Commission's Catalogue of Publications; included are reports, command papers, forestry Acts, regulations, bulletins, booklets, leaflets, forest records, guides, and information pamphlets

1135 FORESTRY COMMISSION
Northern Research Station, Roslin, Midlothian EH25 9SY — Tel. 031-445 2176
Government Department

Enquiries to the Librarian

Subject coverage
forestry

Publications
see FORESTRY COMMISSION Forest Research Station, Wrecclesham

FORFAR PUBLIC LIBRARY *see* **ANGUS DISTRICT LIBRARY SERVICE**

1136 FORMAN HOUSE PUBLIC RELATIONS LIMITED
39 Charing Cross Road, London WC2H 0AS — Tel. 01-240 0721
Telex 22150
Public Relations Organization; formerly LPE PR; part of LOPEX Limited (London Press Exchange Limited), 110 St. Martins Lane, London WC2N 4BH

Enquiries to the Managing Director

Subject coverage
public relations

1137 FORMICA INTERNATIONAL LIMITED
68 Lower Cookham Road, Maidenhead, Berkshire SL6 8LA — Tel. 0628 21441
Telex 847545
Company, subsidiary of De la Rue Company Limited; formerly Formica Limited

Enquiries to the Technical Information Officer

Subject coverage
polymer science and technology; surface science; gravure printing; ink rheology; process engineering; web impregnation, coating and drying; laminations; extrusion; cure kinetics; paper; gel permeation chromatography; instrumental analysis techniques

1138 FORT BOVISAND UNDERWATER CENTRE
Plymouth, Devonshire PL9 0AB — Tel. 0752 42570
Underwater Training Centre, of Plymouth Ocean Projects Limited

Enquiries to the Secretary

Subject coverage
commercial diver training, including the use of underwater tools, cutting gear, inspection and non-destructive testing equipment

Publication
Fort Bovisand Newsletter

FOSECO MINSEP LIMITED *see* **PROTIM LIMITED**

1139 FOSTER WHEELER POWER PRODUCTS LIMITED
Greater London House, Hampstead Road, London NW1 7QN Tel. 01-388 1212
Telex 263984

Company, subsidiary of Foster Wheeler Corporation (U.S.A.); formerly Foster Wheeler-John Brown Boilers of above address

Enquiries to the Information Officer

Subject coverage
industrial, marine and nuclear boilers; welding; stress analysis; materials data; heat transfer; relevant standards

1140 FOUNDRY EQUIPMENT AND SUPPLIES ASSOCIATION LIMITED
21 John Adam Street, London WC2N 6JH Tel. 01-839 6171
Trade Association; formerly the Foundry Trades Equipment and Supplies Association

Enquiries to the Secretary

Subject coverage
foundry trades; metals casting

1141 FOUNDRY INDUSTRY TRAINING COMMITTEE
50–54 Charlotte Street, London W1P 2EL Tel. 01-580 0575
Industrial Training Board; Statutory Committee of the Engineering Industry Training Board

Enquiries to the Information Officer

Subject coverage
general training and specialist training for the cast metals industry, its manpower structure, occupational and career information and employment conditions

Publications
Recommendations on Training Standards
Guidelines on Training Plans
Guidebooks
Statistical Reviews
Information Bulletins
Publications List available

FRANCE, EMBASSY *see* **FRENCH EMBASSY**

FRASERBURGH BURGH LIBRARY *see* **NORTH EAST OF SCOTLAND LIBRARY SERVICE**

1142 FRAZER-NASH GROUP LIMITED
Burgoyne House, Lower Teddington Road, Kingston-upon-Thames, Tel. 01-977 0051
Surrey KT1 4EX Telex 929947
Company; consisting of five parts: Frazer-Nash Limited (design and development), Frazer-Nash (Consultancy) Limited, Frazer-Nash (Electronics) Limited, Frazer-Nash (Engineering) Limited and Frazer-Nash P.E.D. Limited

Enquiries to the Companies are dealt with on a commercial basis

Subject coverage
design, consultancy and manufacture in mechanical, electronic, hydraulic and pneumatic engineering; activities include offshore hydraulic technology; document handling equipment; postal mechanization; machining, fabrication and welding; automatic test equipment; weapons release systems; meteorological recording systems; computing; low-cost automation; weighbridges

Publications

Brochures and leaflets on projects available on request

1143 FREIGHT TRANSPORT ASSOCIATION LIMITED

Hermes House, St. Johns Road, Tunbridge Wells, Kent TN4 9UZ Tel. 0892 26171

Trade Association; formerly Traders Road Transport Association; having five regional offices

Enquiries to the Chief Information Officer

Subject coverage

freight transport, including transport law; costs and rates; education and training; vehicle maintenance; international transport

Publications

Freight (monthly)
FTA Yearbook
Designing for Deliveries
Delivering the Goods
Planning for Lorries
Living with the Lorry

1144 FREIGHTLINERS LIMITED

43 Cardington Street, London NW1 2LR Tel. 01-388 0611
Telex 24743

Company; owned jointly by the National Freight Corporation and the British Railways Board

Enquiries to the Communications Manager

Subject coverage

road/rail container operations and equipment; planning of road/rail container interchange facilities

1145 FRENCH EMBASSY

Scientific Office, 41 Parkside, London SW1X 7JP Tel. 01-245 9456

Government Department

Enquiries to the Scientific Department

Subject coverage

French science and technology

1146 FRESHWATER BIOLOGICAL ASSOCIATION

Ferry House, Far Sawrey, Ambleside, Cumbria LA22 0LP Tel. 096-62 2468/9

Grant-aided Research Association of the Natural Environment Research Council

Enquiries to the Librarian or the Director

Subject coverage

limnology; freshwater biology (hydrobiology); freshwater algae; microbiology; fish; invertebrates; physics and chemistry of lakes and rivers

Special collection

the Fritsch Collection of illustrations of the freshwater algae

Publications

Annual Report
Keys for the identification of freshwater organisms
Occasional publications

1147 FRESHWATER FISHERIES LABORATORY

Faskally, Pitlochry, Perthshire, Scotland PH16 5LB Tel. 0796 2060

Government Research Laboratory, of the Department of Agriculture and Fisheries for Scotland

Enquiries to the Officer-in-Charge

Subject coverage

freshwater biology; freshwater fisheries; salmon fisheries; fisheries management; fish rearing; pollution

Publications
Annual Reports to 1972
Triennial Reports from 1976

1148 FROME COLLEGE
Park Road, Frome, Somerset BA11 1EU Tel. 0373 2456
College of Further Education; formerly North East Somerset Technical College; associated with Frome College (secondary education), Bath Road, Frome

Enquiries to the Librarian

Subject coverage
general and science

FROME DISTRICT LIBRARY *see* **SOMERSET COUNTY LIBRARY**

FRUIT AND VEGETABLE CANNERS ASSOCIATION *see* **FOOD MANUFACTURERS FEDERATION INCORPORATED**

FRUIT AND VEGETABLE PRESERVATION RESEARCH ASSOCIATION *now* **CAMPDEN FOOD PRESERVATION RESEARCH ASSOCIATION,** *q.v.*

FRUIT IMPORTERS ASSOCIATION *see* **COVENT GARDEN MARKET AUTHORITY**

1149 FRYS METALS LIMITED
Tandem Works, Merton Abbey, London SW19 2PD Tel. 01-648 7020
Telex 265732

Company; formerly Fry's Metal Foundries Limited

Enquiries to the Information Officer

Subject coverage
soldering and brazing; uses of casting metals, type metals and bearing metals, *i.e.* the field of non-ferrous metals except aluminium

Publications
Technical booklets on solders and fluxes; automatic soldering machines; printing metals; bearing metals, casting metals and bronzes

1150 FULMER RESEARCH INSTITUTE LIMITED
Stoke Poges, Slough, Buckinghamshire SL2 4QD Tel. 028-16 2181
Telex 848314

Contract Research Organization, wholly owned by the Institute of Physics, *q.v.*, connected with Yarsley Research Laboratories, *q.v.* and Yarsley Testing Laboratories

Enquiries to the Librarian

Subject coverage
materials; metals; plastics and polymers; physics and chemistry

Publications
Polymerics (abstracts journal)
Additives for Polymers
Fulmer Materials Optimiser
Disposals of Plastics
Register of Consulting Scientists and Contract Research Organizations

1151 FURNITURE AND TIMBER INDUSTRY TRAINING BOARD
31 Octagon Parade, High Wycombe, Buckinghamshire HP11 2JA Tel. 0494 32751
Industrial Training Board, of the Training Services Agency, *q.v.*

Enquiries to the Librarian or Public Relations Officer

Subject coverage
training of operatives within the furniture and timber industries; safety

Publications
Instruction Manuals
Training Notes
Training Recommendations
Training Guide
Annual Report
Preventing Accidents in the Furniture Trade and Allied Industries
Training Grant Schemes
Wood Machining Safely (film, for hire or sale)
Research Reports

1152 FURNITURE INDUSTRY RESEARCH ASSOCIATION (FIRA)
Maxwell Road, Stevenage, Hertfordshire SG1 2EW Tel. 0438 3433
Research Association; associated with the Furniture Development Council, of the same address

Enquiries, generally from members only, to the Librarian, or to the Technical Services Department, for submission to specialist advisors

Subject coverage
furniture design and manufacturing methods; tests for furniture materials and complete items of furniture; upholstery; fault investigations; market research and marketing; consultancy in product costing, factory layout, etc.; machinery and material selection; statistics for the industry

Publications
Statistical digests/market survey reports
U.K. and European furniture statistics
Research and technical journals
F.I.R.A. Bulletin (quarterly)

1153 FURZEBROOK RESEARCH STATION
Wareham, Dorset BH20 5AS Tel. 092-93 361/2
Research Station, of the Institute of Terrestrial Ecology, *q.v.*; formerly of the Nature Conservancy

Enquiries to the Librarian

Subject coverage
ecology, particularly of Dorset and the Isle of Purbeck

Special collection
Diver memorial collection (Captain Cyril Diver's collections and records relating to the South Haven Peninsula, at Studland)

FYLDE DISTRICT CENTRAL LIBRARY *see* **LANCASHIRE LIBRARY**

GALASHIELS DISTRICT LIBRARY *see* **BORDERS REGIONAL LIBRARY**

GALVANIZERS ASSOCIATION *see* **ZINC DEVELOPMENT ASSOCIATION**

1154 GAME CONSERVANCY
Fordingbridge, Hampshire SP6 1EF Tel. 0425 52381
Research and Advisory/Registered Charity, formed by the amalgamation of the Eley Game Advisory Station and the Game Research Association

Enquiries to the Information Officer

Subject coverage
game rearing and conservation; habitat requirements; game diseases; partridge survival; wildfowl in wet gravel pits

GAME RESEARCH ASSOCIATION *now* **GAME CONSERVANCY,** *q.v.*

GARAGE EQUIPMENT ASSOCIATION *see* **SOCIETY OF MOTOR MANUFACTURERS AND TRADERS LIMITED**

1155 GAS BEARING ADVISORY SERVICE
Department of Mechanical Engineering, The University, Southampton SO9 5NH — Tel. 0703 559122, Telex 47661
Professional Consultants

Enquiries to the Manager

Subject coverage
utilization of fluid film bearings, specially gas bearings; application of gas bearings to machine tools and metrological instruments; latterly the application of self-acting oil or grease bearings to rotating mechanisms

1156 GAS KINETICS DATA COMPILATION AND EVALUATION GROUP
Department of Chemistry, The University, Birmingham B15 2TT — Tel. 021-472 1301
University Department, supported by the Science Research Council

Enquiries to the Head, Department of Chemistry

Subject coverage
kinetics of gas phase reactions

Publications
Second Supplementary Tables of Bimolecular Gas Reactions, University of Birmingham, 1972
Evaluated Kinetic Data on Gas Phase Addition Reactions, Butterworths, 1973
Evaluated Kinetic Data on Gas Phase Hydrogen through Reactions of Methyl Radicals, Butterworths, 1976

GAS REFRACTORY AND COKE OVEN CONTRACTORS ASSOCIATION *see* **REFRACTORY USERS FEDERATION**

1157 GATESHEAD PUBLIC LIBRARIES & ARTS DEPARTMENT
Central Library, Prince Consort Road, Gateshead, County Durham NE8 4LN — Tel. 0632 773478, Telex 537379
Public Library

Enquiries to the Borough Librarian

Subject coverage
general and a railways collection

1158 GEC HIRST RESEARCH CENTRE
East Lane, Wembley, Middlesex HA9 7PP — Tel. 01-904 1262 ext. 219, Telex 923429

Industrial Research Laboratory

Enquiries to the Librarian

Subject coverage
telecommunications; electronics; physics and chemistry; metallurgy; engineering

Publication
G.E.C. Journal of Science and Technology (quarterly)

1159 GEC—MARCONI ELECTRONICS
Marconi Research Laboratories Limited, West Hanningfield Road, Great Baddow, Essex CM2 8HN — Tel. 0245 73331, Telex 99201
Company, part of the General Electric Company Limited

Enquiries to the Chief Librarian and Information Officer

Subject coverage
electronics, covering communications, radar and avionics; theoretical sciences including computer software, antennas, solid state physics, materials; mechanical engineering; applied physics

Special collection
Marconi Historical Collection

Publications
Marconi Review
Aerial
Communication and Broadcasting

1160 GEC POWER ENGINEERING LIMITED
Cambridge Road, Whetstone, Leicester LE8 3LH
Company; formerly English Electric; houses the Nuclear Power Company (Whetstone) Limited

Enquiries to the Chief Librarian

Subject coverage
mechanical and nuclear engineering, including materials, particularly metals; gas turbines

Publications
Thesaurofacet: thesaurus and faceted classification for engineering and related subjects 1969
Bibliographies and Reading Lists

GEC LIMITED *see also*
PAXMAN DIESELS LIMITED
RUSTON DIESELS LIMITED
SALFORD ELECTRICAL INSTRUMENTS LIMITED

GEM TESTING LABORATORY *see* **DIAMOND, PEARL AND PRECIOUS STONE TRADE SECTION**

1161 GEMMOLOGICAL ASSOCIATION OF GREAT BRITAIN
St. Dunstans House, Carey Lane, London EC2V 8AB Tel. 01-606 5025
Trade Association

Enquiries to the Secretary

Subject coverage
minerals and substances used in the jewellery trade; gemmology and the identification of natural from synthetic and imitation counterparts

Publications
Journal of Gemmology
Proceedings of the Gemmological Association of G.B.

1162 GENERAL ACCIDENT FIRE AND LIFE ASSURANCE CORPORATION
General Buildings, Perth PH1 5TP Tel. Perth 21202
Telex 76237

Company

Enquiries to the Company Secretary

Subject coverage
insurance; pension schemes; executor and trustee services

1163 GENERAL FOODS LIMITED
Banbury, Oxfordshire OX16 7QU Tel. 0295 4433
Telex 83196

Manufacturing Company, part of General Foods Corporation (U.S.A.)

Enquiries to the Information Officer, Marketing Library

Subject coverage
U.K. food trade and marketing

GENERAL REFRACTORIES LIMITED *now* **GR STEIN REFRACTORIES LIMITED,** *q.v.*

GENERAL REGISTER OFFICE *now* **OFFICE OF POPULATION CENSUSES AND SURVEYS,** *q.v.*

1164 GEO ABSTRACTS LIMITED
University of East Anglia, Norwich NR4 7TJ Tel. 0603 26327
Company, formerly Geomorphological Abstracts, then Geographical Abstracts

Enquiries to the Company

Subject coverage
environmental sciences, especially geography, planning, geology, geophysics, ecology, geomorphology

Publications
Geophysical Abstracts (7 parts, each 6 issues per annum)
Ecological Abstracts (6 issues per annum)
Symposia Series
Bibliographies
Concepts and Techniques in Modern Geography Series
Technical Bulletins
Publications List available

GEOCOMP LIMITED *see* **SOIL MECHANICS LIMITED**

1165 GEOGRAPHICAL ASSOCIATION
343 Fulwood Road, Sheffield S10 3BP Tel. 0742 61666
Association to further study and teaching of geography

Enquiries to the Information Officer

Subject coverage
geography

Publications
Geography (periodical)
Teaching Geography Series
British Landscape through Maps Series
Geography in Education: a bibliography of British sources, 1870–1970
Aerial photographs

1166 GEOLOGICAL SOCIETY OF LONDON
Burlington House, Piccadilly, London W1V 0JU Tel. 01-734 2356
01-734 5673 (Library)

Private Learned Society

Enquiries, general, to the Executive Officer; bibliographical, to the Librarian

Subject coverage
geology and allied sciences

Special collections
Rare Book Collection
Murchison Letters and Diaries

Publications
Journal of the Geological Society (6 issues per annum)
Quarterly Engineering Journal
Memoirs
Special Publications
Special Reports
Annual Report
Newsletter (6 issues per annum)
Miscellaneous Papers

1167 GEOLOGISTS ASSOCIATION
23 Green Dragon Lane, Flackwell Heath, Buckinghamshire HP10 9JZ
Registered Charity; the Association's Library is housed in the Library of University College, London

Enquiries to the General Secretary

Subject coverage
geology and allied sciences

Publications
Proceedings (quarterly)
Monthly Circulars
Geological Guides (over 30 published; others in preparation)
Pamphlets
Publications List

1168 GEOMET SERVICES
Cox Lane, Chessington, Surrey KT9 1SJ
Department of Company, Borax Consolidated Limited, *q.v.*

Enquiries to the Information Officer

Subject coverage
evaluation and processing of industrial minerals

1169 GEOSYSTEMS
P.O. Box 1024, Westminster, London SW1P 2JL Tel. 01-222 7305
Telex 21120

Company, part of Lea Associates Limited

Enquiries to the Director (fees payable by non-members)

Subject coverage
geoscience, including mining, petroleum, oceanography, geology, geophysics, geochemistry; information and computer science applied to database construction and manipulation

Publications
Geotitles Weekly
Geocom Bulletin
Geoscience Documentation
Bibliography of Vertebrate Paleontology

1170 GERMAN CHAMBER OF INDUSTRY AND COMMERCE IN THE UNITED KINGDOM
11 Grosvenor Crescent, London SW1X 7EE Tel. 01-235 0691
Telex 919442

Chamber of Commerce

Enquiries to the Information Desk

Subject coverage
information, in German or English, about the economy, trade, industry and investment opportunities in the United Kingdom and in the Federal Republic of Germany; specialist departments for British Market, German Market, agency and cooperation, law and publicity

Publications
List, covering above subjects, available

1171 Sir Alexander GIBB & PARTNERS
Standard House, London Street, Reading RG1 4PS Tel. 0734 586171
Telex 847404

Company/Consultants

Enquiries to the Librarian, Technical Intelligence Department

Subject coverage
civil engineering

1172 GILLETTE RESEARCH & DEVELOPMENT LABORATORY
454 Basingstoke Road, Reading, Berkshire RG2 0QE Tel. 0734 85222
Company, subsidiary of Gillette Company, U.S.A. Telex 848339

Enquiries to the Librarian

Subject coverage
metallurgy; toiletries

GILLINGHAM DIVISIONAL LIBRARY *see* **KENT COUNTY LIBRARY**

1173 GIRLING LIMITED
Kings Road, Tyseley, Birmingham B11 2AH — Tel. 021-706 3371
Telex 338631

Company, subsidiary of Lucas Industries

No enquiry service

Subject coverage
brakes for cars, tractors, commercial vehicles and railways; shock absorbers

GIRVAN AREA LIBRARY *see* **KYLE AND CARRICK DISTRICT LIBRARIES**

1174 G K N GROUP TECHNOLOGICAL CENTRE
Birmingham New Road, Wolverhampton, West Midlands WV4 6BW — Tel. 0902 34361
Telex 339724

Company; formerly G K N Group Research Centre

Enquiries to the Information Officer

Subject coverage
metalworking; ferrous metallurgy; fasteners

GLACIOLOGICAL SOCIETY *now* **INTERNATIONAL GLACIOLOGICAL SOCIETY,** *q.v.*

GLAMORGAN COUNTY LIBRARIES *now* **MID GLAMORGAN COUNTY LIBRARY,** *q.v.*

GLAMORGAN POLYTECHNIC *now* **POLYTECHNIC OF WALES,** *q.v.*

1175 GLASGOW CHAMBER OF COMMERCE AND MANUFACTURES
30 George Square, Glasgow G2 1EQ — Tel. 041-202 2121
Telex 77667

Chamber of Commerce; houses the Secretariat of the Scottish Export Committee

Enquiries to the Information Officer

Subject coverage
Scottish industry and commerce; Glasgow and West of Scotland firms and sources of supply of goods and services; markets and market research (probably chargeable); statistics; commercial legislation, regulations, documentation

Special collection
Colquhoun Library (commercial and industrial history of Glasgow)

Publications
Annual Report
The Journal (monthly)
Industrial Index to Glasgow and the West of Scotland
Reports

1176 GLASGOW COLLEGE OF NAUTICAL STUDIES
21 Thistle Street, Glasgow G5 9XB — Tel. 041-429 3201
Nautical College

Enquiries to the Librarian

Subject coverage
maritime studies; marine engineering; navigation; marine radio, electronics and radar; maritime law and economics; meteorology; oceanography

1177 GLASGOW COLLEGE OF TECHNOLOGY
20 North Hanover Place, Glasgow G4 0BA — Tel. 041-332 7090
Telex 779341

College of Technology

Enquiries to the Periodicals Librarian

Subject coverage
ophthalmic optics

1178 GLASGOW DISTRICT LIBRARIES
Mitchell Library, 201 North Street, Glasgow G3 7DN Tel. 041-248 7121
Telex 778732

Public Libraries, formerly Glasgow Corporation Public Libraries

Enquiries to the Director

Subject coverage
general

Special collection
North British Locomotive Collection (photographic official records of the Company)

1179 GLASGOW SMALL FIRMS INFORMATION CENTRE
57 Bothwell Street, Glasgow G2 6TU Tel. 041-248 6014
Telex 779334

Government Information Centre of the Department of Industry

Enquiries to the Manager

Subject coverage
business studies and problems; management

Publications
Pamphlets on financial and business subjects

1180 GLASGOW UNIVERSITY
Adam Smith Library, 8 Bute Gardens, Glasgow G12 8RT Tel. 041-339 8855
University Library

Enquiries to the Librarian

Subject coverage
economics; town and regional development planning

Special collections
James Bonar Collection
Smart Memorial Collection

1181 GLASGOW UNIVERSITY LIBRARY
Hillhead Street, Glasgow G12 8QE Tel. 041-334 2122
Telex 778421

University Library

Enquiries to the Librarian, by letter only

Subject coverage
accountancy; aeronautics and fluid mechanics; agricultural chemistry, economics, technology and zoology; anatomy; animal developmental biology; animal nutrition, astronomy, bacteriology and immunology; biochemistry; biology; botany; cell biology; chemical physics; chemistry; civil engineering; computing science; conveyancing; economics; electronics and electrical engineering; genetics; geology; history of science; management studies; mathematics; mechanical engineering; mercantile law, microbiology, naval architecture; ocean engineering; parasitology; pathology; pharmacology; physics; physiology; statistics; taxation; topographic science; town and regional planning; virology; zoology

Special collections
Ferguson Collection (8,000 volumes on the history of chemistry)
Hunterian Collection (history of medicine and anatomy)
Library of the Institution of Engineers and Shipbuilders in Scotland
Foreign periodicals of the Geological Society of Glasgow

Publications
Directory of Departmental Libraries
Current Scientific Periodicals held in Departments
various bibliographies

GLASGOW UNIVERSITY *see also* **BUILDING SERVICES RESEARCH UNIT**

1182 GLASS AND ALLIED TRADES ASSOCIATION LIMITED
London Chamber of Commerce and Industry, 69 Cannon Street, London EC4N 5AB Tel. 01-248 4444
Telex 888941

Trade Association

Enquiries to the Secretary

Subject coverage
glass and allied trades

1183 GLASS MANUFACTURERS FEDERATION
19 Portland Place, London W1N 4BH Tel. 01-580 6952
Trade Association; houses and provides secretarial services for the British Lampblown Scientific Glassware Manufacturers Association, the European Glass Container Manufacturers Association, and the Association of Glass Container Manufacturers

Enquiries to the Information Officer or Director

Subject coverage
glass industry, including commercial, economic, statistical, technical, educational and training, and legislative information; safety; recycling; specifications

Publications
various general and specialised publications—a list available

1184 GLASS TEXTILE ASSOCIATION
King Edward House, New Street, Birmingham B2 4QP Tel. 021-643 5494
Trade Association

Enquiries to the Secretary

Subject coverage
glass yarns and glass textiles

1185 GLASSFIBRE REINFORCED CEMENT ASSOCIATION
Farthings End, Dukes Ride, Gerrards Cross, Buckinghamshire SL9 7LD Tel. 49 82606
Trade Association

Enquiries to the Secretary

Subject coverage
sources of supplies and technical advice concerning glassfibre reinforced cement

Publications
Codes of Practice (in preparation)
Technical Information (in preparation)

1186 GLASSHOUSE CROPS RESEARCH INSTITUTE
Worthing Road, Rustington, Littlehampton, West Sussex BN16 3PU Tel. 090 644481
State-aided Research Institute, of the Agricultural Research Council

Enquiries to the Scientific Information Officer

Subject coverage
cultivation of glasshouse crops and mushrooms and of bulbs, flowers, and shrubs grown in the open

Publications
Annual Report
Growers Bulletin
Proceedings of the National Glasshouse Conferences

1187 GLAXO LABORATORIES LIMITED AND GLAXO RESEARCH LIMITED
891–995 Greenford Road, Greenford, Middlesex UB6 0HE Tel. 01-422 3434
Telex 22134

Company, of Glaxo Holdings Limited; there are laboratories also at Ulverston, Cumbria and at Barnard Castle, Durham; another Research Department at Sefton Park, Stoke Poges, Bucks., *q.v.*

Enquiries to the Librarian

Subject coverage
chemistry; medicine; the use of antibiotics, corticosteroids and immunologicals; veterinary science; biological sciences; industrial and laboratory hazards

1188 GLAXO RESEARCH LIMITED
Sefton Park, Stoke Poges, Buckinghamshire SL2 4DZ Tel. 028-16 2121
Phamaceutical Company, subsidiary of Glaxo Holdings Limited

Enquiries to the Librarian

Subject coverage
antibiotics (excluding clinical information); fermentation; microbiology; biochemistry; plant physiology; food technology; nutrition

1189 GLENROTHES AND BUCKHAVEN TECHNICAL COLLEGE
Stenton Road, Glenrothes, Fife KY6 2RA Tel. Glenrothes 772233
Technical College; formerly Glenrothes Technical College

Enquiries to the Librarian

Subject coverage
mechanical engineering (craft level); electrical engineering; electronics; industrial studies; mining; commerce

GLENROTHES GROUP LIBRARY *see* **KIRKCALDY AND NORTH EAST FIFE DISTRICT LIBRARIES**

1190 GLOSTER DESIGN SERVICES (c & b) LIMITED
Gloucester Trading Estate, Hucclecote, Gloucester GL3 4AA Tel. 0452 69433
Company

Enquiries to the Director

Subject coverage
engineering design; light-weight structures

Publications
technical literature

1191 GLOUCESTER CITY COLLEGE OF TECHNOLOGY
Brunswick Road, Gloucester GL1 1HU Tel. 0452 35881 ext. 20
College of Further Education; part of the Gloucester Institute of Higher Education; formerly Gloucester Technical College

Enquiries to the Librarian

Subject coverage
building; business studies; electrical engineering; home economics; mechanical and motor vehicle engineering; wood science

1192 GLOUCESTER COUNTY LIBRARY
Shire Hall, Quayside, Gloucester GL1 2HY Tel. 0452 21444
Public Library system; main libraries at Cheltenham, Cinderford, Cirencester, Gloucester, Moreton-in-Marsh, Stroud

Enquiries to the County Librarian

Subject coverage
general; commercial information

Special collection
Day Collection of Natural History

1193 GLOUCESTER TECHNICAL INFORMATION SERVICE (GTIS)
205 Gloucester Road, Cheltenham GL51 8NJ Tel. 0242 55422/28782
Telex 43321

Interlibrary Cooperative Scheme

Enquiries to the Secretary

Subject coverage
general, technical

Publication
Contents List Service

1194 J. GLOVER & SONS LIMITED
Leacroft Works, Queens Road, Egham, Surrey TW20 9RU Tel. 903 3971
Company

Enquiries to the General Manager

Subject coverage
mobile steel shelving

Publications
illustrated brochures

GLYNDWR AREA LIBRARY *see* **CLWYD COUNTY LIBRARY SERVICE**

GOLBORNE GROUP LIBRARY *see* **WIGAN METROPOLITAN BOROUGH REFERENCE LIBRARIES**

GOLF BALL MANUFACTURERS CONFERENCE *see* **FEDERATION OF BRITISH MANUFACTURERS OF SPORTS AND GAMES LIMITED**

1195 GOOD HOUSEKEEPING INSTITUTE
Chestergate House, Vauxhall Bridge Road, London SW1V 1HF Tel. 01-834 2331
Consumer Research and Advice Organization

Enquiries to the Director

Subject coverage
consumer rights and law; cookery; home management; domestic appliances

1196 GOSPORT LIBRARY
High Street, Gosport, Hampshire PO12 1BT Tel. 070-17 80432
070-17 87952
Telex 86359

Public Library; Branch of Hampshire County Library *q.v.* and central library of Hampshire's Gosport District

Enquiries to the Librarian

Subject coverage
highway transport; history of technology; electric batteries; road and highway engineering; pavements; enamels and enamelling; protective and decorative coatings

1197 GOTHARD HOUSE GROUP OF COMPANIES LIMITED
Gothard House, Henley-on-Thames, Oxfordshire RG9 1AJ Tel. 049-12 3602
Publishers and Booksellers

Enquiries to the Information Officer

Subject coverage
technical, scientific and medical publishing and bookselling; information and library services; library stocking; typesetting and printing; information in most areas of research

Publications
Lists available
International Bibliographical Service in Human Medicine, Veterinary Medicine, Zoology and Chemistry (weekly card service)

1198 GOVERNMENT COMMUNICATION HEADQUARTERS
Priors Road, Cheltenham, Gloucestershire GL52 5AJ — Tel. 0242 21491
Telex 43612

Government Department, of the Foreign and Commonwealth Office

Enquiries, preferably by letter, to the Librarian

Subject coverage
telecommunications; electronic engineering; linguistics

GOVERNMENT SOCIAL SURVEY *now* **OFFICE OF POPULATION CENSUSES AND SURVEYS,** *q.v.*

1199 GR-STEIN REFRACTORIES LIMITED
Central Research Laboratories, Sandy Lane, Worksop, — Tel. 0909 2291
Nottinghamshire S80 3EU — Telex 54585
Private Company; formerly General Refractories Limited; subsidiary of Hepworth Ceramic Holdings Limited

No enquiry service

Subject coverage
refractory materials

1200 W.R. GRACE LIMITED
Technical Centre, Cromwell Road, St. Neots, — Tel. 0480 73141
Cambridgeshire PE19 1QL — Telex 32156
Company

Enquiries to the Information Officer

Subject coverage
cans and closures; shrink film; automotive sealants

1201 GRADUATE BUSINESS CENTRE
City University, 23 Goswell Road, London EC1M 7BB — Tel. 01-253 4399
Business School within the City University

Enquiries to the Librarian/Information Officer

Subject coverage
business studies; management; European business law; internal auditing; corporate strategy

Publications
Business Quest (journal, available on subscription)
Annual prospectus
Books in business and management

1202 GRAND METROPOLITAN LIMITED
Metropolitan House, 6–9 Stratford Place, London W1A 4YU — Tel. 01-629 6618
Company

Enquiries to the Press Officer

Subject coverage
hotels; restaurants; discotheques; brewing; distilling; milk products; industrial catering

1203 GRASSLAND RESEARCH INSTITUTE

Hurley, Maidenhead, Berkshire SL6 5LR Tel. 062-882 3631

Grant-aided Research Institute, of the Agricultural Research Council; houses also the Commonwealth Bureau of Pastures and Field Crops, *q.v.*, and the British Grassland Society

Enquiries to the Librarian

Subject coverage

grassland for agriculture, and all related subjects

Publications

Annual Report
Technical reports
Information leaflets

GRAVESEND PUBLIC LIBRARY *now* **GRAVESHAM DIVISIONAL LIBRARY** *see* **KENT COUNTY LIBRARY**

GRAVESHAM DIVISIONAL CENTRAL LIBRARY *see* **KENT COUNTY LIBRARY** *see also* **LIBRARY INFORMATION SERVICE TO INDUSTRY AND COMMERCE**

1204 GRAY LABORATORY OF THE CANCER RESEARCH CAMPAIGN

Mount Vernon Hospital, Northwood, Middlesex HA6 2RN Tel. 65 28611

Research Laboratory funded by Cancer Charity; there are Cancer Research Campaign Laboratories also at the University of Nottingham

Enquiries to the Director

Subject coverage

radiation biology applied to cancer treatment; pulse radiolysis

Publication

Annual Report

1205 GREAT YARMOUTH DIVISIONAL LIBRARY

Tolhouse Street, Great Yarmouth, Norfolk NR30 25H Tel. 0493 4551

Public Library, Divisional Library of Norfolk County Library

Enquiries to the Divisional Librarian

Subject coverage

general

1206 GREATER LONDON COUNCIL

Civil Engineering Library, Room G.09, Broadway Buildings, 50–64 Broadway, London SW1 Tel. 01-839 8822 ext. 3

Local Government Organization; part of the GLC Research Library, *q.v.*

Enquiries to the Information Officer

Subject coverage

civil engineering, particularly road and bridge works

1207 GREATER LONDON COUNCIL

Research Library, Intelligence Unit, Policy Studies and Intelligence Branch, Director General's Department, Greater London Council, Room 513/4, County Hall, London SE1 7PB Tel. 01-633 7343 and 6483/7169/7530/7007 Telex 919443

Local Government Organization; the above address also houses the Scientific Library, Room 755B (tel. 01-633 2207)

Enquiries to the Information Officer or Librarian; fees may be chargeable to external enquirers

Subject coverage

urban planning; transport problems and traffic planning and control; public health; housing; pollution, etc. statistics

Publications
Urban Abstracts (monthly, annual indexes)
Research Bibliographies (about 12 per annum, list available)
London Topics (about 6 per annum)
Computer Services (including COM indexes, retrospective searches, SDI information)
Research Memoranda List (monthly)
Greater London Intelligence Quarterly (technical journal)

1208 GREATER LONDON COUNCIL STAFF ASSOCIATION
164–168 Westminster Bridge Road, London SE1 7RW Tel. 01-633 5576
Trade Union

Enquiries to the Secretary

Subject coverage
pay and conditions of work of Greater London Council Staff

Publication
London Town

GREENOCK PUBLIC LIBRARIES *now* **INVERCLYDE DISTRICT LIBRARIES,** *q.v.*

1209 W. GREENWELL & COMPANY LIMITED
Bow Bells House, Bread Street, London EC4M 9EL Tel. 01-236 2040
Telex 883006

Company

Enquiries to the Librarian

Subject coverage
investment techniques; economics; statistics; information on companies and industries in general

1210 GREENWICH LIBRARIES
203–207 Woolwich Road, London SE10 0RL Tel. 01-858 6656
Public Libraries, including Plumstead Library

Enquiries to the Librarian

Subject coverage
industrial technology in general; inventions; patents; trade marks; materials and materials testing; energy, mechanical and electrical engineering; nuclear technology; hydraulics; steam engineering; naval engineering; foundation, tunnelling, bridge, railway and road engineering; river, port, harbour and dam engineering etc.

Special collection
British Standards (at Woolwich Library)

1211 GRIMSBY COLLEGE OF TECHNOLOGY
Nuns Corner, Grimsby, South Humberside Tel. 0472 79292
College of Further Education

Enquiries to the Tutor Librarian

Subject coverage
food science and technology; refrigeration; fishing; building; management

1212 GRIMSBY DIVISIONAL LIBRARY
Town Hall Square, Grimsby, Lincolnshire DN31 1HX Tel. 0472 59161
Public Library, Division of the Humberside County Leisure Services Department; formerly Grimsby Borough Libraries and part of the Lindsey County Libraries

Enquiries to the Divisional Leisure Services Officer

Subject coverage
fisheries; general

1213 GRINDLAYS BANK LIMITED
23 Fenchurch Street, London EC3 3DD Tel. 01-626 0545
Bank; formerly National and Grindlays Bank; affiliated to Lloyds Bank and Citibank N.A.

Enquiries to the Press Officer or Economics Department Librarian

Subject coverage
overseas banking, in Africa, Middle East, Far East and Indian sub-continent

GROCERS INSTITUTE *now* **INSTITUTE OF GROCERY DISTRIBUTION**, *q.v.*

GTIS *see* **GLOUCESTER TECHNICAL INFORMATION SERVICE**

1214 GUARDIAN ROYAL EXCHANGE ASSURANCE
Royal Exchange, London EC3V 3LS Tel. 01-283 7101
Assurance Company

Enquiries to the Company will be dealt with as helpfully as possible

Subject coverage
all classes of insurance business

GUERNSEY STATES HEADQUARTERS LIBRARY *see* **PRIAULX LIBRARY**

1215 GUILD OF ARCHITECTURAL IRONMONGERS
15 Soho Square, London W1V 5FB Tel. 01-439 1753
Trade Association; affiliated to the British Hardware Federation and the National Federation of Builders and Plumbers Merchants, *q.v.*

Enquiries to the Secretary

Subject coverage
architectural ironmongery

GUILD OF BRITISH NEWSPAPER EDITORS *see* **NEWSPAPER SOCIETY**

GUILD OF METAL PERFORATORS *see* **PERFORATED METAL EXPORT GROUP**

1216 GUILD OF SURVEYORS
The Lodge, Eastbury Farm, 33 Batchworth Lane, Northwood, Middlesex HA6 3EQ Tel. 84 27755
Guild and Technical Advisory Panel

Enquiries to the Honorary General Secretary

Subject coverage
all fields of surveying

Publication
Survey (3 times per annum)

GUILDFORD BRANCH LIBRARY *see* **SURREY COUNTY LIBRARY**

1217 GUILDFORD COUNTY COLLEGE OF TECHNOLOGY
Stoke Park, Guildford, Surrey GU1 13Z Tel. 0483 73201
Polytechnic, formerly Guildford County Technical College

Enquiries to the Librarian

Subject coverage
building construction; civil, electrical and mechanical engineering; catering; physical and natural sciences

Publication
Quarterly Abstracts

1218 Arthur GUINNESS AND COMPANY LIMITED
Park Royal Brewery, London NW10 7RR Tel. 01-965 7700
Telex 23498

Company; associated with Guinness Superlatives Limited

Enquiries to the Information Officer

Subject coverage
brewing

1219 GUISBOROUGH AGRICULTURAL CENTRE
Avenue Place, Guisborough, Cleveland TS14 6AX
Agricultural Centre

Enquiries to the Head of the Centre

Subject coverage
home economics and country crafts

1220 GUN TRADE ASSOCIATION
75 Harborne Road, Birmingham B15 3DH Tel. 021-454 6171 ext. 290
Trade Association

Enquiries to the Secretary

Subject coverage
firearms and shooting; legal aspects

Publication
summary of the Law relating to the Possession and Use of Firearms and Ammunition

1221 GWENT COLLEGE OF HIGHER EDUCATION
Library of the Faculty of Science and Technology and the Faculty of Management and Administration, Allt-yr-yn Avenue, Newport, Gwent NPT 5XA Tel. 0633 51525
College of Higher Education; formerly Newport and Monmouthshire College of Technology

Enquiries to the Librarian

Subject coverage
management; science and technology

Special collection
British Standards

1222 GWENT COUNTY LIBRARY
Cambria House, Caerleon, Gwent NP6 1XG Tel. 0633 421018
Public Library system; having five regional libraries: Blaenau (at Ebbw Vale), Islwyn, Monmouth, Newport and Torfaen

Enquiries to the County Librarian

Subject coverage
general

1223 GWYNEDD LIBRARY SERVICE
Headquarters Library, Maesincla, Caernarfon, Gwynedd LL55 1LH Tel. 0286 4441 & 61565
Public Library Service, formed by the amalgamation of the former seven authorities: Caernarfonshire, Anglesey and Merioneth County Libraries, Bangor City Library, Caernarfon, Conwy and Llandudno Public Libraries; Area Libraries are at Aberconwy, Arfon/Dwyfor, Meirionnydd and Anglesey

Enquiries to the Librarian at County H.Q. or at any of the Area Libraries

Subject coverage
general

1224 HACKNEY CENTRAL LIBRARY
Mare Street, Hackney, London E8 1HG Tel. 01-985 8262
Public Library Service; includes Homerton, Shoreditch, *q.v.* and Stoke Newington Libraries

Enquiries to the Librarian

Subject coverage
transport engineering; road vehicles; shipbuilding, ships and boats; aeronautical engineering, aircraft; astronautics

1225 HACKNEY COLLEGE
Keltan House, 89/115 Mare Street, London E8 4RG Tel. 01-985 8484
Technical College; includes the Poplar Centre, formerly Poplar Technical College, which, with Hackney Technical College and Hackney & Stoke Newington College of Further Education, was part of the merger which formed the present Hackney College

Enquiries to the Librarian

Subject coverage
horology; marine engineering; mechanical engineering; housing management

1226 HACKNEY COLLEGE (POPLAR CENTRE)
112 Poplar High Street, London E14 0AF Tel. 01-987 4205
College; formerly Poplar Technical College

Enquiries to the Librarian

Subject coverage
marine engineering; foundry and patternmaking; naval architecture

1227 HAIGH & HOCHLAND LIMITED
Precinct Centre, Oxford Road, Manchester M13 9QA Tel. 061-273 4156
Booksellers

Enquiries to the Bibliography Section

Subject coverage
availability and bibliographical details of English and European books in technical and medical fields

1228 HAIRDRESSING MANUFACTURERS AND WHOLESALERS ASSOCIATION LIMITED
69 Cannon Street, London EC4N 5AB Tel. 01-248 4444
Telex 888941

Trade Association

Enquiries to the Secretary

Subject coverage
supply of hairdressing equipment and accessories

HALDIS *see* **CALDIS**

HALE PUBLIC LIBRARY *see* **TRAFFORD BOROUGH LIBRARY SERVICE**

HALESOWEN DISTRICT LIBRARY *see* **DUDLEY PUBLIC LIBRARIES**

HALIFAX AND DISTRICT INFORMATION SERVICE (HALDIS) *now* **CALDERDALE INFORMATION SERVICE,** *q.v.*

HALIFAX CENTRAL LIBRARY *now* **CALDERDALE CENTRAL LIBRARY**
see **CALDERDALE METROPOLITAN DISTRICT LIBRARIES**

1229 HALL GREEN TECHNICAL COLLEGE
Cole Bank Road, Birmingham B28 8ES Tel. 021-777 6251 ext. 28
Technical College

Enquiries to the Tutor Librarian

Subject coverage
building; engineering; motor vehicle engineering

1230 HALTON COLLEGE OF FURTHER EDUCATION
Kingsway, Widnes, Lancashire WA8 7QQ Tel. 051-423 1391
College of Further Education; formerly Widnes Technical College *or* Widnes College of Further Education

Enquiries to the Tutor Librarian

Subject coverage
mechanical engineering; electrical engineering; instrument engineering; chemistry

1231 HAMILTON DISTRICT LIBRARIES
98 Cadzow Street, Hamilton, Lanarkshire ML3 6HQ Tel. 05522 21188
Public Library

Enquiries to the Chief Librarian

Subject coverage
general

1232 HAMMERSMITH AND WEST LONDON COLLEGE
Greyhound Road, London W14 9SE Tel. 01-385 7183
College of Further and Higher Education

Enquiries to the Librarian

Subject coverage
business studies

1233 HAMMERSMITH PUBLIC LIBRARIES
Central Library, Shepherds Bush Road, Hammersmith, London W6 7AT Tel. 01-748 6032
Public Libraries

Enquiries to the Librarian

Subject coverage
general

1234 HAMMERSMITH SCHOOL OF BUILDING
Lime Grove, London W12 8EB Tel. 01-743 3321
College of Further and Higher Education

Enquiries to the Librarian

Subject coverage
construction industry

1235 HAMPSHIRE COUNTY LIBRARY
County Library Headquarters and Central Reference Library, Tel. 0962 3301–3
81 North Walls, Winchester, Hampshire SO23 8BY Telex 47121
Public Library system; principal District Libraries at Andover, *q.v.*, Basingstoke, *q.v.*, Eastleigh, Fareham, Farnborough, *q.v.*, Fleet, Gosport, *q.v.*, Havant, Lymington, Petersfield, Portsmouth, *q.v.*, Southampton, *q.v.* and Winchester, *q.v.*; Administrative Centre of HATRICS (Hampshire Area Technical, Research, Industrial and Commercial Service), *q.v.*

Enquiries to the Librarian

Subject coverage
pure science; mathematics (including computers); palaeontology; botanical sciences; electrical engineering and generation; electric traction; forestry

Special collection
British Standards

1236 HAMPSHIRE TECHNICAL RESEARCH INDUSTRIAL COMMERCIAL SERVICE (HATRICS)
Hampshire County Library Headquarters, 81 North Walls, Winchester SO23 8BY — Tel. 0962 3301/2/3, 0962 62171/2/3, Telex 47121

Interlibrary and Interorganizational Cooperative Scheme

Enquiries to the Librarians of Portsmouth Central Library, Southampton Central Library (Reference Library) or Winchester Central Reference Library

Subject coverage
commercial, scientific, technical

Publications
H.A.T.R.I.C.S.: Directory of Resources, 6th edition 1975.
News Bulletin
Bibliographies:
A bibliography of fibreoptics 1971.
Containerization: a bibliography 2nd ed. 1969.
Marketing in the sixties 1968.
Numerical control of machine tools 1970.
Urban transport innovation: a bibliography (revised 1976)

1237 HANDSWORTH TECHNICAL COLLEGE
Whitehead Road, Aston, Birmingham B6 6EU — Tel. 021-327 1493
Technical College; formerly Handsworth and Erdington Technical College; includes a Centre at Golds Hill Road, Handsworth

Enquiries to the Tutor Librarian

Subject coverage
electrical engineering; automobile engineering; clothing technology; economics; commerce

1238 HANNAH RESEARCH INSTITUTE
Kirkhill, Ayr KA6 5HL — Tel. 0292 77292
Research Institute, formerly Hannah Dairy Research Institute

Enquiries to the Information Officer

Subject coverage
production and utilization of milk, including herbage production and conservation; milk composition; milk protein; milk analysis; hygiene of milk production; processing characteristics of milk and milk powder; climate-related aspects of animal productivity

Publication
Research Report (annual)

1239 HARINGEY LIBRARIES, MUSEUM AND ARTS DEPARTMENT
Bruce Castle, Lordship Lane, Tottenham, London N17 8NU — Tel. 01-808 8772, Telex 263257 (Hornsey Library)

Public Library Service; including Hornsey Public Library

Enquiries to the Controller of Libraries or to any library service point

Subject coverage
general; mining; naval engineering and technology; civil and structural engineering; railway and road engineering; hydraulic engineering and construction; inland water, rivers, ports, harbours, coast works and dams; water supply; lighting

1240 HARLAND AND WOLFF LIMITED
Queen's Island, Belfast BT3 9DU — Tel. 0232 58456, Telex 74396

Company

Enquiries to the Public Affairs Manager

Subject coverage
shipbuilding

1241 HARLOW TECHNICAL COLLEGE
College Gate, The High, Harlow, Essex CM20 1LT Tel. 0279 20131 ext. 47
College of Further Education

Enquiries to the Librarian

Subject coverage
mechanical and electrical engineering; management; journalism; catering

Special collection
Spagnoletti Collection on management

1242 HARPER ADAMS AGRICULTURAL COLLEGE
Newport, Shropshire TF10 8NB Tel. 0952 811280
College of Agriculture; incorporating the National Institute of Poultry Husbandry; main centre for the West Central Region of the National Institute of Agricultural Botany

Enquiries to the Director of Studies

Subject coverage
feeding and management of cattle, pigs, and poultry; cropping experiments (potato, sugar beet, grass, cereal, maize, peas, beans, brassica); NIAB variety trials (general information); agricultural education

Publication
Farm Guide (annual)

HARRIS COLLEGE *now* **PRESTON POLYTECHNIC,** *q.v.*

1243 HARRIS TWEED ASSOCIATION LIMITED
Station Square, Inverness IV1 1LE Tel. 0463 31270
Trade Association

Enquiries to the Secretary

Subject coverage
Harris tweed industry

HARROGATE DIVISIONAL LIBRARY *see* **NORTH YORKSHIRE COUNTY LIBRARY**

1244 HARROW COLLEGE OF TECHNOLOGY & ART
Northwick Park, Watford Road, Harrow, Middlesex HA1 3TP Tel. 01-864 4411 ext. 43
College of Technology

Enquiries to the Librarian

Subject coverage
information graphics; fashion; pottery; applied photography; engineering; management

1245 HARROW PUBLIC LIBRARIES
P.O. Box 4, Civic Centre, Harrow, Middlesex HA1 2UU Tel. 01-863 5611
Telex 923826
Public Reference and Lending Library; Branch at Gayton Road, Harrow

Enquiries to the Librarian

Subject coverage
general

1246 HARTLEPOOL DISTRICT LIBRARY
Clarence Road, Hartlepool, Cleveland TS24 7EW Tel. 0429 72905 *and* 63778
Telex 58617
Public Library; formerly Hartlepool Public Libraries; now one of the District Libraries of Cleveland County Library Service

Enquiries to the District Librarian

Subject coverage
general

Special collection
British Standards

HARWOOD PUBLIC LIBRARY *see* **BOLTON METROPOLITAN BOROUGH CENTRAL LIBRARY**

1247 HASTINGS AREA LIBRARY
Brassey Institute, 13 Claremont, Hastings, Sussex TN34 1HA Tel. Hastings 420501
Public Library, part of East Sussex County Library; formerly Hastings Public Library

Enquiries to the Area Librarian

Subject coverage
general

Special collection
Brassey Collection, including books relating to the work of Thomas Brassey, the railway contractor

1248 HATFIELD POLYTECHNIC
P.O. Box 110, College Lane, Hatfield, Hertfordshire AL10 9AD Tel. 070-72 68100
Telex 262413
Technical College; formerly Hatfield College of Technology; including the National Reprographic Centre for Documentation, *q.v.*; providing the Headquarters of the Hertfordshire Technical Information Service (HERTIS) *q.v.*

Enquiries to the Chief Information Officer or Polytechnic Librarian

Subject coverage
civil, electrical, mechanical and production engineering; computer science; management sciences and business studies; biology; chemistry; mathematics and statistics; operational research; astronomy; economics

Publications
Further and Higher Education Review (fortnightly abstract series)
Polytechnic Research Report (annual)

1249 HATRA
7 Gregory Boulevard, Nottingham NG7 6LD Tel. 0602 623311
Research Association, formerly Hosiery and Allied Trades Research Association

Enquiries to the Information Officer

Subject coverage
knitting; lace; hosiery; clothing manufacture; textiles and dyeing

Publication
Hosiery Abstracts (monthly)

HATRICS *see* **HAMPSHIRE TECHNICAL RESEARCH INDUSTRIAL COMMERCIAL SERVICE**

1250 HAUGHLEY RESEARCH FARMS LIMITED
Walnut Tree Manor, Haughley, Stowmarket, Suffolk IP14 3RS
Company, part of the Pye Research Centre, *q.v.*

Enquiries to the Director

Subject coverage
experimental farm husbandry

HAVANT DISTRICT LIBRARY *see* **HAMPSHIRE COUNTY LIBRARY**

1251 HAVERING CENTRAL LIBRARY
St. Edwards Way, Romford, Essex RM1 3AR Tel. 0708 44297
Public Library

Enquiries to the Borough Librarian or Reference Librarian

Subject coverage
all subjects

Publication
LOGA (Local Government Abstracts) is edited from the Havering Library address

1252 HAVERING TECHNICAL COLLEGE LIBRARY
42 Ardleigh Green Road, Hornchurch, Essex RM11 2LL Tel. 49 55011
College of Further Education

Enquiries to the Tutor-Librarian

Subject coverage
mechanical engineering; motor vehicle engineering; electrical engineering; radio and television engineering; physics; chemistry; biology; business studies; banking; accounting; management; exporting

1253 HAWKER SIDDELEY AVIATION LIMITED
Richmond Road, Kingston-upon-Thames, Surrey KT2 5QZ Tel. 01-546 7741
Telex 23726
Company; there are libraries at the Company's installations at Brough, Yorkshire; Hatfield, Hertfordshire; and Woodford, Stockport, Cheshire

Enquiries to the Information Officer

Subject coverage
aircraft engineering; aerodynamics; metallurgy and materials

Special collections
AIAA, NASA, SAWE, ARC, RAE literature

Publication
Hawker Siddeley News

1254 HAZARD CONTROL LIMITED
61 High Street, Barnet, Hertfordshire EN5 5UR Tel. 01-449 3580
Telex 264880

Company, part of G.C. Davis & Company Limited, *q.v.*

Enquiries to the Technical Director

Subject coverage
control of toxic and explosive atmospheres

1255 HAZARDOUS MATERIALS SERVICE
Atomic Energy Research Establishment, Harwell, Didcot, Oxfordshire OX11 0RA Tel. 0235 24141
Government Centre, within the United Kingdom Atomic Energy Authority

Enquiries to the Information Officer

Subject coverage
hazardous materials, chemicals; accidents, spillages; safety

HAZLETON MEMORIAL LIBRARY *see* **PRODUCTION ENGINEERING RESEARCH ASSOCIATION (PERA)**

1256 HEALDERS AND TWISTERS TRADE AND FRIENDLY SOCIETY
20 Uppergate, Hepworth, Huddersfield HD7 1TG Tel. 048 489 4509
Trade Union

Enquiries to the General Secretary

Subject coverage
industrial relations in wool textiles; wool textile industry

1257 HEALTH AND SAFETY EXECUTIVE
H.Q. Library, Baynards House, 1 Chepstow Place, London W2 4TY Tel. 01-229 3456 Ext. 497
Government Department, formerly Directorate of Occupational Safety and Health; includes the Alkali and Clean Air Inspectorate, the Mines and Quarries Inspectorate, the Factory Inspectorate, the Nuclear Installations Inspectorate, Units for Agricultural Safety and Safety of Diving and Offshore Installations, and the Committee of Experts on Major Hazards

Enquiries to the Librarian

Subject coverage
pollution; occupational health and safety; mining and quarrying; chemical hazards; engineering hazards; electrical hazards; nuclear hazards; dust hazards; noise hazards; ventilation; factory processes; legislation

Publication
Hazard (a proposed new journal)

HEALTH AND SAFETY EXECUTIVE *see also*
BRITISH APPROVAL SERVICE FOR ELECTRICAL EQUIPMENT IN FLAMMABLE ATMOSPHERES
EMPLOYMENT MEDICAL ADVISORY SERVICE
INDUSTRIAL AND SAFETY CENTRE
SAFETY IN MINES RESEARCH ESTABLISHMENT

HEALTH PHYSICS AND NUCLEAR MEDICINE UNIT *see* **SCOTTISH UNIVERSITIES RESEARCH AND REACTOR CENTRE**

1258 HEALTH VISITORS ASSOCIATION
36 Eccleston Square, London SW1V 1PF Tel. 01-834 9523
Professional Association/Trade Union

Enquiries to the Secretary for Public Relations and Research

Subject coverage
general information on the profession

Publication
Health Visitor (monthly)

1259 HEARING AID COUNCIL
40A Ludgate Hill, London EC4M 7DE
Registration Council set up by the Hearing Aid Council Act 1968

Enquiries to the Registrar, but advice on aids not given

Subject coverage
hearing aids register membership

1260 HEAT TRANSFER AND FLUID FLOW SERVICE
Atomic Energy Research Establishment, HTFS, Building 392, Harwell, Oxfordshire OX11 0RA Tel. 0235 24141 Telex 83135
Government Research Laboratory

Enquiries to the Information Officer

Subject coverage
heat transfer; condensation; boiling; evaporation; general fluid flow; cryogenic fluids; combustion; heat transfer in nuclear reactors

Publications
HTFS Digest
HTFS Information Sheets

1261 HEATING AND VENTILATING CONTRACTORS ASSOCIATION
ESCA House, 34 Palace Court, London W2 4JG Tel. 01-229 2488
Trade Association

Enquiries, from members only, to the Information Officer

Subject coverage
heating, ventilating and air-conditioning industry

Publications
Annual Report
Heating, Ventilating, and Air Conditioning Year Book
Wage Agreement Information
Technical, contractual, educational, and industrial relations matters publications (over 100) are available to members only

HEATING AND VENTILATING RESEARCH ASSOCIATION *now* **BUILDING SERVICES RESEARCH AND INFORMATION ASSOCIATION,** *q.v.*

1262 HEBBURN TECHNICAL COLLEGE
Mill Lane, Hebburn, South Tyneside NE31 2ER Tel. 0632 832741
Technical College

Enquiries to the Librarian

Subject coverage
general

HEBDEN BRIDGE PUBLIC LIBRARY *see* **CALDERDALE METROPOLITAN DISTRICT LIBRARIES**

1263 W. HEFFER & SONS LIMITED
20 Trinity Street, Cambridge CB2 3NG Tel. 0223 58351
Telex 81298

Company/Booksellers

Enquiries to the General Manager

Subject coverage
books and periodicals in major academic disciplines

1264 H.J. HEINZ COMPANY LIMITED
Hayes Park, Hayes, Middlesex UB4 8AL Tel. 01-573 7757 ext. 457
Telex 261477

Company

Enquiries to the Information Officer

Subject coverage
food processing

HEMEL HEMPSTEAD CENTRAL LIBRARY *see* **HERTFORDSHIRE LIBRARY SERVICE**

HENDON COLLEGE OF TECHNOLOGY *now* **MIDDLESEX POLYTECHNIC,** *q.v.*

1265 HENLEY CENTRE FOR FORECASTING LIMITED
27 St. Johns Square, London EC1M 2DP Tel. 01-251 3841
Company (Consultants); formerly James Morrell & Associates Limited; associated with the Administrative Staff College, Greenlands, Henley-on-Thames, Oxfordshire RG9 3AU

Enquiries to the Director

Subject coverage
economic and business forecasting; environmental forecasting; forecasting systems and methods

Publications
Framework Forecasts for the U.K.
Forecasts of Exchange Rate Movements
Director's Guide
Costs and Prices
Framework Forecasts for the E.E.C. Economies
Forecasts for the Stock Market
A Measure for Portfolio Performance
Catalogue of Publications/Services

1266 HERBERT WHITLEY TRUST
190 Totnes Road, Paignton, Devonshire Tel. 0803 58189
Educational Charity

Enquiries to the Managing Trustee

Subject coverage
biology; zoos; horticulture

1267 HEREFORD & WORCESTER COUNTY LIBRARY
Loves Grove, Worcester WR1 3BY Tel. 0905 23400
Public Library Service; Divisional Libraries: Hereford Division at Hereford, North East Worcestershire at Redditch, North West Worcestershire at Kidderminster, South Worcestershire at Worcester

Enquiries to the Librarians

Subject coverage
general

1268 HEREFORD COLLEGE OF AGRICULTURE
Holme Lacy, Hereford Tel. 043-273 282/316
Agricultural College; formerly Herefordshire School of Agriculture; library facilities staffed and administered by the Hereford and Worcester County Libraries

Enquiries to the Librarian

Subject coverage
agriculture; horticulture, environmental studies and domestic economy

HEREFORD DIVISIONAL LIBRARY *see* **HEREFORD AND WORCESTER COUNTY LIBRARY**

1269 HEREFORDSHIRE TECHNICAL COLLEGE
Folly Lane, Hereford HR1 1LS Tel. 0432 67311 ext. 65
Technical College

Enquiries to the Tutor-Librarian

Subject coverage
catering; building; engineering; motor vehicle engineering

Special collection
British Standards

1270 HERIOT-WATT UNIVERSITY LIBRARY
Chambers Street, Edinburgh EH1 1HX Tel. 031-225 8432
University Library; also at Riccarton, Currie, Edinburgh EH14 4AS, the address of the Institute of Offshore Engineering and the Syntex Research Centre *qq.v.*

Enquiries to the Librarian

Subject coverage
biological sciences; brewing; computer science, pharmacy; building; chemical and process engineering; electrical and electronic engineering; offshore engineering

1271 HERRING INDUSTRY BOARD
Sea Fisheries House, 10 Young Street, Edinburgh EH2 4JQ — Tel. 031-225 2515, Telex 727225

Statutory Government Body; H.Q. office of the White Fish Authority, *q.v.*

Enquiries to the Public Relations Officer

Subject coverage
U.K. fishery matters

Publications
Annual Report
Story of the Herring
The Herring Book
All about the Kipper
Versatile Herring in Catering
Filmstrip List

1272 HERTFORD COLLEGE
Cattle Street, Oxford OX1 3BW — Tel. 0865 41434
University

Enquiries to the Librarian

Subject coverage
general, for first degree courses

1273 HERTFORDSHIRE COLLEGE OF AGRICULTURE AND HORTICULTURE
Oaklands, St. Albans, Hertfordshire AL4 0JA — Tel. 56 50651
College of Agriculture

Enquiries to the Librarian

Subject coverage
science, husbandry and economics of British agriculture and horticulture; European agriculture

Special collection
Barley Collection (illustrated, rare or antiquarian books on agriculture and horticulture)

Publication
Periodicals Index

1274 HERTFORDSHIRE COLLEGE OF BUILDING
St Peters Road, St Albans, Hertfordshire AL1 3RX — Tel. 56 54273
College of Further Education; formerly St. Albans College of Further Education *and* Hertfordshire College of Building

Enquiries to the Librarian

Subject coverage
construction, building services, engineering services, civil engineering, building management, building economics, quantity surveying, building crafts, furniture crafts, machine woodworking, architecture, town planning, education of construction technicians, building regulations, building law

Special collections
British Standards
Trade literature on building materials and components

Publication
Safety in the Construction Industry

1275 HERTFORDSHIRE LIBRARY SERVICE
County Hall, Hertford, Hertfordshire SG13 8EJ — Tel. 099-25 4242 ext. 5485, Telex 81272

Public Library Serivce, formerly Hertfordshire County Library; Divisional Libraries: Mid-Herts at Welwyn Garden City, East Herts at Stevenage, and West Herts at Hemel Hempstead

Enquiries to the Librarian

Subject coverage
general; (at the Hertford Branch), architecture; town planning and highway engineering

1276 HERTFORDSHIRE LIBRARY SERVICE
Technical Book Service, Central Library, Southgate, Stevenage, Hertfordshire SG1 1HD — Tel. 0438 4500, Telex 826723
Public Library

Enquiries to the Librarian

Subject coverage
science and technology

1277 HERTFORDSHIRE TECHNICAL LIBRARY AND INFORMATION SERVICE (HERTIS)
P.O. Box 110, Hatfield Polytechnic, Hatfield, Hertfordshire AL10 9AD — Tel. 940 68100 ext. 321 *or* 326, Telex 262413

Interlibrary Cooperative Scheme, based on libraries of all the Hertfordshire Colleges; comprising the Industrial Services (to members in Hertfordshire and adjacent counties) and the Bureau of Research and Consultancy

Enquiries to the Chief Information Officer

Subject coverage
technical and commercial

Publications
Hertis News (free to members)
Hertis: a guide for industrial members
Directory of Resources for Research and Consultancy
Directory of Consultancy Services
Bibliographies (list available)

HERTIS *see* **HERTFORDSHIRE TECHNICAL LIBRARY AND INFORMATION SERVICE**

HEXHAM PUBLIC LIBRARY *now* **TYNEDALE BRANCH LIBRARY**
see **NORTHUMBERLAND COUNTY LIBRARY**

HEYWOOD AREA LIBRARY *see* **ROCHDALE LIBARIES AND ARTS SERVICES**

1278 HIGH DUTY ALLOYS LIMITED
89 Buckingham Avenue, Slough SL1 4PA — Tel. 0753 23901, Telex 848134

Company, member of Hawker Siddeley Group

Enquiries to the Information Services Officer

Subject coverage
aluminium alloys; die casting and extrusion of aluminium alloys; forging of aluminium, steel, titanium and nickel base alloys

Publications
Publications on the products

1279 HIGH PRESSURE TECHNOLOGY ASSOCIATION
Department of Chemical Engineering, Imperial College, London SW7 2AZ — Tel. 01-589 5111
Scientific Association

No enquiry service

Subject coverage
high pressure science and engineering, including safety

Publications
High Pressure Safety Code
Directory of High Pressure Work in the British Isles

1280 HIGH SPEED STEEL TOOL BIT ASSOCIATION
3 Melbourne Avenue, Sheffield S10 2QJ Tel. 0742 663084
Trade Association; member of the Natural Federation of Engineers Tool Manufacturers

Enquiries to the Secretary

Subject coverage
manufacture of high speed tool bits

HIGH WYCOMBE COLLEGE OF TECHNOLOGY AND ART *now* **BUCKINGHAMSHIRE COLLEGE OF FURTHER EDUCATION,** *q.v.*

HIGH WYCOMBE DIVISIONAL LIBRARY *see* **BUCKINGHAMSHIRE COUNTY LIBRARY**

HIGHAM FERRERS DISTRICT LIBRARY *see* **NORTHAMPTONSHIRE LIBRARIES**

1281 HIGHBURY TECHNICAL COLLEGE
Dovercourt Road, Cosham, Portsmouth, Hampshire PO6 2SA Tel. 070-18 83131
Technical College

Enquiries to the Librarian

Subject coverage
building construction; catering; commerce; computer science; domestic science; electrical engineering; hotel-keeping; management; marine engineering; mechanical engineering

1282 HIGHLAND REGION LIBRARY SERVICE
Regional Buildings, Glenurquhart Road, Inverness TV3 5NX Tel. 0463 34121
Public Library Service; formed by the merger of Caithness, Sutherland, Ross & Cromarty and Inverness County Libraries and Inverness Public Library; its 3 Divisional Libraries are at Inverness, Dingwall (Ross & Cromarty) and Wick (Caithness/Sutherland)

Enquiries to the Regional Librarian or the Divisional Librarians

Subject coverage
general and Scottish Highlands

1283 HIGHLANDS AND ISLANDS DEVELOPMENT BOARD
Bridge House, 27 Bank Street, Inverness IV1 1QR Tel. 0463 34171
Telex 75267
Government Agency, of the Scottish Economic Planning Department

Enquiries to the Secretary

Subject coverage
regional development; industrial development and marketing; fisheries, including fish farming; boatbuilding; land use; tourism; transport; agriculture

Publications
North 7 (3 or 4 times per annum)
Annual Report
Surveys, Studies and Occasional Papers
Highlands and Islands in Print (publications list)

HIGHWAY AND TRAFFIC TECHNICIANS ASSOCIATION LIMITED *see* **INSTITUTION OF HIGHWAY ENGINEERS**

1284 HILL FARMING RESEARCH ORGANISATION
Bush Estate, Penicuik, Midlothian EH26 0PY Tel. 031-445 3401
Independent grant-aided Research Institute, of the Agricultural Research Council

Enquiries to the Information Officer

Subject coverage
performance of sheep in hill and upland environments; synthesis of hill and upland farming systems; beef cattle in hill and upland environments; pasture production; husbandry of red deer

Publication
Triennial Report

1285 HILLINGDON PUBLIC LIBRARY
22 High Street, Uxbridge, Middlesex UB8 1JN — Tel. 89 37446, Telex 934224

Public Library

Enquiries to the Librarian

Subject coverage
general

HINCKLEY AREA LIBRARY *see* **LEICESTERSHIRE LIBRARIES AND INFORMATION SERVICE**

1286 HIRST ELECTRIC INDUSTRIES LIMITED
Gatwick Road, Crawley, Sussex RH10 2SA — Tel. 0293 25721/5, Telex 87424

Company, subsidiary of BOC Limited

Enquiries to the Marketing and Sales Manager

Subject coverage
precision resistance welding of ferrous, non-ferrous and dissimilar metals components; thermocompression bonders and microwelders for semiconductor manufacture; permanent magnets; moisture analysis; drying techniques by microwave heating; power supplies, transformers, and rectifiers

HITCHIN COLLEGE *now* **NORTH HERTS COLLEGE,** *q.v.*

1287 H.M. CUSTOMS & EXCISE LIBRARY & INFORMATION SERVICES
Kings Beam House, 39–41 Mark Lane, London EC3R 7HE — Tel. 01-626 1515 ext. 2509
Government Department

Enquiries to the Librarian

Subject coverage
indirect taxation; trade statistics; general fiscal matters, economics, and revenue history

Special collections
Under the terms of the Public Records Act 1958, a wide range of manuscript material is available for bona fide research into the history of commerce, sea ports, shipping, H.M. Customs & Excise, etc

Publications
H.M. Customs and Excise tariff and overseas trade classification
Annual Statement of trade of the U.K.
Guide to the classification for overseas trade statistics
VAT News

1288 H.M. NAUTICAL ALMANAC OFFICE
Royal Greenwich Observatory, Herstmonceux Castle, Hailsham, East Sussex BN27 1RP — Tel. 032-181 3171, Telex 87451
Government Department; of the Royal Greenwich Observatory under the direction of the Science Research Council, funded through the Department of Education and Science

Enquiries to the Superintendent

Subject coverage
astronomical ephemerides, such as coordinates of the sun, moon, and planets, phases of the moon, eclipses; times of sunrise, sunset, twilight, moonrise, moonset, for particular places; calendarial information

Publications
Astronomical Ephemeris and Explanatory Supplement (annual)
Air Almanac (annual)
Nautical Almanac (annual)
Star Almanac for Land Surveyors (annual)
Various Navigational and Mathematical tables

1289 H.M. STATIONERY OFFICE
Atlantic House, Holborn Viaduct, London EC1P 1BN Tel. 01-248 9876 ext. 6151
Telex 22805

Government Department

Enquiries, on government publications, to PM2B, H.M.S.O., as above

Subject coverage
publication for Parliament, and Government Departments; agency for United Nations, E.E.C. and other international organizational publications

Publications
Daily, Monthly, Annual and Sectional Lists of official publications

1290 H.M. STATIONERY OFFICE
Sovereign House, Botolph Street, Norwich NR3 1DN Tel. 0603 22211 ext. 7376
Government Departmental Library

Enquiries to the Librarian

Subject coverage
printing; typography; management training; public administration

1291 HOECHST PHARMACEUTICALS LIMITED
Hoechst House, Salisbury Road, Hounslow, Middlesex TW4 6JH Tel. 01-570 7712
Manufacturing Company, Division of Hoechst U.K. Limited

Enquiries to Medical Services (Information)

Subject coverage
general medicine; biochemstry; pharmacology; toxicology of drugs; methodology of drug evaluation

Special collection
Symposia Medica Hoechst

HOLBORN COLLEGE OF LAW, LANGUAGES AND COMMERCE *now* **POLYTECHNIC OF CENTRAL LONDON,** *q.v.*

1292 HOLBORN LIBRARY
32/38 Theobalds Road, London WC1X 8PA Tel. 01-405 2705
Telex 24314

Public Library, of the London Borough of Camden Libraries and Arts Department

Enquiries to the Lending Librarian; for commercial reference, to the Reference Librarian

Subject coverage
commerce and transport (to 1975)

Publication
Commercial Library Bulletin (irregular)

1293 HOLLINGS COLLEGE
Old Hall Lane, Fallowfield, Manchester M14 6HR Tel. 061-224 7341
College of Further Education

Enquiries to the Librarian

Subject coverage
catering; food technology; clothing design and manufacture

HOLTON PARK DISTRICT LIBRARY *see* **OXFORDSHIRE COUNTY LIBRARIES**

1294 HOME GROWN CEREALS AUTHORITY
Hamlyn House, Highgate Hill, London N19 5PR Tel. 01-272 4812
Telex 27615

Statutory Authority

Enquiries to the Research Officer

Subject coverage
cereals marketing

Publications
Annual progress reports

HOME LAUNDERING CONSULTATIVE COUNCIL *see* **BRITISH MAN-MADE FIBRES FEDERATION**

1295 HOME OFFICE CENTRAL RESEARCH ESTABLISHMENT
Aldermaston, Reading, Berkshire RG7 4PN Tel. 07356 3022
Government Department

Enquiries to the Director

Subject coverage
forensic science; biology; study of blood and human tissues; chemistry; toxicology

Special collections
data of analytical characteristics
Footprints Collection in kind, photographs and documents
Headlamp Collection in kind, photographs and documents

Publication
Abstracts for operational forensic science laboratories (Home Office use only)

HOME OFFICE *see also* **POISONS BOARD**

1296 HOME TIMBER MERCHANTS ASSOCIATION OF ENGLAND AND WALES
1 Warwick Street, Leamington Spa, Warwickshire CV32 5LW Tel. 0926 29905
Trade Association

Enquiries to the Secretary

Subject coverage
British sawmilling industry

HOMERTON PUBLIC LIBRARY *see* **HACKNEY CENTRAL LIBRARY**

1297 HONG KONG GOVERNMENT OFFICE
6 Grafton Street, London W1 Tel. 01-499 9821 ext. 26
Foreign Government Representational Organization

Enquiries to the Librarian

Subject coverage
Hong Kong affairs

1298 HONG KONG TRADE DEVELOPMENT COUNCIL
14 Cockspur Street, London SW1Y 5DP Tel. 01-930 7955
Telex 916923

Trade Promotion Council

Enquiries, trade, to the Trade Enquiry Section; others, to the Information Officer

Subject coverage
Hong Kong—U.K. trade

Publications
Hong Kong Enterprise (monthly)
Apparel (2 per annum)
Toys (annual)
Dateline Hong Kong (monthly)

1299 HOOVER LIMITED
Perivale, Greenford, Middlesex UB6 8DX — Tel. 01-997 3311, Telex 05445

Company

Enquiries to the Librarian

Subject coverage
domestic appliances, especially washing and floor cleaning equipment

1300 HOPS MARKETING BOARD
61 Maidstone Road, Paddock Wood, Kent TN12 6BY — Tel. 089-283 3415
Statutory Board

Enquiries to the Secretary

Subject coverage
cultivation and marketing of English hops

HORBURY LIBRARY *see* **WAKEFIELD METROPOLITAN DISTRICT LIBRARIES**

HORNSEY PUBLIC LIBRARY *see* **HARINGEY LIBRARIES, MUSEUM AND ARTS DEPARTMENT**

1301 HORSTMANN CLIFFORD MAGNETICS LIMITED
Newbridge Works, Newbridge Road, Bath, Somerset BA1 3EF — Tel. 0225 21141, Telex 44897

Company, part of the Horstmann Gear Company Limited

Enquiries to the Manager

Subject coverage
advanced technology basic timing mechanism research and development; quartz crystal oscillator and similar electronic timing mechanisms; magnetic escapements; tuning fork timing mechanisms

HORTICULTURAL AND CONTRACTORS TOOL ASSOCIATION *see* **FEDERATION OF BRITISH HAND TOOL MANUFACTURERS**

HORTICULTURAL EDUCATION ASSOCIATION *see* **PERSHORE COLLEGE OF HORTICULTURE**

HOSIERY AND ALLIED TRADES RESEARCH ASSOCIATION *see* **HATRA**

HOSPITAL ENGINEERING RESEARCH UNIT *now* **BUILDING SERVICES RESEARCH UNIT,** *q.v.*

1302 HOTEL AND CATERING INDUSTRY TRAINING BOARD
Ramsey House, Central Square, Wembley, Middlesex HA9 7AP — Tel. 01-902 8865
Industrial Training Board, of the Training Service Agency

Enquiries to the Information Officer

Subject coverage
training and training aids for the hotels and catering industry; careers information

Publications
Service (ten issues per annum)
Training Recommendations
Research reports
Training packages
Careers information

HOTEL AND CATERING INSTITUTE *now* **HOTEL CATERING AND INSTITUTIONAL MANAGEMENT ASSOCIATION,** *q.v.*

1303 HOTEL CATERING AND INSTITUTIONAL MANAGEMENT ASSOCIATION
191 Trinity Road, London SW17 7HN Tel. 01-672 4251
Professional Association; includes the National Association of School Meals Organisers; formed by the merger of the former Institutional Management Association and the Hotel and Catering Institute

Enquiries to the Information Officer

Subject coverage
hotel and catering industry; careers in the industry

Publications
HCIMA Journal (monthly)
HCIMA Review (twice per annum)
HCIMA Research Register (updated annually)
Administrative Employment in Residential Establishments

1304 HOUGHTON POULTRY RESEARCH STATION
Houghton, Huntingdon PE17 2DA Tel. 0480 64101
Research Station

Enquiries to the Librarian

Subject coverage
poultry science

Publication
Annual Report

1305 HOULDSWORTH SCHOOL OF APPLIED SCIENCE
Library, Leeds University, Leeds LS2 9JT Tel. 0532 31751 ext. 457
University Departmental Library

No enquiry service

Subject coverage
ceramics; fuel and combustion science; chemical engineering; metallurgy

1306 HOUNSLOW BOROUGH COLLEGE
London Road, Isleworth, Middlesex TW7 6PE Tel. 01-568 0244
College of Further Education; formerly Isleworth Polytechnic and Chiswick Polytechnic

Enquiries to the Librarian

Subject coverage
graphic design; business studies; electrical and mechanical engineering; economics; geography

1307 HOUNSLOW LIBRARY SERVICE
Administrative Headquarters, Civic Centre, Lampton Road, Hounslow, Middlesex TW3 4DN Tel. 01-570 7728
Public Library Service; district libraries at Chiswick, Feltham and Hounslow

Enquiries to the Librarian in Charge of Information Services, Reference Department, Chiswick District Library, Dukes Avenue, London W4 2AB (01-994 5295)

Subject coverage
general

1308 HOUSE-BUILDERS FEDERATION
82 New Cavendish Street, London W1A 8AD Tel. 01-580 4041
Trade and Employers Association, formerly Federation of Registered Housebuilders

Enquiries to the Secretary

Subject coverage
building; land; planning; statistics

Publication
Housebuilder and Estate Developer

1309 HOUSEMAN HEGRO LIMITED
The Priory, Burnham, Slough SL1 7LS Tel. 06286 4488
Telex 848252

Company, formerly Houseman & Thompson Limited; part of Portals Water Treatment

Enquiries to the Advertising Manager

Subject coverage
chemicals; water treatment services and equipment

Publication
Good Water Guide

1310 HOVE AREA LIBRARY
Church Road, Hove, Sussex BN3 2EG Tel. 0273 70472
Public Library, of East Sussex County Library Service, *q.v.*

Enquiries to the Area Librarian

Subject coverage
general

HUDDERSFIELD PUBLIC LIBRARY *see* **KIRKLEES LIBRARIES**

1311 HUDDERSFIELD POLYTECHNIC
Queensgate, Huddersfid, West Yorkshire HD1 3DH Tel. 0484 30501
Polytechnic, formerly the Huddersfield College of Technology,Oastler College of Education, Huddersfield College of Education (Technical)

Enquiries to the Librarian

Subject coverage
architecture; building; catering; chemistry; civil, electrical and mechanical engineering; computing; mathematics; business and management; physics; textile industries

Special collection
G.H. Wood collection of nineteenth century books and pamphlets on sociology and economics

1312 HUDDERSFIELD TECHNICAL COLLEGE
New North Road, Huddersfield, Yorkshire HD1 5NN Tel. 0484 36521
Technical College, of Kirklees Metropolitan Council; formerly Ramsden Technical College

Enquiries to the Tutor-Librarian

Subject coverage
engineering; construction; science; catering; business studies; matters relating to the Technician Education Council and the Business Education Council; staff and curriculum development in Further Education

HULL CITY LIBRARIES *now* **HUMBERSIDE LIBRARIES,** *q.v.*

1313 HULL COLLEGE OF HIGHER EDUCATION
Cottingham Road, Hull, North Humberside HU6 7RT Tel. 0482 41451
College of Higher Education; formed by an amalgamation of six previous Hull colleges

Enquiries to the College Librarian

Subject coverage
architecture; biology; botany; building; business studies; catering; ceramics; chemistry; communications; computer science; dyeing; ecology; economics; engineering (aeronautical, chemical, civil, electrical, marine, mechanical, production, systems); fishing; geography; geology; management; mathematics; meteorology; printing; surveying; textiles; zoology

HULL FISHING INDUSTRY ASSOCIATION *see* **HULL FISHING VESSEL OWNERS ASSOCIATION LIMITED**

1314 HULL FISHING VESSEL OWNERS ASSOCIATION LIMITED
Saint Andrews Dock, Hull HU3 4PJ Tel. 0482 27586
Trade Association, allied to Hull Fishing Industry Association and Hull Fishing Vessel Owners Trading Company Limited; affiliated to British Trawlers Federation

Enquiries to the General Manager or Secretary

Subject coverage
fishing industry

Publication
Hull Fishing Handbook (bi- or triennial)

HULL UNIVERSITY LIBRARY *see* **BRYNMOR JONES LIBRARY**

HULTIS *see* **HUMBERSIDE LIBRARIES TECHNICAL INTERLOAN SCHEME**

1315 HUMBER LABORATORY OF THE TORRY RESEARCH STATION
Wassand Street, Hull HU3 4AR Tel. 0482 27879
Research Station, of the Ministry of Agriculture, Fisheries and Food

Enquiries to the Officer in Charge

Subject coverage
use of fish as food; fish processing technology; fish handling; utilization of fishery bi-products

Publications
Annual Report
Contributions to Torry Research Station series of Advisory notes

1316 HUMBERSIDE LIBRARIES
Library of Science, Technology and Commerce, Central Library, Albion Street, Hull HU1 3TF Tel. 0482 224040 Telex 52211
Public Library Service; Headquarters of Hultis, *q.v.*; formerly Hull City Libraries; the three Divisional Libraries are at Beverley, Grimsby and Scunthorpe, *qq.v.*

Enquiries to the Director

Subject coverage
all the sciences, technologies, commerce and law. Special attention paid to local interests including food technology, fish and fishing industry, paint and organic chemicals, edible oils, port working and transport, pharmaceuticals, building industry

1317 HUMBERSIDE LIBRARIES TECHNICAL INTERLOAN SCHEME (HULTIS)
Library of Science, Technology and Commerce, Central Library, Albion Street, Hull HU1 3TF Tel. 0482 223344 exts. 37, 38, 39 Telex 52211
Interlibrary Cooperative Scheme; over 60 members; formerly Hull Technical Interloan Scheme

Enquiries to the Honorary Secretary

Subject coverage
technical and commercial; special subjects are fishing, whaling, shipping, timber, and commerce; subjects covered by members are: organic chemicals; pharmaceuticals; non-ferrous metals; edible oils; docks and harbour engineering; food; iron and steel; marine engineering

Special collections
British Patent specifications, 1901— ; abridgements, 1617—
United States Patent Specifications (20 year file)
Derwent Belgian, French and German Patent Abstracts, 1964—
Derwent Soviet Inventions, 1959—
British Standards
ASTM Specifications
World Index to Trade Marks
1″ Geological Survey, old and new series, England, Wales, and Scotland
1″ Land Utilization Survey, England, Wales and Scotland
1″ Agricultural Land Classification Survey, England and Wales

Publications
Humberside Libraries Commercial and Technical Bulletin (monthly, July & August combined)
Checklist of Members Periodicals (annual; half yearly supplement)
Members Handbook and Directory
Annual Report and Statistics
HULTIS: this is your Library Service
Abstracts and Indexes in Hultis Members Libraries

1318 HUMPHREYS & GLASGOW LIMITED
22 Carlisle Place, London SW1P 1JA Tel. 01-828 1234
Telex 261821
Company

Enquiries to the Publicity Manager

Subject coverage
contracts and consultancy in the chemical, petrochemical, oil, gas, fertiliser, pharmaceutical, food and drinks industries

HUNTINGDON DISTRICT LIBRARY *see* **CAMBRIDGESHIRE LIBRARIES**

1319 HUNTINGDON RESEARCH CENTRE
Huntingdon, Cambridgeshire PE18 6ES Tel. 0480 890431
Telex 32100

Contract Research Organization

Enquiries, to the Librarian (tel. 0480 52522)

Subject coverage
toxicology; environmental science; pesticide science; pathology; pharmacology; microbiology; cell biology; metabolic studies; pharmacokinetics; analytical chemistry; animal science

Publication
HRC Gazette

1320 HUNTINGDON TECHNICAL COLLEGE
California Road, Huntingdon PE18 7BL Tel. 0480 52346 ext. 37
Technical College; its Library was formerly the Huntingdon and Peterborough County Technical Library

Enquiries to the Librarian

Subject coverage
business studies; building science; automobile engineering; natural sciences

HYDE PUBLIC LIBRARY *see* **TAMESIDE LIBRARIES**

1321 HYDRAULIC ASSOCIATION OF GREAT BRITAIN
P.O. Box 219, 13 Catherine Street, London SW1 Tel. 01-222 2029
Trade Association; member of the Metallurgical Plant Makers Association, *q.v.*

Enquiries to the Director

Subject coverage
hydraulic plant actuated by pressures above 500 lbs per square inch; supply sources of such equipment for special applications

1322 HYDRAULICS RESEARCH STATION
Wallingford, Oxfordshire OX10 8BA Tel. 0491 35381
Government Research Laboratory, of the Department of the Environment

Enquiries to the Librarian

Subject coverage
civil engineering hydraulics; flow of water over weirs and spillways; flood relief works; diffusion and dispersion of heat and pollutants; silting of rivers and estuaries; sea-defence works; design of harbours and offshore structures

Publications
Annual Report
Research reports, papers and brochures

1323 HYDROCARBON SOLVENTS ASSOCIATION LIMITED
Owletts, Woodlands Road, Bickley, Bromley, Kent BR1 2AR Tel. 01-467 4920
Trade Association, affiliated to the Chemical Industries Association Limited, *q.v.*

Enquiries to the General Secretary

Subject coverage
hydrocarbon solvent trade; health and safety aspects of these solvents

HYDROGEOLOGICAL ENQUIRY SERVICE *see* **CENTRAL WATER PLANNING UNIT**

1324 HYDROGRAPHIC SOCIETY
North East London Polytechnic, Walthamstow, London E17 4JB Tel. 01-527 2272
Learned Society

Enquiries to the Honorary Secretary

Subject coverage
hydrography; hydrographic surveying and techniques; developments; careers, employment therein; applied oceanography; marine geophysics

Publication
Hydrographic Journal (twice per annum)

HYDROLOGICAL RESEARCH UNIT *now* **INSTITUTE OF HYDROLOGY,** *q.v.*

HYNDBURN DISTRICT CENTRAL LIBRARY *see* **LANCASHIRE LIBRARY**

1325 IBM UNITED KINGDOM LIMITED
Technical Information Centre, 17 Addiscombe Road, Croydon CR9 6HS Tel. 01-686 0621
Company

Enquiries to the Librarian

Subject coverage
computer science; data processing

1326 IBM UNITED KINGDOM LIMITED
U.K. Scientific Centre, Neville Road, Peterlee, County Durham SR8 1BY Tel. 078-323 863322
Telex 537275
Company

Enquiries to the Communications Officer

Subject coverage
computer applications in general, and specifically in modelling techniques in planning, particularly regional and local authority planning; and in data base management, particularly the design, implementation and evaluation of high level data base systems, with emphasis on the relational model of data

Publications
Report series
Annual Report
List of publications

1327 IBM UNITED KINGDOM LABORATORIES LIMITED
Hursley Park, Hursley, Winchester, Hampshire SO21 2JN Tel. 0962 4433
Telex 47645

Company Development Laboratory

Enquiries to the Manager, Library and Information Retrieval Services, by letter only

Subject coverage
data processing; computers; programming

ICAM *see* **BRITISH ASSOCIATION OF GRAIN SEED FEED AND AGRICULTURAL MERCHANTS LIMITED**

ICE CREAM FEDERATION *see* **FOOD MANUFACTURERS FEDERATION INCORPORATED**

1328 ICI LIMITED
Agricultural Division, Research and Development Department, P.O. Box 6, Billingham, Cleveland TS23 1LB — Tel. 0642 553601, Telex 58443
Company

Enquiries to the Intelligence Section Manager

Subject coverage
physics; chemistry; agriculture; nitrogen industry; fertilizers; catalysts

1329 ICI LIMITED
Central Toxicology Laboratory, Alderley Park, Nr. Macclesfield, Cheshire SK10 4TJ — Tel. 099-66 2711, Telex 66152
Company Laboratory, formerly Industrial Hygiene Research Laboratories

Enquiries to the Librarian or Information Officer

Subject coverage
toxicology; occupational and industrial health; pesticides; cancer; food legislation; pollution

1330 ICI LIMITED
Corporate Laboratory, P.O. Box 11, The Heath, Runcorn, Cheshire WA7 4QE — Tel. 029-85 73456, Telex 62655
Company Laboratory, formerly Petrochemical & Polymer Laboratory

Enquiries to the Information Officer, by letter only

Subject coverage
catalysis chemistry, systems engineering, process technology, chemical engineering, polymer science, inorganic chemistry, solid state science, surface science, molecular genetics, plant science, biomaterials science, cell biology

1331 ICI LIMITED
ICI Fibres, Hookstone Road, Harrogate, Yorkshire HG2 8QN — Tel. 0423 68021, Telex 57947

Company Division, formerly ICI Fibres Limited

Enquiries to the Librarian and Information Officer

Subject coverage
synthetic fibres; textile technology; polymer chemistry

Publications
Trade Names of Non-Cellulosic Man-made Fibres, Polynosic Fibres and Textured Yarns

1332 ICI LIMITED
Mond Division, P.O. Box 8, Runcorn, Cheshire WA7 4QD — Tel. 092-85 73456, Telex 62655

Manufacturing Company

Enquiries, in writing, to the Librarian

Subject coverage
soda ash and associated alkali by-products of the ammonia-soda process, inorganic fillers and water treatment chemicals; chlorine and caustic soda by electrolysis of brine; salt, lime and limestone; sulphur, fluorine and cyanide derivatives; titanium; sodium; organic petrochemicals including vinyl and acrylic monomers for the plastics industry; chlorinated and fluorinated hydrocarbons and derivatives, namely solvents such as trichlorethylene, refrigerants, aerosol propellants, anaesthetics

and fire-fighting agents; chlorinated polymers, waxes and rubber; pyridine derivatives and other plant protection products; metal degreasing and heat treatment

Publications
technical booklets

1333 ICI LIMITED
Organics Division, Hexagon House, Blackley, Manchester M9 3DA Tel. 061 740 1460
Telex 667841/2/3
Company Division; the Organics Division was formerly known as the Dyestuffs Division

Enquiries to the Manager, Information & Library Services Department

Subject coverage
chemistry and technology of dyestuffs and pigments; auxiliary products for use with textiles, rubbers and plastics; polyurethanes and polyurethane chemicals

1334 ICI LIMITED
Paints Division, Hyde and Wallcoverings Groups, Newton Works, Hyde, Cheshire SK14 4EJ Tel. 061-368 4000
Telex 668411
Company Division

Enquiries to the Librarian

Subject coverage
coated fabrics; plastic film and sheet, particularly pvc; wallcoverings; pollution control

1335 ICI LIMITED
Petrochemicals Division, P.O. Box 90, Wilton, Middlesbrough, Cleveland TS6 8JE Tel. 064-95 5522
Telex 58522
Company Division, formerly the Heavy Organic Chemicals Division; houses Phillips-Imperial Petroleum Limited and Engineering Services (Wilton) Limited

Enquiries, in writing, to the Intelligence Section Manager, the Information Unit Co-ordinator or the Division Librarian

Subject coverage
petrochemicals; North Sea oil and gas; energy

1336 ICI LIMITED
Pharmaceuticals Division, Library and Information Unit, P.O. Box 25, Alderley Park, Macclesfield, Cheshire SK10 4TG Tel. 09966 2828
Telex 669095/669588
Company Division

Enquiries to the Head, Literature Services Section

Subject coverage
chemistry; biochemistry; applied chemistry; biology; pharmacology; physiology; pathology; human and veterinary medicine; pharmacy; medical aids; economics; commerce; management; statistics; packaging; the pharmaceutical industry

1337 ICI LIMITED
Plant Protection Division, Jealotts Hill Research Station, Bracknell, Berkshire RG12 6EY Tel. 0344 24701 ext. 261/260
Telex 668411
Company Division, formerly Agricultural Division and then Plant Protection Limited

Enquiries to the Librarian

Subject coverage
agriculture and agricultural chemicals; crop protection; biology; chemistry (but not inorganic); crop production; soil science; animal husbandry; ecology; environment

Special collection
Nuptown House Collection (pre-1850 books on agriculture)

Publications
Outlook on Agriculture
Guide to Field Experiments and Farm Projects

1338 ICI LIMITED
Plant Protection Division, Fernhurst, Haslemere, Surrey GU27 3JE — Tel. 0428 4061, Telex 858270, 858512

Company Division, formerly Plant Protection Limited

Enquiries to the Librarian

Subject coverage
crop protection chemicals

Publication
Outlook on Agriculture (journal)

1339 ICI LIMITED
Plastics Division, Bessemer Road, Welwyn Garden City, Hertfordshire AL7 1HD — Tel. 96 23400
Company Division

Enquiries to the Librarian

Subject coverage
plastics moulding powders, film and sheet; plastics processing, fabrication, properties and uses; chemistry and engineering related to plastics

Publications
Technical booklets

ICI LIMITED *see also*
BRIXHAM LABORATORY
IMPERIAL METAL INDUSTRIES LIMITED
SCOTTISH AGRICULTURAL INDUSTRIES LIMITED

ILFORD CENTRAL LIBRARY *see* **REDBRIDGE PUBLIC LIBRARIES**

ILKESTON PUBLIC LIBRARY *see* **DERBYSHIRE COUNTY LIBRARY**

ILKLEY DISTRICT LIBRARY *see* **BRADFORD LIBRARIES**

1340 ILLUMINATING ENGINEERING SOCIETY
York House, 199 Westminster Bridge Road, London SE1 7UN — Tel. 01-928 7110
Professional and Learned Society

Enquiries to the Secretary (not consulting)

Subject coverage
light sources and applications; daylight

Publication
Lighting Research and Technology (quarterly, includes abstracts)

IMPERIAL CHEMICAL INDUSTRIES LIMITED *see* **ICI LIMITED**

IMPERIAL COLLEGE OF SCIENCE AND TECHNOLOGY LIBARY *see*
LYON PLAYFAIR LIBRARY
ROYAL SCHOOL OF MINES

1341 IMPERIAL METAL INDUSTRIES (KYNOCH) LIMITED
P.O. Box 216, Witton, Birmingham B6 7BA — Tel. 021-356 4848, Telex 336771

Company, wholly-owned subsidiary of Imperial Metal Industries Limited which is partially owned by ICI Limited

Enquiries to the Librarian

Subject coverage
non-ferrous metals, particularly copper, titanium and zirconium; sporting ammunition; heat exchange equipment; zip fasteners; fluid power products

1342 IMPERIAL SMELTING PROCESSES LIMITED
St. Andrews Road, Avonmouth, Bristol BS11 9HP Tel. 02752 3631
Telex 44256
Company, part of Rio Tinto Zinc Corporation; has a Research Group at the above address (tel. 02752 5371)

Enquiries to the Chief Executive or Engineering Director

Subject coverage
process research and design in the field of non-ferrous extractive metallurgy; environmental studies

Publications
Descriptive Brochure
Reprints of technical publications in the subject fields given

1343 IMPERIAL TOBACCO LIMITED
Research Department, Raleigh Road, Ashton Gate, Bristol BS3 1QX Tel. 0272 666961
Company,formerly Imperial Tobacco Company Limited and Imperial Tobacco Group Limited; part of Imperial Group Limited

Enquiries to the Librarian

Subject coverage
tobacco science and technology; analytical chemistry; precise air conditioning

Publication
Tobacco Bibliography (fortnightly)

1344 INBUCON/AIC MANAGEMENT CONSULTANTS LIMITED
Knightsbridge House, 197 Knightsbridge, London SW7 1RN Tel. 01-584 6171
Company, formerly Associated Industrial Consultants Limited; subsidiary of Reliance Group, Incorporated, U.S.A.

Enquiries to the Information Officer

Subject coverage
company development and policy; administration; finance; management information systems; marketing; personnel and training; distribution; production

Publications
Salary Surveys of U.K., Scotland and Ireland, Europe
International Taxation and Living Costs

1345 INCOMTEC BUSINESS EDUCATION AND TRAINING COMPANY
InComTec House, 7 High Street, Camberley, Surrey Tel. 0276 62677
Company

Enquiries to the General Manager

Subject coverage
management training; in-company training

Publications
Brochures

INCORPORATED ADVERTISING MANAGEMENT ASSOCIATION *see* **ADVERTISING ASSOCIATION**

1346 INCORPORATED ASSOCIATION OF ARCHITECTS AND SURVEYORS
29 Belgrave Square, London SW1X 8QF Tel. 01-235 3755
Professional Institution, providing the Secretariat for the Joint Examinations Board for Building Control Surveyors

Enquiries to the Secretary

Subject coverage
surveying, building control, building regulations

Publications
Architect and Surveyor (bi-monthly)
List of Members
Codes of Conduct
Scales of Professional Charges

INCORPORATED ASSOCIATION OF COST AND INDUSTRIAL ACCOUNTANTS *now* **SOCIETY OF COMPANY AND COMMERCIAL ACCOUNTANTS,** *q.v.*

1347 INCORPORATED BREWERS GUILD
8 Ely Place, Holborn, London EC1N 6SD Tel. 01-405 4565
Professional Association

Enquiries to the Secretary

Subject coverage
careers in brewing

Publication
The Brewer (monthly)

INCORPORATED BRITISH INSTITUTE OF CERTIFIED CARPENTERS *now* **INSTITUTE OF CARPENTERS,** *q.v.*

1348 INCORPORATED GUILD OF HAIRDRESSERS, WIGMAKERS AND PERFUMERS
4 The Broadway, Woodbridge Road, Guildford, Surrey GU1 1DY Tel. 0483 67922
Trade Association

Enquiries to the General Secretary

Subject coverage
hairdressing and ancillary trades

Publication
Guild Hairdresser (quarterly)

INCORPORATED INSTITUTE OF BRITISH DECORATORS AND INTERIOR DESIGNERS *now* **BRITISH INSTITUTE OF INTERIOR DESIGN,** *q.v.*

1349 INCORPORATED PRACTITIONERS IN RADIO AND ELECTRONICS (IPRE) LIMITED
32 Kidmore Road, Caversham, Reading RG4 7LU Tel. 0734 473809
Professional Institution; merged with the Radio and Electronics Association; member of the Standing Conference for Technician Engineers and Technicians Limited

Enquiries to the Secretary

Subject coverage
status and professional recognition of the technician engineer and technician in electronics

Publication
IPRE Review (3 times per annum; formerly Radar and Electronics Association Journal)

1350 INCORPORATED SOCIETY OF BRITISH ADVERTISERS LIMITED
2 Basil Street, London SW3 1AG Tel. 01-584 5221
Advertising Association

Enquiries to the Information Officer

Subject coverage
advertising in the U.K. and overseas; voluntary controls; legislation; terms and conditions of business in all advertising media

Publications
Guides to Direct Mail
Industrial Publicity

Advertising Overseas
Exhibiting in U.K. and Overseas
Advertising Research Guides

1351 INCORPORATED SOCIETY OF VALUERS AND AUCTIONEERS
3 Cadogan Gate, London SW1X 0AS Tel. 01-235 2282
Professional Society

Enquiries to the Education Officer

Subject coverage
valuation; auctioneering; estate agency

Publication
The Valuer

1352 INDEPENDENT BROADCASTING AUTHORITY
70 Brompton Road, London SW3 1EY Tel. 01-584 7011
Telex 24345

Public Authority, formerly Independent Television Authority

Enquiries to the Information Office

Subject coverage
television and radio broadcasting and associated engineering; control of broadcasting advertising

Special collection
Press Cuttings on Broadcasting

Publications
Annual Report
TV and Radio (annual guide)
Independent Broadcasting (quarterly)
IBA Technical Review (occasional)

INDEPENDENT TELEVISION AUTHORITY *now* **INDEPENDENT BROADCASTING AUTHORITY,** *q.v.*

1353 INDEPENDENT WASTE PAPER PROCESSORS ASSOCIATION (U.K.)
16 High Street, Brampton, Huntingdon, Cambridgeshire PE18 8TU Tel. 0480 55249
Telex 32546

Trade Association

Enquiries to the Secretary

Subject coverage
waste paper reclamation

1354 INDIA HOUSE LIBRARY
India House, Aldwych, London WC2 Tel. 01-836 8484 ext. 114
Governmental Body of the Indian Ministry of External Affairs

Enquiries to the Librarian when they concern India; press enquiries and those relating to U.K./India affairs, to the Information Officer

Subject coverage
most aspects of Indian interest; Indian Government official publications

1355 INDUSTRIAL AERODYNAMICS UNIT
Department of Aeronautics and Astronautics, The University, Southampton SO9 5NH Tel. 0703 555995
Telex 47661
Industrial Consulting Unit

Enquiries to the Manager

Subject coverage
evaluation of marine and engineering structures, etc.

1356 INDUSTRIAL AIDS LIMITED
Terminal House, 52 Grosvenor Gardens, London SW1W 0AU Tel. 01-730 5288
Company

Enquiries to the Managing Director

Subject coverage
industrial market research, company acquisitions, diversification, new product searches and licensing; plastics, packaging, chemical and allied process industries including fertilisers, herbicides, paints, pigments, printing inks, adhesives and sealants, and fragrances, rubbers, fibres, detergents, food industry, recycling and reclamation industries, industrial wastes and pollution problems

Publications
U.K. Industry Digests:
No. 1 Polishes (July 1971)
No. 2 Flavours and Fragrances (July 1971)
No. 3 Rubber (February 1972)
No. 4 Fire and Flame Retardants (February 1972)
No. 5 Food Additives (January 1974)
No. 6 Cleaning and Maintenance Chemicals (April 1974)
U.K. Depth Studies:
Injection Moulding in the U.K. (January 1975)
Adhesives Industry (January 1975)
Reclamation and Recycling: Solvent Recovery (September 1975)
Engineering Thermoplastics in the U.K. (planned January 1977)
Published Data on European Industrial Markets, 1976 (lists over 1,000 surveys available and other guides to sources in all European countries)
Other European Studies and other Digests available

1357 INDUSTRIAL AND TRADE FAIRS LIMITED
Radcliffe House, Blenheim Court, Solihull, West Midlands B91 2BG Tel. 021-705 6707
Telex 337073

Company, members of the Association of Exhibition Organisers, *q.v.*

Enquiries to the Company Secretary

Subject coverage
organisation of exhibitions

1358 INDUSTRIAL CENTRE FOR DESIGN AND MANUFACTURING ENGINEERING
University of Salford, Salford M5 4WT Tel. 061-736 8921–3
Telex 668680

University Department for industrial consultancy; the associated limited company is Salford University Industrial Centre Limited

Enquiries to the General Manager or the Commercial Managers

Subject coverage
industrial noise and vibration; industrial design; ion-plating; manufacturing technology; manufacture and design of bowl feeders and other mechanized assembly operations

1359 INDUSTRIAL CLEANING MACHINE MANUFACTURERS ASSOCIATION
Leicester House, 8 Leicester Street, London WC2H 7BN Tel. 01-437 0678
Trade Association; member of BEAMA, *q.v.*

Enquiries to the Director

Subject coverage
manufacture and marketing of industrial cleaning equipment

INDUSTRIAL CO-PARTNERSHIP ASSOCIATION *now* **INDUSTRIAL PARTICIPATION ASSOCIATION,** *q.v.*

1360 INDUSTRIAL DEVELOPMENT (BANGOR)
University College of North Wales, Dean Street, Bangor, Gwynedd LL57 1UT — Tel. 0248 51151 ext. 757/8

Engineering Company, wholly owned by the University College of North Wales

Enquiries to the Director

Subject coverage
industrial instrumentation, including infra red techniques, opto-electronic devices, telemetry, electrostatic systems; system analysis and control, including pattern recognition, logic circuitry; device construction and applications, including radio navigation, electron beam devices, magnets and electromagnets, linear motors; diagnostic techniques, including microscopy; materials preparation and evaluation

Publications
Summary of Recent Projects
Brochure

1361 INDUSTRIAL DIAMOND INFORMATION BUREAU
Charters, Sunninghill, Ascot, Berkshire SL5 9PX — Tel. 0990 23456, Telex 848021

Company, part of de Beers Industrial Diamond Division Limited

Enquiries to the Information Officer

Subject coverage
all applications of industrial diamond tools, including metalworking, civil engineering, glass, ceramics and mining industries; sources of supply of industrial diamond and of tools for specific applications; tool use

Publications
Industrial Diamond Review (incorporating Industrial Diamond Abstracts; monthly)
Industrie Diamanten Rundschau (in German; quarterly)
Diamond Research (annually)

1362 INDUSTRIAL GAS CLEANING ASSOCIATION
15 Tooks Court, London EC4A 1LA — Tel. 01-831 7581, Telex 23485

Trade Association; formerly Electrostatic Precipitators Association

Enquiries to the Secretary

Subject coverage
pollution control equipment; electrostatic precipitators, fabric collectors, scrubbers, mechanical collectors

Publications
G2—Proposal Data Sheet: a comprehensive schedule of information which the user should provide to the supplier
EP1—Terminology of Electrostatic Precipitators
EP2—Evaluation Form for Electrostatic Precipitators
F2—Proposal Evaluation Form for Fabric Dust Collectors

1363 INDUSTRIAL HEALTH AND SAFETY CENTRE
97 Horseferry Road, London SW1P 2DY — Tel. 01-828 9255

Government Department, of the Health and Safety Executive; formerly within the Department of Employment

Enquiries to the Director

Subject coverage
technical and legal aspects of safety at work

Publications
H.M.S.O. Sectional List 18 for publications of the Health and Safety Executive

INDUSTRIAL HYGIENE RESEARCH LABORATORIES *now* **ICI LIMITED, Central Toxicology Laboratory,** *q.v.*

1364 INDUSTRIAL LAW SOCIETY
c/o The Secretary, 28 Boundary Road, Sidcup, Kent Tel. 01-850 3725
British Section of the International Society for Labour, Law and Social Legislation

Enquiries to the Secretary

Subject coverage
industrial law

Publication
Quarterly Journal

1365 INDUSTRIAL LOCOMOTIVE SOCIETY
28 Duncroft Road, Hucclecote, Gloucester GL3 3AS
Club and Study Group

Enquiries to the Secretary

Subject coverage
railway locomotives, locomotive builders and owners, other than Main Line

Publications
Industrial Locomotive (quarterly)
Occasional books (e.g. Birchenwood and its Locomotives)

1366 INDUSTRIAL MARKET RESEARCH LIMITED
17 Buckingham Gate, London SW1E 6LN Tel. 01-834 7814
Telex 917036

Company, subsidiary of Audits of Great Britain Company

No enquiry service

Subject coverage
market research, acquisition studies, diversification and forecasting for industrial, consumer, travel and other service industry clients

1367 INDUSTRIAL MARKETING ASSOCIATION
9 Aston Road, Nuneaton, Warwickshire CV11 5EL Tel. 0682 67161
Professional Association; member of the Industrial Marketing Council, *q.v.* the European Council for Industrial Marketing; the European Marketing Association, *q.v.* and la Commission Internationale de Marketing; houses the European Industrial Marketing Research Society, linked with the Society for the Development of Techniques in Industrial Marketing *q.v.*

Enquiries to the Secretary or External Liaison Officer

Subject coverage
market research; European markets; marketing

Publications
Marketing Intelligence Service
European Marketing Newsletter
International Marketing Directory
Directory and Yearbook of Industrial Marketing in Europe
Journal of International Marketing and Marketing Research

1368 INDUSTRIAL MARKETING COUNCIL
9 Aston Road, Nuneaton, Warwickshire CV11 5EL Tel. 0682 67161
Committee of the Professional Marketing Organizations; member of la Commission Internationale de Marketing and the European Council for Industrial Marketing

Enquiries to the Director-General

Subject coverage
marketing information sources; training

Publications
New market research reports

1369 INDUSTRIAL PARTICIPATION ASSOCIATION
25–28 Buckingham Gate, London SW1E 6LP Tel. 01-828 8754
Company and Registered Charity; formerly Industrial Co-Partnership Association

Enquiries to the Association

Subject coverage
industrial democracy; employee participation; profit sharing; employee shareholding; joint consultation; job enrichment; work re-structuring; job involvement; communication in industry; worker directors; common ownership companies; co-operatives; provision of information

Publications
IPA Commentary
Industrial Participation (formerly Co-partnership) continuous since 1894)
Study Papers
Resource Papers
Books

INDUSTRIAL PEST CONTROL ASSOCIATION *now* **BRITISH PEST CONTROL ASSOCIATION,** *q.v.*

1370 INDUSTRIAL POLICE AND SECURITY ASSOCIATION
7 Bluewaters Drive, Broadsands, Paignton, Devonshire TQ4 6JE Tel. 080-44 2326
Trade Association; houses the Institution of Industrial Security, *q.v.*

Enquiries to the National Secretary

Subject coverage
industrial and commercial security

Publication
Security and Protection Journal

1371 INDUSTRIAL POLLUTION ABATEMENT LIMITED
21 Inner Park Road, London SW19 6ED Tel. 01-789 0841
Company

Enquiries to the Information Officer

Subject coverage
industrial pollution; pulp and paper industry; effluent treatment; sewage treatment works

1372 INDUSTRIAL RELATIONS RESEARCH UNIT
Warwick University, Coventry CV4 7AL Tel. 0203 24011
Academic Research Unit, of the Social Science Research Council

Enquiries to the Administrative Officer

Subject coverage
industrial relations; labour economics; industrial sociology

Publications
Notes on Research Projects
Monographs and reprints series

1373 INDUSTRIAL SAFETY (PROTECTIVE EQUIPMENT) MANUFACTURERS ASSOCIATION
69 Cannon Street, London EC4N 5AB Tel. 01-248 4444
Telex 888941

Trade Association

Enquiries to the Secretary

Subject coverage
production and marketing of safety equipment

Publication
Reference Book of Protective Equipment (buyers' guide)

1374 INDUSTRIAL SOCIETY
48 Bryanston Square, London W1H 8AH — Tel. 01-262 2401
Charitable Trust

Enquiries to the Information Department or the Publicity Department

Subject coverage
leadership; management; management-union relations and participation; communication; conditions of employment

Publications
Notes for Managers (26 practical guides)
Legislation Guides (on relevant Acts of Parliament)
Industrial Society (monthly)

1375 INDUSTRIAL TRAINING RESEARCH UNIT
32 Trumpington Street, Cambridge CB2 1QY — Tel. 0223 51576 & 66814
University Research Unit, of London University; formerly Research Unit into Problems of Industrial Retraining; grant-aided by the Training Services Agency

Enquiries to the Director

Subject coverage
development of industrial training and selection methods; autonomous working groups; management team composition; problems of older workers

Publications
Research papers
Booklets
Publications List

1376 INDUSTRON LIMITED
Industron House, 2267 Coventry Road, Sheldon, Birmingham B26 3PD — Tel. 021-742 4141/2/3
Telex 338024

Private Company; Consultants

Enquiries to the Projects Director

Subject coverage
industrial marketing and research; export marketing; production engineering; personnel selection; lithographic printing; platemaking; photography

INFESTATION CONTROL LABORATORY *now* **PEST INFESTATION CONTROL LABORATORY,** *q.v.*

1377 INFORMATION CENTRE ON HIGH TEMPERATURE PROCESSES
Leeds University, Department of Fuel and Combustion Science, Leeds LS2 9JT — Tel. 0532 31751
University Centre

Enquiries to the Information Officer

Subject coverage
flames and combustion; arcs and sparks; lasers; shock waves and detonations; plasmas, high temperature chemistry; refractory materials; techniques of measurement of high temperature; high temperature apparatus; radiation and spectra; transport phenomena

1378 INFORMATION RESEARCH LIMITED
Bond Street House, 14 Clifford Street, London W1X 1RE — Tel. 01-491 7693
Company

Enquiries to the Information Officer

Subject coverage
techno-economic aspects of the chemical and chemical processing industries (U.K. and Europe)

Publications
Profile Reports
Marketing Research Studies
List available

1379 INFORMATION RETRIEVAL LIMITED
1 Falconberg Court, London W1V 5FG — Tel. 01-437 5362
Telex 28398

Company, of the Anthony Woolcott Group, and including Information Printing Limited

Enquiries are not accepted; information published as abstracts

Subject coverage
amino-acid peptide and proteins; animal behaviour; applied ecology; aquatic sciences and fisheries; biological membranes; calcified tissues; chemoreception; entomology; feeding weight and obesity; genetics; immunology; microbiology (bacteriology, algology, mycology and protozoology); nucleic acids; oncology; virology

Special collection
over 1,000,000 abstracts in above subjects, from 1965, worldwide

Publications
Abstract Journals covering all the above subjects (monthly or quarterly)
Bibliographies
Publications List available

1380 INFOTECH INTERNATIONAL LIMITED
Nicholson House, Maidenhead, Berkshire SL6 1LD — Tel. 0628 32588
Telex 847319

Company; formerly Infotech Limited

Enquiries to the Information Officer

Subject coverage
computing and computer systems; systems and programming; operations; data bases; teleprocessing; measurement and tuning; reliability; security

Publications
Reports on the state of the art in computing

1381 INLAND REVENUE LIBRARY
Somerset House, Strand, London WC2R 1LB — Tel. 01-438 6325
Government Department, formerly Inland Revenue Board's Library

Enquiries, loan requests only, to the Librarian

Subject coverage
taxation (U.K. and foreign)

INLAND WATERWAYS AMENITY ADVISORY COUNCIL *see* **BRITISH WATERWAYS BOARD**

1382 INLAND WATERWAYS ASSOCIATION
114 Regents Park Road, London NW1 8UQ — Tel. 01-586 2556 & 2510
Limited Company/Registered Charity

Enquiries to the General Secretary

Subject coverage
restoration, retention and development of inland waterways in the British Isles; commercial and recreational use

1383 INLAND WATERWAYS PROTECTION SOCIETY
25 Market Place, Chapel-en-le-Frith, via Stockport, Cheshire
Registered Charity

Enquiries to the Honorary Secretary

Subject coverage
preservation and development of all inland waterways in the British Isles for commercial and recreational purposes

1384 INPACT (INTERNATIONAL POWDER ADVISORY CENTRE)
Thames Polytechnic, Wellington Street, Woolwich, London SE18 6PF — Tel. 01-854 2030 ext. 361
Information and Consultancy Service
Enquiries to the Director

Subject coverage
bulk solids handling technology; measurement of solids velocity; particle degradation; rotary valve design; gravity transport systems; design of components, systems and costs of pneumatic handling and associated processes; testing services and assessment of equipment performance, pipeline materials

1385 INPLAN LIMITED
Fillongley, Coventry, Warwickshire CV7 8DP — Tel. 0676 40580
Company
Enquiries to the Director

Subject coverage
industrial market research

Publications
multi-client market research reports

1386 INSPEC (INTERNATIONAL INFORMATION SERVICES FOR THE PHYSICS AND ENGINEERING COMMUNITIES)
Station House, Nightingale Road, Hitchin, Hertfordshire SG5 1RJ — Tel. 0462 53331
Publishing, Information and Abstracting Service; department of the Institution of Electrical Engineers, *q.v.*
Enquiries, on publication matters, to the Marketing Department, Inspec; other requests to the Librarian of the Institution

Subject coverage
information processing, primarily in physics, electrical engineering; electronics; control engineering; computing

Publications
Physics Abstracts (twice monthly)
Electrical and Electronic Abstracts (monthly)
Computer and Control Abstracts (monthly)
Current Papers in Physics (monthly)
Current Papers in Electrical and Electronics Engineering (monthly)
Current Papers in Computers and Control (monthly)
Key Abstracts (six titles; monthly)

INSPECTORATE OF MINES AND QUARRIES *see* **H.M. INSPECTORATE OF MINES AND QUARRIES**

1387 INSTITUTE FOR FISCAL STUDIES
62 Chandos Place, London WC2N 4HH — Tel. 01-836 2141
Research Institute
Enquiries to the Director

Subject coverage
research in the fiscal régime; *not* individual tax matters

Publications
Conference proceedings
Research papers

1388 INSTITUTE FOR MARINE ENVIRONMENTAL RESEARCH
67–69 Citadel Road, Plymouth, Devonshire PL1 3DH Tel. 0752 20681
Research Institute, of the Natural Environment Research Council; formed by incorporation of the SMBA Oceanographic Laboratory (Edinburgh), the NERC Fisheries Helminthology Research Unit (St. Albans), and the NERC Seals Research Unit (Lowestoft)

Enquiries to the Director

Subject coverage
marine ecology, especially of estuaries; plankton of the North Atlantic and North Sea; seals ecology; environmental stress and pollution

Publications
Bulletin of Marine Ecology (irregular)
Annual Report

1389 INSTITUTE FOR OPERATIONAL RESEARCH
4 Copthall House, Station Square, Coventry CV1 2PP Tel. 0203 20201/2/3
Research Institute; offices also in London and Edinburgh

Enquiries to the Librarian

Subject coverage
use of operational research in health & social services; government (local and central) and industry

Publications
List available

1390 INSTITUTE FOR RESEARCH ON ANIMAL DISEASES
Compton, near Newbury, Berkshire RG16 0NN Tel. 070-131 411
Research Institute, of the Agricultural Research Council

Enquiries to the Librarian/Information Officer

Subject coverage
diseases, of economic importance, in farm animals; enteritis, mastitis, production diseases, respiratory diseases; wildlife diseases; infertility; parasites; protozoal infections; metabolic pathology

Publication
Report on the Institute

1391 INSTITUTE FOR SCIENTIFIC INFORMATION (ISI)
132 High Street, Uxbridge, Middlesex UB8 1DP Tel. 89 30085
Company, subsidiary of ISI, Philadelphia, USA

Enquiries to the Director

Subject coverage
bibliographic searching in all areas of pure and applied sciences and in social sciences; current awareness services and on-line services

Publications
Current Contents (6 editions)
Science Citation Index
Current Abstracts of Chemistry and Index Chemicus
Index to Scientific Reviews

1392 INSTITUTE OF ACOUSTICS
47 Belgrave Square, London SW1X 8QX Tel. 235 6111
Telex 918453

Professional Institute

Enquiries to the Secretary

Subject coverage
acoustics; noise; vibration; ultrasonics

Publications
Proceedings of the Institute of Acoustics
Year Book
Education and Careers in Acoustics
Acoustics Bulletin

1393 INSTITUTE OF ACTUARIES
Staple Inn Hall, High Holborn, London WC1V 7QJ Tel. 01-242 0106
Professional Institute

Enquiries to the Secretary

Subject coverage
actuarial science; life assurance; superannuation and pension funds; risk theory; statistics; demography; economics

Publications
Journal of the Institute of Actuaries (3 times per annum)
Year Book (including list of members)

1394 INSTITUTE OF ADMINISTRATIVE ACCOUNTING LIMITED
Walter House, 418–422 Strand, London WC2R 0PW Tel. 01-240 3106
Professional Qualifying Institute; formerly the Institute of Book-keepers and Related Data Processing Limited

Enquiries to the Secretary-General

Subject coverage
accounting and business practice

Publication
Administrative Accounting (quarterly)

1395 INSTITUTE OF ADMINISTRATIVE MANAGEMENT
205 High Street, Beckenham, Kent BR3 1BA Tel. 01-658 0171/5
Professional Institute and Examining Body; formerly Institute of Office Management

Enquiries to the Information Officer

Subject coverage
administrative management

Publications
Guide to Effective Office Supervision
Effective Use of Secretarial Services
Office Salaries Analysis 1975
Other books and pamphlets, some in their second editions

1396 INSTITUTE OF ADVANCED ARCHITECTURAL STUDIES
York University, Kings Manor, York Tel. 0904 24919
University Institute; comprising the Research Section and the Building Science Research Development Unit; houses the York Centre for continuing Education of the Building Professions

Enquiries to the Secretary, or Research Director, or Librarian

Subject coverage
conservation education

INSTITUTE OF AGRARIAN AFFAIRS *now* **INSTITUTE OF AGRICULTURAL ECONOMICS,** *q.v.*

1397 INSTITUTE OF AGRICULTURAL ECONOMICS
Oxford University, Dartington House, Little Clarendon Street, Oxford OX1 2HP Tel. 0865 52921
University Department; the former Institute of Agrarian Affairs was merged with the Agricultural Economics Research Institute, which then changed its name to that given above; the building houses the Editorial Office of the International Association of Agricultural Economists, as well as the

separately financed and organised Agricultural Economics Bureau; the Plunkett Foundation for Co-operative Studies, *q.v.*, occupies an adjacent building

Enquiries to the Librarian or Director

Subject coverage
agricultural economics, particularly concerned with national, international and developing country problems

Publication
Oxford Agrarian Studies (bi-monthly)

1398 INSTITUTE OF AGRICULTURAL SECRETARIES
1 Main Street, Elloughton, Brough, North Humberside HU15 1JN — Tel. 0482 667306
Professional Body

Enquiries to the Secretary

Subject coverage
careers, education and training in farm secretaryship

1399 INSTITUTE OF ANIMAL PHYSIOLOGY
Babraham, Cambridge CB2 4AT — Tel. 0223 832312
Government Research Establishment, of the Agricultural Research Council

No enquiry service

Subject coverage
basic work to extend knowledge of the physiology and biochemistry of farm livestock

Publication
Biennial Report

1400 INSTITUTE OF ARBITRATORS
75 Cannon Street, London EC4N 5BH — Tel. 01-236 8761
Professional Body; houses the London Court of Arbitration

Enquiries to the Secretary

Subject coverage
training of arbitrators; provision of arbitration facilities for commercial and other disputes, U.K. domestic, international or small-claims; law and practice of arbitration at home and abroad

Publication
Arbitration (quarterly)

1401 INSTITUTE OF ASPHALT TECHNOLOGY
25 Lower Belgrave Street, London SW1W 0LS — Tel. 01-997 7574
Technical Institute, with seven regional offices

Enquiries are not accepted from the public

Subject coverage
asphalt technology

INSTITUTE OF ASTRONOMY *see* **CAMBRIDGE UNIVERSITY, Institute of Astronomy Library**

INSTITUTE OF AUTOMOBILE ENGINEER ASSESSORS *see* **INSTITUTION OF MECHANICAL ENGINEERS**

1402 INSTITUTE OF BIOLOGY
41 Queens Gate, London SW7 5HU — Tel. 01-589 9076
Professional Institute

Enquiries to the General Secretary

Subject coverage
sources of biological information; training and employment of biologists

Publications
Biologist
Journal of Biological Education (bi-monthly)

INSTITUTE OF BIOLOGY *see also* **SOCIETY FOR THE BIBLIOGRAPHY OF NATURAL HISTORY**

INSTITUTE OF BOOK-KEEPERS AND RELATED DATA PROCESSING LIMITED *now* **INSTITUTE OF ADMINISTRATIVE ACCOUNTING LIMITED,** *q.v.*

1403 INSTITUTE OF BRITISH GEOGRAPHERS
1 Kensington Gore, London SW7 2AR Tel. 01-584 6371
Learned Society

Enquiries to the Administrative Assistant

Subject coverage
geography of rural and urban areas; medical, transport and population geography; bio-geography; geomorphological geography

Publications
Area
Transactions of the IBG

INSTITUTE OF BUILDERS MERCHANTS *see* **NATIONAL FEDERATION OF BUILDERS AND PLUMBERS MERCHANTS**

1404 INSTITUTE OF BUILDING
Englemere, Kings Ride, Ascot, Berkshire SL5 8BJ Tel. 0990 23355
Professional Institution

Enquiries to the Technical Information Officer

Subject coverage
building management

Publication
Abstract Bulletin

1405 INSTITUTE OF CARPENTERS
24 Ormond Street, Richmond, Surrey Tel. 01-948 4151
Craft Association; formerly Incorporated British Institute of Certified Carpenters; 17 branches

Enquiries, from members, in writing, to the Secretary; enquiries concerning examinations to the Registrar, 37 Holbeck Avenue, Brookfield, Middlesbrough, Teesside TS5 8DS

Subject coverage
education and training in carpentry

Publication
House Journal (to members only)

1406 INSTITUTE OF CERAMICS
Federation House, Station Road, Stoke-on-Trent, Staffordshire ST4 2RT Tel. 0782 44840
Professional Qualifying Body; formerly the Institute of Ceramics Limited

Enquiries to the Secretary

Subject coverage
education and careers in ceramic technology, including pottery, refractories, bricks, electrical porcelain, glass and cement

Publication
Newsletter (to members only)

1407 INSTITUTE OF CHARTERED ACCOUNTANTS IN ENGLAND AND WALES
Chartered Accountants Hall, Moorgate Place, London, EC2R 6EQ Tel. 01-628 7060
Professional Body

Enquiries to the Secretary

Subject coverage
accountancy; auditing; taxation; management consultancy; financial planning, etc.

Publications
Publications list
Current Accounting Literature (annual)

1408 INSTITUTE OF CHARTERED ACCOUNTANTS OF SCOTLAND
Edinburgh Library, 27 Queen Street, Edinburgh EH2 1LA Tel. 031-225 3687
Professional/Teaching Institute, having a library also in Glasgow

Enquiries to the Librarian

Subject coverage
Accountancy; economics; management; taxation

Special collection
Antiquarian collection of some 700 items on accounting and related topics, 1494–1930

Publications
Accountants Magazine (monthly)
Catalogue of the Antiquarian Collection (3rd ed. in prep.)

1409 INSTITUTE OF CHARTERED SECRETARIES AND ADMINISTRATORS
16 Park Crescent, London W1N 4AH Tel. 01-580 4741
Professional Institute, formerly Chartered Institute of Secretaries

Enquiries to the Librarian and Information Officer

Subject coverage
company law and company secretarial practice; accounts; taxation; management and related topics

Special collection
Company histories

Publications
Professional Administration (11 times per annum)
Administrators' Handbooks

1410 INSTITUTE OF CHARTERED SHIPBROKERS
25 Bury Street, London EC3A 5BA Tel. 01-283 1361
Telex 8812708
Professional Institute, member of the Federation of National Associations of Shipbrokers and Agents of the same address

Enquiries to the Secretary
Subject coverage
ship broking

Publication
The Shipbroker (periodical)

INSTITUTE OF CLAYWORKERS *see* **NATIONAL FEDERATION OF CLAY INDUSTRIES**

1411 INSTITUTE OF CLERKS OF WORKS OF GREAT BRITAIN INCORPORATED
41 The Mall, Ealing, London W5 3TJ Tel. 01-579 2917 & 2918
Professional Institution

Enquiries to the General Secretary

Subject coverage
any aspects of the construction industry relating to site supervision; in particular, the role of the Clerk of Works

Publication
Journal of the Institute of Clerks of Works (monthly, since 1883)

INSTITUTE OF COASTAL OCEANOGRAPHY AND TIDES now **INSTITUTE OF OCEANOGRAPHIC SCIENCES,** *q.v.*

INSTITUTE OF COMPANY ACCOUNTANTS LIMITED *now* **SOCIETY OF COMPANY AND COMMERCIAL ACCOUNTANTS,** *q.v.*

INSTITUTE OF CORN AND AGRICULTURAL MERCHANTS LIMITED *see* **BRITISH ASSOCIATION OF GRAIN SEED FEED AND AGRICULTURAL MERCHANTS LIMITED**

1412 INSTITUTE OF COST AND MANAGEMENT ACCOUNTANTS
63 Portland Place, London W1N 4AB Tel. 01-637 4716
Professional Association, formerly Institute of Cost and Works Accountants

Enquiries to the Librarian and Information Officer

Subject coverage
cost and management accounting; terotechnology; general management

Publications
Textbooks and general books on accountancy
Examination papers

INSTITUTE OF COST AND WORKS ACCOUNTANTS *now* **INSTITUTE OF COST AND MANAGEMENT ACCOUNTANTS,** *q.v.*

1413 INSTITUTE OF CREDIT MANAGEMENT
12 Queen Square, Brighton, Sussex BN1 3FD Tel. 0273 26644
Professional Institute

Enquiries to the Secretary or Registrar

Subject coverage
all aspects of credit management

Publication
Credit Management (quarterly)

1414 INSTITUTE OF DATA PROCESSING LIMITED
Walter House, 418–422 Strand, London WC2R 0PW Tel. 01-240 3106
Enquiries to the Secretary-General

Subject coverage
data processing and computing within a commercial and industrial and general business environment

Publication
Data Processing Practitioner (quarterly)

1415 INSTITUTE OF DIRECTORS
10 Belgrave Square, London SW1X 8PW Tel. 01-235 3601
Representational and Educational Body; houses the British Executive Service Overseas

Enquiries to the Secretary

Subject coverage
boardroom responsibilities; finance; languages; effective speaking; retirement advice; industrial relations; executive health; non-executive directorships; taxation

Special collection
Business reference library

Publication
The Director (monthly)

1416 INSTITUTE OF ECONOMIC AFFAIRS
2 Lord North Street, London SW1P 3LB Tel. 01-799 3745
Educational Charity

Enquiries, from Subscribers only, to the Institute

Subject coverage
economics

1417 INSTITUTE OF ECONOMICS AND STATISTICS
Oxford University, St Cross Building, Manor Road, Oxford OX1 3UL Tel. 0865 49631
University Department

Enquiries to the Librarian or the Secretary

Subject coverage
economics, including economic statistics

Publication
Oxford Bulletin of Economics and Statistics (quarterly)

1418 INSTITUTE OF EMPLOYMENT CONSULTANTS LIMITED
120 Baker Street, London W1M 2DE Tel. 01-486 6905
Limited Company/Educational & Training Body

Enquiries to the Secretary

Subject coverage
employment agency techniques; interviewing techniques; employment legislation

Publications
Selection (quarterly)
Newsletter (monthly)
Institute Manual for Employment Agencies

1419 INSTITUTE OF ENGINEERS AND TECHNICIANS
11 Barry Parade, Barry Road, London SE22 0JA Tel. 01-699 8707/1255
Professional and Qualifying Body

Enquiries to the Honorary Librarian

Subject coverage
professional registration and qualifications

Publications
Quarterly Journal
Occasional Reports

1420 INSTITUTE OF EXPLOSIVES ENGINEERS
141 London Road, Leicester LE2 1EF Tel. 0533 536167
Trade Association
Enquiries to the Secretary
Subject coverage
explosives; blasting

Publication
Membership Brochure

1421 INSTITUTE OF EXPORT
World Trade Centre, London E1 9AA Tel. 01-488 2400
Telex 884671

Professional Institute

Enquiries to the Director-General

Subject coverage
sources of information on all aspects of export trading

Publications

Export (10 times per annum)
Specimen Agency Agreements (advisory booklet)
Thinking managerially about Exports (book)
Legal Aspects of Export Sales (book)

INSTITUTE OF FOOD DISTRIBUTION *now* **INSTITUTE OF GROCERY DISTRIBUTION,** *q.v.*

1422 INSTITUTE OF FOOD SCIENCE AND TECHNOLOGY OF THE UNITED KINGDOM
3A Hoskins Road, Oxted, Surrey Tel. Oxted 3699
Incorporated Professional Qualifying Body

No enquiry service

Publications

Journal of Food Technology (bi-monthly)
IFST Proceedings (quarterly)

1423 INSTITUTE OF FOOD TECHNOLOGISTS, BRITISH SECTION NO. 40
c/o RHM Research Limited, Spicer Building, Lincoln Road, Cressex, High Wycombe, Buckinghamshire HP12 3QR Tel. 0494 26191
Technical Institute; part of the Institute of Food Technologists, Chicago, Illinois, USA

Enquiries to the Secretary

Subject coverage

food science and technology

Publications

Food Technology
Journal of Food Science (both published by the USA Institute)
Newsletter (6 or 7 per annum for the British Membership)

1424 INSTITUTE OF FORESTERS OF GREAT BRITAIN
6 Rutland Square, Edinburgh EH1 2AU Tel. 031-229 4010
Professional Institute; formerly Society of Foresters of Great Britain

Enquiries to the Assistant Secretary

Subject coverage

forest management and planning; silviculture; arboriculture; investment in woodlands; timber marketing and harvesting; game and wildlife management in woods; inventories; woodland landscaping; recreational use; farm shelterbelts; forest nursery technology; tree pests and diseases; woodland taxation; timber processing

Publication

Forestry (twice per annum)

1425 INSTITUTE OF FREIGHT FORWARDERS LIMITED
9 Paradise Road, Richmond, Surrey TW9 1SA Tel. 01-948 3141
Professional Body and Trade Association, formerly Institute of Shipping and Forwarding Agents

Enquiries to the Institute, for routing to appropriate department

Subject coverage

international freight forwarding

Publication

Freight Forwarder (periodical)

1426 INSTITUTE OF FUEL
18 Devonshire Street, Portland Place, London W1N 2AU Tel. 01-580 7124
Professional Body/Scientific Institute

Enquiries to the Institute

Subject coverage
technical, scientific and economic aspects of all types of fuel; nuclear applications; pollution; engineering

Publication
Fuel Abstracts (monthly)

1427 INSTITUTE OF GEOLOGICAL SCIENCES
Exhibition Road, South Kensington, London SW7 2DE Tel. 01-589 3444
Research Institute, government funded, of the Natural Environment Research Council; Northern England and Wales Office in Halston, Leeds LS15 8TQ (Tel. 0532 649161); Scotland Office, West Mains Road, Edinburgh (Tel. 031-667 1000)

Enquiries to the Librarian

Subject coverage
all aspects of the earth sciences

Special collection
National geological archives

Publications
see H.M.S.O. Sectional List No. 45
Ordnance Survey maps catalogue – geological survey maps

1428 INSTITUTE OF GROCERY DISTRIBUTION
Grange Lane, Letchmore Heath, Watford WD2 8DQ Tel. 779 7141
Company, formed by the merger of the Grocers Institute and the Institute of Food Distribution

Enquiries to the Librarian

Subject coverage
food retailing and distribution

Publications
Digest of Statistics (with annual up-dating)
Research Index
Distribution and Retailing in the Eighties
Reports and Studies
Publications List

1429 INSTITUTE OF HEALTH SERVICE ADMINISTRATORS
75 Portland Place, London W1N 4AN Tel. 01-580 5041
Professional Association; formerly Institute of Hospital Administrators

Enquiries to the Secretary

Subject coverage
health service administration

Publications
Hospitals and Health Services Yearbook
Hospital and Health Services Review (monthly)
Hospital and Health Services Purchasing (monthly)
Subject Index to Statutory Instruments and Official Memoranda and Circulars
Reports (occasional)

1430 INSTITUTE OF HOSPITAL ENGINEERING
20 Landport Terrace, Southsea, Hampshire PO1 2RG Tel. 0705 23186
Learned Society

Enquiries to the Secretary

Subject coverage
Hospital engineering

Publication
Hospital Engineering (monthly)

1431 INSTITUTE OF HYDROLOGY
Maclean Building, Crowmarsh Gifford, Wallingford, Tel. 0491 38800
Berkshire OX10 8BB Telex 849365
Research Institute, of the Natural Environment Research Council; formerly Hydrological Research Unit; houses the Editorial Office of the International Association of Hydrological Sciences

Enquiries to the Information Officer or Librarian

Subject coverage
scientific hydrology

Publications
Annual Report (free)
Research Reports (free)
Hydrological Research in the U.K. 1970–75 (free)
Flood Studies Report, 5 vols, 1975 (NERC £40.00)

1432 INSTITUTE OF INDUSTRIAL TRAINING
Kingston Lane, Hillingdon, Middlesex Tel. 89 37188
University Institute, of Brunel University

Enquiries to the Director

Subject coverage
industrial training and careers; research and statistics; sandwich degree courses

Special collection
Statistics on Sandwich Degree Courses for the 9 technological universities

Publication
Research Projects on Industrial Training

1433 INSTITUTE OF INFORMATION SCIENTISTS
657 High Road, Tottenham, London N17 8AA Tel. 01-808 6399
Professional, Qualifying Body

Enquiries to the Secretary

Subject coverage
information science: careers and qualifications therein

Publications
Information Scientist
Inform

1434 INSTITUTE OF INVENTORS
19 Fosse Way, Ealing, London W13 0BZ Tel. 01-998 3540 & 4372
Professional Association/Examining and Qualifying Body

Enquiries, brief only, to the President; other enquiries from non-members are chargeable

Subject coverage
the sponsorship of all stages of sound, private inventions (design, development, prototype construction and mass production); provision of invention services (sifting, patenting, technical and legal advice, etc.)

Publication
List of inventions (to business members only)

1435 INSTITUTE OF LANDSCAPE ARCHITECTS
12 Carlton House Terrace, London SW1Y 5AH Tel. 01-839 4044
Professional Association; it is proposed to change the name to Landscape Institute

Enquiries to the Librarian or Registrar

Subject coverage
landscape architecture

Publications
Landscape Design (quarterly)
Reports, Symposia, etc. (available from RIBA bookshops)

1436 INSTITUTE OF LINGUISTS
Loyds Bank Chambers, 91 Newington Causeway, London SE1 6BN Tel. 01-407 4755 & 3871
Professional Organization; the Translators' Guild of the Institute is affiliated to the Fédération Internationale des Traducteurs

Enquiries, lexical to the Librarian; examination to the Examinations Officer; membership to the Secretary; all other to the Information Officer

Subject coverage
language learning; courses; methods; availability and training of translators and interpreters; qualifications; language grammar books and dictionaries; employment of translators; examinations in languages; careers with languages; language in general

Publication
Incorporated Linguist (quarterly)

1437 INSTITUTE OF LONDON UNDERWRITERS
40 Lime Street, London EC3M 5DA Tel. 01-623 9991
Telex 884165

Marine Insurance Association

Enquiries to the Manager or Secretary

Subject coverage
marine, aviation and transport insurance

1438 INSTITUTE OF MANAGEMENT CONSULTANTS
23–24 Cromwell Place, London SW7 2LG Tel. 01-584 7285
Professional Organization

Enquiries to the Secretary
Subject coverage
management consulting practice and careers

Publications
Management Symposium (bi-annual)
List of Members (annual)

1439 INSTITUTE OF MANPOWER STUDIES
Sussex University, Mantell Building, Fulmer, Brighton BN1 9RF Tel. 0273 686751
Research, Advisory, and Teaching Institution

Enquiries to the Administration Manager or Publications Assistant

Subject coverage
manpower planning; use of computers and models; conducting of manpower data surveys; measurement of manpower behaviour; labour market studies including professions and industries

Publications
Summary of annual IMS Manpower Survey (500,000 employees in 40 organisations)
Annual Handbook
Quarterly Newsletter
Advisory Manuals
Research reports
Conference and occasional papers
Course teaching material

1440 INSTITUTE OF MARINE ENGINEERS
76 Mark Lane, London EC3R 7JN Tel. 01-481 8493
Telex 886841

Learned Society; affiliated to the Chartered Engineers Institute; the Marlib Information Service is a unit of the Institute of Marine Engineers

Enquiries to the Director of Information Services

Subject coverage
marine engineering; ocean technology

Publication
Marine Engineer's Review

1441 INSTITUTE OF MARKET OFFICERS
The Abattoir, Cricket Inn Road, Sheffield S2 5BD Tel. 0742 20316
Administrative Institute

Enquiries, from Members and Public Authorities only

Subject coverage
markets, fairs, abbatoirs and cold stores: administration, management

1442 INSTITUTE OF MARKETING
Moor Hall, Cookham, Berkshire SL6 9QH Tel. 062-85 24922
Professional Institute; includes the College of Marketing

Enquiries to the Information Services Officer or the Librarian

Subject coverage
marketing; market research; salary scales for marketing staff; education and training; industry analyses

1443 INSTITUTE OF MATERIALS HANDLING
St. Ives House, St. Ives Road, Maidenhead, Berkshire SL6 1RB Tel. 0628 28011
Technical Institute

Enquiries to the Executive Officer

Subject coverage
materials handling; plant layout; materials management; storage and warehousing

1444 INSTITUTE OF MATHEMATICS AND ITS APPLICATIONS
Maitland House, Warrior Square, Southend-on-Sea, Essex SS1 2JY Tel. 0702 612177
Professional Institution

Enquiries, by letter only, to the Assistant Secretary

Subject coverage
mathematics and mathematical education

Publications
Bulletin (monthly, house journal)
Research Journal (bi-monthly)

1445 INSTITUTE OF MEASUREMENT AND CONTROL
20 Peel Street, London W8 7PD Tel. 01-727 0083/5
Telex 916226

Learned and Professional Society

Enquiries to the Secretary

Subject coverage
measurement; control theory; instrumentation and control engineering; computers; automation; process control

Publications
Measurement and Control (monthly)
Conference Proceedings
Monographs

1446 INSTITUTE OF MEDICAL LABORATORY SCIENCES
12 Queen Anne Street, London W1M 0AU Tel. 01-636 8192/5
Professional Body; formerly Institute of Medical Laboratory Technology

Enquiries to the Information Department

Subject coverage
careers in medical laboratory science; medical laboratory scientific information

Publications
Gazette (monthly; news, etc.)
Medical Laboratory Sciences (quarterly, scientific)

1447 INSTITUTE OF METAL FINISHING
178 Goswell Road, London EC1V 7DU Tel. 01-253 4775
Technical and Scientific Society; eight regional branches; three technical groups

No enquiry service

Subject coverage
metal finishing; printed circuits; anodizing; coating

Publications
Transactions of the Institute (quarterly)
Symposia

INSTITUTE OF METALLURGICAL TECHNICIANS *see* **INSTITUTION OF METALLURGISTS**

INSTITUTE OF METALS *now* **METALS SOCIETY,** *q.v.*

1448 INSTITUTE OF MUNICIPAL BUILDING MANAGEMENT
57 Marine Drive, Rhos-on-Sea, Colwyn Bay Tel. Colwyn Bay 49373
Professional Organization

Enquiries to the General Secretary

Subject coverage
direct labour building

Publication
Municipal Building Management (quarterly)

1449 INSTITUTE OF NAVAL MEDICINE
Alverstoke, Gosport, Hampshire PO12 2DL Tel. 0705 22351 ext. 41530/41531/41533
Government Department, of the Ministry of Defence, Medical Directorate (Naval)

Enquiries to the Medical Officer in Charge

Subject coverage
underwater medicine; survival medicine; habitability, heat, cold, toxicology; nuclear medicine and radiological protection; audiology and hearing conservation; submarine medicine and experimental physiology; dental research and preventive dentistry; occupational medicine and hygiene; medical statistics

Publications
Annual Report
Reports and Technical Memoranda

1450 INSTITUTE OF OCCUPATIONAL MEDICINE
8 Roxburgh Place, Edinburgh EH8 9SU Tel. 031-667 5131
Charitable Foundation, associated with the National Coal Board; houses the Asbestosis Research Foundation

Enquiries to the Director

Subject coverage
occupational hygiene; pulmonary function testing in industry; radiological surveys in industry; epidemiological investigations; animal exposure facilities; techniques in dust measurement; methods of counting asbestos fibres; tissue culture

Publications
papers in the open literature

1451 INSTITUTE OF OCEANOGRAPHIC SCIENCES
Wormley, Godalming, Surrey GU8 5UB Tel. 042-879 2122
Research Laboratory; created by the amalgamation of the former National Institute of Oceanography, the Institute of Coastal Oceanography and Tides, the British Oceanographic Data Service (which retains its title within the new Institute), and the Unit of Coastal Sedimentation; the Institute is one of the Natural Environment Research Council Institutes

Enquiries to the British Oceanographic Data Service

Subject coverage
all aspects of marine science

Special collection
Discovery Collection

Publications
Annual Report
Collected Reprints (annually)
Discovery Reports (irregular)

INSTITUTE OF OFFICE MANAGEMENT *now* **INSTITUTE OF ADMINISTRATIVE MANAGEMENT,** *q.v.*

1452 INSTITUTE OF OFFSHORE ENGINEERING
Heriot-Watt University, Riccarton, Currie, Edinburgh EH14 4AS Tel. 031-449 5111
Research Institute, of Heriot-Watt University

Enquiries to the Information Officer

Subject coverage
offshore engineering; marine technology; oil and gas activities

Publication
Guide to Information Sources in Marine Technology

1453 INSTITUTE OF OPHTHALMOLOGY
Judd Street, London WC1H 9GS Tel. 01-387 9621
Research Institute, of the University of London

Enquiries to the Librarian

Subject coverage
ophthalmology; visual science including visual optics

Publications
Ophthalmic Literature (abstracting journal)
Annual Report

1454 INSTITUTE OF PACKAGING
Fountain House, 1a Elm Park, Stanmore, Middlesex HA7 4BZ Tel. 01-954 6277
Professional Society

Enquiries to the Secretary

Subject coverage
packaging education and qualification; overseas contacts; exhibitions

Publications
packaging textbooks and monographs

1455 INSTITUTE OF PATENTEES AND INVENTORS
Whiteley Building, 165 Queensway, London W2 4SB Tel. 01-229 2246
Semi-professional Institute; member of the Royal Society of Arts; houses the International Federation of Inventors' Associations

Enquiries, limited, except to subscribing members, to the Secretary

Subject coverage
national and international patents; registered designs; trade marks; copyright; the furtherance, protection and exploitation of inventions through to industrial innovation

Publications
The Inventor
New Patents (abstracts for members)

1456 INSTITUTE OF PERSONNEL MANAGEMENT
Central House, Upper Woburn Place, London WC1H 0HX Tel. 01-387 2844
Professional Institute

Enquiries, from members and post-graduate research students only, to the Secretary

Subject coverage
management; personnel management; manpower planning; industrial training; employee participation; job analysis and enrichment, etc.; recruitment

Publications
IPM Management Books (complete list)

1457 INSTITUTE OF PETROLEUM
61 New Cavendish Street, London W1M 8AR Tel. 01-636 1004
Telex 264380
Professional Society; houses the World Petroleum Congress European Co-ordinating Committee

Enquiries to the Information Officer or Librarian

Subject coverage
petroleum technology; petroleum geology, exploration, production, refining, transportation; physical and chemical properties of hydrocarbons; methods of analysis; petroleum products and petrochemicals; statistics

Publications
Petroleum information booklets
Technical papers
Petroleum Review (monthly)

1458 INSTITUTE OF PHYSICS
47 Belgrave Square, London SW1X 8QX Tel. 01-235 6111
Telex 918453
Learned Society and Professional Institution, formerly Institute of Physics and the Physical Society; houses also the following 9 bodies: Association of Consulting Scientists, *q.v.*, British Society for the History of Science, British Vacuum Council, Council of Science and Technology Institutes, Hospital Physicists Association, Institute of Acoustics, *q.v.* International Union of Vacuum Science and Technology, R and D Society, *q.v.*, United Kingdom Crystallographic Council

Enquiries to the Executive Secretary

Subject coverage
physics

Publications
A very large number of publications are listed in an annual Publications Catalogue

1459 INSTITUTE OF PLUMBING
Scottish Mutual House, North Street, Hornchurch, Essex RM11 1RU Tel. 49 51236
Professional Organization; amalgamated with the former Registered Plumbers Association

Enquiries to the Executive Director

Subject coverage
plumbing technology *not* trading or pricing matters

Publications
Plumbing and Associated Mechanical Services (quarterly)
Booklist

1460 INSTITUTE OF POLYMER TECHNOLOGY
Loughborough University of Technology, Loughborough, Leicestershire LE11 3TU — Tel. 0509 63171 ext. 5228/9; Tel. 34319
Postgraduate Training Body

Enquiries to the Director

Subject coverage
processing and use of plastics and rubbers

Publication
Journal of the Institute of Polymer Technology (irregular)

1461 INSTITUTE OF PRACTITIONERS IN WORK STUDY, ORGANISATION AND METHODS
9/10 River Front, Enfield, Middlesex EN1 3TE — Tel. 01-363 7452/7
Professional Body, created by the merger of the former Institute of Work Study Practitioners and the Organisation and Methods Society

Enquiries to the Technical Information Officer

Subject coverage
work study; organization and methods and related disciplines

Publications
Management Services (monthly, free to members, or by subscription)
Monographs on technical subjects
Problem Solving for Management (book)
Work Measurement (book)

1462 INSTITUTE OF PRINTING LIMITED
10/11 Bedford Row, London WC1R 4DZ — Tel. 01-405 1176
Professional Body

Enquiries to the Secretary

Subject coverage
printing technology; management; design; education

Publication
Professional Printer (on subscription to non-members)

INSTITUTE OF PUBLIC CLEANSING *now* **INSTITUTE OF SOLID WASTES MANAGEMENT,** *q.v.*

1463 INSTITUTE OF PURCHASING AND SUPPLY
York House, Westminster Bridge Road, London SE1 7UT — Tel. 01-928 1851
Professional Institute; the address also of the National Industrial Materials Recovery Association, *q.v.*

Enquiries to the Education and Training Manager

Subject coverage
materials management; purchasing; stores; materials handling and supplies

1464 INSTITUTE OF QUALIFIED PRIVATE SECRETARIES LIMITED
126 Farnham Road, Slough SL1 4XA — Tel. 75 22395
Professional Institute

Enquiries to the Assistant Secretary

Subject coverage
private secretarial training, qualifications and employment

Publication
Journal of the Institute

1465 INSTITUTE OF QUALITY ASSURANCE
54 Princes Gate, Exhibition Road, London SW7 2PG Tel. 01-584 9026
Professional Institution, formerly Institution of Engineering Inspection

Enquiries to the Secretary

Subject coverage
quality assurance

Publications
Quality Assurance (quarterly)
Quality Assurance News (monthly; for members only)

1466 INSTITUTE OF QUANTITY SURVEYORS
98 Gloucester Place, London W1H 4AT Tel. 01-935 1895 *or* 4048
Professional Association

Enquiries to the Librarian

Subject coverage
quantity surveying; construction costs

Publications
Quantity Surveyor (monthly)
Occasional research reports

1467 INSTITUTE OF REFRIGERATION
272 London Road, Wallington, Surrey SM6 7DJ Tel. 01-647 7033
Professional Society

Enquiries to the Secretary
Subject coverage
refrigeration

INSTITUTE OF REGISTERED ARCHITECTS *now* **FACULTY OF ARCHITECTS AND SURVEYORS LIMITED,** *q.v.*

1468 INSTITUTE OF REPROGRAPHIC TECHNOLOGY
52–55 Carnaby Street, London W1V 1PF Tel. 01-734 6584
Professional Institute

Enquiries to the Honorary Technical Officer

Subject coverage
photocopying and duplicating; office systems; reproduction of engineering drawings; in-plant printing; mechanised addressing and mailing; microfilms; miniaturisation; photography; visual aids

Publications
Reprographic Management Handbook
Basics of Reprography
Electrostatics in Reprography
35 mm Microfilming for Drawing Offices

1469 INSTITUTE OF ROAD TRANSPORT ENGINEERS
1 Cromwell Place, London SW7 2JF Tel. 01-589 3744
Professional Institute

Enquiries to the Secretary

Subject coverage
road transport engineering

Publication
Transport Engineer (bi-monthly)

1470 INSTITUTE OF SCIENCE AND TECHNOLOGY (UMIST)
Manchester University, P.O. Box 88, Sackville Street, Manchester M60 1QD — Tel. 061-236 3311
University Institution, of academic affiliation only

Enquiries, bibliographic, to the Librarian; technical, to the Director of Industrial Liaison

Subject coverage
science, engineering, management (including European aspects)

Special collection
Joule Collection (books collected by J.P. Joule 1818–1889)

Publication
Annual Report

1471 INSTITUTE OF SCIENCE AND TECHNOLOGY (UWIST)
University of Wales, King Edward VII Avenue, Cardiff CF1 3NU — Tel. 0222 42522
University Institute; formerly Welsh College of Advanced Technology

Enquiries to the Librarian

Subject coverage
Science, technology, economics, management, accountancy, architecture, town planning

1472 INSTITUTE OF SCIENCE TECHNOLOGY
345 Grays Inn Road, London WC1X 8PX — Tel. 01-837 2207
Professional Institute

Enquiries to the Secretary

Subject coverage
careers, education, examination of science laboratory technicians

1473 INSTITUTE OF SCIENTIFIC AND TECHNICAL COMMUNICATORS LIMITED
17 Bluebridge Avenue, Brookmans Park, Hatfield, Herts AL19 7RY — Tel. 77 55392
Professional Institution

Enquiries to the Secretary

Subject coverage
technical and scientific communication

Publication
Communicator of Scientific and Technical Information (quarterly, *known as* The Communicator)

INSTITUTE OF SHIPPING AND FORWARDING AGENTS *now* **INSTITUTE OF FREIGHT FORWARDERS LIMITED,** *q.v.*

1474 INSTITUTE OF SHOPS ACTS ADMINISTRATION
c/o The Health Department, Borough of Reigate and Banstead, 24 Hatchlands Road, Redhill RH1 6AR — Tel. 91 61265
Association of Local Government Enforcement Officers

Enquiries, by letter, to the Secretary

Subject coverage
Health and Safety at Work Act 1974; Young Persons Employment Acts; the Shops Acts 1950–1965; the Offices, Shops and Railway Premises Act 1963; Licensing; Consumer Protection Act

Publication
The Inspector (monthly)

1475 INSTITUTE OF SOLID WASTES MANAGEMENT
28 Portland Place, London W1N 4DE — Tel. 01-580 5324
Professional Institute, formerly Institute of Public Cleansing; has five regional Centres

Enquiries to the Director

Subject coverage
solid waste management

Publication
Solid Wastes

1476 INSTITUTE OF SOUND AND VIBRATION RESEARCH

The University, Southampton SO9 5NH Tel. 0703 559122
Telex 47661

University Institute; associated with the Wolfson Unit for Noise and Vibration Control, *q.v.*

Enquiries to the Director

Subject coverage
acoustics; structural dynamics; audiology; fluid dynamics; automotive engineering; instrumentation; random process analysis; human response to noise and vibration; hearing conservation; urban planning and noise; vibration engineering and control; machinery noise and vibration, etc.

Special collection
Literature on the human response to vibration

Publication
Annual Report

1477 INSTITUTE OF STATISTICIANS

36 Churchgate Street, Bury St. Edmunds, Suffolk IP33 1RD Tel. 0284 63660
Professional and Examining Body; member of the International Statistical Institute

Enquiries to the Secretary, who will refer them to Members

Subject coverage
statistics; operational research, market research

Publications
The Statistician (quarterly)
List of Members (annually)
Newsletter and Notice of Vacancies (monthly)
Beveridge Memorial Lectures
Statistical Teaching Aids Book
Examiners Reports

1478 INSTITUTE OF SUPERVISORY MANAGEMENT

22 Bore Street, Lichfield, Staffordshire WS13 6LP Tel. 054-32 51346
Independent Professional Body

Enquiries to the Director

Subject coverage
management; educational and training of professional supervisors; effective writing for supervisors

Publication
Supervisory Management (quarterly)

1479 INSTITUTE OF TAXATION

3 Grosvenor Crescent, London SW1X 7EL Tel. 01-235 8847
Professional Body

Enquiries are not accepted from the public

Subject coverage
U.K. taxation

Publications
Monthly Magazine
Annotated Taxing Statutes

1480 INSTITUTE OF TERRESTRIAL ECOLOGY
Headquarters, 68 Hills Road, Cambridge CB2 1LA Tel. 0223 69745
Research Institute, of the Natural Environment Research Council; most of the nine research stations were formerly part of the Nature Conservancy; also includes the Culture Centre for Algae and Protozoa, *q.v.*

Enquiries, scientific, to the Liaison Officer; bibliographical, to the Librarian, Merlewood Research Station, q.v.

Subject coverage
factors determining the structure, composition and processes of terrestrial ecological systems and the abundance and performance of individual species and organisms; scientific bases for predicting and modelling future environmental trends, human impact, and the protection and management of the environment

Publication
Annual Report

1481 INSTITUTE OF TERRESTRIAL ECOLOGY
Edinburgh Laboratories (Bush), Bush Estate, Penicuik, Midlothian EH26 0QB Tel. 031-445 4343/6
Research Laboratories, including the former Institute of Tree Biology and the Bryophyte Project Group

Enquiries to the Librarian

Subject coverage
genetics; physiology of trees

1482 INSTITUTE OF TERRESTRIAL ECOLOGY
Edinburgh Laboratories (Hope Terrace), 12 Hope Terrace, Edinburgh EH9 2AS Tel. 031-447 4784/6

Enquiries to the Librarian

Subject coverage
freshwater and peatland ecology

INSTITUTE OF TERRESTRIAL ECOLOGY *see also*
CULTURE CENTRE FOR ALGAE AND PROTOZOA
FURZEBROOK RESEARCH STATION
MERLEWOOD RESEARCH STATION
MONKS WOOD EXPERIMENTAL STATION

INSTITUTE OF THE FURNITURE WAREHOUSING AND REMOVING INDUSTRY *see* **BRITISH ASSOCIATION OF REMOVERS**

1483 INSTITUTE OF THE MOTOR INDUSTRY INCORPORATED
Fanshaws, Brickendon, Hertford, Hertfordshire SG13 8PQ Tel. 099-286 282
Professional Institute

Enquiries to the Secretary

Subject coverage
automobile engineering; education and training in the retail motor industry; management techniques

Publication
Motor Management (bi-monthly)

INSTITUTE OF THE RUBBER INDUSTRY *now* **PLASTICS AND RUBBER INSTITUTE,** *q.v.*

1484 INSTITUTE OF TRADING STANDARDS ADMINISTRATION
Estate House, 319D London Road, Hadleigh, Benfleet, Essex SS7 2BN Tel. 0702 558179/558170
Professional Institute, formerly Institute of Weights and Measures Administration

Enquiries to the Information Officer

Subject coverage
fair trading; consumer protection; advice to consumers and traders; legal, technical, scientific, practical and general information relative to the purpose of the Administration

Special collection
Museum of Measuring Instruments

Publications
Monthly Review
Measuring Instrument Treatise
Weights and Measures Handbook
Criminal Process in Scotland
Food and Drugs Handbook

1485 INSTITUTE OF TRAFFIC ADMINISTRATION
8 Cumberland Place, Southampton SO1 2BH — Tel. 0703 31380
Professional Institute

Enquiries to the National Secretary

Subject coverage
use and provision of transport by road, rail, air and sea; education and training of members

Publications
Transport Management (quarterly, free to members)

INSTITUTE OF TRANSPORT *now* **CHARTERED INSTITUTE OF TRANSPORT,** *q.v.*

INSTITUTE OF TREE BIOLOGY *now* **INSTITUTE OF TERRESTRIAL ECOLOGY, Edinburgh Laboratories (Bush),** *q.v.*

1486 INSTITUTE OF WATER POLLUTION CONTROL
Ledson House, London Road, Maidstone, Kent ME16 8JH — Tel. 0622 62034
Professional Institute

Enquiries to the General Secretary

Subject coverage
water pollution control; treatment and disposal of sewage and trade wastes; prevention of river pollution

Publications
Water Pollution Control (bi-monthly)
Conferences and Symposia proceedings
Manuals of British practice in water pollution control

INSTITUTE OF WEIGHTS AND MEASURES ADMINISTRATION *now* **INSTITUTE OF TRADING STANDARDS ADMINISTRATION,** *q.v.*

INSTITUTE OF WELDING *now* **WELDING INSTITUTE,** *q.v.*

1487 INSTITUTE OF WELFARE OFFICERS
73 Penrhyn Road, Kingston upon Thames, Surrey — Tel. 01-546 4550
Professional Institute

Enquiries to the General Secretary

Subject coverage
welfare and the interests of welfare officers

Publication
Welfare Officer (bi-monthly)

1488 INSTITUTE OF WOOD SCIENCE LIMITED
62 Oxford Street, London W1 — Tel. 01-580 3185
Company

Enquiries to the Secretary or the Editor

Subject coverage
wood science and technology

Publication
Institute of Wood Science Journal

INSTITUTE OF WORK STUDY PRACTITIONERS *now* **INSTITUTE OF PRACTITIONERS IN WORK STUDY, ORGANISATION AND METHODS,** *q.v.*

1489 INSTITUTION OF AGRICULTURAL ENGINEERS
West End Road, Silsoe, Bedford MK45 4DU Tel. 0525 61096
Professional Organisation/Learned Society

Enquiries to the Institution Secretary

Subject coverage
agricultural engineering

Publication
Agricultural Engineer (quarterly)

1490 INSTITUTION OF BRITISH ENGINEERS
Regency House, 3 Marlborough Place, Brighton, Sussex Tel. 0273 61399
Telex 877534

Professional Institution

Enquiries to the Secretary

Subject coverage
all aspects of engineering

Publication
British Engineer (bi-monthly)

1491 INSTITUTION OF BUYERS
Concorde House, 24 Warwick New Road, Royal Leamington Spa, Warwickshire CV32 5JH Tel. 0926 37621
Professional Institution; member of Sales Augmentation Limited, of the same address

Enquiries to the Director-General, the Membership Registrar or the Courses Registrar

Subject coverage
purchasing; stock control; sourcing; management techniques; purchasing training

Publication
Journal (monthly)

1492 INSTITUTION OF CHEMICAL ENGINEERS
Library and Information Service, 15 Belgrave Square, London SW1 Tel. 01-235 3647
Learned Society; Headquarters at 165–171, Railway Terrace, Rugby CU21 3HQ (Tel. 0788 78214)

Enquiries to the Information Officer

Subject coverage
chemical engineering; loss prevention

Special collections
Loss Prevention Collection
Filtration Society Collection

Publications
Chemical Engineer (monthly)
Transactions of the Institution (monthly)
Loss Prevention Bulletin
Diary

1493 INSTITUTION OF CIVIL ENGINEERS

1–7 Great George Street, London SW1P 3AA Tel. 01-839 3611

Learned Society; houses the British Nuclear Energy Society, *q.v.* the Society of Civil Engineering Technicians, and the Building Services Engineering Society

Enquiries to the Secretary

Subject coverage

engineering, particularly civil engineering, and related theoretical and applied sciences

Special collection

B.L. Vulliamy Horological Library

Publications

Proceedings (2 parts per quarter)
Abstracts (10 per annum)
New Civil Engineer (weekly)
Géotechnique (quarterly)
Offshore Engineer (monthly)
BNES Journal (quarterly)
Civil Engineering Technician (quarterly)

1494 INSTITUTION OF ELECTRICAL ENGINEERS

Savoy Place, London WC2R 0BL Tel. 01-240 1871
Telex 261176

Learned Society, parent body of INSPEC, *q.v.*

Enquiries to the Librarian (technical enquiries sometimes charged)

Subject coverage

electrical, electronic and control engineering; computer science; information science

Special collections

Sir Francis Ronalds Collection (19th century rare books and manuscripts on electricity)
Thompson Collection (rare books and manuscripts)

Publications

Proceedings of the IEE (monthly, 3 sections; Electronics Record, Power Record, Control & Science Record)
Electronics and Power (monthly)
Electronics Letters (fortnightly)
see also INSPEC (publications)

1495 INSTITUTION OF ELECTRICAL & ELECTRONICS TECHNICIAN ENGINEERS LIMITED

2 Savoy Hill, London WC2R 0BS Tel. 01-836 3357

Learned Society and Qualifying Body

Enquiries to the Secretary

Subject coverage

electrical and electronics engineering

Publications

Electrotechnology (quarterly)
Bulletin (monthly)

1496 INSTITUTION OF ELECTRONIC AND RADIO ENGINEERS

8–9 Bedford Square, London WC1B 3RG Tel. 01-637 2771

Scientific and Technical Institution; member of the Council of Engineering Institutions, *q.v.*

Enquiries to the Librarian

Subject coverage

electronics; computer science; engineering; radio; telephony; telegraphy; audio engineering; medical engineering

Publication

Electronic and Radio Engineer

1497 INSTITUTION OF ENGINEERING DESIGNERS
Courtleigh, Westbury Leigh, Westbury, Wiltshire BA13 3TA — Tel. 0373 822801
Professional Body

Enquiries to the Secretary

Subject coverage
engineering design; engineering drawing; design; design education

Publications
Guide to Engineering Design Courses in the U.K.
Engineering Designer (monthly)
Conference proceedings, etc.

INSTITUTION OF ENGINEERING INSPECTION *now* **INSTITUTE OF QUALITY ASSURANCE,** *q.v.*

1498 INSTITUTION OF ENGINEERS AND SHIPBUILDERS IN SCOTLAND
183 Bath Street, Glasgow G2 4HT — Tel. 041-248 3721/2
Learned Institution

Enquiries to the Secretary

Subject coverage
science and practice of engineering and shipbuilding; civil, mechanical and electrical engineering; metallurgy; naval architecture

Publications
Transactions of the Institution
Abstracts

1499 INSTITUTION OF ENVIRONMENTAL SCIENCES LIMITED
14 Princes Gate, Hyde Park, London SW7 1PU — Tel. 01-584 6262
for information 0254 64321
Professional and Learned Society

Enquiries to the Honorary Director, c/o College of Technology, Feilden Street, Blackburn BB2 1LH

Subject coverage
all aspects of environmental problems; pollution; urban and population problems; ecology; public health; genetics; noise; nutrition

Publications
Papers delivered at Conferences are usually published in the *independent* Journal of Environmental Studies

1500 INSTITUTION OF FIRE ENGINEERS
148 New Walk, Leicester LE1 7QB — Tel. 0533 59171
Professional Institute, part of the Federation of British Fire Organisations

Enquiries to the General Secretary

Subject coverage
fire engineering

Publication
Institution of Fire Engineers Journal (quarterly)

1501 INSTITUTION OF GAS ENGINEERS
17 Grosvenor Crescent, London SW1X 7ES — Tel. 01-245 9811
Professional Association, member of the International Gas Union

Enquiries to the Librarian

Subject coverage
gas engineering, manufacture, transmission and distribution; gas utilization; natural gas; LNG; gas by-products; gas industry administration and personnel

Publications
Gas Engineering and Management (house journal)
Communications Series (research papers)
Recommendations for Transmission, Distribution, Safety and Measurement
Publications List

1502 INSTITUTION OF GENERAL TECHNICIAN ENGINEERS
33 Ovington Square, London SW3 Tel. 01-589 9648
Technical Institution, formerly Junior Institution of Engineers; member of Engineers Registration Board

Enquiries to the Secretary

Subject coverage
engineering; careers advice and support

Publication
General Engineer (10 issues per annum)

1503 INSTITUTION OF HEATING AND VENTILATING ENGINEERS
49 Cadogan Square, London SW1X 0JB Tel. 01-235 7671
Professional Institution

Enquiries to the Technical Department

Subject coverage
heating; ventilating; air conditioning; buildings services including sanitary services, water, fire protection, lighting, electrical services, acoustics; refrigeration; combustion; internal transport (lifts, etc.)

Publication
Building Services Engineer (monthly)

1504 INSTITUTION OF HIGHWAY ENGINEERS
14 Queen Annes Gate, London SW1H 9AF Tel. 01-839 3582
Learned Society, in close association with the Highway and Traffic Technicians Association Limited

Enquiries to the Technical Adviser

Subject coverage
highway engineering; transportation; traffic engineering

Publication
The Highway Engineer

1505 INSTITUTION OF INDUSTRIAL SAFETY OFFICERS
222 Uppingham Road, Leicester LE5 0QG Tel. 0533 768424
Professional Association; some 20 regional and district Branches

Enquiries to the Secretary

Subject coverage
industrial health and safety; occupational hygiene and health hazards; training; legislation; environmental problems

Publications
Protection (monthly, except August)
Protection Directory of Industrial and Environmental Safety Personnel (publisher A. Osborne)

1506 INSTITUTION OF INDUSTRIAL SECURITY
7 Blue Waters Drive, Broadsands, Paignton, Devonshire TQ4 6JE Tel. 080-44 2326
Professional Institution; linked with the Industrial Police and Security Association, *q.v.*

Enquiries to the Secretary

Subject coverage
industrial and commercial security

Publication
Security and Protection Journal

1507 INSTITUTION OF MECHANICAL ENGINEERS
1 Birdcage Walk, Westminster, London SW1H 9JJ Tel. 01-839 1211
Telex 917944

Professional Learned Society, member of the Council of Engineering Institutions, *q.v.*; having an Automobile Division and a Railway Division; housing daughter societies as follows: Society for Underwater Technology, *q.v.*, British Society of Audiology, Institute of Automobile Engineer Assessors, Diecasting Society and National Council for Quality and Reliability

Enquiries, normally from Members only, to the Librarian

Subject coverage
mechanical engineering and related fields

Publications
Automotive Engineer (bi-monthly)
Chartered Mechanical Engineer (monthly)
Engineering in Medicine (quarterly)
International Journal of Mechanical Engineering Education (quarterly)
Journal of Mechanical Engineering Science (6 times per annum)
Journal of Strain Analysis for Engineering Design (quarterly)
Marine Technology (6 times per annum)
Mechanical Engineering News (weekly)
Proceedings of the Institution (separate papers or annual volume)
Heat and Fluid Flow (twice per annum)
Conference publications

1508 INSTITUTE OF MEDICAL LABORATORY SCIENCES
12 Queen Anne Street, London W1M 0AU Tel. 01-636 8192
Professional Institute; formerly Institute of Medical Laboratory Technology

Enquiries, bibliographical, to the Librarian; medical laboratory sciences, to the General Secretary

Subject coverage
qualification and training in the medical laboratory sciences, including histopathology, clinical chemistry, virology, medical microbiology, serology, haematology, blood transfusion; immunology; microscopy; laboratory administration and management

Special collection
Theses submitted for Fellowship of the Institute

Publications
Medical Laboratory Sciences (quarterly)
Gazette of the Institute of Medical Laboratory Sciences (monthly)

1509 INSTITUTION OF METALLURGISTS
Northway House, High Road, Whetstone, London N20 9LW Tel. 01-446 2251
Professional Association; includes the Institute of Metallurgical Technicians and the Metals and Metallurgy Trust

Enquiries to the Assistant Registrar or Education Officer

Subject coverage
metallurgy (jobs, education, careers)

Publications
Course manuals
Monographs and books

1510 INSTITUTION OF MINING AND METALLURGY
44 Portland Place, London W1N 4BR Tel. 01-580 3802
Professional Institution, a constituent member of the Council of Engineering Institutions, *q.v.*, houses the Council of Commonwealth Mining and Metallurgical Institutions and the Mineral Industry Research Organisation

Enquiries to the Librarian and Information Officer

Subject coverage
economic geology; mining and processing of minerals other than coal; non-ferrous extractive metallurgy

Special collection
the history of mining and metallurgy

Publications
IMM Abstracts
Bulletin of the Institution of Mining and Metallurgy
Transactions: Section A, mining industry
Section B, applied earth science
Section C, mineral processing & extractive metallurgy

1511 INSTITUTION OF MINING ENGINEERS
Hobart House, Grosvenor Place, London SW1X 7AE Tel. 01-235 3691
Professional Body; associated with the North of England Institute of Mining and Mechanical Engineers, *q.v.*

Enquiries to the Secretary

Subject coverage
mining of stratified deposits

Publications
Mining Engineer
Proceedings of Symposia

1512 INSTITUTION OF MUNICIPAL ENGINEERS
25 Eccleston Square, London SW1V 1NX Tel. 01-834 5082
Professional Body, member of the Council of Engineering Institutions

Enquiries to the Secretary

Subject coverage
municipal engineering and local government

Publications
Chartered Municipal Engineer (monthly)
Monographs on protection of the environment

1513 INSTITUTION OF NUCLEAR ENGINEERS
1 Penerley Road, London SE6 Tel. 01-698 1500
Qualifying Body/Professional Institution

Enquiries to the Secretary

Subject coverage
any and all peaceful aspects of nuclear technology; members are attached to other disciplines and therefore it is in electronic/nuclear, mechanical/nuclear, nuclear physics, nuclear mathematics, that the greatest part of the expertise of this Institution lies; its journal carries a section on hematology

Publication
Journal of the Institution of Nuclear Engineers, formerly Nuclear Energy (bi-monthly)

1514 INSTITUTION OF PLANT ENGINEERS
138 Buckingham Palace Road, London SW1W 9SG Tel. 01-730 0469
Professional Institution

Enquiries, from members only, to the Secretary

Subject coverage
plant engineering; maintenance; terotechnology

Publication
Plant Engineer (monthly)

1515 INSTITUTION OF PRODUCTION ENGINEERS
Rochester House, 66 Little Ealing Lane, London W5 4XX Tel. 01-579 9411
Professional Institution; member of the Council of Engineering Institutions, *q.v.*, houses the British Numerical Control Society, *q.v.* and the United Kingdom Hovercraft Society

Enquiries to the Librarian, Hazleton Memorial Library, c/o PERA, Melton Mowbray, Leicester LE13 0PB

Subject coverage
production engineering

Publications
Production Engineer (monthly)

1516 INSTITUTION OF PROFESSIONAL SALESMEN
Concorde House, 24 Warwick New Road, Royal Leamington Spa, Warwickshire CV32 5JH Tel. 0926 37621

Professional Institution; member of Sales Augmentation Limited, of the same address

Enquiries to the Director-General or the Membership Executive

Subject coverage
salesmanship; sales management; sales training

Publication
Journal (monthly)

1517 INSTITUTION OF PUBLIC HEALTH ENGINEERS
32 Eccleston Square, London SW1V 1PB Tel. 01-834 3017
Professional Institution

Enquiries to the Secretary

Subject coverage
water supply and treatment; sewerage and the disposal of sewage and trade wastes; sanitation

Publications
Public Health Engineer (bi-monthly)
Year Book
Proceedings of Symposia
Public Health Engineering – career opportunities (free)

1518 INSTITUTION OF RAILWAY SIGNAL ENGINEERS
21 Avalon Road, Earley, Reading, Berkshire RG6 2NS
Tel. 0734 65904 (in business hours 01-262 3232 ext. 5734)

Company

Enquiries to the Honorary General Secretary

Subject coverage
railway signal engineering

Publications
Proceedings (annual)
Technical booklets (list available)

1519 INSTITUTION OF SALES ENGINEERS
Concorde House, 24 Warwick New Road, Royal Leamington Spa, Warwickshire CV32 5JH Tel. 0926 37621

Professional Institution; member of Sales Augmentation Ltd., of the same address; houses also the Institution of Buyers and the Institution of Professional Salesmen, *qq.v.*

Enquiries to the Director-General, the Membership Executive or the Courses Registrar

Subject coverage
sales engineering; sales management; training

Publication
Journal (monthly)

1520 INSTITUTION OF STRUCTURAL ENGINEERS
11 Upper Belgrave Street, London SW1X 8BH Tel. 01-235 4535
Professional Institution; member of the Council of Engineering Institutions; houses the International Association for Bridge and Structural Engineers London Office

Enquiries to the Librarian

Subject coverage
structural engineering

Publication
Structural Engineer (monthly)

INSTITUTION OF THE RUBBER INDUSTRY *see* **PLASTICS AND RUBBER INSTITUTE**

1521 INSTITUTION OF TRAINING OFFICERS
5 Baring Road, Beaconsfield, Buckinghamshire HP9 2NX Tel. 04946 3994
Professional Association, affiliated to the International Federation of Training and Development Organizations

Enquiries to the Information Officer

Subject coverage
training in industry and commerce

Publications
Training (10 issues per year)

1522 INSTITUTION OF WATER ENGINEERS AND SCIENTISTS
6–8 Sackville Street, London W1X 1DD Tel. 01-734 5422
Professional Institution, formerly Institution of Water Engineers

Enquiries to the Secretary

Subject coverage
all aspects of the water cycle

Publications
Journal of the Institution (8 issues per annum)
Manual of British Water Engineering Practice, 3 vols
Reports and Symposia Proceedings

1523 INSTITUTION OF WORKS MANAGERS
45 Cardiff Road, Luton, Bedfordshire LU1 1RQ Tel. 0582 37071
Professional Institution

Enquiries to the Management Services Department

Subject coverage
industrial management and management education

Publication
Works Management (monthly)

INSTITUTIONAL MANAGEMENT ASSOCIATION *now* **HOTEL CATERING AND INSTITUTIONAL MANAGEMENT ASSOCIATION,** *q.v.*

1524 INSULATION GLAZING ASSOCIATION
6 Mount Row, London W1Y 6DY Tel. 01-629 8334
Trade Association

Enquiries to the Information Officer

Subject coverage
glazing; double glazing; thermal insulation

Publication
Double Glazing Technical Standard

1525 INSURANCE TECHNICAL BUREAU
Albany House, Petty France, London SW1H 9EA — Tel. 01-222 3104
Company; small research organization, supported by ten major insurance Groups

Enquiries to the Information Officer

Subject coverage
industrial fire and explosion hazards

Publications
Reports of investigations into fire and explosion hazards in various industries

1526 INTERCOMPANY COMPARISONS LIMITED
81 City Road, London EC1Y 1BD — Tel. 01-253 0063
Telex 23678

Company

Enquiries to the Director

Subject coverage
industry and individual company financial information; analysis of such information including publication of over 200 annual surveys; presentation of business information by audio-visual methods

Publications
Annual ICC Business Ratio Reports (over 60 titles)
Annual ICC Financial Surveys (over 140 titles)
Industry Performance Analysis (annual)

1527 INTERGOVERNMENTAL MARITIME CONSULTATIVE ORGANIZATION
101–104 Piccadilly, London W1V 0AE — Tel. 01-499 9040
Agency of the United Nations

Enquiries to the Information Officer

Subject coverage
international regulations concerning safety of navigation; prevention and control of marine pollution caused by ships; international law concerning marine pollution and some aspects of merchant shipping

Publications
International Maritime Conventions
Codes of Maritime Practice
Technical Manuals
Catalogue

1528 INTERIOR DECORATORS AND DESIGNERS ASSOCIATION
24 Ormond Road, Richmond, Surrey TW10 6TH — Tel. 01-948 4151
Trade Association

Enquiries, only for names of decorators and designers to undertake work, to the Secretary, in writing

Subject coverage
decorating and design services

1529 INTERMEDIATE TECHNOLOGY DEVELOPMENT GROUP LIMITED
9 King Street, Covent Garden, London WC2E 8HN — Tel. 836 6379
Limited Company/Registered Charity

Enquiries (engineering only) to the Information Officer

Subject coverage
low-cost and small-scale manufacturing processes in a wide range of engineering disciplines, suitable for the under-developed countries

Publications
Appropriate Technology (quarterly)
Aid and Self-help
Disaster Technology: an annotated bibliography
Numerous publications in building, chemistry, health, energy, etc.

1530 INTERNATIONAL ASBESTOS INFORMATION CONFERENCE STANDING COMMITTEE
114 Park Street, London W1Y 4AB Tel. 01-499 6022
International Information Association

Enquiries to the Chairman

Subject coverage
health and safety in the manufacture and use of asbestos materials

INTERNATIONAL ASSOCIATION FOR BRIDGE AND STRUCTURAL ENGINEERS *see* **INSTITUTION OF STRUCTURAL ENGINEERS**

INTERNATIONAL ASSOCIATION FOR EARTHQUAKE ENGINEERING *see* **SOCIETY FOR EARTHQUAKE AND CIVIL ENGINEERING DYNAMICS**

INTERNATIONAL ASSOCIATION FOR RADIATION RESEARCH *see* **ASSOCIATION FOR RADIATION RESEARCH**

INTERNATIONAL ASSOCIATION OF AGRICULTURAL ECONOMISTS *see* **INSTITUTE OF AGRICULTURAL ECONOMICS**

1531 INTERNATIONAL ASSOCIATION OF BIOLOGICAL STANDARDIZATION
Sutton House, Iford, Lewes, East Sussex BN7 3EU Tel. 079-16 6477
Scientific Society; member of the International Association of Microbiological Societies; Records Office and Treasurer at Biostandards, Case Postale 109, CH-1211 Geneva 4, Switzerland

Enquiries to the Secretary-General

Subject coverage
development and use of standard preparations for biological products in medical and veterinary disciplines; production and control methods for these preparations: cooperation with international authorities such as WHO and FAO

Publication
Journal of Biological Standardization (Academic Press)

INTERNATIONAL ASSOCIATION OF HYDROLOGICAL SCIENCES *see* **INSTITUTE OF HYDROLOGY**

INTERNATIONAL ASTRONAUTICAL FEDERATION *see* **BRITISH INTERPLANETARY SOCIETY**

1532 INTERNATIONAL BEE RESEARCH ASSOCIATION
Hill House, Chalfont St. Peter, Gerrards Cross, Tel. 49 85011
Buckinghamshire SL9 0NR
Company limited by guarantee, formerly Bee Research Association

Enquiries, from members only, to Director

Subject coverage
bees, all species; apiculture; bee products (honey, beeswax, pollen, royal jelly, bee venom, propolis, etc); substances used by bees (nectar, pollen, honeydew); pollination (especially by bees)

Special collections
Morland Bequest of classical papers and books
Essinger Bequest of early beekeeping books
Picture Collection and Slide Collection
Collection of Historical and Contemporary Beekeeping material

Publications
Apicultural Abstracts (quarterly)
Journal of Apicultural Research (quarterly)
Bee World (quarterly)
Publications List

INTERNATIONAL BUSINESS COMMUNICATIONS LIMITED *now* **OYEZ INTERNATIONAL BUSINESS COMMUNICATIONS LIMITED** *q.v.*

1533 INTERNATIONAL CARGO HANDLING CO-ORDINATION ASSOCIATION
Abford House, 15 Wilton Road, London SW1V 1LX Tel. 01-828 3611
Telex 261106
International Association, having consultative status with the United Nations and observer status with the International Labour Organization and the International Standardization Organization

Enquiries, from members only, to the Technical Secretary

Subject coverage
cargo handling technology in all modes of transport

Publications
Cargo Systems International (monthly)
Useful Publications: a bibliography
Progress in Cargo Handling: proceedings of ICHCA Conferences
Reports and papers

1534 INTERNATIONAL COFFEE ORGANISATION
22 Berners Street, London W1P 4DD Tel. 01-580 8595
Intergovernmental Organization

Enquiries, research only, to the Director

Subject coverage
economic aspects of production, consumption and trade of coffee

1535 INTERNATIONAL COMMISSION ON RADIOLOGICAL PROTECTION
Clifton Avenue, Sutton, Surrey SM2 5PU Tel. 01-642 4680
Non-governmental International Commission; member of the International Congress of Radiology

Enquiries to the Scientific Secretary

Subject coverage
all aspects of radiation protection (ionizing radiations only)

Publications
Reports and Recommendations of the International Commission on Radiation Protection (approximately 2 new volumes per annum, published by Pergamon Press)

1536 INTERNATIONAL COMMISSION ON ZOOLOGICAL NOMENCLATURE
c/o British Museum (Natural History), Cromwell Road, London SW7 Tel. 01-589 6323 ext. 387
International Commission

Enquiries to the Secretary

Subject coverage
zoological nomenclature; maintenance and interpretation of the International Code of Zoological Nomenclature

Publications
International Code of Zoological Nomenclature
Bulletin of Zoological Nomenclature
Official lists and indexes of names and works in zoology

1537 INTERNATIONAL COMMODITIES CLEARING HOUSE LIMITED
Roman Wall House, 1/2 Crutched Friars, London EC3N 1AN Tel. 01-488 3200
Telex 887234

Company; Subsidiary of United Dominions Trust Limited, *q.v.*

Enquiries to the Managing Director

Subject coverage
commodity futures markets

INTERNATIONAL CONFEDERATION OF FREE TRADE UNIONS *see* **TRADES UNION CONGRESS**

INTERNATIONAL CONGRESS OF MARITIME MUSEUMS *see* **NATIONAL MARITIME MUSEUM**

INTERNATIONAL CONGRESS OF RADIOLOGY *see* **INTERNATIONAL COMMISSION ON RADIOLOGICAL PROTECTION**

INTERNATIONAL CONSULTANTS FOUNDATION *see* **CARGILL ATTWOOD AND THOMAS LIMITED**

1538 INTERNATIONAL COPPER RESEARCH ASSOCIATION INCORPORATED
Orchard House, Mutton Lane, Potters Bar, Hertfordshire EN6 3AP Tel. 77 50711
Telex 27711

Contract Research Management Organisation; shares premises with the Copper Development Association, *q.v.*

Enquiries to the Information Officer, Copper Development Association

Subject coverage
copper and copper mining industry

Publications
INCRA Research Reports
Project Status (report on INCRA research)
INCRA monographs
List of available INCRA literature

INTERNATIONAL COUNCIL OF GRAPHIC DESIGN ASSOCIATIONS *see* **SOCIETY OF INDUSTRIAL ARTISTS AND DESIGNERS LIMITED**

INTERNATIONAL COUNCIL OF SOCIETIES OF INDUSTRIAL DESIGN *see* **SOCIETY OF INDUSTRIAL ARTISTS AND DESIGNERS LIMITED**

INTERNATIONAL DAIRY FEDERATION *see* **UNITED KINGDOM DAIRY ASSOCIATION**

1539 INTERNATIONAL DEEP DRAWING RESEARCH GROUP
Queensway House, 2 Queensway, Redhill, Surrey RH1 1QS Tel. 91 68611
Telex 948669

International Cooperative Research Group

Enquiries to the Secretary General

Subject coverage
forming and testing of sheet metals and allied subjects

Publication
Biennial Proceedings

INTERNATIONAL ENVIRONMENTAL BUREAU *see* **BNF METALS TECHNOLOGY CENTRE**

INTERNATIONAL FEDERATION FOR MEDICAL AND BIOLOGICAL ENGINEERING *see* **BIOLOGICAL ENGINEERING SOCIETY**

INTERNATIONAL FEDERATION OF AIRWORTHINESS *see* **SOCIETY OF LICENSED AIRCRAFT ENGINEERS AND TECHNOLOGISTS**

INTERNATIONAL FEDERATION OF INTERIOR DESIGNERS *see* **SOCIETY OF INDUSTRIAL ARTISTS AND DESIGNERS LIMITED**

INTERNATIONAL FEDERATION OF INVENTORS ASSOCIATIONS *see* **INSTITUTE OF PATENTEES AND INVENTORS**

INTERNATIONAL FEDERATION OF OPERATIONAL RESEARCH SOCIETIES *see* **OPERATIONAL RESEARCH SOCIETY**

INTERNATIONAL FEDERATION OF THE PERIODICAL PRESS *see* **PERIODICAL PUBLISHERS ASSOCIATION LIMITED**

INTERNATIONAL FEDERATION OF TRAINING AND DEVELOPMENT ORGANISATIONS *see* **INSTITUTION OF TRAINING OFFICERS**

INTERNATIONAL FLAME RESEARCH FOUNDATION *see* **BRITISH FLAME RESEARCH COMMITTEE**

1540 INTERNATIONAL FLUIDICS SERVICES LIMITED
Carlton, Bedford MK43 7JS Tel. 0234 720479
Company

Enquiries to the Managing Director

Subject coverage
production engineering; automation; industrial robots; materials handling; warehousing; fluid controls

Publications
Industrial Robot Journal (quarterly, including abstracts)
Proceedings Conference on Industrial Robot Technology (CIRT, 3rd, 1976)
Proceedings International Conference on Automation in Warehousing (ICAW, 2nd, 1977)

1541 INTERNATIONAL FOOD INFORMATION SERVICE (IFIS)
Lane End House, Shinfield, Reading RG2 9BB Tel. 0734 883895
Telex 847204
International Cooperative Organization; sponsored by the Commonwealth Agricultural Bureaux, Institut für Dokumentationswesen (Frankfurt), PUDOC (Wageningen) and Institute of Food Technology (Chicago)

Enquiries to the Editor or Director

Subject coverage
food science and technology; food engineering and processing; food additives and packaging; food microbiology, toxicology, hygiene; food legislation and standards; food economics

Publications
Food Science and Technology Abstracts
Annotated Bibliographies

1542 INTERNATIONAL FUR TRADE FEDERATION
69 Cannon Street, London EC4N 5AB Tel. 01-248 4444
Trade Association; includes the British Fur Trade Association

Enquiries are accepted only from members; non-members should enquire of the British Fur Trade Association

Subject coverage
fur trade

INTERNATIONAL GAS UNION *see* **INSTITUTION OF GAS ENGINEERS**

1543 INTERNATIONAL GLACIOLOGICAL SOCIETY
Lensfield Road, Cambridge CB2 1ER Tel. 0223 55974
Scientific Society; formerly Glaciological Society; associated with the Scott Polar Institute, *q.v.*

Enquiries to the Secretary General

Subject coverage
glaciology: snow and ice studies in the fields of geomorphology, geology, oceanography, engineering, avalanches, glaciers and ice sheets

Publications
Journal of Glaciology
Ice, News Bulletin of the Society

1544 INTERNATIONAL INSTITUTE FOR COTTON
17–19 Maddox Street, London W1R 9LE — Tel. 01-493 7841, Telex 21316

Intergovernmental Agency (Headquarters in Brussels); supports a Technical Research Division at Kingsbury Road, Didsbury, Manchester

Enquiries to the Information Officer, London or Manchester

Subject coverage
raw cotton production and consumption; cotton processing; cotton end use markets; cotton promotion

Publications
Market and technical research papers

1545 INTERNATIONAL INSTITUTE OF WELDING
54 Princes Gate, Exhibition Road, London SW7 2PG — Tel. 01-584 8556/9
International non-governmental organization

Enquiries to the Secretary General; enquiries from within member countries are normally directed to their national delegations

Subject coverage
welding and allied processes; testing and inspection of welds; health and safety precautions; welding education

Publications
Welding in the World (bi-monthly)
Multilingual Collection of Terms in 18 Languages
Collections of Radiographs of Welds
Specialised books

INTERNATIONAL MASTER PRINTERS ASSOCIATION *see* **BRITISH PRINTING INDUSTRIES FEDERATION**

1546 INTERNATIONAL MEEHANITE METAL COMPANY LIMITED
38 Albert Road North, Reigate, Surrey RH2 9EH — Tel. 74 44786, Telex 28700

Company (consultants and licensors)

Enquiries to the Technical Information Officer

Subject coverage
castings; metallurgy, non-destructive testing; foundries; meehanite

INTERNATIONAL MYCOLOGICAL ASSOCIATION *see* **BRITISH LICHEN SOCIETY**

1547 INTERNATIONAL NICKEL LIMITED
European Research and Development Centre, Research and Technical Development Laboratory, Wiggin Street, Birmingham B16 0AJ — Tel. 021-454 4871, Telex 336626
Company

Enquiries, by letter only, to the Head of Technical Information Services

Subject coverage
metallurgy of nickel and of ferrous and non-ferrous metals containing nickel; precious metals; general metallurgy; applications of nickel and nickel-containing materials

Publications
Nickel Topics
Basic data and applicational publications

1548 INTERNATIONAL PAINT COMPANY LIMITED

International Marine Coatings, Stoneygate Lane, Felling, Gateshead, Tyne and Wear NE10 0JY — Tel. 0632 696111, Telex 537264

Company Divisional Factory and Research Laboratories; Head Office, 9 Henrietta Place, London W1A 1AD; subsidiary of Courtaulds

Enquiries, paint schemes, Marketing Department; prevention of corrosion and/or marine fouling, etc., to the Research & Development Laboratory

Subject coverage
paint, for whatever use needed; corrosion, its prevention; marine fouling, identification and prevention; yacht paint specialization

Special collection
Collection of fouling specimens (at the Marine Biological Laboratory, Newton Ferrers, South Devon)

Publications
Brochures on paint
Catalogues

1549 INTERNATIONAL PETROLEUM INDUSTRIES ENVIRONMENTAL CONSERVATION ASSOCIATION

110 Euston Road, London NW1 — Tel. 01-387 8251
(about to move to Bucklersbury House, Cannon Street, London EC4)
Industry Association of twenty-eight companies

Enquiries to the Executive Secretary

Subject coverage
environmental matters having an impact on oil industry operations

INTERNATIONAL POWDER ADVISORY CENTRE *see* **INPACT**

1550 INTERNATIONAL RESEARCH AND DEVELOPMENT COMPANY LIMITED

Fossway, Newcastle-upon-Tyne NE6 2YD — Tel. 0632 650451, Telex 537086

Private Contract Research Organization, owned equally by Reyrolle Parsons Limited and Vickers Limited

Enquiries to the Librarian

Subject coverage
electrical and mechanical engineering; materials science; biotechnology; applied physics

Publication
Newsletter (quarterly)

INTERNATIONAL ROAD FEDERATION *see* **BRITISH ROAD FEDERATION**

INTERNATIONAL SILK ASSOCIATION *see* **SILK ASSOCIATION LIMITED**

INTERNATIONAL SOCIETY FOR ROCK MECHANICS *see* **BRITISH GEOTECHNICAL SOCIETY**

1551 INTERNATIONAL SOCIETY FOR SOIL MECHANICS AND FOUNDATION ENGINEERING

c/o King's College, Strand, London WC2R 2LS — Tel. 01-836 5454 ext. 2643
International Conference Body

Enquiries are not accepted

Subject coverage
soil mechanics; foundation engineering; geotechnology

Publications
Conference Proceedings
Geotechnical Abstracts (monthly)

INTERNATIONAL STATISTICAL INSTITUTE *see* **INSTITUTE OF STATISTICIANS**

1552 INTERNATIONAL STEEL TRADE ASSOCIATION
London Chamber of Commerce and Industry, 69 Cannon Street, London EC4N 5AB — Tel. 01-248 4444, Telex 888941

Trade Association; formerly Iron and Steel International Trade Section of the London Chamber of Commerce and Industry

Enquiries to the Secretary

Subject coverage
international iron and steel trade

1553 INTERNATIONAL SUGAR ORGANIZATION
Haymarket House, 28 Haymarket, London SW1Y 4SP — Tel. 01-930 3666

Inter-governmental Organization; formerly the International Sugar Council

Enquiries to the Executive Director

Subject coverage
statistics on production, consumption, exports and imports of sugar in all countries of the world

Publications
Statistical Bulletin (monthly)
Sugar Year Book (annual)
Press Summary
World Sugar Economy, Structure and Policies (new edition in preparation)

1554 INTERNATIONAL SYSTEMS RESEARCH LIMITED
Stratton House, Piccadilly, London W1X 6DD — Tel. 01-629 8886, Telex 261223

Company; subsidiary of British Electric Traction Company Limited

Enquiries are not accepted from the public

Subject coverage
public transport services; planning physical distribution systems; management of industrial R & D

INTERNATIONAL TIN RESEARCH COUNCIL *see* **TIN RESEARCH INSTITUTE**

INTERNATIONAL UNION OF AIR POLLUTION PREVENTION ASSOCIATIONS *see* **NATIONAL SOCIETY FOR CLEAN AIR**

INTERNATIONAL UNION OF PURE AND APPLIED CHEMISTRY *see* **IUPAC**

INTERNATIONAL UNION OF SPELEOLOGY *see* **BRITISH CAVE RESEARCH ASSOCIATION**

INTERNATIONAL UNION OF VACUUM SCIENCE AND TECHNOLOGY *see* **INSTITUTE OF PHYSICS**

1555 INTERNATIONAL WATER SUPPLY ASSOCIATION
1 Queen Annes Gate, London SW1H 9BT — Tel. 01-930 3100, Telex 918518

International Service Association

Enquiries to the Secretary General

Subject coverage
water supply

Publications
Proceedings of the International Water Supply Congress (every 2 or 3 years)
Papers on corrosion, etc.
Aqua (quarterly, free to members, or, by subscription, to others)

1556 INTERNATIONAL WHEAT COUNCIL
28 Haymarket, London SW1Y 4SS Tel. 01-930 4128
Telex 916128

International Commodity Organization, administering the Wheat Trade Convention; providing administrative services for the Food Aid Committee which administers the Food Aid Convention, both of the International Wheat Agreement 1971

Enquiries to the Executive Secretary

Subject coverage
world wheat market; statistics on production, stocks, trade, and prices

Publications
World Wheat Statistics (annual)
Review of World Wheat Situation (annual)
Market Report (monthly)
Annual Report
Secretarial papers (occasional)

1557 INTERNATIONAL WOOL SECRETARIAT
Wool House, 6 Carlton Gardens, London SW1Y 5AE Tel. 01-930 7300
Telex 263926

Promotion and Research Organization; having a Technical Centre in Ilkley, Yorkshire, *q.v.*

Enquiries to the Librarian

Subject coverage
economics and statistics of wool and wool textiles; market research

Publications
Wool Science Review (about 3 per annum)
Occasional papers

1558 INTERNATIONAL WOOL SECRETARIAT
Technical Centre, Valley Drive, Ilkley, West Yorkshire LS29 8PB Tel. 094-33 5555
Telex 51457

Research Centre of the Organization

Enquiries to the Librarian

Subject coverage
wool technology; textiles; textile chemistry, processing, design

1559 INTERNATIONAL WOOL TEXTILE ORGANISATION, BRITISH NATIONAL COMMITTEE
Lloyds Bank Chambers, Hustlergate, Bradford, West Yorkshire BD1 1PF Tel. 0274 22612

Trade Association

Enquiries to the Secretary

Subject coverage
international trade practice and technical specifications relating to the raw materials, intermediate products and end products of the wool textile industry

1560 INTERNATIONAL WROUGHT COPPER COUNCIL
6 Bathurst Street, London W2 2SD Tel. 01-723 7465
Telex 23556

Representative Council of a manufacturing industry

Enquiries to the Secretariat

Subject coverage
non-ferrous metals in relation to the environment (noise, air pollution, effluents) and to safety and health

Publications
The Environmental Series of manuals

1561 INTERPLANETARY SPACE TRAVEL RESEARCH ASSOCIATION (UNITED KINGDOM)
15 Nealden Street, London SW9 9QX Tel. 01-720 7394
Charitable Association; affiliated to the Interplanetary Space Travel and Research Groups (International)

Enquiries to the Information Officers for Space, or Astronomy, or Ufology, or Science Fiction; in writing with a s.a.e.

Subject coverage
space news worldwide; astronomy; ufology

Publications
Interplanetary News (monthly)
ISTRA Journal (quarterly)
Newsletter (monthly)
Challenge from Space
Project reports

1562 INTERVENTION BOARD FOR AGRICULTURAL PRODUCE
Steel House, Tothill Street, London SW1H 9LU Tel. 01-273 3696
Government Department

Enquiries to the Press Officer

Subject coverage
implementation in the United Kingdom of the support arrangements of the E.E.C. Common Agricultural Policy, and aspects relating to the guarantee sector of the European Agricultural Guidance and Guarantee Fund

Publication
Annual Report (Command Paper)

1563 INVERCLYDE DISTRICT LIBRARIES
Central Library, Clyde Square, Greenock, Renfrewshire PA15 1NA Tel. 0475 26211/2
Public Library, formerly Greenock Public Libraries

Enquiries to the Chief Librarian

Subject coverage
general

1564 INVERESK RESEARCH INTERNATIONAL
Inveresk Gate, Musselburgh, Midlothian, Scotland EH21 7UB Tel. 031-665 6881
Contract Research Organization; formerly Arthur D.Little Research Institute

Enquiries to the Information Officer

Subject coverage
biochemistry; chemistry; consumer products; toxicology (general, developmental, inhalation); metabolic studies; pathology; pharmacology

INVERNESS COUNTY LIBRARY *now* **HIGHLAND REGION LIBRARY SERVICE,** *q.v.*

INVERNESS DIVISIONAL LIBRARY *see* **HIGHLAND REGION LIBRARY SERVICE**

INVERURIE BURGH LIBRARY *see* **NORTH EAST OF SCOTLAND LIBRARY SERVICE**

1565 IPC MAGAZINES LIMITED
Marketing Information Services Unit, Kings Reach Tower, Stamford Street, London SE1 9LS Tel. 01-261 5000
Publishing Company

Enquiries to the Marketing Information Manager

Subject coverage
advertising; marketing; market research; consumer magazine publishing

IPEC (POLYMERS) LIMITED *now* **YARSLEY POLYMER ENGINEERING CENTRE,** *q.v.*

1566 IPSWICH CHAMBER OF COMMERCE AND SHIPPING INCORPORATED
17/19 Museum Street, Ipswich, Suffolk IP1 1HF Tel. 0743 59201
Telex 987703

Trade Association

Enquiries to the Assistant

Subject coverage
trade; commerce; shipping

Publications
News Letter
List of Members

1567 IPSWICH CIVIC COLLEGE
Rope Walk, Ipswich, Suffolk IP4 1LT Tel. 0473 55885
College of Further and Higher Education

Enquiries to the Tutor Librarian

Subject coverage
engineering; construction; nursing; management; domestic studies

IPSWICH DISTRICT LIBRARY *see* **SUFFOLK COUNTY LIBRARY**

1568 IPSWICH PORT AUTHORITY
Old Custom House, Key Street, Ipswich IP4 1BY Tel. 0473 56011
Telex 98642

Port Authority; formerly Ipswich Dock Commission

Enquiries to the Chief Executive

Subject coverage
port facilities, particularly of Ipswich

1569 IRANIAN EMBASSY (IMPERIAL IRANIAN EMBASSY)
16 Princes Gate, London SW7 1PX Tel. 01-584 8101
Government Department

Enquiries to the Press Section

Subject coverage
Iranian affairs

1570 IRISH ASSOCIATION OF DOCUMENTATION AND INFORMATION SERVICES
c/o National Library of Ireland, Kildare Street, Dublin 2 Tel. (01) 765521
Forum for special libraries and information centres

Enquiries to the Honorary Secretary

Subject coverage
information sources in Ireland

Publication
Union List of current periodicals and serials in Irish libraries

1571 IRISH CENTRAL LIBRARY FOR STUDENTS
53–54 Upper Mount Street, Dublin 2 Tel. 0382 761167
0382 761963
Telex 5733

National Headquarters of Library Co-operation

Enquiries to the Librarian or Director

Subject coverage
material of Irish interest; bibliographical enquiry service

1572 IRISH LINEN GUILD
Morley House, 314 Regent Street, London W1R 6PB — Tel. 01-636 1794
Trade Association

Enquiries to the Public Relations Officer

Subject coverage
manufacture and marketing of Irish linen

IRON AND STEEL CONSUMERS COUNCIL *now* **BRITISH IRON AND STEEL CONSUMERS COUNCIL,** *q.v.*

1573 IRON AND STEEL INDUSTRY TRAINING BOARD
4 Little Essex Street, London WC2R 3LH — Tel. 01-240 2044
Industrial Training Board, of the Training Services Agency, *q.v.*

Enquiries to the Information Officer

Subject coverage
training within the iron and steel industry

Publications
Recommendations and related guidance material
Information Bulletins

IRON AND STEEL INSTITUTE *now* **METALS SOCIETY,** *q.v.*

1574 IRONFOUNDERS NATIONAL ASSOCIATION
4 Southampton Place, London WC1A 2DA — Tel. 01-242 9737
Telex 25293

Trade Association, part of the Council of Ironfoundry Associations, *q.v.*

Enquiries to the Secretaries

Subject coverage
ironfounders of the U.K.

1575 IRONMAKING AND STEELMAKING PLANT CONTRACTORS ASSOCIATION
7 Ludgate Broadway, London EC4V 6DX — Tel. 01-248 1543
Trade Association; member of the Metallurgical Plantmakers Federation, *q.v.*

Enquiries to the Secretary

Subject coverage
structure and nature of turn-key contracts; all areas of ironmaking and steelmaking contracts for plant including iron ore handling and preparation plant, coke ovens, blast furnaces, continuous casting machines, tonnage oxygen plant, power plant, etc.

1576 ISLE OF MAN CHAMBER OF TRADE, COMMERCE AND INDUSTRY
8 Prospect Hill, Douglas, Isle of Man — Tel. 0624 4941
Chamber of Trade, etc.

Enquiries to the Secretary

Subject coverage
trade, commerce and industry within the Isle of Man, and general information on the Island including communications, taxation, constitution etc.

Publication
Annual Classified Directory of Members

ISLE OF MAN PUBLIC LIBRARY *see* **DOUGLAS PUBLIC LIBRARY**

1577 ISLE OF WIGHT COLLEGE OF ARTS AND TECHNOLOGY LIBRARY
Hunnyhill, Newport, Isle of Wight PO30 5TA Tel. 098-381 6631
Education Authority Department of the Isle of Wight County Council; formerly Isle of Wight Technical College

Enquiries to the Tutor Librarian

Subject coverage
engineering; construction; agriculture; business studies; food; fashion

1578 ISLE OF WIGHT COUNTY LIBRARY
Parkhurst Road, Newport, Isle of Wight Tel. 098-381 2324
098-381 4541

Public Library, formerly County Seely Library

Enquiries to the Director of Cultural Services

Subject coverage
television; manufacturing; architecture; photography

Special collection
Museum of Isle of Wight geology

ISLEWORTH POLYTECHNIC *now* **HOUNSLOW BOROUGH COLLEGE,** *q.v.*

1579 ISLINGTON LIBRARIES
2 Fieldway Crescent, London N5 1PF Tel. 01-607 4038 ext. 3
Telex 263674

Public Libraries

Enquiries to the Chief Librarian and Curator

Subject coverage
pure electricity; electronics; magnetism; physics; photography

Publication
Information News Sheet (quarterly)

ISLWYN REGIONAL LIBRARY *see* **GWENT COUNTY LIBRARY**

ISOTOPE GEOLOGY UNIT *see* **SCOTTISH UNIVERSITIES RESEARCH AND REACTOR CENTRE**

1580 ITT CREED LIMITED
5 Crowhurst Road, Hollingbury, Brighton, Sussex BN1 8AL Tel. 0273 507111
Telex 87169

Company; associated with ITT Business Systems Group, of the same address

Enquiries to the Technical Information Officer

Subject coverage
teleprinters; telecommunications; data processing; automation; data terminals

Publications
Abstracts Journal
Research Projects List

1581 IUPAC THERMODYNAMICS TABLES PROJECT CENTRE
Imperial College of Science and Technology, Chemistry Department, Tel. 01-589 5111 ext. 1905
Prince Consort Road, South Kensington, London SW7 2BY Telex 261503
Numerical Data Centre, of the International Union of Pure and Applied Chemistry (IUPAC)

Enquiries to the Director

Subject coverage
thermodynamic properties of pure fluids and the critical assessment and correlation of experimental data on them

Publications
International Thermodynamic Tables of the Fluid State (a single fluid to each volume. Pergamon Press)
Argon, Ethylene, *published*
Carbon Dioxide, Helium 4, *in the press*
Nitrogen, Methane, Oxygen, etc., *in preparation*

1582 IVORY COAST EMBASSY
1 Upper Belgrave Street, London SW1X 8BJ Tel. 01-235 6991
Telex 23906

Diplomatic Mission

Enquiries to the Information Officer

Subject coverage
economic, commercial, scientific information concerning the Ivory Coast

Publication
News of the Ivory Coast (monthly)

1583 J.B. MORRELL LIBRARY
York University, Heslington, York YO1 5DD Tel. 0904 59861
Telex 57933

University Library

Enquiries to the Librarian

Subject coverage
biochemistry; biology; chemistry; computer science; mathematics; physics

Publication
Periodicals Catalogue

1584 JAPAN TRADE CENTRE
19–25 Baker Street, London W1M 1AE Tel. 01-486 6761
Telex 262520

Semi-governmental Trade Organization

Enquiries to the Centre

Subject coverage
trade; trade statistics; trade fairs and exhibitions; joint venture and overseas investment

Publications
JETRO Journal
Focus Japan
JETRO Marketing Series
JETRO Business Information Series
Japan's Industrial and Technical Information

JEALOTTS HILL RESEARCH STATION *see* **ICI LIMITED, Plant Protection Division**

1585 JERSEY STATES LIBRARY SERVICE
Royal Square, St. Helier, Jersey, Channel Islands Tel. 0534 33201
Government Department, formerly Jersey Public Library (or Libraries)

Enquiries to the Chief Librarian

Subject coverage
general; marine and local history

James A. JOBLING LIMITED *now* **CORNING LIMITED,** *q.v.*

JOHN DALTON LIBRARY *see* **MANCHESTER POLYTECHNIC**

1586 JOHN INNES INSTITUTE
Colney Lane, Norwich NR4 7UH Tel. 0603 52571
Grant-aided Research Institute, of the Agricultural Research Council

Enquiries to the Director

Subject coverage
plant breeding; genetics of bacteria and higher plants; biochemistry and biophysics of viruses; electron microscopy; ultrastructure of organisms

Publications
Annual Report
Proceedings of John Innes Symposia

1587 JOHN LEWIS PARTNERSHIP
4 Old Cavendish Street, London W1A 1EX Tel. 01-637 3434
Co-operative Society of Producers within the framework of a group of companies

Enquiries to the Librarian

Subject coverage
retailing; industrial democracy

Publication
Gazette of the John Lewis Partnership

1588 JOHN RYLANDS UNIVERSITY LIBRARY OF MANCHESTER
Oxford Road, Manchester M13 9PP Tel. 061-273 3333
Telex 668932
University Library

Enquiries, by letter only, to the Director

Subject coverage
biochemistry; botany; chemistry; computer science; electrical engineering; geology; mathematics; metallurgy; pharmacy; physics; zoology

Special collections
History of Science
Partington History of Chemistry

1589 JOHNSON MATTHEY RESEARCH CENTRE
Blount's Court, Sonning Common, Reading RG4 9NH Tel. 073-525 2811
Company Research Centre; formerly Johnson Matthey and Company Limited Research Laboratories

Enquiries to the Librarian

Subject coverage
platinum group metals; gold; silver

Publication
Platinum Metals Review (quarterly)

1590 JOINT CONTRACTS TRIBUNAL FOR THE STANDARD FORM OF BUILDING CONTRACT
66 Portland Place, London W1N 4AD Tel. 01-580 5533
Advisory Body, formed of representatives of eleven organisations concerned with surveying, architecture, building, building contracts, Metropolitan and District Councils

Enquiries to the Joint Secretaries
Subject coverage
production of the standard form of building contract, popularly but inaccurately known as the RIBA form of contract

JOINT FIRE RESEARCH ORGANIZATION *now* **FIRE RESEARCH STATION,** *q.v.*

JOINT INDUSTRIAL COUNCIL FOR THE BISCUIT INDUSTRY *see* **CAKE AND BISCUIT ALLIANCE LIMITED**

1591 JOINT LIBRARY OF GLASS TECHNOLOGY
Elmfield, Northumberland Road, Sheffield N10 2TZ Tel. 0742 78555 ext. 131
Library; jointly of a Sheffield University Department and the Society of Glass Technology, *q.v.*

Enquiries to the Librarian

Subject coverage
ceramics; glasses; polymers

1592 JORDAN & SONS LIMITED
Jordan House, 47 Brunswick Place, London N1 6EE Tel. 01-253 3030
Telex 261010

Company, associated with Jordan Dataquest Limited, *q.v.*, both subsidiaries of Jordan Group Limited

Enquiries to the Information Division

Subject coverage
company information, formation of new companies, commercial credit status

Publications
Pamphlets on the information services

1593 JORDAN DATAQUEST LIMITED
Jordan House, 47 Brunswick Place, London N1 6EE Tel. 01-253 3030
Telex 261010

Company, formerly Finance Analysis Group Limited, associated with Jordan & Sons Limited, *q.v.*, both subsidiaries of Jordan Group Limited

Enquiries to the Managing Director

Subject coverage
analysis of company information; industrial surveys; financial studies

Publications
Financial studies of major British and foreign-owned companies
Surveys by industrial sector

JUNIOR INSTITUTION OF ENGINEERS *now* **INSTITUTION OF GENERAL TECHNICIAN ENGINEERS,** *q.v.*

1594 JUTE IMPORTERS ASSOCIATION LIMITED
71 Meadowside, Dundee DD1 1EE Tel. 0382 21683
Trade Association

Enquiries to the Secretary

Subject coverage
the importation of raw jute

KADIS *now* **KIS,** *q.v.*

KANTHACK LIBRARY *see* **CAMBRIDGE UNIVERSITY, Department of Pathology**

KEIGHLEY DISTRICT LIBRARY *see* **BRADFORD LIBRARIES**

1595 KEIGHLEY TECHNICAL COLLEGE
Cavendish Street, Keighley, West Yorkshire BD21 3DF Tel. 053-52 4248
College of Further Education

Enquiries to the Librarian

Subject coverage
engineering; construction

1596 KEMPS GROUP (PRINTERS & PUBLISHERS) LIMITED
1–5 Bath Street, London EC1V 9QA Tel. 01-253 5314
Private Limited Company, wholly-owned subsidiary of Number Nine Investments Limited

Enquiries to the Manager

Subject coverage
free general information on trade names, trade marks, identities of manufacturers and merchants, sources of supplies in specialist industries, etc.

Special collections
List of clothing exporters
List of technicians and suppliers to the film and television industry and the music and recording industry

Publications
Kemps Director (2 vols)
London Directory
Clothing Export Council of G.B. Directory for the Clothing Industry
Many other Directories, Buyers Guides etc. (list available)

1597 KENSINGTON AND CHELSEA CENTRAL LIBRARIES AND ARTS SERVICE
Phillimore Walk, London W8 7RX Tel. 01-937 2542
Public Library Service; Branch Library in Chelsea, Manresa Road, London SW3 7LU

Enquiries to the Borough Librarian

Subject coverage
general

1598 KENT COUNTY LIBRARY
Springfield, Maidstone, Kent ME14 2LH Tel. 0622 54371
Telex 965212
Public Library Service; Divisional Libraries at Ashford, Canterbury, Dartford, Dover, Gillingham, Gravesham, Maidstone, Medway, Sevenoaks, Shepway, Swale, Thanet, Tonbridge, Tunbridge Wells

Enquiries to the County Reference Librarian or County Technical Librarian

Subject coverage
general; railways; printing; diseases

Publication
Kent Union List of Periodicals

1599 KENT UNIVERSITY LIBRARY
Canterbury, Kent CT2 7NU Tel. 0227 66822
Telex 965449
University Library

Enquiries, by post, to the Librarian; telephone enquiries to the Science Information Officer

Subject coverage
biochemistry; microbiology; chemistry; physics; electronics; mathematics; economics; finance and accounting; statistics

Special collection
European Documentation Centre

1600 KENYAN HIGH COMMISSION
45 Portland Place, London W1 4AS Tel. 01-636 2371
Telex 262551

High Commission

Enquiries to the Information Officer

Subject coverage
commercial, agricultural education, tourist and immigration sections provide information on Kenya

KETTERING DISTRICT LIBRARY *see* **NORTHAMPTONSHIRE LIBRARIES**

KIDDERMINSTER DIVISIONAL LIBRARY *see* **HEREFORD AND WORCESTER COUNTY LIBRARY**

1601 KILBURN POLYTECHNIC
Library, Priory Park Road, London NW6 1YB Tel. 01-624 0022
College of Further Education; Department of Engineering and Science and Department of Fashion, Food, and Community Studies are at 373 Edgware Road, Colindale, London NW9 6NH

Enquiries to the Librarian

Subject coverage
engineering and science; fashion, food and community studies

KILLINGWORTH AREA LIBRARY *see* **NORTH TYNESIDE METROPOLITAN DISTRICT LIBRARIES**

1602 KILMARNOCK AND LOUDOUN PUBLIC LIBRARY
Dick Institute, Elmbank Avenue, Kilmarnock, Ayrshire KA1 3BU Tel. 0563 26401
Public Library

Enquiries to the Librarian

Subject coverage
geology; natural history; early printing; arms and armour; archaeology

KINCARDINE BURGH LIBRARY *see* **NORTH EAST OF SCOTLAND LIBRARY SERVICE**

1603 KINGS COLLEGE
London University, Stand, London WC2R 2LS Tel. 01-836 5454
College of the University of London

Enquiries, by letter only, to the Librarian

Subject coverage
natural sciences; medical science, preclinical; civil, electrical, electronic and mechanical engineering

Special collections
Early scientific works (particularly 19th century)
Wheatstone Library (Sir Charles Wheatstone's own library, the background to his researches on the electric telegraph)
Ruggles Gates Collection (Library and manuscript notes of Professor R. Ruggles Gates on genetics and ethnology)
Coulson Collection (on science and religion)

1604 KINGS LYNN DIVISIONAL LIBRARY
London Road, Kings Lynn, Norfolk PE30 5EZ Tel. 0553 2568
Public Library, Division of Norfolk County Library

Enquiries to the Divisional Librarian

Subject coverage
general

1605 KINGSTON POLYTECHNIC
Penrhyn Road, Kingston upon Thames, Surrey KT1 2EE Tel. 01-549 1366
Telex 928530
Institute of Higher Education, formed from the Kingston Regional College of Technology and Kingston College of Art; comprises four sites: Canbury Park Centre, Knights Park Centre, New Malden Centre (Kingston Regional Management Centre) and Gipsy Hill Centre

Enquiries to the Librarian

Subject coverage
physics; chemistry; geography, geology, computer science; electrical engineering; business studies; mathematics; graphic design; interior design, estate management; quantity surveying; management

Special collection
British Standards

Publications
Research Report (annual)
Kingston Geological Review (two per annum)

1606 KINGSTON-UPON-THAMES CENTRAL LIBRARY
Fairfield Road, Kingston-upon-Thames, Surrey KT1 2PS Tel. 01-549 0226
01-546 8905
Telex 928544

Public Library; district libraries at New Malden and Surbiton

Enquiries to the Librarian

Subject coverage
natural history

KINGSWINFORD DISTRICT LIBRARY *see* **DUDLEY PUBLIC LIBRARIES**

KINGSWOOD/NORTHAVON DISTRICT LIBRARY (Yate) *see* **AVON COUNTY LIBRARY**

KINROSS COUNTY LIBRARY *see* **PERTH AND KINROSS DISTRICT LIBRARIES**

KIRKBY LIBRARY *see* **KNOWSLEY BOROUGH LIBRARIES**

1607 KIRKCALDY AND NORTH EAST FIFE DISTRICT LIBRARIES
Headquarters, East Fergus Place, Kirkcaldy, Fife KY1 1XT Tel. 0592 68386
Public Library service; formerly Kirkcaldy Public Library and Fife County Library; Group Libraries at Kirkcaldy, St. Andrews, Glenrothes, and Methil

Enquiries to the District Librarian

Subject coverage
general

1608 KIRKCALDY TECHNICAL COLLEGE
St Brycedale Avenue, Kirkcaldy, Fife KY1 1EX Tel. 0592 61686
Technical College

Enquiries to the Librarian

Subject coverage
mechanical and production engineering; management; mining engineering

1609 KIRKLEES INFORMATION SERVICE (KIS)
Kirklees Libraries and Museums Service, Princess Alexandra Walk, Huddersfield HD1 2SU Tel. 0484 21356
Telex 517463
Interlibrary Co-operative Service

Enquiries to the Liaison Officer

Subject coverage
commercial, scientific, technical and management information

Publication
KIS Bulletin (occasional)

1610 KIRKLEES LIBRARIES & MUSEUMS SERVICE
Princess Alexandra Walk, Huddersfield, Yorkshire HD1 2SU Tel. 0484 21356
Telex 517463
Public Library service, formerly Kirklees Public Library; now comprises Batley, Dewsbury, Huddersfield, and Spenborough Public Libraries

Enquiries to the Chief Librarian

Subject coverage
general; textiles; textile engineering; chemical and mechanical engineering

KIS *see* **KIRKLEES INFORMATION SERVICE**

1611 KITSON COLLEGE OF TECHNOLOGY
The R.L. Wilkinson Library, Cookridge Street, Leeds LS2 8BL Tel. 0532 30381
College of Further Education, formerly Kitson College of Engineering and Science

Enquiries to the Tutor Librarian

Subject coverage
pure and applied sciences

1612 KNITTED TEXTILE DYERS FEDERATION
Charnwood Chambers, Market Place, Loughborough, Leicestershire LE11 3EF Tel. 05093 63079
Trade Association

Enquiries to the Secretary

Subject coverage
dyeing and finishing of hosiery and knitwear; terms and conditions of employment

KNITTING CRAFT GROUP *see* **BRANDED HAND KNITTING ASSOCIATION LIMITED**

1613 KNITTING INDUSTRIES FEDERATION LIMITED
7 Gregory Boulevard, Nottingham NG7 6NB Tel. 0602 61081
Trade/Employers Association, with North Midlands and North of England Regional Councils; houses the British Jersey Fabric Board

Enquiries to the Secretary

Subject coverage
knitting industry statistics, legislation, industrial relations, U.K. and E.E.C.

Publication
Annual Report

1614 KNITTING, LACE & NET INDUSTRY TRAINING BOARD
4 Hamilton Road, Sherwood Rise, Nottingham NG1 5AU Tel. 0602 61075
Training Board, of the Training Services Agency

Enquiries to the Information Officer

Subject coverage
training within the knitting industries

Publications
List available

1615 KNOWSLEY METROPOLITAN BOROUGH LIBRARIES
Reference and Information Services, Kirkby Branch Library, Newtown Gardens, Kirkby, Liverpool L32 8RR Tel. 051-547 3414
Public Library Service

Enquiries to the Principal Librarian, Reference and Information Services

Subject coverage
general subjects; local affairs

1616 KODAK LIMITED
Chemical Division Research Laboratories, Acornfield Road, Kirkby Industrial Estate, Kirkby, Liverpool, Lancashire L33 7UF Tel. 051-546 2101 Telex 62640
Company, subsidiary of Eastman Kodak Company

Enquiries to the Information Officer

Subject coverage
fine chemicals; dyes; polymers

1617 KODAK LIMITED
Kodak House, P.O. Box 66, Station Road, Hemel Hempstead, Hertfordshire HP1 1JU — Tel. 0442 61122
Company

Enquiries to the Public Relations Department

Subject coverage
company photographic products and services

Publications
catalogues
instructional and promotional material

1618 KODAK LIMITED
Research Division, Headstone Drive, Harrow, Middlesex HA1 4TY — Tel. 01-427 4380
Telex 21925

Company

Enquiries to the Research Librarian

Subject coverage
photographic science and technology

Publications
catalogues
instructional and promotional material

1619 KYLE AND CARRICK DISTRICT LIBRARIES
Public Library, 12 Main Street, Ayr KA8 8ED — Tel. 0292 81511 ext. 229
Public Library service; formed by the amalgamation of Ayr Public Library and part of Ayr County Library; urban Area Library at above address, rural Area Library at Girvan

Enquiries to the Director of Library Services

Subject coverage
general

1620 LAAS INTERNATIONAL
5 Holyport Road, Fulham, London SW6 6LY
Voluntary Amateur Aviation Society

Enquiries to the Honorary General Secretary

Subject coverage
history of transport aircraft 1945 to present day; airline and air taxi operator fleets worldwide, particularly U.K. and European operations; other aviation topics including aircraft accidents since 1945, history of Concorde, etc.

Publications
Aviation News and Review (monthly, illustrated)
British Independent Airlines since 1945 (4 vols)
Vickers Turbine Transports: history of Viscount and Vanguard airlines

LABORATORY ANIMALS CENTRE *see* **MEDICAL RESEARCH COUNCIL LABORATORIES**

1621 LABORATORY OF THE GOVERNMENT CHEMIST
Cornwall House, Stamford Street, London SE1 9NG — Tel. 01-928 7900
Government Body, of the Department of Industry, *q.v.*; includes the Pesticide Residue Analysis Information Service

Enquiries, by letter only, to the Director

Subject coverage
analytical chemistry; advice on methods of analysis; chemical nomenclature; wines, soft drinks, spirits, beer, tobacco, sugar composites, foods, pesticide formulations and residues; drug analysis; fusion products in water; water analysis; identification of textile fibres; rocks and minerals; background

information on a wide variety of products, including paints, plastics, chemicals, hydrocarbon and essential oils; safety and health

Publication

Annual Report of the Government Chemist (H.M.S.O.)

1622 LACE RESEARCH ASSOCIATION

7 Gregory Boulevard, Nottingham NG7 6LD Tel. 0602 623311

Research Body

Enquiries to the Director of Research

Subject coverage

all technical matters concerning the lace industry

1623 LACKHAM COLLEGE OF AGRICULTURE

Lacock, Chippenham, Wiltshire Tel. 0249 50812

Agricultural College

Enquiries to the Librarian

Subject coverage

agriculture; agricultural economics; horticulture; home economics

LADSIRLAC *see* **LIVERPOOL AND DISTRICT SCIENTIFIC, INDUSTRIAL AND RESEARCH LIBRARY ADVISORY COUNCIL**

1624 John LAING RESEARCH AND DEVELOPMENT LIMITED

Manor Way, Borehamwood, Hertfordshire WD6 1LN Tel. 01-953 6144

Company, part of John Laing and Son Limited; at the same address, Ground Engineering Limited, a subsidiary

Enquiries to the Librarian

Subject coverage

building; civil engineering; concrete and other building materials

1625 LAMBEG INDUSTRIAL RESEARCH ASSOCIATION

Lambeg, Lisburn, County Antrim BT27 4RJ Tel. 023-82 2255/6

Research Association, formerly the Linen Industry Research Association

Enquiries to the Information Officer

Subject coverage

textiles (long staple fibres, preparing, spinning, fabric production and finishing), linen, jute, development of non-flam textiles and test methods, polymer extrusion and processing, polymer characterisation and testing, civil engineering uses of specially developed textile materials, carpets, catalytic methods of pollution control (odours, organic vapours, intractable effluents) member service and testing, trouble shooting, consultancy, development of instrumentation, engineering design and prototype construction, energy conservation and recycling, utilization of textile and polymer wastes, environmental conditions

Publications

Annual Report

for members only:

Progress Research Reports

Technical Reports

Journal Scan

1626 LAMBETH REFERENCE LIBRARY

Tate Central Library, Brixton Oval, London SW2 1JQ Tel. 01-274 7451

Public Reference Library; includes LINK, Lambeth Information Network, *q.v.*

Enquiries to the Scientific Librarian

Subject coverage
chemical technology; chemicals; explosives; fireworks; matches; fuel technology; coal technology (not mining); food technology; beverages; oils, fats and waxes; petroleum technology; gas technology; (including North Sea developments); ceramics and clay industry; cleaning, dyeing and related industries; inks; protective coatings; soaps; adhesives; plastics; synthetic agricultural chemicals; perfumery; metallurgy & metal manufactures; timber; pulp; paper; textiles; rubbers

Publications
Bibliographies on food technology and plastics

1627 LAMBETH INFORMATION NETWORK (LINK)
Reference Library, Tate Central Library, Brixton Oval, London SW2 1JQ — Tel. 01-274 7451, Telex 25821
Information Service for industry and commerce in Lambeth; 380 members

Enquiries to the Scientific Librarian/LINK Liaison Officer

Subject coverage
general, commercial, industrial; value added tax; health and safety at work; business and management; courses and meetings

Special collection
Metropolitan Special Collection of Chemical Technology

Publications
Publicity Brochure
Newsletter (bi-monthly)
Bibliographies (in trade and commerce, about 14 titles to date)

1628 LAMINATED PLASTICS FABRICATORS ASSOCIATION LIMITED
c/o 3–4 Cardale Street, Rowley Regis, Warley, West Midlands B65 0LX — Tel. 021-559 1819
Trade Association

Enquiries to the Information Officer

Subject coverage
fabrication of decorative laminates

1629 LAMSAC (LOCAL AUTHORITIES MANAGEMENT SERVICES AND COMPUTER COMMITTEE)
3 Buckingham Gate, London SW1E 6JH — Tel. 01-828 2333
Local Government Advisory Body

Enquiries to the Director or the Information Officer

Subject coverage
local government management services; computing and computer services

Publications
Reports of Working Parties and Research Projects
Quarterly News Sheet

LANARKSHIRE COUNTY LIBRARIES *now* **STRATHCLYDE REGIONAL LIBRARY AND RESOURCE SERVICE, Lanark Division,** *q.v.*

1630 LANCASHIRE COLLEGE OF AGRICULTURE
Myerscough Hall, Bibborrow, Preston PR3 0RY — Tel. 099-54 40611
Agricultural College, houses the Myerscough Trial Grounds of the National Institute of Agricultural Botany, *q.v.*

Enquiries to the Principal

Subject coverage
agriculture, soil science, amenity horticulture, arboriculture

1631 THE LANCASHIRE LIBRARY
County Library Headquarters, 143 Corporation Street, Preston, Lancashire PR1 8RH — Tel. 0772 54868 ext. 319; Telex 63749
Public Library Service; fourteen District Central Libraries; Blackburn, Blackpool, Burnley, Chorley, Fylde, Hyndburn, Lancaster, Ormskirk, Pendle, Preston, Ribble Valley, Rossendale, South Ribble, Wyre

Enquiries to the County Librarian

Subject coverage
all aspects of science, technology and commerce; technical information centre at County Library Headquarters

Special collections
Sets of British Standards at Headquarters, and at Blackburn, Burnley and Preston District Central Libraries

LANCASTER DISTRICT CENTRAL LIBRARY *see* **LANCASHIRE LIBRARY**

1632 LANCASTER UNIVERSITY LIBRARY
Bailrigg, Lancaster, Lancashire LA1 4YH — Tel. 0524 65201; Telex 65111

University Library

Enquiries to the Librarian

Subject coverage
usual fields of university study, excluding law and medicine, but including business studies

Publications
Occasional Papers series

LANCASTER UNIVERSITY *see also* **LANCORD LIMITED**

1633 LANCHESTER POLYTECHNIC
Priory Street, Coventry, Warwickshire CV1 5FB — Tel. 0203 24166; Telex 31469
Polytechnic, formed from three colleges, the former Lanchester College of Technology, the Coventry College of Art and the Rugby College of Engineering Technology

Enquiries, bibliographical, to the Librarian; technical to the Industrial Liaison Officer

Subject coverage
accountancy; biological sciences; building; business; chemistry; communication studies; computing; economics; engineering (civil, electrical, mechanical, production); geography; industrial design/transportation; management, materials, mathematics; metallurgy; operational research; physics; statistics

Publication
Research Report

1634 LANCORD LIMITED
Lancaster University, Cartmel, Bailrigg, Lancaster, Lancashire LA1 4YH — Tel. 0524 65201
Company, wholly-owned by the University

Enquiries to the Secretary

Subject coverage
operational research; management science

1635 LAND ADVISORY GROUP
c/o Chris Yarrow and Associates, 56 High Street, Lewes BN7 1XE — Tel. 07916 6291
Consulting Group of Independent Advisors

Enquiries to the Secretary

Subject coverage
forestry; soil and plant analysis; soil management; land drainage; farm management; farm office/management; crop husbandry; animal husbandry; landscape architecture; garden design; planning appeals

Publication
Descriptive Brochure

1636 LAND AND PROPERTY DEVELOPMENT (SOUTH WALES) LIMITED
58 Park Place, Cardiff CF1 3AT Tel. 0222 21782/26494
Company/Consultants

Enquiries to the Managing Director

Subject coverage
building; civil engineering; land development; insurance

1637 LAND AND WATER MANAGEMENT LIMITED
88a Girton Road, Cambridge CB3 0LN Tel. 0223 76002 or 76898
Company

Enquiries to the Librarian

Subject coverage
agricultural land appraisal and management improvements; industrial land reclamation and restoration of mineral workings; field engineering and soil physics including drainage, irrigation, soil & water conservation; turf and grass culture in sports field construction; research and development particularly on soil blades and implements

Publications
Technical Notes
Catalogues

1638 LAND INSTITUTE LIMITED
93 High Street, Epsom, Surrey KT19 8EG Tel. 037-27 22582
Research and Publishing Organisation

Enquiries to the Secretary

Subject coverage
land acquisition, disposal, planning, management; statutes affecting land

1639 LAND RESOURCES DIVISION
Ministry of Overseas Development, Tolworth Tower, Surbiton, Surrey KT6 7DY Tel. 01-399 5281
Government Department, formerly of the Directorate of Overseas Surveys

Enquiries to the Information Officer

Subject coverage
land resources assessment in tropical developing countries; agriculture, soil science, forestry, water resources; geology; geomorphology; meteorology; hydrology; vegetation studies; land use; land capability

Publications
Land Resource Studies
Technical Bulletins
Progress Reports
Land Resource Reports and Bibliographies

LANDSCAPE INSTITUTE *see* **INSTITUTE OF LANDSCAPE ARCHITECTS**

LANGLEY DISTRICT LIBRARY *see* **SANDWELL PUBLIC LIBRARIES**

1640 LANKRO CHEMICALS LIMITED
Eccles, Manchester M30 0BH Tel. 061-789 7300
Telex 667725

Company

Enquiries to the Librarian

Subject coverage
polyurethanes; plastics additives; surface active agents

1641 LANSING BAGNALL
Kingsclere Road, Basingstoke, Hampshire RG21 2XJ Tel. 0256 3131
Telex 858120

Private Manufacturing Company

Enquiries to the Public Relations Officer

Subject coverage
materials handling using industrial trucks, including freight, warehousing, high density storage; fork truck operation and maintenance; rental and leasing

Publications
Handling and Storage (bi-monthly)
Using Industrial Trucks for Materials Handling (book)
Technical data sheets and catalogues

1642 LAPORTE INDUSTRIES LIMITED
Moorfield Road, Widnes, Halton, Cheshire WA8 0JU Tel. 051-424 5555
Company

Enquiries to the Librarian

Subject coverage
chemicals; water treatment

1643 LAPORTE INDUSTRIES LIMITED
Organics and Pigments Division, P.O. Box 26, Grimsby, Tel. 0469 73171
South Humberside DN37 8DP
Company Division

Enquiries to the Information Officer, Research Department

Subject coverage
the chemistry, physics and chemical engineering of titanium dioxide pigments; applications in paints plastics and paper

Special collection
Patents mainly on titanium mineral processing and titanium dioxide manufacture

LARD ASSOCIATION *see* **FOOD MANUFACTURERS FEDERATION INCORPORATED**

LASER LABORATORY *see* **RUTHERFORD LABORATORY**

1644 LAUDER TECHNICAL COLLEGE
North Fod, Halbeath, Dunfermline, Fife KY11 5DY
Technical College

Enquiries to the College Librarian

Subject coverage
building; catering; commerce; electrical and mechanical engineering; nursing; mining

Publications
subject bibliographies

1645 LEAD DEVELOPMENT ASSOCIATION
34 Berkeley Square, London W1X 6AJ Tel. 01-499 8422
Telex 261286

Trade Association

Enquiries to the Information Officer

Subject coverage
building; batteries; coatings; environment; health and safety; extraction, refining and production; noise insulation

Publications
Lead Abstracts
Technical booklets, etc.
Films

LEAD SHEET AND PIPE EXPORT GROUP *see* **BRITISH LEAD MANUFACTURERS ASSOCIATION**

LEAD SMELTERS AND REFINERIES ASSOCIATION *see* **BRITISH LEAD MANUFACTURERS ASSOCIATION**

LEAMINGTON SPA PUBLIC LIBRARY *see* **WARWICKSHIRE COUNTY LIBRARY**

1646 LEASCO SOFTWARE LIMITED
Reliance House, 150 Bath Road, Maidenhead, Berkshire SL6 4LD Tel. 0628 23391
Telex 848557

Company, formerly Leasco Systems and Research Limited; subsidiary of Reliance Group Incorporated

Enquiries to the Information Officer

Subject coverage
communications (data, message or speech); computing applications

Publications
Newsletter
Technical papers

1647 LEATHER PRODUCERS ASSOCIATION
82 Borough High Street, London SE1 1LL Tel. 01-407 1522
Trade Association

Enquiries to the Secretary

Subject coverage
employment matters in the leather trades; leather technology

Publication
Leather Technician's Handbook

1648 LEEDS CITY LIBRARIES
Library of Commerce, Science and Technology, Central Library, Calverley Street, Leeds LS1 3AB Tel. 0532 31301 ext. 2065/6
Telex 556237
Public Library

Enquiries to the Librarian

Subject coverage
all aspects of commerce, science; especially clothing manufacture, wool textiles, statistics, mining

Special collections
Patent specifications (over 8,000,000 items): British, U.S., German, French, Belgian and abstracts of Canadian and Russian
British Standards
ISO, IEC, DIN, ASTM and other standards
UNESCO publications
Ohio University Engineering Experiment Station Reports
U.S. Bureau of Mines Reports

1649 LEEDS SMALL FIRMS INFORMATION CENTRE
5 Royal Exchange House, City Square, Leeds LS1 5PQ Tel. 0532 445151
Telex 557687

Government Information Centre of the Department of Industry

Enquiries to the Manager

Subject coverage
business studies and problems

Publications
Pamphlets on financial and business subjects

1650 LEEDS POLYTECHNIC
Calverley Street, Leeds LS1 3HE Tel. 0532 41101
Technical College, formerly Leeds Central Colleges

Enquiries to the Librarian

Subject coverage
Management sciences; trade and marketing; accounting and finance; applied economics; transport; sociology and psychology (industrial applications); mathematics; computing; building; civil engineering; mechanical and production engineering; chemistry; electrical engineering; physics; speech therapy; nutrition and dietetics; applied biology

1651 LEEDS UNIVERSITY LIBRARY
Leeds LS2 9JT Tel. 0532 31751
University Library, formerly referred to as the Brotherton Library; now comprises the Brotherton Library and the new South Library

Enquiries to the Librarian

Subject coverage
agriculture; architecture; astronomy; biophysics; botany; ceramics; chemical engineering; chemistry; civil engineering; dyeing; economics; electrical engineering; engineering (general); food science; fuel; general biology; general science; geography; geology; leather; mathematics; mechanical engineering; metallurgy; meteorology; mining; palaeontology; physics; psychology; seismology; technology (general); textiles; transport; zoology

Special collections
All Souls and Chaston Chapman Collections in early Science
Yorkshire Geological Society Library

Publication
Current Periodicals in the University Libraries

LEEDS UNIVERSITY *see also*
ASTBURY DEPARTMENT OF BIOPHYSICS
COOKRIDGE RADIATION RESEARCH CENTRE
HOULDSWORTH SCHOOL OF APPLIED SCIENCE
INFORMATION CENTRE ON HIGH TEMPERATURE PROCESSES

LEEK DISTRICT LIBRARY *see* **STAFFORDSHIRE COUNTY LIBRARY**

LEICESTER CENTRAL LIBRARY *see* **LEICESTERSHIRE LIBRARIES AND INFORMATION SERVICE**

LEICESTER POLYTECHNIC *see also* **U.K. MECHANICAL HEALTH MONITORING GROUP**

1652 LEICESTERSHIRE LIBRARIES AND INFORMATION SERVICE
Lee Circle, Leicester LE1 3SH Tel. 0533 22012
Telex 34307

Public Library Service, formed from the seven Leicestershire libraries and the branches; Area Libraries: Central, at Leicester; North, at Loughborough; East, at Oakham; South East, at Oadby; South, at Wigston Magna; South West, at Hinckley; West, at Coalville; North West, at Syston

Enquiries to the County Librarian

Subject coverage
general

Special collection
Stretton Collection on Railways

Publication
SCAN Series of current awareness abstracts (governmental, local governmental, parliamentary)

1653 LEICESTER POLYTECHNIC
Technology Library, Hawthorn Building, P.O. Box 143, Leicester LE1 9BH
Tel. 0533 50181 ext. 2321/2159
Technical College; formerly City of Leicester Polytechnic and City of Leicester College of Education of Scraptoft Campus, Leicester LE7 9SU

Enquiries to the Librarian

Subject coverage
economics; mathematics; physics; chemistry; biology; pharmacy; electrical and mechanical engineering; business management; textile technology; polymers; computing

Publication
Leicester Polytechnic Research Report

1654 LEICESTER UNIVERSITY LIBRARY
University Road, Leicester LE1 7RH Tel. 0533 50000
Telex 341198
University Library; houses the Library of the Mathematical Association, *q.v.*

Enquiries to the Librarian

Subject coverage
general, including engineering

Special collection
Transport History collection

Publications
Periodicals List (annual)
Leicester University Press publications

LEIGH LIBRARY *see* **WIGAN METROPOLITAN BOROUGH REFERENCE LIBRARIES**

1655 LEITH NAUTICAL COLLEGE
59 Commercial Street, Leith, Edinburgh EH6 6NH Tel. 031-554 1650
Nautical College

Enquiries to the Librarian

Subject coverage
marine engineering; navigation; marine radio and radar

LETCHWORTH COLLEGE *now* **NORTH HERTS COLLEGE,** *q.v.*

1656 LETCOMBE LABORATORY
Letcombe Regis, Wantage, Oxfordshire OX12 9JT Tel. 023-57 3327
Research Institute, of the Agricultural Research Council

Enquiries to the Head, Scientific Information Section

Subject coverage
plant growth in relation to soil conditions; methods of cultivation including direct drilling; effects of water-logging; behaviour of fertilizer nitrogen in soil; radioactive and stable isotope techniques; environmental radioactivity and contamination of human diet and milk

Publication
Annual Report

1657 LEVINGTON RESEARCH STATION
Fisons Fertiliser Division, Levington, Ipswich, Suffok IP10 0LU Tel. 0743 76911
Telex 98140

Company; includes the North Wyke Experimental Station, North Wyke, Devonshire

Enquiries to the Head of Library Services

Subject coverage
manufacture and use of fertilizers

Publications
Fisons Fertilizer and Agricultural News
Fisons Technical Bulletin

1658 LEWES TECHNICAL COLLEGE
Mountfield Road, Lewes, Sussex BN7 2XH Tel. 079-16 6121
Technical College

Enquiries to the Librarian

Subject coverage
general

1659 LEWISHAM LIBRARY SERVICE
Commercial and Technical Reference Library, Deptford Library, Tel. 01-692 1162
Lewisham Way, London SE14 6PF Telex 25830
Public Reference Library; member of the South East Area Libraries Information Service (SEAL)

Enquiries to the Librarian

Subject coverage
commercial, technical, economic and management information; statistics; bank reviews; standards and specifications

Publications
Contech (8 times per annum—information for local, particularly small, firms)
Precis (current awareness service for local government officers)

1660 LIBRARIES OF NORTH STAFFORDSHIRE AND SOUTH CHESHIRE IN COOPERATION (LINOSCO)
Horace Barks Reference Library, Bethesda Street, Hanley, Tel. 0782 25108
Stoke-on-Trent ST1 3RS Telex 36132
Interlibrary Co-operative Scheme; resources of twenty-five libraries

Enquiries to the Honorary Secretary

Subject coverage
general, technical, commercial

Publications
Union List of Periodicals (jointly with MISLIC)

1661 LIBRARY ASSOCIATION
7 Ridgmount Street, Store Street, London WC1E 7AE Tel. 01-636 7543
Telex 21897

Professional Association

Enquiries to the Information Officer

Subject coverage
librarianship; libraries; education for the profession; salaries and conditions of service

Publications
Guide to Reference Material, 3 vols
Manuals in library and information studies, buildings and history (list available)
British Technology Index (monthly)
Journal of Librarianship (quarterly)
Library and Information Science Asbtracts (bi-monthly)

1662 LIBRARY INFORMATION SERVICE FOR TEESSIDE (LIST)
Reference Department, Central Library, Victoria Square, Middlesbrough, Cleveland TS1 2AY — Tel. 0642 45294/5/6, Telex 58439
Interlibrary Cooperative Scheme

Enquiries to the Honorary Secretary

Subject coverage
general, technical, commercial

Special collections
British Standards
British Patents
Foreign Patents and Standards

Publications
Steel, Oil and Chemicals: select bibliography on the future direction of industry in Cleveland
Current information sheets (to members only)

1663 LIBRARY INFORMATION SERVICE TO INDUSTRY AND COMMERCE (LISIC)
Gravesham Divisional Central Library, Windmill Street, Gravesend, Kent DA12 1AQ — Tel. 0474 52758
Library service to small firms; Division of Kent County Library, *q.v.*; incorporated in the South East Area Library Information Service

Enquiries to the Librarian

Subject coverage
technical and commercial

Special collection
British Standards

1664 LIBRARY OF JAPANESE SCIENCE AND TECHNOLOGY
24 Duke Street, Whitley Bay, Northumberland NE26 3PP — Tel. 089-44 34392
Technical Library; formerly H.A.S. Technical Library

Enquiries to the Librarian

Subject coverage
Japanese serial literature; Japanese technology and science in general

Special collection
1,700 Japanese serial titles including publications of colleges and universities

Publications
Bibliographies of Japanese articles (chargeable)

LICHFIELD DISTRICT LIBRARY *see* **STAFFORDSHIRE COUNTY LIBRARY**

1665 LIFE OFFICES ASSOCIATION
Aldermary House, Queen Street, London EC4P 4JD — Tel. 01-248 4477, 01-236 5117

Trade Association

Enquiries to the Information Officer

Subject coverage
life assurance; pensions

Publication
Annual Statistics Summary

1666 LIFTING EQUIPMENT MANUFACTURERS ASSOCIATION
430 Barking Road, London E13 8HJ — Tel. 01-476 2958
Trade Association

Enquiries to the Secretary

Subject coverage
all types of lifting and winching equipment, hand- or power-operated; hydraulic jacks; light duty overhead cranes; other cranes; hoists and slings; conveyors, handling equipment; lifts; vacuum lifting equipment

Publication
Handbook of Members & Products

1667 LIGHT RAILWAY TRANSPORT LEAGUE
4 Madge Hill, Church Road, Hanwell, London W7 3BW — Tel. 01-567 2297
Subscribing Members Society

Enquiries to the Honorary Secretary, at the above address, or, to the Honorary Planning Officer, 37 Wellesley Road, Ilford 1GI 4JX

Subject coverage
applications of modern light rapid rail transit, electrically operated, particularly for urban areas

Publications
Modern Tramway and Rapid Transit Review (monthly)
Tramway Review (quarterly)
Publications on light rapid transit and tramway history

1668 LILLY RESEARCH CENTRE LIMITED
Erl Wood Manor, London Road, Windlesham, Surrey GU20 6PH — Tel. 0276 73631
Company, affiliated to Eli Lilly and Company, Indianapolis, U.S.A.

Enquiries to the Librarian

Subject coverage
analytical, organic, and pharmaceutical chemistry; pharmacology; toxicology; metabolism; biochemistry; microbiology; veterinary medicine; plant science, especially fungicides and selective weed killers: in general, the discovery and application of products for use in human medicine, animal health and agriculture

LIMEHOUSE AREA LIBRARY *see* **TOWER HAMLETS LIBRARIES DEPARTMENT**

LIMESTONE FEDERATION *now* **BRITISH QUARRYING & SLAG FEDERATION,** *q.v.*

LINCOLN DIVISIONAL LIBRARY *see* **LINCOLNSHIRE LIBRARY SERVICE**

1669 LINCOLNSHIRE LIBRARY SERVICE
Brayford House, Lucy Tower Street, Lincoln LN1 1XN — Tel. 0522 26287
Public Libraries; the service formed from Lindsey and Holland and Kesteven County Libraries, and Boston, Gainsborough, *q.v.*, Grantham, Lincoln and Stamford Public Libraries; present four Divisional Libraries are at Lincoln, Spalding, Sleaford and Louth

Enquiries to the County Librarian

Subject coverage
general; medicine; agriculture

Special collections
Medical Library at Lincoln County Hospital
Medical Library at Pilgrim Hospital, Boston

1670 LINEAR MOTORS (LINTROL) LIMITED
Empress Road, Loughborough, Leicestershire LE11 1SR — Tel. 05093 31876
Telex 34408
Company, part of H. Morris Limited Group; formerly Lintrol Systems (U.K.) Limited

Enquiries to the Manager

Subject coverage
linear induction motors; low speed transport systems; instrumentation for linear motion

LINEN INDUSTRY RESEARCH ASSOCIATION *now* **LAMBEG INDUSTRIAL RESEARCH ASSOCIATION,** *q.v.*

1671 LINEN SEWING THREAD MANUFACTURERS ASSOCATION OF GREAT BRITAIN AND NORTHERN IRELAND
Hilden, Lisburn, County Antrim BT27 4RR — Tel. 023 82 2791, Telex 74442

Trade Association

Enquiries to the Secretary

Subject coverage
linen thread manufacture

LINK *see* **LAMBETH INFORMATION NETWORK**

1672 LINNAEAN SOCIETY OF LONDON
Burlington House, Piccadilly, London W1V 0LQ — Tel. 01-734 1040
Learned Society

Enquiries, limited, bibliographical and biographical, not scientific, to the Librarian; no scientific enquiry service available

Subject coverage
natural history; biology, botany, zoology; taxonomy

Special collections
Linnaeus Collection, the natural history collections, personal library and manuscripts
Collections of correspondence and manuscripts of 18th and 19th century naturalists, their portraits and engravings

Publications
Botanical Journal (8 times per annum)
Zoological Journal (8 times per annum)
Biological Journal (quarterly)

LINOSCO *see* **LIBRARIES OF NORTH STAFFORDSHIRE AND SOUTH CHESHIRE IN CO-OPERATION**

LINTROL SYSTEMS (U.K.) LIMITED *now* **LINEAR MOTORS (LINTROL) LIMITED,** *q.v.*

LISIC *see* **LIBRARY INFORMATION SERVICE TO INDUSTRY AND COMMERCE**

LIST *see* **LIBRARY INFORMATION SERVICE FOR TEESSIDE**

1673 LISTER INSTITUTE OF PREVENTIVE MEDICINE
Dagger Lane, Elstree, Hertfordshire WD6 3AX — Tel. 01-953 6191
Independent, Registered Charity; comprising the Vaccines and Sera Laboratories and the Blood Products Laboratory (Plasma Fractionation Laboratory, Oxford)

Enquiries to the Directors of the Laboratories

Subject coverage
Vaccines and Sera Laboratories: immunization against infectious diseases; Blood Products Laboratory: methods of preparing fractions of human sera for use in medicine and surgery

Publications
Annual Report
Catalogue of Vaccines and Sera

1674 LIVERPOOL AND DISTRICT SCIENTIFIC, INDUSTRIAL AND RESEARCH LIBRARY ADVISORY COUNCIL (LADSIRLAC)
Liverpool City Library, William Brown Street, Liverpool L3 8EW Tel. 051-207 1937/8
Telex 62500

Interlibrary Cooperative Scheme

Enquiries to the Liaison Officers

Subject coverage
industrial, scientific, commercial information

Publications
Regional Services for Industry and Commerce (irregular)
Annual Report
Newsletter (quarterly)

1675 LIVERPOOL CITY LIBRARIES
William Brown Street, Liverpool, Lancashire L3 8EW Tel. 051-207 2147
Telex 62500

Public Libraries; includes LADSIRLAC Technical Information Centre and Industrial Library Services, *q.v.*

Enquiries to the City Librarian

Subject coverage
science, technology and medicine; commercial and social sciences; statistics; trade names, etc.

Special collections
Complete sets ASA, ASTM, BSI, DEF, DTD, DIN and ISO standard specifications
Patent specifications of twelve countries

Publications
LADSIRLAC Newsletter
MRLS Bulletin (for municipal research staff)

1676 LIVERPOOL POLYTECHNIC
Engineering and Science Library, Byrom Street, Liverpool L3 3AF Tel. 051-207 3581
Polytechnic Library Service; formerly Liverpool Regional College of Technology Library

Enquiries to the Librarian

Subject coverage
biology; chemistry; biochemistry; pharmacy; mechanical engineering; marine engineering; production engineering; control engineering; maritime studies; mathematics; physics

1677 LIVERPOOL SCHOOL OF TROPICAL MEDICINE
Pembroke Place, Liverpool L3 5QA Tel. 051-709 7611
Telex 627095

Limited Company, owned by the University of Liverpool

Enquiries to the Dean

Subject coverage
all aspects of human and veterinary medicine of the tropics and sub-tropics, including parasitology, entomology, community health and paediatrics

Special collections
Reference collections of trypanosomes of man and animals, rodent malaria parasites, and *Leishmania*

Publications
Annals of Tropical Medicine and Parasitology
Annual Report

1678 LIVERPOOL UNIVERSITY LIBRARY
P.O. Box 123, Liverpool L69 3DA Tel. 051-709 6022
Telex 627095

University Library

Enquiries to the Librarian

Subject coverage
commerce; economics; management; geography; building; civil, electrical, electronic and mechanical engineering; metallurgy; materials science; biochemistry; botany; chemistry; genetics; geology; geophysics; history of science; marine biology; computer science; oceanography; physics; zoology; medical and veterinary science

Special collections
Campbell Brown Collection (400 books, 16th–19th century, on alchemy and chemistry)
Fraser Collection (900 items on Nicotiniana)
Salisbury Collection (340 scientific books of 19th century)
Whale Collection (309 items, 19th & 20th centuries on finance and banking)

LIVERPOOL UNIVERSITY *see also* **LIVERPOOL SCHOOL OF TROPICAL MEDICINE**

1679 LLANDRILLO TECHNICAL COLLEGE
Llandudno Road, Rhos-on-Sea, Colwyn Bay LL28 4H2 Tel. 0492 44216
Technical College

Enquiries to the Librarian

Subject coverage
particularly hotel-keeping, catering and tourism; engineering; construction; nursing; domestic science

LLANDRINDOD WELLS AREA LIBRARY *see* **POWYS COUNTY LIBRARY**

1680 LLANELLI BOROUGH LIBRARY
Vaughan Street, Llanelli, Dyfed SA15 3TY Tel. 05542 3538
Public Library

Enquiries to the Librarian

Subject coverage
industrial history of East Carmarthenshire

1681 LLANELLI TECHNICAL COLLEGE
Alban Road, Llanelli, Dyfed SA15 1NG Tel. 05542 59165
Technical College

Enquiries to the Principal

Subject coverage
mechanical and electrical engineering; electronics; construction technology; management; business studies; mathematics; computer studies

1682 LLOYDS BANK INTERNATIONAL LIMITED
Economics Department, 100 Pall Mall, London SW1Y 5HP Tel. 01-930 2313 ext. 118
Telex 888421/2
International Bank; formerly Lloyds and Bolsa, and before that, Bank of London and South America Limited

Enquiries to the Librarian

Subject coverage
Latin American countries—political, economic and statistical information; other countries—general economic information

Publication
Bank of London & South America Review

1683 LLOYDS INSURANCE BROKERS ASSOCIATION
3–4 Lime Street, London EC3M 7DQ Tel. 01-623 2855
Trade Association; organizations operating from this address are: the British Insurance Brokers Association, the U.K. Credit Insurance Brokers Committee, the U.K. Insurance Brokers European Committee, and the Bureau International des Producteurs d'Assurances et de Réassurances

Enquiries to the Secretary

Subject coverage
insurance and ancillary matters

1684 LLOYDS/LLOYDS REGISTER SHIPPING INFORMATION SERVICES
4 Lloyds Avenue, London EC3N 3ED — Tel. 01-709 9166
Telex 888379

Information Service; joint concern of Lloyds Register of Shipping and Lloyds of London

Enquiries to the Information Service; charges related to work involved

Subject coverage
shipping data; shipping movements; vessel histories

Publications
Information on magnetic tape, computer print-out, or microfiche

1685 LLOYDS MOTOR UNDERWRITERS ASSOCIATION
Lloyds Building, Leadenhall Street, London EC3M 7DQ — Tel. 01-626 7235
01-626 7006

Trade Association

Enquiries to the Secretary

Subject coverage
motor insurance

1686 LLOYDS REGISTER OF SHIPPING
71 Fenchurch Street, London EC3M 4BS — Tel. 01-709 9166
Telex 888379

Classification: Society and Independent Inspection Agency; see also other Lloyds Register entries; Lloyds Register Research Laboratory and Printing House are at Manor Royal, Crawley, West Sussex RH10 2QN (tel. 0293 26404) for publications; Industrial Services are at Croydon

Enquiries, shipping, to the Shipping Information Services; general, to the Information Officer

Subject coverage
ships: classification, specification and advisory service, international conventions, Register Book (full details of all known merchant ships of the world over 100 tons dwt), statistics, technical records; offshore services: certification and classification in connection with steel and concrete, submersibles and underwater habitats, welding, linepipe, etc.; land-based industry: nuclear power stations, thermal and hydro-electric power stations, oil refineries and chemical plants, freight containers, and general engineering; other services include yachts, cargo gear, docks, etc.; instrumentation; refrigeration and cold stores; mass-produced machinery; computer services

Special collections
Complete set of Register Books from the 16th century, (less first edition which is in the British Museum)
Complete set of Register of Yachts from the 19th century

Publications
Lloyds Register Book
Register of Yachts
Register of American Yachts
Rules and Regulations for the Construction and Classification of Steel Ships
Rules for Inland Waterway Vessels
Rules for Yachts
Many other guides, test requirements, lists of approved equipment, rules, certification schemes, etc. (list available)

1687 LLOYDS REGISTER OF SHIPPING
Yachts and Small Craft, Lloyds Register House, 69 Oxford Street, Southampton SO1 1DL — Tel. 0703 20353
Telex 477261

Independent Inspection Agency

Enquiries to the Information Officer

Subject coverage
yachts and small craft

LLOYDS REGISTER INDUSTRIAL SERVICES *see* **LLOYDS REGISTER OF SHIPPING**

LLOYDS REGISTER OFFSHORE SERVICES GROUP *see* **LLOYDS REGISTER OF SHIPPING**

LLOYDS REGISTER RESEARCH LABORATORY *see* **LLOYDS REGISTER OF SHIPPING**

LOCAL AUTHORITIES MANAGEMENT SERVICES AND COMPUTER COMMITTEE *see* **LAMSAC**

LOCAL GOVERNMENT OPERATIONAL RESEARCH UNIT *see* **ROYAL INSTITUTE OF PUBLIC ADMINISTRATION**

LOCOMOTIVE AND ALLIED MANUFACTURERS ASSOCIATION *now* **RAILWAY INDUSTRY ASSOCIATION,** *q.v.*

1688 LONDON AND DISTRICT SCALING EMPLOYERS ASSOCIATION
Blackwall Engineering Works, Blackwall Way, London E14 9QD — Tel. 01-987 2404
Trade Association

Enquiries to the Honorary Secretary

Subject coverage
marine and industrial de-scaling; boiler cleaning; chemical cleaning and deslagging

LONDON AND MIDDLESEX ARCHAEOLOGICAL SOCIETY *see* **BISHOPSGATE INSTITUTE LIBRARY**

1689 LONDON ASSOCIATION OF MASTER DECORATORS
24 Ormond Road, Richmond, Surrey — Tel. 01-948 4151
Trade Association; member of British Decorators Association, *q.v.*

Enquiries, in writing, to the Secretary, but only for names and addresses of members undertaking work

Subject coverage
painting contractors and master decorators

1690 LONDON ASSOCIATION OF MASTER STONEMASONS
82 New Cavendish Street, London W1M 8AD — Tel. 01-580 4041
Trade Association; member of the National Federation of Building Trades Employers

Enquiries to the Secretary

Subject coverage
stonework

LONDON BOROUGHS *see*

BARKING
BARNET
BEXLEY
BRENT
BROMLEY
CAMDEN
CITY OF LONDON
CROYDON
EALING
ENFIELD
GREENWICH
HACKNEY
HAMMERSMITH
HARINGEY
HARROW
HAVERING
HILLINGDON
HOUNSLOW
ISLINGTON
(ROYAL) KENSINGTON & CHELSEA
(ROYAL) KINGSTON UPON THAMES
LAMBETH
LEWISHAM
MERTON
NEWHAM
REDBRIDGE
RICHMOND
SOUTHWARK
SUTTON
TOWER HAMLETS
UPPER NORWOOD
WALTHAM FOREST
WANDSWORTH
WESTMINSTER

LONDON BUSINESS SCHOOL *see* **LONDON GRADUATE SCHOOL OF BUSINESS STUDIES**

1691 LONDON CHAMBER OF COMMERCE AND INDUSTRY
69 Cannon Street, London EC4N 5AB Tel. 01-248 4444
Telex 888941

Chamber of Commerce, affiliated to the Association of British Chambers of Commerce, *q.v.*

Enquiries to the Head of Information Department, answered free to members of the London Chamber of Commerce and to organisations. Fee to others is £10.00

Subject coverage
commerce and industry in general

Publications
Home and Economics Affairs Bulletins (fortnightly, members only)
Commerce International (monthly)
Trade Contacts in Eastern Europe
Arab Trade Contacts
Eastern European Bulletin

1692 LONDON COLLEGE OF FASHION
20 John Prince's Street, London W1M 9HE Tel. 01-493 8341/5
Specialist College, of the Inner London Education Authority; formerly College of Fashion and Clothing Technology

Enquiries to the Chief Librarian

Subject coverage
fashion design; light clothing manufacture; tailoring; embroidery; furriery; millinery; hairdressing; beauty therapy; clothing management

1693 LONDON COLLEGE OF FURNITURE
41–71 Commercial Road, London E1 1LA Tel. 01-247 1953
Specialist College

Enquiries to the Librarian

Subject coverage
furniture production and history; cabinet making and woodwork; upholstery and furnishings; interior design; musical instrument technology; toymaking; timber and plastics

1694 LONDON COLLEGE OF PRINTING
Elephant and Castle, London SE1 6SB Tel. 01-735 8484
Specialist College

Enquiries to the Librarian

Subject coverage
printing, management, art and design; photography; film and television; typography; reprography; audio-visual material

Special collections
Historical material and printed ephemera
Audio-visual material

LONDON CONSTRUCTION SAFETY GROUP *now* **CONSTRUCTION HEALTH AND SAFETY GROUP,** *q.v.*

1695 LONDON GRADUATE SCHOOL OF BUSINESS STUDIES
Sussex Place, Regents Park, London NW1 4SA Tel. 01-262 5050
Telex 27461

Academic Institution; affiliated to London University

Enquiries to the Librarian

Subject coverage
management and business, including management education, marketing, production, finance and accounting, personnel and industrial relations, economics, industries, organisational behaviour, business law, management science, operational research and statistics, computers and data processing

Special collection
Corporate Library: company information including annual reports of about 2,500 British, European and American companies; Extel and McCarthy cards, etc.

Publications
London Business School Journal
London Classification of Business Studies
Periodicals in the Library of LBS (annual)
Sources of Information (short bibliographical guides)
Contents of Current Journals

1696 LONDON HEMP ASSOCIATION
c/o Wigglesworth and Company Limited, 30–34 Mincing Lane, London EC3 — Tel. 01-626 6471
Trade Association

Enquiries to the Secretary

Subject coverage
Indian hemp trade

1697 LONDON JUTE ASSOCIATION
London Chamber of Commerce and Industry, 69 Cannon Street, London EC4N 5AB — Tel. 01-248 4444, Telex 888941
Trade Association

Enquiries to the Secretary

Subject coverage
trade in raw jute

1698 LONDON MASTER PLASTERERS ASSOCIATION
82 New Cavendish Street, London W1M 8AD — Tel. 01-580 4041
Trade Association; member of the National Federation of Building Trades Employers

Enquiries to the Secretary

Subject coverage
plaster and plastering in building

LONDON MATHEMATICAL SOCIETY *see* **ROYAL ASTRONOMICAL SOCIETY**

1699 LONDON NATURAL HISTORY SOCIETY
142 Harborough Road, Streatham, London SW16 2XW
Voluntary Society; its Library is housed at Imperial College, Kensington, London

Enquiries to the Secretary

Subject coverage
natural history to scientific level; research, statistics, identification and classification of species; observation and conservation; botany; ecology; geology; ornithology

Publications
London Naturalist (annual)
London Bird Report (annual)
Newsletters (to members)

LONDON PRESS EXCHANGE LIMITED *now* **FORMAN HOUSE PUBLIC RELATIONS LIMITED,** *q.v.*

LONDON PRINTING INDUSTRIES ASSOCIATION *see* **BRITISH PRINTING INDUSTRIES FEDERATION**

LONDON SCHOOL OF ECONOMICS LIBRARY *see* **BRITISH LIBRARY OF POLITICAL AND ECONOMIC SCIENCE**

1700 LONDON SCHOOL OF HYGIENE AND TROPICAL MEDICINE
Keppel Street, London WC1E 7HT Tel. 01-636 8636
Postgraduate Medical School, of the University of London; houses the Bureau of Hygiene and Tropical Diseases, the Public Health Laboratory Service Mycological Reference Laboratory, the MRC Arbovirus Unit, the Environmental Physiology Research Unit and Organization of Medical Care Unit; incorporates the Ross Institute of Tropical Hygiene, *q.v.* and the TUC Centenary Institute of Occupational Health, *q.v.*

Enquiries to the Dean, the Head of Department or the Librarian

Subject coverage
community and occupational health; industrial hygiene and toxicology; epidemiology; medical statistics; tropical medicine and public health, human genetics; human nutrition; environmental physiology; medical microbiology, parasitology, entomology and mycology

Special collections
Reece Collection (on vaccination against smallpox)
Ross Archives (Sir Ronald Ross papers on the transmission of malaria)
Manson Collection (documents, etc., of Sir Patrick Manson, founder of the School)
Brownlee Collection (books from 16th century onwards, on epidemiology)

Publications
Annual Report
Journal of Helminthology (quarterly)
Memoir Series (occasional)
Ross Institute Information Bulletins (occasional)

1701 LONDON SISAL ASSOCIATION
London Chamber of Commerce and Industry, 69 Cannon Street, London EC4N 5AB Tel. 01-248 4444
Telex 888941

Trade Association

Enquiries to the Secretary

Subject coverage
sisal trade

1702 LONDON SMALL FIRMS INFORMATION CENTRE
65 Buckingham Palace Road, London SW1W 0QX Tel. 01-828 2384
Telex 917920

Government Information Centre of the Department of Industry

Enquiries to the Manager

Subject coverage
business studies and problems

Publications
Pamphlets on financial and business subjects

LONDON TOPOGRAPHICAL SOCIETY *see* **BISHOPSGATE INSTITUTE LIBRARY**

1703 LONDON TRANSPORT EXECUTIVE
55 Broadway, London SW1H 0BD Tel. 01-222 5600
Statutory Public Authority; responsibility for finance and policy with the Greater London Council; formerly London Transport Board

Enquiries to the Public Relations Officer

Subject coverage
public passenger transport; supporting engineering and administration

Special collection
London Transport Collection (vehicles, etc.)

Publications
Annual Report
LT News (internal circulation)
Guide books, etc.
Books on transport

1704 LONDON TRANSPORT PASSENGERS COMMITTEE
Room 33, 26 Old Queen Street, London SW1H 9HP Tel. 01-930 8019
Independent Consultative Committee, appointed by Greater London Council

Enquiries to the Secretary

Subject coverage
suggestions and complaints about London transport services; matters affecting services and facilities; (problems arising should first be submitted to the appropriate authority such as the London Transport Executive, the Greater London Council, etc.)

Publications
Annual Report
Information Leaflet

1705 LONDON UNIVERSITY
Department of Photogrammetry and Surveying, University College, Gower Street, London WC1E 6BT Tel. 01-387 7050
University Department, housing also the Library of the Photogrammetric Society

Enquiries to the Librarian or the Head of the Department

Subject coverage
photogrammetry, particularly non-topographic applications, plotting instrument design and aerial triangulation; land surveying; survey computations and statistics

Publications
Photogrammetric Record (2 per annum)
Survey Review (quarterly)
Directory of Research and Development Activities in the United Kingdom in the Fields of Land Survey, Geodesy, Photogrammetry and Hydrographic Surveying

1706 LONDON UNIVERSITY
School of Pharmacy, Library, 29–39 Brunswick Square, London WC1N 1AX Tel. 01-837 7651
University Department Library

Enquiries to the Librarian

Subject coverage
pharmaceutics; pharmaceutical chemistry; pharmaceutical engineering science; pharmacognosy; pharmacology; rheology; organic chemistry; analytical chemistry; biology; microbiology; biochemistry

Publications
Library Guide, with notes for preparing dissertations
Library Bulletin (quarterly)

1707 LONDON UNIVERSITY OBSERVATORY
Department of Physics and Astronomy, University College, 553 Watford Way, London NW7 Tel. 01-959 1618
University Department

Enquiries, from researchers or teachers only, to the Librarian

Subject coverage
astronomy and astrophysics

Publications
University of London Observatory Communications

LONDON UNIVERSITY *see also*
BEDFORD COLLEGE
BRITISH LIBRARY OF POLITICAL AND ECONOMIC SCIENCE (LONDON SCHOOL OF ECONOMICS)
CENTRE FOR EUROPEAN AGRICULTURAL STUDIES
CHELSEA COLLEGE
INDUSTRIAL TRAINING RESEARCH UNIT
INSTITUTE OF OPHTHALMOLOGY
KINGS COLLEGE
LONDON GRADUATE SCHOOL OF BUSINESS STUDIES
LONDON SCHOOL OF HYGIENE AND TROPICAL MEDICINE
LONDON UNIVERSITY OBSERVATORY
LYON PLAYFAIR LIBRARY (IMPERIAL COLLEGE)
QUEEN ELIZABETH COLLEGE
QUEEN MARY COLLEGE
ROYAL SCHOOL OF MINES
UNIVERSITY COLLEGE
WESTFIELD COLLEGE
WYE COLLEGE

1708 D.F. LONG & COMPANY (TRANSLATIONS) LIMITED
68 Newington Causeway, London SE1 6DQ — Tel. 01-407 3385, Telex 888123

Company

Enquiries to the Managing Director

Subject coverage
technical translation (engineering)

1709 LONG ASHTON RESEARCH STATION
Long Ashton, Bristol BS18 9AF — Tel. 027-580 2181
State-aided Research Institute, of the Agricultural Research Council, within the University of Bristol Department of Agriculture and Horticulture; houses the National Fruit and Cider Institute

Enquiries to the Librarian

Subject coverage
fruit culture; plant nutrition, physiology and pathology; ecology of pests and beneficial insects, etc.; spray application; microclimatology of orchards; technology of cider and fruit juices; home preservation and storage of foods

Special collection
antiquarian books on cider and horticulture

Publications
Annual Report
Occasional publications

1710 LORD RANK RESEARCH CENTRE
RHM Research Limited, Lincoln Road, High Wycombe, Buckinghamshire HP1Z 3QR — Tel. 0494 26191, Telex 837445
Company, part of Ranks Hovis McDougall Limited

Enquiries to the Information Officer

Subject coverage
food science and technology; crop science; cereal chemistry; electron microscopy; microbial biochemistry; food analysis and microbiology; protein chemistry; process engineering

1711 LOUGHBOROUGH CONSULTANTS LIMITED
University of Technology, Loughborough, Leicestershire LE11 3TU — Tel. 0509 30426, Telex 34319

Company/Consultancy, wholly owned by Loughborough University

Enquiries to the Managing Director or the Business Manager

Subject coverage
chemical engineering; chemistry; civil engineering; computer studies; economics; electrical and electronic engineering and design; engineering mathematics, production, and design; management; materials technology; mechanical engineering; physics; polymer technology; transport technology

LOUGHBOROUGH LIBRARY *see* **LEICESTERSHIRE LIBRARIES AND INFORMATION SERVICE**

1712 LOUGHBOROUGH RECREATION PLANNING CONSULTANTS LIMITED
1 The Coneries, Loughborough, Leicestershire

Company/Consultants

Enquiries to the Planning Services Manager

Subject coverage
sports centres; leisure centres; golf and country clubs; squash courts; swimming pools; parks; feasibility studies; financial studies; construction supervision; management; materials testing; marketing in recreation

1713 LOUGHBOROUGH UNIVERSITY OF TECHNOLOGY LIBRARY
Radmoor, Ashby Road, Loughborough, Leicestershire LE11 3TU Tel. 050-93 63171
Telex 34319

University Library; the University also houses the Particle Science and Technology Information Service, *q.v.* in the Department of Chemical Engineering

Enquiries to the Librarian

Subject coverage
chemical engineering; chemistry; civil engineering; computer studies; economics; electrical and electronic engineering; engineering mathematics and production engineering; human biology and ergonomics; management; materials technilogy; mathematics; mechanical engineering; physics; polymer engineering; transport technology

Publications
Research Reports on library automation projects

LOUGHBOROUGH UNIVERSITY OF TECHNOLOGY *see also*
INSTITUTE OF POLYMER TECHNOLOGY
LOUGHBOROUGH CONSULTANTS LIMITED
PARTICLE SCIENCE AND TECHNOLOGY INFORMATION SERVICE

LOUTH DIVISIONAL LIBRARY *see* **LINCOLNSHIRE LIBRARY SERVICE**

LOWESTOFT AREA LIBRARY *see* **SUFFOLK COUNTY LIBRARY**

LUDLOW DISTRICT LIBRARY *see* **SHROPSHIRE COUNTY LIBRARY**

LUTIS *see* **LUTON INFORMATION SERVICE**

1714 LUTON COLLEGE OF HIGHER EDUCATION
Park Square, Luton, Bedfordshire LU1 3JU Tel. 0582 34111
Telex 825995

College of Higher Education, formerly Luton College of Technology; now includes Putteridge Bury College of Education

Enquiries to the Librarian

Subject coverage
business studies, including management, industrial relations, personnel management, secretarial work; mechanical, automotive, electronic and electrical engineering; industrial design, metallurgy; mathematics and computing; geology; geography, biology, biochemistry; mineralogy; physics, building, including wood treatment and construction; painting and decorating

1715 LUTON DISTRICT LIBRARY
Bridge Street, Luton, Bedfordshire LU1 2NG — Tel. 0582 30161, Telex 82347

Public Library; formerly Luton Public Library; part of Bedfordshire County Library, *q.v.*

Enquiries to the District Librarian

Subject coverage
general; specialization in automobile engineering and automotive industries in general; internal combustion engines; commercial information

1716 LUTON INFORMATION SERVICE (LUTIS)
Central Reference Library, Bridge Street, Luton LU1 2NG — Tel. 0582 30161 ext. 389, Telex 82347

Interlibrary Cooperative Scheme

Enquiries to the Assistant Librarian

Subject coverage
general, technical, commercial; use of commercial reference material (courses)

Publications
LUTIS Newsletter and Commercial Bulletin
Publicity Material
Occasional papers for local Chamber of Commerce Monthly Journal
Bibliographies for Chamber of Commerce International Trade Group

1717 LUTON SMALL FIRMS INFORMATION CENTRE
35 Wellington Street, Luton, Bedfordshire LU1 2SB — Tel. 0582 29215, Telex 826115

Government Information Centre of the Department of Industry

Enquiries to the Manager

Subject coverage
business studies and problems

Publications
Pamphlets on financial and business subjects

LYMINGTON LIBRARY *see* **HAMPSHIRE COUNTY LIBRARY**

1718 LYON PLAYFAIR LIBRARY
Imperial College of Science and Technology, South Kensington, London SW7 2AZ — Tel. 01-589 5111 ext. 2100, Telex 261503

University Library, of London University; includes sixteen departmental libraries; houses the Libraries of the London Natural History Society, the Operational Research Society and the Tensor Society of Great Britain, *qq.v.*

Enquiries to the Librarian

Subject coverage
aeronautics; chemical engineering and chemical technology; chemistry; civil enginering; computer and control engineering; electrical engineering; geology; history ot science; life sciences (including biochemistry, botany and plant technology, zoology, applied entomology); management; mathematics; mechanical engineering; metallurgy and materials science; mining and mineral technology; physics

Special collections
Annan Collection (history of metals, mining and metallurgy)
Computing and Control Collection (formerly the Library of the Institution of Computer Sciences)

Publications
Union List of Periodical and Serial Holdings for Imperial College
Series of Guides to Bibliographic Aids and Information Sources
KWIC Indexes to Review Publications and to Abstracting and Indexing Publications

1719 J. LYONS & COMPANY LIMITED
Group Information Service, 149 Hammersmith Road, London W14 0QU — Tel. 01-603 2040
Company

Enquiries, selected, to Manager or Information Departments

Subject coverage
production and marketing of food products

Publications
Current Awareness Bulletins (internal circulation only)

LYTHAM ST ANNES CENTRAL LIBRARY *now* **FYLDE DISTRICT CENTRAL LIBRARY** *see* **LANCASHIRE LIBRARY**

1720 3M UNITED KINGDOM LIMITED
3M House, Wigmore Street, London W1 — Tel. 01-486 5522
Telex 28155
Company, part of Minnesota Mining and Manufacturing Company, St. Paul, Minnesota, U.S.A.

Enquiries to the Chief Librarian, 3M Library and Information Services

Subject coverage
Manufacture and marketing of adhesive tape, sound recording and instrumentation tapes, medical products, coated abrasives, adhesives, copying and microfilm products, reflective, printing & photographic products, electrical products, fluorchemicals, reinforced plastics, nuclear products and all-weather surfacing

1721 MABEL FLETCHER TECHNICAL COLLEGE
Sandown Road, Liverpool L15 4JB — Tel. 051-733 7211
College of Further Education

Enquiries to the Librarian

Subject coverage
health studies, including occupational health; clothing and textiles

1722 MACALISTER CARVALL LIMITED
9–11 Stem Lane Industrial Estate, New Milton, Hampshire — Tel. 0425 617333
Company; Member of the Carvall Group

Enquiries to the Company

Subject coverage
ferrocement; fishing boats; amateur yachts

1723 MACAULAY INSTITUTE FOR SOIL RESEARCH
Craigiebuckler, Aberdeen AB9 2QJ — Tel. 0224 38611
State-aided Institute of the Agricultural Research Council; grant administered by Department of Agriculture and Fisheries for Scotland

Enquiries to the Librarian

Subject coverage
soil; its physical chemistry, organic chemistry, microbiology, fertility; mineralogy; spectrochemical techniques of soil analysis; plant physiology; peat and forest soils; soil survey and cartography; statistical techniques in soil research

Publications
Annual Report
Collected Papers
Soil Survey of Scotland (HMSO, Edinburgh; in continuation) consists of monographs and soil maps

1724 McCARTHY INFORMATION LIMITED
Manor House, Ash Walk, Warminster, Wiltshire BA12 8PY Tel. 098-52 5151
Company

Enquiries to the Marketing Manager or Managing Director

Subject coverage
company and industrial information

Special collections
five-year files of newspaper articles on companies and industries

1725 MACCLESFIELD LIBRARY
Park Lane, Macclesfield, Cheshire Tel. Macclesfield 22512
Public Library, part of the Cheshire County Library, *q.v.*

Enquiries to the Librarian

Subject coverage
clothing and clothing trades

1726 MACDATA (MATERIALS AND COMPONENTS DEVELOPMENT AND TESTING ASSOCIATION)
47 High Street, Paisley PA1 2BE Tel. 041-887 5737 & 1241
Telex 778951

Consultancy Unit, of Paisley College of Technology, *q.v.*

Enquiries to the Director

Subject coverage
construction; mechanical engineering; metallurgy; management; chemistry; computing

Publication
descriptive brochure

1727 MACHINE MADE CHAIN MANUFACTURERS ASSOCIATION
168 Lower High Street, Stourbridge, West Midlands DY8 1TL Tel. 03843 5684
Trade Association

Enquiries to the Secretary

Subject coverage
British and International Standards and general information relating to machine-made (electric-welded) chain

1728 MACHINE TOOL INDUSTRY RESEARCH ASSOCIATION
Hulley Road, Hurdsfield, Macclesfield, Cheshire SK10 2NE Tel. 0625 25421
Research Association

Enquiries to the Information Officer

Subject coverage
machine tool design, manufacture, testing and use, including foundations, structures, bearings, slideways, etc.; machine noise measurement and reduction; control systems, computer-aided design; manufacturing procedures; marketing and supplier information; production engineering generally

Publications
Machine Tool Research (quarterly, to Members only)
Library Bulletin (monthly, compilation of production engineering titles, chargeable to non-members)

1729 MACHINE TOOL TRADES ASSOCIATION
62 Bayswater Road, London W2 3PH Tel. 01-402 6671
Telex 27829

Trade Association

Enquiries, general, to the Head of Information Services; technical to the Head of Trade Promotion

Subject coverage

exhibitions overseas; trade missions to and from U.K.; tariffs; manufacture under licence; export credit facilities; agencies; statistics; manpower resources and training; standardization of components; health and safety; environmental problems; standards; press and public relations; advertising

Publications

British Machine Tools and Equipment
Imported Machine Tools and Equipment
Electrical Equipment of Machine Tools
Standards and booklets
Publications List

1730 MACHINERY PUBLISHING COMPANY LIMITED

New England House, New England Street, Brighton BN1 4HN — Tel. 0273 61334
Publishing Company

Enquiries, from journal subscribers only, to Machinery's Enquiry Bureau, 17a Queens Road, Southend-on-Sea SS1 1LT

Subject coverage

mechanical and production engineering; machine tools

Publications

Machinery and Production Engineering (weekly)
Machinery's Annual Buyers Guide

1731 MADE-UP TEXTILES ASSOCIATION LIMITED

Kandahar House, 71 Meadowside, Dundee DD1 1EE — Tel. 0382 25881
Trade Association; formerly Canvas Goods and Made-up Textiles Association Limited

Enquiries to the Secretary

Subject coverage

the making-up industry of heavy industrial textiles into marquees, tarpaulins, covers, sails, tents, etc.

Publication

Members Trade Directory

1732 MAGEE UNIVERSITY COLLEGE

Northland Road, Londonderry, Northern Ireland BT48 7JL — Tel. 0504 65621
University College, of the Ulster New University, *q.v.*

Enquiries to the Librarian

Subject coverage

public administration (most subjects relate to volume 2 of the Directory)

1733 MAGNESITE AND CHROME BRICKMAKERS ASSOCIATION

301 Glossop Road, Sheffield S10 2HN — Tel. 0742 21071
Telex 54170

Trade Association

Enquiries to the Secretaries

Subject coverage

refractory bricks for the lining of industrial furnaces

1734 MAGNESIUM ELEKTRON LIMITED

P.O. Box 6, Lumns Lane, Clifton Junction, Swinton, Manchester M27 2LS — Tel. 061-794 2511
Telex 667817

Company, associated with British Aluminium Company Limited and Tube Investments Limited

Enquiries to the Librarian

Subject coverage

magnesium alloy technology; inorganic zirconium chemicals

1735 MAIDENHEAD CENTRAL LIBRARY
St Ives Road, Maidenhead, Berkshire SL6 1QU Tel. 0628 25657
Telex 849 319
Public Library; District Library of Berkshire County Library Service, and as such Central Library of the Royal Borough of Windsor and Maidenhead; houses the local Tourist Information Centre

Enquiries to the District Librarian

Subject coverage
general

MAIDSTONE DIVISIONAL LIBRARY *see* **KENT COUNTY LIBRARY**

MALARIA REFERENCE LABORATORY *see* **ROSS INSTITUE OF TROPICAL MEDICINE**

1736 MALAYSIAN RUBBER PRODUCERS RESEARCH ASSOCIATION
Brickendonbury, Hertford SG13 8NP Tel. 32 54966
Development Association; formerly the Natural Rubber Producers Research Association

Enquiries to the Librarian

Subject coverage
rubber, especially natural rubber, (free technological and engineering consultancy services for natural rubber)

Publications
Thesaurus of Rubber Technology
MRPRA Publications 1938–1974: an author bibliography
NR Technology (quarterly, free, includes abstracts of new publications)

1737 MALTA HIGH COMMISSION
24 Haymarket, London SW1 4DJ Tel. 01-930 9851
Telex 261102
Malta Government Department; houses also the Malta Government Tourist Office, and Air Malta Company Limited

Enquiries to the Information Attaché

Subject coverage
Malta trade and tourism

Publications
Literature about Malta in general

1738 MAMMAL SOCIETY
Harvest House, 62 London Road, Reading RG1 5AS
Learned Society

Enquiries, by letter, to the Assistant Secretary

Subject coverage
biology of British mammals, their distribution and status; Specialist Groups of the Society deal with particular activities and groups of animals, including the Bat Group, the Carnivore Group, the Otter Survey; the Harvest Mouse Survey, etc.

Publications
Mammal Review (quarterly)
Notes from the Mammal Society (twice per annum)
Newsletter (quarterly)

1739 MANAGEMENT CENTRE
University of Bradford, Heaton Mount, Keighley Road, Bradford, West Yorkshire BD9 4JU Tel. 0274 42299
University Unit; for Management Development Programmes, formerly Post Experience Programmes

Enquiries to the Director

Subject coverage
general management; business policy; corporate strategy; marketing; personnel and organization development; contract and construction management; finance and accounting

Publication
Manual of Readings

1740 MANAGEMENT CONSULTANTS ASSOCIATION
23–24 Cromwell Place, London SW7 2LG Tel. 01-584 7283
Trade Association

Enquiries to the Executive Director

Subject coverage
management consulting; selection of firms; codes of practice; statistics; exports

Publications
Annual Report
Various brochures

1741 MANCHESTER BUSINESS SCHOOL
Booth Street West, Manchester M15 6PB Tel. 061-273 8228
Telex 668354

Business School, of the University of Manchester

Enquiries to the Librarian

Subject coverage
management; marketing; finance; personnel management; sociology; economics; operational research; computers; statistics

Publications
Working Papers
Register of Research
Contents Pages in management
Research Reports

1742 MANCHESTER CHAMBER OF COMMERCE AND INDUSTRY
Ship Canal House, P.O. Box 559, King Street, Manchester M60 8AH Tel. 061-832 5574
Telex 667822
Chamber of Commerce and Industry; the Chamber of Commerce Testing House is at Barlow Moor Road, Didsbury, Manchester

Enquiries to the Trade Enquiries Department

Subject coverage
sources of supply of goods and services, particularly those of the area; addresses, trade marks, trade fairs, customs duties in all countries of the world; import and export controls; exchange regulations; shipping documentary requirements

Special collection
Chamber Archives from 1820

Publications
Manchester Chamber of Commerce and Industry Record (bi-monthly)
Manchester Chamber of Commerce and Industry Year Book Directory of Members
Manchester Chamber of Commerce and Industry Monthly Bulletin

1743 MANCHESTER COLLEGE OF BUILDING
Lower Hardman Street, Manchester M3 3ER Tel. 061-834 2285
Specialist College

Enquiries to the Librarian

Subject coverage
construction industry

1744 MANCHESTER COMMERCIAL LIBRARY
Central Library, St Peters Square, Manchester M2 5PD — Tel. 061-236 9422
Public Library

Enquiries to the Commercial Librarian

Subject coverage
commercial information

Publication
Brief Guides to Business Sources

1745 MANCHESTER SCIENTIFIC AND TECHNICAL LIBRARY AND INFORMATION SERVICE
Central Library, St. Peters Square, Manchester M2 5PD — Tel. 061-236 9422
Public Library

Enquiries to the Information Officer

Subject coverage
all fields of science, technology and medicine

Special collections
Patents Depository collection, (British, U.S., Irish and Australian); Atomic Energy Depository, (British, U.S., and European)

1746 MANCHESTER TECHNICAL INFORMATION SERVICE (MANTIS)
Central Library, St. Peters Square, Manchester M2 5PD — Tel. 061-236 9422
Telex 667149/669475

Interlibrary cooperative scheme

Enquiries to the Librarian, Scientific and Technical Library

Subject coverage
technical and commercial

Special collection
British Patent Specifications

Publications
Bibliographies and Reading Lists

1747 MANCHESTER POLYTECHNIC LIBRARY
All Saints, Manchester M15 6BX — Tel. 061-228 2351
Telex 667915

Polytechnic; created by the merger of the John Dalton College of Technology and the Manchester College of Commerce; houses the John Dalton Library

Enquiries to the Librarian

Subject coverage
general science and technology

Special collection
Manchester Society of Architects Library

1748 MANCHESTER SHIP CANAL COMPANY
Ship Canal House, King Street, Manchester M2 4WX — Tel. 061-872 2411
Telex 669025

Company, member of the British Ports Association, *q.v.*

Enquiries to the Public Relations Officer

Subject coverage
the port of Manchester

Publications
Notes on the Port of Manchester
Resolution and Achievement
Various booklets, plans, maps, and a film

1749 MANCHESTER SMALL FIRMS INFORMATION CENTRE
Peter House, Oxford Street, Manchester M1 5AN — Tel. 061-832 5282, Telex 667952

Government Information Centre of the Department of Industry

Enquiries to the Manager

Subject coverage
business studies and problems

Publications
Pamphlets on financial and business subjects

MANCHESTER UNIVERSITY LIBRARY *now* **JOHN RYLANDS UNIVERSITY LIBRARY OF MANCHESTER,** *q.v.*

MANCHESTER UNIVERSITY *see also*
CONTROL SYSTEMS CENTRE
INSTITUTE OF SCIENCE AND TECHNOLOGY (UMIST)
MANCHESTER BUSINESS SCHOOL
NUFFIELD RADIO ASTRONOMY LABORATORIES

1750 MANDER COLLEGE
Cauldwell Street, Bedford MK42 9AH — Tel. 0234 45151
College of Further Education; will be involved in a merger with Bedford College of Education and Bedford College of Physical Education to form the Bedford College of Higher Education

Enquiries to the Tutor-Librarian

Subject coverage
agriculture; horticulture; biology; construction; engineering, electrical, mechanical, and production; home economics; management; mathematics; office practice

Special collection
British Standards

1751 MANDOVAL LIMITED
Index House, St. Georges Lane, Ascot, Berkshire SL5 7EU — Tel. 0990 25011, Telex 848819
Company, subsidiary of RTZ Services Limited; also houses the Vermiculite Information Service

Enquiries to the Marketing Manager

Subject coverage
crude vermiculite ore; exfoliated vermiculite; vermiculite fire protective products; vermiculite sound absorption and anti-condensation treatments

Publications
Vermiculite Handbook
Carcinogenic Screening of Vermiculite
Brochures on products

1752 MAN-MADE FIBRES PRODUCERS COMMITTEE
41/42 Dover Street, London W1X 4DS — Tel. 01-493 7446
Trade Association; linked with British Man-Made Fibres Federation, *q.v.*

Enquiries to the British Man-Made Fibre Federation

Subject coverage
statistics of the industry; sources of supply

1753 MAN-MADE FIBRES PRODUCING INDUSTRY TRAINING BOARD
3 Pond Place, London SW3 6QR — Tel. 01-589 9008/9
Industrial Training Board, of the Training Services Agency

Enquiries to the Administration Officer or the Training Adviser

Subject coverage
training within the man-made fibres industry

Publications
Annual Report
Training Recommendations

1754 MANPOWER LIMITED
National Westminster House, The Grove, Slough, Berkshire Tel. 97 38911
Work Contractor

Enquiries to the Librarian

Subject coverage
contract work of every kind: facts, research, exclusive surveys, with special reference to efficiency/productivity and to contract cleaning; stocktaking; design draughting; plant installation; relocation; maintenance

Publications
Manpower Management Journal (quarterly)
Manpower Research Council (quarterly)

MANPOWER SERVICES COMMISSION *see*
PROFESSIONAL AND EXECUTIVE RECRUITMENT
TRAINING SERVICES AGENCY

1755 MANPOWER SOCIETY
c/o The Secretary, Shell (U.K.) Oil, P.O. Box 148, Strand, London WC2R 0DX Tel. 01-438 2609
Registered Charity; sponsored by the Institute of Personnel Management and the Operational Research Society, *qq.v.*

Enquiries to the Secretary

Subject coverage
manpower planning, particularly at company level

Publications
Newsletter (monthly, to members only)
Manpower Society Reports

MANSFIELD CENTRAL LIBRARY *see* **NOTTINGHAMSHIRE COUNTY LIBRARY**

MANTIS *see* **MANCHESTER TECHNICAL INFORMATION SERVICE**

MARBLE AND GRANITE ASSOCIATION *now* **FEDERATION OF STONE INDUSTRIES** *q.v.*

MARCH DISTRICT LIBRARY *see* **CAMBRIDGESHIRE LIBRARIES**

1756 MARCHWOOD ENGINEERING LABORATORIES
Central Electricity Generating Board, Marchwood, Southampton SO4 4ZB Tel. 042-16 5711 Telex 47338
Research Division of Nationalized Industry

Enquiries to the Librarian

Subject coverage
generation and transmission of electricity; electrical, mechanical, nuclear engineering; welding

1757 MARCONI ELLIOTT AVIONIC SYSTEMS LIMITED
Elstree Way, Borehamwood, Hertfordshire WD6 1RX Tel. 01-953 2030 Telex 22777

Company, part of the General Electric Company

Enquiries to the Technical Reference Officer (ext. 3733)

Subject coverage
civil and military avionics; laser technology; security systems; neutron technology; mobile radar

1758 MARCONI ELLIOTT AVIONIC SYSTEMS LIMITED
Technical Library and Information Services, Airport Works, Rochester, Kent ME1 2XX — Tel. 0634 44400 ext. 48 *and* 369
Company, formerly Elliott Flight Automation

Enquiries to the Chief Librarian

Subject coverage
aviation electronics (avionics)

1759 MARCONI INSTRUMENTS LIMITED
Longacres, St. Albans, Hertfordshire AL4 0JN — Tel. 0727 59292
Telex 23350

Company, part of GEC-Marconi Electronics Group

Enquiries to the Librarian

Subject coverage
electronic instrumentation and measurements; telecommunications

1760 MARCONI RADAR SYSTEMS LIMITED
New Parks, Leicester LE3 1WF — Tel. 0533 871331
Telex 34551
Company; part of G.E.C. Limited; formerly Associated Electrical Industries Limited (Electronics Group)

Enquiries to the Librarian

Subject coverage
atmospherics; oceanic sciences; electrical and mechanical engineering; electronics; aerospace, automatic control; industrial safety

MARCONI RESEARCH LABORATORIES LIMITED *see* **GEC–MARCONI ELECTRONICS**

1761 MARCONI SPACE & DEFENCE SYSTEMS LIMITED
The Grove, Warren Lane, Stanmore, Middlesex HA7 4LY — Tel. 01-954 2311
Telex 22616

Research Establishment of the General Electric Company

Enquiries to the Librarian

Subject coverage
electronics, aerospace engineering and technology

MARGARINE AND SHORTENING MANUFACTURERS ASSOCIATION *see* **FOOD MANUFACTURERS FEDERATION INCORPORATED**

MARGATE CENTRAL LIBRARY *now* **THANET DIVISIONAL LIBRARY** *see* **KENT COUNTY LIBRARY**

1762 MARINE BIOLOGICAL ASSOCIATION OF THE UNITED KINGDOM
The Laboratory, Citadel Hill, Plymouth, Devonshire PL1 2PB — Tel. 0752 21761
Research Laboratory, grant-aided, of the Natural Environment Research Council; housing the Marine Pollution Information Centre, *q.v.* and the Aquatic Sciences and Fisheries Information System (ASFIS), *q.v.*; the Association is responsible for the U.K. input to ASFIS

Enquiries to the Librarian

Subject coverage
marine and estuarine biology; oceanography; fisheries; marine and estuarine pollution

Publications
Journal of the Marine Biological Association of the U.K. (quarterly)
Marine Pollution Research Titles (monthly)
Bibliographies

MARINE ENGINE AND EQUIPMENT MANUFACTURERS ASSOCIATION *see* **SHIP AND BOAT BUILDERS NATIONAL FEDERATION**

1763 MARINE EXPLORATION LIMITED

Marex House, High Street, Cowes, Isle of Wight — Tel. 098-382 4731
Telex 86262

Company

Enquiries: state nature of enquiry to telephone operator

Subject coverage

oceanography; instrumentation; data processing and analysis; Arctic studies

1764 MARINE INDUSTRIES CENTRE

Newcastle-upon-Tyne University, 24 Claremont Place, Newcastle-upon-Tyne NE2 4AA — Tel. 0632 610757

Company, supported by the University of Newcastle upon Tyne

Enquiries to the Director

Subject coverage

marine industry; automation and control system design; ship and machinery performance analysis under dynamic conditions; propeller testing; digital computer applications for marine systems; instrumentation; equipment and techniques; marine/mechanical/electrical engineering consultancy

1765 MARINE LABORATORY

P.O. Box 101, Victoria Road, Torry, Aberdeen AB9 8DB — Tel. 0224 29944
Telex 73587

Government Research Laboratory, of the Department of Agriculture and Fisheries for Scotland

Enquiries to the Librarian

Subject coverage

marine biology; oceanography; fisheries; fishing methods and gear

Special collection

Ogilvie Collection on Diatomaceae

Publications

Fisheries of Scotland Report
Marine Research Series
Scottish Fisheries Bulletin
Scottish Fisheries Research Reports
Scottish Sea Fisheries Statistical Tables
Shellfish Pamphlets

1766 MARINE POLLUTION INFORMATION CENTRE

Marine Biological Association of the United Kingdom, Citadel Hill, Plymouth, Devonshire PL1 2PB — Tel. 0752 21761

Information Centre, sponsored by the Natural Environment Research Council

Enquires to the Librarian

Subject coverage

marine and estuarine pollution; detection, analysis, and removal of pollutants; levels of pollutants in seawater, sediments and organisms; biological effects of pollutants

Publications

Marine Pollution Research Titles (monthly)
Bibliography on Marine and Estuarine Pollution 1971 and Supplement 1975
Bibliography on Marine and Estuarine Pesticide Pollution 1976

MARINE SCIENCE LABORATORIES *see* **UNIVERSITY COLLEGE OF NORTH WALES, Bangor**

1767 MARINE SOCIETY

Mansbridge House, 207 Balham High Road, London SW17 7BH — Tel. 01-673 8866

Voluntary Society; includes the Seafarers Education Service and College of the Sea

Enquiries to the Secretary

Subject coverage

Merchant Navy; Ship adoption

Special collection

Merchant Navy Collection

Publications

The Seafarer (quarterly)
Occasional books, pamphlets and wall charts

1768 MARINE TECHNOLOGY SUPPORT UNIT

Atomic Energy Research Establishment, Harwell, Didcot, — Tel. 0235 24141
Oxfordshire OX11 0RA — Telex 83135

Government Advisory and Executive Support Unit, of the United Kingdom Atomic Energy Authority, for the Departments of Energy and Industry

Enquiries to the Head of the Unit

Subject coverage

research and development in marine and offshore technology; exploitation of the continental shelf; underwater engineering; submersibles; structural materials: diving; underwater inspection and testing, ship operation

MARINE TRADES ASSOCIATION *see* **SHIP AND BOAT BUILDERS NATIONAL FEDERATION**

1769 MARITIME TRANSPORT RESEARCH

21 Grosvenor Place, London SW1X 7JE — Tel. 01-235 5131
Telex 22797

Research Unit, part of the Shipbuilders and Repairers National Association; formerly British Shipbuilding Exports

Enquiries to the Information Officer

Subject coverage

research into future demand for ships

Publications

Research Projects
List of publications available

1770 MARKET RESEARCH SOCIETY

51 Charles Street, London W1X 7PA — Tel. 01-499 1913

Professional Society

Enquiries to the Secretary

Subject coverage

market research

Publications

MRS Newsletter (monthly)
Journal of the Market Research Society (quarterly)
Market Research Abstracts (2 issues per annum)
Market Research Society Yearbook
International Directory of Market Research Organisations
Directory of Syndicated Services, vol. 1, Europe

1771 MARKETING CONSULTANCY SERVICES LIMITED

Churchill House, 87 Jesmond Road, Newcastle upon Tyne NE2 1NH — Tel. 0632 812257

Company

Enquiries to the Managing Director or the Planning Director

Subject coverage
consumer trade and industrial market research throughout the United Kingdom; desk research and specialised list building and mailing

1772 MARLEY LIMITED
London Road, Riverhead, Sevenoaks, Kent — Tel. 0732 55255
Company

Enquiries to the Press, P.R. and Publications Officer

Subject coverage
roof tiles; contract and domestic floor coverings; D.I.Y. products

Publications
Marley News
Tile Talk

MARLIB INFORMATION SERVICE *see* **INSTITUTE OF MARINE ENGINEERS**

MARSHALL LIBRARY OF ECONOMICS *see* **CAMBRIDGE UNIVERSITY, Marshall Library of Economics**

1773 MARTONAIR LIMITED
128 St Margarets Road, Twickenham, Middlesex TW1 1RJ — Tel. 01-892 4411
Company

Enquiries to the Information Officer

Subject coverage
pneumatic control systems and associated equipment

Publication
Journal of Applied Pneumatics (2 or 3 times per annum, free)

1774 MASIUS, WYNNE-WILLIAMS AND D'ARCY-MacMANUS
2 St James's Square, London SW1Y 4JY — Tel. 01-839 3422, Telex 21915

Company; formerly Masius Wynne-Williams

Enquiries to the Information Officer

Subject coverage
advertising; marketing

1775 MASS SPECTROMETRY DATA CENTRE
Building A8 1A, PE(MOD), Atomic Weapons Research Establishment, Reading, Berkshire RG7 4PR — Tel. 07356 4111, Telex 848104/5
Government Department, of the Department of Industry

Enquiries to the Manager or Information Officer

Subject coverage
mass spectrometry

Special collection
17000 full mass spectra on magnetic tape
31000 abbreviated mass spectra on magnetic tape
39000 full spectra available to on-line search systems

Publication
Mass Spectrometry Bulletin (monthly)

1776 MASTIC ASPHALT COUNCIL AND EMPLOYERS FEDERATION
24 Grosvenor Gardens, London SW1W 0DH — Tel. 01-730 7175
Trade Association; member of the Federation of Associations of Specialists and Sub-contractors

Enquiries to the Director

Subject coverage
mastic asphalt in building construction, roofing, flooring and tanking; waterproofing of bridge decks

Publications
Application of Mastic Asphalt (handbook)
Flooring with Mastic Asphalt (booklet)
Technical Information Sheets
European Mastic Asphalt Association Trilingual Bibliography of Terms (English, French, German)

MATERIALS AND COMPONENTS DEVELOPMENT AND TESTING ASSOCIATION *see* **MACDATA**

1777 MATERIALS RESEARCH COMPANY LIMITED
St. Johns Estate, Tylers Green, Penn, High Wycombe, Buckinghamshire HP10 8HR — Tel. 049-481 5154, Telex 837346
Company, subsidiary of Materials Research Corporation, New York

Enquiries to the Company

Subject coverage
high purity materials; thin film deposition techniques

Publication
Basics of Sputtering (booklet)

1778 MATERIALS SCIENCE CLUB
c/o Division of Materials Applications, National Physical Laboratory, Teddington, Middlesex TW11 0LW — Tel. 01-977 3222, Telex 262344
Informal Professional Society; member of the British National Committee on Materials and of the U.K. Crystallographic Council, *qq.v.*

Enquiries to the Honorary Secretary

Subject coverage
all fields of materials science and technology; all types of materials (metals, plastics, ceramics, etc.); relationships between structure/property/use

Publication
Monthly Bulletin

1779 MATERIALS TECHNOLOGY BUREAU
Atomic Energy Research Establishment, Building 393, Harwell, Didcot, Oxfordshire OX11 0RA — Tel. 0235 24141 ext. 4230, Telex 83135
Government-funded Centre, of the United Kingdom Atomic Energy Authority

Enquiries to the Director

Subject coverage
materials, including metallic and non-metallic, their properties, fabrication, etc

Publication
Harwell Material Development News (about 3 per annum)

1780 MATHEMATICAL ASSOCIATION
259 London Road, Leicester LE2 3BE — Tel. 0533 703877
Educational Association

Enquiries to the Executive Secretary; Library housed in the Leicester University Library, q.v.

Subject coverage
mathematics and the teaching of mathematics

Publications
Mathematical Gazette (quarterly)
Mathematics in School (bi-monthly)

1781 MAY & BAKER LIMITED
Rainham Road South, Dagenham, Essex RM10 7XS Tel. 01-592 3060
Telex 28691
Company, part of Rhône-Poulenc S.A, Paris

Enquiries to the Librarian

Subject coverage
chemistry and biomedical sciences related to drugs, veterinary and agricultural sciences; photographic chemistry

Publications
Pharmaceutical Bulletin
Medical films

1782 MCB COMPANY (LUPUS) LIMITED
Lupus Works, Industrial Estate, Winsford, Cheshire CW7 3QB Tel. 060-62 2055
Company

Enquiries to the Personal Assistant to the Managing Director

Subject coverage
miniature, earth leakage and moulded case circuit breakers; their correct integration into distribution networks; discrimination and back-up protection

Publication
Catalogues

1783 MEAT AND LIVESTOCK COMMISSION
P.O. Box 44, Queensway House, Bletchley, Milton Keynes, MK2 2EF Tel. Milton Keynes 74941 ext. 265
Government Body

Enquiries to the Librarian

Subject coverage
meat and livestock production

Publication
Index of MLC Research

MEAT MANUFACTURERS ASSOCIATION *see* **FOOD MANUFACTURERS FEDERATION INCORPORATED**

1784 MEAT RESEARCH INSTITUTE
Langford, Bristol BS18 7DY Tel. 0934 852661
Research Institute, of the Agricultural Research Council

Enquiries to the Librarian or Information Officer

Subject coverage
meat science and technology; butchery; chilling and freezing; packaging; microbiology; preservation; spoilage; hygiene; meat structure and evaluation of quality

Special collections
Reprints of Meat Research Institute
Reprints of Meat Industry Research Industry of New Zealand (incomplete)
Proceedings of European meetings of Meat Research Workers

Publication
Annual Report
Symposium Proceedings
Reports and Memoranda
Biennial List of Staff Publications

MECHANICAL HANDLING ENGINEERS ASSOCIATION *see*
ENGINEERING INDUSTRIES ASSOCIATION
METALLURGICAL PLANTMAKERS FEDERATION

1785 MEDICAL INFORMATION SERVICE
British Council, 10 Spring Gardens, London SW1A 2BN Tel. 01-930 8466
Information Service, formerly the Medical Library, of the British Council Medical Department

Enquiries to the Head of the Service

Subject coverage
medicine, nursing, psychology, social services

Publications
British Medicine (monthly)
British Medical Publications, 4th ed.

1786 MEDICAL RESEARCH COUNCIL LIBRARY
National Institute for Medical Research, The Ridgeway, Tel. 01-959 3666
Mill Hill, London NW7 1AA Telex 922666
Research Council

Enquiries to the Librarian

Subject coverage
basic medical science

Publications
Annual Report
MRC Handbook
NIMR Report

1787 MEDICAL RESEARCH COUNCIL LABORATORIES
Woodmansterne Road, Carshalton, Surrey SM5 4EF Tel. 01-643 8000
Government Department; part of the National Institute for Medical Research, The Ridgeway, Mill Hill, NW7; includes the Laboratory Animals Centre

Enquiries, Laboratories, to the Librarian; Laboratory Animals Centre, to the Information Officer

Subject coverage
husbandry and breeding of laboratory animals; nutrition; toxicology; biochemistry

Publications
Mouse Newsletter
Guinea Pig Newsletter

MEDICAL RESEARCH COUNCIL *see also*
ARBOVIRUS UNIT
BIOMEDICAL INSTRUMENTATION ADVISORY SERVICE
ENVIRONMENTAL HAZARDS UNIT
FAST ACCESS INFORMATION RETRIEVAL
PNEUMOCONIOSIS UNIT
RADIOBIOLOGY UNIT

1788 MEDLARS (U.K.) (Medical Literature Analysis and Retrieval System)
British Library Lending Division, Boston Spa, Wetherby, Tel. 0937 843434
West Yorkshire LS23 7BQ
Data Base, founded by U.S. National Library of Medicine

Enquiries to the U.K. Medlars Service by annual subscription

Subject coverage
biomedicine, medicine and related sciences; (over two million articles, since 1963, from over 2800 journals)

Publications
Index Medicus
Current Awareness (monthly print-outs) to specific selection

1789 MEDWAY AND MAIDSTONE COLLEGE OF TECHNOLOGY
Horsted, Maidstone Road, Chatham, Kent ME5 9UQ Tel. 0634 41001–4
Technical College; a unit also at Oakwood Park, Maidstone; houses a Business Advisory Centre

Enquiries to the Manager, Business Advisory Centre

Subject coverage
building and civil engineering; commerce; data processing; electrical and electronic engineering; mechanical and marine engineering; management

MEDWAY DIVISIONAL LIBRARY *see* **KENT COUNTY LIBRARY**

MEIRIONNYDD AREA LIBRARY *see* **GWYNEDD LIBRARY SERVICE**

1790 MERCHANT NAVY COLLEGE
Greenhithe, Kent DA9 9NY Tel. 0322 845050
College of Further Education/Nautical College

Enquiries to the Librarian

Subject coverage
careers and training for the Merchant Navy, particularly for deck and radio officers

1791 MERCK SHARP & DOHME LIMITED
Hertford Road, Hoddesdon, Hertfordshire EN11 9BU Tel. 099-24 67123
Manufacturing Company, of Merck and Company, Inc., N.J., U.S.A.

Enquiries to the Librarian

Subject coverage
pharmaceuticals, particularly for the treatment of arthritis, rheumatism, hypertension, parkinsonism

Publications
Merck Manual of Diagnosis and Therapy
Merck Veterinary Manual
Merck Index

1792 MERLEWOOD RESEARCH STATION
Grange-over-Sands, Cumbria LA11 6JU Tel. 044-84 2234/6
Research Station, of the Institute of Terrestrial Ecology, *q.v.*; formerly of the Nature Conservancy

Enquiries to the Librarian

Subject coverage
grasslands research

1793 MERRIST WOOD AGRICULTURAL COLLEGE
Worplesdon, Nr Guildford, Surrey GU3 3PE Tel. 048-631 2424
Agricultural College

No enquiry service

Subject coverage
agriculture

1794 MERTHYR TYDFIL BOROUGH COUNCIL PUBLIC LIBRARIES
Central Library, High Street, Merthyr Tydfil, Mid-Glamorgan CF47 8AF Tel. 0685 3057
Public Library Service; formerly County Borough of Merthyr Tydfil Public Libraries

Enquiries to the Librarian

Subject coverage
general; local industrial history

1795 MERTON LIBRARIES SERVICE
Merton Cottage, Church Path, Merton Park, London SW19 3HH Tel. 01-542 6211
Public Library Service; includes Mitcham, Morden and Wimbledon Libraries, *qq.v.*

Enquiries to the Librarian

Subject coverage
general

1796 MERTON TECHNICAL COLLEGE
Morden Park, London Road, Morden, Surrey SM4 5QX Tel. 01-640 3001
Technical College, formerly Wimbledon Technical College

Enquiries to the College Librarian

Subject coverage
electrical and electronic engineering, including automatic control, computers, telecommunications; mechanical and production engineering including motor cycle engineering; sociology; science. The Annexe covers business studies, management, catering, home economics

Special collection
on musical instrument technology

1797 METAL BOX LIMITED
Research and Development Department, Twyford Abbey Road, London NW10 7XQ Tel. 01-965 8800
Company, formerly Metal Box Company Limited

Enquiries to the Information Officer or Librarian

Subject coverage
packaging, printing, coating, food, plastics and paper converting technologies; microbiology; metallurgy of sheet metals; mechanical, electronic, heating, and polymer engineering; analytical, physical, and polymer chemistry; biological safety

Publications
Bibliographies
Information Surveys (both occasional)

1798 METAL CLOSURES GROUP LIMITED
14–28 Brunswick Park Road, London N11
Company

Enquiries to the Information Officer/Librarian

Subject coverage
packaging; metals; plastics

1799 METAL CUTTING BANDSAW ASSOCIATION
Light Trades House, Melbourne Avenue, Sheffield S10 2QJ Tel. 0742 663084
Trade Association; Member of the National Federation of Engineers Tool Manufacturers

Enquiries to the Secretary

Subject coverage
metal cutting bandsaw industry

1800 METAL FORMING MACHINERY MAKERS ASSOCIATION
21 John Adam Street, London WC2N 6JH Tel. 01-839 6171
Trade Association, formerly British Power Press Manufacturers Association Ltd

Enquiries to the Secretary

Subject coverage
metal forming machinery trade

1801 METAL ROOFING CONTRACTORS ASSOCIATION
Hamlyn House, Highgate Hill, London N19 5PS Tel. 01-272 0233
Trade Association

Enquiries, limited, to the Secretary

Subject coverage
fully-supported metal roofing in copper, zinc, aluminium, stainless steel

1802 METAL WINDOW FEDERATION LIMITED
13 Upper High Street, Epsom, Surrey KT17 4QY Tel. 78 29191
Trade Association, comprising the Aluminium Window Association, the Steel Window Association, and the Patent Glazing Conference, *qq.v.*

Enquiries to the Directors of the component bodies

Subject coverage
metal windows and patent glazing

1803 METALLURGICAL PLANTMAKERS FEDERATION
7 Ludgate Broadway, London EC4V 6DX Tel. 01-248 1543
Telex 8812908
Federation of Trade Associations, including the British Metalworking Plant Makers Association, a section of the Control and Automation Manufacturers Association, a section of the Federation of Manufacturers of Construction Equipment and Cranes, the Hydraulic Association of Great Britain, the Ironmaking and Steelmaking Plant Contractors Association; also a section of the Mechanical Handling Engineers Association and the Society of Industrial Furnace Engineers, *qq.v.*

Enquiries to the Director or Secretary

Subject coverage
iron and steel plantmaking industry as a whole; relationship between the plantmakers and the British Steel Corporation; interest and involvement of the plantmakers in the Corporation's investment programme

METALS AND METALLURGY TRUST *see* **INSTITUTION OF METALLURGISTS**

1804 METALS SOCIETY
1 Carlton House Terrace, London SW1Y 5DB Tel. 01-839 4070
Learned/Technical Society, formed 1974 from the Iron and Steel Institute *and* Institute of Metals

Enquiries to the Assistant Secretary, Library and Information Services

Subject coverage
metallurgy; iron and steel

Publications
Iron and Steel Profiles (ISIP)
Abstract and Book Title Index Card Service for Iron and Steel (ABTICS)
British Industrial and Scientific Translation Service of the Metals Society (BISITS)
Metals Abstracts
World Calendar of Forthcoming Meetings: metallurgical and related fields

1805 METEOROLOGICAL OFFICE
London Road, Bracknell, Berkshire RG12 2SZ Tel. 0344 20242
Telex 848160, 847010

Government Department, of the Ministry of Defence

Enquiries to the Director-General

Subject coverage
meteorology; climatology; oceanography; hydrology

Special collections
original British climatological data, land and maritime
material on expeditions

Publications
are listed in HMSO Sectional List No. 37 and in Meteorological Office Leaflet No. 1a

1806 METEOROLOGICAL OFFICE
231 Corstorphine Road, Edinburgh EH12 7BB Tel. 031-334 9721
Government Department, branch of National Meteorological Office

Enquiries to the Superintendent

Subject coverage
meteorology, hydrology, agricultural meteorology, weather, climate, rainfall

Special collection
climatological and rainfall information for the whole of Scotland

METHIL GROUP LIBRARY *see* **KIRKCALDY AND NORTH EAST FIFE DISTRICT LIBRARIES**

1807 METRA CONSULTING GROUP LIMITED
22 Lower Belgrave Street, London SW1W 0NS Tel. 01-730 0855
Telex 919173

Company

Enquiries to the Information Officer

Subject coverage
industrial market research; planning; computer consultancy; product planning

1808 METRICATION BOARD
22 Kingsway, London WC2B 6LE Tel. 01-242 6828
Government Department, of the Department of Prices and Consumer Protection

Enquiries to the Information Officer

Subject coverage
the metric system and general aspects of metrication and its adoption

Publications
Going Metric (quarterly)
List of publications and posters available

METROPOLITAN BRADFORD LIBRARIES *see* **BRADFORD LIBRARIES**

1809 METROPOLITAN POLICE FORENSIC SCIENCE LABORATORY
109 Lambeth Road, London SE1 7JH Tel. 01-230 6255
Fringe Government Organization

Enquiries, general or routine, to the Librarian; technical or special services, to the Director

Subject coverage
analytical techniques for small quantities of drugs, paint, glass, metals, body fluids, etc.; grouping systems on dried blood and body secretions; high pressure chromatography applied to drugs and lubricating oils; gas liquid chromatography for identification of drugs, petrols and solvents; use of scanning electron microscopy for identification of very small particles; identification of synthetic fibres and fibres of living origin (plant and animal)

MEXBOROUGH TECHNICAL COLLEGE *now* **DONCASTER METROPOLITAN INSTITUTE OF HIGHER EDUCATION,** *q.v.*

MICHELL BEARINGS *now* **VICKERS LIMITED MICHELL BEARINGS,** *q.v.*

1810 MICROBIOLOGICAL RESEARCH ESTABLISHMENT
Porton Down, Salisbury, Wiltshire Tel. 0980-61 391
Government Department, formerly of the Ministry of Defence, Procurement Executive

Enquiries to the Director

Subject coverage
microbiology; biochemistry of microorganisms; non-clinical aspects of infectious diseases

Publication
MRE Abstracts Booklet

1811 MICROFILM ASSOCIATION OF GREAT BRITAIN
1/2 Trinity Churchyard, High Street, Guildford, Surrey GU1 3RW Tel. 048-68 6653
Non-profit Association, whose Secretariat and information resources are provided by G.G. Baker and Associates, *q.v.*

Enquiries to the Director-General (complex enquiries may involve fees)

Subject coverage
micrographics, including computer output microfilm

Publications
Microdoc (quarterly, fee to members, on subscription to others)
COM Applications in Libraries
Directory of British Photoreproduction Services for Libraries
Information Methods for Microfilm Systems
Microfilm Points the Way to Harnessing the Information Explosion
Microfilm Saves Money
National Micrographics Association of America publications are available from MAGB

1812 MICROINFO LIMITED
Post House, High Street, Alton, Hampshire GU34 1EF Tel. 0420 84300
Company; U.K. Representative of the United States Department of Commerce National Technical Information Service

Enquiries to the Director

Subject coverage
microfilm information handling techniques for business systems, engineering design, micropublishing, library activities, etc., and as an EDP peripheral. Conventional and Computer Output Microfilm (COM) methods are covered. Energy-related subjects, particularly further sources of data; pollution-related subjects, particularly further sources of data

Publications
News Bulletins on energy and pollution
International Microfilm Source Book
International File of Micrographic Equipment and Accessories
Microinfo (monthly newsletter)
FT Abstracts in Science and Technology
NTIS ... Microinfo Technology Report Series
Technologymart Technology Transfer News Bulletin

1813 MICROMATION LIMITED
Croft House, High Street, Aldridge, Staffordshire WS9 8NL Tel. 0922 55221
Company

Enquiries to the Director

Subject coverage
document microfilm equipment and supplies, computer output microfilm (COM) equipment, supplies, software

Publications
Microfilm Equipment Guide
Specification Sheets

1814 MICROMEDIA LIMITED
Telford Road, Bicester, Oxfordshire OX6 0UP Tel. 08692 45711
Microfilm Bureau, Member of Blackwells Group; a C.O.M. Unit in Bristol

Enquiries to the Managing Director

Subject coverage
micropublishing

1815 MID AND SOUTH STAFFORDSHIRE LIBRARIES IN COOPERATION (MISLIC)
Staffordshire County Library, Friars Terrace, Stafford ST17 4AY Tel. 0785 3121 ext. 8350
Interlibrary Cooperative Scheme, of 52 members

Enquiries to the Secretary

Subject coverage
general, technical, commercial

Publications
Union List of Periodicals
Union List of Standard Specifications
MISLIC Brochure

1816 MIDDLE EAST ASSOCIATION
33 Bury Street, St. James's, London SW1Y 6AX Tel. 01-839 2137
Trade Association

Enquiries from members only; others to the Committee on Middle East Trade, q.v.

Subject coverage
Middle East trade

Publication
Fortnightly Digest

MIDDLESBROUGH CENTRAL LIBRARY *see* **CLEVELAND COUNTY LIBRARY**

1817 MIDDLESEX POLYTECHNIC
Queensway, Enfield EN3 4SF Tel. 01-804 8131
Institute of Higher Education, comprising the former Enfield College of Technology, Hendon College of Technology, Hornsey College of Art, New College of Speech and Drama and Trent Park College of Education

Enquiries to the Polytechnic Librarian

Subject coverage
civil, electrical and mechanical engineering; sociology; business mathematics; economics, business studies; microwaves; computers; gas engineering; chemistry

MIDDLETON AREA LIBRARY *see* **ROCHDALE LIBRARIES AND ARTS SERVICES**

1818 MID-GLAMORGAN COUNTY LIBRARY
Coed Parc, Park Street, Bridgend, Glamorgan CF31 4BA Tel. 0656 57451
Public Libraries; with West Glamorgan and South Glamorgan was formed from the former Glamorgan County Libraries; District Libraries at Bridgend, Rhymney Valley, Pontypridd

Enquiries to the Technical Librarian

Subject coverage
general; specializing in physics, chemistry, mathematics, geology; mechanical, civil and electrical engineering; agriculture; management; industrial processes; economics of industries

Special collection
British Standards

1819 MID-GLOUCESTERSHIRE TECHNICAL COLLEGE
Stratford Road, Stroud, Gloucestershire GL5 4AH Tel. 045-36 3424/5
Technical College

Enquiries to the Librarian

Subject coverage
building; commerce; domestic science; engineering; science

Special collection
Library of the Plastics Institute, South Western Branch

1820 MIDLOTHIAN DISTRICT LIBRARY
Fisherrow School, South Street, Musselburgh EH21 6AU Tel. 031-665 2931
Public Library, formerly Midlothian County Library

Enquiries to the Librarian

Subject coverage
general

1821 MILITARY VEHICLES AND ENGINEERING ESTABLISHMENT
Chobham Lane, Chertsey, Surrey KT16 0EE Tel. 0990 23366
Telex 848442
Government Research Establishment, Procurement Executive, Ministry of Defence; formerly Fighting Vehicles Research and Development Establishment

Enquiries to the Information Officer or Librarian, normally only accepted from Government Departments and the Armed Services

Subject coverage
automobile engineering; military applications of engineering

1822 MILITARY VEHICLES AND ENGINEERING ESTABLISHMENT (CHRISTCHURCH)
Barrack Road, Christchurch, Dorset BH23 2BB Tel. 020-15 4431
Government Research Establishment, Procurement Executive, Ministry of Defence

Enquiries to the Librarian

Subject coverage
military engineering, including civil and mechanical engineering aspects; military bridge design, analysis, construction and testing; general structural testing; metallurgical and fatigue problems of structures; structural stability; marine equipment; earth-moving plant; pre-fabricated airfield surfaces; mechanical handling equipment; water supply and filtration; fuel supply, terrain evaluation and soil mechanics; plastics and composite materials; civil testing of construction plant

Publication
Technical brochures

1823 MILK MARKETING BOARD OF ENGLAND AND WALES
Thames Ditton, Surrey KT7 0EL Tel. 01-398 4101
Telex 928239

Producers' Cooperative

Enquiries to the Librarian

Subject coverage
economics of milk production; dairy farming including cattle breeding, artificial insemination; cattle husbandry including feeding and disease control; transport of milk; dairy products; utilization of waste; agriculture; agricultural marketing; dairy industries of the world, especially the EEC; food industry

Publications
Milk Producer (monthly)
United Kingdom Dairy Facts and Figures
EEC Dairy Facts and Figures
Reports and brochures on breeding and production, farm management, and marketing
List available

1824 MILKING MACHINE MANUFACTURERS ASSOCIATION
3 Eden Hall, 52 Albemarle Road, Beckenham, Kent BR3 2HR Tel. 01-650 5879
Trade Association

Enquiries to the Secretary

Subject coverage
milking machinery

1825 MILLBANK COLLEGE OF COMMERCE
Bankfield Road, Liverpool L13 0BQ Tel. 051-220 4661
College

Enquiries to the Librarian

Subject coverage
business studies; management; secretarial studies; languages

1826 MILLBANK TECHNICAL SERVICES LIMITED
North House, Great Peter Street, London SW1P 3LN Tel. 01-222 8090 exts. 287/234
Telex 916205
Company; subsidiary of the Crown Agents for Oversea Governments and Administrations, *q.v.*

Enquiries to the Secretariat (company business only)

Subject coverage
export contracting for the public sector, mainly with Iran

MILLINERY DISTRIBUTORS ASSOCIATION *see* **FEDERATION OF WHOLESALE AND INDUSTRIAL DISTRIBUTORS**

1827 MILLING CUTTER AND REAMER ASSOCIATION
Light Trades House, Melbourne Avenue, Sheffield S10 2QJ Tel. 0742 663084
Trade Association; member of the National Federation of Engineers Tool Manufacturers, *q.v.*

Enquiries to the Secretary

Subject coverage
manufacture of milling cutters and reamers

1828 MILTON KEYNES DEVELOPMENT CORPORATION
Wavendon Tower, Wavendon, Milton Keynes, Buckinghamshire MK17 8LX Tel. 0908 74000
Development Corporation

Enquiries to the Information Unit Manager

Subject coverage
town planning, design, implementation and management

Publications
Literature on the City's development

MINERAL INDUSTRY RESEARCH ORGANISATION *see* **INSTITUTION OF MINING AND METALLURGY**

1829 MINERALOGICAL SOCIETY OF GREAT BRITAIN AND IRELAND
41 Queens Gate, London SW7 5HR Tel. 01-584 7516
Scientific Society

Enquiries to the Society

Subject coverage
mineralogy; petrology

Publication
Mineralogical Abstracts (quarterly)

1830 MINERALS ENGINEERING SOCIETY
2 Alder Grove, Stapenhill, Burton on Trent, Staffordshire DE15 9QR
Professional Society; formerly Coal Preparation Society

Enquiries to the Honorary Secretary

Subject coverage
minerals engineering; coal preparation; education and training of minerals engineers

Publications
Papers in the journal Mine and Quarry (monthly)

MINES AND QUARRIES INSPECTORATE *see* HEALTH AND SAFETY EXECUTIVE

1831 MINING INSTITUTE OF SCOTLAND
National Coal Board, Green Park, Greenend, Edinburgh EH17 7PZ Tel. 031-663 2811
Professional Association, branch of the Institution of Mining Engineers, *q.v.*

Enquiries to the Secretary

Subject coverage
mining engineering

Publication
Journal

1832 MINING RESEARCH AND DEVELOPMENT ESTABLISHMENT
Ashby Road, Stanhope Bretby, Burton-on-Trent, Staffordshire DE15 0QD Tel. 028-387 6161 Telex 341741
Research and Development Establishment of the National Coal Board; formerly the Central Engineering Establishment, with which the former mining Research Establishment was merged

Enquiries to the Information Officer

Subject coverage
underground mining research and development; coal winning machines; underground transport; rock cutting machines; roof supports; rock mechanics; strata control; the underground environment; electronic and hydraulic control systems; respirable dusts; coal preparation

Publication
Annual Report

1833 MINISTRY OF AGRICULTURE, FISHERIES AND FOOD
Great Westminster House, Horseferry Road, London SW1P 2AE Tel. 01-216 7343 & 7444 Telex 21271
Government Department; Library is a Branch of the Ministry's Main Library; formerly Food and Nutrition Library

Enquiries to the Librarian

Subject coverage
human nutrition; food science, food standards; food engineering and processing; dietetics

Publications
see MINISTRY, Whitehall Place entry

1834 MINISTRY OF AGRICULTURE, FISHERIES AND FOOD
Government Buildings, Hook Rise South, Tolworth, Surbiton, Surrey KT6 7NF Tel. 01-337 6611 Telex 22203
Government Department; Library is a Branch of the Ministry's Main Library

Enquiries to the Librarian

Subject coverage
animal health; vertebrate pest biology and control

Publications
see MINISTRY, Whitehall Place entry

1835 MINISTRY OF AGRICULTURE, FISHERIES AND FOOD
3/8 Whitehall Place, London SW1A 2HH Tel. 01-839 7711
Telex 22856

Government Department; Main Library at above address; Branches at Horseferry Road, London and Tolworth, Surrey, *qq.v.*

Enquiries to the Librarian

Subject coverage
agriculture; fisheries; food; particularly temperature agriculture

Special collections
Cowan and Cotton Collection on Apiculture
Pannett Collection on Poultry Genetics

Publications
ADAS Quarterly review
Plant pathology (quarterly)
Experimental horticulture (semi-annually)
Experimental husbandry (semi-annually)
Plant varieties & seeds gazette (monthly)
Agricultural statistics (annually)
Sea fisheries statistical tables (annually)
Advisory leaflets, bulletins, mechanisation leaflets, technical bulletins
Fishery investigation series. Notices together with a wide range of publications produced by the Ministry itself and not through HMSO
Full details are given in HMSO Sectional lists 1 (Agriculture and Food), 23 (Fisheries) and in a Ministry publication "Agriculture, fisheries and food ... Catalogue of departmental publications"

MINISTRY OF AGRICULTURE, FISHERIES AND FOOD *see also*
CENTRAL VETERINARY LABORATORY
DIRECTORATE OF FISHERIES RESEARCH
HUMBER LABORATORY
PEST INFESTATION CONTROL LABORATORY
PLANT PATHOLOGY LABORATORY
ROYAL BOTANIC GARDENS
TORRY RESEARCH STATION

1836 MINISTRY OF DEFENCE LIBRARY SERVICE
Old War Office Building, Whitehall, London SW1A 2EU Tel. 01-218 0139
Government Department, formerly Ministry of Defence Library (Central and Army)

Enquiries, by letter only, to the Chief Librarian, Ministry of Defence Library Service, Room 0046/A, address as above

Subject coverage
scientific and technical, and other subjects necessary in the work of administering the armed services

Publications
scientific and technical bibliographies

1837 MINISTRY OF DEFENCE LIBRARY SERVICE
St. Giles Court, 1–13 St. Giles High Street, London WC2H 8LD Tel. 01-632 3773
Telex 22241

Government Department, formerly Ministry of Technology

Enquiries, by letter only, to the Chief Librarian, Ministry of Defence Library Service, Room 0046/A, Old War Office Building, Whitehall, London SW1A 2EU

Subject coverage
aero and space technology; electronics; metallurgy; management; mechanical engineering

1838 MINISTRY OF DEFENCE (NAVY)
Hydrographic Department, Taunton, Somerset TA1 2DN — Tel. 0823 87900, Telex 46274

Government Department

Enquiries to the Librarian

Subject coverage
navigation; geodesy; photogrammetry; cartography; geophysics; oceanography; meteorology; shipping and ports; computing

Special collections
Historical archives of hydrographic surveying
Libraries of tidal, oceanographic, geodetic and wreck data

Publications
Catalogue of Admiralty Charts and other hydrographic publications

MINISTRY OF DEFENCE *see also*
ADMIRALTY COMPASS OBSERVATORY
ADMIRALTY EXPERIMENTAL DIVING UNIT
ADMIRALTY MARINE ENGINEERING ESTABLISHMENT
ADMIRALTY MATERIALS LABORATORY
ADMIRALTY RESEARCH LABORATORY
ADMIRALTY SURFACE WEAPONS ESTABLISHMENT
ADMIRALTY UNDERWATER WEAPONS ESTABLISHMENT
AEROPLANE AND ARMAMENT EXPERIMENTAL ESTABLISHMENT
ATOMIC WEAPONS RESEARCH ESTABLISHMENT
CHEMICAL DEFENCE ESTABLISHMENT
DEFENCE RESEARCH INFORMATION CENTRE
EXPLOSIVES RESEARCH AND DEVELOPMENT ESTABLISHMENT
INSTITUTE OF NAVAL MEDICINE
METEOROLOGICAL OFFICE
MICROBIOLOGICAL RESEARCH ESTABLISHMENT
MILITARY VEHICLES AND ENGINEERING ESTABLISHMENT
NATIONAL GAS TURBINE ESTABLISHMENT
NAVAL AIRCRAFT MATERIALS LABORATORY
NAVAL CONSTRUCTION RESEARCH ESTABLISHMENT
ROYAL AIRCRAFT ESTABLISHMENT
ROYAL MILITARY COLLEGE OF SCIENCE
ROYAL NAVAL COLLEGE
ROYAL NAVAL ENGINEERING COLLEGE
ROYAL NAVAL PHYSIOLOGICAL LABORATORY
ROYAL SIGNALS AND RADAR ESTABLISHMENT

MINNESOTA MINING & MANUFACTURING COMPANY *see entry* 1720

MISLIC *see* **MID AND SOUTH STAFFORDSHIRE LIBRARIES IN CO-OPERATION**

1839 MITCHAM DISTRICT LIBRARY
London Road, Mitcham, Surrey CR4 2YR — Tel. 01-648 4070 *and* 6516
Public Library, district library of the Merton Libraries Service *q.v.*

Enquiries to the Librarian

Subject coverage
general; cricket

MITCHELL LIBRARY *see* **GLASGOW DISTRICT LIBRARIES**

1840 MLH CONSULTANTS LIMITED
148 Grosvenor Road, London SW1V 3JY Tel. 01-821 9141/5
Telex 24170

Company; housing also Productivity and Management Services Limited, a subsidiary

Enquiries to the Managing Director

Subject coverage
corporate and strategic planning; business appraisal and investigation; financial and management information systems; total industry studies; feasibility studies; marketing and selling; distribution; production planning and scheduling; shop floor and junior supervision training

Publications
National Prices Commission Dublin: Animal feedstuffs industry
National Prices Commission Dublin: Flour industry
Occasional Papers

1841 MOBIL OIL COMPANY LIMITED
54/60 Victoria Street, London SW1E 6QB Tel. 01-828 9777
Telex 22288

Company; Affiliate of Mobil Oil Corporation, New York; its Technical Library is at the Research and Technical Services Laboratory, Stanford-le-Hope, Essex (tel. 03756 3355)

Enquiries to the Information Officer

Subject coverage
petroleum and petroleum products

1842 MOBILE RADIO USERS ASSOCIATION
P.O. Box 15, London SW1V 1DT
Trade Association

Enquiries, from Members only, to the Association

Subject coverage
mobile radio

Publication
Talk Through Magazine (for Members)

1843 MODEL ENGINEERING TRADE ASSOCIATION
139 Parkside Drive, Withycombe Park, Exmouth, Devonshire EX8 4LX Tel. 039-52 71420
Trade Association

Enquiries to the Honorary Secretary

Subject coverage
model railway engineering

1844 MODEL RAILWAY CLUB
4 Calshot Street, London N1 9AT
Club

Enquiries to the Librarian/Archivist

Subject coverage
railway history, especially aspects of engineering in the U.K.

1845 MODULAR SOCIETY FOR ADVANCEMENT IN BUILDING
24 Ormond Road, Richmond, Surrey TW10 6TH Tel. 01-948 4151
Learned Society

Enquiries, in writing, to the Secretary

Subject coverage
modular construction

Publications
List available

MOIR LIBRARY *see* **SCOTTISH BEEKEEPERS ASSOCIATION**

1846 MONOPOLIES AND MERGERS COMMISSION
Room 567, 48 Carey Street, London WC2A 2JT Tel. 01-831 6111 ext. 2075
Government Department; formerly Monopolies Commission

Enquiries to the Librarian

Subject coverage
monopolies; mergers; anti-trust matters

Publications
Reports on matters referred to the Commission, listed in HMSO Sectional List 3

MONMOUTH REGIONAL LIBRARY *see* **GWENT COUNTY LIBRARY**

1847 MONKS WOOD EXPERIMENTAL STATION
Abbots Ripton, Huntingdon, Cambridgeshire PE17 2LS Tel. 04873 381
Research Station, of the Institute of Terrestrial Ecology, *q.v.*; formerly of the Nature Conservancy

Enquiries to the Librarian

Subject coverage
lowlands farming; southern chalk grasslands; East Anglian fens

1848 MONKLANDS DISTRICT LIBRARIES
Wellwynd, Airdrie, Lanarkshire ML6 0AG Tel. 02366 63221
Public Libraries, formerly Airdrie Public Library *and* Coatbridge Public Library, *q.v.*

Enquiries to the Librarian

Subject coverage
general

1849 MONSANTO LIMITED
London Information Centre, Monsanto House, Victoria Street, London SW1 Tel. 01-222 5678
Company, formerly Monsanto Chemical Company Limited (Ruabon and Newport); now part of Monsanto Europe S.A., affiliated to Monsanto Company, St. Louis, U.S.A.

Enquiries to the Information Officer

Subject coverage
physics; chemistry (especially organic); chemical engineering; analytical methods; polymer science; rubber and plastics technology

MONTROSE PUBLIC LIBRARY *see* **ANGUS DISTRICT LIBRARY SERVICE**

1850 MOTHERWELL BRIDGE ENGINEERING LIMITED
P.O. Box 4, Motherwell, Lanarkshire ML1 3NP Tel. 0698 66111
Telex 77197
Company; formerly Motherwell Bridge and Engineering Company Limited

Enquiries to the Librarian

Subject coverage
structural, mechanical, civil and chemical engineering; bulk storage including cryogenic storage; materials; welding

1851 MORAY DISTRICT LIBRARY
Grant Lodge, Cooper Park, Elgin, Moray IV30 1HS Tel. 0343 2746
Public Library; formerly Moray and Nairn County Library

Enquiries to the Director of Libraries

Subject coverage
general

1852 MORDEN DISTRICT LIBRARY
Morden Road, London SW19 3DA Tel. 01-542 1701 *and* 2842
Public Library, district library of Merton Libraries Service, *q.v.*

Enquiries to the Librarian

Subject coverage
general; macroeconomics

MOREDUN INSTITUTE *see* **ANIMAL DISEASES RESEARCH ASSOCIATION**

MORETON-IN-MARSH PUBLIC LIBRARY *see* **GLOUCESTER COUNTY LIBRARY**

MORPETH LIBRARY *see* **NORTHUMBERLAND COUNTY LIBRARY**

MORRELL LIBRARY (YORK UNIVERSITY) *see* **J.B. MORRELL LIBRARY**

1853 MORTAR PRODUCERS ASSOCIATION LIMITED
274 High Street, Slough, Buckinghamshire Tel. 75 36936
Trade Association

Enquiries to the Secretary

Subject coverage
technical information about mortar

Publication
Data sheets

1854 MOTHERWELL DISTRICT COUNCIL PUBLIC LIBRARIES
Hamilton Road, Motherwell, Lanarkshire ML1 3BZ Tel. 0698 51311
Public Library Service; formerly Motherwell and Wishaw Public Libraries

Enquiries to the Chief Librarian

Subject coverage
iron and steel

1855 MOTOR CYCLE ASSOCIATION OF GREAT BRITAIN LIMITED
Starley House, Eaton Road, Coventry CV1 2FH Tel. 0203 27427
Trade Association; together with the Bicycle Association of Great Britain, *q.v.*, of the same address, it formed the original Cycle and Motor Cycle Associated, now dissolved

Enquiries to the Director

Subject coverage
structure of the British motor cycle industry; manufacture; imports; accessories, statistics

MOTOR FACTORS ASSOCIATION *see* **FEDERATION OF WHOLESALE AND INDUSTRIAL DISTRIBUTORS**

1856 MOTOR INDUSTRY RESEARCH ASSOCIATION
Watling Street, Nuneaton, Warwickshire CV10 0TU Tel. 0682 68541
Telex 311277
Research Association/Consultancy

Enquiries to the Information Officer

Subject coverage
automobile engineering; problems applicable to motor vehicles including noise, vibration, comfort, safety, air pollution

Publications
Automobile Abstracts
Research Reports
Indexes to MIRA publications
Translations

1857 MOTOR INSURANCE REPAIR RESEARCH CENTRE
Colthrop Lane, Thatcham, Berkshire Tel. 0635 62555
Research Organization, sponsored by Members of the British Insurance Association and Lloyds Syndicates

Enquiries to the Information Officer

Subject coverage
vehicle repair: cost control and standards improvement

Publications
Repair manuals
Thatcham News (both to members only)

1858 JOHN MOWLEM & COMPANY LIMITED
Westgate House, Ealing Road, Brentford, Middlesex TW8 0QZ Tel. 01-568 9111
Telex 24414

Company

Enquiries to the Librarian or Public Relations Manager

Subject coverage
rock and soil mechanics, construction industry testing equipment, epoxy resins, ground stabilisation, tunnelling, diaphragm walling, building design, construction plant design, corrosion inhibition (for construction industry); engineering and resources consultancy

1859 MULLARD RESEARCH LABORATORIES
Cross Oak Lane, Redhill, Surrey RH1 5HA Tel. 0293-4 5544
Telex 877261

Company, subsidiary of Philips Industries

Enquiries to the Librarian

Subject coverage
circuit physics; electronic systems; solid state physics; vacuum and electron beam physics

Publications
Philips Research Reports and Supplements
Philips Technical Review
Philips Electronic Applications
Mullard Technical Communications

1860 MULLARD SPACE SCIENCE LABORATORY
Department of Physics and Astronomy, (University College, London), Holmbury St. Mary, Dorking, Surrey RHS 6MS Tel. 030-670 292
Telex 859185
University Department

Enquiries to the Director

Subject coverage
X-ray astronomy; solar X-ray studies; ionospheric/magnetospheric studies

MUREX WELDING PROCESSES LIMITED *now* **BOC MUREX,** *q.v.*

1861 MUSEUM OF MANKIND
6 Burlington Gardens, London W1X 2EX Tel. 01-437 2224
National Museum, the Ethnography Department of the British Museum; holds the former Library of the Royal Anthropological Institute; the Institute's Librarian may be reached via the Museum's Library

Enquiries to the Museum of Mankind

Subject coverage
library facilities and bibliographical information on all branches of anthropology and archaeology from any part of the world; primitive art, culture and technology of village cultures world-wide

Special collections
Sir Eric Thompson Library (Maya archaeology)
Burton Library
RAI Manuscript and Photographic Collections

Publications
Occasional handbooks

1862 MUSHROOM GROWERS ASSOCIATION
Agriculture House, Knightsbridge, London SW1X 7NJ Tel. 01-235 5077 ext. 329
Trade Association, specialist branch of the National Farmers Union

Enquiries to the Secretary

Subject coverage
mushroom production in all its forms

Publication
Mushroom Journal

1863 MUSIC PUBLISHERS ASSOCIATION LIMITED
73–75 Mortimer Street, London W1N 7TB Tel. 01-580 3399
01-636 6027

Trade Association

Enquiries to the Secretary

Subject coverage
music publishing and related activities

Publications
List of Members
Introduction to Music Publishing

MYERSCOUGH TRIAL GROUNDS *see* **LANCASHIRE COLLEGE OF AGRICULTURE**

NANTIS *see* **NOTTINGHAM AND NOTTINGHAMSHIRE TECHNICAL INFORMATION SERVICE**

1864 NAPIER COLLEGE OF COMMERCE AND TECHNOLOGY
Colinton Road, Edinburgh EH10 5DT Tel. 031-447 7070
College of Further Education; formerly Napier College of Science and Technology; name changed as above upon merger with Edinburgh College of Commerce

Enquiries to the Librarian

Subject coverage
industrial design; biological sciences; ergonomics; information science; hotel-keeping; electronic engineering; printing history

Special collection
Edward Clark Collection on printing and book production

Publication
North Sea Oil 1973: select list of newspaper & periodical articles

1865 NAPIER COLLEGE OF COMMERCE AND TECHNOLOGY
Sighthill Court, Edinburgh EH11 4BN Tel. 031-443 6061 ext. 42 (Library)
College of Further Education, formerly Edinburgh College of Commerce; merged with Napier College of Science and Technology and took name as given above

Enquiries to the Librarian

Subject coverage
economics; finance; management

Publication
North Sea Oil Bibliography, 1972–74 (economic and financial aspects)

NAPIER SHAW LIBRARY *see* **CAVENDISH LABORATORY**

1866 NARROW GAUGE RAILWAY SOCIETY
47 Birchington Avenue, Birchencliffe, Huddersfield HD3 3RD Tel. 04227 4526
Independent Amateur Society

Enquiries to the Secretary

Subject coverage
history and development of narrow gauge rail transport in U.K. and abroad, and of the manufacture of locomotive and rolling stock for such railways; modelling of narrow gauge railways

Publications
Narrow Gauge News (bi-monthly)
Narrow Gauge (quarterly)

1867 NATHANIEL LICHFIELD & PARTNERS
13 Chalcot Gardens, Englands Lane, London NW3 4YB Tel. 01-586 2057
Telex 21879

Company, formerly Nathaniel Lichfield & Associates

Enquiries to the Librarian

Subject coverage
work done by the firm in planning, transport, economics and development

NARROW FABRICS FEDERATION *see*
TAPE MANUFACTURERS ASSOCIATION
WEBBING FABRICS FEDERATION

NATIONAL AGRICULTURAL CENTRE *see* **ROYAL AGRICULTURAL SOCIETY OF ENGLAND**

NATIONAL AND GRINDLAYS BANK LIMITED *now* **GRINDLAYS BANK LIMITED,** *q.v.*

1868 NATIONAL AND MIDLAND IRONFOUNDERS ASSOCIATION
136 Hagley Road, Edgbaston, Birmingham B16 9PN Tel. 021-454 4141
Trade Association, affiliated to the Council of Ironfoundry Associations, *q.v.*

Enquiries to the Secretary

Subject coverage
supply of grey iron castings

1869 NATIONAL ASSOCIATION OF AGRICULTURAL CONTRACTORS
140 Bensham Lane, Thornton Heath, Croydon CR4 7YU Tel. 01-684 2973
Trade Association

Enquiries to the Secretary

Subject coverage
general agricultural contracting; land drainage; crop spraying (ground/air); liquid fertilizer application; lime spreading; farm staff supplying

NATIONAL ASSOCIATION OF BOLT AND NUT STOCKHOLDERS *now* **NATIONAL ASSOCIATION OF FASTENER STOCKHOLDERS,** *q.v.*

1870 NATIONAL ASSOCIATION OF BRITISH MARKET AUTHORITIES
3 St. Judes Avenue, Mapperley, Nottingham NG3 5FG Tel. 0602 621248
Association of Local and Public Authorities

Enquiries to the Secretary

Subject coverage
organization and administration by local authorities of markets of all kinds (e.g. open retail markets, market halls, wholesale fruit, vegetable, flower, fish and meat markets, livestock markets; public abattoirs, cold stores and pleasure fairs

NATIONAL ASSOCIATION OF BUILDING CENTRES *see* **BUILDING CENTRE**

NATIONAL ASSOCIATION OF CHARCOAL MANUFACTURERS *see* **SHIRLEY ALDRED AND COMPANY LIMITED**

1871 NATIONAL ASSOCIATION OF CITIZENS ADVICE BUREAUX
26 Bedford Square, London WC1B 3HU Tel. 01-636 4066
Independent Advisory Body/Registered Charity; formerly National Citizens Advice Bureaux Council

Enquiries, from professional bodies, to the Association are answered at the NACAB discretion; from members of the public, they are referred to local bureaux

Subject coverage
legal, social, and consumer fields

Publication
Information Service (may be purchased)

1872 NATIONAL ASSOCIATION OF COLLIERY OVERMEN DEPUTIES AND SHOTFIRERS
29–31 Euston Road, London NW1 2SP Tel. 01-837 0908
Trade Union; twelve Area Associations

Enquiries to the National Secretary

Subject coverage
trade union services within the colliery industries

NATIONAL ASSOCIATION OF CREAMERY PROPRIETORS *see*
ASSOCIATION OF BUTTER BLENDERS AND BUTTER AND CHEESE PACKERS
ASSOCIATION OF CHEESE PROCESSORS

1873 NATIONAL ASSOCIATION OF DROP FORGERS AND STAMPERS
245 Grove Lane, Birmingham B20 2HB Tel. 021-554 3311
Trade Association; houses the Drop Forging Training Group

Enquiries to the Director

Subject coverage
drop forging industry, commerce and technology; safety and welfare; audiometry

Publications
Buyers Guide
Drop Forging Technical Bulletin
Statistical Bulletin

1874 NATIONAL ASSOCIATION OF EXHIBITION CONTRACTORS
Palace Gate House, Hampton Court, East Molesey, Surrey KT8 9BN Tel. 01-979 9046
Employers Association

Enquiries to the Secretary

Subject coverage
the exhibition contracting industry in Great Britain; as the Employers' Side of the two National Joint Councils, guidance on the Working Rule Agreements which govern pay and working conditions in the industry; as an Employers' Association, a service to Members on relevant Government legislation, industrial procedures and developments within the industry etc.

1875 NATIONAL ASSOCIATION OF EXHIBITORS
Hambutts Barn, Edge Lane, Painswick, Gloucestershire Tel. 0452 813559
Professional Association/Limited Company; formerly Association of Exhibitors and Conference Managers

Enquiries to the Secretary

Subject coverage
advice to companies and others participating in exhibitions

1876 NATIONAL ASSOCIATION OF FASTENER STOCKHOLDERS
Lennig House, Masons Avenue, Croydon CR9 3NU Tel. 01-686 7957
Trade Association, formerly the National Association of Bolt and Nut Stockholders

Enquiries to the Secretariat

Subject coverage
sources of supply of fasteners, including bolts and nuts

NATIONAL ASSOCIATION OF FROZEN FOOD PRODUCERS *now* **UNITED KINGDOM ASSOCIATION OF FROZEN FOOD PRODUCERS,** *q.v.*

NATIONAL ASSOCIATION OF FURNITURE WAREHOUSEMEN AND REMOVERS *now* **BRITISH ASSOCIATION OF REMOVERS,** *q.v.*

1877 NATIONAL ASSOCIATION OF GOLDSMITHS OF GREAT BRITAIN AND IRELAND
St Dunstans House, Carey Lane, London EC2V 8AB Tel. 01-606 5025
Trade Association; houses the Gemmological Association of Great Britain, *q.v.*

Enquiries to the Secretary

Subject coverage
the retail jewellery trade

1878 NATIONAL ASSOCIATION OF INLAND WATERWAYS CARRIERS
Bishop Lane Staithe, High Street, Hull HU1 1PW Tel. 0482 27281
Trade Association

Enquiries to the Secretary

Subject coverage
canal carrying

1879 NATIONAL ASSOCIATION OF INVESTMENT CLUBS LIMITED
17 Harrington Street, Liverpool L2 9QF Tel. 051-227 5272
Company; member of the World Federation of Investment Clubs

Enquiries to the Secretary

Subject coverage
information and advisory services for affiliated Investment Clubs, including nominee facilities; income, corporation and capital gains taxes matters associated with Inland Revenue; formation of regional groups; promotion and interest in the investment club movement

Publication
Investment Club Manual

1880 NATIONAL ASSOCIATION OF LIFT MAKERS
8 Leicester Street, London WC2H 7BN Tel. 01-437 0678
Trade Association

Enquiries to the Director

Subject coverage
lifts; escalators; passenger conveyors; safety, design and standardization

1881 NATIONAL ASSOCIATION OF MALLEABLE IRONFOUNDERS
136 Hagley Road, Edgbaston, Birmingham B16 9PN Tel. 021-454 4141
Trade Association; member of the Council of Ironfoundry Associations, *q.v.*

Enquiries to the Secretaries

Subject coverage
malleable iron castings

Publications
Buyers Guide
Design for Malleable Iron Castings
Engineering Data in SI Units

1882 NATIONAL ASSOCIATION OF MARINE ENGINEBUILDERS
21 Grosvenor Place, London SW1X 7SE Tel. 01-235 5131
Telex 22797
Trade Association; affiliated to the Shipbuilders and Repairers National Association

Enquiries to the Information Officer

Subject coverage
U.K. marine enginebuilding

1883 NATIONAL ASSOCIATION OF MASTER BAKERS, CONFECTIONERS & CATERERS
50 Alexandra Road, Wimbledon SW19 7LB Tel. 01-947 7781
Trade Association

Enquiries to the Assistant Director

Subject coverage
bread; confectionery

Publication
Bakers Review

1884 NATIONAL ASSOCIATION OF MASTER MASONS
Admin House, Market Square, Leighton Buzzard, Bedfordshire Tel. 05253 75252
Trade Association

Enquiries to the General Secretary

Subject coverage
memorial masonry trade

1885 NATIONAL ASSOCIATION OF PHARMACEUTICAL DISTRIBUTORS
176 Northolt Road, South Harrow, Middlesex HA2 0EL Tel. 01-864 0443
Trade Association, affiliated to the Association of the British Pharmaceutical Industry

Enquiries to the Secretary

Subject coverage
pharmaceutical distribution

1886 NATIONAL ASSOCIATION OF PLUMBING, HEATING AND MECHANICAL SERVICES CONTRACTORS
6 Gate Street, London WC2A 3HX Tel. 01-405 2678
Trade Association; formerly the National Federation of Plumbers and Domestic Heating Engineers

Enquiries to the Secretary

Subject coverage
plumbing and mechanical engineering services; industrial agreements; training

1887 NATIONAL ASSOCIATION OF PRINCIPAL AGRICULTURAL EDUCATION OFFICERS
Hampshire College of Agriculture, Sparsholt, Nr. Winchester, Hampshire SO21 2NF Tel. 096-272 441
Professional Association

Enquiries to the Secretary

Subject coverage
agricultural, horticultural and countryside careers and courses

1888 NATIONAL ASSOCIATION OF RETAIL FURNISHERS
3 Berners Street, London W1P 4JP Tel. 01-636 1778
Trade Association

Enquiries to the Secretary or Head of Studies

Subject coverage
furniture trade from retailers viewpoint; training of staff; survey of Operating Experience (fees chargeable to non-members)

Publications
Monthly Bulletin
Training Aids

1889 NATIONAL ASSOCIATION OF ROPE AND TWINE MERCHANTS
First Floor, 251 Brompton Road, London SW3 2EP Tel. 01-584 5552
Trade Association

Enquiries to the Secretary

Subject coverage
supply of rope and twine

Publication
Cordage, Canvas and Jute World (monthly)

1890 NATIONAL ASSOCIATION OF SCAFFOLDING CONTRACTORS
82 New Cavendish Street, London W1M 8AD Tel. 01-637 4771
Telex 265763
Trade Association; member of the National Federation of Building Trades Employers

Enquiries to the Director

Subject coverage
all aspects of the scaffolding industry

1891 NATIONAL ASSOCIATION OF SOFT DRINKS MANUFACTURERS LIMITED
The Gatehouse, 2 Holly Road, Twickenham, TW1 4EF Tel. 01-892 8082
Trade Association

Enquiries to the Secretary

Subject coverage
soft drinks industry

Publications
Soft Drinks Trade Journal (monthly)
Soft Drinks Industry Legal Handbook

1892 NATIONAL ASSOCIATION OF STEEL STOCKHOLDERS
Lennig House, Masons Avenue, Croydon CR9 3NU Tel. 01-686 7957
Trade Association; houses the National Association of Fastener Stockholders, the South Eastern Association of Steel Stockholders and the Tinplate Stockholders Association

Enquiries to the Secretariat

Subject coverage
sources of supply of steels

Publication
Annual Statement
Illustrated Brochure

1893 NATIONAL ASSOCIATION OF WASTE DISPOSAL CONTRACTORS (NAWDC)
Suite 1, 14 Uxbridge Road, Ealing, London W5 2BP Tel. 01-579 5355/6
Trade Association

Enquiries to the Secretary

Subject coverage
Disposal of industrial waste

Publications
NAWDC Handbook, including Trade Directory, Codes of Conduct and Practice, and Conditions of Trading
NAWDC News (bi-monthly)

NATIONAL ASSOCIATION OF WHOLESALE DISTRIBUTORS OF FROZEN FOODS *now* **BRITISH FROZEN FOODS FEDERATION,** *q.v.*

1894 NATIONAL BEDDING FEDERATION LIMITED
251 Brompton Road, London SW3 2EZ Tel. 01-589 4888
Trade Association

Enquiries to the Assistant Director

Subject coverage
all aspects of the bedding manufacturing industry

NATIONAL BOAT SHOWS LIMITED *see* **SHIP AND BOAT BUILDERS NATIONAL FEDERATION**

1895 NATIONAL BRASS FOUNDRY ASSOCIATION
5 Greenfield Crescent, Birmingham B15 3BE Tel. 021-454 2177
Trade Association; member of the National Building and Allied Hardware Manufacturers Federation, *q.v.*

Enquiries to the Director

Subject coverage
industrial relations; wages; working conditions; trade information; interpretation of government legislation

1896 NATIONAL BUILDING AGENCY
7 Arundel Street, London WC2R 3DZ Tel. 01-836 4488
Telex 268312

Limited Company/Government Agency

Enquiries to the Information Officer or Secretary

Subject coverage
management consultancy; capital works programming; contract procedures; cost planning; construction monitoring and maintenance; Government policy implementation; communications; construction industry generally; metrication

Publications
Bulletins, books, pamphlets
NBA Publications (list)

1897 NATIONAL BUILDING AND ALLIED HARDWARE MANUFACTURERS FEDERATION
5 Greenfield Crescent, Birmingham B15 3BE Tel. 021-454 2177
Trade Association

Enquiries to the Director

Subject coverage
technical and marketing information in building and allied hardware

Publications
Annual Report
List of members

1898 NATIONAL BUILDING COMMODITY CENTRE LIMITED
London Building Centre, 26 Store Street, London WC1E 7BT Tel. 01-637 8361
Telex 261446

Company; member of the Builder Group, Building Centre Group, and National Building Agency

Enquiries to the Information Officers or the Librarian

Subject coverage
building and construction; regulations; manufacturers product information; "Data Express" information to specifiers

Publication
NBA & 'Building' Commodity File, 6 volumes (regulations and analyses of manufacturers products)

1899 NATIONAL CARAVAN COUNCIL LIMITED
43–45 High Street, Weybridge, Surrey KT13 8BT Tel. Weybridge 51376
Telex 928800

Trade Association, member of the European Caravan Federation

Enquiries to the Director General

Subject coverage
caravanning; production statistics; operation of caravan parks

Publication
List of members

NATIONAL CASH REGISTER COMPANY LIMITED *now* **NCR LIMITED,** *q.v.*

1900 NATIONAL CATTLE BREEDERS ASSOCIATION
Jenkins Lane, St. Leonards, Nr. Tring, Hertfordshire Tel. 024-029 544
Breeders Association

Enquiries to the Secretary

Subject coverage
cattle, live or dead

NATIONAL CAVING ASSOCIATION *see* **BRITISH CAVE RESEARCH ASSOCIATION**

NATIONAL CENTRE FOR SCHOOLS TECHNOLOGY *see* **TRENT POLYTECHNIC**

1901 NATIONAL CENTRE OF TRIBOLOGY
United Kingdom Atomic Energy Authority, Risley, Warrington, Lancashire Tel. 0925 31244
Telex 62301
Consultancy, Research, and Testing Organization, within the UKAEA Risley Engineering and Materials Laboratory

Enquiries to the Manager

Subject coverage
all aspects of tribology, *i.e.* friction, lubrication, and wear, as applied to all machine elements (bearings, gears, seals, etc.)

Publications
Quarterly Newsletter
National Centre of Tribology (pamphlet on activities)

1902 NATIONAL CHAMBER OF TRADE
Enterprise House, Henley-on-Thames, Oxford RG9 1TU Tel. 04912 6161
Telex 848715

Trade Association; houses the Trade and Professional Alliance

Enquiries to the Director General

Subject coverage
retail distribution, particularly the small firm; trading and business communities

Publications
Intercom (monthly)
Subject booklets for distributive and service information

NATIONAL CHEMICAL EMERGENCY CENTRE *see* **HAZARDOUS MATERIALS SERVICE**

1903 NATIONAL CLAYWARE FEDERATION
7 Castle Street, Bridgwater, Somerset TA6 3DT Tel. 0278 8251
Trade Association

Enquiries to the Secretary

Subject coverage

manufacture of unglazed flue linings; chimney terminals; ridge tiles, air bricks and other clayware goods

1904 NATIONAL COAL BOARD

Hobart House, Grosvenor Place, London SW1X 7AE — Tel. 01-235 2020, Telex 22398

Nationalised Industry, which includes the Mining Research and Development Establishment, the Coal Research Establishment, and the Institute of Occupational Medicine, *qq.v.*

Enquiries to the Librarian

Subject coverage

coal mining

Publications

Abstracts A, Technical Coal Press
Abstracts C, Coal Mining and Geology
Abstracts D, Fluid Mechanics
Information Bulletin—Coal Processing and Combustion

1905 NATIONAL COLD STORAGE FEDERATION

272 London Road, Wallington, Surrey SM6 7DJ — Tel. 01-647 8778

Trade Association; formerly National Federation of Cold Storage and Ice Trades; shares premises with the Institute of Refrigeration, *q.v.*

Enquiries to the Secretary

Subject coverage

cold storage

Publication

Year Book

NATIONAL COLLEGE FOR HEATING, VENTILATING, REFRIGERATION AND FAN ENGINEERING *now* **POLYTECHNIC OF THE SOUTH BANK,** *q.v.*

1906 NATIONAL COLLEGE OF AGRICULTURAL ENGINEERING

Silsoe, Bedford MK45 4DT — Tel. 0525 60428

Agricultural College; part of the School of Agricultural Engineering of Cranfield Institute of Technology; houses the Institution of Agricultural Engineers and the agricultural section of the Intermediate Technology Development Group, *qq.v.*

Enquiries to the Librarian

Subject coverage

agricultural engineering; agricultural machinery design; irrigation and drainage; soil conservation; environmental control; crop processing; agricultural mechanization; tillage problems and practices; land resource planning

Publications

Occasional Papers

1907 NATIONAL COLLEGE OF FOOD TECHNOLOGY

Reading University, St Georges Avenue, Weybridge, Surrey KT13 0DE — Tel. 0932 43991

University Department

Enquiries to the Librarian

Subject coverage

food technology; biotechnology; industrial microbiology; fermentation technology

NATIONAL COMMITTEE FOR AUDIO-VISUAL AIDS IN EDUCATION *see* **ASSOCIATION FOR PROGRAMMED LEARNING AND EDUCATIONAL TECHNOLOGY**

NATIONAL COMPUTER INDEX *see* **PEDDER ASSOCIATES LIMITED**

1908 NATIONAL COMPUTING CENTRE LIMITED
Oxford Road, Manchester M1 7ED Tel. 061-228 6333
Telex 668962
Company Limited by guarantee; non-profit distributing, government sponsored by Department of Industry

Enquiries to the Information Operations Centre

Subject coverage
all aspects of computing, particularly of the U.K.; computing equipment, programmes, education, services, training, consultancy, standards, good practice

Publications
Computing Journal Abstracts (weekly)
Working Papers (available to members only):
1. D.P. Efficiency Monitoring
2. User Experience with DBMS in the U.K.
3. Project Planning and Control for DP
Books listed in NCC Book Catalogue

1909 NATIONAL COOPERAGE FEDERATION
c/o Leith Chamber of Commerce, 27 Queen Charlotte Street, Leith, Edinburgh EH6 6AH Tel. 031-554 3055
Trade Association

Enquiries to the Secretary

Subject coverage
cooperage industry

1910 NATIONAL CORROSION SERVICE
National Physical Laboratory, Teddington, Middlesex TW11 0LW Tel. 01-977 3222
Telex 262344
Government Agency, of the Department of Industry

Enquiries to the Head of the Service

Subject coverage
corrosion control and prevention; design and selection of materials; coating systems; cathodic protection; environmental factors; failure investigations; advisory and consultancy services

NATIONAL COUNCIL FOR EDUCATIONAL QUALIFICATIONS IN SALESMANSHIP *see* **UNITED COMMERCIAL TRAVELLERS ASSOCIATION LIMITED**

NATIONAL COUNCIL FOR EDUCATIONAL TECHNOLOGY *now* **COUNCIL FOR EDUCATIONAL TECHNOLOGY FOR THE UNITED KINGDOM,** *q.v.*

NATIONAL COUNCIL FOR QUALITY AND RELIABILITY *see* **INSTITUTION OF MECHANICAL ENGINEERS**

1911 NATIONAL COUNCIL FOR THE OMNIBUS INDUSTRY
25 New Street Square, London EC4A 3AP Tel. 01-583 9177
Joint Wage Negotiating Council; houses the Conference of Omnibus Companies

Enquiries to the Joint Secretary (Employers Side)

Subject coverage
industrial relations in the omnibus industry

1912 NATIONAL COUNCIL OF AVICULTURE
Midda Beck, Mill Lane, Aldringham, Leiston, Suffolk IP16 4PZ Tel. 0728 830887
Advisory Body

Enquiries to the Joint Secretaries

Subject coverage
all aspects of cage and aviary birds and their Societies; construction of aviaries, etc.; show organization; liaison between the membership and government departments, transport organizations and local authorities

1913 NATIONAL COUNCIL OF BUILDING MATERIAL PRODUCERS
26 Store Street, London WC1E 7BT Tel. 01-580 3344
Confederation of Trade Associations; houses the Building Materials Export Group, *q.v.*

Enquiries to the Secretary

Subject coverage
building materials industry in general, and non-specialist information on availability and sources of materials; forecasts of construction industry output; statistics, legislation

Publications
BMP Information (fortnightly)
BMP Statistical Bulletin (monthly)
Annual Report
Occasional special reports

NATIONAL DAIRY COUNCIL *see* **NATIONAL MILK PUBLICITY COUNCIL**

NATIONAL DISPLAY EQUIPMENT ASSOCIATION *now* **SHOP AND DISPLAY EQUIPMENT ASSOCIATION,** *q.v.*

NATIONAL DIVING COUNCIL FOR SCOTLAND *see* **SCOTTISH SUB-AQUA CLUB**

1914 NATIONAL ECONOMIC DEVELOPMENT OFFICE
Millbank Tower, Millbank, London SW1P 4QX Tel. 01-211 3000
Quasi-Governmental Department, comprising a large number of Economic Development Committees, *q.v.*

Enquiries to the Secretary

Subject coverage
economic situation and prospects of individual industries or larger industry groupings

Publications
List available from NEDO Bookshop, 1 Steel House, Tothill Street, London SW1

NATIONAL EDIBLE OIL DISTRIBUTORS ASSOCIATION *see* **FOOD MANUFACTURERS FEDERATION INCORPORATED**

1915 NATIONAL EGG PACKERS ASSOCIATION LIMITED
No 1, London Bridge, London SE1 9SZ Tel. 01-407 0738
Trade Association; houses the Scottish Federation of Egg Packers Limited

Enquiries to the Secretary

Subject coverage
packing and marketing of eggs

1916 NATIONAL EGG PRODUCERS RETAILERS ASSOCIATION
40 Sudley Road, Bognor Regis, Sussex PO21 1ER Tel. (Robophone) 24897 *or* 25778
Trade Association; two separate companies operate under the above name, at the same address; the National Egg Producers Retailers Association Limited and N.E.P.R.A. Commercial Limited

Enquiries to the Company Secretary

Subject coverage
egg production and retailing industry market intelligence

Publication
Market Report (weekly, for members only)

1917 NATIONAL ELECTRONICS COUNCIL
Abell House, John Islip Street, London SW1P 4LN — Tel. 01-211 6671 *or* 3066
Company

Enquiries to the Secretary

Subject coverage
social impact of electronics—non-technical

Publication
National Electronics Review (bi-monthly)

1918 NATIONAL ENGINEERING LABORATORY
East Kilbride, Glasgow G75 0GU — Tel. 035-52 20222
Telex 77588

Government Research and Development Establishment, of the Department of Industry; incorporates the former Birniehill Institute which was also known as IAMTACT or Institute for Advanced Machine Tools and Control Technology (all those names now discontinued)

Enquiries to the Librarian

Subject coverage
advisory services on engineering metrology; machine tools, including programming of numerically controlled machine tools; gearing; bearings; control of noise & vibration in machinery; properties & strength of engineering materials, including fatigue, creep & resistance to wear and the application of this information to the design of components; structural analysis; metal forming operations including extrusion; pumps & water turbines; fans & blowers; flow measurement; heat exchangers; heat pipes; and the physical properties of fluids, including their thermodynamic & transport properties; testing & calibration of flow-meters & valves to BCS specifications; cavitation and performance tests on pumps and water turbines; performance tests on fans; dynamic calibration of fatigue machines; creep & fatigue tests on engineering materials; full scale service loading tests on structures, vehicles and components; life tests on bearing materials; measurement of noise from mechanisms; engineering metrology; efficiency tests on mechanical & hydraulic transmissions; and performance tests on heat exchangers

Publications
NEL Reports series (gratis)
NEL Research Summaries (gratis)
NEL Research and Test; services to industry (gratis)
Conference and Symposia Proceedings (priced)
Other publications through H.M.S.O. (see H.M.S.O. Sectional List No 3)

1919 NATIONAL FARMERS UNION OF ENGLAND AND WALES
Agriculture House, 25–31 Knightsbridge, London SW1X 7NJ — Tel. 01-235 5077
Telex 919669

Trade Association, housing also the British Farm Produce Council, the Mushroom Growers Association, and Agricultural Cooperation and Marketing Services Ltd, *qq.v.*

Enquiries to the Librarian

Subject coverage
agriculture and horticulture; land use; trade in agricultural products

Publications
British Farmer and Stockbreeder (fortnightly)
NFU Handbook (annual)
NFU Showguide (annual)
NFU Guide to Prices and Services
Various other guides, reports, and Common Market publications

NATIONAL FEDERATED ELECTRICAL ASSOCIATION *see* **ELECTRICAL CONTRACTORS ASSOCIATION**

1920 NATIONAL FEDERATION OF BEER BOTTLERS
Newton Place, Hockley, Birmingham B18 5LL Tel. 021-554 9886
Trade Association

Enquiries to the Secretary

Subject coverage
beer bottling

1921 NATIONAL FEDERATION OF BUILDERS AND PLUMBERS MERCHANTS
15 Soho Square, London W1V 5FB Tel. 01-439 1753
Trade Association; houses the Guild of Architectural Ironmongers, *q.v.*, the National Federation of Roofing Contractors, *q.v.* and the Institute of Builders Merchants

Enquiries, from members only, to the Director

Subject coverage
sources of materials, etc.

NATIONAL FEDERATION OF BUILDING TRADES EMPLOYERS *see*
BUILDING ADVISORY SERVICE
NATIONAL ASSOCIATION OF SCAFFOLDING CONTRACTORS

1922 NATIONAL FEDERATION OF CLAY INDUSTRIES
Weston House, West Bar Green, Sheffield, South Yorkshire S1 2DA Tel. 0742 730261
Telex 54453

Trade Association; houses the Institute of Clayworkers

Enquiries to the Secretary

Subject coverage
bricks; refractories; clay pipes; floor tiles

NATIONAL FEDERATION OF COLD STORAGE AND ICE TRADES *now* **NATIONAL COLD STORAGE FEDERATION,** *q.v.*

1923 NATIONAL FEDERATION OF DEMOLITION CONTRACTORS LIMITED
141 London Road, Leicester LE2 1EF Tel. 0533 536167
Trade Association

Enquiries to the Secretary

Subject coverage
demolition

Publications
Membership Brochure
Form of Direct Contract
Working Rule Agreement
Bibliography

1924 NATIONAL FEDERATION OF ENGINEERS TOOL MANUFACTURERS
Light Trades House, Melbourne Avenue, Sheffield S10 2QJ Tel. 0742 663084
Telex 54208

Trade Association, of eight member associations; the above address also houses the Federation of British Hand Tool Manufacturers, *q.v.*

Enquiries to the Secretary General

Subject coverage
tool industry; exports, standardization; metrication and commercial matters

Publication
British Tools Directory

1925 NATIONAL FEDERATION OF FISHMONGERS
Queensway House, 2 Queensway, Redhill, Surrey RH1 1QS Tel. 91 68611
Trade Federation

Enquiries to the Secretary

Subject coverage
problems of fishmongers

1926 NATIONAL FEDERATION OF FRUIT AND POTATO TRADES LIMITED
Russell Chambers, Covent Garden, London WC2E 8AD Tel. 01-836 0036/7/8/9
Telex 22207
Trade Association

Enquiries to the Secretary

Subject coverage
the importing and wholesaling of fresh fruit, vegetables, potatoes and flowers

NATIONAL FEDERATION OF MASTER PAINTERS AND DECORATORS OF ENGLAND AND WALES *now* **BRITISH DECORATORS ASSOCIATION,** *q.v.*

1927 NATIONAL FEDERATION OF MASTER STEEPLEJACKS AND LIGHTNING CONDUCTOR ENGINEERS
141 London Road, Leicester LE2 1EF Tel. 0533 536167
Trade Association

Enquiries to the Secretary

Subject coverage
steeplejacking

Publications
Membership List
History
Day Work Charges

NATIONAL FEDERATION OF PLUMBERS AND DOMESTIC HEATING ENGINEERS *now* **NATIONAL ASSOCIATION OF PLUMBING HEATING AND MECHANICAL SERVICES CONTRACTORS,** *q.v.*

NATIONAL FEDERATION OF PUBLICITY ASSOCIATIONS *see* **ADVERTISING ASSOCIATION**

1928 NATIONAL FEDERATION OF ROOFING CONTRACTORS
15 Soho Square, London W1V 5FB Tel. 01-439 1753
Trade Association; member of the Federation of Associations of Specialists and Sub-Contractors

Enquiries, from members only, to the General Secretary

Subject coverage
wage rates and conditions of employment within the industry; contract and legal matters; training; safety

Publications
Yearbook
Roofing Contractor (bi-monthly)

NATIONAL FEDERATION OF SAILING SCHOOLS *see* **SHIP AND BOAT BUILDERS NATIONAL FEDERATION**

1929 NATIONAL FEDERATION OF TERRAZZO MOSAIC SPECIALISTS
First Floor, 251 Brompton Road, London SW3 2EP Tel. 01-584 5552
Trade Association; member of the Federation of Associations of Specialists and Sub-Contractors

Enquiries to the Secretary

Subject coverage
the laying of terrazzo and mosaic; investigation of complaints

1930 NATIONAL FEDERATION OF VEHICLE TRADES
3 Shakespeare Road, Finchley, London N3 1XE Tel. 01-349 2066/7
Employers Association, member of, and sharing address with, the United Kingdom Joint Wages Board of Employers for the Vehicle Building Industry

Enquiries to the General Secretary

Subject coverage
working conditions and wages in the vehicle building industry

1931 NATIONAL FEDERATION OF WHOLESALE GROCERS AND PROVISION MERCHANTS
18 Fleet Street, London EC4Y 1AS Tel. 01-353 8894/5
Trade Association

Enquiries to the Secretary

Subject coverage
wholesale food distribution

Publication
Yearbook

NATIONAL FIRE BRIGADES ASSOCIATION *now* **BRITISH FIRE SERVICES ASSOCIATION,** *q.v.*

1932 NATIONAL FIREPLACE MANUFACTURERS ASSOCIATION
P.O. Box 35, Hanley, Stoke-on-Trent ST1 3RG Tel. 0782 29031
Trade Association

Enquiries to the Executive Officer

Subject coverage
fireplaces

1933 NATIONAL FOOD AND DRINK FEDERATION
Federation House, 17 Farnborough Street, Farnborough, Hampshire GU14 8AG Tel. 0252 515001/2
Trade Association; created by the merger of the former National Grocers Federation and the National Off-Licence Federation

Enquiries to the Chief Executive

Subject coverage
retail food trade; off-licence trade

Publication
Grocery Trade Handbook (annual)

NATIONAL FRUIT AND CIDER INSTITUTE *see* **LONG ASHTON RESEARCH STATION**

1934 NATIONAL GAS TURBINE ESTABLISHMENT
Pyestock, Farnborough, Hampshire GU14 0LS Tel. 0252 44411
Telex 85231
Government Research Establishment, of the Procurement Executive, Ministry of Defence

Enquiries to the Librarian

Subject coverage
gas turbine engines of all types but principally transport applications

1935 NATIONAL GRAPHICAL ASSOCIATION (NGA)
63–67 Bromham Road, Bedford MK40 2AG Tel. 0234 51521
Trade Union

Enquiries to the Secretary

Subject coverage
printing trade conditions

Publication
Print

NATIONAL GROCERS FEDERATION *now* **NATIONAL FOOD AND DRINK FEDERATION,** *q.v.*

1936 NATIONAL ILLUMINATION COMMITTEE OF GREAT BRITAIN
c/o Building Research Establishment, Garston, Watford, Hertfordshire WD2 7JR — Tel. 09273 74040, Telex 923220
Independent Committee, supported by Government, Public, Trade, Professional and Academic Bodies; member of the Commission Internationale de l'Eclairage (CIE)

Enquiries to the Honorary Secretary

Subject coverage
all aspects of lighting and applied visual science, including photometry, colorimetry, sources, actinic effects, daylighting, relation to architecture, visual signalling

1937 NATIONAL INDUSTRIAL FUEL EFFICIENCY SERVICE LIMITED (NIFES)
Orchard House, 14 Great Smith Street, London SW1P 3BU — Tel. 01-222 0961
Company; branches at Altrincham, Birmingham, Buntingford, Dundee, Glasgow, Newcastle, Nottingham and Yeadon

Enquiries to the Secretary

Subject coverage
fuel efficiency; energy conservation; instrumented surveys; energy audits; service visiting; training in energy conservation; consultancy in energy-intensive new mechanical and electrical projects; commissioning and testing of newly installed plant

Publications
Introducing NIFES
NIFES Energy Consultants to Industry and Commerce
Project Design
Boiler Operations Handbook

1938 NATIONAL INDUSTRIAL MATERIALS RECOVERY ASSOCIATION
York House, Westminster Bridge Road, London SE1 7UT — Tel. 01-928 5715
Trade Association; having 8 Regional Councils; houses the Institute of Purchasing and Supply, *q.v.*

Enquiries to the Secretary General

Subject coverage
conservation; disposal of waste; reclamation of waste; anti-pollution

Publications
Industrial Recovery (monthly)
Technical leaflets on reclamation, pollution, etc
Collated Conference Lectures (booklet)

1939 NATIONAL INSPECTION COUNCIL FOR ELECTRICAL INSTALLATION CONTRACTING
Alembic House, 93 Albert Embankment, London SE1 7TB — Tel. 01-582 7746
Non-profit-making Consumer Protection Organization/Registered Charity

Enquiries to the Chief Engineer

Subject coverage
electrical installation; electrical equipment and components; safety; reliability; regulations

Publications
Roll of Approved Electrical Contractors
Electrician's Handbook, section 1, Faults and Remedies
Electrician's Handbook, section 3, Electrical Installations for Petrol Filling Stations
Newsletter (monthly)
Various pamphlets on wiring, etc.

1940 NATIONAL INSTITUTE FOR BIOLOGICAL STANDARDS AND CONTROL
Holly Hill, Hampstead, London NW3 6RB Tel. 01-435 2232
Telex 21911

Research Institution, government-sponsored; formerly National Institute for Medical Research (Hampstead Laboratories); designated a World Health Organization International Laboratory for Biological Standards

Enquiries to the Librarian

Subject coverage
standardization and control of antibiotics, bacterial products, blood products, hormones, viral products and allergens; biomedical science relevant to the foregoing subjects

NATIONAL INSTITUTE FOR MEDICAL RESEARCH (HAMPSTEAD LABORATORIES) *now* **NATIONAL INSTITUTE FOR BIOLOGICAL STANDARDS AND CONTROL,** *q.v.*

1941 NATIONAL INSTITUTE FOR RESEARCH IN DAIRYING
Church Lane, Shinfield, Reading, Berkshire RG2 9AT Tel. 0734 883895

State-aided Research Institute, at the University of Reading, of the Agricultural Research Council; houses the Commonwealth Bureau of Dairy Science and Technology, *q.v.* and the International Food Information Service, *q.v.*

Enquiries to the Information Officer

Subject coverage
dairying; dairy farming; endocrinology of lactation

Publications
Biennial Reports
Biennial Reviews

1942 NATIONAL INSTITUTE OF AGRICULTURAL BOTANY
Huntingdon Road, Cambridge CB3 0LE Tel. 0223 76381

Independent Research and Development Organization; includes the Official Seed Testing Station for England and Wales

Enquiries, bibliographical and publication, to the Librarian; technical, to the Scientific Officer

Subject coverage
variety testing of most agricultural and horticultural crops (except fruit); advice on choice of variety; seed certification; seed testing procedures; botanical description of varieties; plant pathology

Publications
List available

1943 NATIONAL INSTITUTE OF AGRICULTURAL ENGINEERING
Wrest Park, Silsoe, Bedfordshire MK45 4NS Tel. 0525 60000

Research Institute of the Agricultural Research Council, *q.v.*

Enquiries to the Librarian

Subject coverage
agricultural and horticultural engineering

Publications
Annual Report
Programme of Research

1944 NATIONAL INSTITUTE OF ECONOMIC AND SOCIAL RESEARCH
2 Dean Trench Street, Smith Square, London SW1P 3HE Tel. 01-222 7665

Research Institute

Enquiries to the Librarian

Subject coverage
economic research, particularly short term forecasting

Publications
National Institute Economic Review
Annual Report
Monographs, various series
Occasional Papers series

1945 NATIONAL INSTITUTE OF HARDWARE
10 Leam Terrace, Leamington Spa, Warwickshire CV31 1BD — Tel. 0926 21284
Trade Association

Enquiries to the Director

Subject coverage
hardware commodities, management and training

Publications
Training manuals on commodities and retail law
Hardware Training News

1946 NATIONAL INSTITUTE OF INDUSTRIAL PSYCHOLOGY
c/o North East London Polytechnic, Livingstone House, Livingstone Road, London E15 2LJ — Tel. 01-534 7825
Research Association, not-for-profit

Enquiries to the Librarian or the Assistant Director

Subject coverage
occupational psychology, including occupational or vocational guidance, personnel selection, attitude studies, morale, motivation, safety, fatigue; communication, etc

Special collection
the Charles Myers Library

NATIONAL INSTITUTE OF OCEANOGRAPHY *now* **INSTITUTE OF OCEANOGRAPHIC SCIENCES,** *q.v.*

NATIONAL INSTITUTE OF POULTRY HUSBANDRY *see* **HARPER ADAMS AGRICULTURAL COLLEGE**

1947 NATIONAL JOINT COMMITTEE FOR THE BRUSH AND BROOM AND HAIR, FIBRE AND BASS INDUSTRIES
Baptist Church House, 4 Southampton Row, London WC1B 4AB — Tel. 01-242 1799
Negotiating Body

Enquiries to the Secretary

Subject coverage
wages and conditions in the brush, broom, etc., industries

NATIONAL JOINT COUNCIL FOR MATERIALS HANDLING *now* **NATIONAL MATERIALS HANDLING CENTRE,** *q.v.*

1948 NATIONAL JOINT INDUSTRIAL COUNCIL FOR THE GLASS CONTAINER INDUSTRY
Employers Secretary: 19 Portland Place, London W1N 4BH — Tel. 01-580 6952
Trade Union Secretary: Transport House, Smith Square, London SW1P 3JB — Tel. 01-828 7788
Negotating Body

Enquiries to the Secretaries

Subject coverage
wages and conditions in the glass container industry

1949 NATIONAL JOINT COUNCIL FOR THE THERMAL INSULATION CONTRACTING INDUSTRY
57 Atwood Road, Didsbury, Manchester M20 0TB Tel. 061-445 1173
Joint Wage Negotiating Body

Enquiries to the Secretary, in writing

Subject coverage
wages and conditions in the thermal insulation contracting industry

NATIONAL JOINT INDUSTRIAL COUNCIL FOR THE PAINT, VARNISH AND LACQUER INDUSTRY *see* **PAINTMAKERS ASSOCIATION OF GREAT BRITAIN LIMITED**

1950 NATIONAL LEATHERSELLERS COLLEGE
176 Tower Bridge Road, London SE1 Tel. 01-407 2544
Technical College

Enquiries to the Librarian

Subject coverage
leather manufacture; tanning; leather chemistry

NATIONAL LIBRARY OF IRELAND *see* **IRISH ASSOCIATION OF DOCUMENTATION AND INFORMATION SERVICES**

1951 NATIONAL LIBRARY OF SCOTLAND
George IV Bridge, Edinburgh EH1 1EW Tel. 031-226 4531
Telex 72638

National Library of over 3,000,000 books and pamphlets; Copyright Deposit Library; housing SCOLCAP, Scottish Libraries Co-operative Automation Project; Lending Services also in Edinburgh

Enquiries to the Librarian

Subject coverage
general; official and governmental documents; books; manuscripts; maps; for special subjects, *see Special collections*

Special collections
Combe collection in phrenology
Wordie collection in Arctic and Antarctic exploration
Macadam collection in baking and confectionery
Townley collection of 7,500 postcards on early 20th century topography and railways
Lyle collection in ships and shipping
Tait collection in civil engineering
Graham Brown Alpine *and* Lloyd collections of alpine and mountaineering literature
Macdonald collection of 1,200 colour slides illustrating town planning
Warden collection in shorthand
Birkbeck collection in printing and topography
Collections in the Department of Manuscripts include the John Rennie Papers, archives of Scottish publishers and printers, trade unions, the Society of Arts, and other commercial papers relating to mining and to individual scientists

Publications
Catalogues of exhibitions
Commemorative publications
Annual Report
List of publications for sale

1952 NATIONAL LIBRARY OF SCOTLAND LENDING SERVICES
George IV Bridge, Edinburgh EH1 1EW Tel. 031-226 4531
Telex 72638

National Library, formerly the Scottish Central Library; Headquarters for Scottish Inter-Library Co-operation; houses the Scottish Union Catalogue

Enquiries to the Superintendent of Lending Services

Subject coverage
general; also scarce and expensive books to supplement the reserves of Scottish public libraries

Publication
Out of Print Books and Manuscripts on microfilm, 1969

1953 NATIONAL LIBRARY OF WALES
Penglais, Aberystwyth, Cardiganshire SY23 3BU — Tel. 0970 3816/9, Telex 35165

Copyright and Reference Library; home of the Wales Regional Library Bureau

Enquiries to the Librarian

Subject coverage
life, history and literature of Wales (the largest collection in the world relating to Wales)

Publication
National Library of Wales Journal

1954 NATIONAL MARITIME INSTITUTE
Faggs Road, Feltham, Middlesex TW14 0LQ — Tel. 01-977 3222, Telex 263118

Government Department, of the Department of Industry; formerly Ship Division, National Physical Laboratory; having units at Queens Road, Teddington, formerly the Division of Maritime Science, National Physical Laboratory, and at St. Johns Street, Hythe

Enquiries to the Director

Subject coverage
ships, including hydrodynamics, seakeeping, manoeuvring, propulsion, structural vibration, wind forces, safety; navigational safety; marine traffic systems; operations in ports and harbours; loading, including wind loading, and response of offshore structures, buildings and bridges; fluid dynamics; wave characteristics; instrumentation; trials at sea; hovercraft

1955 NATIONAL MARITIME MUSEUM
Romney Road, Greenwich, London SE10 9NF — Tel. 01-858 4422
National Museum; houses the International Congress of Maritime Museums

Enquiries to the Secretary

Subject coverage
maritime history especially of Great Britain, covering Royal Navy, merchant shipping, commercial fishing, pleasure sailing, ship archaeology, navigation, time keeping at sea, hydrography, dockyards, ports and harbours (History of astronomy at Greenwich—Old Royal Observatory)

Special collections
many and vast collections of documents, maps, charts, prints, drawings, ships' plans, registers, news cuttings, shipping company records, records of ships and shipwrecks, as well as the museum objects collections

Publications
Catalogues of books, atlases, etc.
Inventory of Instruments
Monographs on maritime history, etc.

1956 NATIONAL MATERIALS HANDLING CENTRE
Cranfield Institute of Technology, Cranfield, Bedfordshire MK43 0AL — Tel. 0234 750323, Telex 825072
National Independent non-profit-making Organization, formerly National Joint Council for Materials Handling

Enquiries to the Librarian

Subject coverage
materials handling; warehouse design including cold stores; physical distribution; pallet testing; freight transport; logistics; ergonomics; kinetics; consultancy and market research services

Special collection
extensive collection of trade literature on materials handling equipment

Publications
International Distribution and Handling Review (abstract journal)
Conference proceedings, reports, and bibliographies (list available)

1957 NATIONAL MILK PUBLICITY COUNCIL
5–7 John Princes Street, London W1M 0AP Tel. 01-499 7822
Trade Association; composed of the Milk Marketing Board and the Dairy Trade Federation, *qq.v.* and housing also the National Dairy Council and the English Country Cheese Council

Enquiries to the Information Officer

Subject coverage
consumption of milk and dairy products

1958 NATIONAL MUSEUM OF WALES (LIBRARY)
Cathays Park, Cardiff CF1 3NP Tel. 0222 397951
National Library, part of the National Museum; houses the Cardiff Naturalists Society Library *q.v.* and the Cambrian Archaeological Association Library

Enquiries to the Librarian

Subject coverage
archaeology; botany; geology; industry; zoology

Special collections
Willoughby-Gardner Collection (early scientific books)
Tomlin Collection (conchology)

1959 NATIONAL NUCLEAR CORPORATION LIMITED
c/o GEC Limited, 1 Stanhope Gate, London W1 Tel. 01-493 8484
Telex 22451
Holding Company, including Nuclear Power Company Limited, *q.v.* of the United Kingdom Atomic Energy authority

Enquiries to the Public Relations Officer, NCC, Cambridge Road, Whetstone, Leicester LE8 3LH (tel. 053-729 3434, ext. 764)

Subject coverage
design, construction and commissioning of nuclear power reactors and power plants; associated consultancy

NATIONAL OFF-LICENCE FEDERATION *now* **NATIONAL FOOD AND DRINK FEDERATION,** *q.v.*

1960 NATIONAL PHARMACEUTICAL UNION
321 Chase Road, London N14 6JN Tel. 01-886 6544
Trade Association; houses also the Chemists Defence Associations Limited, the Chemists Mutual Insurance Company Limited, and the Chemists Sickness and Provident Society

Enquiries to the Head of Information Department

Subject coverage
retail pharmacy; medicines

1961 NATIONAL PHYSICAL LABORATORY
Teddington, Middlesex TW11 0LW Tel. 01-977 3222
Telex 262344
Government Research and Standards Laboratory, of the Department of Industry

Enquiries to the Director; telephone enquiries to the Technical Enquiries Officer, ext. 3057

Subject coverage
National and international standards in physics, chemistry and engineering, including electrical, mechanical and optical standards and standards of radioactivity and measurement of ionizing

radiations; physical acoustics and noise; application of computers and information technology; numerical analysis and computing; materials

Publications

Technical reports and memoranda
Specialist books and booklets (H.M.S.O.)

1962 NATIONAL PIG BREEDERS ASSOCIATION

49 Clarendon Road, Watford, Hertfordshire WD1 1HT Tel. 92 34377
Breed Society

Enquiries to the Secretary

Subject coverage

pig breeding

Publication

Pig Breeders Gazette

1963 NATIONAL PORTS COUNCIL

Commonwealth House, 1–19 New Oxford Street, London WC1A 1DZ Tel. 01-242 1200
Statutory Body

Enquiries to the Senior Information Officer; disclosure of information is subject to certain restrictions

Subject coverage

management, maintenance, and improvement of harbours; provision of access by road and rail; national planning for the development of ports; statistics of the ports industry

Publications

Annual Digest of Port Statistics
National Ports Council Bulletins
Port Approach Design, 2 vols
Reports on port progress, trade, costs, engineering, navigation, etc

1964 NATIONAL RADIOLOGICAL PROTECTION BOARD

Harwell, Didcot, Oxfordshire OX11 1RQ Tel. 023-583 600
Government (fringe) Organization; formed partly from the former Radiological Protection Service of the Medical Research Council and the Radiological Protection Division of the United Kingdom Atomic Energy Authority

Enquiries to the Information Officer

Subject coverage

radiological protection, including health and safety aspects of nuclear power, biological/medical effects of ionising radiations, non-ionising radiations (microwaves and lasers), radioactivity in consumer protection, radioactivity in fallout and in man; dosimetry

Publications

Radiological Protection Bulletin (quarterly)
Technical Reports (series NRPB-R)
Three-yearly Report
Codes of Practice
Living with Radiation (layman's guide)

NATIONAL REGISTER OF ENGINEER SURVEYORS *now* **BUREAU OF ENGINEER SURVEYORS,** *q.v.*

1965 NATIONAL REPROGRAPHIC CENTRE FOR DOCUMENTATION (NRCd)

Hatfield Polytechnic, Endymion Road Annexe, Hatfield, Hertfordshire AL10 8AU Tel. 30 66144
Research Centre, Department of Hatfield Polytechnic, grant-aided by the British Library Research and Development Department

Enquiries, from members only, to the Information Officer

Subject coverage
micrographics; micrographic cameras; microform readers and reader-printers; computer output microfilm; micrographic applications to information systems

Special collection
microfiche and hardcopy collection of monographs, articles, directories and papers on micrographics

Publications
Reprographics Quarterly (includes abstracts)
Directory of Commercial Microfilm Services in the U.K.
Thesaurus of Micrographic Terms
List of publications available

1966 NATIONAL SAWMILLING ASSOCIATION
Clareville House, Whitcomb Street, London WC2H 7DL Tel. 01-839 1891
Trade and Employers Association, member of the Timber Trade Federation; houses the Hardwood Flooring Manufacturers Association and the Wood Floor Manufacturers Committee

Enquiries to the Secretary

Subject coverage
industrial relations and trade matters in the sawmilling and imported timber industries

1967 NATIONAL SHEEP ASSOCIATION
Groves Jenkins Lane, St Leonards, Tring, Hertfordshire Tel. 968-29 544
Trade Association

Enquiries to the Secretary

Subject coverage
sheep industry

Publications
Sheep Farmer (quarterly)
British Sheep (5-yearly book)

1968 NATIONAL SOCIETY FOR CLEAN AIR
134–137 North Street, Brighton BN1 1RG Tel. 0273 26313
Limited Company and Charity, affiliated to the International Union of Air Pollution Prevention Associations

Enquiries to the Information Officer

Subject coverage
clean/polluted air and its relationship with the total environment

Publications
Clean Air (3 issues per annum)
NSCA Yearbook (annual)
Technical reports

1969 NATIONAL SOCIETY OF MASTER PATTERNMAKERS
39 Bennetts Hill, Birmingham B2 5SN Tel. 021-236 6674
Trade Association

Enquiries to the Secretary

Subject coverage
pattern-making

Publication
British Pattern and Mould Maker (quarterly)

NATIONAL SOCIETY OF POTTERY WORKERS *now* **CERAMIC AND ALLIED TRADES UNION,** *q.v.*

NATIONAL SULPHURIC ACID ASSOCIATION *see* **CHEMICAL INDUSTRIES ASSOCIATION LIMITED**

1970 NATIONAL SUPERVISORY COUNCIL FOR INTRUDER ALARMS
73/79 Rochester Row, London SW1P 1LQ Tel. 01-828 7582
National Inspectorate

Enquiries to the Director-General

Subject coverage
intruder alarm installation and maintenance to British Standards

1971 NATIONAL TELEVISION RENTAL ASSOCIATION LIMITED
295 Regent Street, London W1R 7YA Tel. 01-637 4591
Trade Association, formerly Electronic Rentals Associates Limited; houses the Cable Television Association of Great Britain, *q.v.*

Enquiries to the Association

Subject coverage
television rental industry

1972 NATIONAL TEROTECHNOLOGY CENTRE
Cleeve Road, Leatherhead, Surrey KT22 7SA Tel. 037-23 78242
Telex 264045
Independent Advisory Centre; part of ERA Limited, *q.v.*

Enquiries to the Information Officer

Subject coverage
terotechnology; maintenance management; reliability; condition monitoring; maintainability; life-cycle costing; investment appraisal; faults diagnosis

Publications
Terotechnology News
Maintenance Management Newsletter
Terotechnology Bibliography

NATIONAL TYRE DISTRIBUTORS ASSOCIATION *see* **FEDERATION OF WHOLESALE AND INDUSTRIAL DISTRIBUTORS**

1973 NATIONAL UNION OF BANK EMPLOYEES
Sheffield House, Portsmouth Road, Esher, Surrey KT1D 9BH Tel. 78 66624
Trade Union

Enquiries to the Publicity Officer

Subject coverage
industrial relations in banking and finance

Publication
NUBE News

1974 NATIONAL UNION OF MINEWORKERS
222 Euston Road, London NW1 2BX Tel. 01-387 7631
Trade Union

Enquiries to the Secretary

Subject coverage
trade unionism in the mining industry

1975 NATIONAL UNION OF SEAMEN
Maritime House, Old Town, Clapham, London SW4 0JP Tel. 01-622 5581
Trade Union; houses the International Transport Workers Federation, of which the Union is a member

Enquiries to the Research Officer

Subject coverage
shipping, with special reference to the employment conditions of seamen

Special collection
Union journals and reports since 1912
Publication
The Seaman (monthly)

1976 NATIONAL UNION OF TAILORS AND GARMENT WORKERS
Radlett House, West Hill, Aspley Guise, Milton Keynes MK17 8DT Tel. 0908 583099
Trade Union

Enquiries to the General Secretary

Subject coverage
trade union services to the clothing industry

Publication
Garment Worker

1977 NATIONAL UNION OF WALLCOVERINGS, DECORATIVE AND ALLIED TRADES
223 Bury New Road, Whitefield, Manchester M25 6GW Tel. 061-766 3645
Trade Union

Enquiries to the Assistant General Secretary

Subject coverage
trade union involvement in the manufacture and distribution of wallcoverings, etc.

Publication
Decor (periodical)

1978 NATIONAL VEGETABLE RESEARCH STATION
Wellesborne, Warwick CV35 9EF Tel. 0789 840382
Government Research Station

Enquiries to the Librarian

Subject coverage
horticulture, botany, soil science, chemistry, biochemistry, pesticides, weed control, entomology, plant pathology

Special collection
historical books on horticulture

Publications
Annual Report
Annual publications record

1979 NATIONAL WATER COUNCIL
1 Queen Anne's Gate, London SW1H 9BT Tel. 01-930 3100
Telex 918518

Statutory Body, formed 1974, from British Waterworks Association, Association of River Authorities and Water Supply Industry Training Board; responsible for the Water Information Centre; also houses the Water Space Amenity Commission; supporting the ten regional water authorities

Enquiries to the Information Officer

Subject coverage
water industry policy and organisation, including finance, manpower, training, and testing of water fittings

Special collections
full sets of publications of the British Waterworks Association and of the Association of River Authorities

Publications
National Water Council Bulletin (weekly)
Water (bi-monthly)
Who's Who in the Water Industry (annual)
Bibliographies and reports

NATIONAL WATER SAFETY COMMITTEE *see* **ROYAL SOCIETY FOR THE PREVENTION OF ACCIDENTS**

1980 NATIONAL WOOLSORTERS SOCIETY
40 Little Horton Lane, Bradford, West Yorkshire BD5 0AL Tel. 0274 20392
Trade Union

Enquiries to the Secretary

Subject coverage
wool textile trade conditions

NATIONAL YACHT HARBOUR ASSOCIATION *see* **SHIP AND BOAT BUILDERS NATIONAL FEDERATION**

1981 NATIONAL ZOOLOGICAL ASSOCIATION OF GREAT BRITAIN
Stowlangtoft, Bury St Edmunds, Suffolk IP31 3JW Tel. 0359 30623
Trade Association

Enquiries to the Secretary

Subject coverage
all matters connected with wild animals in captivity

1982 NATURAL ENVIRONMENT RESEARCH COUNCIL
Alhambra House, 27–33 Charing Cross Road, London WC2H 0AX Tel. 01-930 9232
Telex 916472

Research Council, State-aided through the Department of Education and Science; component Institutes and Units, *q.v.*, are listed for reference, following this entry

Enquiries, general, to the Information Officer; technical, to the appropriate Institute; research grants and studentships, to the University Support Section

Subject coverage
earth sciences; terrestrial ecology; marine sciences; marine biology; inland waters; Antarctic research; atmosphere; pollution

Publications
Annual Report
NERC News Journal (2 or 3 times per annum)
Policy Reviews
Scientific Reports
University Support
Occasional Publications
List of Publications

NATURAL ENVIRONMENT RESEARCH COUNCIL GRANT-AIDED UNITS *see*
FRESHWATER BIOLOGICAL ASSOCIATION
MARINE BIOLOGICAL ASSOCIATION OF THE UNITED KINGDOM
SCOTTISH MARINE BIOLOGICAL ASSOCIATION

NATURAL ENVIRONMENT RESEARCH COUNCIL INSTITUTES *see*
BRITISH ANTARCTIC SURVEY
INSTITUTE FOR MARINE ENVIRONMENTAL RESEARCH
INSTITUTE OF GEOLOGICAL SCIENCES
INSTITUTE OF HYDROLOGY
INSTITUTE OF OCEANOGRAPHIC SCIENCES
INSTITUTE OF TERRESTRIAL ECOLOGY

NATURAL RUBBER PRODUCERS RESEARCH ASSOCIATION *now* **MALAYSIAN RUBBER PRODUCERS ASSOCIATION,** *q.v.*

1983 **NATURE CONSERVANCY COUNCIL**
19/20 Belgrave Square, London SW1X 8PY Tel. 01-235 3241
Statutory Body, grant-aided by the Department of the Environment; formerly a constituent body of the Natural Environment Research Council; its research wing became the Institute of Terrestrial Ecology, *q.v.*

Enquiries to the Librarian

Subject coverage
nature conservation; ecology; natural history; rural land use; protection of the natural environment; geology

Publications
Annual Report (H.M.S.O.)
General, advisory and site leaflets (list available)
Nature Conservancy Staff Research Publications List (on microfiche)
Reading lists
Information sheets

NAUTICAL ALMANAC OFFICE *see* **H.M. NAUTICAL ALMANAC OFFICE**

1984 **NAUTICAL COLLEGE**
Broadwater, Fleetwood, Lancashire F77 8JZ Tel. 039-17 2772
Nautical College, of Lancashire Education Committee

Enquiries to the Tutor-Librarian

Subject coverage
shipping and related subjects; marine radio, radar, and electronics; fishing; coastal and offshore yachting

1985 **NAUTICAL INSTITUTE**
Alderman's House, Alderman's Walk, London EC2M 3UU Tel. 01-283 7340
Professional Body

Enquiries to the Secretary

Subject coverage
all nautical matters

Publications
Seaway (members' bulletin)
Nautical Review (bi-monthly)
Conference Proceedings

1986 **NAVAL AIRCRAFT MATERIALS LABORATORY**
Royal Naval Aircraft Yard, Fleetlands, Gosport, Hampshire PO13 0AW Tel. 0705 22351 ext. 44879 Telex 86164
Government Department, of the Ministry of Defence (Navy)

Enquiries to the Officer-in-Charge

Subject coverage
aircraft materials, metallic and non-metallic; corrosion prevention; spectrometric oil analysis; systems health monitoring generally; vibration analysis; aviation fuels and lubricants; hydraulic fluid cleanliness standards and measuring techniques; non-destructive testing

1987 **NAVAL CONSTRUCTION RESEARCH ESTABLISHMENT**
St. Leonards Hill, Dunfermline, Fifeshire KY11 5PW Tel. 0383 21346 Telex 72363

Government Department

Enquiries to the Superintendent

Subject coverage
heavy structural design and testing; pressure vessel design; submersibles for ocean engineering; glass-reinforced plastic ships; development and fabrication of high-strength steels; underwater demolition problems; oil rigs; engineering valve design; anti-vibration and shock mounts; measures against structural-borne noise

1988 NAYLOR BENZON & COMPANY LIMITED
35 Seething Lane, London EC3N 4HA Tel. 01-481 8241
Telex 888956

Company

Enquiries to the Information Officer

Subject coverage
minerals and ores; refractories; iron, manganese and chromium mining

1989 NCR LIMITED
206 Marylebone Road, London NW1 6LY Tel. 01-723 7070
Telex 263931

Company, subsidiary of NCR Corporation, Dayton, Ohio, U.S.A.; formerly National Cash Register Company Limited

Enquiries to the Manager, Advertising and Public Relations

Subject coverage
use of computers and terminals in commerce and industry, retail organizations, banking and government; microform systems; accounting systems; sales registers

NEATH BRANCH LIBRARY *see* **WEST GLAMORGAN COUNTY LIBRARY**

1990 NEATH TECHNICAL COLLEGE
Dwryfelin Road, Neath, West Glamorganshire SA10 7RF Tel. 0639 3723
Technical College

Enquiries to the Librarian

Subject coverage
general, in commerce, construction, science and engineering

NECTA LIMITED *see* **ELECTRICAL CONTRACTORS ASSOCIATION**

NELSON PUBLIC LIBRARY *now* **PENDLE DISTRICT CENTRAL LIBRARY**
see **LANCASHIRE LIBRARY**

NEPRA COMMERCIAL LIMITED *see* **NATIONAL EGG PRODUCERS RETAILERS ASSOCIATION**

1991 NETHERLANDS—BRITISH CHAMBER OF COMMERCE
307–308 High Holborn, London WC1 7LS Tel. 01-405 1358
Chamber of Commerce

Enquiries to the Information Officer

Subject coverage
Dutch-British trade

Publications
Informatiebronnen in Groot Britannie
Gids voor import en distributie in het V.K.
Penetratie van de Britse markt
Dutch Companies with their U.K. Agents/Distributors
500 bedrijven in Noordwest Engeland
500 bidrijven in Schotland
In Touch
Information Contacts in the Netherlands
Various Market Reports

NETWORK OF PROGRAMMED LEARNING CENTRES *see* **ASSOCIATION FOR PROGRAMMED LEARNING AND EDUCATIONAL TECHNOLOGY**

NEUTRON BEAM RESEARCH UNIT *see* **RUTHERFORD LABORATORY**

NEW MALDEN DISTRICT LIBRARY *see* **KINGSTON UPON THAMES CENTRAL LIBRARY**

1992 NEW ZEALAND HIGH COMMISSION
New Zealand House, Haymarket, London SW1Y 4TQ Tel. 01-930 8422
Governmental High Commission, having a Scientific Branch (formerly New Zealand Scientific Liaison Office) and a Trade Branch

Enquiries to the Scientific Adviser or the Trade Commissioner

Subject coverage
scientific services, research and development in government, industry, universities, institutes and associations; trade involving exports, imports, promotion, tariffs

NEWARK DISTRICT LIBRARY *see* **NOTTINGHAMSHIRE COUNTY LIBRARY**

NEWBURY DISTRICT LIBRARY *see* **BERKSHIRE COUNTY LIBRARY**

1993 NEWCASTLE SMALL FIRMS INFORMATION CENTRE
22 Newgate Shopping Centre, Newcastle upon Tyne NE1 5RH Tel. 0632 25353
Telex 537429

Government Information Centre of the Department of Industry

Enquiries to the Manager

Subject coverage
business studies and problems; management

Publications
Pamphlets on financial and business subjects

NEWCASTLE UNDER LYME DISTRICT LIBRARY *see* **STAFFORDSHIRE COUNTY LIBRARY**

1994 NEWCASTLE UPON TYNE CENTRAL LIBRARY
Princess Square, Newcastle upon Tyne, Northumberland NE99 1MC Tel. 0632 610691
Telex 53373

Public Library, of the Newcastle upon Tyne City Libraries system; Headquarters of the Tyneside Association of Libraries for Industry and Commerce (TALIC), *q.v.*; houses also the Northern Regional Library Bureau

Enquiries to the City Librarian

Subject coverage
commerce and technology; trade statistics; specifications and standards

Special collections
British and foreign trade and professional directories
Technical and commercial foreign language dictionaries
BSI, DEF, ASTM, SMMT, DIN specifications
U.K. Patent Specifications since 1933
U.S.A. Patent Specifications since 1954

1995 NEWCASTLE UPON TYNE COLLEGE OF ARTS & TECHNOLOGY
Maple Terrace, Newcastle upon Tyne NE4 7SA Tel. 0632 30216
Technical College; created by the amalgamation of the Charles Trevelyan Technical College and the College of Further Education

Enquiries to the Librarian

Subject coverage
building services and construction; public health; business studies; catering and bakery; electrical engineering; mechanical engineering; printing

Special collection
British Standards

1996 NEWCASTLE UPON TYNE POLYTECHNIC
Ellison Place, Newcastle-upon-Tyne NE1 8ST Tel. 0632 26002
College of Higher and Further Education; created by the merger of the former Newcastle Colleges of Art, Commerce, and Education, the Rutherford College of Technology and the Northern Counties College of Education

Enquiries to the Librarian

Subject coverage
accountancy; building; business; chemistry; civil engineering; commerce; electrical engineering; geography; industrial design; management; marketing; materials science; mathematics; mechanical engineering; surveying

1997 NEWCASTLE UPON TYNE UNIVERSITY LIBRARY
Queen Victoria Road, Newcastle upon Tyne NE1 7RU Tel. 0632 28511
University Library

Enquiries to the Librarian

Subject coverage
architecture; pure and applied science; economic and social studies; agriculture; medicine; dentistry

NEWCASTLE UPON TYNE UNIVERSITY *see also*
DOVE MARINE LABORATORY
MARINE INDUSTRIES CENTRE
PALAEONTOLOGICAL ASSOCIATION

1998 NEWHAM PUBLIC LIBRARIES
Stratford Reference Library, Water Lane, London E15 Tel. 01-534 4545 ext. 334
Public Library Service; includes East Ham Library

Enquiries to the Assistant Borough Librarian, Reference and Local Studies

Subject coverage
specialization in pharmacology and therapeutics

NEWINGTON DISTRICT LIBRARY *see* **SOUTHWARK LIBRARY SERVICES**

NEWLAND PARK COLLEGE OF EDUCATION *now* **BUCKINGHAMSHIRE COLLEGE OF FURTHER EDUCATION,** *q.v.*

NEWPORT AND MONMOUTHSHIRE COLLEGE OF TECHNOLOGY *now* **GWENT COLLEGE OF HIGHER EDUCATION,** *q.v.*

NEWPORT REGIONAL LIBRARY *see* **GWENT COUNTY LIBRARY**

1999 NEWSCLIP (U.K.) LIMITED
69 Fleet Street, London EC4Y 1NS Tel. 01-353 7191
Company

Enquiries to the Manager

Subject coverage
press-cutting services; all subjects and categories, U.K. and overseas; (1,600 U.K. publications alone)

2000 NEWSPAPER PUBLISHERS ASSOCIATION LIMITED
6 Bouverie Street, London EC4Y 8AY Tel. 01-583 8132/9
Trade Association, member of FIEJ, Fédération Internationale des Editeurs de Journaux et Publications, and of CAEJ, Communauté des Associations d'Editeurs de Journaux de la CEE

Enquiries to the Director

Subject coverage
distribution, advertising, marketing, newsprint, training and industrial relations in the national newspaper industry

2001 NEWSPAPER SOCIETY
Whitefriars House, Carmelite Street, London EC4Y 0BL Tel. 01-353 4722
Trade Association and Employers Organization; houses also the Guild of British Newspaper Editors, the Young Newspapermen's Association and the Newspaper Conference

Enquiries to the Head of Information

Subject coverage
all aspects of the regional press in the U.K. except Scotland

NEWTOWN AREA LIBRARY *see* **POWYS COUNTY LIBRARIES**

NEWTOWNABBEY DIVISIONAL LIBRARY *see* **NORTHERN IRELAND, NORTH EASTERN EDUCATION AND LIBRARY BOARD**

2002 NOISE ABATEMENT SOCIETY
6 Old Bond Street, London W1X 3TA Tel. 01-493 5877/8/9
Telex 262350

Registered Charity

Enquiries to the Chairman

Subject coverage
noise reduction in engines, plant, machinery, appliances and vehicles

Publications
Noise News Digest
'Hush'

2003 NOISE ADVISORY COUNCIL
Department of the Environment, Queen Annes Chambers, 28 Broadway, London SW1H 9JU Tel. 01-273 3771
Government Advisory Council

Enquiries to the Secretariat

Subject coverage
noise prevention and abatement

Publications
Reports on aircraft, traffic and neighbourhood noise, 1971–1974 (seven titles)
Noise in the Next Ten Years, H.M.S.O., 1974
Noise in Public Places, H.M.S.O., 1974
Noise Units, H.M.S.O., 1975
Bothered by Noise? H.M.S.O., 1975

2004 NON-DESTRUCTIVE TESTING CENTRE
Atomic Energy Research Establishment, Building 149, Harwell, Didcot, Oxfordshire OX11 0RA Tel. 0235 24141 ext. 2470
Telex 83135
Government-funded Centre, of the United Kingdom Atomic Energy Authority

Enquiries to the Director

Subject coverage
all aspects of non-destructive testing

Publication
NDT Info

NON-DESTRUCTIVE TESTING SOCIETY OF GREAT BRITAIN *now* **BRITISH INSTITUTE OF NON-DESTRUCTIVE TESTING,** *q.v.*

NON-FERROUS HOT STAMPERS ASSOCIATION *see* **BRITISH NON-FERROUS METALS FEDERATION**

2005 NORFOLK COLLEGE OF AGRICULTURE AND HORTICULTURE
Easton, Norwich, Norfolk NR9 5DX Tel. 0603 742105
College of Agriculture, formerly Norfolk School of Agriculture; houses the Norfolk County Beekeeper, the Norfolk Farm Machinery Club and the Norfolk Federation of Young Farmers Clubs

Enquiries, to the Director or the Librarian; agricultural advice cannot be given

Subject coverage
agricultural and horticultural education; agriculture; horticulture; related subjects

2006 NORFOLK COUNTY LIBRARY
County Hall, Martineau Lane, Norwich NR1 2DH Tel. 0603 611122
Public Library Service; Divisional Libraries at Norwich, Great Yarmouth and King's Lynn, *qq.v.*

Enquiries to the Divisional Librarians (see the Divisional Library entries)

Subject coverage
general

2007 NORMALAIR-GARRETT LIMITED
Yeovil, Somerset BA20 2YD Tel. 0935 5181
Telex 46132

Company; subsidiary of Westland Aircraft Limited

Enquiries to the Marketing Manager

Subject coverage
aircraft air conditioning, pressure control, temperature control and oxygen equipment; aircraft and marine hydraulics; ground support equipment; ice detection equipment; flight and cockpit voice recorders; data loggers; digital panel meters; tape translators; automatic weather stations; gas mixture analysers

Publications
product leaflets and brochures

NORMANTON LIBRARY *see* **WAKEFIELD METROPOLITAN DISTRICT LIBRARIES**

2008 NORTH EAST COAST INSTITUTION OF ENGINEERS AND SHIPBUILDERS
Bolbec Hall, Westgate Road, Newcastle-upon-Tyne NE1 1TB Tel. 0632 20289
Learned Society

Enquiries to the Secretary

Subject coverage
shipbuilding; naval architecture; marine engineering

Publications
Transactions of the N.E. Coast Institution of Engineers and Shipbuilders (annually, in six parts)

NORTH EAST ESSEX TECHNICAL COLLEGE *now* **COLCHESTER INSTITUTE OF HIGHER EDUCATION,** *q.v.*

2009 NORTH EAST LONDON POLYTECHNIC
Romford Road, London E15 4LZ Tel. 01-555 0811
Higher Education Institute; an amalgamation of the Waltham Forest Technical College, the West Ham College of Technology and Barking Regional College

Enquiries, consultancy and research, to the Assistant Director; others, to the Registrar

Subject coverage
business studies; banking; computing; market research; architecture; building; estate management; land administration; biology; pharmacology; biophysical science; biometry; chemical energetics; radiation science; management studies (all branches)

Publication
NELP Newsletter (contract research and consultancy)

2010 NORTH EAST LONDON POLYTECHNIC
Department of Land Surveying, Walthamstow, London E17 4JB Tel. 01-527 2272
Polytechnic Department; associated with the Hydrographic Society, and the Association of British Geodesists, *qq.v.*

Enquiries to the Head or the Librarian

Subject coverage
land, hydrographic, quantity surveying

2011 NORTH EAST LONDON POLYTECHNIC
Engineering and Business Studies Libraries, Longbridge Road, Dagenham, Essex RM8 2AS
Polytechnic

Enquiries to the Librarian

Subject coverage
engineering (mechanical, electrical, production, chemical); business studies, including ergonomics

2012 NORTH EAST LONDON POLYTECHNIC
Environmental Studies Library, Forest Road, London E17 4JB
Polytechnic

Enquiries to the Librarian

Subject coverage
environmental sciences, including architecture, general surveying, land surveying, civil engineering

2013 NORTH EAST LONDON POLYTECHNIC
Mathematics and Social Sciences Library, Livingstone House, Livingstone Road, London E15 2LJ Tel. 01-534 7825
Polytechnic; houses the Charles Myers Library of the National Institute of Industrial Psychology, *q.v.*

Enquiries to the Librarian

Subject coverage
mathematics; industrial psychology

2014 NORTH EAST LONDON POLYTECHNIC
Science Library, Maryland House, Manby Park Road, Stratford, London E15 1EY Tel. 01-555 8131
Polytechnic

Enquiries to the Librarian

Subject coverage
mathematics; physics; chemistry; biology; underwater technology

NORTH EAST LONDON POLYTECHNIC *see also* **ANGLIAN REGIONAL MANAGEMENT CENTRE**

2015 NORTH EAST OF SCOTLAND LIBRARY SERVICE
14 Crown Terrace, Aberdeen AB9 2BH Tel. 0224 572658/9
Public Library and Museum Service; formerly Aberdeen County Library, including Kincardine, Peterhead, Fraserburgh and Inverurie Burgh Libraries, and part of Banff County Library

Enquiries to the Chief Librarian

Subject coverage
general; oil industry

2016 NORTH EAST SCOTLAND DEVELOPMENT AUTHORITY (NESDA)
20 Union Terrace, Aberdeen AB1 1NN Tel. 0224 55971
Local Government Development Service; the Industrial Development Department of the Grampian Regional Council

Enquiries to the Secretary

Subject coverage
industrial development organisation, and for N.E. Scotland in particular

NORTH EAST SOMERSET TECHNICAL COLLEGE *now* **FROME COLLEGE,** *q.v.*

2017 NORTH EAST SURREY COLLEGE OF TECHNOLOGY
Reigate Road, Ewell, Surrey KT17 3DS Tel. 01-394 1731
Technical College; formerly Ewell County Technical College

Enquiries to the Tutor Librarian

Subject coverage
applied biology; building and construction; home economics

2018 NORTH EAST WALES INSTITUTE OF HIGHER EDUCATION
Kelsterton College, Connah's Quay, Deeside, Clwyd CH5 4BR Tel. Deeside 817531
Technical College; formerly Flintshire College of Technology; Aston College and Cartrefle College (Wrexham) are component parts of NEWI

Enquiries to the Librarian

Subject coverage
chemistry; computer studies; physics; metallurgy; management; business studies

2019 NORTH EASTERN TRADERS ASSOCIATION
133 Norton Road, Stockton-on-Tees, Cleveland TS18 2B9 Tel. 0642 67127
Trade Association

No enquiry service

Subject coverage
consumer and commercial credit; company status

Publication
Brochure on the Association's services

2020 NORTH GLOUCESTER COLLEGE OF TECHNOLOGY
The Park, Cheltenham, Gloucestershire GL50 2RR Tel. 0242 28021
College of Technology

Enquiries to the Librarian

Subject coverage
mechanical, production and electrical engineering; building; surveying; business studies; mathematics including computing; food technology

2021 NORTH HERTS COLLEGE
Broadway, Letchworth, Hertfordshire SG6 3PB Tel. 046-26 3911
College of Further Education; formerly Letchworth College of Technology which merged with Hitchin College

Enquiries to the Tutor Librarian

Subject coverage
catering; mathematics; physics; chemistry; mechanical and electrical engineering; management

2022 NORTH LINDSEY COLLEGE OF TECHNOLOGY
Kingsway, Scunthorpe, South Humberside DN17 1AJ Tel. 0724 55022
College of Technology; formerly North Lindsey Technical College

Enquiries to the Librarian

Subject coverage
metallurgy; engineering; construction

2023 NORTH OF ENGLAND DEVELOPMENT COUNCIL
Bank House, Carliol Square, Newcastle upon Tyne NE1 6XE Tel. 0632 610026
Telex 537212

Development Council; formerly North East Development Council

Enquiries to the Information Officer

Subject coverage
economic and industrial information on the Northern region of England

Publications
Annual Report
Buyers Guide to North East Industry
Oilfield Directory
Briefing booklets

2024 NORTH OF ENGLAND INSTITUTE OF MINING AND MECHANICAL ENGINEERS
Neville Hall, Westgate Road, Newcastle upon Tyne NE1 1TD Tel. 0632 22201
Professional Institute, affiliated to the Institution of Mining Engineers, *q.v.*

Enquiries to the Librarian

Subject coverage
mining and allied subjects

Special collections
MSS collections—
London Lead Court Minutes and Plans
Watson Collection
Bell Collection
Buddle Collection

Publication
Transactions, in association with the Institution of Mining Engineers

2025 NORTH OF SCOTLAND COLLEGE OF AGRICULTURE
581 King Street, Aberdeen AB9 1UD Tel. 0224 40291
Agricultural College; the Library also serves the School of Agriculture of the University of Aberdeen

Enquiries to the Librarian

Subject coverage
agriculture

Publications
Annual Report
Research Investigations
Field Trials

2026 NORTH OXFORDSHIRE TECHNICAL COLLEGE & SCHOOL OF ART
Broughton Road, Banbury, Oxfordshire OX16 9QA Tel. 0295 52221
Technical College

Enquiries to the Librarian/Resources Officer

Subject coverage
general

2027 NORTH REGIONAL PLANNING COMMITTEE
Municipal Buildings, Middlesbrough, Cleveland TS1 2QH Tel. 0642 248155
Joint Committee of County Councils

Enquiries to the Secretary of the Committee or to the Director of the Environment, Tyne and Wear County Council, Sandyford House, Newcastle upon Tyne NE2 1ED

Subject coverage
regional strategy, including trends and changes in the economy of the region, in various industries, in population, in settlement, health, etc.

Publications
technical and progress reports
Working papers
(on subjects as given above)

NORTH RIDING COUNTY LIBRARY *now* **NORTH YORKSHIRE COUNTY LIBRARY,** *q.v.*

NORTH SHIELDS CENTRAL LIBRARY *see* **NORTH TYNESIDE METROPOLITAN DISTRICT LIBRARIES**

2028 NORTH STAFFORDSHIRE POLYTECHNIC
College Road, Stoke-on-Trent, Staffordshire ST4 SDE Tel. 0782 45531
Polytechnic; includes a Branch at Beaconside, Stafford; formed by the merger of the North Staffordshire College of Technology and the Staffordshire College of Technology

Enquiries to the Deputy Librarian, Information Services, Beaconside

Subject coverage
ceramics; mining; electrical and mechanical engineering; computing; chemistry; physics

2029 NORTH TRAFFORD COLLEGE
Talbot Road, Stretford, Manchester M32 0XH Tel. 061-832 3731
College of Further Education; formerly Stretford Technical College

Enquiries to the Tutor Librarian

Subject coverage
general; gas engineering; chemical process plant operation

2030 NORTH TYNESIDE METROPOLITAN DISTRICT LIBRARIES
Central Library, Northumberland Square, North Shields, Tel. 089-45 82811
Tyne and Wear NE30 1QU Telex 53134
Public Library Service; Area Libraries at Wallsend, Whitley Bay and Killingworth

Enquiries to the Librarians

Subject coverage
general

2031 NORTH WEST INDUSTRIAL DEVELOPMENT ASSOCIATION
Brazenose House, Brazenose Street, Manchester M2 5AZ Tel. 061-834 6778
Telex 667822

Industrial Development Body

Enquiries to the Director

Subject coverage
industrial development, expansion and relocation; vacant industrial property; government aid

2032 NORTH WEST KENT COLLEGE OF TECHNOLOGY
Miskin Road, Dartford, Kent DA1 2LU Tel. 0322 25471 ext. 31
College of Technology; an associated College at Isaac Newton Building, Peckham Road, Gravesend

Enquiries to the Librarian

Subject coverage
electronics; engineering; catering; business and secretarial studies

Special collection
British Standards

2033 NORTH WEST LEICESTERSHIRE TECHNICAL COLLEGE
Bridge Road, Coalville, Leicestershire LE6 2QR Tel. 0530 36136
Technical College

Enquiries to the Tutor Librarian

Subject coverage
engineering and mining; business and management

2034 NORTH YORKSHIRE COUNTY LIBRARY
21 Grammar School Lane, Northallerton, North Yorkshire DL6 1DF Tel. 0609 5381
Telex 58257

Public Library Service; formed by the amalgamation of parts of the North Riding, West Riding and East Riding County Libraries, and the Public Libraries of Harrogate, Scarborough, Skipton and York

Enquiries to the County Librarian

Subject coverage
general

NORTH WYKE EXPERIMENTAL STATION *see* **LEVINGTON RESEARCH STATION**

2035 NORTHAMPTON DEVELOPMENT CORPORATION
Cliftonville House, Bedford Road, Northampton NN4 0AY Tel. 0604 34734
New Town Development Corporation

Enquiries to the Librarian, Architects Department

Subject coverage
building; architecture; town and country planning (particularly of new towns); landscape architecture; quantity surveying; housing

Special collections
Collection of Slides on British and European shopping centres
Collection of photographs and slides on expansion and development of Northampton
Collection of trade literature (c. 5000 manufacturers)

Publications
Bibliographies
Promotional literature

NORTHAMPTON DISTRICT LIBRARY *see* **NORTHAMPTONSHIRE LIBRARIES**

2036 NORTHAMPTONSHIRE COUNTY TECHNICAL LIBRARY
George Street, Corby, Northamptonshire NN17 1PZ Tel. 053-66 3695
Public Library, part of the Northamptonshire Libraries Service

Enquiries to the Technical Librarian

Subject coverage
most technical subjects; especially metallurgy and management

2037 NORTHAMPTONSHIRE LIBRARIES
27 Guildhall Road, Northampton NN1 1EF Tel. 0604 34833
Public Library Service; District Libraries at Corby, Daventry, Higham Ferrers, Kettering, Northampton, Towcester and Wellingborough; *see also* Northamptonshire County Technical Library

Enquiries to the Librarian

Subject coverage
general

Special collection
Leather and Footwear Collection

Publication
Catalogue of the Leather and Footwear Collection

2038 NORTHERN CARPET TRADE UNION
22 Clare Road, Halifax, Yorkshire HX1 2HX Tel. 0422 60492
Trade Union

Enquiries to the General Secretary

Subject coverage
organization in the carpet industry

2039 NORTHERN COKE RESEARCH LABORATORY
School of Chemistry, Newcastle upon Tyne University, Newcastle upon Tyne NE1 7RU Tel. 0632 28511 ext. 3085
University Laboratory

Enquiries to the Director

Subject coverage
fundamental science of coke formation from coals and of the manufacture of needle-cokes and graphites; structure of carbons and graphites; gasification mechanism of carbons, cokes and graphites; porosity in solids; electron microscopy of cokes, carbons and graphites;

Publications
List of research publications available

2040 NORTHERN FOODS LIMITED
Beverley House, St Stephens Square, Hull HU1 3XG Tel. 0482 25432 Telex 527149

Company; formerly Northern Dairies Limited

Enquiries to the Public Relations Manager

Subject coverage
milk processing and retailing; manufacture of milk-based products, prepacked and bulk; dairy engineering; milling and baking (bread and cakes); brewing; wines and spirits; public houses; hire purchase finance

Publication
Northern News (company newspaper)

2041 NORTHERN IRELAND DEPARTMENT OF ENVIRONMENT
Stormont, Belfast BT4 3SS
Government Department; formerly Ministry of Development for Northern Ireland

Enquiries to the Information Office

Subject coverage
planning, roads, housing, local government, water, sewerage, transport

2042 NORTHERN IRELAND INFORMATION SERVICE
Stormont Castle, Belfast BT4 3ST Tel. 0232 63011 Telex 74272

Government Department

Enquiries to the Publications Section

Subject coverage
government matters concerning agriculture, health and social services, environment, commerce, manpower services etc.

Publications
Ulster Year Book
Notes on Northern Ireland
Ulster Commentary (monthly)
Facts at Your Fingertips

2043 NORTHERN IRELAND NORTH EASTERN EDUCATION AND LIBRARY BOARD
County Library, Demesne Avenue, Ballymena, Co. Antrim BT43 7BG Tel. 0266 41531/2/3
Telex 747371

Public Library; formerly Antrim County Library; Divisional Libraries at Coleraine and Newtownabbey

Enquiries to the Librarian

Subject coverage
general

Special collection
British Standards

2044 NORTHERN IRELAND, SOUTH EASTERN EDUCATION AND LIBRARY BOARD
H.Q. Library, Windmill Hill, Ballynahinch, Co. Down BT24 8DH Tel. 023-856 2639
Telex 747325

Public Library Service; formerly Down County Library Service

Enquiries to the Librarian

Subject coverage
general and local

2045 NORTHERN IRELAND, SOUTHERN EDUCATION AND LIBRARY BOARD
Library Headquarters, Brownlow Road, Legandry, Craigavon, Tel. 42312/4
Northern Ireland BT65 8DP Telex 747528
Public Library Service; formed by the merging of Armagh County Library with parts of other systems

Enquiries to the Information Service, Library Headquarters, Charlemont Gardens, Armagh

Subject coverage
general

2046 NORTHERN IRELAND, WESTERN EDUCATION AND LIBRARY BOARD
Headquarters, Dublin Road, Omagh, County Tyrone Tel. 0662 2107
Public Library Service; District Libraries at Londonderry, Omagh and Enniskillen/County Fermanagh

Enquiries to the Librarian

Subject coverage
general

2047 NORTHERN IRELAND TOURIST BOARD
River House, 48 High Street, Belfast BT1 2DS Tel. 0232 31221
Tourist Board

Enquiries to the Information Officer

Subject coverage
Irish tourist industry

Publications
Annual Report
Occasional Surveys
Quarterly Newspaper

2048 NORTHERN MINE RESEARCH SOCIETY
38 Main Street, Sutton, via Keighley, West Yorkshire
Records Society, formerly Northern Cavern and Mine Research Society

Enquiries to the Librarian or to the Central Records Office

Subject coverage
past and present mining of minerals in U.K.; some aspects of University field work

Publications
Transactions, 1960–1964
Memoirs, 1964–1975
British Mining, 1976–
Surveys series

NORTHERN REGIONAL LIBRARY BUREAU *see* **NEWCASTLE UPON TYNE CENTRAL LIBRARY**

NORTHERN WOOL BUYERS ASSOCIATION *now* **WOOL BUYERS ASSOCIATION OF GREAT BRITAIN,** *q.v.*

2049 NORTHUMBERLAND COLLEGE OF AGRICULTURE
Kirkley Hall, Ponteland, Newcastle upon Tyne NE20 0AQ Tel. 0661 24141
College of Agriculture; Headquarters of Northumberland Young Farmers Clubs

Enquiries to the Principal

Subject coverage
agricultural and horticultural practice and management; home economics; careers

2050 NORTHUMBERLAND COUNTY LIBRARY
The Willows, Morpeth, Northumberland NE61 1TA Tel. 0670 2385
Telex 53439
County Library System; District Libraries at Alnwick, Ashington, Berwick, Blyth, Morpeth; Technical Library Service from Cramlington Library

Enquiries to the County Librarian

Subject coverage
general; all aspects of commerce, management, science and technology particularly from the Technical Library Service

Special collection
British Standards

2051 NORTHUMBERLAND COUNTY TECHNICAL COLLEGE
College Road, Ashington, Northumberland Tel. 067-081 3248
Technical College

Enquiries to the Tutor Librarian

Subject coverage
general; particularly, mining including geology and surveying; building (technical service available to firms); engineering (motor vehicle, workshop, electrical and mechanical); commerce; business studies; catering; biological sciences

Special collection
British Standards

2052 NORWICH CITY COLLEGE
Ipswich Road, Norwich, Norfolk NR2 2LJ Tel. 0603 60011
College of Further Education

Enquiries to the Librarian

Subject coverage
management; science; electrical, mechanical and production engineering; construction; printing; catering

Special collection
British Standards

2053 NORWICH DIVISIONAL LIBRARY
Bethel Street, Norwich NR2 1NJ Tel. 0603 22233 ext. 644
Public Library, Division of Norfolk County Library

Enquiries to the Divisional Librarian

Subject coverage
general

2054 NORWICH UNION INSURANCE GROUP
P.O. Box 4, Norwich NR1 3NG Tel. 0603 22200
Insurance Company; houses Eastern Region Information Office of the British Insurance Association and the Secretariat of the Insurance Institute of Norwich

Enquiries to the Public Relations Manager

Subject coverage
life insurance and associated investment plans; pensions provision; fire, accident, motor and marine insurance

2055 NORWOOD HALL INSTITUTE OF HORTICULTURAL AND AGRICULTURAL EDUCATION
Norwood Green, Southall, Middlesex Tel. 01-574 2261
Further Education Institute

Enquiries to the Principal

Subject coverage
agricultural and horticultural education

2056 NOTTINGHAM AND NOTTINGHAMSHIRE TECHNICAL INFORMATION SERVICE (NANTIS)
Nottinghamshire County Council Leaisure Services Department, County Hall, West Bridgford, Nottingham NG2 7QP Tel. 0602 863366
Interlibrary Co-operative Scheme

Enquiries to the Honorary Secretary, Central Library, South Sherwood Street, Nottingham NG1 4DA (tel. 0602 43591)

Subject coverage
emphasis on business information, and the needs of small firms

Publications
Annual Report
Directory of Members
NANTIS News (monthly)
Directory of Translators

NOTTINGHAM CITY LIBRARY *see* **NOTTINGHAMSHIRE COUNTY LIBRARY**

2057 NOTTINGHAM SMALL FIRMS INFORMATION CENTRE
48–50 Maid Marian Way, Nottingham NG1 6GF Tel. 0602 49791
Telex 377313

Government Information Centre of the Department of Industry

Enquiries to the Manager

Subject coverage
business studies and problems; management

Publications
Pamphlets on financial and business subjects

2058 NOTTINGHAM UNIVERSITY MEDICAL LIBRARY
University Hospital and Medical School, Clifton Boulevard, Nottingham NG7 2UH Tel. 0602 700111
Telex 37346
University Library, *with* the School of Agriculture Library and the Science Library, *qq.v.*

Enquiries to the Librarian

Subject coverage
basic medical sciences; nursing

Special collections
F.H. Jacob History of Medicine Collection
Nottingham Medico-Chirurgical Society Collection

2059 NOTTINGHAM UNIVERSITY SCHOOL OF AGRICULTURE LIBRARY
Sutton Bonington, Loughborough, Leicestershire LE12 5RD Tel. 050-97 2386
Telex 341788

University Library with the Medical Library and the Science Library, *qq.v.*

Enquiries to the Librarian

Subject coverage
agriculture, horticulture, farm management, food science, biophysics, biochemistry, biology, physiology, environmental sciences

2060 NOTTINGHAM UNIVERSITY SCIENCE LIBRARY
University Park, Nottingham NG7 2RD Tel. 0602 56101 ext. 2583 *or* 2571
Telex 37346

University Library, *with* the Medical Library and the School of Agriculture Library, *qq.v.*

Enquiries to the Librarian

Subject coverage
physical sciences, including geology; life sciences, including pharmacy and psychology; engineering, including mining, metallurgy, materials science

Special collection
Porter Collection (on ornithology)

NOTTINGHAM UNIVERSITY *see also* **BRITISH SOCIETY FOR CELL BIOLOGY**

2061 NOTTINGHAMSHIRE COLLEGE OF AGRICULTURE
Brackenhurst, Southwell, Nottinghamshire NG25 0QF Tel. 0636 812252
College of agriculture

Enquiries to the Librarian

Subject coverage
agriculture; horticulture; home economics; food technology; agricultural merchanting

2062 NOTTINGHAMSHIRE COUNTY LIBRARY
County Hall, West Bridgford, Nottinghamshire NG2 7QP Tel. 0602 863366
Telex 37662

Public Library Service; District Libraries at Ashfield, Bassetlaw, Broxtowe, Gedling, Mansfield, Newark, Nottingham, Rushcliffe

Enquiries to the Librarians

Subject coverage
general

2063 NUCLEAR ENTERPRISES (G.B.) LIMITED
Bankill Crossway, Sighthill, Edinburgh EH11 4EY Tel. 031-443 4060
Telex 72333

Industrial Company

Enquiries to the Librarian

Subject coverage
nuclear physics instrumentation; ultrasonic diagnostic scanning (medical)

NUCLEAR INSTALLATIONS INSPECTORATE *see* **HEALTH AND SAFETY EXECUTIVE**

2064 NUCLEAR POWER COMPANY (RISLEY) LIMITED
Warrington Road, Risley, Warrington WA3 6BZ Tel. 0925 51291
Telex 627727

Company; operating company of the National Nuclear Corporation Limited, United Kingdom Atomic Energy Authority; formerly Nuclear Power Group Limited

Enquiries to the Librarian or Public Relations Officer

Subject coverage
design and construction of nuclear power stations

NUFFIELD INSTITUTE OF COMPARATIVE MEDICINE *see* **ZOOLOGICAL SOCIETY OF LONDON**

2065 NUFFIELD RADIO ASTRONOMY LABORATORIES
Jodrell Bank, Macclesfield, Cheshire SK11 9DL Tel. 047-77 321
Telex 36149

Part of the Physics Department, University of Manchester

Enquiries to the Public Relations Officers

Subject coverage
astronomy; radio astronomy techniques—long and short base line interferometry; computing techniques, including design and construction for real-time computers for telescope control; galactic structure; hydrogen line observations; radio sources and source surveys and identifications; polarization; pulsars; flare stars; quasars

Publications
Astronomical Contributions from the University of Manchester Series I
Jodrell Bank Annals

NUNEATON PUBLIC LIBRARY *see* **WARWICKSHIRE COUNTY LIBRARY**

2066 NUTRITION SOCIETY
Chandos House, 2 Queen Anne Street, London W1M 9LE Tel. 01-580 5753
Company

No enquiry service

Subject coverage
nutrition

Publications
Proceedings of the Nutrition Society
British Journal of Nutrition

OADBY LIBRARY *see* **LEICESTERSHIRE LIBRARIES AND INFORMATION SERVICE**

OAKHAM LIBRARY *see* **LEICESTERSHIRE LIBRARIES AND INFORMATION SERVICE**

2067 OCCUPATIONAL HEALTH UNIT
Central Middlesex Hospital, 249 Acton Lane, London NW10 7NS Tel. 01-965 5733 ext. 275
Government Department; N.H.S. Hospital Unit; above address is also the home of a Clinical Unit for Occupational Medicine and Nursing

Enquiries to the Information Officer

Subject coverage
occupational health; medicine; nursing; health hazards; toxic substances; safety equipment; immunization and control of infection

2068 OCCUPATIONAL MEDICINE AND HYGIENE LABORATORIES
403/405 Edgware Road, Cricklewood, London NW2 6LN Tel. 01-450 8911
Government Department, of the Health and Safety Executive; formerly of the Department of Employment; the library is associated with the Safety in Mines Research Establishment library service

Enquiries to the Librarian

Subject coverage
analytical testing of dusts and fumes; flammable liquids and solids; industrial hygiene; noise and vibration; industrial control; radiation sources in industry

Publications
see Health and Safety Executive

2069 OFFICE MACHINES AND EQUIPMENT FEDERATION
16 Wood Street, Kingston-upon-Thames, Surrey Tel. 01-549 7699
Trade Association

Enquiries to the Director

Subject coverage
office machines and equipment

Publication
Office Pride (bi-monthly)

2070 OFFICE OF FAIR TRADING
Field House, Breams Buildings, London EC4 1PR Tel. 01-242 2858
Telex 2175

Government Department; formerly Office of the Registrar of Restrictive Trading Agreements; includes the Consumer Credit Licensing Branch at Government Buildings, Bromyard Avenue, Acton W3 7BB, the Office of Fair Trading, 9 Hope Street, Edinburgh EH2 4EL, and the two public registers: 1. Consumer Credit Licenses and 2. Restrictive Trading Agreements, both at the Office of Fair Trading, 53 Chancery Lane, London WC2A 1SP

Enquiries to the Director General

Subject coverage
consumer affairs; consumer credit; monopolies, mergers and restrictive trade practices

Publications
Annual Report (H.M.S.O.)
Publicity and educational material on the work of the Office

OFFICE OF HEALTH ECONOMICS *see* **ASSOCIATION OF BRITISH PHARMACEUTICAL INDUSTRY**

2071 OFFICE OF POPULATION CENSUSES AND SURVEYS (OPCS)
St Catherines House, 10 Kingsway, London WC2B 6JP Tel. 01-242 0262
Government Department, formed by the merger of the General Register Office and Government Social Survey

Enquiries to the Librarian or Information Officer, exts. 2237 or 2235

Subject coverage
population censuses; vital statistics; social survey reports; registration of births, deaths and marriages

Publications
see Government Publications Sectional List 56 (H.M.S.O.)
Registrar General's Statistical Review of England and Wales (annual)
Population Trends (quarterly)
OPCS Monitors (irregular)

OFFICE OF THE QUEEN'S AWARD TO INDUSTRY *now* **QUEEN'S AWARDS OFFICE,** *q.v.*

2072 OFFICE PLANNING CONSULTANTS LIMITED
6 Mercer Street, Covent Garden, London WC2H 9QG Tel. 01-836 9597
Telex 24861

Company; formerly Office Planning Limited

Enquiries to the Marketing Director

Subject coverage
organisation and methods, (including relocation surveys); space planning; interior design; telecommunications; construction management

OFFSHORE ENERGY TECHNOLOGY BOARD *see* **DEPARTMENT OF ENERGY**

2073 OFFSHORE INFORMATION LITERATURE
30 Baker Street, London W1M 2DS Tel. 01-486 5353
Publishing Company

Enquiries to the Editor, 3/15 Kings Gardens, Hove, Sussex BN3 2PG (tel. 0273 733241); fees chargeable

Subject coverage
offshore oil and gas technology; processes, research and new developments in the industry

Publication
Offshore Abstracts (bi-monthly)

2074 OFFSHORE SUPPLIES OFFICE
Alhambra House, 45 Waterloo Street, Glasgow G2 6AS Tel. 041-221 8777
Telex 779379

Government Department, a Division of the Department of Energy

Enquiries to the Librarian

Subject coverage
the market in goods and services for the exploration and development of oil fields on the U.K. Continental Shelf and world-wide; capability of U.K. industry to supply these markets

Publication
Offshore Oil and Gas: summary of orders placed by operators of oil and gas fields on the U.K. Continental Shelf (H.M.S.O., annual)

2075 OIL AND CHEMICAL PLANT CONSTRUCTORS ASSOCIATION
112 Jermyn Street, London SW1Y 4UR Tel. 01-930 0865
Employers Association

Enquiries to the Information Officer

Subject coverage
industrial relations and related matters on oil and petrochemical construction sites; safety

Publication
Safety manual (in association with Kluwer Harrap)

2076 OIL AND COLOUR CHEMISTS ASSOCIATION
967 Harrow Road, Wembley, Middlesex HA0 2SF Tel. 01-908 1086
Telex 922670

Learned society

Enquiries to the Secretary

Subject coverage
raw materials, plant, equipment and services for the paint, ink, resins, varnishes, drying oils, lacquers, adhesives, soap, linoleum and treated fabrics industries; surface coatings in general; testing

Publications
Paint Technology manuals (seven titles but only 2 in print at the time of going to press)
Introduction to Paint Technology (3rd edition in preparation)
History of the Association
Ultraviolet Curing
Journal of the Oil and Colour Chemists Association (monthly)

2077 OIL APPLIANCE MANUFACTURERS ASSOCIATION
75 Harborne Road, Birmingham B15 3DH Tel. 021-454 6171 ext. 290
Trade Association

Enquiries to the Secretary

Subject coverage
use of portable domestic paraffin heaters

Publications
Safety leaflets, etc. (from Public Relations Officer, Counsel Ltd., 15 Thayer Street, London W1M 5LD)

2078 OLDHAM COLLEGE OF TECHNOLOGY
Rochdale Road, Oldham, Lancashire OL9 6AA — Tel. 061-624 5214
Technical College

Enquiries to the Librarian

Subject coverage
mechanical, electrical, and production engineering; building; textiles; chemistry; physics; mathematics

2079 OLDHAM LIBRARIES
Commercial and Technical Library, Union Street, Oldham, Lancashire OL1 1DN — Tel. 061-624 3633, Telex 667779
Public Library

Enquiries to the Director

Subject coverage
local companies; general

Special collection
British Standards

Publication
Oldham Companies (classified directory)

OLIVER GATTY LIBRARY *see* **CAMBRIDGE UNIVERSITY Department of Biochemistry**

2080 OMNIBUS SOCIETY
103a Streatham Hill, London SW2 — Tel. 01-674 5280
Independent Society of individual members

Enquiries to the Secretary

Subject coverage
road passenger transport; traffic, engineering and methods of operation of buses, coaches, etc.

Publication
Omnibus Magazine (bi-monthly)

2081 OPEN UNIVERSITY LIBRARY
Walton Hall, Milton Keynes MK7 6AA — Tel. 0908 74066, Telex 826739
University Library

Enquiries to the Director of Information Services, the Director of Consultancy Services, or the Director of Marketing

Subject coverage
general; specialist interest in non-book media

Publications
Course textbooks
Films and tapes

2082 OPENSHAW TECHNICAL COLLEGE
Whitworth Street, Openshaw, Manchester M11 2WH — Tel. 061-223 8282
Technical College

No enquiry service

Subject coverage
jewellery; horology; heating and ventilating engineering; vehicle body work; radio; television; telephony; safety courses

2083 OPERATIONAL RESEARCH SOCIETY
6th Floor, Neville House, Waterloo Street, Birmingham B2 5TX — Tel. 021-643 0236
Learned Society/Company; Member of the International Federation of Operational Research Societies; Society's Library is housed at Imperial College, London

Enquiries to the Secretary

Subject coverage
operational research as applicable to: banking and finance, construction industries, forecasting (with marketing), health and welfare services, inventory and production control, mathematical programming, simulation, systems dynamics, transportation, distribution; operational research techniques

Publications
Monthly Newsletter (members only)
Operational Research Quarterly (members only)
(International Abstracts in Operations Research, published by the International Federation, obtainable through the Society)

2084 OPTICAL INFORMATION COUNCIL
Walter House, 418–422 Strand, London WC2R 0PB Tel. 01-836 2323
Trade Association

Enquiries to the Press/Information Office

Subject coverage
eyecare and ophthalmic optics

Publication
Insight: layman's guide to eyes and eyecare (free)

2085 ORCHID SOCIETY OF GREAT BRITAIN
28 Felday Road, Lewisham, London SE13 7HJ Tel. 01-690 4519
Horticultural Society

Enquiries to the Secretary

Subject coverage
growing, conservation and identification of orchids

Special collection
library of 35 mm slides of orchids

Publications
Quarterly Journal (members only)
Handbook of Orchid Culture

2086 ORDNANCE SURVEY
Romsey Road, Maybush, Southampton SO9 4DH Tel. 0703 775555
Independent Sub-Unit of the Department of the Environment

Enquiries, by letter only, to the Director

Subject coverage
cartography; geodesy; surveying (field and geodetic); photogrammetry; printing; satellite geodesy; archaelogy; survey and mapping of Great Britain

Publications
Professional and technical papers
Map catalogues
Services leaflets
Descriptive guides
Small and large scale maps
Administrative maps
Geological and Soil Survey maps
Archaeological and Historical maps

ORGANISATION AND METHODS SOCIETY *now* **INSTITUTE OF PRACTITIONERS IN WORK STUDY, ORGANISATION AND METHODS,** *q.v.*

2087 ORGANISATION OF EUROPEAN ALUMINIUM SMELTERS
Technical Secretariat, 288 Terminal House, 52 Grosvenor Gardens, London SW1W 0AU — Tel. 01-730 2078
Trade Association

Enquiries to the Information Officer

Subject coverage
secondary aluminium

Publication
Annual Review

2088 ORGANON LABORATORIES LIMITED
Crown House, London Road, Morden, Surrey SM4 5DZ — Tel. 01-542 6611
Company

Enquiries to the Librarian

Subject coverage
endocrinology

ORMSKIRK DISTRICT CENTRAL LIBRARY *see* **LANCASHIRE LIBRARY**

ORPINGTON DISTRICT LIBRARY *see* **BROMLEY PUBLIC LIBRARIES**

2089 OSIRIS SURVEY PROJECTS LIMITED
Port Causeway, Bromborough, Merseyside LC2 4SY — Tel. 051-645 2293, Telex 62470

Company, formerly Dredging Investigations Limited

Enquiries to the Director

Subject coverage
geophysical surveys and geotechnical site investigations for civil engineering projects; hydrographic and topographic surveys; electronic survey systems; dredging technology

Publications
commercial marketing brochures

OSSETT LIBRARY *see* **WAKEFIELD METROPOLITAN DISTRICT LIBRARIES**

OSWESTRY DISTRICT LIBRARY *see* **SHROPSHIRE COUNTY LIBRARY**

OTAR *see* **OVERSEAS TARIFFS AND REGULATIONS SECTION**

2090 OVERALL MANUFACTURERS ASSOCIATION OF GREAT BRITAIN
42 Castle Street, Liverpool L2 7LF — Tel. 051-227 3383
Trade Association

Enquiries to the Secretary

Subject coverage
manufacture of protective clothing and leisure wear; supplies and materials for such manufacture

OVERSEAS DEVELOPMENT ADMINISTRATION *see*
CENTRE FOR OVERSEAS PEST RESEARCH
LAND RESOURCES DIVISION
TROPICAL PRODUCTS INSTITUTE

2091 OVERSEAS DEVELOPMENT INSTITUTE
10–11 Percy Street, London W1P 0JB — Tel. 01-637 3622
Limited Company/Registered Charity/Research Institute

Enquiries to the Librarian

Subject coverage
overseas development, with particular reference to aid, international trade and finance, and agricultural development; regional emphasis on Asia and Africa

Publications
Booklets
Research studies, in collaboration with Croom Helm

2092 OVERSEAS MINING ASSOCIATION
40 Holborn Viaduct, London EC1P 1AJ Tel. 01-353 1545
Trade Association

Enquiries to the Secretary

Subject coverage
mining operations outside the United Kingdom of businesses administered from the United Kingdom; for members only, general representation and coordinated action

Publications
Metal Seekers
International Mining

2093 OVERSEAS TARIFFS AND REGULATIONS SECTION (OTAR)
Export House, 50 Ludgate Hill, London EC4M 7HU Tel. 01-248 5757
Telex 886143

Government Department; of the Department of Trade, a section of Export Services and Promotions Division, *q.v.*, Export Data Branch

Enquiries to the Section, specifying countries of interest

Subject coverage
tariffs and customs regulations of overseas countries, including import duties, taxes, import licensing, documentation, health regulations for livestock, animal products, plants and seeds, foodstuffs, drugs, marking and labelling, legislation

Special collection
Tariffs and Customs Laws and Regulations, for nearly all overseas countries, updated

2094 OXFORD CENTRE FOR MANAGEMENT STUDIES
Kennington Road, Oxford OX1 5NY
Management Education Centre; associated with Oxford University

Enquiries, by letter only, to the Librarian

Subject coverage
management studies for senior managers, postgraduate teaching and research

Special collection
Lubbock Bequest

Publication
O.C.M.S. Brochure

2095 OXFORD UNIVERSITY
Department of Agricultural Science Library, Parks Road, Oxford OX1 3PF Tel. 0865 57245
University Department Library

Enquiries to the Librarian

Subject coverage
agriculture; application of forest sciences and economics to farming systems; research in animal, plant and soil sciences in relation to agriculture

Special collection
Sibthorpian Collection

2096 OXFORD POLYTECHNIC
Gipsy Lane, Headington, Oxford OX3 0BP Tel. 0865 64777
Polytechnic; formerly Oxford College of Technology; Lady Spencer Churchill College of Education at Wheatley, Oxford, is associated with the Polytechnic

Enquiries to the Librarian

Subject coverage
architecture; planning; engineering; science; catering management

Special collection
British Standards

2097 OXFORD UNIVERSITY
Botany, School, South Parks Road, Oxford OX1 3RQ
University Department

Enquiries to the Librarian

Subject coverage
botany; biochemistry; genetics; cytology; ecology; physiology; taxonomy

2098 OXFORD UNIVERSITY
Department of Astrophysics, University Observatory, South Parks Road, Oxford OX1 3RQ Tel. 0865 59878
0865 52676
University Department

Enquiries to the Director, by letter only

Subject coverage
astronomy, optics, spectroscopy

Special collections
National Geographic Society and Palomar Observatory Sky Survey

Publications
Departmental documents

2099 OXFORD UNIVERSITY
Department of Biochemistry, South Parks Road, Oxford OX1 3QU Tel. 0865 59214
Telex 83681

University Research Department

Enquiries to the Librarian

Subject coverage
biochemistry; immunology; microbiology

Publications
List of publications of Staff Members

2100 OXFORD UNIVERSITY
Department of Geology and Mineralogy, Library, Parks Road, Oxford OX1 3PR Tel. 0865 54511
University Department Library

Enquiries, from undergraduates, and research workers only, to the Librarian

Subject coverage
geology; mineralogy; geochemistry; rock structure; geochronology

2101 OXFORD UNIVERSITY
Elton Library, Animal Ecology Research Group, Department of Zoology, South Parks Road, Oxford OX1 3PS Tel. 0865 56789 ext. 298
University Department Reference Library

No enquiry service; reference library only

Subject coverage
ecology

2102 OXFORD UNIVERSITY
Engineering Laboratory, Parks Road, Oxford OX1 3PJ Tel. 0865 59988
University Department

Enquiries to the Librarian

Subject coverage
engineering science

Publications
List of Research Projects

2103 OXFORD UNIVERSITY
Physical Chemistry Laboratory, South Parks Road, Oxford OX1 3QZ Tel. 0865 53324
University Department

Enquiries to the Head of the Department

Subject coverage
physical chemistry

2104 OXFORD UNIVERSITY
Zoology Department Library, South Parks Road, Oxford OX1 3PS Tel. 0865 56789
University Department Library, part of the Radcliffe Science Library, *q.v.*

Enquiries to the Librarian

Subject coverage
zoology; ecology; ornithology; molecular biology; genetics; cell biology; biophysics; behaviour

OXFORD UNIVERSITY *see also*
BODLEIAN LIBRARY
OXFORD CENTRE FOR MANAGEMENT STUDIES
RADCLIFFE SCIENCE LIBRARY

2105 OXFORDSHIRE COUNTY LIBRARIES
Central Library, Westgate, Oxford OX1 1DJ Tel. 0865 815656
Telex 837439

Public Libraries, system created by the amalgamation of the former Oxfordshire County Library, Oxford City Libraries and Banbury Public Library; District Libraries also at Witney and Holton Park

Enquiries to the County Librarian

Subject coverage
accountancy and book-keeping; motor vehicle engineering; hydraulic engineering; inland waterways; internal combustion engines; timber manufactures

2106 OYEZ INTERNATIONAL BUSINESS COMMUNICATIONS LIMITED
1 Hills Place, London W1R DB Tel. 01-437 1416
Company, formerly International Business Communications Limited

Enquiries to the Secretary

Subject coverage
commercial and private law

Publication
Cassette Law Library

OYSTER MERCHANTS AND PLANTERS ASSOCIATION *now* **SHELLFISH ASSOCIATION OF GREAT BRITAIN,** *q.v.*

2107 PA COMPUTERS AND TELECOMMUNICATIONS (PACTEL)
Rutland House, Rutland Gardens, Knightsbridge, Tel. 01-235 6060
London SW7 1BY Telex 27874
Company/Consultants; part of PA International Management Consultants Limited, *q.v.*

Enquiries to the Director

Subject coverage

application of computers, telecommunications, and operational research in commerce, industry and government; systems work and programming; use of forecasting, statistical analysis and mathematical modelling; management information systems and data-based management

2108 PA INTERNATIONAL MANAGEMENT CONSULTANTS LIMITED

Personnel Services Group, Hyde Park House, 60a Knightsbridge, London SW1X 7LE — Tel. 01-235 6060, Telex 27874

Company/Consultants

Enquiries to the Director

Subject coverage

availability of executives in the U.K. and other parts of the world; costs of recruitment and advertising; recommended remuneration and company remuneration structure; recommended conditions of service; job evaluation techniques; house styles and corporate image for recruitment advertising

2109 PA INTERNATIONAL MANAGEMENT CONSULTANTS LIMITED

U.K. Consulting Groups, Hyde Park House, 60a Knightsbridge, London SW1X 7LE — Tel. 01-235 6060, Telex 27874

Company/Consultants

Enquiries to the Director

Subject coverage

corporate policy and structure; marketing; distribution; manufacturing; materials management; capital projects; administration and services; management accounting and information systems; management development; human and industrial relations

2110 PA TECHNOLOGY AND SCIENCE CENTRE (PATSCentre)

Back Lane, Melbourn, Royston, Herts SG8 6DP — Tel. 763 61222, Telex 81561

Company/Consultants, part of PA International Management Consultants Limited, *q.v.*

Enquiries to the Director

Subject coverage

advice to companies on the extension of product ranges, diversification, technological problems; electronics engineering; mechanical sciences; material sciences; applied and engineering physics; advance production technology; mechanisation; small batch production of new products

2111 PADDINGTON COLLEGE

Paddington Green, London W2 1NB — Tel. 01-402 6221

Technical College; formed from the amalgamation of Paddington Technical College and Paddington College for Further Education

Enquiries to the College Librarian or to the Librarian at Saltram Crescent, W9 (Tel. 01-969 2391, ext. 28)

Subject coverage

engineering (production, electronic, mechanical, electrical, radio and television, gas, heating and ventilating, and motor vehicle); medical laboratory science; bacteriology; immunology; medical microbiology; haematology; histopathology; applied biology; animal technology; science laboratory technology; glassworking; photographic technology

Special collection

Management Projects of the Institute of Medical Laboratory Sciences, *q.v.*

PAINT AND PAINTING INDUSTRIES LIAISON COMMITTEE *see* **PAINTMAKERS ASSOCIATION OF GREAT BRITAIN LIMITED**

2112 PAINT RESEARCH ASSOCIATION

Waldegrave Road, Teddington, Middlesex TW11 8LD — Tel. 01-977 4427, Telex 928720

Research Association; formerly Research Association of British Paint, Colour & Varnish Manufacturers, Paint Research Station

Enquiries to the Information Department (fees possibly chargeable to non-members)

Subject coverage

paint science and technology; corrosion; deterioration and biodeterioration of materials; pigments; oils; resins; polymers; paint application; health hazards and toxicology; industrial hazards and anti-pollution legislation; organic and inorganic chemistry; analytical chemistry; anti-fouling technology; spectroscopy; rheology; colour science and colorimetry; paint testing; powder coatings; microbiology; building materials; standards, specifications, reports and patents

Publications

World Surface Coatings Abstracts (monthly, with SDI Service)
Paint Titles (weekly, current awareness service)
Annual Report
Bibliographies

2113 PAINTMAKERS ASSOCIATION OF GREAT BRITAIN LIMITED

Alembic House, 93 Albert Embankment, London SE1 7TU — Tel. 01-735 8201

Trade Association; houses the Paint and Painting Industries Liaison Committee and the National Joint Industrial Council for the Paint, Varnish and Lacquer Industry

Enquiries to the Information Officer

Subject coverage

paint selection; testing; suppliers; technical training

2114 PAISLEY COLLEGE OF TECHNOLOGY

High Street, Paisley, Renfrewshire PA1 2BE — Tel. 041-887 1241
Telex 778951

College of Technology, central government-financed; houses the Materials and Component Development and Testing Association (MACDATA), *q.v.*, the Local Government Information Centre and the Scottish School of Non-Destructive Testing

Enquiries to the Librarian, or to the Director of the Centre for Liaison with Industry and Commerce

Subject coverage

land economics; economics and management; mathematics; computing; physics; chemistry; biology; marine ecology; mechanical, civil and electrical engineering; building; chemic technology

Publication

List of Serial Holdings

PAISLEY PUBLIC LIBRARIES *see* **RENFREW DISTRICT LIBRARIES**

2115 PALAEONTOGRAPHICAL SOCIETY

Institute of Geological Sciences, Exhibition Road, — Tel. 01-589 3444
South Kensington, London SW7 2DE

Learned Society

Enquiries to the Secretary

Subject coverage

British fossils; study of geology in relation to fossils particularly by publications upon them

Publications

Monographs of British fossils

2116 PALAEONTOLOGICAL ASSOCIATION

c/o Department of Geology, The University, Newcastle upon Tyne NE1 7RU — Tel. 0632 28511

Learned Society

Enquiries to the Secretary

Subject coverage

palaeontology

Publications

Palaeontology (quarterly)
Special Papers in Palaeontology (1 or 2 per annum)
List of British Palaeontologists

PALMERS GREEN MAIN LIBRARIY *see* **ENFIELD LIBRARY SERVICE**

2117 PAPER AND PAPER PRODUCTS INDUSTRY TRAINING BOARD
Star House, Potters Bar, Hertfordshire EN6 2PG — Tel. 98 50211
Industrial Training Board, of the Training Services Agency

Enquiries to the Training Information Officer, the Librarian, or the Information Assistant

Subject coverage
training recommendations, standards and guidelines for the paper and paper products industry; including paper and board making; carton making; corrugated case making; bag making; flexible packaging; stationery; wallcoverings

Publications
Training Recommendations and Guides
Publications List

2118 PAPER MAKERS ALLIED TRADES ASSOCIATION
c/o CPC (United Kingdom) Limited, Trafford Park, Manchester M17 1PA — Tel. 061-872 2571, Telex 667022
Trade Association

Enquiries to the Honorary Secretary

Subject coverage
machinery and chemicals for the paper industry

Publications
Catalogues

2119 PAPER TRADE PROTECTION AGENCY
12–18 Station Road, Sidcup, Kent DA15 7EH — Tel. 01-300 6815, Telex 262859
Trade Protection Association; Member of the British Mercantile Agency Limited, *q.v.*

Enquiries to the Director

Subject coverage
commercial debt collecting and status enquiries in the paper trade

2120 C.A. PARSONS & COMPANY LIMITED
Heaton Works, Shields Road, Newcastle-upon-Tyne NE6 2YL — Tel. 0632 650411, Telex 53109
Company; part of the Reyrolle Parsons Group

Enquiries, involving only published literature within his field, to the Librarian

Subject coverage
design and production of turbo generators and auxiliary plant

Publication
Reyrolle Parsons Review

2121 PARSONS PEEBLES LIMITED
East Pilton, Edinburgh EH5 2XT — Tel. 031-552 6261, Telex 72125
Manufacturing Company; member of the Reyrolle Parsons Group

Enquiries, only on matters concerning Company products, to the Publicity Manager

Subject coverage
electric motors; generators; power transformers

2122 PARTICLE SCIENCE AND TECHNOLOGY INFORMATION SERVICE (PSTIS)
University of Technology, Loughborough, Leicestershire LE11 3TU — Tel. 050-93 63171 ext. 5212, Telex 34319
University Department

Enquiries, from subscribers only, to the Information Officer

Subject coverage
particle technology; properties of powders and particle dispersions in liquids and gases; handling of bulk powders; air filtration; production of particles; gaseous effluent control; aerosols

Publication
Current Awareness in Particle Technology, formerly Particulate Information (monthly, annual KWIC index, a continuing bibliography of world wide coverage)

2123 PASSPORT OFFICE
Clive House, 70 Petty France, London SW1H 9HD Tel. 01-222 8010
Government Department, of the Foreign and Commonwealth Office; Branch Offices in Liverpool, Glasgow, Peterborough and Newport, Gwent

Enquiries, written, to the Chief Passport Officer; telephoned, to the General Enquiries Department

Subject coverage
issue of U.K. Passports to British Subjects, citizens of U.K. and Colonies, British Subjects without Citizenship or British Protected Persons; advice to such passport holders regarding travel overseas; grant of return visas to aliens leaving U.K. for short period and wishing to return

2124 PATENT GLAZING CONFERENCE
13 Upper High Street, Epsom, Surrey KT17 4QY Tel. 78 29191
Trade Association, member of the Metal Window Federation Limited

Enquiries to the Director

Subject coverage
patent glazing; roof lights, etc.

Publication
Brochure

2125 PATENT OFFICE AND INDUSTRIAL PROPERTY AND COPYRIGHT DEPARTMENT
25 Southampton Buildings, London WC2A 1AY Tel. 01-405 8721
Government Department, of the Department of Trade

Enquiries to the Industrial Property and Copyright Department

Subject coverage
patents; designs; trade marks; industrial property and copyright

Special collection
Patent specifications (and indexes)

Publications
Trade Marks Journal (weekly)
Official Journal (weekly)
Abridgements of Specifications
Patents: a source of technical information (includes further list of publications)

2126 PATTERN WEAVERS SOCIETY
21 Kaye Lane, Almondbury, Huddersfield MD5 8XP Tel. 0484 25657
Trade Union

Enquiries to the Secretary

Subject coverage
pattern weaving; conditions of service, etc. in the woollen and worsted industry

2127 PEEBLES AREA LIBRARY
Chambers Institution, High Street, Peebles, Tweeddale District, Borders Region, Scotland EH45 8AG Tel. 0721 20123
Public Library, of the Borders Regional Library system; composed of the former Peebles Burgh Library and the Peebles County Library

Enquiries to the Librarian

Subject coverage
general and local

Special collection
Chambers Brothers (publishers) material especially in relation to their home town of Peebles

2128 PAXMAN DIESELS LIMITED
P.O. Box 8, Colchester, Essex CO1 2HW Tel. 0206 5151
Telex 98151
Company; subsidiary of G.E.C. Limited; formerly Ruston Paxman Diesels Limited
Enquiries to the Librarian
Subject coverage
engineering; diesel engines

2129 P E CONSULTING GROUP LIMITED
Park House, Wick Road, Egham, Surrey TW20 0HW Tel. 903 4411
Telex 933783
Company/Consultancy
Enquiries to the Information Section, on a fee-paying basis
Subject coverage
consultancy in management, manufacturing, marketing, industry and commerce

PEA GROWING RESEARCH ORGANISATION LIMITED *now* **PROCESSORS AND GROWERS RESEARCH ORGANISATION LIMITED,** *q.v.*

2130 PEAT MARWICK MITCHELL & COMPANY
11 Ironmonger Lane, London EC2V 8AX Tel. 01-606 8888
Telex 886658
Professional Partnership of Consultants; member of International Group of the same name
Enquiries to the Information Officer
Subject coverage
management; business planning and control; marketing and distribution; data processing; personnel and training; production and inventory planning; transportation and land use; projects involving the foregoing, in many countries and various industries

2131 PEDDER ASSOCIATES LIMITED
51 Portland Road, Kingston-upon-Thames, Surrey KT1 2SH Tel. 01-546 9877
Private Company; editorial office for Computer Survey and office of the National Computer Index
Enquiries to the Senior Information Officer
Subject coverage
computers and computing; users and locations of computer installations in the U.K.; computer hardware in Europe; computer service and computer marketing information; statistics on U.K. computer industry
Special collections
Computer held data bases on computer users, hardware, and service companies
Publications
Computer Survey
Annual Census of U.K. Computer Installations

PEMBROKE DISTRICT LIBRARY *see* **DYFED COUNTY LIBRARY**

PENDLE DISTRICT CENTRAL LIBRARY *see* **LANCASHIRE LIBRARY**

2132 PENNWALT LIMITED
Tower Works, Doman Road, Camberley, Surrey GU15 3DN Tel. 0276 63383
Telex 858283
Company, formerly Pennsalt Limited
Enquiries to the Librarian
Subject coverage
separators for the chemical, food, and process industries; vacuum pumps and processes

PENZANCE DISTRICT LIBRARY *see* **CORNWALL COUNTY LIBRARY**

PERA *see* **PRODUCTION ENGINEERING RESEARCH ASSOCIATION**

2133 PERFORATED METAL EXPORT GROUP
8 St. Bride Street, London EC4A 4DA — Tel. 01-353 3020
Telex 24276

Trade Association; affiliated to the Guild of Metal Perforators

Enquiries may be redirected to member companies

Subject coverage
export of perforated metal products

2134 PERIODICAL PUBLISHERS ASSOCIATION LIMITED
Imperial House, Kingsway, London WC2B 6UN — Tel. 01-836 9204
Trade Association, affiliated to the International Federation of the Periodical Press, of 17 Draycott Avenue, London SW3 3BS, and to La Fédération des Associations d'Editeurs de Périodiques de la CEE, of the Kingsway, London address

Enquiries to the Director General

Subject coverage
periodicals publishing, other than labour relations

Publications
Booklets on periodicals production as follows:
Origination
Paper
Composing
Printing and Finishing

2135 PERKINS ENGINES COMPANY
East Field, Frank Perkins Way, Peterborough PE1 5NA — Tel. Peterborough 67474
Telex 32132

Company, subsidiary of Massey-Ferguson

Enquiries to the Technical Librarian

Subject coverage
diesel engines

PERMANENT COMMITTEE ON GEOGRAPHICAL NAMES *see* **ROYAL GEOGRAPHICAL SOCIETY**

2136 PERMUTIT-BOBY LIMITED
Permutit House, 632–652 London Road, Isleworth, — Tel. 01-560 5199
Middlesex TW7 4EZ — Telex 24440
Company; formerly Permutit Company Limited; subsidiary of Portals Water Treatment Limited

Enquiries to the Public Relations Manager

Subject coverage
water, effluent and process liquids treatment; in particular, engineered industrial treatment plant and processes, including water recovery and re-use

Publications
Treatment Case Histories
Technical article reprints
Catalogues

2137 PERSHORE COLLEGE OF HORTICULTURE
Avonbank, Pershore, Worcestershire WR10 3JP — Tel. 038-65 2227/8
Horticultural College; houses the Secretariat of the Horticultural Education Association; formerly Pershore Institute of Horticulture

Enquiries to the College Librarian

Subject coverage
horticulture; apiculture; pollution; conservation; pedology; entomology; landscape planning and design; forestry; careers in horticulture

Special collection
Apicultural literature (formerly of Hereford and Worcester Public Libraries)

Publication
Proceedings of the Nurseryman's Conference (annual)

2138 PERTH AND KINROSS DISTRICT LIBRARIES
7 Rose Terrace, Perth PH1 5HE — Tel. 0738 22318, 0738 27277

Public Libraries; formerly Perth and Kinross County Library

Enquiries to the District Librarian or the Sandeman Librarian

Subject coverage
local industry and commerce; U.K. and other countries

2139 PERTH TECHNICAL COLLEGE
Crieff Road, Perth PH1 2NX — Tel. 0738 27044
Technical College

Enquiries to the Librarian

Subject coverage
building; mechanical and automobile engineering; catering; business studies; economics

2140 PERUVIAN EMBASSY
52 Sloane Street, London SW1X 9SP — Tel. 01-235 1917
Government Commission

Enquiries to the Economic Counsellor

Subject coverage
commercial and economic matters as they affect Peru

2141 PEST INFESTATION CONTROL LABORATORY
London Road, Slough, Buckinghamshire SL3 7HJ — Tel. 75 34626
Government Research Laboratory, of the Ministry of Agriculture, Fisheries and Food, Agricultural Development and Advisory Service; created by merger of the Ministry of Agriculture's Infestation Control Laboratory and the Agricultural Research Council's Pest Infestation Laboratory; controls laboratories at Tolworth (mammals) and Worplesdon (birds)

Enquiries to the Librarian

Subject coverage
biology and control of vertebrate and invertebrate pests of stored products; moulds on stored products; vertebrate pests of crops; biochemistry; toxicology, and environmental effects of pesticides

Special collections
Stored Product Entomology
Information on Rodents
Living culture collection of most known stored product insects

Publications
Triennial Report
Research papers

PET FOOD MANUFACTURERS ASSOCIATION *see* **FOOD MANUFACTURERS FEDERATION INCORPORATION**

2142 PETERBOROUGH DIVISIONAL LIBRARY
Broadway, Peterborough PE1 1RX — Tel. 0733 69105, Telex 32634

Public Library, of the Cambridgeshire Libraries, *q.v.*

Enquiries to the Reference Librarian or Technical Librarian

Subject coverage
general, commercial and technical

Publication
Directory of Scientific, Technical and Commercial Information Resources in the Peterborough Area 3rd ed., 1976

PETERHEAD BURGH LIBRARY *see* **NORTH EAST OF SCOTLAND LIBRARY SERVICE**

PETERSFIELD LIBRARY *see* **HAMPSHIRE COUNTY LIBRARY**

2143 PETROLEUM INDUSTRY TRAINING BOARD
York House, Empire Way, Wembley, Middlesex HA9 0PT Tel. 01-903 4161
Government Department, of the Training Services Agency; includes the Drilling Technology Training Centre

Enquiries to the Information Department

Subject coverage
training in management, supervision, and industrial relations; metrication; marketing and sales; central heating; safety; fire fighting; drilling; in-company training plans

Publications
Abstract Bulletin
Publications lists

2144 PHARMACEUTICAL SOCIETY OF GREAT BRITAIN
1 Lambeth High Street, London SE1 7JN Tel. 01-735 9141
Professional Body

Enquiries to the Librarian or Information Officer

Subject coverage
pharmaceutical subjects; materia medica; pharmacology; toxicology; chemistry; botany

Special collections
Historical Collection (including many herbals)
London, Edinburgh and Dublin Pharmacopoeias from 1618
Hanbury Library of rare, illustrated, botanical works
Collection on English and foreign proprietary medicines

Publications
British National Formulary
British Pharmaceutical Codex
Calendar of the Pharmaceutical Society
Chemical Nomenclature
Constipation and Allied Disorders
Drug Interactions and their Mechanisms
Dental Practitioners' Formulary
Extra Pharmacopoeia (Martindale)
Frontiers in Pharmacology
Historical Collection: Coloured Postcards
Index of New Products
Isolation and Identification of Drugs
Journal of Pharmacy and Pharmacology
Pharmaceutical Handbook
Pharmacy Law and Ethics
Register of Pharmaceutical Chemists
Restricted Medicines and Poisons
Short History of Surgical Dressings

PHILIP LYLE MEMORIAL RESEARCH LABORATORY *see* **TATE & LYLE LIMITED, Group Research and Development,** *q.v.*

2145 PHILIPPINE EMBASSY
Office of the Commercial Attaché, 9a Palace Green, Kensington, London W8 Tel. 01-937 1898
Telex 24411

Government Department

Enquiries to the Commercial Attaché

Subject coverage
Philippine foreign trade; investment information; import-export opportunities; general economic information on the Philippines

Publications
Brochures on economics or culture
Trade and investment laws

PHOTOELECTRIC SPECTROMETRY GROUP *now* **ULTRA VIOLET SPECTROMETRY GROUP,** *q.v.*

PHOTOGRAMMETRIC SOCIETY *see* **LONDON UNIVERSITY, Department of Photogrammetry and Surveying**

2146 PHOTOGRAPHIC DEALERS ASSOCIATION
238 High Street North, London E12 6SB Tel. 01-471 0941
Trade Association

Enquiries to the Association

Subject coverage
photographic retail trade

Publication
Hot News (weekly)

PHOTOGRAPHIC TRADE PROTECTION AGENCY *see* **BRITISH MERCANTILE AGENCY LIMITED**

PHYSICAL SOCIETY *now* **INSTITUTE OF PHYSICS,** *q.v.*

2147 PIANO PUBLICITY ASSOCIATION LIMITED
30 Eastbourne Terrace, London W2 6LD Tel. 01-723 010538
Telex 23856

Trade Association

Enquiries to Public Relations Department, Infoplan Limited, of same address

Subject coverage
pianos and piano manufacture

2148 PIANO TRADE SUPPLIERS ASSOCIATION LIMITED
18a Northampton Square, London EC1V 0EJ Tel. 01-253 7132/3
Trade Association

Enquiries to the Secretary

Subject coverage
sources of supply for component parts of pianofortes

2149 PICKERING AGRICULTURAL CENTRE
Pickering, Yorkshire YO1 8NE
Agricultural Centre

Enquiries to the Head of the Centre

Subject coverage
home economics and country crafts

2150 PILKINGTON BROTHERS LIMITED
Research and Development Laboratories, Hall Lane, Lathom, Ormskirk, Lancashire L40 5UF — Tel. 0695 73801

Company; part of Pilkington Brothers, St. Helens; provides services to and from the Flat Glass Manufacturers Association, *q.v.*

Enquiries to the Information Officer

Subject coverage
fundamental research in glass; applied research and development of new processes and products in flat glass, pressed and moulded glass, optical and other special glasses, glass fibres and surface-treated glass

PILKINGTON GROUP *see also* **FIBREGLASS LIMITED**

2151 PIPE JACKING ASSOCIATION
Dickens House, 15 Tooks Court, London EC4 1LA — Tel. 01-831 7581
Telex 23485

Trade Association

Enquiries to the Secretaries

Subject coverage
pipe jacking; thrustboring

Publication
Design and Specification Bulletin

2152 PIPELINE INDUSTRIES GUILD
17 Grosvenor Place, London SW1X 7ES — Tel. 01-235 7938
Learned Society

Enquiries to the Technical Officer

Subject coverage
pipeline technology, including oil, gas, water and any other products transported by pipelines

Publication
Quarterly Journal (for members only)

2153 PIRA, RESEARCH ORGANISATION FOR THE PAPER AND BOARD, PRINTING AND PACKAGING INDUSTRIES
Randalls Road, Leatherhead, Surrey KT22 7RU — Tel. 53 76161
Telex 929810

Research Association

Enquiries to the Information Officer

Subject coverage
pulping and pulp evaluation; paper and board making; water and effluent treatment; printing; inks; factory planning; bookbinding; adhesives; packaging; paper and board testing; printing machinery; package development and testing

Publications
Paper and Board Abstracts
Printing Abstracts
Packaging Abstracts
Management and Marketing Abstracts
Pira Annual Review
Pira News
Pira Handbooks
Pira Bibliographies
Pira Instruction Manuals
Pira Reports

2154 PIRELLI GENERAL CABLE WORKS LIMITED
P.O. Box 6, Leigh Road, Eastleigh, Hampshire SO5 5YE Tel. 0703 612261
Telex 47625

Company

Enquiries, in writing, to the Librarian, Engineering Department

Subject coverage
electric power and telephone cable design, manufacture and installation

Publications
Cable Review
Catalogues and technical leaflets

2155 PLANNING FOR GROWTH LIMITED
8a Symons Street, Sloane Square, London SW3 2TJ Tel. 01-730 0137
Management and Business Consultants

Enquiries to the Chairman

Subject coverage
corporate planning; all aspects of management; marketing; including international marketing; new product development; physical distribution

Publications
Books on management and marketing

PLANNING RESEARCH AND SYSTEMS LIMITED *see* **PRS GROUP LIMITED**

2156 PLANT BREEDING INSTITUTE
Maris Lane, Trumpington, Cambridge CB2 2LQ Tel. 022-021 3234
Research Institute of the Agricultural Research Council

Enquiries to the Information Officer

Subject coverage
improvement of agricultural crops by breeding, (cereals, potatoes, brassicas, forage plants, sugar beet); research in new crops, (lupins, sunflowers, maize)

Publication
Annual Report

2157 PLANT GROWTH SUBSTANCES AND SYSTEMIC FUNGICIDES UNIT
Wye College, Wye, Ashford, Kent TN25 5AL Tel. 0233 812401
Research Unit, of the Agricultural Research Council

Enquiries to the Secretary

Subject coverage
hormonal control of plant growth; chemical basis of plant disease resistance

Publications
papers on research findings, in scientific journals

2158 PLANT PATHOLOGY LABORATORY
Hatching Green, Harpenden, Hertfordshire AL5 2BD Tel. 058-27 5241
Government Laboratory, part of the Agricultural Development and Advisory Service of the Ministry of Agriculture, Fisheries and Food

Enquiries to the Librarian

Subject coverage
plant pathology (bacteriology, disease assessment, disease control, mycology, virology); agricultural entomology (general entomology, pest assessment and control, fumigation, insect systematics); crop protection chemistry (biological efficiency, analytical methods for pest formulations and residues in crops, safety to users); general agricultura; botany; systematic zoology (mainly entomology); floras; toxicology; industrial hygiene and medicine; chromatography and microscopy

Publications
Plant Pathology
Pesticide usage survey reports
Approved products for farmers and growers

PLANT PROTECTION LIMITED *now* **ICI PLANT PROTECTION DIVISION,** *q.v.*

2159 PLASTIC COATING RESEARCH COMPANY LIMITED
Swan Lane, Sandhurst, Camberley, Surrey GU17 8DB Tel. 0252 873470
Company; includes Plastic Dipping Company Limited, of the same address; houses Chemical Coatings Limited

Enquiries to the Managing Director

Subject coverage
plastic coating technology; research, formulation and execution of the processes

Publications
Technical Information Booklets on specific plastic coating materials

2160 PLASTICS AND RUBBER INSTITUTE
11 Hobart Place, London SW1W 0HL Tel. 01-245 9555
Professional Society, formed by the merger of the Plastics Institute and the Institute of the Rubber Industry; a Qualifying Body

Enquiries to the Information Officer

Subject coverage
art, science, and technology of plastics, rubber and high polymers; education and training in those fields and in related management, economics and finance

Publications
Members Journal (bi-monthly)
Plastics and Rubber (quarterly)
Series of monographs, books for students, conference papers, general information on the plastics & rubber industry, safety, bibliography, etc.

PLASTICS CRATE MANUFACTURERS ASSOCIATION *see* **ALLIED BREWERY TRADERS ASSOCIATION**

2161 PLASTICS INDUSTRIES ASSOCIATION
Confederation House, Kildare Street, Dublin 2 Telex 4711
Trade Association

Enquiries to the Director

Subject coverage
plastics industry in Ireland

Publication
Plastics in Ireland

PLASTICS INSTITUTE *now* **PLASTICS AND RUBBER INSTITUTE,** *q.v.*

2162 PLASTICS TANKS AND CISTERNS MANUFACTURERS ASSOCIATION
c/o Peat Marwick Mitchell and Company, 7 Ludgate Broadway, Tel. 01-248 1550
London EC4V 6DX Telex 8812908
Trade Association

Enquiries to the Secretary

Subject coverage
installation and fixing of tanks

2163 PLESSEY AEROSPACE
Abbey Works, Titchfield, Fareham, Hampshire PO14 4QA — Tel. 03294 43031, Telex 86214

Company, part of Plessey Company Limited

Enquiries to the Marketing Executive

Subject coverage
electrical, electro-mechanical and mechanical systems for the aerospace industry; small gas turbines

2164 PLESSEY AVIONICS AND COMMUNICATIONS
Martin Road, West Leigh, Havant, Hampshire PO9 5DH — Tel. 07012 6391, Telex 86227

Company, part of Plessey Company Limited; formerly Electronics Group; libraries at above address and at Vicarage Lane, Ilford, Essex

Enquiries to the Librarian, Havant or to Library Liaison Representative, Ilford

Subject coverage
radar communications and airborne electronic systems; antenna design; reliability and quality assurance; flight data recording systems; advanced techniques development; secondary radars; (at Ilford, electronics, specifications and standards)

2165 PLESSEY COMPANY LIMITED
Sopers Lane, Poole, Dorset BH17 7ER — Tel. 020-13 5161, Telex 41272

Company; formerly Plessey Automation; associated with the Company's installation at Vicarage Lane, Ilford, Essex

Enquiries to the Information Officer

Subject coverage
road traffic control; nucleonic instrumentation; numerical control of machine tools; data capture systems; mathematics

2166 PLESSEY POWER SYSTEMS
Crown Works, Eastern Avenue West, Romford, Essex RM7 7NL — Tel. 01-478 3040, Telex 26284

Company, part of the Plessey Company Limited

Enquiries to the Marketing Manager

Subject coverage
power supply equipment; airfield lighting; stepper motors; domestic central heating water circulating pumps

2167 PLESSEY RADAR LIMITED
Addlestone, Weybridge, Surrey KT15 2PW — Tel. 0932 47282, Telex 262329

Company, part of Plessey Company Limited

Enquiries to the Publicity Department

Subject coverage
air traffic control systems, including airfield control radar, primary and secondary surveillance radars, display, data-handling and software systems and services; defence systems, surveillance, display, data-handling, command, control and height-finding systems; naval systems, including action information, coastal defence, weapon control, maritime control and radars for air and surface warning; automatic meteorological systems including hydrological, industrial, oceanographic, upper air and weather radar systems; information processing; communication satellite terminal equipment; metal detectors

Publications
Journals and catalogues

2168 PLESSEY RADAR RESEARCH CENTRE
Technical Information and Library Services, Southleigh Park House, Havant, Hampshire PO9 2PE
Tel. 07012 6391
Telex 86709
Research Centre, part of the Plessey Company Limited

Enquiries to the Technical Information Officer

Subject coverage
radar systems for air defence and air traffic control; microwave and UHF/VHF systems; instrument landing systems; radar sensors, plot extractors and track processors; environmental sensors; acoustics; optics; infrared; magnetics; seismics; scientific computing; image processing; operational research for civil and military resource management

2169 PLESSEY TELECOMMUNICATIONS LIMITED
Edge Lane, Liverpool L7 9NW Tel. 051-228 4830
Telex 62267
Company, part of Plessey Company Limited; formerly Plessey Telecommunications Group

Enquiries to the Manager, Information and Library Services

Subject coverage
telecommunications

2170 PLESSEY TELECOMMUNICATIONS RESEARCH LIMITED
Taplow Court, Taplow, Maidenhead, Berkshire SL6 0ER Tel. 0628 23351
Telex 484119
Private Sector Research Unit, part of Plessey Company Limited

Enquiries to the Information Officer or Librarian

Subject coverage
telephone and data switching and transmission; computer applications relevant to telecommunications; military electronics and communication systems; mathematical studies

Publication
Systems Technology (three times per annum)

2171 PLUMPTON AGRICULTURAL COLLEGE
Plumpton, Lewes, Sussex BN7 3AG Tel. 079-157 890454
Agricultural College, East Sussex County Council; formerly East Sussex School of Agriculture

Enquiries to the Librarian

Subject coverage
agriculture, including livestock and crops; horticulture; agricultural machinery; poultry

2172 PLUNKETT FOUNDATION FOR COOPERATIVE STUDIES
31 St. Giles, Oxford OX1 3LF Tel. 0865 53960/1
Limited Company with Charitable status; housing also the Agriculture Co-operative Managers Association and the Brundrett Trust; the Foundation is partially integrated with the Federation of Agricultural Co-operatives (U.K.) Limited

Enquiries to the Chief Executive Officer

Subject coverage
agricultural cooperation; information, education, consultancy

Publications
Yearbook
Occasional papers, reports and reprints
Bibliography of Co-operation

2173 PLYMOUTH CENTRAL LIBRARY
Drake Circus, Plymouth, Devonshire PL4 8AL Tel. 0752 68000
Telex 145578

Public Library; the West Devon Area Library of the Devon Library Services, *q.v.*; formerly Plymouth City Public Library

Enquiries to the Area Librarian

Subject coverage
general

Special collections
Moxon Collection of Ornithology and Travel
Naval History and Naval Architecture
British Standards
Patent Abridgements from 1855
Extel cards

PLYMOUTH OCEAN PROJECTS LIMITED *see* **FORT BOVISAND UNDERWATER CENTRE**

2174 PLYMOUTH POLYTECHNIC LEARNING RESOURCES CENTRE
Drake Circus, Plymouth, Devonshire PL4 8AA Tel. 0752 21312
Telex 45423

Polytechnic; formerly Plymouth College of Technology

Enquiries to the Head of Learning Resources Centre

Subject coverage
civil, mechanical, electrical and communication engineering; maritime studies; mathematics; physics; chemistry; biology; zoology; architecture; management; business studies

2175 PNEUMOCONIOSIS RESEARCH UNIT
Llandough Hospital, Penarth, South Glamorgan CF6 1XW Tel. 0222 708761
Research Unit, of the Medical Research Council

Enquiries to the Director

Subject coverage
multidisciplinary studies into the effects of industrial dusts and fumes on the lungs, the types of disability caused and the natural history of the associated diseases; studies in epidemiology, lung function, dust physics, chemistry, morbid anatomy, immunology; experimental pathology, biochemistry, radiology, treatment and statistics, as related to industrial diseases of the lung

Special collection
UICC reference samples of asbestos

2176 POISON CENTRE
North Thames Regional Health Authority, Oldchurch Hospital, Romford, Essex RM7 0BE Tel. 0708 46090
Government Department, Regional Centre

Enquiries to the Director

Subject coverage
treatment of poisoning, domestic or occupational/accidental or deliberate/all ages of people; potentiality of poisons, particularly acute poisons; lethal doses; blood levels; all patterns of therapy

Special collections
Card index reference covering 25 years of poisons admissions

2177 POISONS BOARD
Home Office, Romney House, Marsham Street, London SW1P 3DY Tel. 01-212 6571 *or* 6809
Statutory Advisory Body; of the Home Office, to advise the Home Secretary

Enquiries should be made to the Drugs Branch of the Home Office, not *to the Poisons Board*

Subject coverage
sale and supply of substances included in the Poisons List made under the Pharmacy and Poisons Act 1933 and to which the Poisons Rules, also made under the Act, apply

2178 POLITICAL AND ECONOMIC PLANNING
12 Upper Belgrave Square, London SW1X 8BB — Tel. 01-235 5271
Independent Research Organisation

Enquiries cannot be accepted

Publications
Broadsheets (about 10 per annum)
Reports (about 2 or 3 per annum)

2179 POLYTECHNIC OF CENTRAL LONDON
309 Regent Street, London W1R 8AL — Tel. 01-580 2020
Polytechnic; formerly Regent Street Polytechnic, merged with Holborn College of Law, Languages and Commerce and Sidney Webb College of Education

Enquiries to the Chief Librarian

Subject coverage
mathematics; computing; physics; chemistry; biological sciences; electrical and electronic engineering; mechanical and systems engineering; architecture; building; civil engineering; surveying; business studies; economics; statistics; photography; film and television studies; management

2180 POLYTECHNIC OF THE SOUTH BANK
Borough Road, London SE1 0AA — Tel. 01-928 8989
Institute of Higher Education; formed by the amalgamation of the Borough Polytechnic, the Brixton School of Building, the City of Westminster College and the National College for Heating, Ventilating, Refrigeration and Fan Engineering; there is a unit of the Polytechnic at Wandsworth Road

Enquiries to the Chief Librarian

Subject coverage
food technology; applied biology; baking technology; building environmental services (heating, ventilation, lighting, etc.); construction engineering (civil engineering, architecture, building management, etc.)

2181 POLYTECHNIC OF WALES
Llantwit Road, Treforest, Glamorgan — Tel. 0443 405133
Institute of Higher Education; formerly Glamorgan College of Technology and, latterly, Glamorgan Polytechnic; Glamorgan College of Education has been incorporated

Enquiries to the Librarian

Subject coverage
the following branches of engineering: building, mechanical, civil, electrical, electronic, mining, production; estate management; mathematics; computer science; accountancy; economics; management

PONTEFRACT DISTRICT LIBRARY *see* **WAKEFIELD METROPOLITAN DISTRICT LIBRARIES**

PONTYPRIDD CENTRAL LIBRARY *see* **MID GLAMORGAN COUNTY LIBRARY**

POOLE CENTRAL LIBRARY *see* **DORSET COUNTY LIBRARY**

2182 POOLE TECHNICAL COLLEGE
North Road, Poole, Dorset BH14 0LS — Tel. 0202 747600
College of Further Education

Enquiries to the College Librarian

Subject coverage
building; business studies; engineering

POPLAR AREA LIBRARY *see* **TOWER HAMLETS LIBRARIES DEPARTMENT**

POPLAR TECHNICAL COLLEGE *now* **HACKNEY COLLEGE (Poplar Centre),** *q.v.*

PORT SUNLIGHT LABORATORY *see* **UNILEVER RESEARCH PORT SUNLIGHT LABORATORY**

PORT TALBOT BRANCH LIBRARY *see* **WEST GLAMORGAN COUNTY LIBRARY**

2183 PORTSMOUTH CENTRAL LIBRARY
Dorothy Dymond Street, Guildhall Square, Portsmouth, Hampshire PO1 2DX — Tel. 0705 819311–8, Telex 86382
Public Library; Branch of Hampshire County Library, *q.v.*, and central library for Hampshire's Portsmouth District

Enquiries to the Librarian

Subject coverage
electronics; radio; resins; soaps; glues; plastics; welding; electroplating; textiles; celluloid; clothing trade

Special collections
Naval History
British Standards

2184 PORTSMOUTH POLYTECHNIC
Central Library, Cambridge Road, Portsmouth, Hampshire PO1 2LG — Tel. 0705 27681
Polytechnic; formerly Portsmouth College of Technology

Enquiries to the Librarian

Subject coverage
business studies and commerce; engineering and technology; environmental sciences; physical and life sciences

2185 POST OFFICE RESEARCH CENTRE
Martlesham Heath, Ipswich, Suffolk IP5 7RE — Tel. 0473 643171, Telex 98376
Public Corporation Centre, part of the Post Office Telecommunications Headquarters

Enquiries to the Library

Subject coverage
telecommunications; electronics; semiconductor technology; computer technology

Publication
Subject and Author Catalogues of the bookstock

2186 POST OFFICE USERS NATIONAL COUNCIL
Waterloo Bridge House, Waterloo Road, London SE1 8UA — Tel. 01-928 9458, Telex 261969
Government-financed Consumer Organization, with units in Wales, Scotland and Northern Ireland

Enquiries to the Secretary

Subject coverage
representations or complaints about the Post Office services; posts, telephones, telex, other telecommunications services, giro

Publications
Reports on Post Office Proposals
Reports on Post Office Services
Leaflets on the Council's services and activities

2187 POTASSIUM INSTITUTE LIMITED
Nuffield, Henley-on-Thames, Oxfordshire RG9 5SS — Tel. 049-18 658
Company

Enquiries to the Director

Subject coverage
potash; fertilizer use; plant nutrition

2188 POTATO MARKETING BOARD
50 Hans Crescent, London SW1X 0NB — Tel. 01-589 4874
Statutory Marketing Board

Enquiries to the Information Officer

Subject coverage
potato varieties; diseases; production and marketing; storage and cookery

Special collection
British Atlas of Potato Varieties

Publications
Lists of Research Projects
Miscellaneous reports on research

2189 POTTERY AND GLASS WHOLESALERS ASSOCIATION
69 Cannon Street, London EC4N 5AB — Tel. 01-248 4444
Trade Association; member of the Federation of Wholesale and Industrial Distributors, *q.v.*

Enquiries accepted from members only

Subject coverage
pottery, glass

2190 POULTRY CLUB OF GREAT BRITAIN
72 Springfields, Great Dunmow, Essex — Tel. 0371 2935
Non-Trading Society; four regional branches; incorporating the British Bantam Association

Enquiries to the Secretary

Subject coverage
pure breeds of poultry

Publication
Year Book, including Breeders Directory Centenary ed., 1977. (free to members, on sale to non-members)

2191 POULTRY INDUSTRY CONFERENCE LIMITED
52–54 High Holborn, London WC1V 6SX — Tel. 01-242 4683
Telex 28479
Company

Enquiries to the Conference Organising Secretary

Subject coverage
the annual conference only

2192 POULTRY RESEARCH CENTRE
King's Buildings, West Mains Road, Edinburgh EH9 3JS — Tel. 031-667 4461
Government Department, of the Agricultural Research Council

Enquiries to the Liaison Officer or Librarian

Subject coverage
all aspects of the production of poultry for eggs or meat, except infectious disease; and *not* poultry or eggs as human food

Publication
Summary of Research Reports (annual)

POWER ACTUATED SYSTEMS ASSOCIATION *see* **FEDERATION OF BRITISH HAND TOOL MANUFACTURERS**

2193 POWER GENERATION ASSOCIATION
Leicester House, 8 Leicester Street, London WC2H 7BN — Tel. 01-437 0678
Trade Association; member of BEAMA, *q.v.*

Enquiries to the Director

Subject coverage
steam turbines including turbines driving power station boiler feed pumps; gas turbines; condensing and feed heating plant; turbo-type generators; water turbines

2194 POWER LOOM CARPET WEAVERS AND TEXTILE WORKERS ASSOCIATION
Callows Lane, Kidderminster, Worcestershire DY10 2JG Tel. 0562 3192
Trade Union

Enquiries to the General Secretary

Subject coverage
trade unionism; industrial relations

2195 POWYS COUNTY LIBRARIES AND MUSEUMS SERVICE
Cefnllys Road, Llandrindod Wells, Powys LD1 5LD Tel. 0597 2212
Public Libraries; an amalgamation of the former Breconshire, Montgomeryshire and Radnorshire County Library Services; Area Libraries at Brecon and Newton

Enquiries to the County Librarian

Subject coverage
general

PREPACKED FLOUR ASSOCIATION *see* **FOOD MANUFACTURERS FEDERATION INCORPORATED**

2196 PRESSED GLASSMAKERS SOCIETY OF GREAT BRITAIN
11 Oakfield Road, Lobley Hill, Gateshead, Tyne and Wear NE11 0AA Tel. 0632 605099
Trade Association

Enquiries to the General Secretary

Subject coverage
general information on the pressed glassmaking industry

PRESTON DISTRICT CENTRAL LIBRARY *see* **LANCASHIRE LIBRARY**

2197 PRESTON POLYTECHNIC
Corporation Street, Preston, Lancashire PR1 2TQ Tel. 0772 51831
College of Further and Higher Education, formerly Harris College

Enquiries to the Librarian

Subject coverage
chemistry; biology; physics; mathematics; computing science; electrical engineering; electronics; mechanical and production engineering; construction and urban studies; business and administration; law; management

Special collection
Preston Incorporated Law Society collection

PRESTWICH DISTRICT LIBRARY *see* **BURY METROPOLITAN BOROUGH LIBRARY**

2198 PRIAULX LIBRARY
Candie Road, St. Peter Port, Guernsey, Channel Islands Tel. 0481 21998
Public Library

Enquiries to the Librarian

Subject coverage
general; Guernsey affairs

2199 PRICE AND PIERCE GROUP
51 Aldwych, London WC2B 4AZ Tel. 01-240 2494
Company, subsidiary of Tozer Kemsley & Millbourn (Holdings) Limited

Enquiries to the Company Secretary

Subject coverage
woodpulp, paper and board, machinery, timber and sheet materials; international transportation, road haulage, shipping and forwarding, warehousing; business and holiday travel; finance and insurance broking

2200 PRICE COMMISSION
Neville House, Page Street, London SW1P 4LS Tel. 01-222 8020
Telex 917865
Independent Government Agency; having fifteen regional offices, including one each in Wales, Scotland and Northern Ireland
Enquiries to the Headquarters Information Centre, (tel. 01-828 7070) and to the Regional Offices, to the Press Officer or to the Librarian
Subject coverage
guidance to companies on requirements under the Price Code and Associated Orders
Publications
Quarterly Reports to Parliament
Reports on references to the Price Commission, on marketing, prices, distribution, retailers' margins, etc.
Price data sheets
List of publications in H.M.S.O. Sectional List 3

2201 PRINCES RISBOROUGH LABORATORY
Building Research Establishment, Princes Risborough, Aylesbury, Buckinghamshire HP17 9PX Tel. 084-44 3101
Telex 83559
Government Research Establishment, part of Building Research Establishment, of the Department of the Environment; formerly Forest Products Research Laboratory
Enquiries for information to the Advisory Service; for books and journals to the Librarian
Subject coverage
timber including structure and identification, physical and chemical properties, and protection against insects and fungi; utilization, especially for building

2202 PRINTING AND PUBLISHING INDUSTRY TRAINING BOARD
Merit House, Edgware Road, London NW9 5AG Tel. 01-205 0162
Training Board, of the Training Services Agency
Enquiries to the Information Officer
Subject coverage
training facilities in printing, publishing and photography
Publication
Contact

2203 PROCESS PLANT ASSOCIATION
197 Knightsbridge, London SW7 1RS Tel. 01-581 2621
Telex 917984
Trade Association, formed by the amalgamation of the Tank and Industrial Plant Association, British Chemical Plant Manufacturers Association and the Food Manufacturers Association
Enquiries to the Secretary
Subject coverage
process plant industry, including brewery and bottling equipment, food process machinery, packaging machinery, dairy equipment, solid wastes, process pipework

Publications
Steel Data Handbook
Production Control Handbook for the Plate Fabricating Industry
Costing Manual
Scientific Computing
Welding Fume: 2 vols
Noise Control: 3 vols
British Process Plant
British Packaging Machinery

2204 PROCESSED WOODCHIP, SAWDUST AND WOODFLOUR ASSOCIATION
69 Cannon Street, London EC4N 5AB Tel. 01-248 4444
Trade Association

Enquiries accepted from members only

Subject coverage
wood products

2205 PROCESSORS AND GROWERS RESEARCH ORGANISATION LIMITED
The Research Station, Great North Road, Thornhaugh, Peterborough, Northamptonshire PE8 6HJ Tel. Stamford 782585
Research Organization, formerly the Pea Growing Research Organization Limited

Enquiries to the Director

Subject coverage
vegetables for the processing industry; agronomy; weed control; herbicides; pest control; seeds; fertilizers; peas and beans

Publications
Annual Report
Vining Peas in England
Pea and Bean Growing Handbook, 2 vols.
News Letter (monthly)
Papers and advisory leaflets

2206 PRODUCTION ENGINEERING RESEARCH ASSOCIATION
Melton Mowbray, Leicestershire LE13 0PB Tel. 0664 4133
Telex 34684
Research Association; houses the Hazleton Memorial Library of the Institution of Production Engineers

Enquiries, only from members of the Association and of the Institution of Production Engineers, to the Head of Library and Information Services

Subject coverage
metal forming; metal cutting; inspection, measurement and testing; materials and treatments; management; product finishing; plastics technology; assembly; foundry practice ; packaging; powder metallurgy; power transmission; joining methods; noise control; welfare and safety; design engineering; industrial engineering; education and training; communications; marketing

Publications
PERA Bulletin (6 per annum)
Research Reports
Machines and Tooling (monthly)
Russian Engineering Journal (monthly)

2207 PROFESSIONAL AND EXECUTIVE RECRUITMENT
4–5 Grosvenor Place, London SW1X 7SB Tel. 01-235 7030
Government Employment Service, of the Manpower Services Commission; formerly the Professional and Executive Register

Enquiries to the Senior Information Officer

Subject coverage
current condition of the executive employment and recruitment market; supply and demand by geographical area and occupational discipline; level of executive employment; general characteristics of the market; overseas recruitment; trends in recruitment advertising

Publication
Reward (4-monthly salary survey)

PROFESSIONAL FIRE BRIGADES ASSOCIATION *now* **BRITISH FIRE SERVICES ASSOCIATION,** *q.v.*

2208 PROGRAMMES ANALYSIS UNIT
Chilton, Didcot, Oxfordshire OX11 0RF — Tel. 0235 24141 ext. 3066
Telex 83135
Government Agency; jointly sponsored by the Department of Industry and the United Kingdom Atomic Energy Authority

Enquiries to the Information Officer

Subject coverage
techno-economic analysis; project appraisal in aid of decision-making; industrial sector studies; technological forecasting; technology assessment; environmental appraisal

Publications
Programmes Analysis Unit (revised 1976)
M Series' open reports
P.A.U. Papers

2209 PROGRESSIVE RESEARCH SERVICES LIMITED
Wendover, 103 Old Station Road, Hampton-in-Arden, Solihull, Warwickshire B92 0HE — Tel. 067-55 2572
Company (consultants)

No enquiry service

Subject coverage
powder metallurgy, ferrous metallurgy, industrial materials research and development

Publications
surveys of powder metallurgy conferences

2210 PROPERTY CONSULTANTS SOCIETY
133 Hammersmith Road, London W14 0QN — Tel. 01-603 9101
Professional Centre

Enquiries to the Secretary

Subject coverage
property; law of property; landlord and tenant; Rent Acts; estate agency; mortgage and insurance; compulsory purchase

2211 PROPERTY SERVICES AGENCY
Library Service, C Block, Whitgift Centre, Wellesley Road, Croydon, Surrey CR9 3LY — Tel. 01-686 8710 ext. 4560
Telex 55555
Government Department, of the Department of the Environment; includes the Product Information Centre (ext. 4507) and the Photographic Library (tel. 01-703 6380, ext. 469)

Enquiries to the Librarian

Subject coverage
construction industry: design, construction, management, maintenance, estate management, product information

Special collection
Mayson Beeton collection (old, rare books and prints of architecture, etc.)

Publications

Current Information in the Construction Industry (fortnightly)
Construction References (2 per annum)
Thesaurus of Product Terms
Information on Building (abridged U.D.C. Schedule)
Bibliography on Data Coordination in the Construction Industry
Current Information on Maintenance (6 parts)
Other bibliographies and various publications (list available)

2212 PROPRIETARY ARTICLES TRADE ASSOCIATION

4 Margaret Street, London W1N 7LG — Tel. 01-580 4511
Trade Association

Enquiries to the Secretary

Subject coverage

pharmaceutical industry; resale price maintenance

2213 PROTIM LIMITED

Fieldhouse Lane, Marlow, Buckinghamshire SL7 1LS — Tel. 06284 6644, Telex 847057

Limited Company, subsidiary of Foseco Minsep Limited

Enquiries to the Information Officer

Subject coverage

wood preservatives; wood preservation and methods of application; damp proofing materials and allied products

2214 PRS GROUP LIMITED

33 Cork Street, London W1X 1HB — Tel. 01-734 6845, Telex 23442

Company/Consultants; comprising Planning Research and Systems Limited, PRS Management Consultants Limited and Economic Associates Limited

Enquiries to the Managing Director

Subject coverage

business research; corporate planning; economic consultancy; management consultancy

2215 PRUDENTIAL ASSURANCE COMPANY LIMITED

142 Holborn Bars, London EC1N 2NH — Tel. 01-405 9222 ext. 2538
Company

Enquiries to the Librarian, Investment Department

Subject coverage

insurance; investment

2216 PUBLIC HEALTH LABORATORY SERVICE

Central Public Health Laboratory, Colindale Avenue, London NW9 5HT — Tel. 01-205 7041, Telex 922094

Independent Board set up by the Secretary of State for Social Services; part of the Department of Health and Social Security; its Mycological Reference Laboratory is housed in the London School of Hygiene and Tropical Medicine, *q.v.*

Enquiries to the Director of the Public Health Laboratory Service, or to the Directors of the Regional or Reference Laboratories, or to the Librarian of the Service

Subject coverage

microbiology; vaccination; infective diseases; food, milk and water monitoring; disinfection; epidemiology

Publications
National Collection of Type Cultures Catalogue (H.M.S.O.)
Papers published by Staff Members
Books and reports
List available in the annual yearbook

2217 PUBLIC RECORD OFFICE
Chancery Lane, London WC2A 1LR Tel. 01-405 0741
Government Department, with Library; includes the British Transport Historical Records, at Porchester Road, London W2

Enquiries to the Keeper of Public Records

Subject coverage
records of Royal Courts of law and government departments from 11th century to 20th century; related subjects; archive science

Special collections
Collections of private papers, mainly of families or individuals who have been active in public life
Transcripts of records in various foreign archives
Archives of the former British Transport Commission and the British Railways Board

Publications
see H.M.S.O. Sectional List no. 24 British National Archives

2218 PUBLIC RELATIONS CONSULTANTS ASSOCIATION LIMITED
44 Berkeley Square, London SW1X 8QS Tel. 01-235 6225
Trade Association

Enquiries to the Director

Subject coverage
public relations consultancy and code of consultancy practice

2219 PUBLISHERS ASSOCIATION
19 Bedford Square, London WC1B 3HJ Tel. 01-580 6321
Trade Association; having Divisions for General Books, Paperback Books, Children's Books, University, College, & Professional Publishing; including the Book Development Council and the Educational Publishers Council

Enquiries to the Assistant Secretary (normally from publisher members)

Subject coverage
matters affecting publishing

PULTENEY COLLEGE *now* **WESTMINSTER COLLEGE,** *q.v.*

2220 PYE RESEARCH CENTRE
Haughley Research Farms Limited, Walnut Tree Manor, Haughley, Stowmarket, Suffolk IP14 3RS Tel. 044-970 444
Research Institute, Registered Charity

Enquiries to the Director

Subject coverage
agriculture, human ecology, human nutrition

Publication
List of Research Projects

2221 QMC INDUSTRIAL RESEARCH LIMITED
229 Mile End Road, London E1 4AA Tel. 01-790 8425/6
Telex 28905

Contract Research Company; attached to Queen Mary College, University of London; formerly Industrial Materials Research Unit, Queen Mary College; QMC Research Instruments Limited is a subsidiary company; the QMC Wolfson Recycle Unit is also housed at the above address

Enquiries to the Managing Director or to the Information Officer

Subject coverage

materials and composites; fire research; far infra red instrumentation; waste recycle and reuse; prototype engineering; energy and the environment; patents

2222 QUEEN ELIZABETH COLLEGE

Campden Hill Road, London W8 7AH Tel. 01-937 5411

College of the University of London; Library, ext. 378; Periodicals Library, ext. 360

Enquiries, preferably by post, to the College Librarian

Subject coverage

food science; nutrition

2223 QUEEN MARY COLLEGE

Library, Mile End Road, London E1 4NS Tel. 01-980 4811

School of London University

Enquiries to the Librarian

Subject coverage

economics; geography; chemistry; geology; mathematics; computer science; physics; plant biology; microbiology; zoology; comparative physiology; aeronautical, civil, electrical, electronic, mechanical, nuclear, and materials engineering

Special collection

European Documentation Centre (documents on, about, or printed by, the E.E.C.)

QUEEN MARY COLLEGE *see also* **QMC INDUSTRIAL RESEARCH LIMITED**

2224 QUEEN'S AWARDS OFFICE

Williams National House, 11/13 Holborn Viaduct, London EC1 Tel. 01-222 2277
Telex 27366

Government Office, of the Civil Service Department; formerly Office of the Queen's Award to Industry

Enquiries to the Secretary

Subject coverage

the Queen's awards for industry and technology; eligibility; application

2225 QUEENS UNIVERSITY OF BELFAST SCIENCE LIBRARY

Chlorine Gardens, Belfast BT9 5EQ Tel. 0232 661111
Telex 747691

University Branch Library; (the University's Main Library covers art and social sciences only); the University also houses an Agriculture Library and a Medical Library; the Science Library was formerly known as the David Keir Library

Enquiries to the Science Librarian

Subject coverage

architecture; town planning; mathematics; computer science; physics; chemistry; botany; zoology; biochemistry; anatomy; physiology; civil, electrical, mechanical and aeronautical engineering

2226 QUEKETT MICROSCOPICAL CLUB

British Museum, Natural History Museum, Cromwell Road, London SW7

Club

Enquiries to the Librarian

Subject coverage

microscopy, using the optical microscope; techniques; associated natural history

RADCLIFFE DISTRICT LIBRARY *see* **BURY METROPOLITAN BOROUGH LIBRARY**

2227 RADCLIFFE SCIENCE LIBRARY

South Parks Road, Oxford OX1 3QP Tel. 0861 54161
Telex 83656

University and Copyright Library; the Science Section of the Bodleian Library, *q.v.*

Enquiries, limited, to the Keeper of Scientific Books

Subject coverage

science, including medicine and mathematics

Special collections

Acland (medical pamphlets and offprints)
Hardy (mathematical pamphlets and offprints)
Tylor (anthropological pamphlets and offprints

Publication

Union list of serials in the Science Area, Oxford

RADIO AND ELECTRONIC COMPONENT MANUFACTURERS FEDERATION *see* **RADIO INDUSTRY COUNCIL**

RADIO AND ELECTRONICS ASSOCIATION *now* **INCORPORATED PRACTITIONERS IN RADIO AND ELECTRONICS,** *q.v.*

RADIO AND SPACE RESEARCH STATION *now* **APPLETON LABORATORY,** *q.v.*

RADIO AND TELEVISION RETAILERS ASSOCIATION LIMITED *now* **RADIO ELECTRICAL AND TELEVISION RETAILERS ASSOCIATION (RETRA) LIMITED,** *q.v.*

2228 RADIO ELECTRICAL AND TELEVISION RETAILERS ASSOCIATION (RETRA) LIMITED

100 St Martins Lane, London WC2N 4BD Tel. 01-836 1436

Trade Association; formerly Radio and Television Retailers Association (RTRA) Limited

Enquiries to the Secretary

Subject coverage

electrical and electronic retailing, rental, and service

Publication

Electrical and Electronic Dealer (periodical)

2229 RADIO INDUSTRY COUNCIL

20th Century House, 31 Soho Square, London W1V 5DG Tel. 01-734 7471 Telex 27869

Trade Association, comprising three Associations: Electronic Components Board, *q.v.*, Radio and Electronic Component Manufacturers Federation and British Radio Equipment Manufacturers Association, *q.v.*

Enquiries to the Director

Subject coverage

government/industry relations; industry-to-industry talks with Japanese electronics industry; through the Member Associations, the manufacture of consumer electronic products and of electronic components for the total electronics industry

2230 RADIO SOCIETY OF GREAT BRITAIN

35 Doughty Street, London WC1N 2AE Tel. 01-837 8688

National Society

Enquiries to the Information Officer

Subject coverage

amateur radio

Publication

Radio Communication (monthly, to members)

RADIO WHOLESALERS FEDERATION *see* **FEDERATION OF WHOLESALE AND INDUSTRIAL DISTRIBUTORS**

2231 RADIOBIOLOGY UNIT
Harwell, Didcot, Oxfordshire OX11 0RD Tel. 023-583 393 ext. 242
Research Unit, of the Medical Research Council; formerly Radiobiological Research Unit

Enquiries to the Librarian or the Director

Subject coverage
action of ionizing radiations on living cells and animals, with particular attention to high LET (linear energy transfer) radiations and X- and gamma-rays; effects of radiation in the following fields: biophysics, cytogenetics, cell biology, experimental pathology, carcinogenesis, physiology, mammalian genetics; mouse genetics; statistical analysis; laboratory techniques including animal breeding

RADIOCARBON LABORATORY *see* **SCOTTISH UNIVERSITIES RESEARCH AND REACTOR CENTRE**

2232 RADIOCHEMICAL CENTRE LIMITED
White Lion Road, Amersham, Buckinghamshire HP7 9LL Tel. 024-04 4444
Telex 83141
Company, wholly-owned by the United Kingdom Atomic Energy Authority, for the Government

Enquiries to the Librarian

Subject coverage
production and uses of radioactive isotopes and radiation sources; synthetic organic chemistry; nuclear medicine; analytical chemistry; nuclear physics

Publications
Product catalogues, review booklets, medical monographs, etc.

RADIOLOGICAL PROTECTION SERVICE *now* **NATIONAL RADIOLOGICAL PROTECTION BOARD,** *q.v.*

2233 RADIONIC ASSOCIATION LIMITED
Field House, Peaslake, Guildford, Surrey GU5 9SS Tel. 0306 730080
Professional Society

Enquiries to the Secretary

Subject coverage
radionics, radiesthesia; psychoenergetics; alternative medicine

Publication
Radionic Quarterly

2234 RAF INSTITUTE OF AVIATION MEDICINE
Royal Air Force, Farnborough, Hampshire GU14 6SZ Tel. 0252 24461
Government Department

Enquiries to the Commandant

Subject coverage
aviation medicine and psychology

Publications
Reports

2235 RAILWAY CORRESPONDENCE AND TRAVEL SOCIETY
95 Chestnut Avenue, London E7 0JF
Voluntary Society

Enquiries are not accepted

Subject coverage
railways

Publications
Railway Observer (monthly, to members)
Various publications on the locomotives of the Southern Railway, Great Western Railway, London and North Eastern and South Eastern, etc. (list available)

2236 RAILWAY CLUB
112 High Holborn, London WC1V 6JS Tel. (Hon. Sec.) 833 3003
Private Members Club
Enquiries to the Honorary Secretary or the Honorary Librarian
Subject coverage
British railway history; current practice and trends in railway operation
Special collection
railway publications for the last half-century

2237 RAILWAY DEVELOPMENT ASSOCIATION
The Old Vicarage, Piddinghoe, nr. Newhaven, Sussex BN9 9AP Tel. 079-12 4369
Voluntary Association; corporate member of the National Council on Inland Transport
Enquiries to the Honorary Secretary
Subject coverage
transport, especially railways
Publications
Development Report (quarterly)
Other reports occasionally

2238 RAILWAY INDUSTRY ASSOCIATION
9 Catherine Place, London SW1E 6DH Tel. 01-834 1426
Trade Association; formerly the Locomotive and Allied Manufacturers Association
Enquiries to the Director
Subject coverage
all aspects of the railway industry, except labour relations
Publication
Railpower

2239 RALEIGH INDUSTRIES LIMITED
Lenton Boulevard, Nottingham NG7 2DD Tel. 0602 77761
Telex 37681
Manufacturing Company; subsidiary of Tube Investments Limited
Enquiries to the Export Sales and Marketing Director
Subject coverage
bicycle and component manufacturing

RAMSBOTTOM DISTRICT LIBRARY *see* **BURY METROPOLITAN BOROUGH LIBRARY**

RAMSDEN TECHNICAL COLLEGE *now* **HUDDERSFIELD TECHNICAL COLLEGE,** *q.v.*

RANK HOVIS McDOUGALL (RESEARCH) LIMITED *see* **LORD RANK RESEARCH CENTRE**

2240 RANK XEROX (U.K.) LIMITED
Bridge House, Oxford Road, Uxbridge, Middlesex UB8 1HS Tel. 89 51133
Company
Enquiries to Public Relations Department
Subject coverage
copying; duplicating; facsimile transmission; colour copying
Publications
Product brochures

2241 RATING AND VALUATION ASSOCIATION
115 Ebury Street, Belgravia, London SW1W 9QT Tel. 01-730 7258/9
Professional Society

Enquiries to the Secretary

Subject coverage

rating administration; valuation for rating purposes; local authority income; appeals against rating valuations

Publications

Rating and Valuation (monthly)
Texts of Statutes and comments on current legislation
Statistical returns
Publications list (which includes textbooks) is available

RAWTENSTALL PUBLIC LIBRARY *now* **ROSSENDALE DISTRICT CENTRAL LIBRARY** *see* **LANCASHIRE LIBRARY**

RAYLEIGH LIBRARY *see* **CAVENDISH LABORATORY**

David RAYNER ASSOCIATES *now* **EUROLEC,** *q.v.*

READER & SONS LIMITED *see* **SOIL MECHANICS LIMITED**

2242 READING COLLEGE OF TECHNOLOGY

Kings Road, Reading, Berkshire RG1 4HJ — Tel. 0734 583501

College of Further Education

Enquiries to the Librarian

Subject coverage

biology; building; catering; chemistry; electronics; civil, electrical, mechanical, and production engineering; home economics; management; metalworking; photography; printing

2243 READING LIBRARIES

Blagrave Street, Reading, Berkshire RG1 1QL — Tel. 0734 55911, Telex 849421

Public Library; District Library of the Berkshire County Library, *q.v.*

Enquiries to the Borough Librarian

Subject coverage

general

2244 READING UNIVERSITY LIBRARY

Whiteknights, Reading, Berkshire RG6 2AE — Tel. 0734 84331, Telex 847813

University Library

Enquiries to the Librarian

Subject coverage

physical sciences; earth sciences; biological sciences; agriculture

Special collections

Cole Library (history of zoology and comparative anatomy)
Printing history
Agricultural history
Neville collection (mathematical history)
Archive of Farm Records

Publication

Cole library of early medicine and zoology, N.B. Eales, 2 vols

READING UNIVERSITY *see also*
CENTRE FOR AGRICULTURAL STRATEGY
NATIONAL COLLEGE FOR FOOD TECHNOLOGY
REMOTE SENSING SOCIETY
SEDIMENTOLOGY RESEARCH LABORATORY

2245 RECKITT & COLMAN LIMITED
P.O. Box 26, Burlington Lane, Chiswick, London W4 2RW — Tel. 01-994 6464, Telex 21268

Company; formerly Chiswick Products Limited

Enquiries to the Librarian

Subject coverage
management, commercial and business information

2246 RECKITT & COLMAN LIMITED
Kingston Works, Dansom Lane, Hull, North Humberside HU8 7DS — Tel. 0482 26151, Telex 52166

Company; formerly Reckitt & Sons Limited, Hull and J. and J. Colman Limited, Norwich

Enquiries to the Manager, Library and Information Service

Subject coverage
household, cosmetic and pharmaceutical products; pharmacy; pharmacology; organic chemistry; packaging; plastics; veterinary medicine; U.K., E.E.C. and U.S.A. regulations

RECLAMATION ASSOCIATION *see* **BRITISH SCRAP FEDERATION**

RECLAMATION INDUSTRIES COUNCIL *see* **BRITISH SCRAP FEDERATION**

2247 RED DEER COMMISSION
Knowsley, 82 Fairfield Road, Inverness IU3 5LH — Tel. 0463 31751
Government Department

Enquiries to the Secretary

Subject coverage
conservation and control of red deer in Scotland

Publication
Annual Report

RED LEAD AND LITHARGE MANUFACTURERS ASSOCIATION *see* **BRITISH LEAD MANUFACTURERS ASSOCIATION**

2248 REDBRIDGE PUBLIC LIBRARIES
Oakfield Road, Ilford, Essex — Tel. 01-478 0017, Telex 897778

Public Library Service

Enquiries, in writing, to the Borough Librarian; by telephone, to the Reference Librarian or the Head of the Readers Advisory Service

Subject coverage
general; special strength in photography

2249 REDBRIDGE TECHNICAL COLLEGE
Little Heath, Romford, Essex RM6 4XT — Tel. 01-599 5231
Technical College

Enquiries to the Tutor Librarian

Subject coverage
general

REDCAR DISTRICT LIBRARY *see* **CLEVELAND COUNTY LIBRARY**

REDDITCH DIVISIONAL LIBRARY *see* **HEREFORD AND WORCESTER COUNTY LIBRARY**

2250 REDIFFUSION ENGINEERING LIMITED
187 Coombe Lane West, Kingston-upon-Thames, Surrey KT2 7DJ Tel. 01-942 8900 ext. 273
Telex 929984
Company, part of Rediffusion Limited (itself a member of the B.E.T. Group); formerly Rediffusion Research Limited

Enquiries to the Librarian

Subject coverage
radio and television engineering, especially cable systems; telecommunications

2251 REDLAND TECHNOLOGY LIMITED
New Technology Product Development Centre, Graylands, Horsham, West Sussex RH12 4QG Tel. 0403 2351
Company, subsidiary of Redland Limited; formerly Redland Research and Development Limited

Enquiries to the Librarian and Information Officer

Subject coverage
building materials production, testing, and applications; blacktop and anti-skid road surfacing; road markings; industrial waste disposal; incineration

2252 REED ENGINEERING & DEVELOPMENT SERVICES LIMITED
E & D Centre, Aylesford, Maidstone, Kent Tel. 0622 77711
Company; formerly Reed Development Services Limited Telex 96148

Enquiries to the Senior Librarian and Linguist

Subject coverage
technical consultancy, engineering and development work in the pulp, paper and board making fields; packaging; printing; plastics; building materials

Publications
Current Awareness Abstract Bulletin: commercial (fortnightly)
Current Awareness Abstract Bulletin: technical (monthly)
Technical and commercial translations

2253 REFINED BITUMEN ASSOCIATION
24 Grosvenor Gardens, London SW1W 0DH Tel. 01-730 7175
Trade Association

Enquiries to the Secretary

Subject coverage
the promotion of research into the use of bitumen; the interests of suppliers of bitumen

2254 REFRACTORIES ASSOCIATION OF GREAT BRITAIN
14 Moody Street, Congleton, Cheshire CW12 4AR Tel. 02602 3466
Trade Association

Enquiries to the Honorary Secretary

Subject coverage
refractory materials

Publication
Refractories Journal (bi-monthly)

REFRACTORY CONTRACTORS ASSOCIATION *see* REFRACTORY USERS FEDERATION

2255 REFRACTORY USERS FEDERATION
4th Floor, 112 Jermyn Street, London SW1 Tel. 01-930 0866
Employers Association; composed of the Refractory Contractors Association, the Society of Industrial Furnace Engineers and the Gas Refractory and Coke Oven Contractors Association

Enquiries to the Secretary

Subject coverage
industrial relations, terms and conditions of employment for refractory bricklayers and labourers; training

Publications
Blue Booklet Agreement (for refractory bricklayers)
Red Booklet Agreement (for bricklayers labourers)

REGENT STREET POLYTECHNIC *now* **POLYTECHNIC OF CENTRAL LONDON,** *q.v.*

REGISTERED PLUMBERS ASSOCIATION *now* **INSTITUTE OF PLUMBING,** *q.v.*

REGISTRAR OF RESTRICTIVE TRADING AGREEMENTS *now* **OFFICE OF FAIR TRADING,** *q.v.*

2256 REGISTRY OF BUSINESS NAMES
Pembroke House, 40–56 City Road, London EC1Y 2DN Tel. 01-253 9393
Government Department, linked with the Companies Registration Office, *q.v.*; address for Scotland: 102 George Street, Edinburgh; address for Northern Ireland: Department of Commerce, 43–47 Chichester Street, Belfast

Enquiries to the Registrar

Subject coverage
details of persons or firms trading under names other than the true name(s) of the proprietor(s), *e.g.* the true names, the addresses of principal places of business and the nature of the business

REIGATE BRANCH LIBRARY *see* **SURREY COUNTY LIBRARY**

2257 REINDEER COUNCIL OF THE UNITED KINGDOM
Newton Hill, Harston, Cambridge CB2 5NZ
Advisory and Research Body

Enquiries to the Honorary Secretary

Subject coverage
reindeer breeding and reindeer products

Publication
Annual Report

2258 REINSURANCE OFFICES ASSOCIATION
Aldermary House, Queen Street, London EC4N 1ST Tel. 01-248 4477
Trade Association/Representative Body

Enquiries to the Director

Subject coverage
reinsurance

Publications
Reports on technical reinsurance subjects
Earthquakes: six studies, by region

RELAY SERVICES ASSOCIATION OF GREAT BRITAIN *now* **CABLE TELEVISION ASSOCIATION OF GREAT BRITAIN,** *q.v.*

2259 REMOTE SENSING SOCIETY
Department of Geography, University of Reading, TOB2, Earley Gate, Whiteknights, Reading RG6 2AB Tel. 0734 85123, exts. 6387, *or* 6389
Learned Society

Enquiries to the Secretary

Subject coverage
remote sensing; types of sensors; image processing equipment; platforms (satellites, rockets, aircraft) for Earth Resource Survey; applications of remote sensing in land use, crops, soils and geological and hydrological surveying; monitoring of pollution and natural hazards

Publications
Newsletter (quarterly) includes lists of publications

2260 RENFREW DISTRICT LIBRARIES
Marchfield Avenue, Paisley, Renfrewshire PA3 2RJ Tel. 041-887 2468/9
Public Libraries; formerly Renfrew County Library and merged with Paisley Public Library

Enquiries to the District Librarian

Subject coverage
general

2261 RENOLD LIMITED
Renold House, Styal Road, Wythenshawe, Manchester M22 5WL Tel. 061-437 5221
Telex 669052

Company

Enquiries to the Manager, Central Library

Subject coverage
All aspects of mechanical power transmission, including: roller chains, wheels and pinions; conveying and elevating chains and wheels; gears; worm gear speed reducers; worm gear sets; spur, helical and spiral bevel gearboxes; shaft mounted gear units; geared motors; variable speed drives, hydraulic, mechanical and electrical; couplings, clutches and brakes; sprag clutches for over-running, indexing and backstopping; vibratory shaker drives; power transmission accessories
Additionally, machine tools; helical rotors for air compressors; tablet-making and other machinery for the pharmaceutical, confectionery and similar industries; hammered steel forgings and copper base alloy castings and machined components

Special collection
Fully classified and catalogued collection of archival material relating to the establishment of the power transmission industry in the U.K. in the late 19th century

2262 RENTOKIL GROUP LIMITED
Felcourt, East Grinstead, Sussex RH19 2JY Tel. 0342 23661
Telex 95456

Company

Enquiries to the Librarian

Subject coverage
industrial and domestic pests; pest control; industrial hygiene; timber preservation; fumigation; fire retardants; property maintenance; thermal insulation; rising damp in buildings

Publications
promotional leaflets

RESEARCH ASSOCIATION OF BRITISH PAINT, COLOUR AND VARNISH MANUFACTURERS *now* **PAINT RESEARCH ASSOCIATION,** *q.v.*

2263 RESEARCH MANAGEMENT DIVISION
Department of the Environment, 2 Marsham Street, London SW1P 3EB Tel. 01-212 8431
Government Department

Enquiries to the Head of R.M.D.

Subject coverage
management of DOE H.Q. extra-mural research programme; handling of research reports

RESEARCH ORGANISATION OF SHIPS COMPOSITIONS MANUFACTURERS LIMITED *now* **BRITISH SHIP RESEARCH ASSOCIATION,** *q.v.*

RESEARCH UNIT INTO PROBLEMS OF INDUSTRIAL RETRAINING *now* **INDUSTRIAL TRAINING RESEARCH UNIT,** *q.v.*

RESTRICTIVE TRADING AGREEMENTS REGISTER *see* **OFFICE OF FAIR TRADING**

2264 RETAIL CONFECTIONERS AND TOBACCONISTS ASSOCIATION
53 Christchurch Avenue, North Finchley, London N12 0DH Tel. 01-445 6344–5
Trade Association; formed by the amalgamation of the Retail Confectioners Association and the Federation of Retail Tobacconists

Enquiries to the Executive Director or Assistant Director

Subject coverage
all aspects of the retail distribution of confectionery, ice cream, soft drinks, snack food, tobacco products

Publications
Retail Confectioner, Tobacconist (monthly)
Confectioner, Tobacco and Newsagency Buyers Guide (annually)

2265 RETAIL CREDIT FEDERATION
192a Nantwich Road, Crewe, Cheshire CW2 6BP Tel. 0270 3399
Trade Association; member of the Retail Alliance

Enquiries to the Secretary

Subject coverage
consumer credit

Publications
Newsletter (quarterly)
Membership Directory (annual)

2266 RETAIL TRADING STANDARDS ASSOCIATION INCORPORATED
360–366 Oxford Street, London W1N 0BT Tel. 01-629 9314/5
Trade Association

Enquiries to the Secretary

Subject coverage
product description and definition; quality standards; test methods; testing facilities; opinion on complaints matters available to members and consumers

Publications
Annual Report (includes publications list)

2267 RETREAD MANUFACTURERS ASSOCIATION
P.O. Box 498, 12 Booth Street, Manchester M60 2ED Tel. 061-239 9721
Trade Association

Enquiries to the Secretaries

Subject coverage
retreading of tyres; names and addresses of manufacturers building to British Standards and of suppliers to the industry

Publication
Manual of Operational Standards

2268 REUTERS LIBRARY
85 Fleet Street, London EC4 Tel. 01-353 6060
International News Agency

Enquiries, in writing, from subscribers to the Reuter News Service, to the Library; non-subscribers are charged

Subject coverage
worldwide news coverage of political, cultural, sports, economic and scientific matters and events

2269 REVERTEX CHEMICALS LIMITED
Temple Fields, Harlow, Essex CM20 2AH Tel. 0279 29555
Telex 81318

Company; formerly Revertex Holdings Limited

Enquiries to the Business Development Manager, or, for books, to the Librarian

Subject coverage

synthetic resin emulsions; synthetic and natural rubber latices; polyvinyl alcohol; noise control products; GRP tanks and pipes; corrosion protection; metal pickling plants

REYROLLE PARSONS LIMITED *see*
INTERNATIONAL RESEARCH AND DEVELOPMENT COMPANY LIMITED
PARSONS PEEBLES LIMITED

RHUDDLAN AREA LIBRARY *see* **CLWYD COUNTY LIBRARY SERVICE**

RHYMNEY VALLEY DISTRICT LIBRARY *see* **MID-GLAMORGAN COUNTY LIBRARY**

RIBBLE VALLEY DISTRICT CENTRAL LIBRARY *see* **LANCASHIRE LIBRARY**

2270 RICARDO CONSULTING ENGINEERS LIMITED

Bridge Works, Shoreham by Sea, Sussex BN4 5FG Tel. 079-17 5611
Telex 87383

Company

Enquiries, limited, to the Librarian/Information Officer

Subject coverage

internal combustion engineering research; diesel engines; gas turbines; petrol engines; automotive engineering; noise; combustion; exhaust emissions; fuel technology; lubrication

2271 RICHMOND-UPON-THAMES COLLEGE

Egerton Road, Twickenham, Middlesex TW2 7SS Tel. 01-892 6656
Tertiary College; formerly Twickenham College of Technology

Enquiries to the Librarian

Subject coverage

mechanical and electrical engineering; production engineering; construction and civil engineering, (including carpentry and joinery, painting and decorating, plumbing); sciences, (including mathematics and statistics, biology, chemistry, physics, environmental sciences, geology); art and graphic design, (including illustration, printing, photography and cinematography, lettering, textiles, book crafts, graphic and exhibition work); business, (including law, accounting, computing, management, secretarial subjects, economics, geography)

Special collections

slides, filmstrips, filmloops, microforms, mounted illustrations; audio tapes and cassettes

Publications

Library Newsletters
Index to Projects and Essays
Handlists

2272 RICHMOND-UPON-THAMES LIBRARIES SERVICE

Administration Headquarters, The Retreat, Retreat Road, Tel. 01-940 0031
Richmond, Surrey TW9 1PH Telex 917174
Public Libraries; District Libraries at Twickenham and East Sheen

Enquiries to the Reference Librarian, Richmond Central Library, Little Green, Richmond, Surrey TW9 1QL Tel. 01-940 9125

Subject coverage

general; specialist subjects are heat, and environmental planning

2273 RIVERSDALE COLLEGE OF TECHNOLOGY

Riversdale Road, Liverpool L19 3QR Tel. 051-427 1227 ext. 36
College of Further Education; formerly Riversdale Technical College

Enquiries to the College Librarian

Subject coverage
electronic and radio engineering; marine engineering; navigation/maritime studies; building construction; general and automobile engineering

2274 ROAD HAULAGE ASSOCIATION LIMITED
Roadway House, 22 Upper Woburn Place, London WC1H 0ES Tel. 01-387 9711
Trade Association

Enquiries to the Association

Subject coverage
professional road haulage; safety in transporting dangerous chemicals

Publications
Road Way (monthly)
Haulage Manual (annual)

ROAD RESEARCH LABORATORY *now* **TRANSPORT AND ROAD RESEARCH LABORATORY,** *q.v.*

2275 ROAD TRANSPORT INDUSTRY TRAINING BOARD
Capitol House, Empire Way, Wembley, Middlesex HA9 0NG Tel. 01-902 8880
Industrial Training Board, of the Training Services Agency, Manpower Services Commission

Enquiries to the Information Department

Subject coverage
road transport industry management, manpower, training, craft, etc.

Publications
Booklets on Training Recommendations (21 titles)
Training Manuals
Safety Training literature
Annual Report
Other publications listed in an available List

2276 ROBERT GORDONS INSTITUTE OF TECHNOLOGY
St. Andrew Street, Aberdeen AB9 1HG Tel. 0224 22338
Institute of Technology

Enquiries to the Principal Librarian

Subject coverage
chemistry; pharmacy; physics; electrical, electronic, mechanical, offshore engineering; nutritional sciences; home economics; business management; hotel and institutional management

Publication
ANSLICS Bibliography on Oil (2nd ed. in preparation)

2277 ROBERTSON RESEARCH INTERNATIONAL LIMITED
'Tyn-y-Coed', Llanrhos, Llandudno, Gwynedd, North Wales Tel. 0492 81811
Telex 61216

Contract Research Company; formerly Robertson Research Company Limited

Enquiries to the Company

Subject coverage
earth sciences: petroleum, mineral, water exploration and development

E.S. & A. ROBINSON (HOLDINGS) LIMITED *now* **DICKINSON ROBINSON GROUP LIMITED,** *q.v.*

2278 James ROBINSON & COMPANY LIMITED
Hillhouse Lane, Huddersfield, Yorkshire HD1 6BU Tel. 0484 36511
Telex 51191

Limited Company

Enquiries to the Librarian

Subject coverage
sulphur dye manufacture and application

2279 ROCHDALE COLLEGE
St. Marys Gate, Manchester Road, Rochdale, Lancashire OC2 6RY Tel. 0706 40421 ext. 34
Technical College

Enquiries to the Librarian

Subject coverage
mechanical engineering; commerce

2280 ROCHDALE LIBRARIES AND ARTS SERVICES
Area Central Library, Esplanade, Rochdale, Lancashire OL16 1AQ Tel. 0706 47474
Telex 63406

Public Library; the Authority is now the Metropolitan Borough of Rochdale, covering Heywood, Wardle, Middleton, and Rochdale Libraries

Enquiries to the Commercial and Technical Librarian

Subject coverage
brickwork; building law; building quantities; engineering materials; engineering mechanics; management; occupational health; radio and TV engineering; steam engineering; textiles

2281 ROCHE PRODUCTS LIMITED
Broadwater Road, Welwyn Garden City, Hertfordshire AL7 3AY Tel. 070-73 28128
Telex 262098

Manufacturing Company, subsidiary of Hoffmann-La Roche, Basle

Enquiries to the Librarian

Subject coverage
pharmaceutical, medical, veterinary and related sciences; vitamins; agrochemicals

Publications
on the Company's interests and products

ROCK MECHANICS INFORMATION SERVICE *see* **ROYAL SCHOOL OF MINES**

ROCK MECHANICS LIMITED *see* **SOIL MECHANICS LIMITED**

ROLLED THREAD SCREW ASSOCIATION *see* **BRITISH INDUSTRIAL FASTENERS FEDERATION**

2282 ROLLS-ROYCE AND ASSOCIATES LIMITED
P.O. Box 31, Raynesway, Derby DE2 8BJ Tel. 0332 61461
Telex 37616

Company

Enquiries to the Librarian

Subject coverage
nuclear science and technology and related subjects

2283 ROLLS-ROYCE (1971) LIMITED
Aero Division, P.O. Box 31, Moor Lane, Derby DE2 8BJ
Company, formerly Rolls-Royce Limited Aero Engine Division

Enquiries to the Head of Library and Information Services

Subject coverage
gas turbine technology for aircraft propulsion; gas dynamics; combustion; high strength/high temperature materials

2284 ROLLS-ROYCE TECHNICAL COLLEGE
P.O. Box 3, Filton, Bristol BS12 7QE Tel. 0272 693871
Telex 44185/6

Technical College, of Rolls-Royce (1971) Limited Aero Division; formerly Bristol Aeroplane Technical College

Enquiries to the Librarian

Subject coverage
aeronautical engineering craft and technician training

Special collection
NASA Special Publications

2285 ROSKILL INFORMATION SERVICES LIMITED
14 Great College Street, London SW1P 3RZ Tel. 01-735 9034
01-930 8272
Telex 916010

Company, associated with O.W. Roskill Industrial Consultants; the Building Statistical Services Division ceased operations in 1974

Enquiries to the Director (fees may be chargeable)

Subject coverage
economics, supply, demand, and prices of all metals and minerals, world-wide; materials used in building construction in the U.K.; markets for all industrial products, world-wide (*see* subject index for all metals & minerals)

Publications
Building Statistical Services Reports
Roskill's Letter from Japan (summary of items from Japanese metals journals)
Roskill's Reports on Metals and Minerals

ROSS AND CROMARTY COUNTY LIBRARY *now* **HIGHLAND REGION LIBRARY SERVICE,** *q.v.*

2286 ROSS INSTITUTE OF TROPICAL HYGIENE
London School of Hygiene and Tropical Medicine, Keppel Street, London WC1E 7HT Tel. 01-636 8636

University Department; part of the London School of Hygiene and Tropical Medicine and of London University; houses the Malaria Reference Laboratory of Horton Hospital, Epsom, which is now a part of the Institute

Enquiries to the Director

Subject coverage
health problems of industry and agriculture in the tropics, particularly housing, sanitation, water supply, communicable disease control and health services; health precautions for overseas travel or expeditions; expertise in diseases such as cholera, malaria, leishmania; knowledge of specialists in all tropical diseases

Special collections
World Health Organisation International Reference Centre for Anopheline Mosquitoes

Publications
Yearbook and Bulletins (list available)

ROSSENDALE DISTRICT CENTRAL LIBRARY *see* **LANCASHIRE LIBRARY**

2287 ROTATING ELECTRICAL MACHINES ASSOCIATION
Leicester House, 8 Leicester Street, London WC2H 7BN Tel. 01-437 0678
Trade Association; member of BEAMA, *q.v.*

Enquiries to the Director

Subject coverage
rotating electrical machines without limitation of output or voltage, *other than* turbine type machines, traction motors or aircraft machines

2288 ROTHAMSTED EXPERIMENTAL STATION
Harpenden, Hertfordshire AL5 2JQ Tel. 058-27 63133
Research Institute, partly Government, of the Agricultural Research Council, and partly private; houses the Commonwealth Bureau of Soils and the Soil Survey of England and Wales

Enquiries to the Librarian or to the Scientific Information Officer

Subject coverage
agricultural research, (*excluding* animal husbandry, diseases, etc., plant breeding and agricultural economics); agricultural computer work, statistics; pure research on many botanical and biochemical aspects of agriculture; entomology; farms; insecticides and fungicides; nematology; pedology; plant pathology; soil microbiology

Special collections
Agricultural books, 1471–1840
British Farm Livestock, prints and paintings, 1780–1910

Publications
Annual Report
Guide (every three years)
Reports and Conference Papers
List of Current Serials
List of publications available

2289 ROTHERHAM PUBLIC LIBRARIES
Central Library, Rotherham, South Yorkshire S65 1JH Tel. 0709 2121
Public Library Service

Enquiries to the Director of Libraries, Museum and Arts

Subject coverage
general; iron and steel; South Yorkshire potteries

2290 ROUSSEL LABORATORIES LIMITED
Kingfisher Drive, Covingham, Swindon SN3 5BZ Tel. 0793 24411
Company, subsidiary of Roussel UCLAF, Paris, and member of Hoechst Group, Frankfurt

Enquiries to the Information Officer or Librarian

Subject coverage
pharmaceutical chemistry; organic chemistry; physiology, medicine; microbiology; toxicology; chemical patents; information storage and retrieval; chemical hazards and safety

2291 ROWETT RESEARCH INSTITUTE
Bucksburn, Aberdeen AB2 9SB Tel. 022-471 2751
State-aided Scientific Research Institute, of the Department of Agriculture and Fisheries for Scotland; houses the Commonwealth Bureau of Nutrition, *q.v.*

Enquiries to the Librarian

Subject coverage
structure and biosynthesis of lipids and proteins of animal tissues; nutritive value of proteins for ruminants and non-ruminants, of energy-yielding feeds for ruminants, of feeds for pigs; minerals in diet; physiology, biochemistry and nutrition of the new-born animal; physiology of pregnancy and parturition; animal diet and management; microbial degradation of feeds; deer and rabbits as meat-producing animals

Special collection
Agriculture in the 18th and 19th centuries

Publication
Annual Report of Studies in Animal Nutrition and Allied Sciences

2292 ROWNTREE MACKINTOSH LIMITED
Wigginton Road, York YO1 1XY Tel. 0904 53071
Telex 57846
Manufacturing Company; a merger of the former companies, Rowntree and Company Limited and John Mackintosh and Sons Limited

Enquiries to the Public Relations Officer

Subject coverage
confectionery industry; chocolate, sugar and grocery products

Publication
Rowntree Mackintosh News (10 issues per annum)

ROXBURGH DISTRICT LIBRARY *see* **BORDERS REGIONAL LIBRARY**

2293 ROYAL AERONAUTICAL SOCIETY
4 Hamilton Place, London W1V 0BQ Tel. 01-499 3515
Learned Society; Divisions world-wide

Enquiries to the Librarian

Subject coverage
aeronautics; aerospace engineering; aerospace history (*not* space itself); agricultural aviation; air law; air transport; rotorcraft

Special collections
Cuthbert Hodgeson Collection (aeronautical material)
Poynton Collection (scientific theses, etc.)

Publications
Aeronautical Journal (monthly)
Aeronautical Quarterly
Aerospace

2294 ROYAL AGRICULTURAL SOCIETY OF ENGLAND
National Agricultural Centre, Stoneleigh, Kenilworth, Warwickshire CV8 2LZ Tel. 0203 56151
Telex 31697
Advisory Centre/Voluntary Society; London office, 35 Belgrave Square SW1X 8QN

Enquiries to the Public Relations Officer

Subject coverage
agriculture in general; horticulture; crop husbandry; machinery; veterinary problems; entomology

Publications
Annual Journal
NAC News (bi-monthly)
Technical Conference Papers

2295 ROYAL AGRICULTURAL SOCIETY OF THE COMMONWEALTH
Robarts House, Rossmore Road, London NW1 6NP Tel. 01-723 8021
Agricultural Charity

Enquiries to the Honorary Secretary

Subject coverage
practice and science of agriculture; improvement of methods of crop production and breeding of livestock; improvement of efficiency of agricultural implements and machinery

Publications
Reports on Biennial Conferences

2296 ROYAL AIRCRAFT ESTABLISHMENT
Clapham, Bedford MK41 6AE Tel. 0234 55241
Telex 82117
Government Research Establishment; part of the Royal Aircraft Establishment, Farnborough, *q.v.*

Enquiries to the Librarian

Subject coverage
aeronautical research

Publications
see Royal Aircraft Establishment, Farnborough

2297 ROYAL AIRCRAFT ESTABLISHMENT
Farnborough, Hampshire GU14 6TD Tel. 0252 24461
Telex 858134

Government Department, of the Ministry of Defence, Procurement Executive

Enquiries to the Chief Librarian

Subject coverage
aerodynamics; aircraft engineering; chemistry; electrical engineering; instrumentation; mathematics; metallurgy; physics; aviation; electronics; radar; radio engineering; space technology; structures; weapons; materials; navigation

Publications
RAE News (monthly, house journal)
Research Reports (issued through Defence Research Information Centre, St. Mary Cray)

2298 ROYAL ASSOCIATION OF BRITISH DAIRY FARMERS
Robarts House, Rossmore Road, London NW1 6NP Tel. 01-723 8021
Agricultural Charity; Organisers of the Annual Dairy Farming Event

Enquiries to the Secretary

Subject coverage
dairy farming; dairying; feeding and other matters related to dairy cattle; the qualifying National Certificate in Dairying

Publication
Dairy Farming Event Catalogue

2299 ROYAL ASTRONOMICAL SOCIETY
Burlington House, Piccadilly, London W1V 0NL Tel. 01-734 4582
Learned Society; the British Astronomical Association and the London Mathematical Society are housed at this address, although the Library of the latter is at the Library of University College London

Enquiries to the Librarian

Subject coverage
astronomy and geophysics

Special collections
Collection of early astronomical books including the Grove-Hills Collection of pre-1700 books
Photographic Collection (astronomical slides and prints)

Publications
Monthly Notices of the Royal Astronomical Society
Memoirs of the Royal Astronomical Society
Geophysical Journal of the Royal Astronomical Society
Quarterly Journal of the Royal Astronomical Society

2300 ROYAL BOTANIC GARDEN LIBRARY
Inverleith Row, Edinburgh EH3 5LR Tel. 031-552 7171
Government Research Establishment Library, of the Department of Agriculture and Fisheries for Scotland; incorporates the Library of the Botanical Society of Edinburgh, *q.v.*

Enquiries to the Regius Keeper/Librarian

Subject coverage
taxonomic botany; amenity horticulture

Special collections
Archival material, manuscript and printed relating to the history of the Garden, 1670–, and to the Botanical Society of Edinburgh, 1836–
Early printed works, 1489–, on botany, medicine, agriculture, horticulture

Publication
Notes from the Royal Botanic Garden Edinburgh (3 times per annum)

2301 ROYAL BOTANIC GARDENS
Kew, Richmond, Surrey TW9 3AE Tel. 01-940 1171
Government Department, of the Ministry of Agriculture, Fisheries and Food

Enquiries, general, to the Enquiries Unit; on bibliography, history and archives, to the Chief Librarian

Subject coverage
botany; plant taxonomy; plant geography; plant anatomy; plant physiology; cytology; economic botany; horticulture; plant conservation

Special collections
Plant Illustrations, including the Roxburgh Drawings
Botanical Portraits Collection
Adams Collection
Darlington Reprint Collection
Linnaean Collection
Kewensia

Publications
Kew Record of Taxonomic Literature (annual)
Index Kewensis (quinquennial)
Catalogue of the Library (9 volumes)
Catalogue of Periodicals
Kew Bulletin
Index of Living Plant Collections in the British Isles
Volumes on the flora of tropical and other countries, etc., etc.

2302 ROYAL COLLEGE OF VETERINARY SURGEONS
Wellcome Library, 32 Belgrave Square, London SW1X 8QP Tel. 01-235 6568
Professional Registration and Disciplinary Body

Enquiries to the Librarian

Subject coverage
veterinary science

Special collection
Henry Gray Collection (ornithology, late 19th and early 20th centuries)

Publications
Modern Works, 1900–1954, plus supplements
Historical Collection (printed works before 1850) plus supplement

2303 ROYAL (DICK) SCHOOL OF VETERINARY STUDIES LIBRARY
Faculty of Veterinary Medicine, Edinburgh University, Summerhall, Edinburgh EH9 1QH Tel. 031-667 1011 exts. 5275, 5327
University Faculty Library; associated libraries at the Field Station and Centre for Tropical Veterinary Medicine, at Easter Bush, Roslin, Midlothian

Enquiries to the Librarian

Subject coverage
veterinary medicine (including tropical)

Special collection
Historical Collection

Publication
Tropical Animal Health and Production (journal)

2304 ROYAL ECONOMIC SOCIETY
c/o The Economic Journal, Nuffield College, Oxford OX1 1NF
Learned Society

Enquiries to the Editor

Subject coverage
economics

Publications
Economic Journal (quarterly, free to members and by subscription)
Books, including new editions of economics classics (from Allen & Unwin, Macmillan, C.U.P. and North-Holland)

2305 ROYAL ENTOMOLOGICAL SOCIETY OF LONDON
41 Queens Gate, London SW7 5HU Tel. 01-584 8361
Scientific Society

Enquiries to the Librarian, (literature queries only)

Subject coverage
pure entomology

Publications
Physiological Entomology
Systematic Entomology
Ecological Entomology
Symposia proceedings
Proceedings of the Royal Entomological Society
Handbooks for the identification of British insects

2306 ROYAL FORESTRY SOCIETY OF ENGLAND, WALES AND NORTHERN IRELAND
102 High Street, Tring, Hertfordshire HP23 4AH Tel. 044-282 2028
Society/charitable status

Enquiries to the Director

Subject coverage
forestry and arboriculture; technical information and information on careers

Publication
Quarterly Journal of Forestry

2307 ROYAL GEOGRAPHICAL SOCIETY
1 Kensington Gore, London SW7 2AR Tel. 01-589 5466
Learned Society; houses the Permanent Committee on Geographical Names, the Institute of British Geographers *q.v.* and the Royal Institute of Navigation; includes the Map Room (of 600,000 map sheets and 4,000 atlases) which is open to the public

Enquiries to the Map Curator or Librarian

Subject coverage
geography; exploration

Publications
Geographical Journal (currently 3 issues per annum)
Geographical Magazine (monthly)
Royal Geographical Research Series
Books, travellers' guides, expedition pamphlets, etc.
Publications List available

2308 ROYAL GREENWICH OBSERVATORY
Herstmonceux Castle, Hailsham, Sussex Tel. 032-181 3171
Telex 87451
Research Observatory, of the Science Research Council; *see also* H.M. Nautical Almanac Office

Enquiries to the Information Officer or Librarian

Subject coverage
astronomy; astrophysics; geomagnetism; time

Publications

Royal Observatory Bulletins:
Series A—Meridian Observations
Series B—Time service
Series C—Solar Observations
Series D—Magnetic Observations
Series E—Miscellaneous, including astrophysical and astrometric papers
Royal Observatory Annals
Royal Observatory Circulars

2309 ROYAL HIGHLAND & AGRICULTURAL SOCIETY OF SCOTLAND
P.O. Box 1, Ingliston, Newbridge, Midlothian EH28 8NF Tel. 031-333 2444
Agricultural Society

Enquiries to the Librarian or Information Officer

Subject coverage

agriculture in general and the history of agriculture in particular
particular

Publication

Show Guide and Review (annual)

2310 ROYAL HORTICULTURAL SOCIETY
P.O. Box 313, Vincent Square, London SW1P 2PE Tel. 01-834 4333
Scientific Society

Enquiries, on administration, to the Secretary; for advice on cultivation and plant pests and diseases, letters to the Director, R.H.S. Garden, Wisley, Woking, Surrey GU23 6QB

Subject coverage

cultivation of all plants, trees and shrubs, both ornamental and culinary

Publications

The Garden (monthly)
Advisory literature and illustrated books

2311 ROYAL INSTITUTE OF BRITISH ARCHITECTS
66 Portland Place, London W1N 4AD Tel. 01-580 3252
Professional Institute

Enquiries to the Chief Executive

Subject coverage

architectural practice, theory and management

Publications

Journal of Architectural Research and Teaching
RIBA Journal (monthly)
Quarterly Statistical Bulletin

2312 ROYAL INSTITUTE OF CHEMISTRY
30 Russell Square, London WC1B 5DT Tel. 01-580 3482
Professional and Qualifying Body; full amalgamation with the Chemical Society in progress; houses the Association of Public Analysts, *q.v.*, and the Association of Clinical Biochemists

Enquiries to the External Relations and Information Officer

Subject coverage

mutual recognition of qualifications, especially in the European Community; professional status of chemists; manpower statistics;education and training; health and safety; ethical practice and code of conduct'

Publications

Chemistry in Britain (monthly)
Directory of Consulting Practices in Chemistry and Related Subjects
Code of Practice for Chemical Laboratories
Professional Conduct: Guidance for Chemists

2313 ROYAL INSTITUTE OF NAVIGATION
Royal Geographical Society, 1 Kensington Gore, London SW7 2AT Tel. 01-589 5021
Learned Society

Enquiries to the Librarian

Subject coverage
navigation (sea, air, astro-, etc.)

Publication
Journal of Navigation (3 times per annum)

2314 ROYAL INSTITUTE OF PUBLIC ADMINISTRATION
Hamilton House, Mabledon Place, London WC1H 9BD Tel. 01-388 0211
Limited Company; includes the Local Government Operational Research Unit of 201 Kings Road, Reading; houses the N.H.S. Operational Research Group and a Unit for the Retail Planning Institute Limited

Enquiries to the Librarian

Subject coverage
public administration; central and local government; management; planning; Civil Service; training techniques

Publications
Public Administration (quarterly)
Bibliographies (about 90 titles)
Research projects

2315 ROYAL INSTITUTION OF CHARTERED SURVEYORS
12 Great George Street, Parliament Square, London SW1P 3AD Tel. 01-839 5600
Professional Institution; with which the Chartered Auctioneers and Estate Agents Institute and the Chartered Land Agents Society were amalgamated in 1970, and the libraries combined

Enquiries to the Librarian

Subject coverage
land and building economics; land, building and housing law; agricultural holdings; estate agency; planning, development and valuation; housing and property management; compulsory purchase and compensation; agriculture and forestry; land, hydrographic and minerals surveying; quantity surveying; taxation and rating of land and property

Publications
Abstracts and Reviews (monthly)
Weekly Briefing
Chartered Surveyor (monthly)

2316 ROYAL INSTITUTION OF GREAT BRITAIN
21 Albemarle Street, London W1X 4BS Tel. 01-409 2992
Learned Society/Charity/Research Laboratories

Enquiries to the Librarian or the Registrar

Subject coverage
history and philosophy of science; solar energy; teaching of science

Special collections
Spottiswoode Collection of Scientific Instruments
Faraday Museum (Faraday apparatus)
Science Archives (19th and 20th centuries)

Publications
Proceedings of the Royal Institution of Great Britain (several issues per annum)
List of Members
Books on the history of the Institution
Royal Institution Library of Science Series (Elsevier—1970—many volumes)

2317 ROYAL INSTITUTION OF NAVAL ARCHITECTS
10 Upper Belgrave Street, London SW1X 8BQ Tel. 01-235 4622
Professional and Learned Institution

Enquiries to the Librarian or Secretary

Subject coverage
naval architecture; marine engineering, and related sciences

Special collection
Scott Collection, dating back to 1600

Publications
Journal
Transactions
Marine Technology Monographs
Symposia Proceedings
Annual Report

ROYAL INSTITUTE OF NAVIGATION *see* **ROYAL GEOGRAPHICAL SOCIETY**

2318 ROYAL INSTITUTE OF PUBLIC HEALTH AND HYGIENE
28 Portland Place, London W1N 4DE Tel. 01-580 2731
Charitable Organization

Enquiries to the Secretary

Subject coverage
training of post-mortem room technicians; food hygiene education; health and hygiene

Publications
Community Health
Lecture Notes in Food Hygiene

2319 ROYAL METEOROLOGICAL SOCIETY
James Glaisher House, Grenville Place, Bracknell, Berkshire RG12 1BX
Charity, incorporated by Royal Charter; Manchester Centre: Department of Mathematics, Manchester University M13 9BL; Scottish Centre: Meteorological Office, 26 Palmerston Place, Edinburgh EH12 5AN; Welsh Centre: Department of Maritime Studies, UWIST, Cathays Park, Cardiff CF1 3NU

Enquiries to the Executive Secretary; at Regional Centres to the Honorary Secretary

Subject coverage
meteorology and oceanography

Special collections
Society publications, and those of forerunner societies
Early (15th–19th century) books on meteorology and related subjects

Publications
Quarterly Journal
Weather (monthly)

2320 ROYAL MICROSCOPICAL SOCIETY
37/38 St. Clements, Oxford OX4 1AJ Tel. 0865 48768
Learned Society

Enquiries to the Administrator

Subject coverage
microscopy

Publications
Journal of Microscopy (bi-monthly)
Proceedings of the Royal Microscopical Society (bi-monthly)
Miscellaneous papers

2321 ROYAL MILITARY COLLEGE OF SCIENCE
Shrivenham, Swindon, Wiltshire SN6 8LA Tel. 0793 782551
Government Department, of the Ministry of Defence

Enquiries to the Librarian

Subject coverage
military applications of science and engineering; civil, mechanical, electrical and electronic engineering; physics; mathematics; chemistry; metallurgy; management sciences; weapons and vehicles

Publications
Military Science Index
List of Journals
List of College Reports and Papers

2322 ROYAL NATIONAL LIFEBOAT INSTITUTION
West Quay Road, Poole, Dorset BH15 1HZ Tel. 020-13 71133
Telex 41328
Registered Charity; provides the Secretariat for the International Life-boat Conference

Enquiries to the Public Relations Officer

Subject coverage
search and rescue at sea; and its organisation and statistics; design and construction of life-boats and their electronic and other equipment; medical and survival techniques and equipment; life-boat history (since 1824)

Special collections
Photographic Library (life-boats since c.1860)
Life-boat models

Publications
Life-boat (quarterly)
Year Book
Leaflets and posters

2323 ROYAL NATIONAL ROSE SOCIETY
Chiswell Green Lane, St Albans, Hertfordshire AL2 3NR Tel. 56 50461/2
Horticultural Society

Enquiries to the Secretary

Subject coverage
rose growing

Publication
The Rose Annual (for members only)

2324 ROYAL NAVAL COLLEGE
Greenwich, London SE10 9NN Tel. 01-858 2154
Government Department, of the Ministry of Defence

Enquiries to the Librarian

Subject coverage
naval history; defence studies; nuclear science and technology

2325 ROYAL NAVAL ENGINEERING COLLEGE
Manadon, Plymouth, Devonshire PL5 3AQ Tel. 0752 53740
Naval Establishment, of the Ministry of Defence (Navy)

Enquiries to the Librarian

Subject coverage
engineering (control, electrical, electronic, mechanical, materials, marine, aeronautical)

2326 ROYAL NAVAL PHYSIOLOGICAL LABORATORY
Fort Road, Alverstoke, Gosport, Hampshire PO12 2DU Tel. 0705 22351
Government Laboratory, of the Procurement Executive, Ministry of Defence

Enquiries to the Superintendent

Subject coverage
physiology; medicine; bioengineering; ergonomics; computing; electronics; photography; more specifically, research into the following subjects: underwater physiology; diving; submarine escape; air and oxygen-helium decompression schedules; decompression sickness; neurophysiology and special senses; nitrogen narcosis; respiratory mechanics; breathing apparatus; gas emergency man-powered drive methods of CO^2 absorption in submarines; hot and cold weather clothing including diver heating

2327 ROYAL NUMISMATIC SOCIETY
c/o Department of Coins and Medals, British Museum, London WC1B 3DG Tel. 01-636 1555 ext. 404
Learned Society; affiliated to the British Association of Numismatic Societies; *see also* British Numismatic Society

Enquiries are not accepted from the public

Subject coverage
numismatics

Publications
Numismatic Chronicle
Coin Hoards
Numismatic Monographs (occasional, eight issues to date)

2328 ROYAL OBSERVATORY
Blackford Hill, Edinburgh EH9 3HJ Tel. 031-667 3321
Telex 72383
Scientific Establishment, of the Science Research Council

Enquiries to the Librarian or the Secretary

Subject coverage
national astronomical facilities management, including U.K. Schmidt Telescope in Australia, the U.K. Infrared Telescope in Hawaii and the Cosmos measuring system in Edinburgh; research on the physical and chemical properties of interstellar solid particles and the large scale distribution, motions and structure of galaxies of stars

Special collection
Crawford Collection of historical books and manuscripts on astronomy, etc. (c.12,000 items)

Publications
Annals of the Royal Observatory, Edinburgh Vols. 1–15, 1838–1886
Annual report (1959– as: Report) of the Astronomer Royal for Scotland for the year ending 31st March 1892–1939, 1959–1973, 1975
Annual report of the Royal Observatory, Edinburgh for the year ending 30 September 1975–
Communications from the Royal Observatory, Edinburgh No. 1–, 1949–
Edinburgh Astronomical Observations Vols. 1–3, 1902–1910
Geophysical communications from the Royal Observatory, Nos. 1–7, Edinburgh 1963–67
Occasional reports of the Royal Observatory, Edinburgh No. 1– 1976–
Publications of the Royal Observatory Edinburgh Vol. 1– 1939–
Catalogue of the Crawford Library of the Royal Observatory, Edinburgh. Edinburgh, 1890

2329 ROYAL SCHOOL OF MINES
Imperial College of Science and Technology, Prince Consort Road, Kensington, London SW7 2AZ Tel. 01-589 5111
Telex 261503
University Department, of the University of London; houses also the Rock Mechanics Information Service and the Applied Geochemistry Research Group; comprises the Departments of Geology, Mineral Resources Engineering and Metallurgy & Materials Science

Enquiries to the Librarian of the Department concerned

Subject coverage
in the Mineral Resources Engineering Library: mining, mineral technology; mineral resources; environmental engineering; rock mechanics; petroleum and natural gas engineering; in the Geology Library: general and regional geology; stratigraphy; palaeontology; mineralogy; petrology; structural geology; geochemistry; geophysics; photogeology; mining geology; engineering and oil geology

Publications
Rock Mechanics Information Service produces the Geomechanics Abstracts in International Journal of Rock Mechanics and Mining Science (bi-monthly)
Applied Geochemistry Research Group produces Technical Communications

2330 ROYAL SCOTTISH FORESTRY SOCIETY
18 Abercromby Place, Edinburgh EH3 6LB Tel. 031-557 1017
Independent, Representative, Organization

Enquiries to the Secretary

Subject coverage
forestry; forest industry; timber; silviculture; arboriculture; education and training in forestry; forestry exhibitions

Publication
Scottish Forestry (quarterly, free to members and on subscription)

2331 ROYAL SCOTTISH GEOGRAPHICAL SOCIETY
10 Randolph Crescent, Edinburgh EH3 7TU Tel. 031-225 3330
Learned Society

Enquiries to the Secretary

Subject coverage
geography

Publication
Scottish Geographical Magazine

2332 ROYAL SIGNALS AND RADAR ESTABLISHMENT
St. Andrews Road, Malvern, Worcestershire WR14 3PS Tel. 068-45 2733
Telex 339747 *and* 339748
Government Research Establishment; formerly Royal Radar Establishment; of the Procurement Executive, Ministry of Defence

Enquiries to the Librarian

Subject coverage
solid state physics; electronics; communications; radar; computers; electronic materials

2333 ROYAL SIGNALS AND RADAR RESEARCH ESTABLISHMENT
Christchurch, Dorset BH23 4JB Tel. 042-52 71311
Telex 41192
Government Research Establishment, of the Ministry of Defence, Procurement Executive; formerly Signals Research and Development Establishment; associated with the Royal Signals and Radar Research Establishment, Malvern

Enquiries to the Librarian

Subject coverage
telecommunications

2334 ROYAL SOCIETY
6 Carlton House Terrace, London SW1Y 5AG Tel. 01-839 5561
Telex 917876
Learned Society; supporting some thirty National Committees, most of them for Unions and Committees of the International Council of Scientific Unions (ICSU); including one National Committee for the International Centre of Insect Physiology and Ecology and one for the International Institute of Applied Systems Analysis; seven Joint Committees and seven Standing Committees

Enquiries to the Information Officer (ext. 242)

Subject coverage
all science; specific interests of the National and Standing Committees are as follows: (Joint Committees are concerned with scientific education) astronomy; biochemistry, biology; biophysics; chemistry; crystallography; geodesy and geophysics; geography; geology; history of science, medicine and technology; mathematics; nutritional sciences; pharmacology; physics; physiological sciences; radio science; theoretical and applied mechanics; Antarctic research; data for science and technology; geodynamics; oceanic research; problems of the environment; solar-terrestrial physics; space research; global atmospheric research; hydrological sciences; insect physiology and ecology; applied systems analysis; volcanological and seismological research

Publications
Philosophical Transactions of the Royal Society (Series A – Physical, Mathematical and Series B – Biological)
Proceedings of the Royal Society (Series A and B)
Notes and Records of the Royal Society
Year Book of the Royal Society

2335 ROYAL SOCIETY LIBRARY
6 Carlton House Terrace, London SW1Y 5AG Tel. 01-839 5561
Telex 917876

Learned Society Library

Enquiries to the Librarian

Subject coverage
history of science

Special collections
Books by Fellows of the Royal Society
Periodicals of the National Academies of Science
Publications of scientific unions forming the International Council of Scientific Unions (ICSU)

2336 ROYAL SOCIETY FOR THE ENCOURAGEMENT OF ARTS, MANUFACTURES AND COMMERCE
6–8 John Adam Street, London WC2N 6EZ Tel. 01-839 2366

Learned Society

Enquiries to the Curator/Librarian

Subject coverage
arts, manufactures and commerce, particularly 18th and 19th centuries

2337 ROYAL SOCIETY FOR THE PREVENTION OF ACCIDENTS (RoSPA)
Cannon House, The Priory, Queensway, Birmingham B4 6BS Tel. 021-233 2461
Telex 336546

Charity/Limited Company; includes the National Water Safety Committee and other national committees for subject areas given below

Enquiries to the Librarian

Subject coverage
occupational, agricultural, educational, road, home and water safety

Publications
Care on the Road (monthly)
Care in the Home (quarterly)
Occupational Safety and Health (monthly)
Safety Education (termly)
Look Out (quarterly)
Water Safety News

2338 ROYAL SOCIETY FOR THE PROTECTION OF BIRDS
The Lodge, Sandy, Bedfordshire SG19 2DL Tel. 0767 80551

Registered Charity; houses the Farming and Wild Life Advisory Group, *q.v.*

Enquiries, accompanied by stamped addressed envelope, to the Society; (loans to members only)

Subject coverage
all aspects of wildlife having a bearing on bird protection, including environmental education; land management; environmental planning; law enforcement

Publications
Birds (quarterly)
Birdlife (six times per annum)
Sales Catalogue (annual)

2339 ROYAL SOCIETY OF EDINBURGH
22 and 24 George Street, Edinburgh EH2 2PQ Tel. 031-225 6057
Learned Society

Enquiries to the Executive Secretary and Librarian

Subject coverage
science and literature

Special collection
Hume manuscripts

Publications
Year Book
Transactions
Communications
Proceedings A – Mathematics
Proceedings B – Natural environment

2340 ROYAL SOCIETY OF HEALTH
13 Grosvenor Place, London SW1X 7EN Tel. 01-235 9961
Learned Society

Enquiries, primarily from members, to the Secretary

Subject coverage
health in society; food and nutrition; hygiene; mental health; dental services; pharmacy; environment; housing

Publications
Journal (bi-monthly)
Books, reports, Congress papers and reprints

2341 ROYAL SOCIETY OF TROPICAL MEDICINE AND HYGIENE
Manson House, 26 Portland Place, London W1N 4EY Tel. 01-580 2127
Learned Society
Enquiries to the Administrator

Subject coverage
causes, treatment and prevention of human and animal diseases in warm climates

Publication
Transactions of the Royal Society of Tropical Medicine and Hygiene

2342 ROYAL STATISTICAL SOCIETY
25 Enford Street, London W1H 2BH Tel. 01-723 5882
Learned Society

Enquiries, from Fellows and Associate Members only, to the Librarian

Subject coverage
statistical theory, methods and applications

Special collections
Yule Collection (early statistical works, 1630–1820)
Porter Collection (early U.K. and foreign trade statistics, housed at the Business Statistics Office, Newport)

Publications
Journal of the Royal Statistical Society Series A (general)
Journal of the Royal Statistical Society Series B (methodological)
Applied Statistics (JRSS Series C)

2343 ROYAL TELEVISION SOCIETY
Tavistock House East, Tavistock Square, London WC1H 9HR Tel. 01-387 1970/1332
Professional Society

Enquiries, from Members only, to the Director

Subject coverage
arts and sciences of television

Publications
Bulletin (monthly)
Television (bi-monthly)

2344 ROYAL ZOOLOGICAL SOCIETY OF SCOTLAND
Zoological Park, Murrayfield, Edinburgh EH12 6TS Tel. 031-334 9171
Scientific Society

Enquiries to the Director

Subject coverage
management of exotic animals; conservation education; legislation relating to exotic animals; careers in animal-related employment

Publication
Annual Report

2345 RUBBER AND PLASTICS PROCESSING INDUSTRY TRAINING BOARD
950 Great West Road, Brentford, Middlesex TW8 9ES Tel. 01-568 0731
Industrial Training Board, of the Training Services Agency, *q.v.*

Enquiries to the Information Officer or Librarian

Subject coverage
training within the rubber and plastics processing industry

Publications
Recommendations for the Training of Operatives up to management level
Building a Marketing Model (tape/slide presentation)
First Report of the Study Group on the Education and Training of the 16–18 year-old

2346 RUBBER AND PLASTICS RESEARCH ASSOCIATION OF GREAT BRITAIN
Shawbury, Shrewsbury SY4 4NR Tel. 09394 383
Telex 35134
Industrial Research Association/International Technical Centre

Enquiries to the Information Officer

Subject coverage
rubber, plastics and allied fields; synthesis and applications; design; additives; processing; properties and testing; market information; chemical resistance; industrial hazards; thermal transitions; trade names

Special collection
the Porritt and Dawson Collection (on rubbers and plastics)

Publications
RAPRA Abstracts (bi-weekly)
New Trade Names in the Rubber and Plastics Industry
International Polymer Science and Technology (monthly)
Plastics in Horticultural Structures
Recent Literature on Hazardous Environments in Industry
Rapra Members Journal (bi-monthly)
Rapid Information (SDI service)
Bio-medical Applications of Polymers
Current publications list

2347 RUBBER GROWERS ASSOCIATION LIMITED
Cereal House, 58 Mark Lane, London EC3R 7NE Tel. 01-480 5493
Trade Association; houses the Malaysia-Singapore Commercial Association Incorporated, the Indonesia Association Incorporated, and the Crepe Sole Rubber Association of London

Enquiries to the Director or Secretary

Subject coverage
production of tropical crops including rubber and oil palm

2348 RUBBER TRADE ASSOCIATION OF LONDON
Cereal House, 58 Mark Lane, London EC3R 7HP Tel. 01-480 5388
Trade Association

Enquiries to the Secretary

Subject coverage
marketing of natural rubber grades

2349 RUBERY OWEN GROUP SERVICES LIMITED
P.O. Box 10, Darlaston, West Midlands WS10 8JD Tel. 021-526 3131 ext. 621
Company, formerly Rubery Owen and Company Limited

Enquiries to the Librarian

Subject coverage
automobile engineering; structural engineering; management; statistics

Special collections
standards, specifications, and regulations, including British Standards, DIN, DEF, FVRDE, Inter Europe Automotive

Publications
Product catalogues

RUGBY COLLEGE OF ENGINEERING TECHNOLOGY *now* **LANCHESTER POLYTECHNIC,** *q.v.*

RUGBY DIVISIONAL LIBRARY *see* **WARWICKSHIRE COUNTY LIBRARY**

2350 RUMNEY COLLEGE OF TECHNOLOGY
Trowbridge Road, Rumney, Cardiff CF3 8XZ Tel. 0222 78615
Technical College; formerly Rumney Technical College

Enquiries to the Librarian

Subject coverage
mechanical, electrical and automobile engineering

2351 RUNCORN LIBRARY
Egerton Street, Runcorn, Cheshire WA7 1JN Tel. 092-85 74495
Public Library, part of the Cheshire County Library, *q.v.*

Enquiries to the Librarian

Subject coverage
roads and highway engineering; purchasing; management; packaging; stock control and storekeeping; cosmetics; perfumes; fertilizers; computers

RURAL INDUSTRIES BUREAU *now* **COUNCIL FOR SMALL INDUSTRIES IN RURAL AREAS,** *q.v.*

RURAL PLANNING SERVICES LIMITED *see* **ECONOMIC FORESTRY GROUP**

RUSH GREEN TECHNICAL COLLEGE *now* **BARKING COLLEGE OF TECHNOLOGY,** *q.v.*

RUSHCLIFFE DISTRICT LIBRARY *see* **NOTTINGHAMSHIRE COUNTY LIBRARY**

2352 RUSTON DIESELS LIMITED

Research Centre, Beevor Street, P.O. Box 25, Lincoln LN5 7JB — Tel. 0522 21241, Telex 56233

Company, formerly at various times, Ruston Hornsby Limited, English-Electric Diesels Limited and latterly Ruston-Paxman Diesels Limited; now part of GEC Limited

Enquiries to the Information Manager

Subject coverage
internal combustion engines, comprising diesel engines, gas engines, gas turbines

RUTHERFORD COLLEGE OF TECHNOLOGY *now* **NEWCASTLE UPON TYNE POLYTECHNIC,** *q.v.*

2353 RUTHERFORD LABORATORY

Chilton, Didcot, Oxfordshire OX11 0QX — Tel. 0235 21900, Telex 83159

Research Laboratory, of the Science Research Council; formerly Rutherford High Energy Laboratory; the former Atlas Laboratory of the Science Research Council is now the Atlas Computing Division of the Rutherford Laboratory; the Neutron Beam Research Unit and the Laser Laboratory of the Science Research Council are also housed at this address

Enquiries to the Librarian

Subject coverage
high energy physics; elementary particles; cryogenics; superconductivity; computers; lasers; neutron studies

Publication
Annual Report

RUTHIN AREA LIBRARY *see* **GLYNDWR AREA LIBRARY**

2354 RYECOTEWOOD COLLEGE

Priest End, Thame, Oxfordshire OX9 2BR — Tel. 084-421 2501

Technical and Agricultural College

Enquiries to the Librarian

Subject coverage
agriculture and agricultural machinery; furniture design and technology; restoring of antiques

SAALIC *now* **WILCO,** *q.v.*

2355 SAFER GLAZING INFORMATION SERVICE

44 Osnaburgh Street, London NW1 3DN — Tel. 01-388 1816

Company-sponsored Information Service

Enquiries to the Information Officer

Subject coverage
glazing and the safe use of glass, mainly in domestic architecture

Publications
Accident Reports
Safer Glazing in the Home

2356 SAFETY GLAZING ASSOCIATION

6 Mount Row, London W1Y 6DY — Tel. 01-629 8334

Trade Association

Enquiries to the Information Officer

Subject coverage
glazing; safety glazing and glass

2357 SAFETY IN MINES RESEARCH ESTABLISHMENT
Red Hill, Broad Lane, Sheffield S3 7HQ
Government Department, of the Health and Safety Executive; library branches at Harpur Hill, Buxton and, eventually, at Edgware Road, Cricklewood, London

Enquiries to the Librarian

Subject coverage
Sheffield: industrial safety and health; mine safety; pure and applied science
Buxton: industrial safety and health; mine safety; explosions and combustion; electrical equipment in flammable atmospheres
Cricklewood: analytical testing of dusts and fumes; flammable liquids and solids

Special collection
mining regulations and safety

Publications
Safety in Mines Abstracts (bi-monthly)
SMRE Bibliography, 3rd ed.
Annual Report (H.M.S.O.)
SMRE Digests

ST ANDREWS GROUP LIBRARY *see* **KIRKCALDY AND NORTH EAST FIFE DISTRICT LIBRARIES**

2358 ST ANDREWS UNIVERSITY LIBRARY
South Street, St Andrews, Fife Tel. 033-481 4333/4/5
Telex 76213

University Library

Enquiries to the Librarian

Subject coverage
those of the Faculty of Science

Special collections
about 35 collections, of which some of the relevant are as follows:
Beveridge Collection (includes material on bee culture)
Forbes Collection (early and rare books in science)
Mackay Collection (mathematics)
Simson Collection and Wedderburn Collection (medicine)

Publications
Readers Guide (revised periodically)
Current Serials (revised annually)

2359 ST ANNES BOARD MILL COMPANY LIMITED
St. Annes Road, Bristol BS4 4AD Tel. 0272 770431
Telex 44279

Company, Member of the Imperial Group Limited

Enquiries to the Librarian

Subject coverage
paper-board manufacture; on- and off-machine coatings; forming developments; refiner pulp

ST. AUSTELL DISTRICT LIBRARY *see* **CORNWALL COUNTY LIBRARY**

2360 ST. BRIDE PRINTING LIBRARY
St. Bride Institute, Bride Lane, London EC4Y 8EE Tel. 01-353 4660
Public Reference Library; one of the City of London Libraries

Enquiries, preferably by letter, to the Librarian

Subject coverage
technique, design and history of printing and related subjects

Special collections
Loan collection of slides
Typefounders specimens
Documents on very early printing unions

2361 ST. CRISPINS BOOT TRADES ASSOCIATION LIMITED
St. Crispins House, Station Road, Desborough, Ketting, Northamptonshire NN14 2SA — Tel. 0536 760374
National Chamber of Trade

Enquiries to the General Secretary

Subject coverage
shoe repairing

Publication
Shoe Service (monthly)

2362 ST. HELENS CENTRAL LIBRARY
Gamble Institute, Victoria Square, St. Helens, Lancashire WA10 1DY — Tel. 0744 24061 ext. 2246, Telex 627813
Public Library

Enquiries to the Bibliographical Services Officer

Subject coverage
general; subject specialization in diseases of the nervous system; glass (all aspects)

2363 ST. HELENS COLLEGE OF TECHNOLOGY
Brook Street, St. Helens, Lancashire — Tel. 0744 20831
College of Further Education; houses the St. Helens School of Management Studies, a College Department and constituent of the North West Regional Management Centre

Enquiries to the Tutor-Librarian

Subject coverage
economics; electrical, mechanical, mining and production engineering; glass technology

Publications
Guides to specific subject fields

2364 ST. PANCRAS LIBRARY
100 Euston Road, London NW1 2AJ — Tel. 01-278 4444, Telex 24323
Public Library, of the London Borough of Camden Libraries and Arts Department

Enquiries to the Reference Librarian

Subject coverage
general, science and technology

SALE CENTRAL LIBRARY *see* **TRAFFORD BOROUGH LIBRARY SERVICE**

SALES AUGMENTATION LIMITED *see*
INSTITUTION OF BUYERS
INSTITUTION OF PROFESSIONAL SALESMEN
INSTITUTION OF SALES ENGINEERS

2365 SALFORD CITY LIBRARIES
Headquarters, Council Offices, Astley Road, Irlam M30 5LL — Tel. 061-775 3981, Telex 669800
Public Library Service, comprising libraries in the former City of Salford area, the Boroughs of Eccles and Swinton and the Urban Districts of Irlam and Worsley; three Area Libraries: Salford Central, Swinton Central and Eccles Central

Enquiries to Assistant Manager (Libraries)

Subject coverage
general

2366 SALFORD COLLEGE OF TECHNOLOGY
Frederick Road, Salford, Lancashire M6 6PU Tel. 061-736 6541
College of Technology

Enquiries to the Tutor-Librarian

Subject coverage
general

Special collection
British Standards

2367 SALFORD ELECTRICAL INSTRUMENTS LIMITED
Peel Works, Barton Lane, Eccles, Manchester M30 0HL Tel. 061-789 5081
Telex 667711

Company; subsidiary of G.E.C. Limited

Enquiries to the Publicity Manager

Subject coverage
multi-range instrumentation, electrical and electronic components; electronics projects

2368 SALFORD UNIVERSITY LIBRARY
Salford, Lancashire M5 4WT Tel. 061-736 5843
Telex 668680

University Library

Enquiries to the Librarian

Subject coverage
science and technology in general

SALFORD UNIVERSITY *see also* **INDUSTRIAL CENTRE FOR DESIGN AND MANUFACTURING ENGINEERING**

2369 SALISBURY COLLEGE OF TECHNOLOGY
Southampton Road, Salisbury, Wiltshire SP1 2LW Tel. 0722 23711
Technical College; formerly Salisbury and South Wiltshire College of Further Education

Enquiries to the Tutor-Librarian

Subject coverage
building construction and management; mechanical, electrical, electronic, and materials engineering; business management; physics; chemistry; biology and microbiology; computer technology; hotel management; catering

SALISBURY DIVISIONAL LIBRARY *see* **WILTSHIRE COUNTY LIBRARY**

SALMON AND FRESHWATER FISHERIES LABORATORY *see* **DIRECTORATE OF FISHERIES RESEARCH**

2370 SALTERS INSTITUTE OF INDUSTRIAL CHEMISTRY
c/o The Salters' Company, Salters' Hall, Fore Street, London EC2Y 5DE Tel. 01-588 5216
Grant-awarding Body, part of the Salters' Company

Enquiries to the Clerk of the Salters' Company

Subject coverage
Award of Salters Fellowships and Scholarships to industrial chemists; limited information on research subjects undertaken by Salters Fellows and Scholars

Special collection
Theses by past Salters' Fellows and Scholars

Publication
Salters' Institute of Industrial Chemistry booklet

2371 SAND AND GRAVEL ASSOCIATION LIMITED
48 Park Street, London W1Y 4HE Tel. 01-499 8967
Trade Association and Employers Organization

Enquiries to the Information Officer or Technical Officer

Subject coverage
sand and gravel

Publications
SAGA Bulletin (quarterly)
Technical papers

SANDLIME BRICK MANUFACTURERS ASSOCIATION LIMITED *now* **CALCIUM SILICATE BRICK ASSOCIATION LIMITED,** *q.v.*

2372 SANDOZ PRODUCTS LIMITED
Dyes/Chemicals Division, Calverley Lane, Horsforth, Leeds LS18 4RP Tel. 0532 584646
Company, subsidiary of Sandoz Limited, Basle

Enquiries to the Librarian

Subject coverage
dyeing technology and related chemical applications technology

2373 SANDOZ PRODUCTS LIMITED
Pharmaceuticals Division, 98 The Centre, Feltham TW13 4EP Tel. 01-890 1366
Company, subsidiary of Sandoz Limited, Basle

Enquiries to the Medical Information Officer

Subject coverage
pharmaceuticals, with particular reference to chemistry, pharmacology and the clinical usage of company products

2374 SANDWELL PUBLIC LIBRARIES
Central Library, High Street, West Bromwich, West Midlands B70 8DZ Tel. 021-569 2416 Telex 338392
Public Library; the former County Boroughs of Warley and West Bromwich merged to form the Metropolitan Borough of Sandwell; District Libraries at Langley, Tipton, Wednesbury, and Smethwick

Enquiries to the Librarian

Subject coverage
general

2375 SANGAMO WESTON LIMITED
Great Cambridge Road, Enfield, Middlesex EN1 3RX Tel. 01-366 1100 Telex 24724

Company, partly owned by Schlumberger Limited

Enquiries to the Publicity Department

Subject coverage
electricity switches; time switches; central heating programmers; industrial and aircraft instruments; photographic exposure meters

SASLIC *see* **SURREY AND SUSSEX LIBRARIES IN CO-OPERATION**

SATRA *see* **SHOE AND ALLIED TRADES RESEARCH ASSOCIATION**

2376 SAVE AND PROSPER GROUP LIMITED
4 Great St. Helens, London EC3P 3EP Tel. 01-588 1717
Company

Enquiries to the Librarian

Subject coverage
unit trusts; insurance; pensions; investment

Special collection
Unit Trust Prices 1962–

Publication
Save and Prosper Book of Money

2377 SAVINGS BANKS INSTITUTE
Knighton House, 52–66 Mortimer Street, London W1N 7DG Tel. 01-580 0791
Professional Institute

Enquiries to the Secretary-General

Subject coverage
academic preparation for careers in savings banking

Publication
Journal of the Savings Banks Institute (bi-monthly)

2378 SAW ASSOCIATION
3 Melbourne Avenue, Sheffield S10 2QJ Tel. 0742 663084
Trade Association, formerly the Saw Manufacturers Association; Member of the Federation of British Hand Tool Manufacturers

Enquiries to the Secretary

Subject coverage
saws; standardisation

2379 SBA – ASSOCIATION OF INDEPENDENT BUSINESSES
Europe House, World Trade Centre, London E1 9AA Tel. 01-481 8669
Political Association, formerly Smaller Businesses Association

Enquiries to the Association Secretary

Subject coverage
taxation; government legislation

Publications
Privately-owned Businesses and Full Employment in a Free Society
Inflation and the Smaller Business
The Last Bastion

SCARBOROUGH AND RYEDALE DIVISIONAL LIBRARY *see* **NORTH YORKSHIRE COUNTY LIBRARY**

2380 SCHERING CHEMICALS LIMITED
The Brow, Burgess Hill, West Sussex RH15 9NE Tel. 044-46 6011
Telex 87577

Company, subsidiary of Schering AG, Berlin

Enquiries to the Head of Medical Services

Subject coverage
medicine, particularLy endocrinology; pharmacology, particularly steroid hormones

SCHOOL OF APPLIED NON-DESTRUCTIVE TESTING *see* **WELDING INSTITUTE**

2381 SCHOOL OF NAVIGATION LIBRARY
City of London Polytechnic, 100 Minories, London EC3N 1JY Tel. 01-283 1030
Telex 8812073

Polytechnic Library, of the City of London Polytechnic, *q.v.*

Enquiries to the Librarian

Subject coverage
navigation; transport

SCHOOL OF WELDING TECHNOLOGY *see* **WELDING INSTITUTE**

2382 SCIENCE MUSEUM LIBRARY
Imperial Institute Road, South Kensington, London SW7 5NH — Tel. 01-589 6371, Telex 21200

National Library

Enquiries to the Keeper

Subject coverage
science and technology, (excluding medicine, nursing and veterinary science), photography, history of science and technology; some aspects of geography

Special collections
British Standards
British and United States atomic energy reports

Publications
Science Library Bibliographical Series

2383 SCIENCE RESEARCH COUNCIL
State House, High Holborn, London WC1R 4TA — Tel. 01-242 1262
Independent 'fringe' Body

Enquiries to the Librarian

Subject coverage
scientific research, particularly in space, astronomy, nuclear physics; science policy; relationship between science and government

Publications
SRC Research Grants
SRC Studentships and Fellowships
List of Research Grants Current
Occasional Reports

SCIENCE RESEARCH COUNCIL *see also*
APPLETON LABORATORY
DARESBURY NUCLEAR PHYSICS LABORATORY
GAS KINETICS DATA COMPILATION AND EVALUATION GROUP
ROYAL GREENWICH OBSERVATORY
ROYAL OBSERVATORY (Edinburgh)
RUTHERFORD LABORATORY

2384 SCIENTIFIC DOCUMENTATION CENTRE LIMITED
Halbeath House, Dunfermline, Fife KY12 0TZ — Tel. 0383 23535
Research Association

Enquiries to the Director

Subject coverage
analytical, chemical, spectroscopic, computer techniques; air pollution; analogue/digital conversion; digitisation of spectra; asbestos; behaviour of animals; cement; concrete; coatings; finishings; critical path analysis; crystal growth; cybernetics; deuterium; dust; fine particles: dyes; ecology; energy; electron microscopy; epitaxials, etc.; explosives; chemical hazards; fertilisers; forensic science; gas – town and natural; industrial safety; lubrication; machine translation; management; metal-forming; municipal engineering; nomograms; oil; operations research; systems analysis; pattern recognition; peat; pollution; protein metabolism; quality control; sleep; spectroscopic instruments; teaching machines: terpenes: textiles: transport: wood, cork; timber; furnishings; X-ray diffraction

Special collections
SDC Retrospective File of over 1,250,000 references
Collection of spectral data

Publications
Weekly Current Awareness Service (1,400 standard subjects)
SDC Bulletin

2385 SCIENTIFIC EXPLORATION SOCIETY
Mildenhall, Marlborough, Wiltshire Tel. 06725 2664
Charity

Enquiries to the Honorary Secretary

Subject coverage
all aspects of exploration work, both scientific and adventure training

Publications
Newsletter (bi-monthly)

2386 SCIENTIFIC INSTRUMENT MANUFACTURERS ASSOCIATION OF GREAT BRITAIN
Sima House, 20 Peel Street, London W8 7PD Tel. 01-727 2614
Trade Association, member of BEAMA, *q.v.*

Enquiries to the Director or Secretary

Subject coverage
scientific instruments trade, statistics and exhibitions

Publications
Statistics

2387 SCIENTIFIC PERIODICALS LIBRARY
University of Cambridge, Bene't Street, Cambridge CB2 3PY Tel. 0223 58381 ext. 252
Telex 81240
Part of University Library system; formerly Cambridge Philosophical Library; shares premises with the Cambridge Philosophical Society and is also the Society's Library

Enquiries to the Librarian

Subject coverage
mathematics; physics; chemistry; biological sciences, earth sciences; electrical engineering

Special Collection
19th century scientific books

SCOCLIS *see* **STANDING CONFERENCE OF CO-OPERATIVE LIBRARY AND INFORMATION SERVICES**

2388 SCOTT BADER COMPANY LIMITED
Wollaston, Wellingborough, Northamptonshire NN9 7RL Tel. Wellingborough 71100
Telex 31387
Company; formerly Scott Bader and Company Limited

Enquiries to the Information Department

Subject coverage
plastics manufacture and technical applications; emulsion and solution polymers; polyesters; reinforced plastics; surface coatings for paper, textiles and other materials

Publications
"Crystic" monographs (CRYSTIC is a trade name)
Technical trade literature on polymers, polyesters, and plasticisers

2389 SCOTT POLAR RESEARCH INSTITUTE
Lensfield Road, Cambridge CB2 1ER Tel. 0223 66499 ext. 454
Sub-Department within the University of Cambridge Department of Geography; houses the International Glaciological Society, *q.v.* and the World Data Centre in Glaciology

Enquiries to the Director

Subject coverage
Polar regions; Arctic regions; Antarctic regions; snow and ice studies; glaciology; cold regions in general; whaling; sealing

Publications
Polar Record (3 times per annum)
Recent Polar Literature (3 times per annum)
Journal of Glaciology (quarterly, published by the International Glaciological Society)

2390 SCOTTISH AGRICULTURAL INDUSTRIES LIMITED
25 Ravelston Terrace, Edinburgh EH4 3ET Tel. 031-332 2481
Telex 72268

Company, a subsidiary of Imperial Chemical Industries Limited

Enquiries to the Licensing Officer

Subject coverage
fertiliser processes; palletising

Publications
process brochures
catalogues

2391 SCOTTISH AGRICULTURAL INDUSTRIES LIMITED
Research and Development Department, 124 Salamander Street, Edinburgh EH6 7LA Tel. 031-554 3156
Company, subsidiary of Imperial Chemical Industries Limited

Enquiries to the Librarian

Subject coverage
fertilizer manufacture

2392 SCOTTISH ASSESSORS ASSOCIATION
30/31 Queen Street, Edinburgh EH2 1LZ Tel. 031-225 1399
Association of Local Government Officers, formerly the Association of Land Valuation Assessors of Scotland

Enquiries, of a general nature on the operation of the Lands Valuation Acts in Scotland, to the Secretary

Subject coverage
lands valuation for rating purposes

2393 SCOTTISH ASSOCIATION FOR PUBLIC TRANSPORT
113 West Regent Street, Glasgow G2 2RU
Voluntary Body; formerly Scottish Railway Development Association

Enquiries to the Secretary

Subject coverage
all modes of public transport; policy and finance

Publications
Quarterly Newsletter
Memoranda and Study Papers

2394 SCOTTISH ASSOCIATION OF MARINE ELECTRICAL CONTRACTORS
105 West George Street, Glasgow G2 1QP Tel. 041-221 9961
Employers' Association

No enquiry service

Subject coverage
marine electrical contracting

2395 SCOTTISH BEEKEEPERS ASSOCIATION (MOIR LIBRARY)
c/o Central Library, George IV Bridge, Edinburgh EH1 1EG Tel. 031-225 5584
Library of Professional Association

Enquiries to the Librarian

Subject coverage
bees and other hymenoptera; insects and husbandry

Special collection
Insects and husbandry: early English books

Publications
Catalogue, 1950 and Supplement, 1963

2396 SCOTTISH BOAT BUILDERS ASSOCIATION
7 West George Street, Glasgow G2 1BD Tel. 041-248 6161
Trade Association; member of the Ship and Boat Builders National Federation

Enquiries to the Secretary

Subject coverage
boat building

2397 SCOTTISH BUSINESS SCHOOL
Department of Business Studies, Edinburgh University, 50 George Square, Edinburgh EH8 9LJ Tel. 031-667 1011
University Department; the Scottish Business School is a partnership of this Edinburgh University Department with those of the Universities of Glasgow and Strathclyde

Enquiries to the Administrative Assistant

Subject coverage
business and management studies

SCOTTISH CENTRAL FILM LIBRARY *see* **SCOTTISH COUNCIL FOR EDUCATIONAL TECHNOLOGY**

2398 SCOTTISH COLLEGE OF TEXTILES
Netherdale, Galashiels, Selkirkshire TD1 3HF Tel. 0896 3351
Telex 72416
Scottish Central Institution; formerly Scottish Woollen Technical College

Enquiries to the Librarian

Subject coverage
textile industries, technology and design; wool textiles; management studies

2399 SCOTTISH COUNCIL FOR EDUCATIONAL TECHNOLOGY
16 Woodside Terrace, Glasgow G3 7XN Tel. 041-332 9988
Grant-aided Company, comprising the Scottish Centre for Educational Technology and the Scottish Central Film Library; housing also Educational Films of Scotland, the Scottish Film Council and the Scottish Standing Committee on Archive Films; title changed in 1975 from Scottish Film Council

Enquiries to the Director

Subject coverage
educational technology; film culture, production and archive

Publications
Catalogue of Films
Various publications on educational technology

SCOTTISH ECONOMIC PLANNING DEPARTMENT *see* **HIGHLANDS AND ISLANDS DEVELOPMENT BOARD**

2400 SCOTTISH ENGINEERING EMPLOYERS ASSOCIATION
105 West George Street, Glasgow G2 1QL Tel. 041-221 3181
Trade Association, affiliated to the Engineering Employers Federation

Enquiries to the Secretary

Subject coverage
industrial relations, training, health and safety

Publications
Annual Report
Occasional papers on manpower and training problems in the engineering industry

SCOTTISH EXPORT COMMITTEE *see* **GLASGOW CHAMBER OF COMMERCE AND MANUFACTURES**

SCOTTISH FARM BUILDINGS INVESTIGATION UNIT *see* **FARM BUILDINGS INFORMATION CENTRE**

2401 SCOTTISH FEDERATION OF MEAT TRADERS ASSOCIATIONS INCORPORATED
24 George Square, Glasgow G2 1ER Tel. 041-221 6872
Trade Association

Enquiries to the Secretary

Subject coverage
butchery trade

Publications
Handbook (for members)
Reports of meetings

SCOTTISH GRAIN DISTILLERS LIMITED *now* **DISTILLERS COMPANY LIMITED,** *q.v.*

2402 SCOTTISH HORTICULTURAL RESEARCH INSTITUTE
Mylnefield, Invergowrie, Dundee DD2 5DA Tel. 082-67 731
Research Institute

Enquiries, by letter only, to the Librarian

Subject coverage
horticulture in general; special reference to the strawberry and raspberry

2403 SCOTTISH MARINE BIOLOGICAL ASSOCIATION
Dunstaffnage Marine Research Laboratory, P.O. Box 3, Oban, Argyll PA34 4AD Tel. 0631 2244/6
Independent Organization; its Oceanographic Laboratory now part of the Institute for Marine Environmental Research, *q.v.*

Enquiries to the Director

Subject coverage
marine biology and ecology; oceanography; aquaculture

2404 SCOTTISH OFFICE
New St. Andrews House, Edinburgh EH1 Tel. 031-556 8400
Telex 727301

Government Department; the principal Scottish departments included are: Home and Health Department, Development Department, Economic Planning Department, Education Department, Department of Agriculture and Fisheries for Scotland and the Scottish Information Office

Enquiries to the Secretaries of the Departments as appropriate

Subject coverage
wide range of Scottish affairs, such as agriculture and fisheries, development in housing, roads, North Sea oil, transport, electricity

Publications
Listed in the H.M.S.O. Sectional List

2405 SCOTTISH ORNITHOLOGISTS CLUB
21 Regent Terrace, Edinburgh EH7 5BT Tel. 031-556 6042
Voluntary Club; houses an extensive Ornithological Reference Library

Enquiries to the Secretary

Subject coverage
birdwatching in Scotland; ornithology

Publication
Scottish Birds (quarterly, free to members or on subscription)

2406 SCOTTISH POISONS INFORMATION BUREAU
Royal Infirmary, Edinburgh EH3 9YW — Tel. 031-229 2477
Information Centre

Enquiries, from hospitals, other medical bodies or general practitioners only, to the Information Officer

Subject coverage
poisons, connected with drugs, plants, household, agriculture, industries, etc.

2407 SCOTTISH RECORD OFFICE
H.M. General Register House, Edinburgh EH1 3YY — Tel. 031-556 6585
Government Department

Enquiries to the Keeper of the Records of Scotland

Subject coverage
Scottish affairs, history, topography

SCOTTISH RESEARCH REACTOR CENTRE *now* **SCOTTISH UNIVERSITIES RESEARCH AND REACTOR CENTRE,** *q.v.*

SCOTTISH SCHOOL OF NON DESTRUCTIVE TESTING *see* **PAISLEY COLLEGE OF TECHNOLOGY**

2408 SCOTTISH SOCIETY FOR RESEARCH IN PLANT BREEDING
Scottish Plant Breeding Station, Pentlandfield, Roslin, Midlothian, Scotland EH25 9RF — Tel. 031-445 2171
State-aided Research Institute, of the Agricultural Research Council and the Department of Agriculture and Fisheries for Scotland

Enquiries to the Director or Information Officer; very specialised information or advice not available

Subject coverage
plant breeding; potatoes

Special collection
Commonwealth Potato Collection

Publications
Annual Report
Inventory of the Commonwealth Potato Collection

2409 SCOTTISH SUB-AQUA CLUB
16 Royal Crescent, Glasgow G3 7SL — Tel. 041-332 9291
Amateur Sports Organization; houses the National Diving Council for Scotland

Enquiries to the Secretary

Subject coverage
training of amateur divers

Publication
Scottish Diver (bi-monthly)

2410 SCOTTISH TOURIST BOARD
23 Ravelston Terrace, Edinburgh EH4 3EU — Tel. 031-332 2433
Telex 72272

Statutory Board

Enquiries, on policy, to the Chief Executive; for tourist information, to the Information Services Department

Subject coverage
tourism to/in Scotland

Publications
wide range of research books and leaflets

2411 SCOTTISH TRADES UNION CONGRESS
12 Woodlands Terrace, Glasgow G3 6DE Tel. 041-332 4946
Trade Unions Federation, of 79 trade unions and 46 trades councils

Enquiries to the General Secretary

Subject coverage
organization and representation of trade unionists in Scotland, in the economic, social, and employment fields

SCOTTISH TRAWLERS FEDERATION *see* **ABERDEEN FISHING VESSEL OWNERS ASSOCIATION**

2412 SCOTTISH UNIVERSITIES RESEARCH AND REACTOR CENTRE
East Kilbride, Glasgow G75 0QU Tel. 035-52 20222
Telex 77588

University Research Centre; formerly the Scottish Research Reactor Centre; includes the Isotope Geology Unit, the Health Physics and Nuclear Medicine Unit and the Radiocarbon Laboratory

Enquiries to the Director

Subject coverage
reactor physics, nuclear engineering and related topics; radiochemistry; activation analysis; provision of radioactive isotopes; tracer studies; nuclear medicine; health physics; isotope geology; isotope geochemistry; radiocarbon dating

Publications
Annual Report
Scientific reports

2413 SCREW THREAD TOOL MANUFACTURERS ASSOCIATION
Light Trades House, Melbourne Avenue, Sheffield S10 2QJ Tel. 0742 663084
Trade Association; member of the National Federation of Engineers Tool Manufacturers

Enquiries to the Secretary

Subject coverage
screw thread tool manufacturing industry; standardisation; metrication

2414 SCUNTHORPE DIVISIONAL LIBRARY
Carlton Street, Scunthorpe, Lincolnshire DN15 6TX Tel. 0724 60161
Telex 52369

Public Library, Division of the Humberside County Leisure Services Department; formerly the Scunthorpe Public Libraries and part of the Lindsey County Libraries

Enquiries to the Divisional Leisure Services Officer

Subject coverage
metallurgy; commerce

SEAFARERS EDUCATION SERVICE *see* **MARINE SOCIETY**

SEAL (SOUTH EAST AREA LIBRARY INFORMATION SERVICE) *see* **BEXLEY LIBRARIES AND MUSEUMS DEPARTMENT REFERENCE LIBRARY**

2415 SEALE-HAYNE AGRICULTURAL COLLEGE
Newton Abbot, Devonshire TQ12 6NQ Tel. 0626 2323
College of Further Education/Agricultural College

Enquiries to the Librarian

Subject coverage
agriculture; farm management; agricultural economics; food technology; veterinary science

Special collection
Devon County Veterinary Science Collection

2416 SEALOCRETE PRODUCTS LIMITED
Atlantic Works, Hythe Road, London NW10 6RU Tel. 01-969 9111
Telex 27950

Company

Enquiries to the Manager, Sales Office

Subject coverage
concrete admixtures, joint sealants, protective surface coatings, epoxy-resin-based materials

Publications
product technical publications

SEALS RESEARCH UNIT *now* **INSTITUTE FOR MARINE ENVIRONMENTAL RESEARCH,** *q.v.*

2417 SEDDON-ATKINSON VEHICLES LIMITED
P.O. Box 7, Oldham, Lancashire OL2 6HP Tel. 061-624 0566
Company; subsidiary of International Harvester Corporation; formed by the merger of Seddon Diesel Vehicles (Oldham) and Atkinson Vehicles (Preston)

No enquiry service

Subject coverage
heavy vehicles and road commercial vehicles

SEDGEFIELD BRANCH LIBRARY *see* **DURHAM COUNTY LIBRARY**

SEDGLEY DISTRICT LIBRARY *see* **DUDLEY PUBLIC LIBRARIES**

SEDGWICK GEOLOGY LIBRARY *see* **CAMBRIDGE UNIVERSITY, Department of Geology**

2418 SEDIMENTOLOGY RESEARCH LABORATORY
Reading University, Geology Department, Whiteknights, Reading, Berkshire RG6 2AH Tel. 0734 85123
University Department

Enquiries to the Librarian

Subject coverage
geology, including geophysics and geochemistry

Publications
Geological reports

SEED CRUSHERS AND OIL PROCESSORS ASSOCIATION *see* **FOOD MANUFACTURERS FEDERATION INCORPORATED**

SEED TESTING STATION OF ENGLAND AND WALES *see* **NATIONAL INSTITUTE OF AGRICULTURAL BOTANY**

2419 SEFTON METROPOLITAN BOROUGH LIBRARIES AND ARTS SERVICES
Bootle Library, Oriel Road, Bootle, Merseyside L20 7AG Tel. 051-922 4040
Telex 677112
Public Library Service; Sefton Metropolitan Borough is an amalgamation of the Boroughs of Bootle, Southport and Crosby and the Urban District Councils of Formby, Litherland, Aintree and Maghull; Reference Libraries at Southport, Crosby and Bootle

Enquiries to the Bibliographical Services Department, 244–246 Liverpool Road, Birkdale, Southport PR8 4PU (Tel. 0704 60144)

Subject coverage
general

2420 SEPARATION PROCESSES SERVICE
Atomic Energy Research Establishment, SPS, B351.28, Harwell, Oxfordshire OX11 0RA — Tel. 0235 24141 ext. 4652, Telex 83135
Government Service; provided by the Harwell Section and Warren Spring Laboratory, *q.v.*; of the Department of Industry; includes extensive data bank

Enquiries to the Information Officer, mainly from Members

Subject coverage
for the chemical and chemical engineering industries: centrifugation; crystallisation; drying; evaporation; filtration; gas cleaning; gas purification; liquid-liquid extraction; reverse osmosis; ultrafiltration

Publications
Reports and Digest of current information (monthly) for members only

SERVICES ELECTRONICS RESEARCH LABORATORIES *now* **ROYAL SIGNALS AND RADAR ESTABLISHMENT,** *q.v.*

SEVENOAKS DIVISIONAL LIBRARY *see* **KENT COUNTY LIBRARY**

2421 SEWELL'S PROFIT & INFORMATION UNIT
Bridge House, 15 Argyle Street, Bath BA2 4BD — Tel. 0225 60466
Company; formerly Ronald Sewell and Associates Limited

Enquiries to the Information Officer

Subject coverage
motor industry and its future; management

Publications
Books, booklets, reports

2422 SGRD LIMITED
Concord Road, Western Avenue, Acton, London W3 0SE — Tel. 01-992 7784
Company, formerly Simms Group Research and Development Limited; part of Lucas Industries

Enquiries to the Librarian

Subject coverage
automotive research, especially diesels; hydraulics research and testing; exhaust emission research and testing; noise and vibration testing; automated engine test control equipment

2423 SHEFFIELD CENTRE FOR ENVIRONMENTAL RESEARCH
299 Western Bank, Sheffield S10 2UD — Tel. 0742 70607
Company/Registered Charity

Enquiries to the Director

Subject coverage
environmental studies

Publications
List of Research Projects
List of Centre Occasional Papers

2424 SHEFFIELD CENTRE FOR INNOVATION AND PRODUCTIVITY
Sheffield Polytechnic, Halfords House, 16 Fitzalan Square, Sheffield S1 2BZ — Tel. 0742 20911, Telex 54680
Technical and Commercial Centre

Enquiries to the Director

Subject coverage
management and technical aid for small and medium firms; sources of equipment; in-plant training; consultancy

Publications
Journal article reprints
Seminar Notes, Case Studies, etc.
Publications List

2425 SHEFFIELD CITY LIBRARIES
Commerce and Technology Division, Central Library, Surrey Street, Sheffield S1 1XZ — Tel. 0742 734742/3/4 — Telex 54243
Public Library; includes the World Metal Index, *q.v.*; houses the Sheffield Interchange Organisation, *q.v.*

Enquiries to the Director

Subject coverage
in the Business Library: over 4000 British and foreign directories, and information files on overseas countries, local firms, national associations; Patent Office Index of World Trade Marks; in the Science and Technology Library: pure and applied sciences, especially metallurgy; standards

Special collections
U.K. Patents, 1617 to date
U.S. Patents, fifteen year file
British Standards; also ASTM, API, AM, ISO, NCB Standards; other foreign standards mainly on materials
Trade literature on steel and non-ferrous metals

Publications
Bibliographies

2426 SHEFFIELD CITY POLYTECHNIC
Eric Mensforth Library, Pond Street, Sheffield S1 1WB — Tel. 0742 20911 ext. 487 — Telex 54680
Polytechnic; formed by merger of Sheffield College of Technology and Sheffield Polytechnic

Enquiries to the Librarian

Subject coverage
general, scientific, technical, commercial

Special collection
European Documentation

Publications
Polytechnic Annual Research Report
Brief introduction to the major bibliographical tools
Concise guide to research literature, with a note on the structure of scientific and technical literature
Guide to the literature search, with notes on compiling a bibliography and on the structure of social science literature
Annual review series held in Sheffield Polytechnic Libraries
Abstracting and Indexing services
Management sources of information
Guide to the European Documentation Collection

2427 SHEFFIELD INTERCHANGE ORGANISATION (SINTO)
Commerce and Technology Division, Sheffield City Libraries, Central Library, Surrey Street, Sheffield S1 1XZ — Tel. 0742 734742/3/4 — Telex 54243
Interlibrary Co-operative Scheme; 68 members who are libraries of the region concerned with technical information

Enquiries to the Honorary Secretary

Subject coverage
technical, British patent and standards information; government publications; training

Special collections
World Metal Index
British Standards
British Patents

Publications
SINTO News (quarterly)
SINTO Review of Progress (annual)
Union List of Periodicals
Directory of Resources

2428 SHEFFIELD SAWMAKERS PROTECTION SOCIETY
27 Main Avenue, Totley, Sheffield S17 4FH Tel. 0742 361044
Trade Union

Enquiries to the Secretary

Subject coverage
sawmaking industry and conditions

2429 SHEFFIELD SMELTING COMPANY LIMITED
P.O. Box 28, Royds Mills, Windsor Street, Sheffield S4 7WD Tel. 0742 20966
Telex 54311

Company, subsidiary of Engelhard Minerals and Chemicals

Enquiries to the Librarian

Subject coverage
silver brazing alloys

2430 SHEFFIELD SPOON AND FORK BLANK MANUFACTURERS ASSOCIATION
179 Watt Lane, Sheffield S10 5RD Tel. 0742 25792
Trade Association

Enquiries to the Secretary

Subject coverage
manufacture of spoon and fork blanks

2431 SHEFFIELD UNIVERSITY LIBRARY
Western Bank, Sheffield S10 2TN Tel. 0742 78555
Telex 54348

University Library; the Biomedical Information Service is also at this address; the Applied Science Library is at St. Georges Square, Sheffield S1 3JD

Enquiries to the Head of Reader Services or the Information Section

Subject coverage
applied science, including glass technology; medicine and life sciences; architecture and planning; economic studies

Publications
Index to Theses 1920–1970
Guides to sources of information, by subjects
Lists of Journals, by subjects
Librarian's Annual Report

2432 SHEFFIELD UNIVERSITY LIBRARY
Applied Science Library, St. Georges Square, Sheffield S1 3JD Tel. 0742 78555 ext. 41
University Library

Enquiries to the Librarian

Subject coverage
engineering; metallurgy; geology

SHELL CENTRE *see* **SHELL U.K. LIMITED**

2433 SHELL CHEMICALS U.K. LIMITED
Carrington, Urmston, Manchester M31 4AJ Tel. 061-775 2601
Telex 667391

Company, part of Shell International Chemical Company Limited, Shell Centre, London SE1 7PG; the Library at the Carrington address was formerly Shell Research Library

Enquiries to the Manager, Library and Information Services

Subject coverage

polyethylene, polypropylene, and polystyrene plastics; polyolefins and their derivatives; petrochemicals

2434 SHELL RESEARCH LIMITED

Sittingbourne Research Centre, Broad Oak Road, Sittingbourne, Kent ME9 8AG — Tel. 0795 24444, Telex 96181

Company, member of the Royal Dutch Shell Group; Woodstock Laboratory now part of the Sittingbourne Centre, which comprises the Shell Biosciences Laboratory and the Shell Toxicology Laboratory

Enquiries to the Librarian

Subject coverage

agricultural chemicals; pesticides; toxicology; microbiology; biology

2435 SHELL RESEARCH LIMITED

Thornton Research Centre, P.O. Box 1, Chester CH1 3SH — Tel. 051-355 3755, Telex 62304

Company

Enquiries, by letter only, to the Information and Communications Division

Subject coverage

applicational research and development of fuels, lubricants and other petroleum products; combustion; lubrication; storage and transportation of petroleum

2436 SHELL U.K. LIMITED

Shell UK Administrative Services, Central Information and Documentation, UASC/3, Shell Centre, London SE1 7NA — Tel. 01-934 1234, Telex 919651

Company

Enquiries to the Librarian or Information Officer

Subject coverage

petroleum industry, including fuels, bitumen, lubricants; petrochemical industry, including solvents, synthetic detergents, thermoplastics, resins, synthetic rubbers; economic conditions; management

2437 SHELLFISH ASSOCIATION OF GREAT BRITAIN

Fishmongers Hall, London Bridge, London EC4R 9EL — Tel. 01-626 3531

Trade Association, part of the Fishmongers' Company; formerly the Oyster Merchants and Planters Association

Enquiries to the Director

Subject coverage

breeding, cultivation and sale of molluscs and crustacea

Publications

Annual Conference papers

SHEPWAY DIVISIONAL LIBRARY *see* **KENT COUNTY LIBRARY**

2438 SHETLAND LIBRARY

Lower Hillhead, Lerwick, Shetland ZE1 0EL — Tel. Lerwick 3868

Public Library, formerly Zetland County Library

Enquiries to the Chief Librarian

Subject coverage

Shetland; including its geography and agriculture

2439 SHIP AND BOAT BUILDERS NATIONAL FEDERATION
Boating Industry House, Vale Road, Weybridge, Surrey KT13 9NS Tel. 97 54511
Trade Association, of ten regional federated associations; for Group and other Associations, see list which follows; National Boat Shows Limited is housed at the London Offices, 31 Great Queen Street, London WC2B 5AD

Enquiries to the Secretary General

Subject coverage
labour relations; management; statistics; legislation; technical standards and safety; boating facilities

Publications
Statistical Review
Members Handbook
Publications List available

SHIP AND BOAT BUILDERS NATIONAL FEDERATION:
ASSOCIATION OF BRITISH SAILMAKERS
ASSOCIATION OF BRITISH YACHT AGENTS
BRITISH HIRE CRUISER FEDERATION
FISHING BOAT BUILDERS ASSOCIATION
MARINE ENGINE AND EQUIPMENT MANUFACTURERS ASSOCIATION
MARINE TRADES ASSOCIATION
NATIONAL YACHT HARBOUR ASSOCIATION
YACHT BROKERS, DESIGNERS AND SURVEYORS ASSOCIATION
NATIONAL FEDERATION OF SAILING SCHOOLS
YACHT CHARTER ASSOCIATION

2440 SHIP DEPARTMENT LIBRARY
Ministry of Defence (PE), Foxhill, Bath, Somerset BA1 5AB Tel. 6225 6911 ext. 3243
Government Department

Enquiries to the Librarian (as point of contact)

Subject coverage
shipbuilding and repair; marine engineering (electrical and mechanical)

2441 SHIPBUILDERS AND REPAIRERS NATIONAL ASSOCIATION
21 Grosvenor Place, London SW1X 7JE Tel. 01-235 5131
Telex 22797
Employers Association; includes the Maritime Transport Research Unit; houses the National Association of Marine Enginebuilders, *qq.v.*

Enquiries to the Information Officer

Subject coverage
shipbuilding; ship repairing; marine enginebuilding

Publications
Membership Book
Projected Reports on World Ship Demand
Bulletin (monthly)
Reports on maritime transport research

2442 SHIPBUILDING INDUSTRY TRAINING BOARD
Raebarn House, Northolt Road, South Harrow, Middlesex HA2 0DR Tel. 01-422 9581
Statutory Organization

Enquiries (on training matters only) to the Information Officer

Subject coverage
training in ship and boat building and repair

Publication
Training Policy Statement

SHIPLEY DISTRICT LIBRARY *see* **BRADFORD LIBRARIES**

2443 SHIPOWNERS REFRIGERATED CARGO RESEARCH ASSOCIATION

140 Newmarket Road, Cambridge CB5 8HE Tel. 0223 65101
Research Association

Enquiries to the Director

Subject coverage
refrigeration; air conditioning; transport of perishable cargoes; heat transfer

SHIPPING INFORMATION SERVICES *see* **LLOYDS REGISTER OF SHIPPING**

2444 SHIRLEY ALDRED AND COMPANY LIMITED

Sandy Lane, Worksop, Nottinghamshire S80 3EY Tel. 0909 6861/2/3
Telex 54625

Company; housing the Secretariat of the National Association of Charcoal Manufacturers

Enquiries to the Director

Subject coverage
wood carbonisation; charcoal production; wood gas production and distillation by-products; solvent recovery; chemical recovery; general chemical manufacture

SHIRLEY INSTITUTE *see* **COTTON SILK AND MAN-MADE FIBRES RESEARCH ORGANISATION**

2445 SHOE AND ALLIED TRADES RESEARCH ASSOCIATION (SATRA)

Rockingham Road, Kettering, Northamptonshire NM16 9JH Tel. 0536 3151
Telex 34323

Research Association

Enquiries to the Librarian or Information Officer

Subject coverage
shoe research and testing; testing of materials and components for the shoe industry; management and training in the industry

Publications
Footwear Digest (bi-monthly, abstracts)
Modern Shoemaking (bi-monthly)
Shoe Machinery Directory
Shoe Fairs List
Monthly Bulletin
World Footwear Statistical Reviews

2446 SHOP AND DISPLAY EQUIPMENT ASSOCIATION

18 Croydon Road, Caterham, Surrey CR3 6YR Tel. 22 48911
Trade Association, formerly National Display Equipment Association

Enquiries to the Director

Subject coverage
shop and display equipment industry

Publication
Intershop (exhibition catalogue)

2447 SHOREDITCH DISTRICT LIBRARY

Pitfield Street, London N1 6EX Tel 01-739 6981
Public Library of London Borough of Hackney Libraries, *q.v.*

Enquiries to the Librarian

Subject coverage
specialised trades and crafts; instruments; reprographic equipment; musical instruments & sound recording; ironmongery & hardware; furniture & upholstery; saddlery; footwear; gloves; bookbinding; clothing; brushes; fancy goods; toys

SHREWSBURY DISTRICT LIBRARY *see* **SHROPSHIRE COUNTY LIBRARY**

2448 SHREWSBURY TECHNICAL COLLEGE
London Road, Shrewsbury, Shropshire SY2 6PR — Tel. 0743 51544
College of Further Education

Enquiries to the Librarian

Subject coverage
mechanical and electrical engineering; business studies and commercial subjects; building and allied trades; general science and technology

Special collection
British Standards

2449 SHROPSHIRE COUNTY LIBRARY
Column House, 7 London Road, Shrewsbury, Shropshire SY2 6NW — Tel. 0743 52561
Telex 35187

Public Library Service; District Libraries at Bridgnorth, Ludlow, Oswestry, Shrewsbury, Whitchurch, Wrekin/Wellington

Enquiries to the County Librarian

Subject coverage
general

Publication
Shropshire Union List of Periodicals

SIADESIGN INFORMATION SERVICE *see* **SOCIETY OF INDUSTRIAL ARTISTS AND DESIGNERS LIMITED**

SILK AND MAN-MADE FIBRE USERS ASSOCIATION *now* **SILK ASSOCIATION LIMITED,** *q.v.*

2450 SILK ASSOCIATION LIMITED
c/o Rheinbergs Limited, Sovereign Way, Tonbridge, Kent TN9 1RN — Tel. 073-22 61357
Telex 95311

Trade Association; incorporated when the Silk and Man-made Fibre Users Association was liquidated; member of the International Silk Association; the Silk Education Service Unit is at 37 Chinbrook Road, Grove Park, London SE12 9TQ

Enquiries, educational, to the Silk Education Service; general, to the Association

Subject coverage
all aspects of silk, silk trade and promotion

Publication
Serica (monthly)

SIMMS GROUP RESEARCH AND DEVELOPMENT LIMITED *now* **SGRD LIMITED**

2451 SIMON ENGINEERING GROUP
Box 31, Cheadle Heath, Stockport, Cheshire SK3 0RT — Tel. 061-428 3600
Telex 669071

Company

Enquiries to the Head, Information and Library Services, or, for loans, to the Librarian

Subject coverage
chemical engineering; process plant; civil engineering; coal technology including coking; ore treatment; effluent treatment; bulk materials handling; flour milling; animal feed milling; container machinery

2452 SINO-BRITISH TRADE COUNCIL
25 Queen Annes Gate, London SW1 — Tel. 01-930 9545 and 9600
Telex 21332

Trade Council, sponsored by the Confederation of British Industry, London Chamber of Commerce and Industry, Associated British Chambers of Commerce, the China Association

Enquiries to the Secretariat

Subject coverage
promotion of trade between the U.K. and the People's Republic of China

Publication
British Industry (quarterly, in Chinese)
Sino-British Trade (monthly, in English)
Surveys of industry in China

SINTO *see* **SHEFFIELD INTERCHANGE ORGANISATION**

SIR BANNISTER FLETCHER LIBRARY *see* **ROYAL INSTITUTE OF BRITISH ARCHITECTS**

SIR JOHN CASS COLLEGE LIBRARY *now* **CITY OF LONDON POLYTECHNIC LIBRARY,** *q.v.*

SIR JOHN PRIESTMAN LIBRARY *see* **SUNDERLAND POLYTECHNIC**

2453 SIRA INSTITUTE LIMITED
South Hill, Chislehurst, Kent BR7 5EH — Tel. 01-467 2636
Telex 896649

Contract Research Institute; formerly British Scientific Instrument Research Association; includes the Siraid Enquiry Service

Enquiries to the Siraid Enquiry Service

Subject coverage
instrumentation, industrial, scientific, analytical, medical; process control; market research; safety and evaluation of instrumentation; optics, electro-optics and optical engineering

Publications
Techno-economic studies of the instrumentation industries
Market Reviews of countries which are major users of instrumentation

SITTINGBOURNE CENTRAL LIBRARY *now* **SWALE DIVISIONAL LIBRARY** *see* **KENT COUNTY LIBRARY**

SITTINGBOURNE RESEARCH CENTRE *see* **SHELL RESEARCH LIMITED**

2454 SKELMERSDALE DEVELOPMENT CORPORATION
Pennylands, Skelmersdale, Lancashire WN8 8AR — Tel. 0695 04242
Telex 628259

New Town Development Corporation

Enquiries to the Information and Research Officer

Subject coverage
new town development, Skelmersdale in particular

Special collection
Basic Plans of British New Towns (not for loan, but available for reference)

Publications
Brochures on the new town

SKINNERS LIBRARY *see* **CITY UNIVERSITY SKINNERS LIBRARY**

SKIPTON DIVISIONAL LIBRARY *see* **NORTH YORKSHIRE COUNTY LIBRARY**

SLEAFORD DIVISIONAL LIBRARY *see* **LINCOLNSHIRE LIBRARY SERVICE**

2455 SLOUGH COLLEGE OF HIGHER EDUCATION
Wellington Street, Slough, Buckinghamshire SL1 1YG — Tel. 75 34585
College of Higher Education, formerly Slough College of Technology

Enquiries to the Librarian

Subject coverage
management, including marketing, purchasing, personnel management; business, including law, accounting, banking, transport; catering; science; engineering; construction

SLOUGH DISTRICT LIBRARY *see* **BERKSHIRE COUNTY LIBRARY**

2456 SMALL FIRMS INFORMATION SERVICE
Abell House, John Islip Street, London SW1P 4LN Tel. 01-211 5245
Government Department, of the Department of Industry; Small Firms Information Centres in Birmingham, Bristol, Cardiff, Glasgow, Leeds, London, Luton, Manchester, Newcastle and Nottingham, *qq.v.*

Enquiries, general, to the above Division; advice and information from local Centres
Subject coverage
business problems, financial, technical and managerial
Publications
Small Firms Register of Research
Small Firms Information Centres: series of free booklets

SMALL RIVET ASSOCIATION *see* **BRITISH INDUSTRIAL FASTENERS FEDERATION**

SMALLER BUSINESSES ASSOCIATION *see* **SBA—ASSOCIATION OF INDEPENDENT BUSINESSES**

SMETHWICK DISTRICT LIBRARY *see* **SANDWELL PUBLIC LIBRARIES**

2457 SMITH & NEPHEW RESEARCH LIMITED
Gilston Park, Harlow, Essex Tel. 027-96 26751
Telex 81327

Company
Enquiries to the Head of the Information Department
Subject coverage
Organic & analytical chemistry; biomedical engineering; biochemistry; pharmacology; toxicology; pharmacy; microbiology; medicine; surgical dressings; textiles; polymer processing; ophthalmology; contact lenses

2458 SMITH KLINE AND FRENCH LABORATORIES LIMITED
Mundells, Welwyn Garden City, Hertfordshire AL7 1EY Tel. 070-73 25111
Telex 261347

Company, part of Smith Kline Corporation of America
Enquiries to the Librarian
Subject coverage
pharmaceutical sciences
Publications
booklets for the medical profession

2459 SOAP CANDLE AND EDIBLE FAT TRADES EMPLOYERS FEDERATION
P.O. Box 68, 2 Kingscote Street, London EC4P 4BQ Tel. 01-353 7474
Employers Organization
Enquiries to the Secretary
Subject coverage
terms and conditions of employment in the industry; health and safety

SOCIETY FOR ANALYTICAL CHEMISTRY *see* **CHEMICAL SOCIETY**

2460 SOCIETY FOR EARTHQUAKE AND CIVIL ENGINEERING DYNAMICS
Institution of Civil Engineers, 1–7 Great George Street, London SW1P 3AA Tel. 01-839 3611
Learned Society; Member of the International Association for Earthquake Engineering

Enquiries to the Secretary, who would suggest specific sources of help

Subject coverage
earthquakes; seismology etc., (but only indirectly)

Publications
Journal of the International Association for Earthquake Engineering – "Earthquake Engineering and Structural Dynamics" (published Wiley)
Proceedings of the Fourth European Symposium on Earthquake Engineering 1972

2461 SOCIETY FOR EXPERIMENTAL BIOLOGY
Harvest House, 62 London Road, Reading RG1 5AS Tel. 0734 861345
Learned Society

Enquiries to the Secretary

Subject coverage
comparative animal physiology; plant physiology; cell biology; other aspects of experimental biology

Publications
Annual Symposium Proceedings (C.U.P.)
Occasional "Summer Series" symposium volumes (C.U.P.)

2462 SOCIETY FOR GENERAL MICROBIOLOGY LIMITED
Harvest House, 62 London Rd., Reading, Berkshire RG1 5AS Tel. 0734 86134/7
Scientific Society; houses or provides services for a number of Societies, (list follows this entry)

Enquiries to the Executive Secretary or Membership Secretary

Subject coverage
biology and microbiology within the scope of the membership, to whom enquiries are routed

Publications
Journal of General Microbiology (monthly)
Journal of General Virology (monthly)
Proceedings of the Society (quarterly)
Symposia Volumes (annual)

SOCIETY FOR GENERAL MICROBIOLOGY LIMITED
ASSOCIATION FOR THE STUDY OF ANIMAL BEHAVIOUR
BOTANICAL SOCIETY OF THE BRITISH ISLES
BRITISH ECOLOGICAL SOCIETY, *q.v.*
BRITISH PHOTOBIOLOGY SOCIETY
BRITISH SOCIETY FOR PARASITOLOGY
BRITISH SOCIETY OF AUDIOLOGY
FEDERATION OF EUROPEAN MICROBIOLOGICAL SOCIETIES
INTERNATIONAL ASSOCIATION OF ECOLOGY
MAMMAL SOCIETY OF THE BRITISH ISLES, *q.v.*
SOCIETY FOR EXPERIMENTAL BIOLOGY, *q.v.*
WILD FLOWER SOCIETY

2463 SOCIETY FOR THE BIBLIOGRAPHY OF NATURAL HISTORY
British Museum (Natural History), Cromwell Road, London SW7 5BD
Private Society; member of the Institute of Biology, *q.v.*

Enquiries to the Secretary

Subject coverage
bibliography of natural history books, including dates of publications; location of rare books and of natural history manuscripts; biography of natural historians

Publications
Journal of the Society for the Bibliography of Natural History (bi-annual)
Sherborn Facsimile Series (occasional)

SOCIETY FOR THE DEVELOPMENT OF TECHNIQUES IN INDUSTRIAL MARKETING *see* **INDUSTRIAL MARKETING ASSOCIATION**

2464 SOCIETY FOR UNDERWATER TECHNOLOGY
1 Birdcage Walk, London SW1H 9JJ Tel. 01-930 8658
Learned Society

Enquiries to the General Secretary

Subject coverage
offshore, oceanic and underwater environment and technology, including diver training, sea bed engineering, fisheries and fish farming, sea law, submersibles; energy from the sea (wave power or tidal flow power)

Publication
Quarterly Journal
Proceedings of Meetings and Conferences

2465 SOCIETY OF ARCHITECTURAL AND ASSOCIATED TECHNICIANS
1–4 Argyll Street, London W1V 1AD Tel. 01-437 0976
Professional Institute; affiliated to the Royal Institute of British Architects, *q.v.*

Enquiries to the Society

Subject coverage
careers of architectural, quantity surveying and structural engineering technicians; the work involved; training programme

Publication
SAATnews (journal for members)

2466 SOCIETY OF BRITISH AEROSPACE COMPANIES LIMITED
29 King Street, St. James's, London SW1Y 6RD Tel. 01-839 3231
Telex 262274

Trade Association; Organisers of Farnborough Air Show

Enquiries to the Secretary

Subject coverage
aerospace manufacturing industry

Publications
Classified List of Members
Technical Specifications and standards

2467 SOCIETY OF BRITISH GAS INDUSTRIES
56/58 Holly Walk, Leamington Spa, Warwickshire Tel. 0926 34357
Trade Association

No enquiry service

Subject coverage
gas industry

2468 SOCIETY OF BRITISH MATCH MANUFACTURERS
P.O. Box 23, Fairfield Works, Fairfield Road, London E3 2QE Tel. 01-980 4321
Trade Association

Enquiries to the Secretary

Subject coverage
matches and match manufacturing

2469 SOCIETY OF BRITISH PRINTING INK MANUFACTURERS
Alembic House, 93 Albert Embankment, London SE1 7TU Tel. 01-735 3001 ext. 137
Telex 916672

Trade Association/Employers Association; member of the Chemical Industries Association Limited, the European Committee of Paint, Printing Ink and Artists Colours Manufacturers Associations and the U.S. National Association of Printing Ink Manufacturers

Enquiries to the Director

Subject coverage
printing ink industry

Publications
British Ink Maker (Batiste Publications)
Printing Ink Manual (Northwood Publications, new edition in preparation)

2470 SOCIETY OF BUSINESS ECONOMISTS
11 Bay Tree Walk, Watford, Hertfordshire WD1 3RX Tel. 92 37287
Company limited by guarantee

Enquiries to the Honorary Secretary

Subject coverage
business economics; forecasting

Publication
Journal (to members only)

2471 SOCIETY OF CABLE TELEVISION ENGINEERS
10 Avenue Road, Dorridge, Solihull, West Midlands B93 8LD Tel. 05645 4058
Technical Society; formerly Society of Relay Engineers

Enquiries to the Secretary

Subject coverage
cable television engineering

Publication
Cable Television Engineering (3 times per annum)

2472 SOCIETY OF CATERING AND HOTEL MANAGEMENT CONSULTANTS
Four, St. Margarets, Church Lane, Buxted, Uckfield, Sussex TN22 4LT Tel. 081-582 3329
Professional Association

Enquiries to the Secretary

Subject coverage
hotel, catering, tourism; market research; feasibility studies; planning and design; business systems; interior design; wine consultancy; property management; marine catering; oil rig catering; all services available at home and abroad

2473 SOCIETY OF INDUSTRIAL FURNACE ENGINEERS
301 Glossop Road, Sheffield S10 2HN Tel. 0742 21071
Telex 54170
Trade Association; formerly Society of Furnace Builders; Member of Metallurgical Plantmakers Federation, *q.v.* and the European Committee of Industrial Furnace and Heating Associations; associated with the Refractory Users Federation, *q.v.*

Enquiries to the Secretaries

Subject coverage
types of furnaces, kilns, etc.; services available

Publication
Buyers Guide

2474 SOCIETY OF INVESTMENT ANALYSTS
211–213 High Street, Bromley, Kent BR1 1NY Tel. 01-464 1081 1/2
Professional Society; Member of the European Federation of Financial Analysts Societies

Enquiries to the Secretary

Subject coverage
techniques of investment; stocks and shares; investment analysis; fund management; *not* investment advice

Publication
Investment Analyst (journal)

2475 SOCIETY OF LAUNDRY ENGINEERS AND ALLIED TRADES LIMITED
18a Northampton Square, London EC1V 0EJ Tel. 01-253 7132
Trade Association

Enquiries to the Secretary

Subject coverage
laundry and dry cleaning machinery and materials

2476 SOCIETY OF LEATHER TECHNOLOGISTS AND CHEMISTS LIMITED
National Leathersellers College, 176 Tower Bridge Road, London SE1 3LX Tel. 01-407 2544
Professional Society, formerly the Society of Leather Trades Chemists

Enquiries to the Honorary Secretary

Subject coverage
science, production and testing of leather and leather products

Publication
Journal of the Society of Leather Technologists and Chemists (bi-monthly)

2477 SOCIETY OF LICENSED AIRCRAFT ENGINEERS AND TECHNOLOGISTS
Grey Tiles, Kingston Hill, Kingston-upon-Thames, Surrey KT2 7LW Tel. 01-543 3249 *and* 1843
Professional Society; houses the International Federation of Airworthiness

Enquiries to the Secretary

Subject coverage
aircraft maintenance engineering education and training; qualifications; careers and employment matters; safety in aviation

Publications
Tech Air (monthly, free to members)
Guide to the Prospective Aircraft Maintenance Engineer
Engineer's Guide to Technical Writing
Mini-tests for Aircraft Engineers

2478 SOCIETY OF LITHOGRAPHIC ARTISTS, DESIGNERS, ENGRAVERS AND PROCESS WORKERS
55 Clapham Common (South Side), London SW4 9DF Tel. 01-720 7551
Trades Union

No enquiry service

Subject coverage
conditions of employment, etc., within the industry

2479 SOCIETY OF MOTOR MANUFACTURERS AND TRADERS LIMITED
Forbes House, Halkin Street, London SW1X 7DS Tel. 01-235 7000
Telex 21628
Trade Association; secretariat to the Garage Equipment Association, and the Fire Fighting Vehicle Manufacturers Association

Enquiries to the Press and Public Relations Manager

Subject coverage
statistics on vehicle and components sales, production, imports and exports; UK and international vehicle legislation; motor shows

Publications
Motor Industry of GB
Buyers Guide to the Motor Industry
Monthly Statistical Review
Summary of International Vehicle Legislation

2480 SOCIETY OF OCCUPATIONAL MEDICINE
Royal College of Physicians, 11 St Andrews Place, London NW1 4LE Tel. 01-486 2641
Learned Society

Enquiries to the Secretary

Subject coverage
occupational medicine, health technology, toxicology, mental health, hygiene; epidemiology; environmental health

Publications
Journal (quarterly)
Proceedings of Symposia

SOCIETY OF PROFESSIONAL ENGINEERS LIMITED *see* **SOCIETY OF ENGINEERS**

2481 SOCIETY OF RADIOGRAPHERS
14 Upper Wimpole Street, London W1M 8BN Tel. 01-935 5726
Professional Society

Enquiries to the Secretary

Subject coverage
radiography and allied subjects

Publication
Radiography (monthly)

SOCIETY OF RELAY ENGINEERS *now* **SOCIETY OF CABLE TELEVISION ENGINEERS,** *q.v.*

2482 SOCIETY OF SURVEYING TECHNICIANS
Aldwych House, Aldwych, London WC2B 4EL Tel. 01-242 4832
Independent Technical Society; founded by the Royal Institution of Chartered Surveyors

Enquiries to the Secretary

Subject coverage
all branches of surveying, *i.e.* agricultural, building, general practice, hydrographic, land, minerals, quantity; careers and training

Publication
Surveying Technician (bi-monthly)

2483 SOCIETY OF X-RAY TECHNOLOGY
4 Hillcrest, Sevenoaks, Kent TN13 3HN Tel. 0732 54210
Professional Society

Enquiries to the Honorary Secretary

Subject coverage
X-ray and electro-medical engineering

Publication
Bi-annual Journal

2484 SOIL AND WATER MANAGEMENT ASSOCIATION LIMITED
National Agricultural Centre, Stoneleigh, Warwickshire CV8 2LZ Tel. 0203 56151
Telex 31697

Registered Charity

Enquiries to the Technical Secretary

Subject coverage
technology of drainage, irrigation and all aspects of soil and water management; cultivation; farm waste

Publication
Quarterly Journal

2485 SOIL ASSOCIATION
Walnut Tree Manor, Haughley, Stowmarket, Suffolk IP14 3RS Tel. 044-970 235
Registered Charity; includes a Bookshop

Enquiries to the General Secretary

Subject coverage
relationship between soil, plant, animal and man; organic husbandry; horticulture; agriculture

Publications
Garden Compost
Make Your Plants Work For You
Value of Weeds
Self-sufficient Small Holding
Farming Organically

2486 SOIL MECHANICS LIMITED
Foundation House, Eastern Road, Bracknell, Berkshire RG12 2UZ Tel. 0344 24567
Telex 847253
Company; part of John Mowlem & Company Limited, *q.v.*; Engineering and Resources Consultants Limited, Geocomp U.K. Limited, Rock Mechanics Limited and E. Reader & Sons Limited are associated companies

Enquiries to the Librarian/Information Officer

Subject coverage
soil mechanics; rock mechanics; geology, hydrology; hydraulics; agriculture; piling; foundation engineering; mining; quarrying, dredging; tunnelling, cables & pipelines; underground storage; waste disposal; dams and reservoirs; power stations; building construction; site investigation; design services (particularly studies for soil & rock stability, vibration & earthquake); computer applications to foundation engineering; bridges; instrumentation; marine and sea bed investigations; training

Publications
Technical data sheets on Geotechnical Processes
Field testing sheets—soil mechanics
Computing services
Geocomp programmes list
Industrial Training

SOCIETY OF CIVIL ENGINEERING TECHNICIANS *see* **INSTITUTION OF CIVIL ENGINEERS**

SOCIETY OF COMMERCIAL ACCOUNTANTS LIMITED *now* **SOCIETY OF COMPANY AND COMMERCIAL ACCOUNTANTS,** *q.v.*

2487 SOCIETY OF COMPANY AND COMMERCIAL ACCOUNTANTS
40 Tyndalls Park Road, Bristol BS8 1PL Tel. 0272 38261
Professional Association; formed by the merger of the Society of Commercial Accountants, the Institute of Company Accountants and the Incorporated Association of Cost and Industrial Accountants

Enquiries, from members only, to the Secretary

Subject coverage
accounting; costing; financial management

2488 SOCIETY OF CONSULTING MARINE ENGINEERS AND SHIP SURVEYORS
6 Lloyds Avenue, London EC3N 3AX Tel. 01-488 3010
Professional Association

Enquiries to the Secretary

Subject coverage
the interests of consulting engineers, naval architects and ship surveyors; shipbuilding, maritime authorities activities

Publication
List of Members

2489 SOCIETY OF DAIRY TECHNOLOGY
172A Ealing Road, Wembley, Middlesex HA0 4QD Tel. 01-902 4464
Learned Society

Enquiries to the Secretary

Subject coverage
dairy science, technology and research, including husbandry, engineering and education

Publications
Journal of the Society of Dairy Technology (quarterly)
Pasteurising Plant Manual
UHT Processing of Dairy Products
Bottle Washing
Cream Processing Manual
Quality Control of Milk Products
Milk Products of the Future

2490 SOCIETY OF DYERS AND COLOURISTS
Perkin House, P.O. Box 244, 82 Grattan Road, Bradford, West Yorkshire BD1 2JB Tel. 0274 25138
Learned and Professional Society

Enquiries to the Technical and Education Officer

Subject coverage
colour science and technology; dyeing and printing; dye manufacture and application; textiles dyeing and printing

Special collection
Historical records on dye manufacture and use

Publications
Journal of the Society of Dyers and Colourists (includes abstracts on colour technology)
Review of Progress in Coloration and Related Topics (annual)
Colour Index (6-volume reference work on dyes & pigments)

2491 SOCIETY OF ELECTRONIC AND RADIO TECHNICIANS
8–10 Charing Cross Road, London WC2H 0HP Tel. 01-240 1152
Technical Institution; houses the Radio, TV, and Electronics Examination Board

Enquiries to the Secretary

Subject coverage
electronics

Publication
SERT Journal (ten times per annum)

2492 SOCIETY OF ENGINEERS
21/23 Mossop Street, London SW3 2LW Tel. 01-222 7244
Professional Association; houses also the Society of Professional Engineers Limited

Enquiries to the Secretary

Subject coverage
all branches of engineering

Publication
Journal and Transactions (quarterly)

SOCIETY OF FORESTERS OF GREAT BRITAIN *now* **INSTITUTE OF FORESTERS OF GREAT BRITAIN,** *q.v.*

SOCIETY OF FURNACE BUILDERS *now* **SOCIETY OF INDUSTRIAL FURNACE ENGINEERS,** *q.v.*

2493 SOCIETY OF GLASS TECHNOLOGY
20 Hallam Gate Road, Sheffield S10 5BT Tel. 0742 663168
Trade Association

Enquiries to the Librarian, Joint Library of Glass Technology, q.v.

Subject coverage
glass science and technology; chemical analysis; glass-making furnaces; hand-made glassware, physical properties of glass; refractories

Publications
Glass Technology (bi-monthly)
Physics and Chemistry of Glasses (bi-monthly)
Proceedings of the International Congresses on Glass
Bibliography of Glass (published by Dawsons)
Tank Blocks for Glass Furnaces
Glass Melting Tank Furnaces (translation from the German book by R. Gunther)

2494 SOCIETY OF INDUSTRIAL ARTISTS AND DESIGNERS LIMITED
12 Carlton House Terrace, London SW1Y 5AH Tel. 01-930 1911
Professional Organization; Founder Member of the International Council of Societies of Industrial Design and the International Council of Graphic Design Associations; Representative member of the International Federation of Interior Designers; operates the SIA Design Information Service

Enquiries to the Information Officer

Subject coverage
professional practice, copyright problems, arbitration within the profession; terms, conduct regulations, conditions of engagement; careers and training; industrial design, product and services information

Publications
on all subjects above
The Designer (monthly)

SOCIETY OF INDUSTRIAL CIVIL DEFENCE OFFICERS *now* SOCIETY OF INDUSTRIAL EMERGENCY SERVICES OFFICERS, *q.v.*

2495 SOCIETY OF INDUSTRIAL EMERGENCY SERVICES OFFICERS
c/o S.W. Electricity Board, Colston Avenue, Bristol BS1 4TS Tel. 0272 26062
Voluntary Association; formerly the Society of Industrial Civil Defence Officers

Enquiries to the Secretary

Subject coverage
emergency services in industry

SOIL SURVEY OF ENGLAND AND WALES *see* ROTHAMSTED EXPERIMENTAL STATION

SOIL SURVEY OF SCOTLAND *see* MACAULAY INSTITUTE FOR SOIL RESEARCH

2496 SOLARTRON-SCHLUMBERGER
Victoria Road, Farnborough, Hampshire GU14 7PW Tel. 0252 44433
Telex 858245
Private Company; formerly Solartron Electronics Group Limited

Enquiries to the Information Scientist

Subject coverage
electronic instrumentation; simulation for weapons, air traffic control and marine navigation; pressure measurement

2497 SOLIHULL PUBLIC LIBRARIES
Central Library, Homer Road, Solihull, West Midlands B91 3RG Tel. 021-705 1838
Public Library Service, twelve libraries

Enquiries to Chief Librarian

Subject coverage
general

2498 SOLIHULL TECHNICAL COLLEGE
Blossomfield Road, Solihull, West Midlands B91 1SB — Tel. 021-705 6376
Technical College

Enquiries to the Librarian

Subject coverage
business studies; engineering; home economics

2499 SOMERSET COLLEGE OF AGRICULTURE AND HORTICULTURE
Cannington, Bridgwater, Somerset
College of Further Education; formerly Somerset Farm Institute

Enquiries are not accepted

Special collection
amenity plants

2500 SOMERSET COLLEGE OF ARTS AND TECHNOLOGY
Wellington Road, Taunton, Somerset TA1 5AX — Tel. 0823 83403
Educational Establishment; formerly Taunton Technical College of Arts and Technology

Enquiries to the Tutor-Librarian

Subject coverage
building and surveying; business studies; catering and community services; engineering

2501 SOMERSET COUNTY LIBRARY
County Reference Library, Bridgwater Library, Binford Place, Bridgwater, Somerset TA6 3LF — Tel. 0278 2597; Telex 46211
Public Library Service; nine District Libraries; Bridgwater, Chard, Frome, Street, Taunton, Wells, West Somerset/Williton, Wincanton, Yeovil

Enquiries to the County Reference Librarian

Subject coverage
science, technology and commerce; particularly agriculture, chemical technology, architecture, transport, aeronautical engineering

Special collections
British Standards
Motor Car Workshop Manuals (over 1,000)

Publication
Union List of Periodicals in Somerset Libraries

SOMERSET FARM INSTITUTE *now* **SOMERSET COLLEGE OF AGRICULTURE AND HORTICULTURE,** *q.v.*

2502 SONDES PLACE RESEARCH LABORATORIES LIMITED
Sondes Place, Dorking, Surrey RH4 3EF — Tel. 0306 5901
Company, part of Steel Brothers and Company Limited

No enquiry service

Subject coverage
heat bonding of synthetic rubbers; testing of rubber samples and of the adhesive properties of tapes; design and manufacture of environmental test chambers

2503 SOUND RESEARCH LABORATORIES LIMITED
Holbrook Hall, Little Waldingfield, Sudbury, Suffolk CO10 0TH — Tel. 0787-24 595
Company

Enquiries to the Managing Director

Subject coverage
noise and vibration control; traffic noise; vehicle noise; auditoria acoustics; industrial noise control; laboratory testing; product development

Publications
Books:
Noise Control in Mechanical Services
Noise and Vibration Control in Industry
Course Lecture manuals:
Basic Vibration Control
Practical Building Acoustics
Airflow and Acoustic Measurements
Industrial Noise Control
Mechanical Services Noise Control
Technical reports

2504 SOUNDWELL TECHNICAL COLLEGE
St Stephens Road, Soundwell, Bristol BS16 4RL — Tel. 0272 675101
Technical College

Enquiries to the Librarian

Subject coverage
business and management; retailing; basic engineering; printing and packaging; history of railways

2505 SOUTH AFRICAN EMBASSY
Office of the Scientific Counsellor, Chichester House, High Holborn, London WC1V 7HE — Tel. 01-242 1766, Telex 27275
South African Government Statutory Body; of the South African Council for Scientific and Industrial Research; formerly South African Science Office

Enquiries to the Scientific Counsellor

Subject coverage
scientific and industrial research in South African Universities

Publications
South African Council for Scientific and Industrial Research Reports
South African Atomic Energy Board Reports

2506 SOUTH BRISTOL TECHNICAL COLLEGE
Marksbury Road, Bedminster, Bristol BS3 5JL — Tel. 0272 661105
College; formerly South Bristol College of Further Education

Enquiries to the Librarian

Subject coverage
business studies and general studies; engineering and electrical engineering

2507 SOUTH DORSET TECHNICAL COLLEGE
Newstead Road, Weymouth, Dorset DT4 0DX — Tel. 030-57 3133
College of Further Education

Enquiries to the Tutor-Librarian

Subject coverage
catering; construction; business studies; management; electrical and mechanical engineering; biology; chemistry; mathematics; computer studies; physics

SOUTH EAST AREA LIBRARY INFORMATION SERVICE (SEAL) *see* **BEXLEY LIBRARIES AND MUSEUMS REFERENCE DEPARTMENT**

2508 SOUTH EASTERN ASSOCIATION OF STEEL STOCKHOLDERS
Lennig House, Masons Avenue, Croydon CR9 3NU — Tel. 01-686 7957
Trade Association, part of the National Association of Steel Stockholders

Enquiries to the Secretariat

Subject coverage
source of supply of steels

2509 SOUTH EASTERN UNION OF SCIENTIFIC SOCIETIES
53 The Drive, Shoreham-by-Sea, Sussex Tel. 079-17 2478
Group of amateur societies, affiliated to the British Association and other bodies

Enquiries to the Honorary Secretary

Subject coverage
local botany, zoology, archaeology and geology

2510 SOUTH GLAMORGAN COUNTY LIBRARIES
Headquarters, Central Library, The Hayes, Cardiff CF1 2QU Tel. 0222 22116
Telex 497416

Public Library Service; includes the Cardiff Public Libraries

Enquiries to the County Librarian

Subject coverage
general science, technology and commerce, especially industry and commerce in Wales; Welsh manufacturers and products; transport

Special collection
British Standards

2511 SOUTH GLAMORGAN INSTITUTE OF FURTHER AND HIGHER EDUCATION
Colchester Avenue, Cardiff CF3 7XR Tel. 22121
College of Further and Higher Education; formerly College of Food Technology and Commerce

Enquiries to the Librarian

Subject coverage
Food; nutrition; cookery; catering

2512 SOUTH KENT COLLEGE OF TECHNOLOGY
Kingsnorth Gardens, Folkestone, Kent Tel. 0303 56661
Technical College; associated units in Ashford and Dover

Enquiries to the Librarian

Subject coverage
business studies; engineering; construction; catering

2513 SOUTH LONDON BOTANICAL INSTITUTE
323 Norwood Road, London SE24 9AQ Tel. 01-674 5787
Scientific Institute/Limited Company

Enquiries to the Honorary Secretary

Subject coverage
botany

Special collection
An extensive herbarium, including the Beeby Collection from the Orkneys and Shetlands

SOUTH RIBBLE DISTRICT CENTRAL LIBRARY *see* **LANCASHIRE LIBRARY**

SOUTH SHIELDS CENTRAL LIBRARY *now* **SOUTH TYNESIDE LIBRARY,** *q.v.*

2514 SOUTH SHIELDS MARINE AND TECHNICAL COLLEGE
St. Georges Avenue, South Shields, County Durham NE34 6ET Tel. 089-43 60403
Technical College

Enquiries to the Librarian

Subject coverage
navigation; marine engineering; radar and radio; seamanship

2515 SOUTH THAMES COLLEGE
Wandsworth High Street, London SW18 2PP Tel. 01-874 2355
College of Further Education; formerly Wandsworth Technical College

Enquiries to the Librarian

Subject coverage
computer technology; electrical and electronic engineering; mechanical engineering; educational technology

2516 SOUTH TYNESIDE LIBRARY
Catherine Street, South Shields, Tyne and Wear NE33 2PP Tel. 08943 68841
Public Library, formed by the merger of South Shields Public Library with several branches from Durham County Library

Enquiries to the Librarian

Subject coverage
general; shipbuilding

2517 SOUTH WEST LONDON COLLEGE
Tooting Broadway, London SW17 0TQ Tel. 01-672 2441
College for Higher Business Studies

Enquiries to the Librarian

Subject coverage
accountancy; banking; business management; commercial law; company secretaryship; data processing; economics; geography; investment; marketing; office management; personnel administration; statistics; training

2518 SOUTHALL COLLEGE OF TECHNOLOGY
26 Beaconsfield Road, Southall, Middlesex UB1 1DP Tel. 01-571 1740
College of Further Education

Enquiries to the Librarian, Library and Resources Centre

Subject coverage
electrical and electronic engineering; mechanical, production and aeronautical engineering; materials science; plastics technology; construction; educational technology

Special collection
history of civil commercial aviation in the U.K.

2519 SOUTHALL DISTRICT LIBRARY
Osterley Park Road, Southall, Middlesex UB2 4BL Tel. 01-574 3412
Public Library; District Library of the London Borough of Ealing Library Service

Enquiries, by letter, to the District Librarian; by telephone, to the District Reference Librarian

Subject coverage
general; science and technology

Special collection
British Standards

2520 SOUTHAMPTON COLLEGE OF TECHNOLOGY
East Park Terrace, Southampton SO9 4WW Tel. 0703 29381
College of Technology

Enquiries to the Librarian

Subject coverage
civil, production, marine, chemical and mechanical engineering; mathematics; computing; business studies; management; town and country planning; naval architecture; yacht and boatyard management; yacht and boat design

2521 SOUTHAMPTON DISTRICT LIBRARY
Civic Centre, Southampton SO9 4XP Tel. 0703 23855
Telex 47331

Public Library; District Library of Hampshire County Library

Enquiries to the Librarian

Subject coverage
U.K. and international commerce, shipping, marine transport, containerization, ocean and air transport; celestial navigation; nautical almanacks and chronology; petroleum technology; economics; oils; fats; waxes; metallurgy; critical path method

Special collections
Maritime collections, including a collection on the Titanic disaster
Pitt collection of 17th and 18th century scientific books

2522 SOUTHAMPTON SCHOOL OF NAVIGATION
Warsash, Southampton SO3 6ZL Tel. 048-95 6161
Training Establishment for Merchant Navy Officers, administered by Hampshire County Council; formerly part of Southampton University

Enquiries to the Librarian

Subject coverage
navigation; seamanship; cargo handling; marine engineering; marine law; naval architecture; maritime history; marine transport economics; shipping; meteorology; oceanography; yachting; hydrographic surveying

2523 SOUTHAMPTON UNIVERSITY LIBRARY
University Road, Highfield, Southampton SO9 5NH Tel. 0703 559122 ext. 2180 *or* 452
Telex 47661
University Library; includes the Wessex Medical Libraries (University Branch, Medical and Biological Sciences Building, Bassett Crescent East, Southampton SO9 3TU and General Hospital Branch, Southampton General Hospital, Tremona Road, SO9 4XY)

Enquiries to the Sub-Librarian, Reader Service; for the Wessex Medical Libraries, to the Medical Sub-Librarian

Subject coverage
to support the Faculty of Medicine; Faculty of Science with Departments of Biology, Chemistry, Electronics, Geology, Mathematics, Oceanography, Physics, Physiology and Biochemistry; Faculty of Engineering with Departments of Aeronautics and Astronautics, Civil Engineering, Electrical Engineering, Mechanical Engineering, Institute of Sound and Vibration Research

Special collection
Perkins Agricultural Collection (books published before 1901)

Publications
Catalogue of the Perkins Collection
User Guides, *e.g.* Biological Information

SOUTHAMPTON UNIVERSITY *see also*
GAS BEARING ADVISORY SERVICE
INDUSTRIAL AERODYNAMICS UNIT
INSTITUTE OF SOUND AND VIBRATION RESEARCH
WOLFSON ELECTROSTATICS ADVISORY UNIT
WOLFSON MARINE CRAFT UNIT
WOLFSON MATERIALS ADVISORY SERVICE
WOLFSON UNIT FOR NOISE AND VIBRATION CONTROL

SOUTHEND CENTRAL LIBRARY *see* **ESSEX COUNTY LIBRARY**

2524 SOUTHEND COLLEGE OF TECHNOLOGY
Caernarvon Road, Southend-on-Sea, Essex SS2 6LS Tel. 0702 353931
College of Technology

Enquiries to the Librarian

Subject coverage
general and technical

Special collection
British Standards

SOUTHERN BRICK FEDERATION *see* **BRICK DEVELOPMENT ASSOCIATION**

2525 SOUTHERN TESTING LABORATORIES
Herontye, East Grinstead, West Sussex RH19 1RB — Tel. 0342 24442
Company, subsidiary of BMMK and Partners, of the same address

Enquiries to the Company

Subject coverage
road materials, bituminous materials; soil mechanics; civil engineering materials

SOUTHGATE DISTRICT LIBRARY *see* **PALMERS GREEN MAIN LIBRARY**

2526 SOUTHGATE TECHNICAL COLLEGE
High Street, Southgate, London N14 6BS — Tel. 01-886 652
Technical College

Enquiries to the Librarian

Subject coverage
general, technical

Special collection
radio/television service sheets (for reference only)

SOUTHPORT DISTRICT LIBRARY *see* **SEFTON METROPOLITAN BOROUGH LIBRARIES AND ARTS SERVICE**

2527 SOUTHWARK LIBRARY SERVICES
20–22 Lordship Lane, London SE22 8HN — Tel. 01-693 9221
Public Library Services; two District Libraries: Dulwich and Newington

Enquiries to the Librarian

Subject coverage
pure science; mathematics; computer programming; astronomy; leather and tanning industry; geology; zoology

Special collections
in communication and computer programming housed at Newington District Library, 155 Walworth Road, London SE17 1RS (01-703 5529)

SPALDING/BOSTON DIVISIONAL LIBRARY *see* **LINCOLNSHIRE LIBRARY SERVICE**

2528 SPECIAL METALS (FABRICATION) LIMITED
Purdey's Way, Sutton Road, Romford, Essex SS4 1NB — Tel. 0702 545861
Telex 995178

Company; subsidiary of Thermal Syndicate Limited, *q.v.*

Enquiries to the Managing Director

Subject coverage
fabrication of special refractory metals, including tungsten and molybdenum into components for high temperature applications; fabrication of special corrosion-resistant metals and alloys, including tantalum, titanium, zirconium, Hastelloy and nickel alloys, into rod, sheet and wire, for pumps for chemical plant, heat exchangers, condensers and storage vessels, for use at high temperatures; explosive-clad titanium-on-steel vessels

Publications
Catalogues

2529 SPECIAL STEELS USER ADVISORY CENTRE
British Steel Corporation, Swinden House, Moorgate, Rotherham, Yorkshire S60 3AR — Tel. 0709 73661
Telex 547279
Company Advisory Service; replaced the Stainless Steel Development Association

Enquiries to the Commercial Information Officer

Subject coverage
technical, commercial, or marketing information on any aspect of alloy, stainless and special carbon steel rolled products, iron and steel castings, forgings and engineering plant; steel selection properties, performance, fabrication and manipulation; sources of supply

Special collection
Card index of manufacturers of end products in stainless steel

SPENBOROUGH PUBLIC LIBRARY *see* **KIRKLEES LIBRARIES AND MUSEUM SERVICES**

2530 SPERRY GYROSCOPE COMPANY LIMITED
Downshire Way, Bracknell, Berkshire RG12 1QL Tel. 0344 3222
Telex 848129

Company, Division of Sperry Rand Corporation

Enquiries to the Librarian

Subject coverage
navigation guidance control systems for ships, aircraft and guns; memory systems for computers

2531 SPHERE ENVIRONMENTAL CONSULTANTS LIMITED
Knightsbridge House, 197 Knightsbridge, London SW7 1RN Tel. 01-584 6171
Company/Consultancy; part of Inbucon Limited

Enquiries, general, to the Technical Information Department; (detailed enquiries on a fee-paying basis)

Subject coverage
environmental, regional and economic problems; impact studies related to North Sea oil industry, petrochemical and other process industries; planning for New Towns and existing urban areas; airports

2532 SPILLERS LIMITED
Old Change House, 4–6 Cannon Street, London EC4M 6XB Tel. 01-248 5700
Telex 888787

Company

Enquiries to the Group Information Officer

Subject coverage
food industry (product and company information); agriculture

2533 SPORTS TURF RESEARCH INSTITUTE
Bingley, West Yorkshire BD16 1AU Tel. 097-66 5131
Company

Enquiries to the Director

Subject coverage
U.K. and overseas research findings on all aspects of turfgrass (amenity grass) use; construction and maintenance of turfgrass areas, particularly for sport and recreation

Publications
Journal of the Sports Turf Research Institute (annual)
Bulletin of the Sports Turf Research Institute (quarterly)

2534 SPRING RESEARCH AND MANUFACTURERS ASSOCIATION
Henry Street, Sheffield S3 7EQ Tel. 0742 70771
Research and Trade Association; formerly Spring Research Association

Enquiries to the Industrial Liaison Officer or the Commercial Officer

Subject coverage
spring technology; design study and investigation of failures in springs and materials; technical, contract, testing and inspection services; training; metrication; relevant foreign standards

Publications
Spring Journal
Newsletter
Research reports
Springs: materials/design/manufacture (a manual)
Publications List

2535 SPRINGBURN COLLEGE OF ENGINEERING
110 Flemington Street, Glasgow G21 4BX Tel. 041-558 9001
College of Further Education

Enquiries to the Librarian

Subject coverage
electrical, fabrication, automobile, mechanical and industrial engineering

SPRINGFIELDS REACTOR FUEL ELEMENT LABORATORIES *see* **UNITED KINGDOM ATOMIC ENERGY AUTHORITY, Reactor Group**

STAFFORD DISTRICT LIBRARY *see* **STAFFORDSHIRE COUNTY LIBRARY**

2536 STAFFORDSHIRE COUNTY LIBRARY
Friars Terrace, Stafford ST17 4AY Tel. 0785 3121 ext. 8350
Telex 36255

Public Library Service; nine regional/district libraries: Cannock, Lichfield, Brewood, Stafford, Leek, Stoke on Trent, Burton upon Trent, Tamworth, Newcastle-under-Lyme; administrative headquarters for MISLIC and LINOSCO

Enquiries to the County Librarian

Subject coverage
general; coal mining; brewing; pottery and ceramics industry

Special collections
British Standards
Solon Collection (ceramics)

STAINLESS STEEL DEVELOPMENT ASSOCIATION *now* **SPECIAL STEELS USER ADVISORY SERVICE,** *q.v.*

2537 STAINLESS STEEL FABRICATORS ASSOCIATION OF GREAT BRITAIN
75 Harborne Road, Birmingham B15 3DH Tel. 021-454 6171
Trade Association

Enquiries to the Secretary

Subject coverage
fabrication of stainless steel

Publication
List of members and products including technical data

STALYBRIDGE PUBLIC LIBRARY *see* **TAMESIDE LIBRARIES**

STANDARD BOOK NUMBERING AGENCY LIMITED *see* **J. WHITAKER AND SONS LIMITED**

2538 STANDARD TELECOMMUNICATIONS LABORATORIES LIMITED
London Road, Harlow, Essex CM17 9NA Tel. 0279 29531
Telex 81151

Company; subsidiary of International Telephone and Telegraph Corporation, New York

Enquiries to the Chief Technical Information Officer

Subject coverage
electrical and electronic engineering, particularly telecommunication theory and practice; physics; chemistry; metallurgy; rubber; plastics; computers

Publication
Electrical Communication (ITT House Journal)

2539 STANDARD TELEPHONES & CABLES LIMITED
STC House, 190 Strand, London WC2R 1DU Tel. 01-836 8055
Telex 22385
Manufacturing Company; subsidiary of International Telephone and Telegraph Corporation, U.S.A. (ITT); for the Laboratories, *see* Standard Telecommunication Laboratories

Enquiries to the Public Relations Department

Subject coverage
telecommunications; electronics; radio and TV manufacture

Publications
STC News (employee newspaper)
Tie-Line (external magazine)
Electrical Communication (technical journal)
Annual Report

STANDING CONFERENCE FOR TECHNICIAN ENGINEERS AND TECHNICIANS LIMITED *see* **INCORPORATED PRACTITIONERS IN RADIO AND ELECTRONICS LIMITED**

2540 STANDING CONFERENCE OF CO-OPERATIVE LIBRARY AND INFORMATION SERVICES (SCOCLIS)
Technical Library, Central Library, Albion Street, Hull HU1 3TF Tel. 0482 224040
Enquiries to the Honorary Secretary

Subject coverage
local library co-operative schemes; range of activities of such schemes; library service to industry and commerce

Publications
SCOCLIS News (3 times per annum)
SCOCLIS Directory (annual)
SCOCLIS members Publications

STANDISH GROUP LIBRARY *see* **WIGAN METROPOLITAN BOROUGH REFERENCE LIBRARIES**

2541 STANFORD RESEARCH INSTITUTE
Carolyn House, Dingwall Road, Croydon CR9 3QX Tel. 01-681 1751
Telex 946125
Independent, not-for-profit Research Institute, of eight Divisions

Enquiries to the Marketing Director or Business Intelligence Program Director

Subject coverage
business planning; industrial research, finance and economics; management; market assessments

Publications
Reports
Brochures on the activities of the Divisions

2542 R.H.H. STANGER LIMITED
The Laboratories, Fortune Lane, Elstree, Hertfordshire WD6 3HQ Tel. 01-953 1306
Company; Independent Testing Laboratories
Enquiries to the Librarian

Subject coverage
information on, and testing of, concrete, building materials, soils, road and engineering materials, metals, paints, plastics, structures; general chemistry

Publications
Newsletters
Company Brochure

2543 STANILAND HALL ASSOCIATES LIMITED
1A Camden Walk, London N1 8DY Tel. 01-359 6054
Advisory and Consultancy Company

Enquiries to the Director

Subject coverage
economic and business forecasts for corporate planning, etc., including U.K. and other European economics, industrial forecasts, costs and prices, consumer spending by sector, capital spending (especially construction)

Publications
Consumer Spending Forecasts (quarterly, U.K.)
Leaflets on industries and markets

STANLEY BRANCH LIBRARY *see* **DURHAM COUNTY LIBRARY**

2544 STANTON & STAVELEY LIMITED
P.O. Box 72, Stanton, Nottingham NG10 5AA Tel. 060-72 322121
Telex 37671/2

Company, part of the British Steel Corporation

Enquiries to the Technical Librarian (ext. 202)

Subject coverage
technology and manufacture of cast irons, including ductile iron; products made from those irons, including engineering castings, pipes, tunnel linings; concrete pipes and lighting columns; reinforced plastics matrix (RPM) pipes; iron powder components

Publications
Brochures

2545 STATISTICS AND MARKET INTELLIGENCE LIBRARY
Export House, 50 Ludgate Hill, London EC4M 7HU Tel. 01-248 5757 exts. 368/369
Telex 886143

Government Department, of the Department of Industry

Enquiries to the Librarian

Subject coverage
foreign economic statistics, comprehensive for trade, selective elsewhere; published official U.K. statistics; foreign development plans; foreign market research reports; overseas trade catalogues

Publications
Bibliographies (irregular) *in* Sources of Statistics and Market Information Series
National Statistical Offices of Overseas Countries (annual)

2546 STATISTICS GROUP
Cambridge University, Department of Applied Biology, Tel. 0223 58381
Pembroke Street, Cambridge CB2 3DX
Government Research Unit, of the Agricultural Research Council

Enquiries to the Officer-in-charge

Subject coverage
statistics for agricultural and biological research

STAVELEY INDUSTRIES LIMITED *see* **BRITISH SALT LIMITED**

2547 STEEL CASTINGS RESEARCH AND TRADE ASSOCIATION
5 East Bank Road, Sheffield S2 3PT Tel. 0742 28647
Telex 54281

Research Association

Enquiries to the Information Officer

Subject coverage
steelfoundry practice; metallurgy; quality assurance; non-destructive testing; steelmaking; moulding materials; surface treatment; training

STEEL SHEET INFORMATION CENTRE *see* **BRITISH STEEL CORPORATION, Technical Information Systems**

2548 STEEL WINDOW ASSOCIATION
Building Centre, 26 Store Street, London WC1E 7JR Tel. 01-637 3571/2
Trade Association; member of the Metal Window Federation Limited, *q.v.*

Enquiries to the Director

Subject coverage
manufacture, supply and installation of hot-rolled section—hot dip galvanized, standard and purpose-made steel windows

Publications
Specification for Metric Preferred Range W.20 Steel Windows
Guide to Fixing
Specifiers' Guide to Zinc Coated Steel Windows
Strength of Fixings: specifiers' guide
Window Performance: specifiers' guide
Module 100 Standard Steel Windows—metric sizes

2549 STEETLEY COMPANY LIMITED
Research Department, Carlton Road, Worksop, Tel. 0909 3441
Nottinghamshire S81 7QG Telex 54124
Company; formerly Steetly Organization; Berk Spencer Acids Limited (*q.v.*) is a subsidiary

Enquiries to the Information Officer or Librarian

Subject coverage
ceramic and refractories technology and silicate science; acids; fine chemicals; industrial minerals especially clays

STEVENAGE CENTRAL LIBRARY *see* **HERTFORDSHIRE LIBRARY SERVICE, Technical Book Service**

STEVENAGE LABORATORY *see* **WATER RESEARCH CENTRE**

2550 STILTON CHEESE MAKERS ASSOCIATION
Midland Bank Chambers, High Street, Melton Mowbray, Tel. 0664 3606
Leicestershire LE13 0TU
Trade Association; affiliated to the Creamery Proprietors Association

Enquiries to the Secretary

Subject coverage
Stilton cheese: all matters including manufacture, methods of storing and serving; sources of supply

2551 STIRLING DISTRICT LIBRARY
Spittal Street, Stirling FK8 1DY Tel. 0786 3131
Public Library; its constituent parts were formerly Stirling Public Library, Stirling County Library and part of Perth County Library

Enquiries to the Reference Librarian

Subject coverage
general

2552 STIRLING UNIVERSITY LIBRARY
Stirling, Scotland FK9 4LA Tel. 0786 3171
Telex 778874

University Library; houses the Resources Centre

Enquiries to the Librarian

Subject coverage
general

2553 STOCK EXCHANGE
London EC2N 1HP Tel. 01-588 2355
Telex 886557

Authority of Broker Members; Units in Belfast, Dublin, Birmingham, Manchester and Glasgow

Enquiries to Public Relations Departments

Subject coverage
history and functioning of the Stock Exchange; lists of stockbrokers; visits, etc.

Publications
general literature only

2554 STOCKPORT CENTRAL LIBRARY
Wellington Road South, Stockport, Cheshire SK1 3RS Tel. 061-480 2966/3038
Telex 667184

Public Library; two Branch Libraries; Stockport and Cheadle

Enquiries to the Assistant Director

Subject coverage
general; commerce; local government; specialist subjects are—advanced mathematics; mechanics; heat; light; sound; personnel management; dogs, cats, and other pets; paediatrics

Publications
Local Government Information Bulletin (weekly)
Focus (bi-monthly)

2555 STOCKPORT COLLEGE OF TECHNOLOGY
Wellington Road South, Stockport, Cheshire SK1 3UQ Tel. 061-480 7331
College of Technology, formerly Stockport College for Further Education; includes the Industrial Liaison Centre (tel. 061-480 3847)

Enquiries to the College Librarian or to the Industrial Liaison Officer

Subject coverage
civil, mechanical, production and electrical engineering; chemistry; biological sciences; building; management and business studies; information and advice on production problems, processes, design, materials testing, low cost automation

Special collection
British Standards

STOCKTON DISTRICT LIBRARY *see* **CLEVELAND COUNTY LIBRARY**

2556 STOCKTON-BILLINGHAM TECHNICAL COLLEGE
The Causeway, Billingham, Teesside TS23 2DB Tel. 0642 552101
College of Further Education

Enquiries to the Librarian; engineering, construction and *British Standard enquiries to the Librarian at Stockton-Billingham Technical College, Oxbridge Avenue, Stockton-on-Tees, Cleveland (Stockton 62317 ext. 33)*

Subject coverage
management; business studies; food; engineering; construction; nursing; health and occupational health; industrial safety

Special collection
British Standards

STOKE NEWINGTON PUBLIC LIBRARY *see* **HACKNEY CENTRAL LIBRARY**

STOKE-ON-TRENT CITY DISTRICT LIBRARY *see* **STAFFORDSHIRE COUNTY LIBRARY**

STOKE-ON-TRENT COLLEGE OF BUILDING AND COMMERCE *now* **CAULDON COLLEGES OF FURTHER EDUCATION,** *q.v.*

STONEWARE POTTERS ASSOCIATION *now* **BRITISH STONEWARE POTTERS ASSOCIATION,** *q.v.*

2557 STORAGE EQUIPMENT MANUFACTURERS ASSOCIATION
7 Ludgate Broadway, London EC4V 6DX Tel. 01-248 1661
Trade Association

Enquiries to the Secretary

Subject coverage
storage equipment, (racking, shelving, etc.)

Publications
Code of Practice for the Use of Static Racking
Terms and Descriptions of Storage Equipment (terminology)

STOURBRIDGE DISTRICT LIBRARY *see* **DUDLEY PUBLIC LIBRARIES**

2558 STOW COLLEGE
43 Shamrock Street, Glasgow G4 9LD Tel. 041-332 1786
College of Further Education, formerly Stow College of Engineering

Enquiries to the Teacher-Librarian

Subject coverage
mechanical, civil, electrical, and production engineering; biological sciences; mathematics; management; chemistry; physics; metallurgy

STRATFORD-UPON-AVON DIVISIONAL LIBRARY *see* **WARWICKSHIRE COUNTY LIBRARY**

2559 STRATHCLYDE REGIONAL LIBRARY AND RESOURCE SERVICE
Lanark Division, 4 Auchingramont Road, Hamilton ML3 6JU Tel. 069-82 22032
Public Library Service

Enquiries to the Principal Educational Resources Librarian

Subject coverage
school libraries and resources services; general

2560 STRATHCLYDE UNIVERSITY LIBRARY
The Andersonian Library, McCance Building, 16 Richmond Street, Glasgow G1 1XQ Tel. 041-552 4156 Telex 77472
University Library; the University houses the Strathclyde Business School

Enquiries to the University Librarian

Subject coverage
mathematics; physics, chemical and materials sciences; mechanical, chemical, civil, mining, electrical and electronic engineering; naval architecture;applied geology; building science and planning; biological sciences; pharmaceutical sciences; business studies

Special collections
Young Collection (alchemy, chemistry, pharmacy, 16th–19th centuries)
Anderson Collection (Founder's Library, 1726–1796)
Laing Collection (Mathematics, 17th–19th centuries)

Publications
Report on Research (annual)
Research Papers

STRATHCLYDE UNIVERSITY *see also* **CENTRE FOR INDUSTRIAL INNOVATION**

2561 STRATHKELVIN DISTRICT LIBRARIES
170 Kirkintilloch Road, Bishopbriggs, Glasgow G64 2LS Tel. 041-762 0112
Public Library Service, for Kirkintilloch, Bishopbriggs, Lennoxtown and Moodiesburn

Enquiries to the Reference Librarian

Subject coverage
general

STREET DISTRICT LIBRARY *see* **SOMERSET COUNTY LIBRARY**

STRETFORD CENTRAL LIBRARY *see* **TRAFFORD BOROUGH LIBRARY SERVICE**

STRETFORD TECHNICAL COLLEGE *now* **NORTH TRAFFORD COLLEGE,** *q.v.*

2562 STRODE COLLEGE
Church Road, Street, Somerset BA16 0AB Tel. 045-84 2277
Tertiary College; formerly Strode Technical College

Enquiries to the Librarian

Subject coverage
general

STROUD MAIN LIBRARY *see* **GLOUCESTER COUNTY LIBRARY**

2563 STRUCTURAL DYNAMICS LIMITED
18 Carlton Crescent, Southampton SO1 2ET Tel. 0703 35611
Telex 477566

Company; formerly Structural Dynamics (Offshore) Limited

Enquiries to the General Manager

Subject coverage
structural analysis; systems for monitoring structural integrity; machinery health monitoring systems; acoustics

2564 STRUCTURAL INSULATION ASSOCIATION
City Wall House, 14/18 Finsbury Street, London EC2Y 9AQ Tel. 01-628 6441 ext. 14
Trade Association

Enquiries to the Secretary

Subject coverage
thermal and sound insulation

2565 SUFFOLK COUNTY LIBRARY
Technical Library Unit, Ipswich Central Library, Northgate Street, Ipswich IP1 3DE Tel. 0473 53561
Telex 98135
Public Library; Suffolk County Library was created by the merger of the former library authorities of Ipswich Borough, Bury St Edmunds, Lowestoft, West Suffolk and East Suffolk

Enquiries to the Technical Librarian

Subject coverage
general and technical

2566 SULPHUR INSTITUTE
Lynwood House, 24–32 Kilburn High Road, London NW6 5UJ Tel. 01-328 2284/5
Telex 24224

Research and Technical Institute

Enquiries to the Information Specialist

Subject coverage
research and technical information on the use of sulphur and sulphur compounds

Publications
Sulphur Institute Journal
Technical bulletins

2567 SUN LIFE ASSURANCE SOCIETY LIMITED
107 Cheapside, London EC2V 6DU Tel. 01-606 7788
Telex 8811871

Life Assurance Company

Enquiries to the Marketing Department

Subject coverage
all aspects of life assurance, pensions, permanent health insurance; taxation; personal financial planning

2568 SUNDERLAND POLYTECHNIC
Sir John Priestman Library, Green Terrace, Sunderland, Tyne and Wear SR1 3SD — Tel. 0783 76191
College of Higher Education; formerly Sunderland Technical College

Enquiries to the Polytechnic Librarian

Subject coverage
mathematics; computing; pharmacy; biology; physics; chemistry; materials science; civil, mechanical, electrical, electronic and control engineering; town planning; geology; naval architecture

2569 SUNDERLAND PUBLIC LIBRARIES
Borough Road, Sunderland, County Durham SR1 1PP — Tel. 0783 70417
Public Library Service

Enquiries to the Director of Libraries

Subject coverage
general

Publications
Finding out (on specific topics, occasional)
Science Technology and Commerce: (guide to resources and services)
Directory of Organisations, Clubs and Societies

2570 SUNDRIDGE PARK MANAGEMENT CENTRE
Bromley, Kent BR1 3JW — Tel. 01-460 9821
Company/Training Centre/Consultants; part of PA International Managements Consultants, *q.v.*

Enquiries to the Director

Subject coverage
training in company strategy; objectives; mergers; functional training in marketing, production and finance; technique training in capital investment planning, materials management and computer audited production control; training in personal skills—participation, executive development, leadership, presentation

SURBITON DISTRICT LIBRARY *see* **KINGSTON UPON THAMES CENTRAL LIBRARY**

2571 SURGICAL DRESSING MANUFACTURERS ASSOCIATION
c/o Robinson and Sons Limited, Wheat Bridge, Chesterfield S40 2AD — Tel. 0246 31101, Telex 547320
Trade Association

Enquiries to the Secretary

Subject coverage
surgical dressings

2572 SURREY AND SUSSEX LIBRARIES IN COOPERATION (SASLIC)
c/o The Honorary Secretary, East Sussex County Library, Hove Area Library, Church Road, Hove, Sussex BN3 2EG
Inter-library Cooperative Scheme

Enquiries to the Honorary Secretary

Subject coverage
commercial, technical, scientific

Publications
Annual Report
SASLIC Newsletter (quarterly)
Directory of Members
Information for Industry & Commerce (publicity leaflet)
Directory of Course ... Venues
Location Key to Foreign Language Dictionaries
PPBS: a bibliography

2573 SURREY COUNTY LIBRARY
140 High Street, Esher, Surrey KT10 9QR — Tel. 0372 63585, Telex 922061

Public Library; Regional Branches: Central, Ewell; North-West, Woking; Northern, Weybridge; South-Western, Guildford; South-Eastern, Reigate

Enquiries to the County Librarian

Subject coverage
general

Special collection
British Standards

2574 SURREY UNIVERSITY LIBRARY
Guildford, Surrey GU2 5XH — Tel. 0483 71281, Telex 895331

University Library

Enquiries to the Librarian

Subject coverage
engineering, all fields except aero-engineering; mathematics; chemistry; physics; metallurgy; materials technology; biochemistry; biological sciences; nutrition; management of hotels, catering and tourism; economics; home economics

Special collection
Transport Trust Library

SURREY UNIVERSITY *see also* **WOLFSON BIOANALYTICAL CENTRE**

2575 SUSPENDED CEILINGS ASSOCIATION
14 Green End Road, Boxmoor, Hemel Hempstead, Hertfordshire HP1 1QW — Tel. 0442 55024
Trade Association

Enquiries to the Director

Subject coverage
suspended ceilings: manufacture and specialist contracting

2576 SUSSEX UNIVERSITY LIBRARY
Brighton, Sussex BN1 9QL — Tel. 0273 66755, Telex 87394

University Library

Enquiries to the Librarian

Subject coverage
applied science and technology; biological sciences; mathematics; physical sciences; molecular sciences

Special collection
Science Policy Research Unit Collection

SUSSEX UNIVERSITY *see also*
INSTITUTE OF MANPOWER STUDIES
UNIT OF NITROGEN FIXATION

2577 SUTCLIFFE SPEAKMAN & COMPANY LIMITED
Guest Street, Leigh, Lancashire WN7 2HE — Tel. 052-35 72101
Telex 67555

Company

Enquiries to the Research and Development Manager

Subject coverage
active carbon; soda lime solvent recovery (active carbon system); calcium silicate brick plant

SUTHERLAND COUNTY LIBRARY *now* **HIGHLAND REGION LIBRARY SERVICE,** *q.v.*

2578 SUTTON LIBRARIES AND ARTS SERVICES
Central Library, St. Nicholas Way, Sutton, — Tel. 01-643 4461
Surrey SM1 1EA — Telex 946762
Public Library; formerly (London Borough of) Sutton Public Libraries; houses the Citizen's Advice Bureau for Sutton; Branch Libraries at Carshalton, and Wallington

Enquiries to the Subject Specialist in Commerce, Science and Technology

Subject coverage
general; astronomy

SWALE DIVISIONAL LIBRARY *see* **KENT COUNTY LIBRARY**

SWANSEA CENTRAL LIBRARY *see* **WEST GLAMORGAN COUNTY LIBRARY**

2579 SWANSEA COLLEGE OF TECHNOLOGY
Mount Pleasant, Swansea, Glamorgan SA1 6ED
College of Technology, to become part of West Glamorgan Institute of Higher Education, late 1976

Enquiries to the Librarian

Subject coverage
business; management; science; mathematics; engineering; construction

2580 SWANSEA TRIBOLOGY CENTRE
University College of Swansea, Singleton Park, Swansea SA2 8PP — Tel. 0792 24561
University Company for contract research, associated with the Swansea Corrosion Advisory Service

Enquiries to the Director

Subject coverage
wear-resistant materials; lubricant testing and selection; plant failure analysis; plant design; test machines; metrology; analysis and physical testing; corrosion

2581 SWANSEA UNIVERSITY COLLEGE LIBRARY
Singleton Park, Swansea, Glamorgan SA2 8PP — Tel. 0792 25678
Telex 48358

Constituent College of the University of Wales

Enquiries, preferably by letter, to the Librarian or the Sub-Librarian for Science

Subject coverage
physical, natural, and engineering sciences

Special collection
British Standards

Publications
Periodical Holdings
Theses

SWINDON AREA ASSOCIATION OF LIBRARIES OF INDUSTRY AND COMMERCE (SAALIC) *now* **WILTSHIRE LIBRARIES IN CO-OPERATION (WILCO)** *q.v.*

2582 SWINDON COLLEGE
Regent Circus, Swindon, Wiltshire Tel. 0793 29141
College of Further Education; known as the College, Swindon; having some departments at North Star Avenue, Swindon

Enquiries to the Librarian, Regent Circus

Subject coverage
management; home economics; catering; engineering

SWINDON DIVISIONAL LIBRARY *see* **WILTSHIRE COUNTY LIBRARY**

SWINTON CENTRAL AREA LIBRARY *see* **SALFORD CITY LIBRARIES**

2583 SWISS COTTAGE LIBRARY
88 Avenue Road, London NW3 3HA Tel. 01-278 4444
Telex 23909
Public Library, of the London Borough of Camden Libraries and Arts Department

Enquiries to the Special Collection Librarian

Subject coverage
agriculture, veterinary science and domestic science (to 1975)

2584 SWISS EMBASSY
16–18 Montagu Place, London W1H 2BQ Tel. 01-723 0701
Telex 28212
Foreign Government Representation

Enquiries to the Swiss Embassy

Subject coverage
matters relating to Switzerland

2585 SYNTEX PHARMACEUTICALS LIMITED
St. Ives House, St. Ives Road, Maidenhead, Berkshire SL6 1RD Tel. 0628 33191
Company; its Research Unit is at Heriot-Watt University, *q.v.*

Enquiries to the Information Officer

Subject coverage
medicine; pharmaceuticals

2586 SYNTEX RESEARCH CENTRE
Research Park, Heriot-Watt University, Riccarton, Edinburgh EH14 4AS Tel. 031-449 6211
Telex 727234
Company Research Unit, linked with Syntex Pharmaceuticals Limited, *q.v.*

Enquiries to the Information Scientist

Subject coverage
drug effects on the cardiovascular system

SYSTON LIBRARY *see* **LEICESTERSHIRE LIBRARIES AND INFORMATION SERVICE**

TALIC *now* **NETWORK** *see* **NEWCASTLE UPON TYNE CENTRAL LIBRARY**

2587 TAMESIDE LIBRARIES
Central Reference Library, Old Street, Ashton-under-Lyne, Lancashire Tel. 061-330 2151
Public Library; Central Library of the Tameside system; District Libraries at Denton, Droylsden, Hyde, Stalybridge

Enquiries to the Reference and Information Librarian

Subject coverage
general

TAMWORTH DISTRICT LIBRARY *see* **STAFFORDSHIRE COUNTY LIBRARY**

2588 TAPE MANUFACTURERS ASSOCIATION
78/79 Friar Gate, Derby DE1 1FL — Tel. 0332 43709
Trade Association; member of the Narrow Fabrics Federation

Enquiries to the Secretary

Subject coverage
manufacture of tapes and light webs

2589 TATE AND LYLE LIMITED
Group Research and Development, Philip Lyle Memorial Research Laboratory, P.O. Box 68, Whiteknights, Reading, Berkshire RG6 2BX — Tel. 0734 861361, Telex 847915
Company; formerly Tate and Lyle Limited, Research Centre, Keston

Enquiries to the Librarian

Subject coverage
sugar refining and technology; sugar agriculture; carbohydrate chemistry

Publication
Sugar Industry Abstracts (published as an insert in La Sucrerie Belge)

TATE & LYLE RESEARCH CENTRE *now* **TATE & LYLE LIMITED, Group Research and Development,** *q.v.*

TAUNTON DISTRICT LIBRARY *see* **SOMERSET COUNTY LIBRARY**

TAUNTON TECHNICAL COLLEGE OF ARTS AND TECHNOLOGY *now* **SOMERSET COLLEGE OF ARTS AND TECHNOLOGY,** *q.v.*

2590 TAYLOR NELSON GROUP LIMITED
457 Kingston Road, Ewell, Epsom, Surrey KT19 0DH — Tel. 01-394 0191
Company

Enquiries to the Marketing Director

Subject coverage
consumer research; marketing consultancy; medical and pharmaceutical market research; financial market research

2591 TEA BROKERS ASSOCIATION OF LONDON
Sir John Lyon House, Upper Thames Street, London EC4V 3LA — Tel. 01-236 3368/9
Trade Association

Enquiries to the Secretary

Subject coverage
tea

Publication
Tea Market Report (weekly)

2592 TEA BUYERS ASSOCIATION
London Chamber of Commerce and Industry, 69 Cannon Street, London EC4N 5AB — Tel. 01-248 7529, Telex 888941
Trade Association

Enquiries to the Secretary

Subject coverage
packing and distribution of tea

2593 TEA COUNCIL LIMITED
Sir John Lyon House, 5 High Timber Street, Upper Thames Street, London EC4V 3NJ — Tel. 01-248 1024/5

Company; associated with Tea Boards in tea-producing countries and with the U.K. Tea Trade Committee

Enquiries to the Secretary/Campaign Director

Subject coverage
tea, where grown and how manufactured; tea consumption; U.K. statistics on tea consumption trends; types and grades of tea, the buying at auction, blending, packaging, distribution; exports and imports (*not* trade, brand, or company matters)

Publications
Facts About Tea
Good Tea for all occasions
Manual on Vending Tea
Technical Notes on Marketing Tea in the U.K.
Leaflets on the preparation, characteristics, distribution and history of tea
Posters

2594 TECHMATION LIMITED
58 Edgware Way, Edgware, Middlesex HA8 8JP — Tel. 01-958 5636, Telex 262245

Company

Enquiries to the Director

Subject coverage
technical information on laboratory equipment, especially analytical instrumentation; pollution and process control; electronic instruments; offshore applications for instrumentation, especially TV and acoustics

2595 TECHNICAL EDUCATION & TRAINING ORGANIZATION FOR OVERSEAS COUNTRIES
Grosvenor Gardens House, 35/37 Grosvenor Gardens, London SW1W 0BS — Tel. 01-834 3665 *and* 6751

Company/Specialized Agency, with the Ministry of Overseas Development; formerly Council for Technical Education & Training for Overseas Countries

Enquiries to the Secretary

Subject coverage
technical education; industrial training; management development; agricultural education and training

Publications
Annual Report
Reports on overseas assignments (limited circulation)
Book lists for Technical College Libraries

2596 TECHNICAL HELP TO EXPORTERS
British Standards Institution, Maylands Avenue, Hemel Hempstead, Hertfordshire HP2 4SQ — Tel. 0442 3111, Telex 82424

Technical Enquiry Service; part of the British Standards Institution, *q.v.* having liaison with the Department of Trade

Enquiries to Project Engineer or Coordinator concerned; fees charged

Subject coverage
overseas technical regulations, standards and approval systems; interpretation and translation of overseas technical requirements; assistance with technical problems and research projects; assistance in obtaining test certificates or approval for products in overseas markets; U.K. testing and inspection of goods for export

Publications
Surveys, *e.g.* Structural Fire Precaution Requirements in the EEC
USA National Electrical Code
Focus on Nigeria
Translations of major foreign codes
Publications catalogue

2597 TECHNICAL INDEXES LIMITED
Easthampstead Road, Bracknell, Berkshire RG12 1NS Tel. 0344 26311
Telex 849207

Company; subsidiary of the Derritron Group

Enquiries to the Systems Liaison Manager

Subject coverage
supply and manufacture of products, materials and components for electronic engineering, chemical engineering, materials handling, laboratory equipment

Publications
Product catalogues and technical literature

2598 TECHNOLOGY REPORTS CENTRE
St Mary Cray, Orpington, Kent BR5 3RF Tel. 66 32111
Telex 896866

Branch of Government Department; of the Department of Industry; with the change from Ministry of Technology, the defence part of the Centre adopted a new name, *i.e.* Defence Research Information Centre (DRIC), *q.v.*

Enquiries, for reports (subject searches) to the Centre, exts 25 or 255; for specific requests, ext. 245

Subject coverage
all subjects within science and technology, mainly in reports of research and government-sponsored work, U.K. and overseas, particularly U.S. (Access to 5 million references by the ESA Recon system)

Publications
R & D Abstracts (semi-monthly)
Techlink (digests of exploitable new technology)

2599 TEESSIDE POLYTECHNIC
Borough Road, Middlesbrough, Cleveland TS1 3BA Tel. 0642 44176
Polytechnic, formerly Constantine College of Technology

Enquiries to the Librarian, the Publicity Officer, or, for local industry technical queries to the Industrial Liaison Officer

Subject coverage
general

TEESSIDE PUBLIC LIBRARY *now* **CLEVELAND COUNTY LIBRARY,** *q.v.*

2600 TELFORD DEVELOPMENT CORPORATION
Priorslee Hall, Telford, Shropshire TF2 9NT Tel. 0952 613131
Telex 35359

New Town Development Company

Enquiries to the Librarian

Subject coverage
aspects of new town development, physical and social

2601 TENSOR SOCIETY OF GREAT BRITAIN
66 South Terrace, Surbiton, Surrey KT6 6HU Tel. 01-399 2724
Learned Society; the Society's Library is housed at Imperial College, London

Enquiries, regarding membership only, to the Public Relations Officer

Subject coverage
the application of determinants, matrices, vectors, dyadics and tensors

Publication
Matrix and Tensor Quarterly

TERMITE RESEARCH UNIT *now* **CENTRE FOR OVERSEAS PEST RESEARCH,** *q.v.*

2602 TETRONICS RESEARCH AND DEVELOPMENT COMPANY LIMITED
5B Lechlade Road, Faringdon, Oxfordshire SN7 8AJ Tel. 0367 20224
Company; connected with and housing Bionics Research Limited

Enquiries to the Director

Subject coverage
Tetronics Research: mineral processing; coal processing; high temperature furnaces and reactors; development of novel processes
Bionics Research: medical instruments; microscopes

2603 TEXTILE COMMISSION MANUFACTURERS ASSOCIATION
36 Mannville Terrace, Bradford, Yorkshire BD7 1BA Tel. 0274 21877
Trade Association

Enquiries to the Association

Subject coverage
worsted and woollen weaving; information on members equipped to deal with work offered on commission

TEXTILE COUNCIL *now* **TEXTILE STATISTICS BUREAU,** *q.v.*

TEXTILE DISTRIBUTORS ASSOCIATION *see* **FEDERATION OF WHOLESALE AND INDUSTRIAL DISTRIBUTORS**

TEXTILE FINISHING TRADES ASSOCIATION *now* **BRITISH TEXTILE EMPLOYERS ASSOCIATION,** *q.v.*

2604 TEXTILE INSTITUTE
10 Blackfriars Street, Manchester M3 5DR Tel. 061-834 1457/8457
Telex 667822 (messages *must* start "For Text. Inst.")

Professional Qualifying Body

Enquiries to the Information Assistant

Subject coverage
textile technology

Publications
Journal of the Textile Institute (monthly)
Textile Institute and Industry (monthly)
Textile Progress (quarterly)
Technical books

TEXTILE MACHINERY AND ACCESSORY MANUFACTURERS ASSOCIATION *now* **BRITISH TEXTILE MACHINERY ASSOCIATION** *q.v.*

2605 TEXTILE RESEARCH COUNCIL
2 First Avenue, Sherwood Rise, Nottingham NG7 6JL Tel. 0602 623311
Telex 37605

Research Organization, established and maintained by WIRA, HATRA, Shirley Institute, Lambeg Industrial Research Association, Dyers and Cleaners Research Organisation, British Launderers Research Association, Lace Research Association; formerly Textile Research Conference, and before that, Standing Consultative Conference on Textile Research

Enquiries to the Secretary

Subject coverage
research and development in clothing and textile industries

Publications
Annual Report
Occasional technical reports

2606 TEXTILE STATISTICS BUREAU
5th Floor, Royal Exchange, Manchester M2 7ER Tel. 061-832 6193
Telex 666737

Company; formerly the Textile Council

Enquiries to the Librarian

Subject coverage
textile statistics, U.K. and international

Publication
Quarterly Statistical Review

TEXTILES CREDIT PROTECTION LIMITED *see* **BRITISH MERCANTILE AGENCY LIMITED**

2607 THAMES BOARD MILLS LIMITED
Purfleet, Essex RM16 1RD Tel. 04026 5555
Telex 262729

Manufacturing Company, subsidiary of Unilever Limited

Enquiries to the Librarian

Subject coverage
paperboard for packaging; wastepaper

2608 THAMES POLYTECHNIC
Wellington Street, London SE18 6PF Tel. 01-854 2030
Polytechnic; formerly Woolwich Polytechnic, houses the International Powder Advisory Centre, *q.v.* Dartford College of Education is now amalgamated with Thames Polytechnic

Enquiries to the Librarian

Subject coverage
chemistry, physics, mathematics, civil engineering; electrical engineering; mechanical engineering; biology; business and management; geography; economics; architecture; surveying; materials science and physics

Publications
Thames Papers in Political Economy

2609 THAMES WATER AUTHORITY
New River Head, Rosebery Avenue, London EC1R 4TP Tel. 01-837 3300
Government Regional Authority, one of the ten Authorities under the National Water Council; responsible to the Department of the Environment; the Ministry of Agriculture, Fisheries and Food has some powers; the Authority has itself nine Divisions: Metropolitan Water, Metropolitan Public Health, Thames Conservancy, Lea, Chiltern, Cotswold, Lambourn, Southern and Vales

Enquiries to the Librarian, Scientific Services Library

Subject coverage
water supply; water conservation; sewerage and sewage disposal; pollution control; fisheries; land drainage; flood prevention; recreational use of the waters

Publication
Thames Water: a description of the Undertaking

THANET DIVISIONAL LIBRARY *see* **KENT COUNTY LIBRARY**

2610 THANET TECHNICAL COLLEGE
Ramsgate Road, Broadstairs, Kent CT10 1PN Tel. 0843 65111
Technical College, of Kent County Council

Enquiries to the Librarian

Subject coverage
hotel and catering management; welfare; building and engineering; business studies

2611 THERMAL INSULATION CONTRACTORS ASSOCIATION
24 Ormond Road, Richmond, Surrey Tel. 01-948 4151
Trade Association; 4 regional offices

Enquiries, in writing, to the Director

Subject coverage
thermal insulation contracting in the insulation of pipelines, plant, tankage, etc., *not* the insulation of buildings; firms undertaking such work

2612 THERMAL SYNDICATE LIMITED
P.O. Box 6, Wallsend, Tyne and Wear NE28 6DG Tel. 0632 625311
Telex 53614

Company; parent body of Special Metals (Fabrication) Limited, *q.v.*

Enquiries, general, to the Company; technical, to the Sales Promotion Manager

Subject coverage
pure vitreous silica, translucent (made from high purity sands) and transparent (made from high purity quartz crystals and also by flame hydrolysis [synthetic fused silica]); tubing; optical components; chemical plant; scientific equipment; pure oxide ceramics (recrystallized alumina, magnesia and zirconia)

Publications
Catalogues

THOMAS HUXLEY COLLEGE *see* **EALING TECHNICAL COLLEGE, St. Marys Road, W5**

2613 J. WALTER THOMPSON COMPANY LIMITED
40 Berkeley Square, London W1X 6AD Tel. 01-629 9496
Telex 22871

Advertising Agency

Enquiries to the Information Services Manager

Subject coverage
advertising; marketing

2614 THOMPSON HENRY LIMITED
London Road, Sunningdale, Berkshire SL5 0EP Tel. 0990 24615
Company; U.K. Agent for Engineering Index, Biological Information Service of Abstracts, World Meetings Information Centre

Enquiries to the Company

Subject coverage
supply and use of abstracting services listed above

2615 THORN GAS APPLIANCES LIMITED
Angel Road, Edmonton, London N18 3HL Tel. 01-807 3030
Telex 264903

Company; associated companies are Main Gas Appliances Limited, Moffat Gas Appliances Limited, and Parkinson Cowan Appliances Limited

Enquiries to the Marketing Services Manager

Subject coverage
gas cookers, fires, unit heaters, water heaters

Publications
Sales leaflets
Technical Data Sheets
User and service manuals

2616 THORNTON & ROSS LIMITED
Linthwaite Laboratories, Huddersfield, Yorkshire HD7 5QH — Tel. 048-484 2217
Company

Enquiries to the Chief Chemist

Subject coverage
Standard formula drugs

THORNTON RESEARCH CENTRE *see* **SHELL RESEARCH LIMITED**

THREE M UNITED KINGDOM LIMITED *see* entry **1720**

2617 THURROCK TECHNICAL COLLEGE
Woodview, Grays, Essex RM16 4YR — Tel. 0375 71621 ext. 292
Technical College; the Library is part of the Essex County Library

Enquiries to the Librarian

Subject coverage
engineering; business studies; transport, catering

2618 S.B. TIETZ & PARTNERS
10–14 Macklin Street, London WC2B 5NF — Tel. 01-242 8742
Telex 21120

Partnership/Consultancy; includes Associated Planning Consultants

Enquiries, trade, to the Librarian; policy matters, to a Partner

Subject coverage
civil, structural, and traffic engineering, especially industrial construction and leisure developments; Associated Planning Consultants cover advice and design related to construction planning and the built environment

2619 TIMBER DRYING ASSOCIATION
Clareville House, Whitcomb Street, London WC2H 7DL — Tel. 01-839 1891
Trade Association

Enquiries to the Secretary

Subject coverage
kiln drying timber; supply of kiln dried timber

Publication
List of members

2620 TIMBER PACKAGING AND PALLET CONFEDERATION
5 Greenfield Crescent, Edgbaston, Birmingham B15 3BE — Tel. 021-454 2711
Trade Association

Enquiries to the Secretary

Subject coverage
wooden cases and pallets; export packing

2621 TIMBER RESEARCH AND DEVELOPMENT ASSOCIATION
Stocking Lane, Hughenden Valley, High Wycombe, Buckinghamshire HP14 4ND — Tel. 0240-24 3091
Research Association, with nine regional offices

Enquiries to the Chief Information Officer, Librarian, Central Enquiry Department or Regional Office, as appropriate

Subject coverage
timber research and most aspects of timber utilization (excluding furniture), with particular reference to timber in building; fire, finishing, timber engineering, handling; design; testing of structures and components; timber yard operations; timber buildings; education and training; statistics; thermal insulation; timber drying

Publications
Concept in Wood (quarterly)
Publications List (includes over 400 publications)
Library Bibliographies

2622 TIMES NEWSPAPERS LIMITED
Information and Marketing Intelligence Unit, New Printing House Square, London WC1X 8EZ Tel. 01-837 1234
Company; part of the Thomson Organisation Limited, for all sections of which the above Unit undertakes work

Enquiries to the Senior Information Officer or the Manager

Subject coverage
media and publishing information; marketing information; industrial, commercial and consumer industries; advertising statistics

Publications
New Products and Market Trends
Trends in Retailing
Travel Report

2623 TIN RESEARCH INSTITUTE
Fraser Road, Perivale, Greenford, Middlesex UB6 7AQ Tel. 01-997 4254
Research Institute; member of the International Tin Research Council

Enquiries to the Technical Information Officer

Subject coverage
tin and its alloys and compounds and their applications; in particular soldering, tin and tin alloy plating, pewter, bearing metals, tin in cast iron, organotins and other tin chemicals

Publications
Tin and its Uses (quarterly)
Technical publications

2624 TINPLATE STOCKHOLDERS ASSOCIATION
Lennig House, Masons Avenue, Croydon CR9 3NU Tel. 01-686 7957
Trade Association; affiliated to the National Association of Steel Stockholders; formerly the Tinplate Stockholders and Merchants Association

Enquiries to the Secretariat

Subject coverage
tinplate; sources of supply, etc.

TIPTON DISTRICT LIBRARY *see* **SANDWELL PUBLIC LIBRARIES**

2625 TOBACCO RESEARCH COUNCIL
Glen House, Stag Place, London SW1E 5AG Tel. 01-828 2041
Research Organization

Enquiries to the Librarian

Subject coverage
tobacco; smoking and health; statistics

Publications
Series of Research Papers, e.g.
no. 1, Statistics of Smoking in the U.K.
no. 6, Teobacco Consumption in various countries

TONBRIDGE/MALLING DIVISIONAL LIBRARY *see* **KENT COUNTY LIBRARY**

2626 TOOTAL FABRIC DIVISION RESEARCH
P.O. Box 1, Hollingworth, Hyde, Cheshire SK14 8NS Tel. 045-74 61100
Telex 669023

Company Research Department, of Tootal Limited

Enquiries to the Librarian

Subject coverage
textile finishing; covering; desizing; scouring; bleaching; dyeing; printing; finishing and testing

Special collection
textile journals, long runs, some from 1885

TOOTAL GROUP *see also* **ENGLISH SEWING LIMITED**

TORFAEN REGIONAL LIBRARY *see* **GWENT COUNTY LIBRARY**

2627 TORQUAY CENTRAL LIBRARY
Lymington Road, Torquay, Devonshire TQ1 3DT Tel. 0803 25211
Telex 42647
Public Library; the South Devon Area Library of the Devon Library Services, *q.v.*; formerly County Borough of Torbay Library Service

Enquiries to the Area Librarian

Subject coverage
general

2628 TORRY RESEARCH STATION
P.O. Box 31, 135 Abbey Road, Aberdeen AB9 8DG Tel. 0224 877071
Government Department, of the Ministry of Agriculture, Fisheries and Food; associated with the Humber Laboratory, *q.v.*

Enquiries to the Director

Subject coverage
fish processing technology; chilling, freezing and cold storage, mechanization, transport, smoking, drying, salting, thawing, canning; fish meal, fish silage, fish oils; project development, quality assessment

Publications
Annual Report
Advisory Notes

2629 TOTTENHAM COLLEGE OF TECHNOLOGY
High Road, London N15 4RU Tel. 01-802 3111
College of Further Education; formerly Tottenham Technical College

Enquiries to the Librarian

Subject coverage
building; environmental health

TOWCESTER DISTRICT LIBRARY *see* **NORTHAMPTONSHIRE LIBRARIES**

2630 TOWER HAMLETS LIBRARIES DEPARTMENT
Bancroft Road, London E1 4DQ Tel. 01-980 4366
Public Library Service; four Area Libraries: Bethnal Green, Limehouse, Poplar, Whitechapel

Enquiries to the Librarian

Subject coverage
general

Special collections
Bolt Collection (sailing and early steamships)
Commercial and industrial art (in the Whitechapel Area Library)

2631 TRADE MARK OWNERS ASSOCIATION LIMITED
15 Finsbury Circus, London EC2M 7DL Tel. 01-588 7128
Company

Enquiries to the Secretary

Subject coverage
trade mark matters

Publication
Trade Mark Record (reproduction of Trade Marks Journal)

TRADERS ROAD TRANSPORT ASSOCIATION *now* **FREIGHT TRANSPORT ASSOCIATION LIMITED,** *q.v.*

2632 TRADES UNION CONGRESS
Congress House, 23–28 Great Russell Street, London WC1B 3LS Tel. 01-636 4030
Trade Union; member of the International Confederation of Free Trade Unions and of the European Trade Union Confederation

Enquiries to the Information Officer or the Librarian

Subject coverage
trade unions; industrial relations; TUC policy

Publications
Annual Report
Publications List (of about 40 pamphlets and books)
Labour (monthly)

2633 TRADES UNION CONGRESS CENTENARY INSTITUTE OF OCCUPATIONAL HEALTH
London School of Hygiene and Tropical Medicine, Keppel Street, (Gower Street), London WC1E 7HT Tel. 01-580 2386
University Department, of London University

Enquiries to the Information Officer

Subject coverage
occupational health, hygiene and medicine; industrial toxicology

2634 TRAFALGAR HOUSE INVESTMENTS
1 Berkeley Street, London W1X 6NN Tel. 01-499 9020
Group of Companies, including Cementation Research Limited, *q.v.*

Enquiries to the Group Publicity Manager, THIGS Limited, Mitcham House, 681 Mitcham Road, Croydon CR9 3AB

Subject coverage
building; civil engineering; foundation engineering; concrete additives; mine shaft sinking; tunnelling; exploration drilling; shock and vibration control; offshore engineering; bridge building; property development; cargo shipping; hotel operation

Publications
Sales promotion literature on all subjects

2635 TRAFFIC RESEARCH CENTRE
41 Cloth Fair, London EC1 Tel. 01-248 2394
Research and development organization, non-profit-making

Enquiries to the Director (tests on problems and sites at cost)

Subject coverage
traffic engineering; transport engineering; transport planning; regional and national planning; passenger and freight handling; large vehicle manoeuvring requirements and standards

Publications
Notes on Research and Consultancy work

2636 TRAFFORD BOROUGH LIBRARY SERVICE
Birch Avenue, Talbot Road, Manchester M16 0GH Tel. 061-872 6133
Public Library; created from the former Altrincham, Hale, Sale, and Stretford Public Libraries

Enquiries to the Borough Librarian

Subject coverage
general

2637 TRAINING SERVICES AGENCY
162/168 Regent Street, London W1R 6DE Tel. 01-214 6000
01-214 6725 (Library)
Government Agency, of the Manpower Services Commission; formed from the Training Division of the Department of Employment

Enquiries to the Librarian

Subject coverage
training; employment; manpower; management; occupational psychology; industrial relations; vocational education

Publications
Training Information Papers series (HMSO)
Training Research Register (HMSO)

TRAINING SERVICES AGENCY *see also*
AGRICULTURAL TRAINING BOARD
AIR TRANSPORT AND TRAVEL INDUSTRY TRAINING BOARD
CARPET INDUSTRY TRAINING BOARD
CHEMICAL AND ALLIED PRODUCTS INDUSTRY TRAINING BOARD
CLOTHING AND ALLIED PRODUCTS INDUSTRY TRAINING BOARD
CONSTRUCTION INDUSTRY TRAINING BOARD
CONSTRUCTION HEALTH AND SAFETY GROUP
ENGINEERING INDUSTRY TRAINING BOARD
FOOTWEAR, LEATHER AND FUR SKIN INDUSTRY TRAINING BOARD
FURNITURE AND TIMBER INDUSTRY TRAINING BOARD
HOTEL AND CATERING INDUSTRY TRAINING BOARD
INDUSTRIAL TRAINING RESEARCH UNIT
IRON AND STEEL INDUSTRY TRAINING BOARD
KNITTING, LACE AND NET INDUSTRY TRAINING BOARD
MAN-MADE FIBRES PRODUCING INDUSTRY TRAINING BOARD
PAPER AND PAPER PRODUCTS INDUSTRY TRAINING BOARD
PETROLEUM INDUSTRY TRAINING BOARD
PRINTING AND PUBLISHING INDUSTRY TRAINING BOARD
ROAD TRANSPORT INDUSTRY TRAINING BOARD
RUBBER AND PLASTICS PROCESSING INDUSTRY TRAINING BOARD
SHIPBUILDING INDUSTRY TRAINING BOARD
WATER SUPPLY INDUSTRY TRAINING BOARD *now* **NATIONAL WATER COUNCIL,** *q.v.*

TRANSLATORS GUILD *see* **INSTITUTE OF LINGUISTS**

2638 TRANSPORT AND ENVIRONMENTAL STUDIES (TEST)
24 Floral Street, London WC2E 8JS Tel. 01-240 1307
Telex 27706

Independent Consultancy

Enquiries to the Director

Subject coverage
urban, regional, transport and environmental planning; ecological planning; data survey and analysis

Publications
Brochure
Project Reports (when unrestricted)

2639 TRANSPORT AND ROAD RESEARCH LABORATORY
Old Wokingham Road, Crowthorne, Berkshire GU25 4NP Tel. 034-46 3131
Government Research Establishment, of the Department of the Environment; formerly Road Research Laboratory

Enquiries to the Head of Technical Information and Library Services

Subject coverage
highway engineering (planning, design, construction and maintenance of roads and highway structures, particularly bridges and tunnels); traffic engineering and safety (movement of people and goods, including the layout of roads and traffice networks, control of traffic flow, study of road accidents and methods of reducing their frequency and severity); transport planning and land use strategies; assessment and use of existing and projected passenger and freight transport systems; environmental effects of vehicles and traffic

Publications
Laboratory Reports
Supplementary Reports
Digests of the Reports
Part III: Roads and Transport, of the DoE Register of Research

2640 TRANSPORT ASSOCIATION
King Edward House, New Street, Birmingham B2 4QP Tel. 021-643 5494
Trade Association

Enquiries to the Secretary

Subject coverage
road transport

2641 TREE COUNCIL
Room 202, 17–19 Rochester Row, London SW1P 1LN Tel. 01-834 8181 ext. 233
Charity Organization; composed of twenty-eight national member associations

Enquiries to the Secretary

Subject coverage
encouragement of tree planting and maintenance; importance of trees and tree cover for amenity, landscape and ecological reasons

Publications
Reports of Annual Conferences, 1974 and 1976
National Tree Survey
Trees in Towns and the Landscape: method of evaluation

2642 TRENT POLYTECHNIC
Burton Street, Nottingham NG1 4BU Tel. 0602 48248
Telex 377534
Institution of Higher Education; formerly the three Nottingham Colleges, Technology, Art & Design and Education; houses the National Centre for Schools Technology

Enquiries to the Librarian

Subject coverage
accountancy; biology; building; business studies; chemistry; civil engineering; computer science; economics; electrical engineering; management; mathematics; mechanical and production engineering; mining; physics; printing; safety; surveying; textiles

Publications
School Technology
Research Bulletin
Bibliography on Safety

2643 ROBERT TRILLO LIMITED
Broadlands, Brockenhurst, Hampshire SO4 7SX Tel. 05902 2220
Company/Consultants

Enquiries to the Director

Subject coverage
amphibious vehicles; hovercraft; hydrofoils; low speed aerodynamics; marine craft; noise (propeller); ocean technologies; offshore technologies; propellers, air and marine; transport feasibility studies; advanced vehicle technologies

Publications
Bimonthly Bibliography Services:
1. air cushion and hydrofoil systems
2. high-speed ground transportation and urban rapid transport systems

2644 TRINIDAD AND TOBAGO HIGH COMMISSION
42 Belgrave Square, London SW1X 8NT Tel. 01-245 9351
Telex 918910

Diplomatic Mission

Enquiries to the High Commissioner

Subject coverage
Trinidad & Tobago trade and commerce; imports and exports, etc.

TRISIL LABORATORIES LIMITED *see* **CRAFER ASSOCIATES**

TROPICAL PESTICIDES HEADQUARTERS AND INFORMATION UNIT *now* **CENTRE FOR OVERSEAS PEST RESEARCH,** *q.v.*

TROPICAL PESTICIDES RESEARCH UNIT *now* **CENTRE FOR OVERSEAS PEST RESEARCH,** *q.v.*

2645 TROPICAL PRODUCTS INSTITUTE
56–62 Gray's Inn Road, London WC1X 8LU Tel. 01-242 5412
Government Research Organization, of the Ministry of Overseas Development

Enquiries to the Librarian

Subject coverage
The Institute helps less developed countries derive greater benefit from their renewable natural resources and specialises primarily in research and development work on the processing, storage, transportation, quality control, marketing and utilization of the plant and animal products of the tropics and sub-tropics

Special collections
Photographic collection of tropical commodities
U.S. Department of Agriculture Publications
Commodity-based technical index of some 700 000 references

Publications
Technical reports (series)
Tropical Science (quarterly)
Biennial Report
Tropical Stored Products Information (twice yearly)
Tropical Storage Abstracts (six issues per year)
Oil Palm News (twice yearly)
Bibliography of Insecticide Materials of Vegetable Origin (twice yearly)
Crop and Product Digests (series)
Publications List

TUFTED CARPET MANUFACTURERS ASSOCIATION *now* **BRITISH CARPET MANUFACTURERS ASSOCIATION,** *q.v.*

TULLOCH LIBRARY, Dunoon *now* **ARGYLL AND BUTE DISTRICT LIBRARY,** *q.v.*

TUNBRIDGE WELLS DIVISIONAL LIBRARY *see* **KENT COUNTY LIBRARY**

2646 TURNER AND NEWALL LIMITED
77 Fountain Street, Manchester M2 2EA Tel. 061-236 9381
Telex 667664

Company

Enquiries to the Group Public Relations Adviser

Subject coverage
asbestos; plastics; glass fibre; insulation

TURNER AND NEWALL LIMITED *see also*
CORK MANUFACTURING COMPANY LIMITED
FERODO LIMITED

TWICKENHAM COLLEGE OF TECHNOLOGY *now* **RICHMOND UPON THAMES COLLEGE,** *q.v.*

TWICKENHAM DISTRICT LIBRARY *see* **RICHMOND UPON THAMES LIBRARIES SERVICE**

2647 TWIST DRILL ASSOCIATION
Light Trades House, Melbourne Avenue, Sheffield S10 2QJ Tel. 0742 663084
Trade Association; Member of the National Federation of Engineers Tool Manufacturers

Enquiries to the Secretary

Subject coverage
twist drill manufacture

TYNEDALE BRANCH LIBRARY *see* **NORTHUMBERLAND COUNTY LIBRARY**

2648 TYNESIDE ASSOCIATION OF LIBRARIES FOR INDUSTRY AND COMMERCE
Commercial and Technical Library, Central Library, Tel. 0632 610691
Newcastle upon Tyne NE99 1MC Telex 53373
Interlibrary Cooperative Scheme and Information Service; title changed to NETWORK, too late to change the numerical position; *see* NEWCASTLE UPON TYNE CENTRAL LIBRARY

Enquiries to the Librarian

Subject coverage
general

2649 UDT INTERNATIONAL FINANCE LIMITED
51 Eastcheap, London EC3P 3BU Tel. 01-623 3020
Telex 883604

Export Finance House; Subsidiary of United Dominions Trust Limited, *q.v.*

Enquiries to the Managing Director

Subject coverage
finance of exports and international trade

2650 UGANDA HIGH COMMISSION
Uganda House, Trafalgar Square, London WC2N 5DX Tel. 01-839 1963
Telex 262241

Government Representational Office; includes the Uganda Coffee Office

Enquiries to the Information Officer

Subject coverage
general and business matters concerning Uganda

2651 U.K. MECHANICAL HEALTH MONITORING GROUP
Leicester Polytechnic, P.O. Box 143, Leicester LE1 9BH Tel. 0533 50181 ext. 2069/2253
Technical Advisory and Educational Group, within Leicester Polytechnic

Enquiries to the Director

Subject coverage
fault diagnosis; condition monitoring; vibration analysis; contaminant analysis; performance/trends monitoring; non-destructive testing; reliability; maintenance engineering

Publication
Brochure

2652 U.K. WASTE MATERIALS EXCHANGE
P.O. Box 51, Stevenage, Hertfordshire SG1 2DT Tel. 0438 3388
Telex 82250

Government Department, of the Department of Industry; having a link with the Warren Spring Laboratory, *q.v.*

Enquiries to the Manager

Subject coverage
recovery of waste materials

Publication
Bulletin (listing of available materials; approximately bi-monthly)

2653 ULSTER COLLEGE
Jordanstown, Newtownabbey, County Antrim, Northern Ireland BT37 0QB Tel. Whiteabbey 65131
Telex 747493

Institute of Higher Education; the Northern Ireland Polytechnic

Enquiries to the Librarian

Subject coverage
most areas of science and technology except nuclear and medical

2654 ULSTER NEW UNIVERSITY LIBRARY
Coleraine, County Londonderry, Northern Ireland BT52 1SA Tel. 0265 4141
University Library; Magee University College Library, *q.v.*, is part of the New University Library

Enquiries to the Librarian

Subject coverage
physical sciences; biological and environmental sciences

Special collections
Stelfox Natural History Collection
European Documentation Centre

Publication
Serials Catalogue

2655 ULTRA VIOLET SPECTROMETRY GROUP
c/o Pye Unicam Limited, York Street, Cambridge CB1 2PX Tel. 0223 58866
Scientific Society; formerly Photoelectric Spectrometry Group

Enquiries to the Honorary Secretary

Subject coverage
ultra violet spectrometry

Publication
U.V. Spectrometry Group Bulletin (annual)

2656 UNDERWATER INSTRUMENTATION LIMITED
212 Station Road, Addlestone, Surrey KT15 2PH Tel. 97 43871
Telex 928346

Company

Enquiries to the Director

Subject coverage
professional diving equipment and associated underwater instrumentation; breathing gas, compressors and mixing equipment; underwater television and communications equipment; underwater lighting; manned submersible vehicles

Publication
Catalogue

2657 UNIGATE LIMITED
Unigate Technical Centre, Abbey House, Church Street, Bradford-on Avon BA15 1DH   Tel. 02216 5311/5
Company; formerly Unigate Central Laboratory; also known as United Dairies Limited

Enquiries (brief) to the Information Officer

Subject coverage
dairy and other food science and technology

UNIGATE LIMITED *see also* **COW & GATE BABY FOODS**

2658 UNILEVER RESEARCH ISLEWORTH LABORATORY
455 London Road, Isleworth, Middlesex TW7 5AB   Tel. 01-560 1266
Company Research Laboratory, of Unilever Limited; formerly Unilever Research Laboratory

Enquiries, by letter only, to the Information Officer

Subject coverage
basic research on skin, hair and teeth; toiletry products

2659 UNILEVER RESEARCH LABORATORY (COLWORTH)
Greyhope Road, Aberdeen, Scotland AB9 2JA   Tel. 0224 24295
Telex 73181
Company Research Organization; unit of the Colworth House, Bedford, Laboratory

Enquiries to the Information Officer

Subject coverage
biochemistry; chemistry and technology of fish processing; fish and shellfish farming

2660 UNILEVER RESEARCH LABORATORY (Colworth/Welwyn)
Colworth House, Sharnbrook, Bedford   Tel. 0234 55251
Telex 82229
Company Research Organization; the Welwyn Laboratory was formerly a separate unit

Enquiries, by letter only, to the Head of Library and Information, or to the Library Manager

Subject coverage
human and animal nutrition; food technology and related sciences

2661 UNILEVER RESEARCH PORT SUNLIGHT LABORATORY
Port Sunlight, Wirral, Merseyside L62 4XN   Tel. 051-645 2000
Telex 627235
Industrial Research Laboratory; formerly Unilever Research Laboratory

Enquiries, by letter only, to the Manager, Library and Documentation

Subject coverage
soaps and detergents technology

UNILEVER LIMITED *see also*
THAMES BOARD MILLS LIMITED
VINYL PRODUCTS LIMITED

2662 UNION OF CONSTRUCTION, ALLIED TRADES AND TECHNICIANS (UCATT)
Supervisory, Technical, Administrative, Managerial and Professional Section (STAMP), UCATT House, 177 Abbeville House, London SW4 9RL — Tel. 01-622 2442, Telex 917430
Trade Union; formerly Association of Building Technicians

Enquiries, from members only, to the General Secretary

Subject coverage
conditions of work and rates of pay in the construction and allied trades

2663 UNION OF SHOP, DISTRIBUTIVE AND ALLIED WORKERS
188 Wilmslow Road, Fallowfield, Manchester M14 6LJ — Tel. 061-962 4706
Trade Union; affiliated to three International Federations: Food Workers, Chemical Workers, and Commercial and Technical Employees

Enquiries to the Public Relations Officer

Subject coverage
Conditions of work, industrial relations and all Trade Union services to members from the retail and wholesale distributive trades, food manufacturing and chemical processing industries and service trades such as catering, laundries

Publications
Dawn (monthly)
Annual Report

2664 UNIT OF ANIMAL GENETICS
c/o Department of Genetics, University of Edinburgh, West Mains Road, Edinburgh EH9 3JN — Tel. 031-667 1081
Research Unit, of the Agricultural Research Council

Enquiries to the Information Officer

Subject coverage
genetics of agricultural livestock

UNIT OF COASTAL SEDIMENTATION *now* **INSTITUTE OF OCEANOGRAPHIC SCIENCES,** *q.v.*

2665 UNIT OF MUSCLE MECHANISM AND INSECT PHYSIOLOGY
Department of Zoology, Oxford University, South Parks Road, Oxford OX1 3PS — Tel. 0865 56789
Research Unit, of the Agricultural Research Council

Enquiries to the Honorary Director

Subject coverage
physiology; biophysics and biochemistry of muscular contraction; use of small computers for scientific research

Special collection
Large living tropical insects

2666 UNIT OF NITROGEN FIXATION
School of Molecular Sciences, University of Sussex, Falmer, Brighton, East Sussex BN1 9QJ — Tel. 0273 66755
Research Unit, of the Agricultural Research Council

Enquiries occasionally accepted by authors of papers, about their work

Subject coverage
Strategic and basic science in the area of nitrogen fixation: chemistry of dinitrogen, biochemistry of the nitrogenase reaction, and the microbiology and genetics of nitrogen fixing micro-organisms. The Unit is not involved in the study of symbiotic nitrogen fixing bacteria nor immediately applied work

Publications
all the work of the Unit is published in the appropriate primary journals

2667 UNIT OF SOIL PHYSICS
219c Huntingdon Road, Cambridge CB3 0DL Tel. 0223 76190
Research Unit, of the Agricultural Research Council

Enquiries, (not general enquiries), to the Director

Subject coverage
statics and dynamics of water flow in soils

Publication
List of Research Papers

2668 UNIT OF STATISTICS
James Clerk Maxwell Building, Kings Buildings, Mayfield Road, Edinburgh EH9 3JZ Tel. 031-667 1081
Research and Consultancy Unit, of the Agricultural Research Council

Enquiries to the Director

Subject coverage
statistical methodology for agricultural research; experimental design and analysis; sample surveys; *not* descriptive statistics of agriculture, or of agricultural economics or finance

Publications
List of published papers available

2669 UNIT SWIMMING POOLS LIMITED
Pearson Street, Wolverhampton WV2 4HT Tel. 0902 25371
Company

Enquiries to the Sales Director

Subject coverage
swimming pool filtration and ancillary equipment

2670 UNIT TRUST ASSOCIATION
Park House, 16 Finsbury Circus, London EC2M 7JP Tel. 01-628 0871
Trade Association; formerly Association of Unit Trust Managers

Enquiries to the Secretary

Subject coverage
general information on unit trusts and the unit trust industry; types of unit trusts; statistics on the industry; advice to unit-holders on investment; taxation, legislation and regulation

Publications
List of Member Companies
What everyone should know about Unit Trusts
Personal Taxation and Unit Trusts

2671 UNITED COMMERCIAL TRAVELLERS ASSOCIATION LIMITED
Bexton Lane, Knutsford, Cheshire WA16 9DA Tel. 0565 4136
Trade Association, member of International League of Commercial Travellers; houses the National Council for Educational Qualifications in Salesmanship

Enquiries to the Public Relations Executive

Subject coverage
selling and salesmanship; terms and condition of employment; civil and industrial legal matters; education and training

Publication
Selling Today (monthly)

2672 UNITED DOMINIONS TRUST LIMITED
51 Eastcheap, London EC3P 3BU Tel. 01-623 3020
Telex 888291

Finance House

Enquiries to the Manager, Public Relations

Subject coverage
instalment credit

2673 UNITED GLASS LIMITED
Technical Centre, Porters Wood, St. Albans, Hertfordshire AL3 6NY Tel. 0727 59261
Telex 22770
Company

Enquiries to the Information Officer or Librarian

Subject coverage
glass technology; packaging; glass containers and tableware; plastic containers; closures and caps

UNITED KINGDOM AGRICULTURAL SUPPLY TRADES LIMITED *see* **BRITISH ASSOCIATION OF GRAIN SEED FEED AND AGRICULTURAL MERCHANTS LIMITED**

2674 UNITED KINGDOM ASSOCIATION OF FROZEN FOOD PRODUCERS
1 Green Street, Grosvenor Square, London W1Y 3RG Tel. 629 0655 *or* 493 2985
Trade Association, affiliated to the Food and Drink Industries Council; formerly the National Association of Frozen Food Producers

Enquiries to the Secretary General

Subject coverage
frozen foods

Publication
Annual Report

UNITED KINGDOM ASSOCIATION OF MANUFACTURERS OF BAKERS YEAST *see* **FOOD MANUFACTURERS FEDERATION INCORPORATED**

2675 UNITED KINGDOM ASSOCIATION OF PROFESSIONAL ENGINEERS
Wix Hill House, West Horsley, Surrey KT24 6DZ Tel. 0483 222383
Trade Union

Enquiries to the General Secretary

Subject coverage
terms and conditions of employment of professional engineers

Publications
Guide to the Classification of Professional Engineering Responsibility Levels
Recommended Salary Levels for Professional Engineers

2676 UNITED KINGDOM ATOMIC ENERGY AUTHORITY
Library and Information Centre, 11 Charles II Street, London SW1 Tel. 01-930 6262 ext. 587
Headquarters of the Public Board

Enquiries to the Librarian/Information Officer

Subject coverage
research and development in the nuclear field

2677 UNITED KINGDOM ATOMIC ENERGY AUTHORITY, Reactor Group
Atomic Energy Establishment, Winfrith, Dorchester, Dorset DT2 8DH Tel. 0305 3111 ext. 2060
Telex 41231
Government Research Establishment (UKAEA, Public Board)

Enquiries to the Information Officer

Subject coverage
nuclear power; reactor physics, instrumentation and operation

Publications
AEEW Reports and Memoranda (notified in HMSO Daily List)

2678 UNITED KINGDOM ATOMIC ENERGY ESTABLISHMENT, Reactor Group
Dounreay Experimental Reactor Establishment, Thurso, Caithness KW14 7TZ Tel. 0847 2121
Government Research and Development Establishment, (UKAEA, Public Board)

Enquiries to the Information Officer, by letter

Subject coverage
fast reactor operation and development; testing of fuel elements; fuel reprocessing; development of components to operate in sodium environments; irradiation services; materials testing; reactor fuels; health physics and safety

2679 UNITED KINGDOM ATOMIC ENERGY AUTHORITY, Reactor Group
Headquarters, Library and Information Department, Risley, Warrington, Cheshire WA3 6AT — Tel. 0925 31244, Telex 62301
Government Library and Information Department (UKAEA, Publie Board); serves Risley Engineering and Materials Laboratory, British Nuclear Fuels Limited, Nuclear Power Company and the Authority Safety and Reliability Directorate at Culcheth

Enquiries to the Chief of Library and Information Services

Subject coverage
nuclear power technology; reliability engineering; tribology; industrial research

Publications
UKAEA Reading Lists (14, kept up-to-date)
Translations (deposited with BLL)
Brochures

2680 UNITED KINGDOM ATOMIC ENERGY AUTHORITY, Reactor Group
Reactor Development Laboratory, Windscale Works, Sellafield, Seascale, Cumbria CA20 1PF — Tel. 094-02 333, Telex 64140
Government Laboratory/Public Board

Enquiries to the Librarian

Subject coverage
nuclear power, physics and engineering

2681 UNITED KINGDOM ATOMIC ENERGY AUTHORITY, Reactor Group
Reactor Fuel Element Laboratories, Springfields, Salwick, Preston PR4 0RR — Tel. 0772 729351, Telex 67545
Government Laboratories, (UKAEA, Public Board)

Enquiries to the Information Officer

Subject coverage
nuclear fuel technology; materials science; ceramics fabrication and utilization; quality assurance; production process development; assessment of engineering components and designs

UNITED KINGDOM ATOMIC ENERGY AUTHORITY *see also*
ATOMIC ENERGY RESEARCH ESTABLISHMENT
BRITISH NUCLEAR FUELS LIMITED
CULHAM LABORATORY
NATIONAL CENTRE OF TRIBOLOGY
NATIONAL NUCLEAR CORPORATION LIMITED
NATIONAL RADIOLOGICAL PROTECTION BOARD
NUCLEAR POWER COMPANY (RISLEY) LIMITED
PROGRAMMES ANALYSIS UNIT
RADIOCHEMICAL CENTRE LIMITED

2682 UNITED KINGDOM CHEMICAL INFORMATION SERVICE
The University, Nottingham, Nottinghamshire NG7 2RD — Tel. 0602 57411/5, Telex 37488
Information Service (non-profit making); affiliated to the Chemical Society and formerly known as the Chemical Society Research Unit in Information Dissemination and Retrieval; also operates the Biological Information Service

Enquiries to the Service Department

Subject coverage
pure and applied chemistry; chemical engineering and related fields, e.g. chemical hazards, pollution, waste treatment, catalysis, corrosion, ion exchange, radiation chemistry, surface chemistry, etc.; biological sciences

Publications
CA Review Titles (fortnightly, 12 titles, 6 monthly indexes)
Macroprofile Service (fortnightly, 45 subjects)
Biological Information Service (personalised service)

UNITED KINGDOM CRYSTALLOGRAPHIC COUNCIL *see* **INSTITUTE OF PHYSICS**

2683 UNITED KINGDOM CUTLERY AND SILVERWARE MANUFACTURERS ASSOCIATION
Light Trades House, Melbourne Avenue, Sheffield S10 2QJ Tel. 0742 663084
Telex 54208

Trade and Employers Association

Enquiries to the Secretary

Subject coverage
trade marks; patterns; care of cutlery and silverware; sources of supply

2684 UNITED KINGDOM DAIRY ASSOCIATION
Giggs Hill Green, Thames Ditton, Surrey KT7 0EL Tel. 01-398 4101
Trade Association; member of the International Dairy Federation

Enquiries to the Secretary

Subject coverage
scientific, technical and economic aspects of the dairy industry; standards; milk and milk products

2685 UNITED KINGDOM GLYCERINE PRODUCERS ASSOCIATION
Pool Lane, Bebington, Wirral, Cheshire L62 4UF Tel. 051-645 5666
Trade Association
Enquiries to the Secretary

Subject coverage
glycerine; production statistics

UNITED KINGDOM HOVERCRAFT SOCIETY *see* **INSTITUTION OF PRODUCTION ENGINEERS**

2686 UNITED KINGDOM METAL MINING ASSOCIATION
40 Holborn Viaduct, London EC1P 1AJ Tel. 01-353 1545
Trade Association

Enquiries to the Secretary

Subject coverage
mineral industry, excluding coal and oil, in the United Kingdom; for members only, general representation and coordinated action

2687 UNITED KINGDOM SOUTH AFRICA TRADE ASSOCIATION LIMITED
21 Tothill Street, London SW1H 9LL Tel. 01-930 6711
Trade Association

No enquiry service

Subject coverage
climate of trade between the two countries and any restrictions of trade

Publication
Monthly Report (members only)

UNITED KINGDOM TEXTILE MANUFACTURERS ASSOCIATION *now* **BRITISH TEXTILE EMPLOYERS ASSOCIATION,** *q.v.*

2688 UNITED NEWSPAPERS LIMITED
23–27 Tudor Street, London EC4Y 0HR Tel. 01-583 9199
Company

Enquiries to the Information Officer

Subject coverage
marketing associated with the media and advertising

Publications
Provincial morning, evening and weekly newspapers
Farming journals
Periodicals, including Punch and Countryman

2689 UNITED ROAD TRANSPORT UNION
76 High Lane, Chorlton, Manchester 21 Tel. 061-881 6245
Trade Union, affiliated to the International Union Transport, the International Union Food and the Trades Union Council

Enquiries to the General Secretary

Subject coverage
road transport, food and drink industries

Publication
Wheels (periodical, to members only)

2690 UNIVERSITY BOTANIC GARDEN
Cambridge University, 1 Brookside, Cambridge CB2 1JF Tel. 0223 50101 *and* 59466
University Sub-Department, of the Department of Botany; the Library is the Cory Library

Enquiries to the Director

Subject coverage
identification of plants cultivated in the temperate regions; taxonomy of vascular plants; horticulture, and the history of horticulture

Special collection
Indexed collection of living plants

Publication
Seed Exchange List (annual)

2691 UNIVERSITY COLLEGE AT BUCKINGHAM
Bank House, 2 Bridge Street, Buckingham MK18 1EG Tel. 028-02 4161
University College

Enquiries to the Librarian

Subject coverage
law; politics; economics

2692 UNIVERSITY COLLEGE LONDON LIBRARY
London University, Gower Street, London WC1E 6BT Tel. 01-387 7050
University Library

Enquiries to the Reference and Information Services Librarian

Subject coverage
science and engineering, (teaching and research)

Special collections
Graves Early Science Library
Johnston Lavis Vulcanology Library
Geologists Association Library
Hertfordshire Natural History & Field Club Library
London Mathematical Society Library
Malacological Society Library

2693 UNIVERSITY COLLEGE OF NORTH WALES
Science Library, Deiniol Road, Bangor, Gwynedd LL57 2UN Tel. 0248 51151
Telex 61100

University Library; with a Branch Library in the School of Electronic Engineering Science, Dean Street, Bangor LL57 1UT; includes Industrial Development (Bangor), *q.v.* and the Marine Science Laboratories Library

Enquiries to the Assistant Librarian, Bibliographical Services

Subject coverage
physical and molecular science; mathematics; environmental science; forestry; agriculture; marine science; zoology; avionics systems; electronics and electrical materials; computing science

Special collections
Talfourd Jones Collection (works on natural history)
Bangor Forensic Science Society Library

2694 UNIVERSITY MICROFILMS INTERNATIONAL LIMITED
18 Bedford Row, London WC1R 4EJ Tel. 01-242 9485
Telex 8811363

Publishing Company; a Xerox Company; formerly University Microfilms Limited

Enquiries to the Sales Development Department

Subject coverage
micropublishing in all disciplines

Publication
Dissertation Abstracts International – Section C (European Abstracts)

UNIVERSITY OF WALES *see*
ABERYSTWYTH UNIVERSITY COLLEGE
CARDIFF UNIVERSITY COLLEGE
INSTITUTE OF SCIENCE AND TECHNOLOGY

2695 UPPER NORWOOD PUBLIC LIBRARY
Westow Hill, London SE19 1TJ Tel. 01-670 2551 *or* 5468
Public Library

Enquiries to the Librarian

Subject coverage
general

2696 URWICK TECHNOLOGY MANAGEMENT LIMITED
134 Buckingham Palace Road, London SW1W 95A Tel. 01-930 0193/8
Company; part of Urwick, Orr & Partners Limited

Enquiries to the Senior Partner

Subject coverage
studies in technology management, international and U.K., for public bodies and in the private sector

2697 VAN LEER RESEARCH LABORATORIES
Passfield, Liphook, Hampshire GU30 7RN Tel. 042-877 296
Telex 85287

Company, subsidiary of Koninklijke Emballage Industrie Van Leer B.V., Amstelveen, Holland; formerly Van Leer (U.K.) Limited Passfield Research Laboratories

Enquiries to the Librarian

Subject coverage
packaging and packaging materials (plastics, metals)

2698 VEHICLE BUILDERS AND REPAIRERS ASSOCIATION
Belmont House, 102 Finkle Lane, Gildersome, Leeds LS27 7TW Tel. 0532 538333
Trade Association; associated with Scottish National Vehicle Builders Association

Enquiries to the Chief Executive

Subject coverage
vehicle body repairs or commercial vehicle body-building

Publication
Body (monthly)
Directory of Members (annual)

VERMICULITE INFORMATION SERVICE *see* **MANDOVAL LIMITED**

2699 VETERINARY RESEARCH LABORATORIES
Northern Ireland Department of Agriculture, Stormont, Stoney Road, Belfast BT4 3SD — Tel. 0232 63082
Government Department Laboratories; linked with Queen's University, Belfast

Enquiries to the Librarian

Subject coverage
veterinary medicine; veterinary pathology; parasitology; physiology; immunology; bacteriology; biochemistry; virology; agriculture

2700 VICKERS LIMITED DESIGN AND PROJECT DIVISION
P.O. Box 44, Swindon SN3 4RA — Tel. 0793-82 3451, Telex 449398

Company; formerly Design and Procurement Division

Enquiries to the Information Services Manager

Subject coverage
automation systems; mechanical handling systems; electrical power plant; research and test equipment; refuse disposal and waste handling; environment and pollution; water treatment; malting plant

2701 VICKERS LIMITED ENGINEERING GROUP
Elswick Works, Newcastle upon Tyne NE99 1CP — Tel. 0632 38888, Telex 53104

Company

Enquiries to the Technical Librarian

Subject coverage
mechanical engineering; hydraulics; electronics; metallurgy; materials testing

2702 VICKERS LIMITED MICHELL BEARINGS
Scotswood Road, Newcastle upon Tyne NE15 6LL — Tel. 0632 30291, Telex 53397

Company, part of Vickers Limited Engineering Group; formerly Michell Bearings Limited

Enquiries to the Sales Department

Subject coverage
hydrodynamic tilting pad thrust and journal bearings for marine and industrial applications

2703 VICKERS LIMITED SHIPBUILDING GROUP
P.O. Box 6, Barrow-in-Furness, Cumbria LA14 1AB — Tel. 0229 20351, Telex 65171

Company

Enquiries to the Chief Librarian

Subject coverage
shipbuilding; nuclear engineering; offshore engineering; mechanical engineering; submarines

VICKERS LIMITED *see also* **INTERNATIONAL RESEARCH AND DEVELOPMENT COMPANY LIMITED**

2704 VINYL PRODUCTS LIMITED
Mill Lane, Carshalton, Surrey SM5 2JU — Tel. 01-669 4422
Telex 266264

Company; subsidiary of Unilever Limited

Enquiries, limited, to the Information Officer

Subject coverage
polymer chemistry and technology

VITAMINS LIMITED *now* **BEECHAM PHARMACEUTICALS RESEARCH DIVISION** *q.v.*

2705 VITREOUS ENAMEL DEVELOPMENT COUNCIL LIMITED
New House, High Street, Ticehurst, Wadhurst, Sussex TN5 7AL — Tel. 058-07 8252
Trade Association

Enquiries to the Director

Subject coverage
nature and uses of vitreous enamel finishes

2706 VOSPER THORNYCROFT LIMITED
Vosper House, 223 Southampton Road, Paulsgrove, Portsmouth, Hampshire PO6 4QA — Tel. 070-18 79481

Company; formerly Vosper Limited; comprises Shipbuilding, Ship Repairing and Engineering Products Divisions; part of David Brown Holdings Limited

Enquiries to the Group Public Relations Manager

Subject coverage
design and building of surface warships and hovercraft; ship stabilization; machinery control

2707 WAKEFIELD METROPOLITAN DISTRICT LIBRARIES
Balne Lane, Wakefield, West Yorkshire WF2 0DQ — Tel. 0924 71231
Telex 557330

Public Libraries; composed of the former West Riding County Library and Castleford, Horbury, Normanton, Ossett, Pontefract and Wakefield Public Libraries; houses the Yorkshire and Humberside Joint Library Services

Enquiries to the Chief Librarian

Subject coverage
general; labour economics; industrial training; trade unions

2708 WALES GAS
Snelling House, Bute Terrace, Cardiff, Glamorgan CF1 2UF — Tel. 0222 33131
Telex 49416

Regional Unit of the British Gas Corporation; formerly Wales Gas Board

Enquiries to the Librarian

Subject coverage
Welsh gas industry; natural gas technology

2709 WALES TOURIST BOARD
Welcome House, Llandaff, Cardiff CF52 2YZ — Tel. 0222 567701
Telex 497269

Statutory Body; three Regional Councils

Enquiries to the Board

Subject coverage
development, marketing and advisory functions relating to tourism in Wales

Publications
Tourist Guides
Promotional publications
Research reports

WALES, UNIVERSITY of *see* **UNIVERSITY OF WALES**

WALIC *now* **WILCO (Wiltshire Libraries in Co-operation)**

WALLASEY PUBLIC LIBRARY *see* **WIRRAL PUBLIC LIBRARIES**

WALLINGTON PUBLIC LIBRARY *see* **SUTTON LIBRARIES AND ARTS SERVICES**

2710 WALLPAPER, PAINT AND WALLCOVERING RETAILERS ASSOCIATION LIMITED
14 Birmingham Road, Walsall WS1 2NA Tel. 0922 31134
Trade Association, formerly Wallpaper and Paint Retailers Association

Enquiries to the Director

Subject coverage
decorating materials; D.I.Y. techniques and materials

Publication
WPW-Wallpaper Paint & Wallcovering (monthly)

2711 WALSALL CHAMBER OF COMMERCE AND INDUSTRY
Tudor House, Bridge Street, Walsall, West Midlands WS1 1HL Tel. 0922 25671
Telex 338212
Chamber of Commerce; includes the Walsall Chamber of Commerce Engineering Centre Limited

Enquiries to the Director

Subject coverage
exports and imports information; interpretation of legislation; industrial training

2712 WALSALL COLLEGE OF TECHNOLOGY
St. Pauls Street, Walsall, West Midlands WS1 1XN Tel. 0922 25124
College of Further Education; formerly Walsall and Staffordshire Technical College

Enquiries to the Tutor-Librarian

Subject coverage
engineering; building; business studies; catering

2713 WALSALL LIBRARY & MUSEUM SERVICES
Lichfield Street, Walsall, Staffordshire WS1 1TR Tel. 0922 21244 ext. 241
Public Library Service; District Libraries at Aldridge, Bloxwich, Brownhills, Darlaston, Willenhall

Enquiries to the Director

Subject coverage
general; leathercraft, including saddlery and harness manufacture; manufacture of leather including treatment of animal skins; boot and shoe manufacture; history of trades and crafts

Special collection
books, pamphlets & catalogues in connection with the Museum of Leathercraft Collection

WALLSEND AREA LIBRARY *see* **NORTH TYNESIDE METROPOLITAN DISTRICT LIBRARIES**

2714 WALTHAM FOREST COLLEGE
Forest Road, Walthamstow, London E17 4JB Tel. 01-527 2272
College of Further Education; formerly Waltham Forest Technical College; the Library has Annexes at Chingford and Hoe Street, Walthamstow

Enquiries to the Tutor Librarian

Subject coverage
catering; building; motor vehicles; electrical engineering; accounting

2715 WALTHAM FOREST PUBLIC LIBRARIES
High Street, Walthamstow, London E17 7JN Tel. 01-520 3031 *and* 4733
Public Library

Enquiries to the Borough Librarian and Curator

Subject coverage
General; specialization in town planning; land; natural resources and land utilization; furniture and furnishings; interior decoration

WANDPETLS *see* **WANDSWORTH PUBLIC EDUCATIONAL AND TECHNICAL LIBRARY SERVICES**

2716 WANDSWORTH PUBLIC EDUCATIONAL AND TECHNICAL LIBRARY SERVICES (WANDPETLS)

West Hill District Library, West Hill, Wandsworth, London SW18 1RZ
Interlibrary Cooperative Scheme

Enquiries to the Honorary Secretary

Subject coverage
general, commercial, technical

Publications
Newsletter
Handbook of Members

2717 WANDSWORTH PUBLIC LIBRARIES
West Hill District Library, West Hill, London SW18 1RZ Tel. 01-874 1143
Telex 25632

Public Library; includes Balham and Battersea Public Libraries

Enquiries to the Borough Librarian

Subject coverage
general; building and architecture

Publication
Focus (abstract of local government journals)

WANDSWORTH TECHNICAL COLLEGE *now* **SOUTH THAMES COLLEGE,** *q.v.*

WARDLE AREA LIBRARY *see* **ROCHDALE LIBRARIES AND ARTS SERVICES**

2718 WARE COLLEGE
Scotts Road, Ware, Hertfordshire Tel. 0920 5441
College of Further Education

Enquiries to the Senior Librarian

Subject coverage
display work; commercial art; photography

2719 WARLEY COLLEGE OF TECHNOLOGY
Crocketts Lane, Smethwick, Warley, West Midlands B66 3BU Tel. 021-558 4121 ext. 10

College of Further Education

Enquiries to the Tutor-Librarian

Subject coverage
general; technical

2720 WARREN SPRING LABORATORY
Gunnels Wood Road, Stevenage, Hertfordshire SG1 2BX Tel. 0438 3388
Telex 82250

Government Research and Development Contractors, for the Department of Industry

Enquiries to the Director

Subject coverage
minerals processing; metals extraction; process automation and control; bulk materials handling; air pollution including odours; oil pollution; waste materials recycling and recovery

2721 WARRINGTON LIBRARY
Museum Street, Warrington, Lancashire WA1 1JB — Tel. 0925 54359
Public Library, part of the Cheshire County Library, *q.v.*

Enquiries to the Reference Librarian

Subject coverage
soap industry and manufacture; other organic chemical industries; wire manufacture; welding; electroplating; alloys

2722 WARRINGTON TECHNICAL COLLEGE
Winwick Road, Warrington, Lancashire WA2 8QA — Tel. 0925 37311
College of Further Education

Enquiries to the Librarian

Subject coverage
building; engineering; science; business studies

2723 WARWICK UNIVERSITY LIBRARY
Gibbet Hill Road, Coventry, Warwickshire CV4 7AL — Tel. 0203 24011
Telex 31406

University Library

Enquiries to the Librarian

Subject coverage
biological sciences, computer science, engineering, environmental sciences, mathematics, molecular sciences, physics, psychology, statistics; economics, industrial and business studies, law

Special collections
Statistics of finance, trade and industry
Economics Working Papers

Publications
The National Provision of Printed Ephemera in the Social Sciences, by J.E. Pemberton (Occasional Paper, no.1)

2724 WARWICKSHIRE COLLEGE OF AGRICULTURE
Moreton Hall, Moreton Morrell, Warwickshire CU35 9BL — Tel. 092-685 367
College of Further Education

Enquiries to the Librarian

Subject coverage
agriculture; horticulture

2725 WARWICKSHIRE COUNTY LIBRARY
The Butts, Warwick CV34 4SS — Tel. 0926 43431
Telex 31621

Public Library Service; four Divisional Libraries: East Divisional at Rugby, Central Divisional at Leamington Spa, South-West Divisional at Stratford-upon-Avon and North Divisional at Nuneaton

Enquiries to the Librarian

Subject coverage
general; strong commercial section; industry; motor engineering; car manuals; industrial management

Special collection
electrical engineering at Rugby Divisional Library

2726 WASHER MANUFACTURERS ASSOCIATION OF GREAT BRITAIN
136 Hagley Road, Edgbaston, Birmingham B16 9PN — Tel. 021-454 4141
Trade Association

Enquiries to the Secretaries

Subject coverage
manufacture of black, mild steel, heavy pattern, round- or square-holed washers; availability of supply

2727 WASTE MANAGEMENT INFORMATION BUREAU
Atomic Energy Research Establishment, Building 151, Harwell, Didcot, Oxford OX11 0RA — Tel. 0235 24141 ext. 2121, Telex 83135
Information Bureau, associated with the Hazardous Materials Service, United Kingdom Atomic Energy Authority

Enquiries to the Information Officer

Subject coverage
waste treatment, disposal, reclamation; hazardous materials; safety; general chemical hazards

WATCH AND CLOCK IMPORTERS ASSOCIATION *see* **FEDERATION OF WHOLESALE AND INDUSTRIAL DISTRIBUTORS**

2728 WATER COMPANIES ASSOCIATION
15 Great College Street, London SW1P 3RX — Tel. 01-222 0644
Company, to promote efficiency of Water Companies, of whom there are 28 members

Enquiries to the Secretary, but more appropriately to the Water Companies themselves

Subject coverage
water supply

2729 WATER DATA UNIT
Reading Bridge House, Reading, Berkshire RG1 8PS — Tel. 0734 57551
Government Department; of the Department of the Environment; formerly Water Resources Board; housed with the Central Water Planning Unit

Enquiries to the Librarian

Subject coverage
water resources management; collation and publication of data provided by the Water Authorities, as the "Water Archive"

Publication
Water Archive (collected data)

WATER INFORMATION CENTRE *see* **NATIONAL WATER COUNCIL**

WATER POLLUTION RESEARCH LABORATORY *now* **WATER RESEARCH CENTRE STEVENAGE LABORATORY** *q.v.*

WATER RESEARCH ASSOCIATION *now* **WATER RESEARCH CENTRE MEDMENHAM LABORATORY,** *q.v.*

2730 WATER RESEARCH CENTRE MEDMENHAM LABORATORY
P.O. Box 16, Henley Road, Medmenham, Buckinghamshire SL7 2HD — Tel. 049-166 531
Research Association; formerly Water Research Association; now part of the Water Research Centre, whose Administrative Headquarters is at 45 Station Road, Henley-on-Thames, Oxon

Enquiries to the Director

Subject coverage
all aspects of water supply: hydrology; water analysis; hydrobiology; water treatment; water distribution; mathematical modelling; operational research; economics

Publications
WRC Information (weekly, abstracting journal)
Technical Reports (confidential to members)
Proceedings of WRC-sponsored Conferences

2731 WATER RESEARCH CENTRE STEVENAGE LABORATORY
Elder Way, Stevenage, Hertfordshire SG1 1TH — Tel. 0438 2444
Research Association; formerly Water Pollution Research Laboratory which merged with the Water Research Association Medmenham Laboratory, now part of the Centre, whose Administrative Headquarters is at 45 Station Road, Henley-on-Thames, Oxon

Enquiries to the Librarian

Subject coverage
sewage treatment; industrial and trade wastes; pollution of water; effects of pollution on aquatic life

Publication
WRC Information (weekly abstracting journal, formerly Water Pollution Abstracts)

WATER RESOURCES BOARD *now* **CENTRAL WATER PLANNING UNIT,** *q.v.*

WATER SPACE AMENITY COMMISSION *see* **NATIONAL WATER COUNCIL**

WATER SUPPLY INDUSTRY TRAINING BOARD *now* **NATIONAL WATER COUNCIL,** *q.v.*

2732 WATER-TUBE BOILERMAKERS ASSOCIATION
Leicester House, 8 Leicester Street, London WC2H 7BN Tel. 01-437 0678
Trade Association, member of BEAMA, *q.v.*

Enquiries to the Director

Subject coverage
land-based water-tube boiler plant for electricity supply utilities and for the electricity and industrial process requirements of public and private sectors of industry

2733 WATFORD COLLEGE
Hempstead Road, Watford, Hertfordshire WD4 8DD Tel. 0923 41211
College of Technology; Member of Herts Technical Information Service (HERTIS); formerly Watford College of Technology

Enquiries to the College Librarian

Subject coverage
management and business, especially advertising and marketing; printing, including ink, paper, packaging and associated technologies

Publications
Research project reports (on microfiche)
Bibliographies: Computer output microfilm, 1974
Optical character recognition, 1974
Radiation drying, 1973 etc.

2734 WATFORD COLLEGE
Water Lane, Watford, Hertfordshire WD1 2NN Tel. 92 29232
College of Further Education; formerly the George Stephenson College

Enquiries to the Librarian

Subject coverage
automobile, electrical and mechanical engineering; printing

2735 WEBBING MANUFACTURERS ASSOCIATION
P.O. Box 498, Derby House, 12–16 Booth Street, Manchester M60 2ED Tel. 061-236 9721
Trade Association, member of the Narrow Fabrics Federation Limited

Enquiries to the Secretary

Subject coverage
manufacture of webbing

WEDNESBURY COLLEGE OF COMMERCE *now* **WEST BROMWICH COLLEGE OF COMMERCE AND TECHNOLOGY,** *q.v.*

WEDNESBURY DISTRICT LIBRARY *see* **SANDWELL PUBLIC LIBRARIES**

2736 WEED RESEARCH ORGANIZATION
Begbroke Hill, Sandy Lane, Yarnton, Oxford OX5 1PF Tel. 086-75 3761
Research Organization, of the Agricultural Research Council, Department of Education and Science, and Ministry of Agriculture

Enquiries to the Head, Information Department

Subject coverage

weed biology, physiology, cultivation and utilization; susceptibility to herbicides; weed control; herbicides including their chemistry, analysis, persistence of residues, physiological effects, soil and environment relations, economics

Publications

Weed Abstracts (published CAB, bi-monthly)
Plant Growth Regulator Abstracts (published CAB)
Weed Research (published Blackwells)
Weed Control Handbook, 2 vols (published Blackwells)
WRO Reports, Annotated Bibliographies, List of Research Projects, etc.

2737 WEIGHING AND TESTING MACHINE MANUFACTURERS EXPORT GROUP
Alan Pond House, 366–370 Soho Road, Birmingham B21 9QL Tel. 021-523 9296
Trade Association

Enquiries to the Secretary

Subject coverage

export of weighing and materials testing equipment

WEIGHTS AND MEASURES SERVICE *see* **DEPARTMENT OF PRICES AND CONSUMER PROTECTION**

2738 WEIR PUMPS LIMITED
149 Newlands Road, Cathcart, Glasgow G44 4EX Tel. 041-637 7141
Telex 77161/2

Company, part of the Weir Group; formerly G. and J. Weir Limited

Enquiries to the Librarian

Subject coverage

mechanical engineering; fluid mechanics; noise and vibration; pumps (centrifugal, axial); stress analysis

WELLCOME INSTITUTE OF COMPARATIVE PHYSIOLOGY *see* **ZOOLOGICAL SOCIETY OF LONDON**

2739 WELLCOME RESEARCH LABORATORIES
Langley Court, Beckenham, Kent BR3 3BS Tel. 01-658 2211
Telex 23937

Company, part of Wellcome Foundation Limited; Excerpta Medica data base

Enquiries to the Librarian or to the Head of Literature Services

Subject coverage

tropical medicine; chemistry; pharmacology; chemotherapy; virology; immunology; bacteriology; biochemistry

Publications

Foot and Mouth Disease Bulletin
Publications of Wellcome Foundation and Associated Companies (quarterly)

2740 WELLCOME RESEARCH LABORATORIES
Berkhamsted Hill, Berkhamsted, Hertfordshire HP4 2QE Tel. 04427 5681
04427 3333
Telex 825477

Company, part of Wellcome Foundation Limited; formerly Cooper Technical Bureau

Enquiries to the Librarian

Subject coverage

veterinary science; entomology; chemotherapy; control of insects affecting livestock, households, and stored products; dairy hygiene; aerosols

2741 WELDED TOOL MANUFACTURERS ASSOCIATION
Light Trades House, Melbourne Avenue, Sheffield S10 2QJ Tel. 0742 663084
Trade Association; member of the National Federation of Engineers Tool Manufacturers

Enquiries to the Secretary

Subject coverage
welded tools manufacture

2742 WELDING INSTITUTE
Abington Hall, Abington, Cambridge CB1 6AL Tel. 0223 891162
Telex 81183

Research Association and Professional Institution; created by the amalgamation of the British Welding Research Association and the Institute of Welding; includes the School of Applied Non-Destructive Testing and the School of Welding Technology; houses the Certification Scheme for Weldment Inspection Personnel

Enquiries, from Member Companies, to the Information Officer; from other librarians/information officers, to the Librarian

Subject coverage
technology and practice of welding; brazing; soldering; thermal cutting; weld surfacing; metal spraying; inspection and non-destructive testing; welding design; welding metallurgy; performance of welded assemblies (failure, fatigue, brittle fracture, corrosion); fabrication and construction; quality control

Publications
Weldasearch Information Services
1. SDI Monthly Abstracts
2. Specialist Reading Lists
6. Complete Information & Retrieval System
other systems on request
Welding Institute Research Bulletin (monthly, Confidential to Members)
Metal Construction (monthly)
Welding Research International (bi-monthly)
Surfacing Journal (quarterly)

2743 WELDING MANUFACTURERS ASSOCIATION
Leicester House, 8 Leicester Street, London WC2H 7BN Tel. 01-437 0678
Trade Association; member of BEAMA, *q.v.*

Enquiries to the Director

Subject coverage
technical and commercial matters relating to manufacture of arc welding electrodes and consumables; arc welding plant, generators, transformers and rectifiers; resistance welding machines

WELLINGBOROUGH DISTRICT LIBRARY *see* **NORTHAMPTONSHIRE LIBRARIES**

2744 WELLMAN ENGINEERING CORPORATION LIMITED
Parnell House, 25 Wilton Road, London SW1V 1LS Tel. 01-834 6800
Telex 21809

Public Company

Enquiries to the Public Relations Officer

Subject coverage
engineering

WELLS DISTRICT LIBRARY *see* **SOMERSET COUNTY LIBRARY**

WELSH COLLEGE OF ADVANCED TECHNOLOGY *now* **INSTITUTE OF SCIENCE AND TECHNOLOGY,** *q.v.*

2745 WELSH OFFICE LIBRARY
Cathays Park, Cardiff CF1 3NQ Tel. 0222 28066
Telex 49228

Government Department Library

Enquiries to the Librarian

Subject coverage
industrial development; economic planning; public finance; land use planning; highways; transportation; all as related to Wales

Publication
Research, Wales (H.M.S.O., annual)

2746 WELSH PLANT BREEDING STATION
Plas Gogerddan, Aberystwyth, Dyfed SY23 3EB Tel. 0970-87 255
Agricultural Research Institute, Department of the University College of Wales, grant-aided by the Agricultural Research Council

Enquiries to the Director

Subject coverage
improvement of crop plants by selection and breeding; plant genetics; physiology; cytology; pathology

Special collections
seed collections of herbage grasses, legumes, oats and barley, field beans and forage brassicas; strains of *Rhizobium* (nitrogen-fixing bacteria)

Publication
Annual Report

WELWYN GARDEN CITY CENTRAL LIBRARY *see* **HERTFORDSHIRE LIBRARY SERVICE**

2747 WELWYN HALL RESEARCH ASSOCIATION
Laboratories, Edgeworth House, Arlesey, Bedfordshire SG15 6SX Tel. 0462 731292
940 71580
Research Association; registered office at 11 White Lion House, Town Centre, Hatfield AL10 0JL; housing also the British Whiting Federation and the Calcium Silicate Brick Association Limited *qq.v.*

Enquiries to the Director at Arlesey or the Secretary at Hatfield

Subject coverage
manufacture, properties and use of lime, calcium silicate bricks and chalk whiting; powder technology

WESLINK *see* **WEST MIDLANDS LIBRARY AND INFORMATION NETWORK**

WESSEX MEDICAL LIBRARIES *see* **SOUTHAMPTON UNIVERSITY LIBRARY**

WEST BROMWICH CENTRAL LIBRARY *see* **SANDWELL CENTRAL LIBRARY**

2748 WEST BROMWICH COLLEGE OF COMMERCE AND TECHNOLOGY
Woden Road South, Wednesbury, West Midlands WS10 0PE Tel. 021-569 4695
College of Further Education

Enquiries to the Librarian

Subject coverage
foundry technology, metallurgy, welding, marketing, business economics, management, motor vehicle technology, production and mechanical engineering, photography, crafts

Special collection
Diecasting Society Library

2749 WEST BROMWICH COLLEGE OF COMMERCE AND TECHNOLOGY
Management Services Division, Wood Green, Wednesbury, West Midlands WS10 9QN Tel. 021-569 4635
College of Further Education; formerly Wednesbury College of Commerce

Enquiries to the Librarian

Subject coverage
accounting; management; economics

2750 WEST CUMBRIA COLLEGE
Park Lane, Workington Tel. 0900 3527
College of Further Education; formerly Workington College of Further Education and amalgamated with Whitehaven College of Further Education

Enquiries to the Tutor-Librarian

Subject coverage
electrical and mechanical engineering; chemistry; physics; catering; management; building and construction

2751 WEST GLAMORGAN COUNTY LIBRARY
Central Library, Alexander Road, Swansea SA1 5DX Tel. 0792 54065
Public Library Service, formed from the former Public Libraries of Swansea, Port Talbot and Neath

Enquiries to the County Librarian

Subject coverage
general

2752 WEST HAM COLLEGE
Welfare Road, Stratford, London E15 4HT Tel. 01-555 1422 ext. 210
College of Further Education

Enquiries to the Librarian

Subject coverage
craft and technician courses subjects; secretarial and business studies

WEST HILL DISTRICT LIBRARY *see* **WANDSWORTH PUBLIC LIBRARIES**

2753 WEST LONDON INSTITUTE OF HIGHER EDUCATION
The Library, Borough Road College, Isleworth, Middlesex TW7 5DU Tel. 01-560 5991
Institute of Higher Education, comprising the former Borough Road and Maria Grey Colleges and part of the former Chiswick Polytechnic

Enquiries to the Librarians at the Isleworth or Bath Road (Chiswick) sites

Subject coverage
general; health and social studies

2754 WEST LOTHIAN COLLEGE OF FURTHER EDUCATION
Marjoribanks Street, Bathgate, West Lothian EH48 1QJ Tel. 0506 55801/4
College of Further Education; formerly Bathgate Technical College

Enquiries to the Librarian

Subject coverage
engineering; building; business studies

2755 WEST LOTHIAN DISTRICT LIBRARY
Marjoribanks Street, Bathgate, West Lothian EH48 1AN Tel. 0506 52866
Public Library service; formerly West Lothian County Library

Enquiries to the Chief Librarian

Subject coverage
local and general

2756 WEST MIDLANDS LIBRARY AND INFORMATION NETWORK (Weslink)
Science and Technology Department, Central Libraries, Birmingham B3 3HQ Tel. 021-235 4393 Telex 337655
Interlibrary Cooperative Scheme

Enquiries to the Honorary Secretary

Subject coverage
science and technology; local government information

Publications
Members Directory and Union List of Standards, Reports and Patents
Current-awareness abstracts bulletin for local authority councillors (no title)

WEST MIDLANDS PRODUCTIVITY ASSOCIATION *see* **BIRMINGHAM PRODUCTIVITY SERVICE LIMITED**

2757 WEST OF SCOTLAND AGRICULTURAL COLLEGE
Auchincruive, Ayr KA6 5HW Tel. 029-252 331
Agricultural College

Enquiries to the Principal

Subject coverage
agriculture and allied subjects

Publications
Annual Report
Advisory bulletins, leaflets, etc.

2758 WEST OXFORDSHIRE TECHNICAL COLLEGE
Holloway Road, Witney, Oxfordshire OX8 7EE Tel. 0993 3464
College of Further Education; Open University Study Centre

Enquiries to the Tutor Librarian

Subject coverage
general

WEST RIDING COUNTY LIBRARY *now* **NORTH YORKSHIRE COUNTY LIBRARY,** *q.v.* *and* **WAKEFIELD METROPOLITAN DISTRICT LIBRARIES**

2759 WEST SUSSEX COUNTY COUNCIL LIBRARY SERVICE
County Hall, Tower Street, Chichester, Sussex PO19 1QJ Tel. 0243 85100
Telex 86279

Public Library Service; three Divisional Libraries: Chichester, Crawley and Worthing

Enquiries to the Librarians

Subject coverage
general, industrial and commercial

2760 WESTFIELD COLLEGE
London University, Kidderpore Avenue, Hampstead, London NW3 7ST Tel. 01-435 7141
University College

Enquiries to the Librarian

Subject coverage
chemistry; physics; botany; biochemistry; zoology; mathematics; computer science; environmental science

Publication
College Report

WESTHOUGHTON PUBLIC LIBRARY *see* **BOLTON METROPOLITAN BOROUGH CENTRAL LIBRARY**

WESTLAND AIRCRAFT LIMITED *see* **NORMALAIR-GARRETT LIMITED**

2761 WESTMINSTER CITY LIBRARIES
Marylebone Road, London NW1 5PS (Headquarters) Tel. 01-828 8070
Telex 263305

Central Reference Library, St. Martins Street, London WC2H 7HP Tel. 01-930 3274
(for information provision) Telex 261845
Public Library

Enquiries to the City Librarian

Subject coverage
all areas of commerce and technology; medicine (at Marylebone address)

Publication
Medical Library List of Additions (quarterly)

2762 WESTMINSTER COLLEGE
Vincent Square, London SW1P 2PD Tel. 01-828 6951
College of Higher and Further Education; formed by the amalgamation of Westminster Technical College and Pulteney College; new premises are proposed from 1977, but the collection on hotel-keeping and catering will remain at Vincent Square

Enquiries to the Librarian

Subject coverage
specializes in hotel-keeping and catering, including food, wine and catering equipment

2763 WESTMINSTER DREDGING COMPANY LIMITED
Westminster House, Blacknest, Alton, Hampshire GU34 4PU Tel. 042-04 3361
Telex 858 395

Company

Enquiries to the Public Relations Officer

Subject coverage
dredging; hand reclamation; submarine pipelines; single-buoy-moorings; oil platforms; building construction; drilling and blasting; survey projects and feasibility studies

Publication
Cohesion (house magazine)

WESTMORLAND COUNTY LIBRARY *now* **CUMBRIA COUNTY LIBRARY,** *q.v.*

2764 WESTON RESEARCH LABORATORIES LIMITED
644 Bath Road, Taplow, Maidenhead, Berkshire SL6 0PA Tel. 06-286 4741
Company, part of Associated British Foods

No enquiry service

Subject coverage
flour milling; baking; cereals

WESTON-SUPER-MARE DISTRICT LIBRARY *see* **AVON COUNTY LIBRARY**

2765 WESTON-SUPER-MARE TECHNICAL COLLEGE
Knightstone Road, Weston-super-Mare, Avon BS23 2AL Tel. 0934 21301
Technical College

Enquiries to Librarian and Resources Tutor

Subject coverage
general

WEYBRIDGE BRANCH LIBRARY *see* **SURREY COUNTY LIBRARY**

WHIPPLE LIBRARY *see* **CAMBRIDGE UNIVERSITY Whipple Library**

WHIPPLE MUSEUM OF THE HISTORY OF SCIENCE *see* **CAMBRIDGE UNIVERSITY Whipple Museum**

2766 J. WHITAKER AND SONS LIMITED
13 Bedford Square, London WC1B 3JE Tel. 01-636 4748
Publishing Company, including Whitakers Book Listing Services and the Standard Book Numbering Agency

Enquiries are not accepted

Subject coverage
book trade bibliography

Publications
The Bookseller (weekly)
Whitakers Books of the Month & Books to Come (monthly)
Whitakers Cumulative Book List (weekly, monthly, 3-monthly, annual vol.)
British Books in Print

WHITAKERS BOOK LISTING SERVICES LIMITED *see* **J. WHITAKER & SONS LIMITED**

WHITCHURCH CALDECOTT LIBRARY *see* **SHROPSHIRE COUNTY LIBRARY**

2767 WHITE FISH AUTHORITY
Sea Fisheries House, 10 Young Street, Edinburgh EH2 4JQ Tel. 031-225 2515
Telex 727225
Statutory Body, quasi-Governmental; includes the Fishery Economics Research Unit, *q.v.*

Enquiries to the Chief Information Officer

Subject coverage
fishing industry: grant and loan facilities; research and development; fish farming; marine survey; fishery economics research

Publications
Research and Development Bulletins (44 titles)
Special Reports
Annual Report
Fishery Economics Research Unit (FERU) Bulletin (quarterly)
List of Publications

2768 WHITE FISH AUTHORITY
Industrial Development Unit, St Andrews Dock South Side, Hull HU3 4QE Tel. 0482 27837
Telex 527261
Statutory Body; Division of White Fish Authority, Edinburgh, *q.v.*

Enquiries to the Librarian

Subject coverage
fisheries management and design services; fishing technology; fishing vessel design; fisheries training

Publications
see White Fish Authority, Edinburgh, list

WHITE LEAD MANUFACTURERS ASSOCIATION *see* **BRITISH LEAD MANUFACTURERS ASSOCIATION**

WHITECHAPEL AREA LIBRARY *see* **TOWER HAMLETS LIBRARIES DEPARTMENT**

2769 WHITECROFT LIMITED
Blackfriars House, Parsonage, Manchester M3 2HX Tel. 061-834 8181
Company; formerly Bleaching Trade Association or Bleachers Association

Enquiries to the Group Commercial Development Executive

Subject coverage
finishing of woven and non-woven cotton and man-made fibre textiles; bleaching, dyeing, resin treatment and scouring of textiles

WHITEHAVEN PUBLIC LIBRARY *see* **CUMBRIA COUNTY LIBRARY**

WHITLEY BAY AREA LIBRARY *see* **NORTH TYNESIDE METROPOLITAN DISTRICT LIBRARIES**

2770 WHITWOOD MINING AND TECHNICAL COLLEGE
Four Lane Ends, Whitwood, Castleford, West Yorkshire WF10 5NF Tel. 097-75 4571
Technical College

Enquiries to the Librarian

Subject coverage
mining

Special collection
Transactions of the Institution of Mining Engineers (an almost complete set)

2771 WHOLESALE CONFECTIONERS ALLIANCE LIMITED
15 Tooks Court, London EC4A 1LA Tel. 01-831 7581
Telex 23485

Trade Association

Enquiries to the Secretaries

Subject coverage
wholesaling of confectionery

Publication
Year Book

WHOLESALE FLOORCOVERING DISTRIBUTORS ASSOCIATION *see* **FEDERATION OF WHOLESALE AND INDUSTRIAL DISTRIBUTORS**

2772 WHOLESALE FOOTWEAR DISTRIBUTORS ASSOCIATION
69 Cannon Street, London EC4N 5AB Tel. 01-248 4444
Telex 888941

Trade Association, affiliated to the Federation of Wholesale and Industrial Distributors

Enquiries to the Secretary

Subject coverage
footwear wholesaling in the U.K.

WHOLESALE HORTICULTURAL ASSOCIATION *see* **FEDERATION OF WHOLESALE AND INDUSTRIAL DISTRIBUTORS**

2773 WHOLESALE LEATHER DISTRIBUTORS ASSOCIATION
69 Cannon Street, London EC4N 5AB Tel. 01-248 4444
Trade Association

Enquiries accepted from Members only

Subject coverage
leather

2774 WHOLESALE TOBACCO TRADE ASSOCIATION
15 Tooks Court, London EC4A 1LA Tel. 01-831 7581
Telex 23485

Trade Association

Enquiries to the Secretary

Subject coverage
wholesaling of tobacco

Publication
List of Members

WICK DIVISIONAL LIBRARY *see* **HIGHLAND REGION LIBRARY SERVICE**

2775 WICKMAN LIMITED
Banner Lane, Coventry CV4 9GE Tel. 0203 465231
Telex 311521

Company, part of John Brown Group; fourteen Branches and Divisions, including a Central Research and Advanced Design Department, Metal Cutting Division, Metal Forming Division, etc.

Enquiries to the Sales Promotion and Public Relations Manager

Subject coverage
machine tools; machine tool manufacturing; metal cutting; metal forming; automatic assembly; numerically controlled machines

Publications
Catalogues
Wickman News (quarterly)

2776 WIDNES LIBRARY
Victoria Road, Widnes, Cheshire Tel. 051-424 2061
Public Library, part of the Cheshire County Library, *q.v.*

Enquiries to the Librarian

Subject coverage
general

WIDNES TECHNICAL COLLEGE *now* **HALTON COLLEGE OF FURTHER EDUCATION,** *q.v.*

2777 WIGAN COLLEGE OF TECHNOLOGY
Parsons Walk, Wigan, Greater Manchester WN1 1RR Tel. 0942 41711 ext. 14

College; formerly Wigan and District Mining and Technical College

Enquiries to the College Librarian

Subject coverage
mining and geology; general scientific, technical & commercial material

Special collection
major part of the Library of the Manchester Geological Society

Publications
Geology and Mining: books published before 1840
College Periodicals

2778 WIGAN METROPOLITAN BOROUGH REFERENCE LIBRARIES
Wigan Library Reference Department, Rodney Street, Tel. 0942 41387
Wigan WN7 1EB

Public Library Service; includes Leigh Library, Wigan WN7 1EB, and Golborne and Standish Libraries

Enquiries to the Librarians

Subject coverage
general; mining; geology

2779 WIGGINS TEAPE RESEARCH & DEVELOPMENT LIMITED
Butlers Court, Beaconsfield, Buckinghamshire HP9 1RT Tel. 0494 65652
Telex 83612

Company; part of British American Tobacco Company Limited

Enquiries to the Technical Information Officer

Subject coverage
scientific, technical and techno/commercial literature for pulp and paper and related disciplines, *i.e.* instrumentation, process control, quality control, testing and test methods

WIGSTON MAGNA LIBRARY *see* **LEICESTERSHIRE LIBRARIES AND INFORMATION SERVICE**

WILCO *see* **WILTSHIRE LIBRARIES IN CO-OPERATION**

2780 WILD FLOWER SOCIETY
C/o Harvest House, 62 London Road, Reading, Berkshire RG1 5AS Tel. 0734 861345
Private Society, a Charity

Enquiries to the Administrative Office

Subject coverage
British wild flowers, their names and importance

Publications
Wild Flower Magazine (3 times per annum)
Wild Flower Diary

R.L. WILKINSON LIBRARY *see* **KITSON COLLEGE OF TECHNOLOGY**

WILLENHALL DISTRICT LIBRARY *see* **WALSALL LIBRARY AND MUSEUM SERVICES**

2781 WILLESDEN COLLEGE OF TECHNOLOGY
Denzil Road, London NW10 2XD Tel. 01-459 0147/8/9
College of Further Education

Enquiries to the Librarian

Subject coverage
professional building; building crafts; electrical, mechanical, and automobile engineering

2782 WILLIAMS & GLYNS BANK LIMITED
20 Birchin Lane, London EC3P 3DP Tel. 01-623 4356
Bank; of the National and Commercial Banking Group Limited; created by the merger of Williams Deacon's Bank, Glyn Mills & Company and the National Bank

Enquiries to the Advertising Manager

Subject coverage
banking and related financial matters

Publication
Three Banks Review

WILLITON AREA LIBRARY *see* **SOMERSET COUNTY LIBRARY**

2783 W.D. & H.O. WILLS
P.O. Box 244, Hartcliffe, Bristol BS99 7UJ Tel. 0272 664641 exts. 2238 *and* 2477
Telex 44744

Manufacturing Company; subsidiary of Imperial Tobacco Limited

Enquiries to the Head of Library

Subject coverage
tobacco industry

2784 WILMSLOW LIBRARY
South Drive, Wilmslow, Cheshire Tel. 099-64 28977
Public Library, part of the Cheshire Country Library, *q.v.*

Enquiries to the Librarian

Subject coverage
general

WILTSHIRE ASSOCIATION OF LIBRARIES OF INDUSTRY AND COMMERCE (WALIC) *now* **WILTSHIRE LIBRARIES IN CO-OPERATION (WILCO)**

2785 WILTSHIRE COUNTY LIBRARY
Bythesea Road, Trowbridge, Wiltshire Tel. 022-14 3641
Telex 44297
Public Library system; Divisional libraries at Chippenham, Salisbury, Swindon; Agency Library: Thamesdown District

Enquiries to the Librarians

Subject coverage
general

2786 WILTSHIRE LIBRARIES IN COOPERATION (WILCO)
Wiltshire Library and Museum Service, Swindon Divisional Library, Tel. 0793 27211
Regent Circus, Swindon SN1 1QG Telex 44658
Interlibrary Cooperative Scheme; resources of eleven members and the Wiltshire Library Service

Enquiries to the Secretary/Treasurer

Subject coverage
general, commercial, technical

2787 WIMBLEDON DISTRICT LIBRARY
Wimbledon Hill Road, London SW19 7NB Tel. 01-946 7979 *and* 7432
Public Library, district library of Merton Libraries Service, *q.v.*

Enquiries to the Librarian

Subject coverage
general; tennis

WIMBLEDON TECHNICAL COLLEGE *now* **MERTON TECHNICAL COLLEGE,** *q.v.*

George WIMPEY AND COMPANY LIMITED *see*
BMES GROUP LIMITED
WIMPEY LABORATORIES LIMITED

2788 WIMPEY LABORATORIES LIMITED
Beaconsfield Road, Hayes, Middlesex UB4 0LS Tel. 01-573 7744
Telex 935797
Company, Research Unit of George Wimpey & Company Limited; formerly Wimpey Central Laboratory

Enquiries to the Librarian

Subject coverage
soil and rock mechanics; grouting; hydrographic surveys; land and marine site investigations; rock bolting and anchors; hydraulic model research; geophysical, geological, and geochemical surveys; oceanographic studies; building materials tests; concrete and asphalt technology; metallurgical and chemical analysis

Publications
Wimpey News

WINCANTON DISTRICT LIBRARY *see* **SOMERSET COUNTY LIBRARY**

2789 WINCHESTER DISTRICT LIBRARY
Jewry Street, Winchester, Hampshire SO23 8RX Tel. 0962 3909
Public Library; Branch of Hampshire County Library, *q.v.*, and central library of Hampshire's Winchester District

Enquiries to the Librarian

Subject coverage
general

Special collection
The Transport Collection (loan collection, principally on railways, but also on canals, trams, buses, traction engines and theory of transport)

WINDERMERE PUBLIC LIBRARY *now* **CUMBRIA COUNTY LIBRARY,** *q.v.*

WINDSCALE REACTOR DEVELOPMENT LABORATORY *see* **UNITED KINGDOM ATOMIC ENERGY AUTHORITY, Reactor Group**

WINDSOR PUBLIC LIBRARY *see* **MAIDENHEAD/WINDSOR DISTRICT LIBRARY**

WINFRITH ATOMIC ENERGY ESTABLISHMENT *see* **UNITED KINGDOM ATOMIC ENERGY AUTHORITY, Reactor Group**

2790 WIRA
Headingley Lane, Leeds LS6 1BW Tel. 0532 75071
Telex 557189

Industrial Research Association; formerly Wool Industries Research Association; includes the former Wool Textile Research Council

Enquiries to the Librarian

Subject coverage
textiles, particularly woollen and worsted

Publications
Wira News
Wira Reports
Wira Scan (abstracts)

2791 WIRRAL PUBLIC LIBRARIES
Birkenhead Central Library, Borough Road, Birkenhead L41 2XB Tel. 051-652 6106/7/8
Telex 628136

Public Libraries and Information Service, created by the merger of Birkenhead, Wallasey and Bebington Public Libraries

Enquiries to the Chief Librarian

Subject coverage
naval architecture and engineering; food and confectionery manufacture and preservation; insurance; floriculture

WISHART LIBRARY *see* **CAMBRIDGE UNIVERSITY Department of Pure Mathematics and Statistics**

WITNEY DISTRICT LIBRARY *see* **OXFORDSHIRE COUNTY LIBRARIES**

WOBURN EXPERIMENTAL STATION *see* **ROTHAMSTED EXPERIMENTAL STATION**

WOKING BRANCH LIBRARY *see* **SURREY COUNTY LIBRARY**

WOKINGHAM DISTRICT LIBRARY *see* **BERKSHIRE COUNTY LIBRARY**

2792 WOLFSON BIOANALYTICAL CENTRE
University of Surrey, Guildford, Surrey GU2 5XH Tel. 0483 71281
Telex 85331

University Unit

Enquiries to the Director

Subject coverage
analysis, especially organic trace substances (drugs etc.) and biological macromolecule populations; asbestos characterization; biochemistry of cell components; centrifugation (especially gradient methods); chromatography; instrumentation (analytical); environmental and safety testing

Publications
Methodology book series (North-Holland)
Brochure on the Centre

2793 WOLFSON CENTRE FOR MAGNETICS TECHNOLOGY
Department of Electrical and Electronic Engineering, University College, 30 The Parade, Cardiff CF2 3AD — Tel. 0222 44741/2/3
University Research Centre; formerly Wolfson Centre for the Technology of Soft Magnetic Materials

Enquiries to the Deputy Director

Subject coverage
applications and performance of magnetic materials

Publications
List of Research Projects
Annual Report

2794 WOLFSON ELECTROSTATICS ADVISORY UNIT
Department of Electrical Engineering, The University, Southampton SO9 5NH — Tel. 0703 552266, Telex 47661
University Department/Consultancy

Enquiries to the Technical Manager or Deputy Manager

Subject coverage
powder coating and painting; electrostatic precipitation and separation; electrostatic hazards; charge behaviour in liquids; static charge generation and elimination; high voltage generation and testing; electrostatic instrumentation; powder property analysis and particle motion analysis; dielectric measurements

2795 WOLFSON HEAT TREATMENT CENTRE
Aston in Birmingham University, Gosta Green, Birmingham B4 7ET — Tel. 021-359 3611, Telex 336997
University Departmental Information and Advisory Centre, of the Department of Metallurgy and Materials; includes the Wolfson Heat Treatment Centre Engineering Group and the Contract Heat Treatment Association

Enquiries to the Information Officer

Subject coverage
heat treatment of metals

Publication
Heat Treatment of Metals (quarterly)

WOLFSON LABORATORY FOR MOLECULAR PATHOLOGY *see* **BEATSON INSTITUTE FOR CANCER RESEARCH**

2796 WOLFSON MARINE CRAFT UNIT
Department of Aeronautics and Astronautics, The University, Southampton SO9 5NH — Tel. 0703 555995, Telex 47661
University Consultancy Unit for Industry; member of the Ship and Boatbuilders National Federation

Enquiries to the Manager

Subject coverage
Solution of problems of a maritime or fluid dynamic nature either by theoretical analysis or model testing in towing tanks, wind tunnels, or a number of other facilities; assessment of new designs of marine craft, propeller design etc; design or assessment of glass reinforced plastic structures, testing of associated materials etc.

2797 WOLFSON MATERIALS ADVISORY SERVICE
Department of Mechanical Engineering, The University, Southampton SO9 5NH — Tel. 2381 559122, Telex 47661
Industrial Consultancy Unit of Southampton University

Enquiries to the Technical Manager

Subject coverage
materials testing, examination, and analysis; fatigue; creep; fracture; fracture mechanics; stress intensity factors; stress analysis; design; corrosion; wear; surface treatments; heat treatment; welding; significance of defects; plastics; composites; adhesives; strain measurement; electron microscopy; electron microprobe analysis

2798 WOLFSON MICROELECTRONICS LIAISON UNIT
Edinburgh University, School of Engineering Science, Mayfield Road, Edinburgh EH9 3JL — Tel. 031-667 1081 ext. 3277
University Departmental Unit

Enquiries to the Director

Subject coverage
electronics and microelectronics; custom design of integrated circuits, charge-coupled devices, thick and thin film hybrids, surface acoustic wave devices; development of microprocessor systems; special artwork; device failure analysis; computer graphics

Publications
List and details of research topics

2799 WOLFSON MOBILE RADIO PROJECT
School of Electrical Engineering, University of Bath, Claverton Down, Bath BA2 7AY — Tel. 0225 6941
University Research Group

Enquiries to the Director

Subject coverage
civil land mobile radio; UHF and VHF radio systems; radio receivers and transmitters

Publications
research reports

WOLFSON RECYCLE UNIT *see* **QMC INDUSTRIAL RESEARCH LIMITED**

2800 WOLFSON UNIT FOR NOISE AND VIBRATION CONTROL
Institute of Sound and Vibration Research, The University, Southampton SO9 5NH — Tel. 0703 559122, Telex 47661
Consultancy Group, within the University

Enquiries to the Librarian of the Institute of Sound and Vibration Research

Subject coverage
noise; vibration

Publications
Annual Report
Research Reports

2801 WOLVERHAMPTON PUBLIC LIBRARIES
Snow Hill, Wolverhampton, Staffordshire WV1 3AX — Tel. 0902 20109, 26988
Public Libraries

Enquiries to the Librarian

Subject coverage
general

Special collection
British Standards

2802 WOLVERHAMPTON POLYTECHNIC
Wulfruna Street, Wolverhampton, West Midlands WV1 1LY — Tel. 0902 27371
Polytechnic, formerly Wolverhampton College of Technology

Enquiries to the Librarian

Subject coverage
biological sciences; physical sciences; management and business studies; mathematics; computing; building and civil engineering; mechanical, production and electrical engineering

Special collection
European Documentation

2803 WOMEN'S ENGINEERING SOCIETY
Company
25 Fouberts Place, London W1V 2AL Tel. 01-437 5212
Enquiries to the Secretary

Subject coverage
study and practice of engineering among women; education, training and careers advice

Publication
Woman Engineer (quarterly)

2804 WOODALL-DUCKHAM LIMITED
The Boulevard, Crawley, Sussex RH10 1UX Tel. 0293 28755
Telex 87317

Company; Subsidiary of Babcock and Wilcox Limited, *q.v.*

Enquiries to the Librarian

Subject coverage
chemical engineering; chemical processing; gas production; gas purification and handling; fertilizer production

2805 WOODSPRING CENTRAL LIBRARY
The Boulevard, Weston super Mare, County of Avon BS23 1PL Tel. 0934 24133
Telex 449382

Public Library, formerly Weston super Mare Public Library, now Headquarters of Avon County Library

Enquiries to the Librarian

Subject coverage
general reference material

WOODSTOCK AGRICULTURAL RESEARCH CENTRE *now* **SHELL RESEARCH LIMITED Sittingbourne Research Centre,** *q.v.*

2806 WOOL BUYERS ASSOCIATION OF GREAT BRITAIN
Wormalds and Walker Limited, Dewsbury Mills, Dewsbury, Yorkshire Tel. 0924 465675
Telex 557819

Trade Association; formerly Northern Wool Buyers Association

Enquiries to the Secretary

Subject coverage
all aspects of wool; other aspects of the textile industry via the Association's Members

WOOL INDUSTRIES RESEARCH ASSOCIATION *see* **WIRA**

2807 WOOL INDUSTRY BUREAU OF STATISTICS
36 Headingley Lane, Leeds LS6 1BL Tel. 0532 783773
Trade Association, part of the Wool Textile Delegation

Enquiries to the Secretary

Subject coverage
production, consumption and trade statistics for wool textile products

2808 WOOL TEXTILE DELEGATION
Lloyds Bank Chambers, Hustlergate, Bradford BD1 1PE Tel. 0274 21406
Trade Association; member of the British Textile Confederation, *q.v.* the International Wool Textile Organization, *q.v.* and INTERLAINE (Committee of the EEC wool textile industries); 8 member federations, *see* the list which follows

Enquiries to the Director

Subject coverage
United Kingdom wool textile industry

WOOL TEXTILE DELEGATION
BRITISH WOOL CONFEDERATION
DYERS AND FINISHERS ASSOCIATION
NATIONAL ASSOCIATION OF SCOTTISH WOOLLEN MANUFACTURERS
PRESSED FELT MANUFACTURERS ASSOCIATION
WEST OF ENGLAND WOOL TEXTILE EMPLOYERS ASSOCIATION
WOOLLEN & WORSTED TRADES FEDERATION
WOOLLEN YARN SPINNERS FEDERATION
WORSTED SPINNERS FEDERATION LIMITED

WOOL TEXTILE RESEARCH COUNCIL *see* **WIRA**

WOOLWICH POLYTECHNIC *now* **THAMES POLYTECHNIC,** *q.v.*

WORCESTER COUNTY LIBRARY *see* **HEREFORD & WORCESTER COUNTY LIBRARY**

2809 WORCESTER ROYAL PORCELAIN COMPANY LIMITED
Severn Street, Worcester WR1 2NE Tel. 0905 23221
Telex 339842

Company, Subsidiary of Royal Worcester Spode Limited

Enquiries to the Advertising Manager

Subject coverage
Worcester Royal Porcelain, 1751 to the present day

Special collection
Dyson Perrins Collection of Worcester Royal Porcelain

WORCESTER SOUTH DIVISIONAL LIBRARY *see* **HEREFORD AND WORCESTER COUNTY LIBRARY**

2810 WORCESTER TECHNICAL COLLEGE
Deansway, Worcester WR1 2JF Tel. 0905 28383
Technical College

Enquiries to the Tutor Librarian

Subject coverage
building; engineering (mechanical, electrical, radio and television); catering; business studies

WORKINGTON DIVISIONAL LIBRARY *see* **CUMBRIA COUNTY LIBRARY**

2811 WORLD BUREAU OF METAL STATISTICS
7 Highfield Road, Edgbaston, Birmingham B15 3ED Tel. 021-454 7766
Telex 339161

Trade Association, formerly British Bureau of non-ferrous metals statistics

Enquiries to the General Manager

Subject coverage
statistics on production and consumption, world-wide and by country, of the major non-ferrous metals, copper, lead, zinc, tin, aluminium, nickel; some figures for antimony and cadmium

Publications

World Metal Statistics (monthly)
World Flow of Copper (yearly)
World Flow of Zinc (yearly)
World Flow of Lead (yearly)
World Flow of Aluminium (yearly)
World Trade in Copper & Copper Alloy semi-manufacture (yearly)
World Trade in Aluminium Conductors (yearly)
Survey of Planned Increases in World Copper Capacity (bi-annually)
Survey of Planned Increases in World Aluminium Capacity (bi-annually)

WORLD DATA CENTRE IN GLACIOLOGY *see* **SCOTT POLAR RESEARCH INSTITUTE**

WORLD FEDERATION OF INVESTMENT CLUBS *see* **NATIONAL ASSOCIATION OF INVESTMENT CLUBS LIMITED**

2812 WORLD METAL INDEX

Commerce and Technology Division, Sheffield City Libraries, Tel. 0742 734742/3/4
Central Library, Surrey Street, Sheffield S1 1XZ Telex 54243

Public Library Service

Enquiries to the Director of Libraries, World Metal Index

Subject coverage

The Index is a listing by grades, abbreviations, or numbers of the chemical composition and mechanical and physical properties of national, international and commercial grades of metals, originally started to cover steel grades; the index now includes non-ferrous materials. The collection includes material published in book form, together with a comprehensive collection of standards, journals, abstracts, and a large collection of technical literature collected on a world-wide basis

WORLD PETROLEUM CONGRESS *see* **INSTITUTE OF PETROLEUM**

WORLD REFERENCE LABORATORY FOR FOOT AND MOUTH DISEASE *see* **ANIMAL VIRUS RESEARCH INSTITUTE**

2813 WORLD SHIP SOCIETY Tel. 0444 3066

35 Wickham Way, Haywards Heath, West Sussex RH16 1UJ
Voluntary Society

Enquiries, maritime, from members only, to the Central Records Section

Subject coverage

maritime research; shipping company fleets

Publications

Books on maritime subjects
Fleet Lists of specific shipping companies
Warship Supplements

2814 WORSHIPFUL COMPANY OF FOUNDERS

13 St Swithins Lane, London EC4N 8AL Tel. 01-626 4956
City of London Livery Company

Enquiries to the Clerk or Beadle

Subject coverage

the City Livery Companies

2815 WORSHIPFUL COMPANY OF GOLD AND SILVER WYRE-DRAWERS

40a Ludgate Hill, London EC4M 7DE
City of London Livery Company

Enquiries to the Clerk

Subject coverage

the City Livery Companies and their statutory rights

2816 WORSHIPFUL COMPANY OF MASONS
9 New Square, London WC2A 3QN Tel. 01-242 4931
Telex 23294

City of London Livery Company

Enquiries to the Clerk

Subject coverage
City of London; Stonemasonry

2817 WORSHIPFUL COMPANY OF SPECTACLEMAKERS
Apothecaries Hall, Black Friars Lane, London EC4V 6EL Tel. 01-236 2932/8645
City of London Livery Company

Enquiries to the Clerk of the Company

Subject coverage
City Livery companies; professional qualification of ophthalmic opticians and of dispensing opticians; training within the optical industry

2818 WORSHIPFUL COMPANY OF WOOLMEN
192–198 Vauxhall Bridge Road, London SW1V 1HF Tel. 01-834 3631
City of London Livery Company

Enquiries to the Clerk

Subject coverage
Livery Company matters only

2819 WORSHIPFUL SOCIETY OF APOTHECARIES OF LONDON
Apothecaries Hall, Black Friars Lane, London EC4V 6EJ Tel. 01-236 1180
City of London Livery Company and Qualifying Body

Enquiries, Livery Company, to the Clerk; examinations, to the Registrar

Subject coverage
City Livery Companies; matters concerning professional pharmaceutical chemists

WORTHING DIVISIONAL LIBRARY *see* **WEST SUSSEX COUNTY COUNCIL LIBRARY SERVICE**

WREKIN DISTRICT LIBRARY *see* **SHROPSHIRE COUNTY LIBRARY**

WREXHAM MAELOR AREA LIBRARY *see* **CLWYD COUNTY LIBRARY SERVICE**

WREXHAM TECHNICAL COLLEGE *now* **ASTON COLLEGE,** *q.v.*

2820 WRITTLE AGRICULTURAL COLLEGE
Chelmsford, Essex CM1 3RR Tel. 0245 420705
Agricultural College, formerly Essex Institute of Agriculture

Enquiries to the Librarian

Subject coverage
agriculture and horticulture; beekeeping

2821 WROUGHT HOLLOWARE TRADES EMPLOYERS ASSOCIATION
168 Lower High Street, Stourbridge, West Midlands DY8 1TL Tel. 038-43 5684

Trade Association

Enquiries to the Secretary

Subject coverage
general information on the holloware trade

2822 WYE COLLEGE
Wye, Ashford, Kent TN25 5AH Tel. 0233 812401
Department of the University of London, including the Wye College Department of Hop Research and the Centre for European Agricultural Studies, *qq.v.*

Enquiries to the Librarian

Subject coverage
agriculture and horticulture; maize; plant growth substances and systematic fungicides; economics, management and marketing in relation to agriculture and horticulture; environmental and landscape studies; agricultural economics and rural development overseas, especially in Africa and Latin America; information and bibliographic services

Special collection
Early books on agriculture and horticulture

Publication
Annual Report

2823 WYE COLLEGE
Department of Hop Research, Wye, Ashford, Kent TN25 5AH Tel. 0233 812401
University Department, grant-aided by the Agricultural Research Council

Enquiries to the Director

Subject coverage
most aspects of hop production; breeding; pests and diseases; cultural and manurial trials; plant physiology; hop chemistry; engineering

Publication
Annual Report

2824 WYETH LABORATORIES (John Wyeth & Brother Limited)
Huntercombe Lane South, Taplow, Maidenhead, Berkshire SL6 0PH Tel. 75 28311
Telex 847640
Company; subsidiary of American Home Products Corporation, New York

Enquiries to the Librarian

Subject coverage
medicine; pharmacy; pharmacology; toxicology; microbiology; organic chemistry

WYRE DISTRICT CENTRAL LIBRARY *see* **LANCASHIRE LIBRARY**

YACHT BROKERS, DESIGNERS AND SURVEYORS ASSOCIATION *see* **SHIP AND BOAT BUILDERS NATIONAL FEDERATION**

YACHT CHARTER ASSOCIATION *see* **SHIP AND BOAT BUILDERS NATIONAL FEDERATION**

2825 YARSLEY POLYMER ENGINEERING CENTRE
Avis Way, Newhaven, Sussex BN9 7RR Tel. 079-12 4976
Telex 87323
Company Development Laboratory; part of the Fulmer Research Institute Limited, *q.v.*; formerly IPEC (Polymers) Limited

Enquiries to the Development Director

Subject coverage
polymer engineering; product design and application; mould design and manufacture; plastics processing units

2826 YARSLEY RESEARCH LABORATORIES LIMITED
Stoke Poges, Slough SL2 4QD Tel. 028-16 2181
Contract Research Organization; subsidiary of the Fulmer Research Institute, *q.v.*; linked with Yarsley Testing Laboratories, The Street, Ashtead, and with the Yarsley Polymer Engineering Centre, *q.v.*

Enquiries to the Librarian/Information Officer

Subject coverage
plastics and polymers; organic synthesis

Publications
Polymerics (abstract journal monthly)
Additives for Plastics (abstract journal)
Special Reports:
Statistics on Plastics
Disposal of Plastics
Degradable Plastics

YARSLEY TESTING LABORATORIES LIMITED *see* **YARSLEY RESEARCH LABORATORIES LIMITED**

2827 YEOVIL COLLEGE
Ilchester Road, Yeovil, Somerset — Tel. 0935 3921
Tertiary College, formerly Yeovil Technical College

Enquiries to the Tutor Librarian

Subject coverage
engineering in general

YEOVIL PUBLIC LIBRARY *see* **SOMERSET COUNTY LIBRARY**

YORK AND SELBY DIVISIONAL LIBRARY *see* **NORTH YORKSHIRE COUNTY LIBRARY**

YORK CENTRE FOR THE CONTINUING EDUCATION OF THE BUILDING PROFESSIONS *see* **INSTITUTE OF ADVANCED ARCHITECTURAL STUDIES**

YORK UNIVERSITY *see* **INSTITUTE OF ADVANCED ARCHITECTURAL STUDIES**
J.B. MORRELL LIBRARY (YORK UNIVERSITY LIBRARY)

YORKSHIRE AND HUMBERSIDE JOINT LIBRARY SERVICES *see* **WAKEFIELD METROPOLITAN DISTRICT LIBRARIES**

2828 YORKSHIRE GEOLOGICAL SOCIETY
c/o Institute of Geological Sciences, Ring Road, Halton, Leeds LS15 8TQ — Tel. 0532 649161
Voluntary Society

Enquiries, except publications, to the General Secretary at above address; publications queries to the Honorary Librarian, Yorkshire Geological Society, Department of Earth Sciences, University of Leeds

Subject coverage
geology

Publication
Proceedings of the Yorkshire Geological Society

YORKSHIRE, NORTH, COUNTY LIBRARY *see* **NORTH YORKSHIRE COUNTY LIBRARY**

2829 YUGOSLAV ECONOMIC CHAMBER
Trade Promotion Office, Crown Office, 143–147 Regent Street, London W1R 7LB — Tel. 01-734 2581, Telex 27552
Yugoslav Government Body

Enquiries to the Representative

Subject coverage
Yugoslav export possibilities; Yugoslav sources of all kinds of products; industrial cooperation with Yugoslav firms; economic and business environment in Yugoslavia; annual fairs

ZETLAND COUNTY LIBRARY *now* **SHETLAND LIBRARY,** *q.v.*

ZINC ALLOY DIECASTERS ASSOCIATION *see* **ZINC DEVELOPMENT ASSOCIATION**

2830 ZINC DEVELOPMENT ASSOCIATION
34 Berkeley Square, London W1X 6AJ Tel. 01-499 6636
Telex 261286

Trade Association; houses the Zinc Alloy Diecasters Association, the Zinc Pigment Development Association, and the Galvanizers Association

Enquiries to the Information Officer

Subject coverage
zinc coatings, especially hot-dip galvanized coatings; die casting; environment, health and safety; paints and pigments; extraction, refining and production; economics and statistics

Publications
see Zinc/Lead Library
Technical leaflets, brochures, books, films

2831 ZINC/LEAD LIBRARY AND ABSTRACTS
34 Berkeley Square, London W1X 6AJ Tel. 01-499 6636/8422
Telex 261286

Trade Organization; of the Zinc and Lead Associations, *qq.v.*; formerly ZDA/LDA Joint Library and Abstracting Service

Enquiries to the Information Officer

Subject coverage
all aspects of zinc, lead and cadmium technology

Special collection
International Lead Zinc Research Organization research reports (U.K. use only)

Publications
Zinc Abstracts
Lead Abstracts
Zinc: a guide to the literature
Lead: a guide to the literature
Cadmium: a guide to the literature
Range of bibliographies

ZINC PIGMENT DEVELOPMENT ASSOCIATION *see* **ZINC DEVELOPMENT ASSOCIATION**

2832 ZIP FASTENER MANUFACTURERS ASSOCIATION
King Edward House, New Street, Birmingham B2 4QP Tel. 021-643 5494
Trade Association

Enquiries, in writing, to the Secretary, who will forward them to appropriate member manufacturers

Subject coverage
zip fasteners

2833 ZOOLOGICAL MUSEUM
Akeman Street, Tring, Hertfordshire
Public Museum, administered by the British Museum (Natural History)

Enquiries to the Officer-in-Charge

Subject coverage
taxonomic research in ornithology

Special collection
Rothschild Collection

Publications
see **British Museum (Natural History)**

2834 ZOOLOGICAL SOCIETY OF LONDON
Regents Park, London NW1 4RY Tel. 01-722 3333
Learned Society; houses the Fauna Preservation Society, *q.v.*, the Conservation Corps, the Nuffield Institute of Comparative Medicine, the Wellcome Institute of Comparative Physiology

Enquiries, general, to the Librarian; schools and school-children, to the Education Officer; Press and TV, etc., to the Public Relations Officer

Subject coverage
zoology

Publications
Journal of Zoology
Transactions of the Zoological Society
Symposia of the Zoological Society
International Zoo Yearbook
Zoological Record

Subject Index